FEMINIST JUDGMENTS: REWRITTEN TORT OPINIONS

By rewriting both canonical and lesser-known tort cases from a feminist perspective, this volume exposes gender and racial bias in how courts have categorized and evaluated harm stemming from prenatal malpractice, pregnancy loss, domestic violence, sexual assault and harassment, invasion of privacy, and the award of economic and noneconomic damages. The rewritten opinions demonstrate that when confronted with gendered harm to women, courts have often distorted or misapplied conventional legal doctrine to diminish the harm or deny recovery. Bringing this implicit bias to the surface can make law students, and lawyers and judges who craft arguments and apply tort doctrines, more aware of inequalities of race, gender, class, and sexual orientation or gender identity. This volume shows the way forward to make the basic doctrines of tort law more responsive to the needs and perspectives of traditionally marginalized people, in ways that give greater value to harms that they disproportionately experience.

Martha Chamallas, the Robert J. Lynn Chair in Law at Ohio State University, is known for her scholarship on the devaluation of emotional and reproductive harm and on gender and race bias in damages. She is the author of the leading treatise on feminist legal theory and *The Measure of Injury: Race, Gender, and Tort Law* (with Jennifer B. Wriggins).

Lucinda M. Finley, the Raichle Professor of Law at the University of Buffalo, SUNY, is a leading feminist torts scholar whose foundational articles examining tort law from a feminist perspective have influenced new generations of legal scholars. She coedited a leading torts casebook that directly considers issues of gender, racial, class, and sexual identity equity in tort law.

Feminist Judgments Series Editors

Bridget J. Crawford
Elisabeth Haub School of Law at Pace University

Kathryn M. Stanchi
University of Nevada, Las Vegas, William S. Boyd School of Law

Linda L. Berger
University of Nevada, Las Vegas, William S. Boyd School of Law

Advisory Panel for Feminist Judgments Series

Feminist Judgments: Rewritten Tort Opinions

Edited by
MARTHA CHAMALLAS
Ohio State University

LUCINDA M. FINLEY
University of Buffalo, SUNY

CAMBRIDGE
UNIVERSITY PRESS

CAMBRIDGE
UNIVERSITY PRESS

University Printing House, Cambridge CB2 8BS, United Kingdom

One Liberty Plaza, 20th Floor, New York, NY 10006, USA

477 Williamstown Road, Port Melbourne, VIC 3207, Australia

314–321, 3rd Floor, Plot 3, Splendor Forum, Jasola District Centre, New Delhi – 110025, India

79 Anson Road, #06–04/06, Singapore 079906

Cambridge University Press is part of the University of Cambridge.

It furthers the University's mission by disseminating knowledge in the pursuit of education, learning, and research at the highest international levels of excellence.

www.cambridge.org
Information on this title: www.cambridge.org/9781108484299
DOI: 10.1017/9781108613293

First published 2020

A catalogue record for this publication is available from the British Library.

ISBN 978-1-108-48429-9 Hardback
ISBN 978-1-108-70624-7 Paperback

Contents

Notes on Contributors

Jamie R. Abrams is a law professor at the University of Louisville Brandeis School of Law where she teaches torts, women & law, and family law. Her research focuses on reproductive and birthing decision-making, gendered violence, legal protections for immigrant victims of domestic violence, and legal education pedagogy.

Alena Allen is an associate professor at the University of Memphis Cecil C. Humphreys School of Law. She teaches courses in torts, family law, health law, and feminist jurisprudence, and writes about the impact of gender on health policy and legislation. She would like to thank Lucinda Finley for thoughtful and helpful editing, Jan Stone for excellent research assistance, and Lee Harris for encouragement and support.

Taunya Lovell Banks is the Jacob A. France Professor of Equality Jurisprudence at the University of Maryland School of Law where she teaches torts, and seminars on law in popular culture (film or literature), citizenship, and critical race theory. Professor Banks's recent publications explore the continuing impact of gender, race, racial formation, and racial hierarchies on the quest for social equality.

Yifat Bitton is an associate professor of law at the Haim Striks School of Law, College of Management Academic Studies, in Israel. Professor Bitton specializes in tort law, anti-discrimination law, and critical–egalitarian theory of law. She is cofounder and chair of Tmura, the Israeli Anti-discrimination Legal Centre, which advocates for the rights of women who have suffered sexual violence and violations of their economic rights.

Martha Chamallas is the Robert J. Lynn Chair in Law at Ohio State's Moritz College of Law where she teaches torts, gender and the law, and employment discrimination. She is the coauthor of *The Measure of Injury: Race, Gender and Tort Law* (2010) (with Jennifer B. Wriggins) and *Introduction to Feminist Legal Theory* (3rd ed. 2013), as well many foundational articles applying feminist theory to tort law. She received the University Distinguished Scholar Award in 2013. She is a member of the American Law Institute, Torts Consultative Group, and has participated on gender and race bias task forces for the states of Iowa and Pennsylvania.

Sara Cressey received her JD in 2018 from the University of Maine School of Law, and worked as a law clerk for Chief Judge Jon D. Levy at the US District Court for the District of Maine during the 2018–19 clerkship term and is clerking for Judge Kermit Lipez at the First Circuit Court of Appeals during the 2019–20 clerkship term. She graduated *magna cum laude* with a BA from Wheaton College in Norton, MA, where she studied cultural anthropology, and received the Paul F. Cressey Prize for excellence in that field.

E. Christi Cunningham is a professor at the Howard University School of Law and Director of the Education Law Institute. She served as Associate Assistant Secretary for Regulatory Affairs at the Department of Labor as part of the Obama administration (2009–12). She teaches torts, education law, labor and employment law, law and poverty, and gender and the law. In addition to publishing scholarly works in her areas of expertise, she writes plays with the Black Women Playwrights' Group.

Mary J. Davis, Interim Dean and the Ashland-Spears Distinguished Research Professor of Law at the University of Kentucky College of Law, teaches and writes in the field of torts and products liability. She is the coauthor of *Products Liability and Safety: Cases and Materials*, now in its eighth edition, and a four-volume products liability treatise, both with Prof. David Owen, and a first-year torts casebook, *The Law of Torts* (with Profs. Christie, Sanders, and Cardi). She is an elected member of the American Law Institute and serves as an adviser to the Restatement (Third) of Torts: Intentional Torts project.

Laura Dooley, a professor of law at Touro Law Center in New York, has been teaching about the civil justice system for almost thirty years. Professor Dooley has published widely in top-tier academic journals, including the flagship journals at NYU, Vanderbilt, Cornell, and Illinois. Her work has been cited by both federal courts and the popular press, including the *Wall Street Journal*, and most recently *Vice News*.

Maurice R. Dyson is a professor of law at Suffolk University Law School. He has published numerous articles on education, civil rights, criminal justice reform, constitutional law, and critical race theory. He served as the Special Projects team attorney for the US Department of Education Office for Civil Rights (OCR) where he was recognized for his work in inter-district equitable school funding enforcement. He has also served as the Chair of the Association of American Law Schools (AALS) Section on Education Law, and as a national executive board member of the AALS Section of Minority Groups.

Zanita E. Fenton is a professor of law, University of Miami School of Law, where she teaches courses in constitutional law, family law, torts, race and the law, and seminars on critical race feminism, and women and the law stories. Fenton's research interests cover issues of structural inequality and forms of subordination, including those of disability, race, gender, and class. For her contribution to this volume she thanks her colleague Andrew Elmore for his sharp insight, and the library staff at the University of Miami School of Law, particularly Nicholas Mignanelli who is well versed in critical race theory.

Lucinda M. Finley is the Frank Raichle Professor of Law at the University at Buffalo Law School, State University of New York. She researches and teaches in the areas of gender and tort law, feminist legal theory, and reproductive rights and justice. Several of her articles are considered foundational works in applying feminist theory to tort law. She was the coauthor of the second and third editions of *Tort Law & Practice* (Vetri, Levine, Finley, and Vogel), a leading torts casebook that incorporates issues of gender, race, class, and sexual orientation into the study of tort law.

Caroline Forell is a professor emerita at the University of Oregon School of Law. Her teaching and research focused on tort law and gender issues, including the critically acclaimed book: *A Law of Her Own: The Reasonable Woman as a Measure of Man* (2000) (with Donna Matthews). Her articles about the legal and ethical standards appropriate for intimate relationships involving various professionals and those they are responsible for, including attorney–client, faculty–student, and doctor–patient, have spurred law reform and revision of codes of ethical conduct.

L. Camille Hébert is the Carter C. Kissell Professor of Law at Ohio State's Moritz College of Law. Her teaching and research focus on employment discrimination and employment law. She is the author of a leading treatise on employee privacy law, and she makes frequent presentations to academic and professional audiences on issues of sexual harassment and employee privacy. Professor Hébert served as Chair of the Employment Discrimination Section of the Association of American Law Schools.

Anna Lauren Hoffmann is an assistant professor with the Information School at the University of Washington. Her scholarship centers on issues in information, data, and ethics, particularly the ways that discourse, design, and uses of information technology work to promote or hinder the pursuit of equality, respect, and justice. She earned a Ph.D. and an MLIS from the School of Information Studies, University of Wisconsin-Milwaukee. She has published her work in interdisciplinary journals, as book chapters, and conference proceedings.

Jessica Hynes is an associate professor of legal studies at Quinnipiac University, where she teaches and researches in the areas of legal writing and rhetoric, legal history, gender and law, alternative dispute resolution, family law, and education law. She received a BS degree from Cornell University and a JD from Boston College Law School.

Hannah Brenner Johnson is the Vice Dean for Academic and Student Affairs and associate professor of law at California Western School of Law where she teaches torts; gender, power, law, and leadership; and the clinical externship seminar. She studies the perpetration of sexual violence, and the related reporting, investigation, and adjudication, in institutional settings like prisons, the military, and institutions of higher education. She is grateful to Eric Clarkson for exceptional research assistance on her opinion.

Eileen Kaufman is professor emerita at Touro Law School, and her publications focus on civil rights, women's rights, and human rights. She served as copresident of the Society of American Law Teachers, Chair of the Bar Admission and Lawyer Performance Committee of the American Association of Law Schools, cochair of the Committee on Legal Education and Admission to the Bar of the New York State Bar Association, and currently serves as a member of the New York State Bar Association Task Force on the New York Bar Exam.

Elizabeth Kukura is a visiting assistant professor at Drexel University's Thomas R. Kline School of Law. Her scholarship examines laws and policies that affect women's agency to make healthcare decisions, from terminating pregnancies to refusing to undergo procedures such as cesarean sections and episiotomies. Her articles have appeared in journals including *Georgetown Law Journal, Nebraska Law Review, Berkeley Journal of Gender Law & Justice*.

Jill Wieber Lens is an associate professor of law at the University of Arkansas School of Law (Fayetteville). She teaches courses in torts, remedies, products liability, and women and the law. Her current scholarship focuses on legal recognition and treatment of stillbirth, mainly within the contexts of tort law and reproductive justice. She has also written extensively on tort compensatory and punitive damages.

Yvonne ("Yvette") Lindgren is a visiting assistant professor of law at University of San Francisco Law School. She was a postdoctoral fellow at the Center on Reproductive Rights and Justice at Berkeley Law, and was executive editor of *Cases on Reproductive Rights and Justice* (2015), coauthored by Melissa Murray and Kristin Luker. Her research and scholarship focus on reproductive rights and justice, constitutional law, and health law policy. She thanks Maya Manian and Tristin Green for their invaluable feedback on an early draft.

Sharmila Lodhia is an associate professor of women's and gender studies at Santa Clara University. She earned her JD from Hastings College of Law and her Ph.D. in women's studies from the University of California, Los Angeles. Her research examines legal responses to violence against women through a transnational feminist lens, specifically why certain dominant frameworks of legal intervention can hinder rather than advance women's rights. She is the coeditor of *New Directions in Feminisms and Human Rights* (2011), and she is widely published in leading feminist studies and women and the law journals.

Twila L. Perry is a professor of law and Judge Alexander P. Waugh, Sr. Scholar at the S.I Newhouse Center for Law and Justice, Rutgers Law School. Professor Perry writes in the area of family law with a particular interest in the intersection of critical race theory and feminist legal theory. She has published articles on numerous subjects, including transracial and international adoption, the legal obligations of marriage, the black family and family law, no-fault divorce, and alimony.

Lisa R. Pruitt is the Martin Luther King, Jr. Professor of Law at the University of California, Davis, School of Law, where she has taught torts for two decades. Her early scholarship brought a feminist critique to communicative torts, but her more recent work regards rural and working-class white women. She also writes about rural poverty and other aspects of rural–urban difference in relation to the law. She thanks Jacqueline M. Nguyen for excellent research and editorial support of her commentary, and Liliana C. Moore for her indispensable administrative and editorial support.

Shaakirrah Sanders is a professor of law at the University of Idaho College of Law. She teaches courses related to US constitutional law and criminal procedure, and her publications focus on felony sentencing reform; civil and criminal jury trial rights; religious freedom; and agriculture security or "ag-gag" legislation. She formerly chaired the AALS Section on Constitutional Law (2018–19) and currently chairs the Idaho State Advisory Committee for the US Commission on Civil Rights.

Katharine B. Silbaugh is a professor of law at Boston University School of Law. She teaches family law, employment discrimination, women, work, and families, and gender and the law. Widely recognized for her work on gender, family care, and household labor, including the landmark article *Turning Labor into Love: Housework and the Law* for *Northwestern Law Review*, she is also coauthor with Judge Richard Posner of a survey of sexual regulation, *A Guide to America's Sex Laws* (1996), and of *The Essentials of Family Law* (2009) with Katharine K. Baker.

Scott Skinner-Thompson is an associate professor of law at the University of Colorado Law School, where his research and teaching center on constitutional law, civil rights, and privacy law, with a particular focus on LGBTQ and HIV issues. Prior to joining Colorado Law School, he was an acting assistant professor of lawyering at New York University School of Law. In 2014, he was selected as one of the Best LGBT Lawyers under 40 by the National LGBT Bar Association.

Sandra F. Sperino is the Judge Joseph P. Kinneary Professor of Law at the University of Cincinnati College of Law. She teaches in the areas of civil procedure, torts, and employment law, and her scholarship focuses on employment discrimination and on the intersection of tort and discrimination law. Her books include *Unequal: How America's Courts Undermine Discrimination Law* (with Thomas) (2017) and *Employment Discrimination: Cases and Materials* (with Grover and Gonzalez) (2013).

Sarah L. Swan is an assistant professor at Florida State University College of Law. She teaches courses in torts, criminal law, family law, and state and local government law. She received her LLM and JSD degrees from Columbia Law School, and her scholarly work has appeared in the *Duke Law Journal*, the *UCLA Law Review*, and the *Vanderbilt Law Review*, among others. She gratefully acknowledges the contributions of works by Peter F. Lake, Amelia J. Uelmen, and Leslie Bender to the ideas underlying this rewritten judgment.

Christine M. Tamer is Assistant Professor of Law and Assistant Director of Legal Writing at the University of North Texas, Dallas College of Law. She earned her JD from the University of Texas and practiced law with the firm of Baron & Budd, focusing on appellate and motion practice. Her law review articles include: *Arab Americans, Affirmative Action and a Quest for Racial Identity*, 16 *Tex. J. on C.L. & C.R.* 101 (2010) and *Toddlers, Tiaras and Pedophilia: The Borderline Child Pornography Embraced by the American Public*, 13 *Tex. Rev. Ent. & Sports L.* 85 (2012).

Jeffrey E. Thomas is the Daniel L. Brenner Faculty Scholar, Professor of Law, and Associate Dean for International Programs at the University of Missouri – Kansas City School of Law. He received his BA from Loyola Marymount University and earned his JD from University of California, Berkeley. He has been teaching torts for twenty-five years and wishes to thank the editors and his daughter, Leah Thomas, for providing a rich opportunity to learn more about feminist perspectives on tort issues through this project.

Leah Thomas is a senior at Georgetown University studying women and gender studies and computer science. She has been interested in the intersection of marginalized communities since early in her college career. After taking gender and the law at Georgetown, she wanted to continue exploring the topic in a more nuanced way so was pleased to participate in this project. She would like to thank her father, Jeffrey E. Thomas, for including her in this project and for their collaboration.

Cristina Tilley is an associate professor of Law at the University of Iowa College of Law. She writes in the areas of tort and media law, focusing on the appropriate treatment of speech and speech injuries. Her scholarship has appeared in *Yale Law Journal*, *Northwestern University Law Review*, and *University of Pennsylvania Journal of Constitutional Law*. Prior to her law career, she was a news reporter, specializing in business and legal affairs.

Stacey A. Tovino is the Judge Jack and Lulu Lehman Professor of Law at the William S. Boyd School of Law, University of Nevada Las Vegas. She publishes on health law, bioethics, and the medical humanities, with particular expertise in the civil, regulatory, operational, and financial aspects of health law. She is a member of the American Law Institute, and has chaired the AALS Sections on Torts and Compensation Systems, and Law and Mental Disability.

Molly Wilder is a Ph.D. candidate in philosophy at Georgetown University, where she has taught courses on philosophy and the law, political philosophy, ethics, autonomy, friendship and the good life, and ancient ethics. She received her JD from Georgetown Law Center and her BA in linguistics from Swarthmore College. Her dissertation uses feminist philosophy of autonomy to analyze how lawyers promote the autonomy of their clients and what autonomy means in the context of the lawyer–client relationship. She thanks her committee members Robin West and Heidi Li Feldman for their helpful comments on her commentary.

Stephanie M. Wildman is Professor Emerita at Santa Clara University School of Law, where she held the John A. and Elizabeth H. Sutro Chair and directed the Center for Social Justice and Public Service. Author of numerous books on women and the law, race, and social justice, her coauthored book *Privilege Revealed: How Invisible Preference Undermines America* (with Margalynne Armstrong, Adrienne D. Davis, & Trina Grillo) won the 1997 Outstanding Book Award from the Gustavus Meyers Center for Human Rights.

Jennifer B. Wriggins is the Sumner T. Bernstein Professor of Law and Codirector of the Information Privacy Program at the University of Maine School of Law. Her scholarship focuses on race, racism, gender, domestic violence, torts, insurance, and health law. Professor Wriggins is the coauthor of *The Measure of Injury: Race, Gender, and Tort Law* (2010, with Martha Chamallas). She thanks her coauthor, Sara Cressey, as well as the editors of and contributors to this volume.

Preface

What would tort law look like if feminist perspectives had influenced judicial opinions? Would feminist perspectives bring to the surface the implicit bias present in its supposedly neutral doctrines so as to make lawyers and judges who craft arguments and apply tort doctrines more aware of inequalities based on race, gender, class, and sexual orientation or gender identity? And if so, would its basic doctrines be more responsive to the needs and perspectives of traditionally marginalized people, in ways that give greater value to harms that they disproportionately experience? To begin to answer these questions, we brought together a group of scholars, lawyers, and students to rewrite, using feminist reasoning, sixteen tort cases spanning many of the major doctrinal areas of torts: intentional torts, privacy, negligence, duty, vicarious liability, and damages. Some of the rewritten cases are canonical classics, appearing in all major US casebooks and thus influencing generations of law students about the scope and possibilities of tort law. Other cases are ones that have received critical analysis from feminist scholars, or involve issues such as reproductive harm and sexual assault that are of central importance to women.

The sixteen rewritten opinions in this volume demonstrate that the insights of feminist legal theory and methods, when incorporated into the judicial task of interpreting and evaluating facts and precedents and applying policies that influence doctrinal developments, can indeed significantly influence and change tort doctrine. This influence can impact all areas of tort law, from the standards for assessing whether actions are negligent, to whether individuals or business entities owe any legal duty or obligation to protect people against certain types of harm, to determining whether an injury entails physical or emotional harm, to whether all-too-commonplace forms of harassment should be deemed beyond the acceptable bounds of social decency. The rewritten opinions highlight that incorporating feminist theories and methods into tort cases is consistent with judicial duties and accepted methods of legal interpretation – and in many instances is more consistent with standard torts principles, which too often have been distorted by courts to deny redress to women for their commonly experienced harms. The rewritten opinions also demonstrate that much of what have been assumed to be gender-neutral principles and doctrines are neither neutral nor inevitable, and that implicit and explicit biases can be overcome through feminist reasoning. The opinions and commentaries in this volume aid in showing a path forward to make tort law more equitable in its impact on women and other marginalized people, and more accessible as a tool to redress and reduce gendered injuries.

Table of Cases

PART I

Introduction

1

Introduction to *Feminist Judgments: Rewritten Tort Opinions*

MARTHA CHAMALLAS AND LUCINDA M. FINLEY

No one would dispute that torts is a foundational legal subject. It is a required part of the first-year law school curriculum and the course where students first discover the power of courts to declare certain conduct "wrongful" and subject to legal sanctions, even though the conduct may not amount to a crime or constitute a violation of statutory or regulatory law. Beyond the classroom, tort law has become a bedrock feature of US legal culture and has permeated social and political culture as well, to the extent that it is often a subject of intense political and media interest. Tort law provokes and is implicated in a variety of important contemporary debates: about personal responsibility and individual and institutional accountability; about appropriate levels of societal investment in safety and tolerance of risk; about striking the right balance between deterring harmful behavior and economic growth and innovation; and about which human interests and types of injuries are deserving of recognition and protection through tort compensation, to name only a few.

This wider debate, however, is most often couched in gender-neutral terms, with only the rare mention of feminism, the personal identity of the parties to the litigation, or the impact of tort rulings on particular social groups. At a time when tort theory is undergoing somewhat of a resurgence among legal academics,[1] the idea of a feminist tort law is still difficult for many scholars and lawyers to imagine.[2] Despite decades of feminist and critical torts scholarship, juxtaposing feminism and torts still requires explanation and defense. Looming over this volume of rewritten torts opinions is the overarching question: Aside from changing the result in some individual cases, what can feminism possibly bring to tort law?

[1] *See* PHILOSOPHICAL FOUNDATIONS OF THE LAW OF TORTS (John Oberdiek ed., 2018).

[2] *See* MARTHA CHAMALLAS & JENNIFER B. WRIGGINS, THE MEASURE OF INJURY: RACE, GENDER AND TORT LAW 13–21 (2010) (discussing feminism in tort theory).

We start from the premise that tort law is dynamic, malleable, and capable of transformation and view this project as designed to encourage such a transformation. Although the rewritten opinions in this volume are not "real" – in the sense of being delivered by real judges in a court of law – as we see it, the opinion authors and commentators are engaged not only in a hypothetical thought experiment, but in an exercise designed to illustrate and persuade. Indeed, a primary goal of this project is to demonstrate how feminist insights and feminist reasoning could potentially reshape important tort doctrines and influence judges and other legal actors to make the law more equitable, inclusive, and responsive to the needs, interests, and perspectives of women and other marginalized groups.

Although tort law has not been impervious to feminist-inspired reforms, it has clearly lagged behind constitutional law and statutory civil rights law when it comes to placing gender equality front and center, and it often takes a back seat to criminal law in addressing issues of sexual violence. Similarly, feminist and critical theory has barely made a dent in the body of tort theory, which is dominated by law and economics scholarship with its preoccupation with efficiency, and corrective justice scholarship which largely ignores social divisions and inequalities in society, even while purporting to be guided by moral principles. By showing how it might be done, this project is directed toward expanding and accelerating feminist interventions into this crucial body of common law, at a time when feminism is on the rise in the larger society and the #MeToo movement has exposed the failure of existing law to put an end to widespread sexual abuse and injustice.

THE CHANGING FACE OF TORT LAW

Gender and race have always played a key role in shaping US tort law. Prior to the mid-nineteenth century, tort recovery was explicitly linked to the legal and social status of the injured party. The institution of slavery, as well as the legal regime of coverture that denied independent legal rights to married women, prevented most African Americans and women of all races from suing for personal injuries in their own right. Because slaves were the property of their owners, personal injuries to slaves were treated as injuries to the slaveholder, rather than to the slave.[3] During the same period, married women also

[3] *See* Anthony R. Chase, *Race, Culture, and Contract Law: From the Cottonfield to the Courtroom*, 28 CONN. L REV. 1, 22–25 (1995); A. LEON HIGGINBOTHAM, JR., IN THE MATTER OF COLOR: RACE AND THE AMERICAN LEGAL PROCESS 6–10 (1978).

possessed no independent legal status.[4] The doctrine of coverture operated to "merge" a married woman's legal rights with those of her husband; husbands alone had the right to institute suits on behalf of their wives and possessed exclusive property rights in their wives' bodies and labor.

Aside from erecting procedural obstacles to legal redress, the regimes of slavery and coverture affected substantive tort law, resulting in race- and gender-segregated causes of actions. To be recognized in law, personal injury to the slave had first to be translated into pecuniary loss to the slaveholder, ending up with white slaveholding plaintiffs owning both a human being and a valuable tort claim for economic loss in the event of a slave's intentional or accidental injury at the hands of another. A similar legal maneuver affected the rights of married women who were not enslaved. Although married women were not regarded as property itself, coverture also resulted in a denial of substantive rights flowing from personal injury. Thus, when a wife was tortiously injured, it was her husband who had a claim for the material value of her household and sexual services, denominated a "loss of consortium" claim that was denied to the wife when her husband was injured.[5]

With the end of slavery and the formal abandonment of coverture, however, gender and race largely vanished from the face of tort law, and tort law appeared on its face to be increasingly gender and race neutral. Even during the era of racial segregation and "separate spheres" – when gender- and race-specific thinking remained the order of the day – judges opted not to create new gender- and race-specific tort rules. For the most part, however, this change in the law was largely cosmetic. Although legal realist and other progressive torts scholars often criticized this ostensibly neutral body of law for being formalist and under-protective of the interests of plaintiffs, it was not until the 1980s that legal scholars first began to unearth the implicit racial and gender bias in various tort doctrines and in the deep structures of tort law.

FEMINIST AND CRITICAL TORTS SCHOLARSHIP

In retrospect, Professor Richard Delgado's 1982 article, *Words that Wound: A Tort Action for Racial Insults, Epithets and Name Calling*,[6] marked the beginning of a vibrant, if still not voluminous, body of critical torts

4 *See* NORMA BASCH, IN THE EYES OF THE LAW: MARRIAGE, WOMEN, AND PROPERTY IN NINETEENTH-CENTURY NEW YORK 42–69 (1982).

5 Katharine Silbaugh, *Turning Labor into Love: Housework and the Law*, 91 NW. U. L. REV. 1, 41 (1996).

6 17 HARV. C.R.-C. L. REV. 133 (1982).

scholarship. In that article, Delgado criticized courts that had ruled that racial insults and harassment on the job were "mere insults" not actionable under the rubric of intentional infliction of emotional distress and proposed a new tort for racial insults. What set Delgado's article apart from other mainstream critiques of specific tort doctrines was his singling out of torts as a site of inequality and as an area ripe for critical analysis. He employed many of the themes that would subsequently become prominent in critical race theory: that racism and racial insults were endemic in our culture; that racial harassment had a devastating and often cumulative effect on its victims who faced bias in other settings; and that, in the long run, the negative racial stereotypes and imagery communicated by racial insults created a culture that reproduced racial injury in succeeding generations.

Inspired by feminist theory and, in particular, the blossoming of the new field of feminist legal theory, feminist torts scholars in the late 1980s and early 1990s began to expose the hidden (and sometimes not so hidden) male bias in specific tort doctrines as well as in basic torts concepts. In exploratory articles, Leslie Bender and Lucinda Finley, for example, broadly canvassed the domain of torts, looking for marginalized sectors of tort law where the law failed to address recurring injuries that disproportionately affected women.[7] They tried to envision what a more inclusive tort law might look like, imagining, for example, the replacement of the ubiquitous "reasonable man" standard with a more protective standard of care that would require persons to act like responsible neighbors who had a stake in the well-being of others.

This early feminist torts scholarship challenged the conventional wisdom that ostensibly gender-neutral doctrines were actually objective or gender-inclusive or free from gender bias. For example, Martha Chamallas and women's historian Linda K. Kerber employed an interdisciplinary approach to theorize that tort recovery for emotional harm had been stunted by its cognitive association with early negligence claims brought by pregnant women seeking damages for stillbirths and miscarriages and mothers suing for nervous shock as result of seeing their children killed or injured.[8] Their study exposed how an entire category of harm could be devalued because of its link to gender, even in cases brought by men.

7 Leslie Bender, *A Lawyer's Primer on Feminist Theory and Tort*, 38 J. LEGAL EDUC. 3 (1988); Lucinda Finley, *A Break in the Silence: Including Women's Issues in a Torts Class*, 1 YALE J. L. & FEMINISM 41 (1989).

8 Martha Chamallas with Linda K. Kerber, *Women, Mothers and the Law of Fright: A History*, 88 MICH. L. REV. 814 (1990).

Although much of the early feminist torts scholarship centered on gender, critical scholars also built upon Delgado's germinal article and noticed the distance between civil rights norms and ideals and the standards used to determine tort liability for discriminatory behavior. In an early intersectional article, for example, Regina Austin focused on the inadequacies of the tort of intentional infliction of emotional distress to redress dignitary injuries of low-income workers, calling on courts to tackle multidimensional harassment based on race, ethnicity, gender, and "color of collar."[9]

In the decades since, feminist and critical torts scholarship has matured to cover a wider range of topics and to utilize a greater variety of theoretical approaches, mirroring the diversification of feminist legal theory more generally. Feminist and critical writers have critiqued the three major theories of tort liability – liability based on intent,[10] negligence liability,[11] and strict liability[12] – and have argued that the methods courts use to calculate and award both economic and noneconomic damages are infected with gender and race bias.[13] Their scholarship has addressed timely and undertheorized topics, such as tort liability for harms inflicted by domestic violence,[14] rape and sexual harassment,[15] denials of reproductive autonomy and reproductive

9 Regina Austin, *Employer Abuse, Worker Resistance, and the Tort of Intentional Infliction of Emotional Distress*, 41 STAN. L. REV. 1 (1988).

10 *See, e.g.*, Martha Chamallas, *Discrimination and Outrage: The Migration from Civil Rights to Tort Law*, 48 WILLIAM & MARY L. REV. 2115 (2007); Jennifer Wriggins, *Domestic Violence Torts*, 75 S. CAL. L. REV. 121 (2001); Lisa Pruitt, *Her Own Good Name: Two Centuries of Talk about Chastity*, 78 IND. L.J. 965 (2004): Leslie Bender, *Teaching Torts as if Gender Matters: Intentional Torts*, 2 VA. J. SOC. POL'Y & L. 115 (1994).

11 *See, e.g.*, Ellen M. Bublick, *Citizen No-Duty Rules: Rape Victims and Comparative Fault*, 99 COLUM. L. REV. 1413 (1999); Margo Schlanger, *Gender Matters: Teaching a Reasonable Woman Standard in Personal Injury Law*, 45 ST. LOUIS U. L.J. 769 (2001); Martha Chamallas, *Gaining Perspective in Tort Law: A New Take on Third-Party Criminal Attack Cases*, 14 LEWIS & CLARK L. REV. 1351 (2010); Sarah Swan, *Triangulating Rape*, 37 N.Y. U. REV. L. & SOC. CHANGE 403 (2013).

12 *See, e.g.*, Martha Chamallas, *Vicarious Liability in Torts: The Sex Exception*, 48 VAL. U. L. REV. 133 (2013); Anita Bernstein, *Fellow-Feeling and Gender in the Law of Personal Injury*, 18 J.L. & POL'Y 295 (2009).

13 *See e.g.*, Martha Chamallas, *Questioning the Use of Race-Specific and Gender-Specific Data in Tort Litigation: A Constitutional Argument*, 63 FORDHAM L. REV. 73 (1994); Lucinda M. Finley, *The Hidden Victims of Tort Reform: Women, Children and the Elderly*, 53 EMORY L.J. 1263 (2004); Frank M. McClellan, *The Dark Side of the "Tort Reform" Movement: Searching for Racial Justice*, 48 RUTGERS L. REV. 761 (1996); Thomas Koenig & Michael Rustad, *His and Her Tort Reform: Gender Injustice in Disguise*, 70 WASH. L. REV. 1 (1995).

14 *See, e.g.*, Camille Carey, *Domestic Violence Torts: Righting a Civil Wrong*, 62 U. KAN. L. REV. 695 (2014).

15 *See, e.g.*, Sarah L. Swan, *Between Title IX and the Criminal Law: Bringing Tort Law to the Campus Sexual Assault Debate*, 64 U. KAN. L. REV. 963 (2016); Martha Chamallas, *The*

interests,[16] devaluation of caregivers' injuries,[17] as well as bias in the litigation process.[18] Their critiques have drawn upon each of the most prominent strands or brands of feminist legal theory – liberal feminism, dominance feminism, cultural feminism, and intersectional feminism[19] – and have borrowed from critical race theory,[20] and more recently, disability studies[21] and queer and trans theory.[22] Although some of the feminist torts scholarship is theoretical in nature,[23] much of it falls into the category of applied feminist scholarship, applying feminist and critical insights to specific issues.

Many of the recurring themes found in feminist and critical torts scholarship echo those found in the larger body of critical scholarship, adapted to the context of tort law. Thus, for example, we see writers placing importance on gender in analyzing the meaning and effect of current tort doctrines. This gender-aware stance presents a contrast to that of most tort scholars and courts who still proceed in a gender-blind fashion, neglecting to question the gendered origins of a particular rule, the gender implications of a particular doctrine, or what changes would have to be made to avoid or ameliorate gender disadvantage. Feminist and critical scholars often eschew formalist or

Elephant in the Room: Sidestepping the Affirmative Consent Debate in the Restatement (Third) of Intentional Torts to Persons, 10 J. Tort L. (2017).

16 *See, e.g.*, Jill Wieber Lens, *Tort Law's Devaluation of Stillbirth*, 19 Nev. L.J. 955 (2019); Elizabeth Kukura, *Obstetric Violence*, 106 Geo. L.J. 721 (2018); Carolyn A. Goodzeit, *Rethinking Emotional Distress Law: Prenatal Malpractice and Feminist Theory*, 63 Fordham L. Rev. 175 (1994).

17 *See, e.g.*, Regina Graycar, *Before the High Court: Women's Work; Who Cares?*, 14 Sydney L. Rev. 86 (1992).

18 *See, e.g.*, Donald G. Gifford & Brian Jones, *Keeping Cases Away from Black Juries: An Empirical Analysis of How Race, Income Inequality, and Regional History Affect Tort Law*, 73 Wash. & Lee L. Rev. 557 (2016).

19 *See* Martha Chamallas, Introduction to Feminist Legal Theory 19–26 (3d ed. 2012) (discussing brands of feminist legal theory).

20 *See, e.g.*, Camille A. Nelson, *Considering Tortious Racism*, 9 DePaul J. Health Care L. 905 (2005); Jody D. Armour, *Toward a Tort-Based Theory of Civil Rights, Civil Liberties, and Racial Justice*, 38 Loy. L.A.L. Rev. 1469 (2005).

21 *See, e.g.*, Anne Bloom with Steven Paul Miller, *Blindsight: How We See Disabilities in Tort Litigation*, 86 Wash. L. Rev. 709 (2011).

22 Anne Bloom, *To Be Real: Sexual Identity in Tort Litigation*, 88 N. C. L. Rev. 357 (2010); Anne Bloom, *Regulating Middlesex* in Fault Lines: Tort Law as Cultural Practice 148–59 (David M. Engel & Michael McCann eds., 2009); Anita Allen, *Privacy Torts: Unreliable Remedies for LGBT Plaintiffs*, 98 Calif. L. Rev. 1711 (2010); Scott Skinner-Thompson, *Privacy's Double Standards*, 93 Wash. L. Rev. 2051 (2018).

23 *See, e.g.*, Martha Chamallas, *The Architecture of Bias: Deep Structures in Tort Law*, 146 U. Pa. L. Rev. 463 (1998); Joanne Conaghan, *Tort Law and Feminist Critique*, 56 Current Legal Probs. 175 (2003); Anita Bernstein, *Restatement (Third) of Torts: General Principles and the Prescription of the Masculine Order*, 54 Vand. L. Rev. 1367 (2001).

abstract inquiries, preferring contextual analyses that tap into women's lived experiences. The critical lens these scholars bring to the law also tends to make them skeptical of abstract dichotomies which permeate the law (e.g., physical v. emotional harm; economic v. noneconomic damages), and tend to overstate distinctions, mask implicit hierarchies of interests and values, and function to legitimate structural bias in tort law.

In contrast to mainstream theoretical approaches, such as law and economics, which implicitly take the perspective of the legislator or judge, feminist and critical scholars often factor the "victim's perspective" into their analysis and focus attention on those who are subjected or governed by the law. Particularly in recent years, much feminist and critical scholarship has taken an intersectional turn, mindful of the complexities posed by interlocking systems of gender, race, and other forms of oppression and the danger of essentialist overgeneralizing from the experience of one subgroup of women. Finally, feminist and critical scholarship is often wary of a conventional wisdom that asserts that gender equality has already been achieved or that we live in a post-racial society. One familiar move in these writings is to look behind claims of progress to uncover important continuities in the subordinate position of the injured parties and to understand how basic hierarchies are reproduced over time.

THE FEMINIST JUDGMENTS TORTS PROJECT

This feminist judgments torts project is a special kind of applied feminism scholarship that questions, critiques, and revises tort doctrine through the process of rewriting torts opinions issued by state and federal courts. It is one of a growing series of such feminist judgments projects in the United States, now covering both public and private law. The first US volume in the series focused on opinions from the US Supreme Court, tackling important constitutional and statutory issues relating to equality and personal liberty.[24] Other projects have or will address tax law,[25] reproductive justice,[26] family law, employment discrimination law, health law, trusts and estates, property, and criminal law. This is the first volume devoted to an area of law that forms part of the core first-year law school curriculum.

24 Feminist Judgments: Rewritten Opinions of the United States Supreme Court (Kathryn M. Stanchi, Linda L. Berger, & Bridget J. Crawford eds., 2016).

25 Feminist Judgments: Rewritten Tax Opinions (Bridget J. Crawford & Anthony C. Infanti eds., 2017).

26 Feminist Judgments: Reproductive Justice Rewritten (Kimberly M. Mutcherson ed., 2020).

The larger feminist judgments project is a global project. It was originally launched by feminist scholars in Canada and the United Kingdom and has since spawned projects in Ireland, Australia, New Zealand, Scotland, Africa, India, and Mexico as well as a project on international law. The common thread of all the projects is a commitment to demonstrating the difference that feminism might make to the substance and rhetoric of judicial decision-making, even absent large-scale legislative or political reforms. The "ground rules" of the project require opinion writers to limit their citations to sources that were available at the time of the opinions, the idea being to show that feminist outcomes and reasoning were possible even in the distant past before contemporary feminist legal theories had emerged. However, opinion writers are not asked to do the impossible and jettison their own knowledge base and contemporary feminist consciousness when writing their opinions. The result is an intriguing mixture of past and present, allowing the authors and readers to imagine the different trajectories the law might have taken if guided by contemporary feminist values, arguments, and modes of reasoning. This distinctive methodology makes the opinions in the feminist judgments volumes ideal texts for use in the classroom, inviting students to debate whether the rewritten opinions are realistic, persuasive, and accord with their own sense of what the insights of feminism might bring to a particular legal controversy.

In line with other feminist judgments projects, the authors and commentators in the feminist torts project were free to pursue their own feminist visions. As editors, we did not attempt to define "feminism" or restrict writers and commentators to any particular brand or variety of feminist or critical theory. In many instances, opinion writers and commentators ended up having a similar "take" on the case. In those instances, the commentary serves mainly to place the opinion in its legal and cultural context and elaborate on the objectives and particular moves of the feminist judgment. In some cases, however, commentators and authors had differing feminist visions. In addition to introducing and contextualizing the feminist opinion, commentators were free to express their disagreement with the opinion and to indicate how they might rewrite the opinion in a different way.

One of the most challenging and consequential aspects of the project was selecting the particular tort opinions to rewrite. The sixteen cases in this volume came from a longer list of potential cases that we included in a call to potential authors and commentators in which we also sought suggestions for additional cases we might include. We narrowed the list based on author interest and, in a few instances, we added cases that were suggested to us.

The volume contains four "classic" cases that appear in virtually every torts casebook. In perhaps the most explicit way, these cases exemplify how feminist thinking and methods could infiltrate basic tort concepts and debunk the notion that torts is a neutral body of law, divorced from considerations of gender or personal identity. The other twelve cases, however, are not part of the torts canon, although some of them are noteworthy enough to have been the subject of commentary,[27] or included as a principal case or in the notes of a torts casebook. In our view, however, these cases are just as significant as the "classic" cases and deserve equal attention. They reveal how tort law has addressed or neglected to address issues of particular importance to women and other social minorities and suggest that the torts canon itself could be revised along feminist lines.[28] Perhaps not surprisingly, many of these cases involve sexual violence and abuse, violations of reproductive rights and interests, and invasions of sexual privacy. By including these cases in the volume, we hope to bring these marginalized areas, marked by gender and sexuality, closer to the center of tort law.

UNRECONSTRUCTED TORT LAW

In a variety of ways, the opinions in this volume show that despite the facial neutrality of contemporary tort law, gender, race, and the personal identity of plaintiffs still affect the availability of tort claims, the prospects for liability and the measure of damages. Although doctrines change, the updated versions often reproduce gender disadvantages and other inequalities, even if in softer, less explicit forms. Legal historian Reva Siegel has described this phenomenon as "preservation through transformation," a process by which a basic hierarchy may remain intact even though the legal rules and legal rhetoric surrounding it undergo substantial change.[29] In fact, the basic hierarchy is preserved precisely because it has been updated to fit the sensibilities of the time. In law, a regime can soften, admitting more exceptions or providing somewhat more protection to a vulnerable group, without dislodging the basic power structure.

Siegel's rather sober account of the difficulties and limitations of effecting social change through law, however, does not mean that real or meaningful

[27] *See, e.g.*, Mae Quinn, *The Garden Path of Boyles v. Kerr and Twyman v. Twyman: An Outrageous Response to Victims of Sexual Violence*, 4 TEX. J. WOMEN & L. 247 (1995) (discussing *Boyles v. Kerr*).

[28] On the torts canon, see Martha Chamallas, *Vanished from the First Year: Lost Torts and the Deep Structures of Tort Law* 104 in LEGAL CANONS (J. M. Balkin & Sanford Levinson eds., 2000).

[29] Reva B. Siegel, *"The Rule of Love": Wife Beating as Prerogative and Privacy*, 105 YALE L.J. 2117, 2176–88 (1996).

change can never occur. The trick is identifying which interventions at which moments can make an appreciable difference. In a recent book,[30] Catharine MacKinnon employed the metaphor of "butterfly politics" evoking chaos theory[31] to argue that unstable social systems, such as the social system of gender inequality, can sometimes be destabilized, even if they normally tend to return to their starting point when faced with a legal challenge. She maintains that the "right small human intervention in an unstable political system can sooner or later have large reverberations."[32] Interestingly, for MacKinnon, the common law can be a promising site for such a butterfly effect, despite the conventional view of the law as precedent-bound and impervious to radical change. She maintains that the rule of precedent can itself be destabilizing if and when "[a] single breakthrough iterated through many variations ... opens up a complex flood in a distinctive direction, even as the precedential system resists an initial breakthrough."[33]

Many of the opinions in this volume exemplify Siegel's "transformation through preservation" thesis, providing critiques of resilient patterns of inequality that take on a somewhat different shape over time. They show how bias and disadvantage can be reproduced and updated in our ostensibly neutral tort law system. At the same time, however, one of the aspirations of the feminist tort judgments project is to allow scholars to draft opinions that read like one of MacKinnon's breakthrough opinions. Through the rewritten opinions in this volume, we can glimpse what a feminist reconstruction of tort law might look like and can determine whether such precedents would be capable of destabilizing the system of inequality and injecting a greater degree of gender and social justice into this foundational area of law.

The variety of tort cases in this volume suggest that no area of tort law is entirely free of bias. The traces of gender and race bias can be seen in a wide array of contexts, from the iconic *Palsgraf* railroad accident (*Palsgraf v. Long Island R.R.*), to the exploding coke bottle case that produced the revolution in products liability (*Escola v. Coca-Cola Bottling*). However, one significant lesson we take away from our work on this volume is that certain types of cases pose a particular challenge for courts hearing torts cases. Most simply put, tort law has a problem with sex and reproduction. Many of the cases in this

30 Catharine A. MacKinnon, Butterfly Politics (2017).

31 Konrad Lorenz famously coined the term "butterfly effect" to describe how "the flap of a butterfly's wings in Brazil [can] set off a tornado in Texas." *Id.* at 1. The butterfly effect illustrates chaos theory's understanding of the "complex causality in dynamic unstable systems." *Id.*

32 *Id.*

33 *Id.* at 5.

volume demonstrate that courts have often failed to come to grips with injuries caused by sexual violence, abuse, harassment, and invasions of privacy and have failed to understand and value the reproductive interests of women and prospective parents. While these cases most often involve female plaintiffs, they are not restricted to one gender. They are gender-related, but not gender-specific, claims.

These gender-related injuries traverse traditional torts categories. They are not confined to specific doctrinal areas but crop up in intentional tort, negligence, and strict liability cases and spill over into debates about the proper measure of damages. Thus, in this volume, sexual assault is not only the subject of a lawsuit alleging an intentional tort (*Guthrie v. Conroy*), but is the gravamen of negligence litigation against different types of institutional actors (a university and its police department, a commercial lessor, and a hotel) who failed to prevent the sexualized violations from occurring (*Tarasoff v. Regents of the Univ. of California*; *Sharon P. v. Arman, Ltd*; *McCarty v. Pheasant Run, Inc.*). Sexual abuse also underlies a strict vicarious liability claim (*Lisa M. v. Henry Mayo Newhall Hospital*), as well as a challenge to legislative restrictions on noneconomic damages (*Simpkins v. Grace Brethren Church of Delaware*). Sexualized invasions of privacy are at the heart of an intentional tort lawsuit (*Sipple v. Chronicle Publishing Co.*) and form the basis of a negligence claim for emotional distress (*Boyles v. Kerr*). And sexual harassment lurks in the background of an iconic negligence case involving a bystander's duty to rescue or render aid (*Farwell v. Keaton*). Similarly, claims for reproductive injury are not confined to malpractice cases sounding in negligence, where they are most often situated (*Broadnax v. Gonzalez*; *Emerson v. Magendantz*), but also arise in the intentional torts context where plaintiffs allege battery and intentional infliction of emotional distress for physicians' disregard of their reproductive choices (*Robinson v. Cutchin*).

Regardless of the doctrinal framework used for asserting a claim for sexual or reproductive injury, however, there is little doubt that such injuries often are severe in nature and cause long-term harm to the victims. Many of the rewritten opinions recount devastating physical harm, the kind of harm that the torts system generally protects most fully. Yet, for a variety of reasons, courts do not always regard the plaintiffs' injuries in these cases as physical harms, or find other reasons to minimize the harm or limit the available damages. Even in those cases in which the sexualized or reproductive injury does not result in immediate physical harm, however, there is often good reason to predict that the resulting nonphysical damage will be severe, leading to the kind of debilitating injury that mimics severe physical injuries. Yet again, many courts seem reluctant to grant full recovery in such cases.

In addition to the severity of the injury, sex and reproduction tort cases are marked by the fact that they often represent systemic injury. While the particular harm to the plaintiff is individualized, the plaintiffs in many of the cases in the volume have suffered an injury that is common to members of their social group. Many of the rewritten opinions, for example, contain statistics about the prevalence of rape and sexual assault and tell familiar stories about how the injury sustained by the plaintiff is tragic yet commonplace. Similarly, the reproductive injury cases highlight the vulnerability of ordinary women who are pregnant or seeking to avoid pregnancy, a predicament that affects the great majority of women at some point in their lives.

The portrait that emerges from this body of cases is that of a tort system that under-compensates for sexual and reproductive injury, at least if the grievous and systemic nature of the injury is considered a reliable indication of the need for compensation. Indeed, many of the rewritten opinions grapple with the overriding question of how and why this under-compensation has occurred and whether it can be justified. Although the forest can sometimes be lost in all the doctrinal trees embedded in the three theories of tort liability, when viewed under the broad rubric of sexual and reproductive harm, the under-compensation problem becomes increasingly visible and ripe for feminist analysis.

Additionally, from a bird's-eye view, the sex and reproduction cases in this volume suggest that courts' reluctance to compensate in this area has consequences for the larger body of tort law. When courts in tort cases do address issues of sex, sexuality, and reproduction, they often choose not to apply the ordinary doctrinal rules that govern the particular theory of tort liability or not to apply the ordinary rules with the same force as in other settings. Thus, the feminist judgments in this volume repeatedly take issue with the exceptional treatment of sexual and reproductive issues and the distortion of tort doctrine that results. For example, when third-party liability for rape is at stake, the familiar concept of foreseeability can be stretched so out of shape that rape becomes unforeseeable, despite the high incidence of rape in the relevant community (*Sharon P. v. Arman, Ltd.*). Although full recovery for injuries caused by medical malpractice is the norm, in wrongful birth cases, courts have fashioned a hodgepodge of special rules to limit damages, often without articulating a convincing theory for the exceptional treatment (*Emerson v. Magendantz*). The highly specialized set of rules governing recovery for negligent infliction of emotional harm, the framework employed in many sexual and reproductive harm cases, can jeopardize recovery for a mother of a stillborn child, despite the defendant physician's negligence and the plaintiff's obvious suffering (*Broadnax v. Gonzalez*). The result is not only confusion in the law, but a subtle undermining of the basic elements of liability under the three theories of tort liability, as litigators and other legal actors debate whether their case is the exception or the rule. We may have reached a point where our facially neutral tort law disfavors, but does not preclude, recovery for sexual and reproductive harm. But that only raises the question of whether the contemporary regime is so very different from regimes of the past that erected total barriers to recovery.

TECHNIQUES OF BIAS

On a more granular level, the feminist opinions in this volume identify and critique a number of recurring techniques or moves courts have deployed which end up disadvantaging plaintiffs from marginalized groups. Some of the techniques are conceptual in nature, while others amount to rhetorical strategies. Most operate beneath the surface; rarely do the rewritten opinions charge judges with intentional discrimination. Instead, they more often try to tease out implicit bias, looking for clues in the language courts use, their choice of analogies and examples, their empathy (of lack of empathy) for the plaintiff, and the degree of attention courts give to the gender, racial, or other identity dimension of the legal issues presented.

To unearth and call out these judicial techniques typically requires not only a close and critical reading of the original opinion but also some knowledge of the relevant history and social context. Perhaps most importantly, many of the judicial techniques criticized by the feminist opinion writers in this torts volume come from the playbook of feminist and critical theory and are familiar "red flags" to critical scholars outside of the world of torts. In those instances in which feminist opinion writers agree with the results reached by the original opinion, they use feminist and critical theory to provide additional reasons to support the result or deepen the analysis of the original majority opinion.

Although we make no attempt here to catalogue all the techniques identified and analyzed by the opinion writers and commentators, six deserve mention.

A *Use of Gender and Race Stereotypes*

Feminist opinion writers in this volume were alert to the use of racial and gender stereotypes that courts sometimes embed either in their description of the facts or in their rationales for judgment. Whether it is excusing risky masculine behavior as normal (*Palsgraf v. Long Island R.R.*), or assuming that a Hispanic child is less intelligent and has less potential to succeed in life than a white child (*G.M.M. v. Kimpson*), or assuming that an African-American woman who already had several children would neither be harmed nor offended by involuntary sterilization (*Robinson v. Cutchin*), the opinion writers expressed disapproval of the use of overbroad generalizations that purport to describe how members of particular social groups actually behave (i.e., descriptive stereotypes) or how they should behave (i.e., prescriptive stereotypes).

B *Victim Blaming*

In the context of sexual violence, the feminist judgments criticized the common tendency to "blame the victim" and to shift the focus away from the harmful quality of a perpetrator's or a defendant's antisocial or negligent behavior. Although such victim-blaming strategies are ubiquitous, in and outside of tort law, in third-party rape cases predicated on negligence, for example, a feminist opinion writer cautioned that the contributory negligence defense especially invites judges and jurors to scrutinize the behavior of the plaintiff and inject sexist assumptions into the decision-making process (*McCarty v. Pheasant Run, Inc.*).

C *Minimization of Sexualized Injuries*

The judicial tendency to devalue and minimize sexualized injuries was criticized by several feminist opinion writers. From calling an attempted rape a "mishap" (*McCarty v. Pheasant Run, Inc.*), to downplaying the seriousness of repeated sexual harassment in the workplace (*Guthrie v. Conroy*), to dismissing the serious consequences of emotional abuse in the domestic violence context (*Lyman v. Huber*), the feminist opinions critiqued the courts' failure to appreciate the devastating effects of sexual abuse on its victims. Through use of statistics and other evidence, the feminist opinion writers found ways to make these gender-related injuries more salient to readers (*Sharon P. v. Arman, Ltd.*), and in some instances, the feminist opinion and commentary writers were able to reframe the facts of the case and the plaintiffs' injuries to bring a hidden sexual dimension to the forefront (*Tarasoff v. Regents of Univ. of Calif.*; *Farwell v. Keaton*).

D *Misunderstanding Pregnancy and Reproduction*

In the reproductive injury context, feminist opinion writers took courts to task for misunderstanding the physical, emotional, and relational aspects of pregnancy and for devaluing women's reproductive choices and health. Judicial failure to respect and value women's desire not to become pregnant and give birth (*Emerson v. Magendantz*), or the desire to have more children (*Robinson v. Cutchin*), was a prominent theme. At a deeper level, a feminist judgment criticized a court for artificially separating an injury to a fetus *in utero* from the entailed physical injury to the pregnant woman, displaying a masculine failure to imagine the interconnected nature of this kind of harm (*Broadnax v. Gonzalez*).

E *Failure to Incorporate History of Racialized Practices*

Taking a page from critical race theory and its use of history to illuminate the meaning of contemporary racialized practices, a feminist opinion drew upon the historical devaluation of black motherhood in the United States and the history of coerced sterilization of women of color to transform an ordinary case of lack of consent to a medical procedure into a claim of battery and intentional infliction of emotional distress (*Robinson v. Cutchin*). Other opinion writers invoked a race-conscious historical analysis – attentive to the legacy of slavery and racial segregation – to justify providing greater protection for consumers and employees (*Escola v. Coca-Cola Bottling Co.*) and eliminating racial disparities in the award of economic damages (*G.M.M. v. Kimpson*).

F *Use of Gender-Correlated Dichotomies*

Feminist opinion writers expressed skepticism about the judicial use of dichotomies that privilege certain types of injuries and types of damages over others and mask the gender-correlation underwriting the categories. Feminist writers challenged the physical/emotional distinction to argue for fuller protection of emotional injuries stemming from sexual exploitation (*Boyles v. Kerr*) and domestic abuse (*Lyman v. Huber*) and objected to the singling out of noneconomic damages in a damage cap case involving clergy sexual abuse of minors (*Simpkins v. Grace Brethren Church of Delaware*).

SOLUTIONS

In addition to pointing out the various techniques courts in tort cases have used to obscure, minimize, or justify gender-related injuries, several feminist writers and commentators offered strategies and approaches to correct for bias and to steer tort law in a more inclusive and egalitarian direction. The strategies ranged from offering methods for teasing out implicit bias, to identifying discriminatory effects of specific tort doctrines, to broader prescriptions for reform that sought to enlarge the scope of tort protection by borrowing norms and principles from other legal domains.

Five such strategies or approaches stood out as particularly promising.

A *Tailor Doctrines to Lived Experiences*

In several instances, the feminist opinions sought to connect tort doctrine to the actual or lived experiences of the parties, rather than relying on abstract categories or dichotomies to determine rights and the scope of protection. Thus, one opinion writer urged that the right to privacy be tailored to protect LGBT plaintiffs who needed the freedom to be selective about choosing to whom to disclose their sexual orientation (*Sipple v. Chronicle Publishing Co.*). Another writer emphasized that vicarious liability rules ought to take into account the vulnerability of female patients who tend to defer to the advice and instructions of medical professionals (*Lisa M. v. Henry Mayo Newhall Hosp.*). A third urged that the tort concept of outrageous behavior be applied in a way that captures harmful workplace sexual harassment on a flexible case-by-case basis (*Guthrie v. Conroy*).

B *Ameliorate Disparate Impact of Neutral Rules*

In an age in which most explicit gender- and race-based rules have been eliminated, feminist opinion writers broadened their definition of bias to include neutral tort rules that have adverse disparate impact on particular social groups. Their opinions argued that, from a collective perspective, such rules can severely limit the degree of tort protection available to marginalized social groups, even though some atypical members of the group may qualify for recovery. For example, one opinion spelled out the disparate gender impact of capping noneconomic damages, given the disproportionate importance of noneconomic damages to women whose injuries tend to yield lower amounts of economic damages than men (*Simpkins v. Grace Brethren Church of Delaware*). Another writer demonstrated the adverse gender effect of relying on the reasonable person standard to determine the severity of injuries suffered as a result of domestic abuse (*Lyman v. Huber*).

C *Borrow Constitutional and Civil Rights Norms*

To inject a dose of equality and social justice into tort law, feminist opinion writers borrowed from constitutional law and statutory civil rights law, arguing that certain fundamental principles from public law should migrate into tort law. They argued that constitutional and Title VII norms of equality should inform courts' determinations of what qualifies as outrageous conduct (*Guthrie v. Conroy*) and that equal protection principles should shape the contours of the tort privacy claim of public disclosure of private facts (*Sipple v. Chronicle Publishing Co.*). They also relied on equal protection guarantees to call for an end to the use of gender- and race-based data to determine the amount of damages awarded to injured children (*G.M.M. v. Kimpson*). In the reproductive injury context, they relied on the fundamental constitutional right to make one's own determination about whether or not to beget or bear a child as the basis for awarding full tort recovery for all foreseeable harm in wrongful birth cases (*Emerson v. Magendantz*), and for classifying involuntary sterilization as outrageous conduct that can lead to punitive damages (*Robinson v. Cutchin*).

D *Correct the Underutilization of Tort Law*

Some feminist opinion writers contested the view that tort law was an inappropriate domain to adjudicate cases of sexualized injury and objected to the judicial tendency to steer these cases into the criminal law. Stressing many of the advantages of the complaint-driven civil tort system, these writers found no sufficient reason for courts to shy away from providing tort relief in hostile environment sexual harassment cases (*Guthrie v. Conroy*) or in cases of rape and domestic abuse (*McCarty v. Pheasant Run, Inc.*; *Lyman v. Huber*).

E *End Sexual Exceptionalism*

An important observation running throughout many of the feminist critiques of current tort doctrine was that cases alleging sexual and reproductive injury were often treated differently (and less favorably) than other cases litigated under the same tort theory. Feminist opinion writers called for an end to such sexual exceptionalism and urged, for example, that wrongful birth cases be treated the same as ordinary malpractice cases (*Emerson v. Magendantz*), and that cases involving sexual abuse of an enterprise's customers and clients give rise to vicarious liability on the same basis as cases of nonsexual aggression (*Lisa M. v. Henry Mayo Newhall Hosp.*). Their arguments also revealed that the judicial penchant for devising elaborate specialized rules for harms that disproportionately injure women and other marginalized groups often recapitulates older exclusionary doctrines and reproduces inequality (*Boyles v. Kerr*; *Sharon P. v. Arman, Ltd.*).

ORGANIZATION OF THE VOLUME

The cases and commentary in this volume are organized with the first-year torts class in mind. Following this Introduction (Part I), Part II consists of "classic" tort cases arranged in chronological order. Three of the classic cases deal with the all-important element of duty in negligence cases (*Palsgraf v. Long Island R.R. Co.*; *Farwell v. Keaton*; *Tarasoff v. Regents of Univ. of Calif.*). The fourth involves proof of negligence and strict products liability (*Escola v. Coca-Cola Bottling Co.*).

Part III consists of intentional tort cases. One case involves a battery claim (*Robinson v. Cutchin*); three cases involve claims of intentional infliction of emotional distress (*Robinson v. Cutchin*; *Guthrie v. Conroy*; *Lyman v. Huber*) and one is a right to privacy case (*Sipple v. Chronicle Publishing Co.*).

Part IV consists of negligence and vicarious liability claims. They involve duty (*Sharon P. v. Arman, Ltd.*) and breach of duty (*McCarty v. Pheasant Run, Inc.*) in the third-party rape context; negligent infliction of emotional distress (*Broadnax v. Gonzales*; *Boyles v. Kerr*); the tort of wrongful birth (*Emerson v. Magendantz*); and vicarious liability for sexual abuse (*Lisa M. v. Henry Mayo Newhall Hosp.*).

Part V consists of two damages cases. One involves the calculation of economic damages (*G.M.M. v. Kimpson*). The other case is a challenge to a cap on noneconomic damages (*Simpkins v. Grace Brethren Church of Delaware*).

To give a flavor of the contents of the volume, below are one-sentence highlights of the opinions and commentaries.

- *Palsgraf v. Long Island R.R. Co.*: Professor Maurice Dyson's dissent takes on Cardozo's famous "zone of danger" test for its underlying subjectivity, gender, and class bias. Professor Taunya Banks's commentary recounts the little-known backstory of the litigation and discusses the larger social, political, and economic context.
- *Escola v. Coca-Cola Bottling Co.*: Building on Justice Traynor's famous concurrence, Professor Zanita Fenton's opinion provides gender, race, and class rationales for strict products liability, consumer protection, and workplace safety. In her commentary, Professor Mary Davis explains the evolution from negligence to strict products liability and delves into the facts and people behind the *Escola* case.
- *Farwell v. Keaton*: Professor Sarah Swan's rewritten majority opinion replaces the myriad exceptions to the "no duty to rescue" rule with a humanitarian approach based on the circumstantial connection between

the parties in the case. Re-characterizing the case as one involving sexual harassment, Professor E. Christi Cunningham's commentary identifies an alternative feminist basis for imposing a duty to render aid.

- *Tarasoff v. Regents of Univ. of Calif.*: Professors Sharmila Lodhia and Stephanie Wildman reveal the full story of the Berkeley student's stalking and delusional romance and broaden the duty to warn potential victims of gender violence. Professor Jamie Abrams's commentary explains the struggle on the California Supreme Court and the difficulties of holding law enforcement accountable in sexual and domestic violence cases.
- *Robinson v. Cutchin*: Professor Alena Allen builds a legal foundation for holding physicians liable for battery and intentional infliction of emotional distress when they perform sterilization procedures on women of color without securing their consent. The commentary by Professor Yvonne Lindgren unpacks the implicit racialized judgments in the opinion that trade on the stereotype that the reproductive practices of African-American women are deviant and excessive.
- *Guthrie v. Conroy*: Professor Sandra Sperino's dissent explains how courts misuse summary judgment in hostile workplace environment cases and argues for a contextual application of the element of "outrageousness" based on victims' experience of sexual harassment. Professor L. Camille Hébert's commentary catalogues the various techniques courts have used to exclude feminist perspectives in harassment cases and urges a greater role for tort litigation.
- *Lyman v. Huber*: Professor Jeffrey Thomas and Leah Thomas revise the requirements for proving an actionable claim of emotional domestic abuse to bring parity to claims alleging physical and emotional injury. Caroline Forell's commentary argues against use of the objective reasonable person standard to determine the severity of injury in tort cases brought by survivors of domestic abuse.
- *Sipple v. Chronicle Publishing Co.*: Professor Scott Skinner-Thompson's opinion reshapes the right to privacy claim to protect LGBT plaintiffs by incorporating constitutional principles of freedom of association and equality. Anna Lauren Hoffman's commentary paints a portrait of the plaintiff as an involuntary "gay hero" whose life was upended by publicity and reflects on the limitations of law as a vehicle of liberation.
- *Sharon P. v. Arman, Ltd.*: Professor Yifat Bitton unpacks the ubiquitous tort concept of "foreseeability" to uncover hidden gender bias and reshapes the law in third-party rape cases to take women's systemic vulnerability to sexual violence into consideration. The commentary by Professor Jessica Hynes updates developments in third-party sexual assault

cases in California and elsewhere and argues for extending the duty of reasonable care to all such cases.

- *Broadnax v. Gonzalez*: Professors Eileen Kaufman and Laura Dooley reframe the injury suffered by pregnant women when they suffer a miscarriage or stillbirth due to their doctor's negligence and argue for full relief for plaintiffs' physical and emotional suffering. Professor Elizabeth Kukura's commentary critiques the dominant two-patient model of care in which physicians owe a duty to the pregnant woman and the fetus and explains how affording recovery for pregnancy loss does not require recognition of fetal rights or personhood.
- *Boyles v. Kerr*: Professor Cristina Tilley's opinion interprets and modernizes negligence doctrine to expand the concept of injury to include serious emotional and relational harms and demonstrates how courts can disrupt sexual stereotypes about interpersonal relationships between men and women. Professor Lisa Pruitt's commentary narrates the full story behind the sex tape litigation, the history of the negligent infliction tort, and the implications of the case for the digital age.
- *Emerson v. Magendantz*: Professor Katharine Silbaugh underscores the centrality of women's autonomy and reproductive choice to justify recovery of full damages in wrongful birth and conception cases. In her commentary, Professor Lucinda Finley elaborates on how difficult it is for many courts to address the complex reality of pregnancy and avoid moralistic judgments based on romanticized stereotypes of mothering.
- *McCarty v. Pheasant Run, Inc.*: Professor Hannah Brenner Johnson objects to Judge Richard Posner's economic formula for determining the reasonableness of a defendant's behavior and questions use of the contributory negligence defense to limit a plaintiff's recovery in cases of rape and sexual assault. Professor Molly Wilder's commentary charges that Judge Posner's rhetoric and his law and economics philosophy leads him to weigh the economic interests of businesses over women's physical and emotional well-being.
- *Lisa M. v. Henry Mayo Newhall Hospital*: Professor Stacey Tovino's opinion ensures that victims of sexual assault have the same opportunity to invoke vicarious liability as other victims and documents the risk of sexual assault in the healthcare setting. In her commentary, Christine Tamer situates the case at the intersection of sexual violence and women's health and examines how job-created power can makes a patient vulnerable to harm by medical professionals.
- G.M.M. *v. Kimpson*: Professor Jennifer Wriggins and Sara Cressy make the case that basing the amount of tort damages on the race, ethnicity, or

sex of a person violates the US Constitution and cannot justify a lower recovery for a minority child injured by lead paint exposure. Professor Twila Perry explains the history behind the use of race-based and gender-based tables and discusses the complications and trade-offs of the various methods for remedying the violation.

- *Simpkins v. Grace Brethren Church of Delaware*: Professor Shaakirrah Sanders exposes the gender discriminatory impact of caps on noneconomic damages to argue that limiting damages in a case of clergy sexual abuse of a minor child violates equal protection and the right to a jury trial. In her commentary, Professor Jill Wieber Lens explains the tort reform movement and discusses how states could mitigate the harsh effects of damage caps for sexual abuse victims.

PART II
The Classics

2

Commentary on *Palsgraf v. Long Island Railroad Co.*

TAUNYA LOVELL BANKS

INTRODUCTION

The 1928 New York Court of Appeals decision, *Palsgraf v. Long Island Railroad Co.*,[1] remains a central touchstone of American tort law, at least in law schools. Each year tortured first-year law students struggle to understand Chief Judge Benjamin N. Cardozo's opinion and Judge William S. Andrews's dissent. Evidence of *Palsgraf*'s abiding force in legal culture can be found on YouTube where the 1924 accident at the center of the case is reenacted using Legos.[2]

The facts of the case are well known, although there is still considerable dispute and uncertainty about what happened. We know that on Sunday August 24, 1924 a sudden explosion rocked the platform at the East New York Atlantic Avenue Station of the Long Island Railroad (LIRR) Company station in Brooklyn. The explosion was front-page news in the *New York Times*, *New York Herald Tribune*, and *Long Island Daily News*. According to most news accounts, the explosion, described as severe, occurred due to a dropped package containing fireworks. Passengers and bystanders on the platform panicked, some were knocked down by the explosion, others were caught up in a "stampede" and many women fainted. The force of the explosion toppled a large scale of a type commonly found in public places where for a penny people could weigh themselves. The newspapers published the names of the injured, including Helen Palsgraf, who is listed as suffering from shock.[3]

1 Palsgraf v. Long Island R.R. Co., 162 N.E. 99 (N.Y. 1928).
2 Izzy4reel, Lego Law: *Palsgraf v. Long Island Railroad*, YouTube (June 11, 2009), https://www.youtube.com/watch?v=mDEbTudkjhc.
3 This factual account of the case is drawn from William H. Manz, The *Palsgraf* Case: Courts, Laws, and Society in 1920s New York 5 (2005).

The injury occurred when Palsgraf, a ticketed passenger, and her two daughters were standing on a platform headed for a day at Rockaway beach. Palsgraf claimed that the explosion caused the large penny scale to fall hitting her on the arm, hip, and thigh. She was treated on the scene and sent home in a taxi. Although able to walk on her own, she was severely shaken by the experience. The next day the family physician observed small bruises on her shoulder. A few days later she developed a stammer and stutter, which persisted, forcing her to stop working.

Listed variously as age 40 or 43, Palsgraf was a life-long resident of New York City. Although married, her husband had abandoned their family, which included three children, leaving her the sole breadwinner. She supported her family by doing housework and performing janitorial duties at the apartment where she and her children lived. The family's total monthly income was approximately $46, far below what was needed to support a working-class family living in Brooklyn.[4]

Probably hoping that the railroad would settle her claim,[5] Palsgraf waited for two months after the accident before securing legal counsel. She chose Matthew W. Wood, a university-educated solo practitioner with more than twenty years of experience.[6] He filed suit on her behalf alleging that the railroad had a duty to prevent people from bringing explosives on its platform and thus failed to take reasonable steps to protect people who were lawfully on its platform from injury, including Palsgraf.[7] The complaint asked for $50,000 in damages, an amount "frequently used in complaints in negligence actions against common carriers."[8]

THE TRIAL

On May 25, 1927, the case was tried before an all-male jury, women being excluded from jury service in New York at the time.[9] At trial, Wood presented witnesses who testified that while Palsgraf was standing on the platform another train entered the station, and as it was underway, two male passengers, one carrying a bundle, ran toward the train and were assisted in boarding by

4 *Id.* at 5–6.

5 *Id.* at 6–9 (noting that LIRR's "huge increase in passenger traffic brought with it an endless stream of complaints" and these complaints made the railroad a "popular target for politicians and leaders of civic groups").

6 *Id.*

7 *Id.* at 30 (citing the complaint).

8 *Id.*

9 *Id.* at 41 (noting that New York, like most states at the time, excluded women from jury service).

the conductors and an LIRR employee on the platform. In the process the bundle was dislodged from one of the boarding passenger's arms and fell causing a large explosion.[10] The railroad's lawyer argued that Palsgraf was not standing near the explosion and thus there was no evidence of negligence toward her.[11] He presented no witnesses to rebut the plaintiff's case, relying instead on "less than vigorous" cross-examination of plaintiff's witnesses.[12]

In his charge to the jury, the trial judge, Burt Jay Humphrey, stated that there was no factual dispute. Ignoring the testimony of three witnesses who said the package was wedged between the platform and the train, Judge Humphrey told the jury that the package either fell to the platform or onto the track.[13] The judge also instructed the jury that the railroad owed no duty to inspect passengers' packages.[14] Therefore, the sole question for the jurors to consider was whether the railroad employees failed to act with ordinary prudence and care toward people on the platform, including Palsgraf.[15] Two hours and thirty minutes later, the jury returned a verdict for Palsgraf awarding her $6,000 in damages.[16] The judge denied the railroad's motion for a new trial and the railroad appealed.[17]

It is important to note that the jury award, while unsurprising, was approximately fourteen times Palsgraf's annual income.[18] One commentator remarked that "[b]y the beginning of the Twentieth Century railroads were regularly paying (or settling cases) following injuries that could loosely be blamed on the railroads."[19] Thus, railroad lawyers tried to avoid sending cases to the jury.[20]

Undoubtedly the railroad company was concerned about the precedent of a large award for what, in their opinion, was a minor injury. The LIRR, unprofitable for most of its history, was saved from financial collapse in 1900 by the Pennsylvania Railroad which subsidized the company during

10 Palsgraf v. Long Island R.R. Co., 222 A.D. 166 (N.Y. 1927).
11 MANZ, *supra* note 3, at 44–45.
12 *Id.*
13 *Id.* at 49.
14 *Id.*
15 *Id.* at 49–50. (citing Palsgraf Record at 214).
16 *Id.* at 50.
17 The trial judge entered an award against the LIRR for $6,142.45, including costs. *Id.* at 65.
18 JOHN NOONAN, JR., PERSONS AND MASKS OF THE LAW: CARDOZO, HOLMES, JEFFERSON, AND WYTHE AS MAKERS OF THE MASKS 128 (2002).
19 Saul Levmore, *The Wagon Mound Cases: Foreseeability, Causation, and Mrs. Palsgraf*, *in* TORTS STORIES 147 (Robert L. Rabin and Stephen D. Sugarman eds., 2003).
20 Michael I. Krauss, Palsgraf: *The Rest of the Story* in 9 THE GREEN BAG 299, 311–12 (2006).

the first half of the twentieth century.[21] Unlike other railroads at the time of the accident, the LIRR made most of its money from passenger fares, not its freight service.[22] There also had been several railroad accidents involving the LIRR including one that occurred less than a month before the Palsgraf incident.[23] It is unknown whether knowledge of these accidents influenced the jury.

THE FIRST APPEAL: THE APPELLATE DIVISION

On appeal, Palsgraf's lawyer noted that she was a ticketed passenger who had been injured when a railroad employee "forcibly knocked" the package from under a passenger's arm causing the explosion.[24] This negligence, her lawyer argued, was the proximate cause of Palsgraf's injuries.[25] As at trial, the railroad's brief denied that its employees were negligent, especially since the company had no notice of the bundle's contents.[26]

The Appellate Division, in a 3:2 decision, ruled for Palsgraf.[27] The majority noted that as a passenger of a common carrier, she was owed "the highest degree of care,"[28] adding "[i]t is no answer or defense to these negligent acts to say that the defendant's employees were not chargeable with notice that the passenger's bundle contained an explosive."[29] The dissenting judges argued that while the jury might reasonably conclude that the railroad employees' carelessness toward the passenger carrying the bundle caused the explosion, their carelessness "was not a likely or natural cause of the explosion" since the event was unusual, and while the "Defendant's negligence was a cause of plaintiff's injury, [it was] too remote."[30] In other words, even though the railroad's carelessness was the actual cause of Palsgraf's injuries, it was not the proximate cause, and thus recovery should not be allowed.[31] Again the railroad appealed.

21 MANZ, *supra* note 3, at 7.
22 *Id.* at 8.
23 *Id.* at 10–11.
24 *Id.* at 66.
25 *Id.* at 66–67.
26 *Id.*
27 *Palsgraf*, 222 A.D. at 166.
28 *Id.* at 168.
29 *Id.*
30 *Id.* at 169 (Lazansky, P.J. dissenting).
31 MANZ, *supra* note 3, at 69–70.

THE COURT OF APPEALS

On February 23, 1928, oral argument in the *Palsgraf* case was held before the court of appeals, the state's highest court. The railroad company's brief advanced the same arguments as before, that Palsgraf was not injured due to any negligence on the company's part. The brief filed by Palsgraf's lawyer argued that the appeal was inappropriate because it hinged on factual disagreements between the parties, as opposed to legal errors, and the court of appeals only had jurisdiction over the latter. Wood argued that the factual disagreements centered on the actions of the railroad's employees and "whether their actions were the proximate cause of Mrs. Palsgraf's injuries."[32] Wood asserted that proximate cause was a question of fact for the jury, and the Appellate Division court agreed.[33]

On May 29, 1928, the New York Court of Appeals in a split decision ruled for the Long Island Railroad Company.[34] Chief Judge Cardozo wrote the majority opinion. A nationally regarded legal scholar and jurist, Judge Cardozo later served briefly on the United States Supreme Court. He is better known today, however, for his opinions written while on the New York Court of Appeals.[35]

In writing for the majority, Judge Cardozo rejected Palsgraf's claim that the railroad acted carelessly toward her, reasoning that any carelessness by the railroad employees was toward the man carrying the package and not toward Palsgraf, who was "standing far away."[36] He also rejected Wood's proximate cause argument writing: "The law of causation, remote or proximate, is … foreign to the case before us" because the railroad company did not breach any duty of care owed to Palsgraf.[37] Instead, Judge Cardozo decided the case on a theory neither party asserted, that any duty of care under the circumstances was owed the male passenger and his package, not Palsgraf, reasoning that she "must show 'a wrong' to herself … a violation of her own right, and not merely a wrong to someone else," in this case the passenger with the package.[38] Finally, in what in hindsight seems a particularly cruel decision, Judge Cardozo imposed all the court costs on Palsgraf.[39]

32 *Id.* at 94.
33 *Id.* (citing Plaintiff-Respondent's Brief at 5–6).
34 *Palsgraf*, 162 N.E. at 100.
35 Andrew L. Kaufman, Cardozo 4 (1998).
36 *Palsgraf*, 162 N.E. at 99.
37 *Id.* at 101.
38 *Id.* at 100.
39 *Id.* at 101.

Judge Andrews dissented. He characterized the railroad's employee as "negligently" knocking a package from a boarding passenger, resulting in a "violent explosion" disturbing some scales "a considerable distance away."[40] In Judge Andrews's view, the key issue was proximate cause, not negligence,[41] and he took issue with Judge Cardozo's statement that "there is no negligence unless there is in the particular case a legal duty to take care, and this duty . . . is owed to the plaintiff."[42] Instead, Judge Andrews argued that if the act is wrong (i.e., careless), then liability extends not only to those "within the radius of danger" but also "to all who might have been there."[43] As to proximate cause, Judge Andrews acknowledged that public policy considerations influence when to cut off legal liability for negligent events that cause greater consequences than expected, and inquired "what might ordinarily be expected to follow [a] fire or explosion," concluding that injury to Palsgraf was "a natural and continuous sequence."[44]

As legal scholar and jurist John T. Noonan, Jr. noted years later, but for an obligatory personal pronoun, Judge Cardozo's opinion barely acknowledged Palsgraf's gender.[45] Judge Andrews omitted *any* reference to the plaintiff's gender.[46] Neither opinion adds any personal details about the plaintiff at the center of the case or the nature of her injuries.[47] The person at the center of the case was virtually erased.

Palsgraf's lawyer moved for reargument saying that "there was an apparent error in the understanding of the facts of the case," specifically that the plaintiff was closer to the accident than Judge Cardozo's opinion suggested.[48] The court in a per curiam decision rejected this argument, writing tersely that even if the court accepted the plaintiff's factual claim, "she was not so near that injury from a falling package, not known to contain explosives, would be within the range of reasonable prevision."[49]

Palsgraf reportedly never rode the LIRR again, remaining upset about the accident for the rest of her life.[50] Railroad accidents continued to plague the

40 *Id.* at 101–02.
41 *Id.* at 102.
42 *Id.*
43 *Id.*
44 *Id.* at 105.
45 Noonan, *supra* note 18, at 113.
46 *Id.* at 112–13 (emphasis added).
47 *Id.*
48 Manz, *supra* note 3, at 99 (citing Affidavit of Helen Palsgraf at 7) (per curiam).
49 Palsgraf v. Long Island R.R. Co., 164 N.E. 564 (N.Y. 1928).
50 Manz, *supra* note 3, at 117.

LIRR, contributing to its financial problems.[51] In 1965, the state finally took over operation of the line after the company declared bankruptcy.[52]

REACTION TO THE DECISION

Aside from the initial explosion, Palsgraf's case attracted little notice in the press. Following the Appellate Division decision, the *New York Times* briefly summarized the majority and dissenting opinion in the case.[53] After the court of appeals decision, a few students and legal scholars commented on the rule from the case, but a decade later legal commentaries were more critical.[54] By the early 1940s some casebooks included the *Palsgraf* case, and by the 1960s the literature about the case was "enormous."[55] Renowned torts scholar William Prosser characterized the case as "a law professor's dream of an examination question … answered by Cardozo."[56]

More than the substance of the opinion troubled Dean Prosser. In 1953 Prosser, in a *Michigan Law Review* article titled *Palsgraf Revisited*, asserted that Judge Cardozo "improperly discussed the case at an ALI (American Law Institute) advisers meeting."[57] Judge Cardozo allegedly engaged in a debate with professors Warren Seavey, Leon Green, and Francis Bohlen, all noted torts scholars, about a hypothetical where a careless driver misses a pedestrian hitting an unmarked package containing explosives which explodes and the debris hits a window washer working ten stories above the explosion injuring him.[58] According to the ALI conference meeting notes for the October 1927, these parties, including Judge Cardozo, debated another hypothetical involving a driver running over an unmarked package that explodes destroying a house.[59] "Judge Cardozo's position was: 'If I run down the box the only interest invaded is the ownership of that box … I have not been negligent towards any other interest, that is, to the adjoining property.'"[60]

51 *Id.* at 119.

52 *Id.*

53 The author states that the appellate division decision was noted in a few legal journals. *Id.* at 95 (citing *Fireworks Blast Laid to Railroad*, N.Y. Times, Dec. 10, 1927, at 29).

54 Noonan, *supra* note 18, at 114–15.

55 *Id.* at 118–19.

56 *Id.* at 120.

57 Manz, *supra* note 3, at 95 (citing William L. Prosser, *Palsgraf Revisited*, 52 Mich. L. Rev. 1, 4–5 (1953)).

58 *Id.* at 95 n.5 (noting that the date of this discussion is in dispute).

59 *Id.*

60 *Id.* (citing American Law Institute, Torts Conference Minutes, 1, 39–43 (Oct. 23, 1927), *reprinted in* Andrew L. Kaufman, Cardozo 291 (1998)).

In 1976, then Berkeley law professor John T. Noonan, Jr. devoted a chapter in his book *Persons and Masks of the Law* to Judge Cardozo's opinion in the *Palsgraf* case.[61] His theme throughout the book is how seminal legal opinions often erase or deny the humanity of the plaintiff-petitioner in the application and explanation of legal rules. In the *Palsgraf* case, Noonan argues, Judge Cardozo abandoned a people-centered approach to the law asking instead what outcome is best for "the welfare of society."[62] By reducing Helen Palsgraf to a pronoun, the opinion masked the injustice of the decision.[63] He argued that the majority opinion ignored her personal trauma and the high number of annual railroad-related accidents.[64] For Noonan, the abstract fairness of the legal rule announced in *Palsgraf*, seemingly formulated in a social and political vacuum, masked the reality that the rule benefited the economic interests of powerful and moneyed railroad companies.[65]

The most comprehensive history of the *Palsgraf* case and the major actors is William Manz's book, *The* Palsgraf *Case*.[66] In addition to the question of whether Judge Cardozo improperly discussed the case at an ALI meeting, Manz argued that the facts relied on by the judges on the court of appeals in *Palsgraf*, including Judge Andrews, misstated the facts of the case as reflected in the trial transcript. Specifically, he asserted that the trial record suggested that Palsgraf was probably only 10 feet away from the explosion.[67]

The most telling aspect of the case may be the court of appeal's curt dismissal of the motion for reargument, suggesting that Palsgraf's actual proximity to the explosion was immaterial to the majority's decision. Instead, it seems that limiting the legal liability of railroads, an important transporter of commerce in the early twentieth century, was the imperative. Judge Cardozo's duty analysis in *Palsgraf* is reflected in *The Restatement (Second) of Torts*.[68] However,*The Restatement (Third) of Torts* arguably rejects Judge Cardozo's duty analysis and treats the case as turning on the question of proximate cause.[69]

[61] Noonan, *supra* note 18, at 111–51.
[62] *Id.* at 137.
[63] *Id.* at 112–13, 136.
[64] *Id.* at 136–39.
[65] *Id.* at 137–39.
[66] Manz, *supra* note 3.
[67] *Id.* at 4.
[68] *Id.* at 110 n. 78 (citing Richard A. Epstein, Torts § 10.13 (1999) (citing Restatement (Second) of Torts § 281 cmt. c (1979)).
[69] *Id.* at 111.

THE FEMINIST DISSENT

Maurice Dyson's feminist dissent in *Palsgraf* puts the plaintiff, Helen Palsgraf, back at the center of the decision. Unlike Judge Andrews's dissenting opinion, Dyson's dissent spells out in greater detail the facts the New York Appellate Division considered crucial to the resolution of the case. His opinion adopts many of the legal arguments advanced by Palsgraf's lawyer. First, the dissent agrees that proximate cause is a question for the factfinder, in this case, the jury, and not a question of law subject to review by the appellate court. Second, the dissent criticizes the New York Court of Appeals majority for mischaracterizing the facts as reflected in the trial transcript.

Tracking the reasoning of the New York Appellate Division, the feminist dissent emphasizes the "higher" duty owed by common carriers, such as railway companies, to their paying passengers, a point Judge Cardozo does not seriously consider. Instead, in concluding that Palsgraf did not fall within the zone of danger created by any carelessness on the part of the railroad's employees, Judge Cardozo imposed a foreseeability requirement before business invitees like Palsgraf are owed a duty of care. This reasoning, the dissent claims, is inconsistent with prevailing common law. Thus, despite Judge Cardozo's claims to the contrary, the majority decision is not grounded in existing law.

The dissent also exposes the inherent gender bias in Judge Cardozo's opinion. It argues that Judge Cardozo does not treat Palsgraf as sympathetically as other accident victims whose cases he considered. The opinion cites, as an example, a case decided seven years earlier, *Hynes v. New York C.R. Co.*,[70] involving a 16-year-old boy killed when an electrical wire owned by the railroad fell on him as he was diving off a plank into the Harlem River. In that case Judge Cardozo, in reversing the lower court decision in favor of the railroad, employed "colorful, vivid and sympathetic narratives." The explicit suggestion is that Judge Cardozo seemed to identify more with the trespassing teenaged boy rather than with the hard-working mother – a decidedly gendered perspective. The feminist dissent suggests that Judge Cardozo may have had a hard time conceiving of a woman as a business invitee. During this era, judges routinely treated women as second-class citizens whose primary place was in the home, not the public sphere.

Cardozo's failure to mention Palsgraf's injuries illustrate this point. Her injuries were not considered worthy of remedy. Legal feminists have long argued that in calculating damage awards, injuries to men (particularly white

[70] Hynes v. New York C.R. Co., 131 N.E. 898 (N.Y. 1921).

men) are more highly valued than injuries to women of all races and non-white men.[71]

Further, Palsgraf's alleged injuries – stammering and nervousness (largely "shock" or what today we might call post-traumatic stress disorder) – were considered by many men as evidence of women's fragility. The Victorian-era notion of the "fragile woman" applied to white women whose fragility allegedly made them unsuited for public life. Thus, courts and others explicitly or implicitly invoke this notion to justify denying, among other things, women admission to certain professions[72] and prohibiting them from serving on juries.[73]

Judge Cardozo may also have realized that the plight of "abandoned" working-class women with children, such as Palsgraf, if known, might garner public sympathy. Thus, the erasure of Palsgraf the person from the majority opinion's narrative was necessary to make the decision seem fair and neutral. Judge Cardozo's approach to decision-making is consistent with legal formalism, an important legal theory that remains influential today. Legal formalism, espoused by such legal scholars as Christopher Columbus Langdell and Oliver Wendell Holmes, assumed that law is rational, apolitical, and technical. Legal categories and methodologies were defined by what jurists and scholars claimed were neutral standards which made it difficult for analysts to appreciate the rich diversity existing between different groups due to factors like gender, socioeconomic class, or race.[74] Instead, formalist analysis was based on the experiences and thinking of privileged white men. During the *Palsgraf* era, this mainstream or centrist approach to law prevailed as the model taught in law school, without any real organized dissent.[75]

[71] Martha Chamallas, *Questioning the Use of Race-Specific and Gender-Specific Economic Data in Tort Litigation: A Constitutional Argument*, 63 FORDHAM L. REV. 73, 84–89 (1994); Elaine Gibson, *The Gendered Wage Dilemma in Personal Injury Damages*, *in* TORT THEORY 185 (Ken Cooper-Stephenson & Elaine Gibson eds., 1993); Jamie Cassels, *Damages for Lost Earning Capacity: Women and Children Last!*, 71 CAN. B. REV. 445, 456–67 (1992); Jane Goodman et al., *Money, Sex, and Death: Gender Bias in Wrongful Death Damage Awards*, 25 L. & SOC'Y REV. 263 (1991). *See also*, Frank M. McClellan, *The Dark Side of Tort Reform: Searching for Racial Justice*, 48 RUTGERS L. REV. 761, 772–76 (1996) (racial disparities).

[72] *See, e.g.*, Bradwell v. Illinois, 83 U.S. 130 (1873) (denying women the right to practice law).

[73] Ironically, the United States Supreme Court in *Strauder v. West Virginia*, 100 U.S. 303 (1880) ruled that the exclusion of African American males from the jury was unconstitutional, but allowed the rule excluding women jurors to stand. In 1942 the Supreme Court specifically upheld the exclusion of women from the jury in *Glasser v. U.S.*, 315 U.S. 60 (1942).

[74] For a discussion of this point, *see*, Gary Minda, *One Hundred Years of Modern Legal Thought: From Langdell and Holmes to Posner and Schlag*, 28 IND. L. REV. 353, 357–67 (1995).

[75] Legal realism, popular among a small group of progressive legal scholars from the 1920s through the 1940s, was the only attempt to challenge legal formalism. *See* Brian Z. Tamanaha, *Understanding Legal Realism*, 87 TEX. L. REV. 731, 751 (2009). Judge Cardozo, among other

Rejecting the majority's formalist approach, the feminist dissent criticizes the majority for tolerating what Dyson characterizes as the "unreasonably risky masculine behavior" of the railroad's employees in facilitating the boarding of the package-carrying passenger. While the majority treats running after and jumping onto moving trains as normative, the dissent sees this behavior as decidedly masculine conduct that women, because of their clothing alone, could never safely undertake. To the majority, the reasonable person is male, and its application of the reasonable person standard fails to consider important differences between the conduct and perceptions of women and men. In this respect, Dyson's dissent resembles the arguments of feminist scholars who have critiqued the application of the reasonable person standard in hostile work environment cases for failing to consider women's views about appropriate sexual conduct, often resulting in the dismissal of women's claims.[76]

In Dyson's view, Judge Cardozo's application of the facially neutral zone of danger test also demonstrates implicit gender bias. Dyson sees a moving train with its open doors as an open invitation to passengers to race across the station platform in a way that could foreseeably endanger other waiting passengers such as Palsgraf. If the type of harm, including shock, is reasonably foreseeable and linked to the defendant's careless conduct, Dyson argues, it should not matter that the passenger carrying the package accepted the railroad's invitation to engage in careless behavior like jumping on the moving train. As the feminist dissent points out, when Judge Cardozo denies Palsgraf's legally protected interest as a railroad passenger to be free of injury caused by the carelessness of the railroad or its employees, it simultaneously prioritizes the harm to the male passenger's package, an inanimate object, subordinating Palsgraf's right to recover for her personal injury.

In straining to protect the railroad's interests, Judge Cardozo denied that the carelessness of its employees was enough for liability to attach for Palsgraf's injuries. In doing so, he announced and applied a subjective and abstract zone of danger test, a seeming contradiction. In Judge Cardozo's de novo interpretation of the facts, Palsgraf could not recover because she was not sufficiently close to the two male employees and the package-carrying passenger whose actions defined the danger zone. For Dyson, this outcome has some

noted scholars, criticized this movement. BENJAMIN J. CARDOZO, THE NATURE OF THE JUDICIAL PROCESS, 128 (1921).

76 Elizabeth L. Shoenfelt, Allison E. Maue, & JoAnn Nelson, *Reasonable Person versus Reasonable Woman: Does It Matter?*, 10 AM. U. J. GENDER, SOC. POL'Y & L. 633 (2002). Note, some scholars argue that the reasonable woman standard is similarly inadequate. *See* Ann C. McGinley, *Reasonable Men?*, 45 CONN. L. REV.1 (2012) (arguing for a "multidimensional masculinities" approach in sexual harassment cases).

disturbing echoes of a not-too-distant past when a woman's relational ties to men through marriage was a prerequisite to vindication of her right to recover in law.

The dissent ends by calling into question whether the rule announced by the majority will reduce train accidents by encouraging property owners to exercise ordinary care toward customers. As the fate of the Long Island Railway Company illustrates, in the end, the attempt by Judge Cardozo to insulate railroad companies from legal liability for accidents to its passengers failed. Justice was denied and the attempt to protect business economic interests failed as well.

PALSGRAF v. LONG ISLAND RAILROAD CO., 162 N.E. 99 (N.Y. 1928)

JUDGE MAURICE R. DYSON, DISSENTING

This action was originally instituted by plaintiff, Helen Palsgraf, to recover damages for personal injuries alleged to have been caused by the negligent actions of employees of the Long Island Railroad (LIRR) Company, when an explosion erupted on defendant's platform where plaintiff was standing, and she was injured as a result. The medical and personal testimony given at trial indicated that plaintiff suffered bruising over her body, soreness, painful injuries, and hysteria, and that the shock to her nervous system caused stammering and stuttering of speech.[1] Ultimately, plaintiff was rendered practically mute as a consequence of the explosion and is currently unable to work, forced to rely on her children to work to support the family.[2]

[1] Plaintiff's doctor confirmed that the explosion resulting in plaintiff's body being violently thrown up against a partition and metal scales was deemed to be a competent cause of her bruised injuries and the extreme panic, stammering, and dazed nervous shock, *see* Direct Examination of Karl A. Parshall, at 2. Furthermore, despite her doctor's administration of bromides and nerve tonics, plaintiff's nervous condition has persisted for nearly three years since the incident and ostensibly appears to be permanent, *see also* Cross-Examination of Karl A. Parshall, at 2.

[2] Plaintiff's condition after the accident did not enable her to readily speak, at least not without some difficulty. See Transcript of Mr. Wood's Direct Examination of Dr. Graeme M. Hammond at 2 ("Q. Doctor, can you say, with a reasonable degree of certainty in your opinion, whether or not there will be a continuation of these symptoms and this trouble? A. Yes. Q. What is your best opinion on that? A. Well, while her mind is disturbed by litigation she will not recover, but after litigation ceases – I don't mean by that her getting any verdict but as soon as the worry of the trial is over and she knows she doesn't have to go here on the witness stand and undergo cross-examination she should make a fairly good recovery in about three years. Q. Of course that is problematical, is it, doctor? A. Yes, sir. Q. That is, she may recover or

Pending now before the court is defendant's appeal of the judgment of the Appellate Division of the Supreme Court in the Second Judicial Department of New York, which affirmed the trial court's holding that defendant was responsible for the harm to plaintiff. 222 A.D. 166 (1927).

I FACTUAL BACKGROUND

On May 31, 1927, the clerk's office of Kings County entered a judgment in favor of plaintiff, for plaintiff's negligence action against the LIRR. *Palsgraf v. Long I. R. Co.*, 1927 N.Y. App. Div. 7823, 1. A jury found that the railroad employees' acts were negligent and rendered a verdict for $6,000.[3] The trial court denied defendant's motion for a new trial and defendant appealed. The Supreme Court affirmed the previous court's judgment and defendant appealed to this court. The majority of the court reversed and dismissed plaintiff's suit. For the reasons elaborated herein, I dissent from the majority and would affirm the lower courts below.

Helen Palsgraf is a 43-year-old mother of three. An industrious, hard-working woman, she manages to eke out a living on her salary of approximately $10 per month as a janitor in Brooklyn.[4] Separated from her husband, Palsgraf decided to treat her two daughters, Elizabeth, 15 years old, and Lillian, 12 years old, to a Sunday outing at Rockaway Beach.

On that hot summer day, the Palsgraf family took the elevated Brooklyn–Manhattan Transportation (BMT) train southeast from Ridgewood to East New York's Atlantic Avenue station, descended the stairs down to the street from those tracks, then climbed up another flight of stairs to the slightly less elevated adjacent tracks of the LIRR. Once there, Palsgraf purchased tickets, and the family awaited the arrival of the next train to the beach. The railroad

she may not? A. Well, she might be dead. If she lives, she may recover in about three years. Q. Well, doctor, this condition having now persisted for nearly three years already, the symptoms not having diminished in that time, would you say that that would bar her recovery three years from now? A. Yes, her symptoms never would get any better as long as the litigation was pending. She hasn't a chance to get well until this trial is over. Q. But that might take two or three years from now? A. Yes, all of that. Q. Tell the jury, please, in your own way, what you found her condition then to be? A. Yes. I noticed, first, that she stammered quite a good deal, and it was with difficulty that she could talk at all. If she persisted she would get the words out").

3 *See* Trial Record at 35–36. Pursuant to statute, plaintiff also recovered costs of $142.45 which were added to the verdict.

4 In addition to janitorial work, plaintiff also performed supplemental housework duties to make ends meet in order to pay her rent of $14, a considerable sum given her limited means. *See* Plaintiff Direct Examination Transcript, at 2.

station in East Long Island was loud, crowded, and bustling, with dozens of people shuffling about when a whistle blew, an engine began to chug along, and the nearest train started to crawl down the tracks away from the station. A train came, but not the intended one, as it was bound for the opposite direction of Jamaica, Queens, and from there to points north.

Although onlookers realized that it was too late to board the departing train, this apparently did not dissuade two men who, seemingly out of nowhere, darted out of a throng of people and raced toward the locomotive. The train still had its doors open. One of the men reached the platform of the car without mishap, although the train was already moving. The other man, barely able to fully grasp his arm around a large oval-shaped package he was holding, quickly darted across the platform. In his haste to catch the moving locomotive, he hit a nearby passenger, Grace Gerhardt, in the stomach as she was waiting for the train with her husband. He then jumped aboard the moving train car. He seemed unsteady, as if about to fall, according to the LIRR. The conductor on the car held the door open to the moving train, apparently inviting the man's risky attempt to board and then proceeded to reach forward to pull the passenger into the moving train. Still another man, also a conductor on the platform, proceeded to push the man from behind. In the behavior of these two conductors, along with the two men chasing after the train, is where we now find the genesis of the tragic negligence that has befallen plaintiff.

Under the boarding passenger's arm was a sizeable, oval-shaped package roughly 15 inches long wrapped in the morning's newspaper. In fact, what the man was carrying in the package was a bundle of fireworks. Maybe the conductors noticed the package, or maybe they did not. But as the package became dislodged in the course of the tussle of one conductor pushing and the other tugging on the passenger, none could fail to notice the bundled package any longer because its fall onto the train tracks below created a tremendous thunder of explosions when the rear wheel of the train struck it.[5]

Several large explosions, likely six, but perhaps as many as twenty-four, followed that could be heard blocks away, filling the station with a fireball, and plumes of black smoke. The explosions were of such magnitude that after the initial shock of the burst, they violently ripped apart the wooden planks of the train platform. In fact, the platform was so shaken to its core that it managed to shatter the glass in a penny scale, which, according to some news

[5] According to the testimony of one eyewitness, the passenger was carrying the package under his arm in his right hand, and he noticed the package fall when the guard on the outside platform pushed the passenger's right arm. *See* Direct Examination of Herbert Gerhardt, at 1–2.

accounts, was allegedly no more than 10 feet away from where Palsgraf was waiting for her train. *Bomb Blast Injures 13 in Station Crowd*, *N.Y. Times*, Aug 25, 1924, at 1.

Making matters worse, the heavy penny scale, which was roughly the same height as plaintiff, was knocked off its resting place and landed onto her, allegedly knocking her down.[6] While there seems to be speculation about whether it was the scale or the crowd that knocked plaintiff over, we note the trial record is devoid of any evidence from the witnesses present to indicate the crowd was the cause. Indeed, none of the witnesses who testified at trial ever claimed that it was the crowd or a stampede that knocked plaintiff down. In the ensuing melee, however, twelve other persons were injured.

I now turn to the reasons why I believe that the majority has erred in its evaluation of the facts and its determination of the law governing this case.

II THE MAJORITY USURPS THE FUNCTION OF THE JURY BY MAKING FACTUAL DETERMINATIONS UNDER THE GUISE OF DECIDING QUESTIONS OF LAW

When deciding appeals from cases of this sort, we must be mindful not to usurp the function of the jury by directly attacking or indirectly reopening issues of fact for the jury, under the guise of addressing questions of law for the court. Yet that is precisely what our colleague Judge Cardozo, writing for the majority, has done in declaring that "the conduct of the Defendant's guard, if a wrong in its relation to the holder of the package, was not a wrong in relation to plaintiff, standing far away. Relative to her, it was not negligence at all." *Palsgraf v. Long Island R.R.Co.*, 162 N.E. 99, 99 (N.Y. 1928).

To support this contention, the majority proffers a new foreseeable zone of danger test. I write in dissent because I cannot endorse such a test, however intellectually adorned, because it is nothing more than fanciful legal fiction

[6] Plaintiff testified on direct examination that she was standing next to the scale when "flying glass" and a "ball of fire" came toward her and her family such that they were "chocked in smoke." With protective instincts, she quickly told her daughter Elizabeth to turn her back away from the flying glass for fear of getting cut. It was at that time when plaintiff testified that the scale near her blew and hit the left side of her arm, thigh, and leg, bruising her body, as she trembled with shock. In the ensuing chaos of the dark smoke, plaintiff remembered her little daughter, Lillian, crying out "I want my mamma!" She was then assisted in her escape to safety by a police officer. *See* Direct Examination of Helen Palsgraf, at 3–4. Another witness testified that the scales were busted and blown to pieces and laid on the platform. *See* Direct Examination of Herbert Gerhardt, at 2.

and we are not at liberty to rewrite the facts nor supplant existing common law.

It is indisputable that this court has no authority to resolve factual disputes. Whether the LIRR employees' conduct was negligent clearly is such a factual question and it has already been decided by the jury and reviewed by five Appellate Division judges. In evaluating this appeal I therefore accept the jury's finding that the conductors' actions of pulling and pushing the passenger holding the package onto a moving train constituted negligence. As evidenced in the trial record, defendant failed to abide by lawful regulations as well as its own safety procedures and practices regarding its employees' conduct.[7] It is not for this bench perched from on high to pronounce what is fact and what is not with respect to plaintiff's claims and injuries. See *Saugerties Bank v. Delaware & Hudson Co.*, 141 N.E. 904, 905 (N.Y. 1923) ("ordinarily it is to be determined as a question of fact whether there has been such a connection between cause and effect as to make the former proximate"); *Boyce v. Greeley Square Hotel*, 126 N.E. 647, 650 (N.Y. 1920) ("It is a rule in actions for negligence that it must generally be left to the jury to determine under the evidence the natural, proximate and fairly to be apprehended consequences of the negligence. It is likewise a rule that in actions for acts tortious in character it must be generally left to the jury to determine under the evidence the direct consequences of the acts").

III THE MAJORITY USURPS THE FUNCTION OF THE JURY BY MISCHARACTERIZING THE FACTS AND DISTORTING THE FACTUAL RECORD

I must begin by noting that any claim that Palsgraf was "distant," "far away," or "far removed" from the situs of the explosion or the negligence, as suggested by the majority, does not appear to have any basis in the trial record.[8] Nor is there anything in the factual record to support Judge Cardozo's assertion that

[7] *Palsgraf v. Long Island R. R. Co.* Court Transcript at 1064. Plaintiff also alleged that at the time of the incident, between the hours of 10 and 11 on the day in question, when defendant knew there was a habitual custom of passengers to congregate in dangerously large numbers where jostling frequently occurred defendant also "failed to provide a sufficient number of employee guards and agents and to make, promulgate and enforce rules and regulations for the guidance and control of its employees." *See* Plaintiff's Complaint at 3.

[8] When Mr. McNamara, counsel for defendant, asked how far plaintiff stood from the explosion, plaintiff testified she did not know which train car took the explosion given the resulting confusion caused by the explosion noting "[t]he whole station seemed to be in a blaze to me at the time." *See* Defendant Cross-Examination of Helen Palsgraf, at 3.

Palsgraf "stood at the other end of the platform many feet away." *Palsgraf*, 162 N.E. at 99. If something conceivably was said during oral argument, this court has no transcription of it either made during the trial, or in the briefs submitted before us, or from the courts below. However, given that proximity to the explosion is the linchpin upon which the majority rests its newly articulated zone of danger test, it is understandable why such liberties were taken with the facts and I strongly dissent from such a distortion of the record.

It is far from clear that plaintiff was as remote from the danger as the majority would have us believe. It is also evident that the majority has markedly understated the magnitude of damage, the number of victims harmed, and the severity of injuries sustained in the ensuing commotion resulting from defendant's negligence. The record shows that Palsgraf may have been standing no more than 10 feet away from the series of violent multiple explosions that were of such force as to rip apart a station platform and injure twelve others. This distortion of the factual record has the effect of making the causal nexus between defendant's negligence and plaintiff's injury appear dim and indirect, thereby assisting the majority in portraying what happened that tragic day as a freakish, unforeseeable event, rather than the natural and probable consequence of a negligent act. While the majority seeks to proffer a new doctrinal philosophy, I cannot endorse a judicial process where expedient ends are procured by such means.

IV THE MAJORITY'S RENDITION OF THE FACTS EMPLOYS A DOUBLE STANDARD AND DISPLAYS A LACK OF SYMPATHY FOR PLAINTIFF

In its opinion, the majority characterizes Helen Palsgraf as a plaintiff without age, family status, purpose, or occupation. This scant, unsympathetic portrayal of plaintiff, I submit, paves the way for the draconian result in this case, ultimately culminating in denying recovery to an admittedly severely injured woman. In this respect, Judge Cardozo's approach stands in stark contrast to the colorful, vivid, and sympathetic narratives he has employed in other tort cases where he has been willing to find a remedy for the plaintiff. Consider, for instance, his detailed and personalized rendition of the facts relating to the plaintiff, Harvey Hynes, in *Hynes v. New York C.R. Co.*, 131 N.E. 898 (N.Y. 1921). The dispute in that case was whether a diving plank with a fallen electrical wire that Hynes came into contact with was private or public property. In other words, the question was whether the plaintiff was a trespasser to whom no duty was owed.

In *Hynes*, Judge Cardozo referred to the plaintiff as a "young lad," "a lad of sixteen," who "swam with two companions from the Manhattan to the Bronx side of the Harlem river or United States Ship canal, a navigable stream."[9] His willingness in that case to employ a detailed, sympathetic story of traveling boys engaging in youthful mischief allowed him to set the stage for arguing the case for the plaintiff's recovery.

To reach the desired result, Judge Cardozo reasoned that although the plank was technically a fixture, it was so close to the river that the two were inextricable, and to consider the plank strictly private property would be splitting hairs. He further observed that the plank belongs to the private sphere in the technical and artificial sense, to the public sphere in the realistic one, making it clear that the realist's view is to be preferred. But a man's realist view can vary widely from that of a woman's and I caution my brethren to be mindful of our own biases here. Perhaps it is easier for men such as ourselves to see a younger imagined version of ourselves in the boy Harvey Hynes than in Helen Palsgraf. If so, it only lends further weight to my concern that what is a foreseeable duty is in the eye of the beholder who wields the judicial pen. It is regrettable that Judge Cardozo gave more attention to how the law should categorize an inanimate object, such as a plank, than to the legal status and predicament of Palsgraf, who might as well have been a static fixture on the platform with no legal significance. While defendant's breach of duty in the case at bar has tragically produced injuries which have literally rendered plaintiff mute, regrettably, the majority has through its factual distortion and double standard, effectively rendered her claim legally mute.

As faithful stewards of the principled application of law, this court must remain vigilant to exercise with integrity an uncompromising fidelity to applicable precedent. In my view, Helen Palsgraf is just as deserving of our sympathy as Harvey Hynes. As Judge Cardozo has declared, the law should not be taken to such a "dryly logical extreme", *Hynes*, 131 N.E. at 900, and we can similarly state here that "[w]e think that considerations of analogy, of convenience, of policy, and of justice, exclude [Helen Palsgraf] from the field of the Defendant's immunity and exemption, and place [her] in the field of liability and duty." *id.*

9 Harvey Hynes swam with his two companions to the United States Ship canal where the New York Central railroad operated its trains using high tension wires strung on poles and cross arms. Hynes climbed on top of the bulkhead onto a springboard and was poised to leap into the water when a cross arm with electric wires fell from defendant's pole. The falling wires struck him and flung him from the plank, causing him to plunge to his death below. The judgment of the Appellate Division and the Trial Term was reversed, and a new trial was ordered.

V THE MAJORITY IGNORES WELL-ESTABLISHED COMMON-LAW DOCTRINE WITH RESPECT TO THE BUSINESS-INVITEE DUTY

Under the common-law rule, premises holders owe a greater duty to their business invitees than to others on their land for nonbusiness purposes. A person is defined as a business invitee when that person enters the land of another with the owner's knowledge and for their mutual benefit. Defendant here received a benefit because plaintiff purchased three tickets, thereby bestowing the benefit of monetary gain to defendant. Because she was a ticket holder waiting to board the train at the time of the incident, I can only conclude that Palsgraf was a business invitee.[10] I am unconvinced by defendant's suggestion that a duty was owed to plaintiff only after she boarded the train and not while she stood on defendant's platform waiting to board with her ticket in hand. To so distinguish between patrons would be splitting hairs based on legal niceties upon which a determination of duty should not rest.

It is also sometimes said that a landowner cannot be an insurer of every business visitor's safety. Yet the duty owed to an invitee is, in fact, an affirmative duty to seek, detect and remediate even latent defects that may harm all those on its land.[11] Therefore, contrary to the majority, we do not believe the newly articulated foreseeable zone of danger duty should exclude or override all consideration of the common-law business-invitee duty. Indeed, the duty owed is not what is merely observable to the vigilant eye, but, rather, it is the duty to make oneself aware of latent dangers that may not be readily observable. The risk is not limited solely to what one reasonably perceives any more than is the duty limited to that which is within the range of apprehension – it is, in fact, a special relationship which heightens the duty of care to reasonably inspect for the safety of the unsuspecting business traveler.

[10] Having paid her fare and those of her children as she waited for the next train to arrive, we think it is clear that she is not the vicarious beneficiary of a breach of duty to another, but rather the party to whom a duty was directly owed as an invitee.

[11] Furthermore, in a busy hub, such as the one here, it is vital that all objects stationed on a platform be securely bolted down. Thus, even if one were to conclude that the conductors' actions were not negligent in causing plaintiff's injuries, the falling of the scales may be evidence of negligence. Additionally, defendant could have taken the simple, cost-effective precaution of closing the gap between the train and the platform. At trial, both plaintiff and Herbert Gerhardt testified that the gap between the train and platform must have been at least 15–18 inches wide because it was substantial enough for the package to fall through, and indeed was large enough for a small child to be injured as well. The danger posed by these perilous conditions was clear. Leaving such an opening in a train platform should result in liability to the child who falls into it and likewise to the waiting passenger whose injuries are occasioned by it.

Because defendant owed a duty to plaintiff as a business invitee, it was bound not to take or fail to take any action that unreasonably affected her rights or the rights of other business visitors. It is evident that the conductor's acts here unreasonably affected the rights of several of its business visitors, including Palsgraf, Herbert and Grace Gerhardt, and other patrons on the platform who could be knocked down or injured as a result of defendant's operation of a moving train car with open doors and its mishandling of a passenger boarding its train car.

The majority improperly engrafts the requirement that a plaintiff must be foreseeable in order for a duty to arise, even with respect to its business invitees. This is too grave a limitation. This court has never held that a plaintiff must be in zone of danger to be owed a duty when a plaintiff was harmed. *Palsgraf*, 162 N.E. at 103. Delimiting such a zone of danger puts too much discretion in the court to determine proximity for itself, and to decide whether a plaintiff was close enough or too remote from the danger. Whenever a defendant's conduct poses an unreasonable risk, its consequences are not confined to those who might probably or foreseeably be harmed. We know children may recover for the negligent killing of their parent by an errant train, just as a spouse may be compensated for the loss of the other for the same negligence. None of these recoveries were ever prevented on the theory that no duty was owing to the plaintiffs because they were outside the zone of danger. Therefore, I hold to the principle that the common-law duty owed to business invitees similarly must extend to a female passenger's right to safety and we must trace defendant's negligent conduct to its consequences. Instead of placing plaintiffs, such as Palsgraf, outside the zone of danger, the law, properly understood, situates her as a natural and probable victim entitled to recovery upon proof of defendant's negligence.

Why then was this clear invitee duty overlooked in the instant case? I fear that for the majority duty is in the eye of the beholder and that the beholder may at times be blinded by common prejudices and presumptions. Perhaps in this case the majority may have been disinclined to view Palsgraf as a business visitor but instead saw her simply as a mother traveling with her children. But such a view would be patently unfair. I must ask: Is not the purchasing power of Helen Palsgraf's dollar as a business visitor entitled to the same equal weight in the eyes of the majority?[12] It would seem that Judge Cardozo's failure of

[12] We are mindful that, on plaintiff's limited salary, purchasing a ticket for herself and her two daughters, while also being asked to pay for her medical bills and the costs of this suit, is no light matter. While in the eyes of the law, her dollar is equal to that of every business invitee on the platform, hers likely came at a heavier price and with far greater sacrifice attached to it.

imagination tragically resulted in his never truly seeing the business-invitee rights of a woman through any eyes but his own.

VI THE MAJORITY IGNORES WELL-ESTABLISHED COMMON-LAW DOCTRINE WITH RESPECT TO THE COMMON CARRIER-PASSENGER DUTY

The common law has long imposed a duty on common carriers to exercise a high degree of care for the safety of their passengers. This elevated standard of care is based on a recognition that the privilege of serving the public as a common carrier necessarily entails a heavy responsibility and justifies imposing a greater duty toward patrons. In this case, defendant owed a duty to all its passengers to make sure that they were able to board and travel on the train in a reasonably safe manner. In this case, the conductors claimed that when they rushed to push and pull the boarding passenger onto the moving train, they were simply helping or assisting him and exercising care for his safety. What the majority apparently fails to appreciate, however, is the unreasonable danger posed by the conductors' actions. Although the passenger was in a rush to catch the train, instead of pushing him onto the moving train, the conductors could have and should have taken a number of safer alternative actions, such as advising him to catch the next train, or signaling to the train's conductor not to pull off or leave the station with the doors open, or refraining from extending a helping hand to invite the boarding passenger in, or simply not extending a helping hand to push him onto the train. Given the range of alternative, safer courses of action, the jury was permitted to conclude that the railroad breached its duty to exercise a high degree of care for its passengers.

Under the common carrier duty, plaintiff was entitled to no lesser protection than the boarding passenger. A railroad company which allows a moving train to exit without taking reasonable precautions is a wrongdoer toward all passengers and intending passengers injured by its imprudence.

The majority's approach not only rewards the foolhardy actions of the conductors and the boarding passenger, but in the process penalizes innocent parties such as Palsgraf.[13] Indeed, it can be said that the only actor who was clearly not negligent in this entire fiasco was Palsgraf herself. Yet she alone is

[13] It has long been a maxim in tort law that as between two innocent parties, the one who occasions the loss ought to bear it. But, as noted, the only truly innocent party here is plaintiff. It is unconscionable then for the majority to place the burden solely upon her shoulders. In my view, the party that is in the best position to effectuate proper precautions to prevent harm ought to be party that bears the burden of doing so. Whether by failing to engage in proper passenger handling, locomotive safety, crowd control, or remedying the premises defects,

being asked to absorb all the costs of the negligence of these three men. Surely one can see the absurdity and unfairness of such a result.

VII THE MAJORITY DISREGARDS THE FACT THAT PLAINTIFF WAS WITHIN THE SO-CALLED ZONE OF DANGER

Disregarding both the business invitee and common carrier doctrines, the majority proclaims that no duty was owed to plaintiff because it was unforeseeable under the circumstances that she could be injured. However, even if one accepts that a duty of care is owed only to a foreseeable plaintiff, such a duty should clearly extend to an intending passenger on defendant's platform who might well be injured by other passengers who could knock them as they rush aboard a moving train. Surely it is foreseeable that those rushing to board the train could harm those on the platform where plaintiff stood. And, if that is so, the zone of danger must also include her as a passenger.

Consider Grace Gerhardt who, while also waiting for the train, stood on the very same platform, and was hit in the stomach by the careless passenger bearing the package as he quickly ran to board the train. What if the package of firework explosives had fallen and exploded at that point? If harm could befall her, it could certainly also threaten Palsgraf, her two daughters, or any other passenger waiting to board the train, and it is defendant's negligence that made ripe the conditions for such injuries and indeed made them more likely to occur.

Foreseeability of harm was present when those running in haste to catch a departing train confronted a throng of waiting passengers on the platform. From this vantage point, the passengers on the platform, including plaintiff, stood in the zone of danger. Unlike the majority, I am not oblivious to the fact that it was defendant's policy of encouraging passengers to board moving locomotives with open doors that invited the hurried rush and mischief and increased the chances that a calamity would occur. So long as it was foreseeable that Helen Palsgraf could be injured from passenger collisions encouraged by defendant's negligence, the unforeseeable manner of the intervening event is of no consequence.[14] This is a fundamental tenet at the heart of proximate causation that the majority fails to comprehend. Accordingly, we

defendant was in the best position to avoid the harm here and it failed to do so. As such, the burden falls squarely upon it and accrues to the benefit of all passengers, including plaintiff.

[14] While defendant may claim the negligence of the man running for a train while carrying fireworks severed LIRR's alleged negligence from Helen Palsgraf's injury, it is also established law that negligence by third parties does not break the chain of causation. Further, when a defendant's negligent acts invite such third-party negligence, it is foreseeable and thus

are not persuaded by the majority's newly fashioned rules redefining the scope of liability under the so-called zone of danger doctrine that would exclude recovery here. Palsgraf's injuries to her body, mind, and soul, constitute the most vivid evidence that she was within the zone of danger.

VIII THE MAJORITY'S APPROACH TOLERATES UNREASONABLY RISKY MASCULINE BEHAVIOR BY ITS EMPLOYEES AND MISAPPLIES THE EMERGENCY DOCTRINE

In addition to denying that defendant owed a duty of care to plaintiff, defendant and the majority also attempt to excuse defendant's behavior, implying that there was nothing at all unreasonably risky in the conductors' conduct. In its brief, counsel for defendant alleged that the conductors could not have stopped the man from boarding, and that once he had flung himself onto the train, the conductors had little choice but to help him. As they contended, confronted with such an emergency, they cannot be found negligent because they chose to assist the man rather than leave him to fall. Defendant's application of the emergency doctrine, however, is fatally flawed. Although it may be said that conductors were faced with an emergency when the boarding passenger tried to dash onto the train, the emergency doctrine that excuses otherwise negligent conduct is inapposite where, as here, the emergency is of defendant's own making. Thus, there would have been no emergency had defendant operated its train properly and closed the train doors before exiting the station.[15] It cannot now rely on the emergency presented to excuse its own prior negligence.

Moreover, defendant's benign view of the conductors' behavior, as a kind of benevolent rescue, does not correspond to the facts and testimony presented at trial. Instead, the facts reveal that the conductors aided and encouraged the risky behavior of the boarding passenger, actually increasing the risk to the passengers. Yet the majority seems to regard jumping onto a moving train and pushing and pulling a passenger to board under those conditions as entirely reasonable. If such behavior is thought of as reasonable, however, it is only because rash, young men often behave in such a fashion, and many regard it as normal behavior for such men. Such a view of reasonableness, however, is

chargeable to the defendant. *See* Scott v. Shepherd, 2 Wm. Bl 892 (1773); Vanderburgh v. Truax, 4 Denio 464 (1847); Guille v. Swan, 19 John 381 (1822).

[15] Furthermore, defendant had a duty to properly train its employees and to implement procedures to prevent imprudent passengers from jumping onto moving trains. The invocation of the emergency doctrine does not supplant this duty.

tainted by a masculine bias and should not be used to adjudicate the injury and suffering of a woman such as Helen Palsgraf. We can take notice of the fact that female passengers, wearing long dresses and other constrictive clothing, have no option to jump onto trains or even jump out of harm's way in the same manner as some of their male counterparts. Their rights should not be judged by standards that take no account of their daily realities. Moreover, adopting risky masculine standards also exposes men to significant risks for injuries and fatalities and does nothing to advance the safety of our transportation systems. We are not so constrained to adhere to canons of social convention. Habit, however prevalent, does not balance the limits of right and wrong on the scales of justice, for only the weights of prudence and unreasonable risk may tip the scales so.

IX THE MAJORITY'S APPROACH FAILS TO PROMOTE SAFETY OR ACHIEVE JUSTICE FOR THE PARTIES

As stated above, the majority's constrained view of duty finds no warrant in precedent and I very much doubt that the court's disposition today will promote either safety or justice, the central goals underpinning our American tort system of compensation. First, the majority's approach does not promote safety or deterrence because it fails to provide any incentive for a railroad to remain vigilant and to invest adequate resources to ensure that its personnel are properly trained in handling passengers. Given today's ruling, railroads have no reason to take simple, common-sense steps to make sure that other passengers are not injured by failing to close the doors on moving trains or warning boarding passengers not to take unnecessary risks.

Second, the majority approach does not achieve a just or fair result in balancing the interests of the parties. The majority makes much of the fact that because defendant's employees did not know the contents of the exploding package, it would be unjust to hold it responsible for unforeseeable consequences. However, its view of the equities in this case is misguided. To use the analogy employed by the lower courts, a driver whose car negligently strikes a pedestrian carrying a bottle in his pocket would clearly be liable for injuries caused by the broken glass, despite ignorance of the bottle's presence. Why then should defendant escape liability for its negligence here simply because of its employees' alleged ignorance of the contents of the package? Contrary to the majority's conclusion, it is of no consequence whether the conductors knew of the contents of the package and a non sequitur to suggest that defendant should therefore fortuitously escape liability.

To hypothesize that causation is highly attenuated in this case and thus it would be unfair to hold the LIRR liable is to lose sight of the victim and the actual harmful consequences of defendant's negligence. Instead, judges must appreciate that a victim without a remedy is doubly injured. In my view, plaintiff was injured for the second time when the majority concluded that to be fair to the LIRR, its interests must take precedence over plaintiff's interests. At stake was plaintiff's ability to work, to speak tenderly as a mother to her daughters, and indeed to communicate to her fellow beings. While Judge Cardozo's opinion may have advanced a novel theory of tort liability, it does nothing to promote safety, nor to liberate our thinking from ambiguous concepts such as a "foreseeable zone of danger." Rather, it enslaves us further to it. In my view, we would be wise to resist adopting new theories of tort liability that are unmoored from justice or any sound principle of deterrence.

X THE MAJORITY ADVANCES AN ABSTRACT RELATIONAL CONCEPT OF NEGLIGENCE THAT IGNORES THE REAL RELATIONSHIP AMONG THE PARTIES

My colleagues in the majority would have me believe that "negligence, like risk, is thus a term of relation." *Palsgraf*, 162 N.E. at 101. It is not. Negligence is not a term of qualified relation, but a term of reasonable obligation, one that guards against unreasonable risks of dangers caused by acts or omissions. *Polemis Case* (1921, 3 K.B. 560); *Smith v. London Southwestern Ry. Co.* [1870–71] 6 C.P. 14; *Anthony v. Slaid*, 52 Mass. 290 (1846); *Wood v. Penn. R.R.*, 35 S. 699 (Pa. 1896); *Trashansky v. Hershkovitz*, 147 N.E. 63 (N.Y. 1925).

The majority asserts that the only possible source of duty in this case is one that is derivative of the duty owed to the boarding passenger and denies that such a derivative duty even exists in this case. However, as a business invitee and passenger, Palsgraf did not need to base her claim on some relationship to the acts involving the boarding male passenger. To suggest that her claim needs such vicarious validation is the height of male hubris. In this day and age, we should be reluctant to deny recovery to a female plaintiff simply because of the absence of some spatial proximity or relation to the negligence of the men in this case. We are reminded that it was once the law of this land and in England that women could not vindicate their legal rights in court except through a relational tie to a man, namely their husbands. See *I de S et ux. v. W de S.*, at the Assizes, Y.B. Lib. Ass folio 99, placitum 60 (1348); *Gulf, Colorado & Santa Fe Ry. v. Luther*, 90 S.W. 44 (Tex. Civ. 1905).

Because their independent legal rights were not recognized, women were placed on a different, unequal footing compared to their male counterparts which we should take care not to replicate now.[16] It already counts as a formidable achievement that Palsgraf was able to prevail before an all-male jury at the trial below, without further diminishing her chances of recovery through fashioning new theories of negligence designed to limit liability.

Judge Cardozo is of the view that "[n]egligence in the abstract, apart from things related, is surely not a tort." *Palsgraf*, 162 N.E. at 101. However, while he purports to be adopting a concrete "relational" approach, in reality his is an abstract approach predicated on a conceptual idea of a relationship that asks whether one could imagine any injury to Palsgraf given the negligence of the conductors. The relationship the majority seeks to discern operates only at the mental level, i.e., in the mind of the judge when he decides whether plaintiff is in the zone of danger. Tellingly, the majority here proffers an abstract relational approach that fails to take account of the real human relationship that actually existed in this case, i.e., the one between a passenger and a common carrier. It also ignores the real human costs paid. Defendant's negligence has not only robbed Palsgraf of her livelihood and well-being, it has also stolen the innocence and childhood of her three children. I cannot countenance a duty to protect against foreseeable harms that would not also require a common carrier to protect putative passengers from the foreseeable and everlasting psychological effects of negligence that plaintiff must now endure without legal accountability.

XI THE MAJORITY'S RELATIONAL CONCEPT OF NEGLIGENCE OFTEN LEADS TO A BIASED DETACHMENT THAT UNDERMINES PLAINTIFFS' RIGHTS

In the final analysis, this is not a case involving a freakish set of events whereby plaintiff alone suffered as the sole victim or where the ensuing events somehow violated the laws of physics. Instead, it is on our separation and detachment as men on this bench from the everyday experiences and lives of women and men that gives rise to thoughtless assumptions of remoteness which, in turn, can bias our perception of duty and proximate cause if we are not careful. This is not the kind of detachment that we should rightfully laud as

[16] I take exception to the majority's assertion that "if there was a wrong to him [the boarding passenger] at all, which may very well be doubted, it was a wrong to a property interest only, the safety of the package." *Palsgraf*, 162 N.E.2d at 100. Such a myopic view of the legal duty owed silently acquiesces in the proposition that Helen Palsgraf's status and legal right to recovery is subordinated to that of the safety of an inanimate package a man holds while boarding a train. This approach too is reminiscent of the days when women were once regarded the property of a wedded man.

principled, judicious objectivity, since it may disproportionately lead to a finding that a tragic occurrence is a fluke or that the distress of victims is inconsequential. Detachment is a poor proxy for objectivity and an even poorer substitute for experience. At its heart, tort law concerns itself with the protection of personhood against invasions of bodily integrity, even when done negligently, regardless of the gender of the plaintiff.

We challenge the majority's implied assumption that there is only one reality endowed with objective truth that commands and defines the scope of liability in this case. To the contrary, there is the reality of Grace Gerhardt, Helen Palsgraf, and her daughters Lillian and Elizabeth Palsgraf, whose stories have been ignored in the record and who must now watch as their mother grows silent before their eyes.

3

Commentary on *Escola v. Coca-Cola Bottling Co. of Fresno*

MARY J. DAVIS

INTRODUCTION

As the law of torts evolved from its inception in trespass to predominantly being based in negligence, pockets of strict, or no-fault, liability remained. We think of escaping animals, and ultra-hazardous activities. In the early to mid-twentieth century, with the advent of increases in technology and progressive social ideals, calls emerged for recognition of strict liability in cases of personal injury from product failure. These calls were, however, often grounded in theories of breach of contract based on failed promises of product quality, theories which came with contract defenses that inhibited many plaintiffs from recovering.

Negligence, then, was often a more attractive theory of recovery for product failure. Yet negligence was hard to prove. Enter *Escola v. Coca-Cola Bottling Co. of Fresno*[1] in 1944, in which the California Supreme Court elaborated on and expanded the use of the proof doctrine of *res ipsa loquitur*, "the thing speaks for itself," to a broader category of product failure cases.

The lasting impact of *Escola*, however, emerged from the concurring opinion of Justice Roger Traynor in which he took the bold move to advocate openly for strict liability in tort for product injuries. Justice Traynor articulated the policies that paved the way for the dramatic adoption of strict products liability across the country in the 1960s. Today, strict products liability is the most important category of strict liability in contemporary tort law.

[1] Escola v. Coca-Cola Bottling Co., 150 P.2d 438 (Cal. 1944).

ORIGINAL OPINIONS

Gladys Escola worked as a waitress and manager at Tiny's Waffle Shop in Merced, California.[2] One day in August 1941, as she was removing Coca-Cola bottles from a case to place them in the refrigerator, one of the bottles "exploded" in her hand, breaking into jagged pieces, causing a deep 5-inch cut, and severing blood vessels.[3] After the bottle exploded, the top portion of the bottle remained in Escola's hand, and "the lower portion fell to the floor but did not break."[4]

After surgery, her hand appeared deformed, and for a long time, she was unable to do even the most basic of tasks with it.[5] It was a debilitating injury. Escola, who made $18 a day, received $42.60 in workers' compensation for this injury.[6] This amount did not cover either her medical expenses or her lost wages.[7] Escola was one of many women in the post-Depression/pre–World War II era who worked outside the home and for whom available jobs provided low wages and little job security.[8]

A prominent attorney in town came to the Waffle Shop regularly and encouraged her to sue the Coca-Cola Bottling Company of Fresno that had bottled and sold the bottles to her employer.[9] She did – an act of bravery in

2 Much of the detail on the background of *Escola* can be found in Mark Geistfeld, Escola v. Coca-Cola Bottling Co.: *Strict Products Liability Unbound*, in TORTS STORIES (Robert L. Rabin and Stephen D. Sugarman eds., 2003). Another good historical treatment can be found in Kyle Graham, *Strict Products Liability at 50: Four Histories*, 98 MARQ. L. REV. 555 (2014).

3 *Escola*, 150 P.2d at 438.

4 *Id.*

5 David A. Moss, *Risk, Responsibility, and the Role of Government*, 56 DRAKE L. REV. 541, 553 (2008).

6 Geistfeld, *supra* note 2, at 229.

7 *Id.*

8 *See* MAUREEN HONEY, *The "Womanpower" Campaign: Advertising and Recruitment Propaganda during World War II*, *FRONTIERS, J. WOMEN STUD.* (NWSA: Selected Conf. Proc.) (spring–summer, 1980), at 50; Karen Tucker Anderson, *Last Hired, First Fired: Black Women Workers during World War II*, 69 J. AM. HIST. 82, 87 (1982); Claudia D. Goldin, *The Role of World War II in the Rise of Women's Employment*, 81 AM. ECON. REV. 741, 741 (1981); WILLIAM H. CHAFE, THE AMERICAN WOMAN: HER CHANGING SOCIAL, ECONOMIC, AND POLITICAL ROLES, 1920–1970, 135–95 (1972). *See generally* Andrea McArdle, *The Postwar Consumer as Feminized Legal Subject*, 27 LEGAL STUD. F. 221 (2003).

9 Geistfeld, *supra* note 2, at 229. When Escola's attorney, Ray Robinson, was drafted into the Navy in 1943, he associated the soon-to-be "King of Torts," Melvin Belli, on the case. For more on the trial techniques for which Belli would become famous, and his relationship with the evolution of tort law, see Joseph A. Page, *Roscoe Pound, Melvin Belli, and the Personal Injury Bar: The Tale of an Odd Coupling*, 26 T.M. COOLEY L. REV. 637 (2009).

times when jobs were scarce, and many workers might not want to make waves.

Escola sued the Bottling Company in negligence; as an employee who did not purchase the bottles, she was not in privity with the Bottling Company, which barred a warranty claim. Her entire claim was based on the proof doctrine of *res ipsa loquitur*. This doctrine permits an inference of negligence in the absence of specific proof of negligence in situations when the accident that happened is one that typically happens because of negligence by the one who was in exclusive control of the instrumentality of harm, the defendant.[10] No one had saved the pieces of the bottle so Escola was not able to inspect it to identify a flaw, though such an inspection would have been unlikely to produce meaningful evidence. It was 1941 and the techniques that might be available today to inspect failed products were distant in the future. Pressurized bottles were widely known to explode: it was a serious hazard in the 1930s and 1940s.[11] The pressurization could have been excessive, the glass bottles could have had an imperfection, and rough handling or other pre- and post-distribution impact could have played a role.

As most defendants do, the Bottling Company blamed the explosion on some mishandling by Escola or others in the restaurant, after the bottles were delivered. The case of bottles had been delivered by the Bottling Company two days earlier and placed on the floor of the kitchen where they might have been knocked or impacted in some way, causing a fracture in the glass or some other weakness. Escola testified to her careful handling of the bottle, and witnesses concurred.

The defendant's evidence consisted of three witnesses. The manager of the defendant's bottling works described the care taken during the bottling procedures.[12] The defendant's second witness testified that the type of break Escola described was consistent with someone mishandling the bottle, suggesting Escola was at fault. Finally, a glass expert from the bottle manufacturer testified that the manufacturing procedures are "'pretty near' infallible."[13]

[10] *Escola*, 150 P.2d at 438.

[11] Such cases were common in the early to mid-1900s. See Graham, *supra* note 2, at 604 ("Glass beverage bottles were ubiquitous from the early 1900s, when new technologies appeared that allowed for their mass manufacture, through the 1970s . . . Throughout this span, when one of these bottles suddenly ruptured, it was easy for would-be plaintiffs to appreciate that they had suffered an injury attributable to an outside force rather than their own fault"); Geistfeld, *supra* note 2, at 235 ("Every state developed case law on exploding bottle cases").

[12] Appellant's Opening Brief, Escola v. Coca-Cola Bottling Co. of Fresno, 3 Civ. No. 6916, at 12, Cal. Ct. of Appeal, 3d Dist. (Dec. 12, 1942). *See also* Geistfeld, *supra* note 2, at 231.

[13] *Escola*, 150 P.2d at 440.

Defendant sought to show, therefore, that the break was caused by an external force that could only have occurred after defendant delivered the bottle to the restaurant.

The jury awarded Escola compensatory damages of $2,900.[14] The intermediate California Court of Appeals reversed, agreeing with the defendant that prior cases required that Escola present evidence of the post-delivery treatment and condition of the bottle.[15] The use of *res ipsa loquitur* was improper, according to the court of appeals, because there was no proof of the defendant's exclusive control of the instrumentality at the time of the alleged negligence.[16]

The issue on appeal was whether prior California cases supported the use of *res ipsa loquitur* under these circumstances. A significant number of exploding bottle cases preceded *Escola*. Exploding bottle cases had become a regular feature of the tort litigation landscape in the 1930s, and given the difficulty and expense of establishing negligence in the bottling process, *res ipsa loquitur* was a common feature of the litigation. The defendant relied on a substantially similar exploding bottle case in which the use of *res ipsa loquitur* was denied based on the lack of defendant's exclusive control of the instrumentality.[17] This classic legal analysis, using case precedent and analogy, likely would not have grabbed the California Supreme Court's attention had it not been for a dissent in the court of appeals that seemed to have the better of the legal analogical argument. In that regard, *Escola* was an unremarkable case – do the cases support use of *res ipsa loquitur* under these circumstances or not?

Importantly, the California Court of Appeals majority opinion expressed concern that if a manufacturer were to be held liable in these circumstances, "he then becomes an insurer."[18] This reference is interesting not only for the gendered way that the manufacturer is described, though this is unremarkable for the time, but also for the possibility that it might have piqued the interest of Justice Roger Traynor who wrote the now famous concurring opinion for

14 The amount of the damages was not contested, nor an issue on appeal. However, the Respondent's brief made it clear that, while defendant "insinuated rather than requested that this Court pass upon a question of 'excessive damage,'" no evidence or argument was made on the matter. Respondent's Brief, Escola v. Coca-Cola Bottling Co. of Fresno, 3 Civ. No. 6916, at 2, Cal. Ct. App. 3d Dist. (Mar. 22, 1943). The brief is the only place in the record that explains in detail the nature of the pain and permanency of Escola's injuries.

15 Escola v. Coca-Cola Bottling Co., 140 P.2d 107, 110 (Cal. Ct. App. 1943).

16 *Id.*

17 Gerber v. Farber, 129 P.2d 485 (Cal. Ct. App. 1942).

18 *Escola*, 140 P.2d at 108 (Cal. Ct. App. 1943). This "the sky is falling" argument was raised in the Appellant's Closing Brief. *See* Appellant's Closing Brief, Escola v. Coca-Cola Bottling Co., 3 Civ. No. 6916, at 19 (Cal. Ct. App. Dist. 3) (Apr. 13, 1943).

which the case is known that lays out the compelling case for "absolute liability" for defective products.

The California Supreme Court reversed and upheld the use of *res ipsa loquitur*.[19] The court found that there was evidence of probable negligence in any of the ways that could have led to the explosion.[20] Of course, manufacturing processes are not perfect. Even though testimony in the case suggested that the bottle manufacturing process is "pretty near infallible," some bottles were surely produced with flaws that did not stem from the negligence either of the bottle manufacturer, who was not a defendant, or the bottler. But the court did not permit this nagging doubt about whether undetectable flaws occurred in the production of the bottle itself to derail the use of the inference of negligence. Consequently, the use of the *res ipsa* inference permitted in *Escola* is considered by some to be an improper use of the doctrine.[21]

The Traynor concurrence has been described as "both traditional and revolutionary."[22] The opinion seeks to unbind liability without fault from the contract heritage of warranty while grounding the tort theory of recovery in a promise of safety that is not based on negligence either. Justice Traynor uses the classic negligence case of *MacPherson v. Buick Motor Co.*,[23] which rejected the privity limitation in negligence cases, to "pave[] the way for a standard of liability that would make the manufacturer guarantee the safety of his product even when there is no negligence."[24] The opinion masterfully relies on precedent and common-law reasoning to lead the reader to what seems the logical conclusion that the use of either negligence or implied warranty is a thin veil for what is actually strict liability.

Justice Traynor lays out the public policy case for strict liability in the first paragraph, which contains all the classic explanations for strict products liability. Those policies are grounded in the goals of deterrence (or risk reduction), and the distributive justice notion that losses should be allocated to those in the best position to bear them.

> In my opinion it should now be recognized that a manufacturer incurs an absolute liability when an article that he has placed on the market, knowing that it is to be used without inspection, proves to have a defect that causes injury to human beings ... Even if there is no negligence ... public policy

[19] *Escola*, 150 P.2d 440.

[20] *Id.* at 439–40.

[21] Geistfeld, *supra* note 2, at 234.

[22] *Id.* at 236.

[23] 111 N.E. 1050 (N.Y. 1916).

[24] *Escola*, 150 P.2d at 442.

> demands that responsibility be fixed wherever it will most effectively reduce the hazards to life and health inherent in defective products that reach the market. It is evident that the manufacturer can anticipate some hazards and guard against the recurrence of others, as the public cannot. Those who suffer injury from defective products are unprepared to meet its consequences. The cost of an injury and the loss of time or health may be an overwhelming misfortune to the person injured, and a needless one, for the risk of injury can be insured by the manufacturer and distributed among the public as a cost of doing business.[25]

Justice Traynor emphasizes the changes in the way products reach consumers, and the obligation those changes impose on product manufacturers.

> It is to the public interest to discourage the marketing of products having defects that are a menace to the public. If such products nevertheless find their way into the market it is to the public interest to place the responsibility for whatever injury they may cause upon the manufacturer, who, even if he is not negligent in the manufacture of the product, is responsible for its reaching the market. However intermittently such injuries may occur and however haphazardly they may strike, the risk of their occurrence is a constant risk and a general one. Against such a risk there should be general and constant protection and the manufacturer is best situated to afford such protection.[26]

He then carefully deconstructs the bases of negligence and warranty liability alongside the no-fault basis of liability that lurks below. He critiques both the difficulty of establishing negligence under the traditional standards, and the limitations of warranty due to restrictive contract-based doctrines such as privity and disclaimers, which thwart the opportunity to establish a promise of quality required by law. Justice Traynor's concurrence stands today as a classic example of legal reasoning: "a patient craftsmanlike working out of things within the frame of reference he has been given by existing law."[27]

In the penultimate paragraph, he returns to the more openly policy-based support for strict liability to which he alluded in his beginning paragraph. He describes the changing nature of the relationship between manufacturer and consumer, but he does not explain nor explore further the social, political, or economic context of his time. He argues that the consumer "no longer has means or skill enough to investigate for himself the soundness of a product . . . and his erstwhile vigilance has been lulled by the steady efforts of

[25] *Id.* at 440–41 (Traynor, J. concurring).

[26] *Id.* at 441.

[27] Geistfeld, *supra* note 2, at 236 (quoting Harry Kalven, Jr., *Torts: The Quest for Appropriate Standards*, 53 Cal. L. Rev. 189, 191 (1965)).

manufacturers to build up confidence by advertising and marketing devices such as trade-marks."[28] His reference to the practices of manufacturers that "lull" consumers into ill-informed product choices with poor, or no, information about risk is as close as the Justice gets to laying boldly the policy groundwork that some legal realists may have preferred.[29] His opinion was one of the first attempts to explain the loss-allocating/risk-distributing bases for "enterprise liability." The importance of this opinion laying the groundwork for what would become one of the most important doctrinal changes in tort law, strict products liability, should not be underestimated. No other justice joined Traynor's concurrence, until now.

THE FEMINIST JUDGMENT

Professor Zanita Fenton, writing as Justice Fenton, chooses not to alter or amend either Justice Traynor's concurring opinion or Chief Justice Phil S. Gibson's majority opinion. She prefers to let each one stand on its own, concurring in both while setting the context for each, and enhancing and clarifying the reasons for each. In her opinion, concurring in the majority, she does not tarry on the underlying *res ipsa loquitur* debate, but rather provides further explanation for the importance of using this proof doctrine expansively in products liability cases. As she notes, Chief Justice Gibson's opinion does a thorough job setting the stage for an expanded use of that proof doctrine, which is supported both by the underlying goal of easing burdens of proof in some cases, and the need to expand liability in cases in which product manufacturers hold all the cards.[30] Easing burdens of proof has the effect of benefiting classes of plaintiffs who have not historically been able to amass evidence of liability, sometimes due to its costs but often because of the burden on already overburdened parties who have neither the resources nor the inherent power to conduct extensive litigation. This situation has also been chronicled in feminist literature, including that of Professor Leslie Bender who explores the power imbalances inherent in our justice system that benefit powerful corporate defendants over injured plaintiffs.[31]

[28] *Escola*, 150 P.2d at 443 (Traynor, J. concurring).

[29] Legal realist scholars such as Fleming James had been advocating for no-fault products liability since the 1930s. *See* George L. Priest, *The Invention of Enterprise Liability: A Critical History of the Intellectual Foundations of Modern Tort Law*, 14 J. LEGAL STUD. 461 (1985).

[30] For an additional discussion of the importance that exploding bottle cases had on the move toward strict liability, *see* Graham, *supra* note 2, at 600–13.

[31] Leslie Bender, *Feminist (Re)Torts: Thoughts on the Liability Crisis, Mass Torts, Power, and Responsibilities*, 1990 DUKE L.J. 848, 885–94.

Professor Fenton's opinion concurring in Justice Traynor's compellingly makes the social, political, and economic case for strict products liability that Justice Traynor did not do directly.[32] Throughout her analysis, she approaches the female plaintiff in the case as both a worker and a product user. Her opinion does not seek to embellish Justice Traynor's analysis of the doctrinal landscape. Rather, she builds on his classic common-law reasoning and enhances it with information about the social, economic, and cultural context in which the doctrine operates to the detriment of many.

The opinion is best characterized as an example of critical race feminism with attention to class.[33] In describing the social, economic, and cultural context, Justice Fenton is careful to consider and mention race and class in addition to gender. By grappling with three dimensions of personal identity, Justice Fenton goes beyond Traynor's impulse to protect the ordinary citizen and analyzes how tort doctrines have a disproportionate impact on certain groups in society. For example, worker safety and consumer protections can be particularly important to low-income workers and consumers, many of whom are women and members of minority groups.

The Fenton opinion moves skillfully through the social context and the dramatic changes wrought by the Great Depression and World War II, to the vast technological changes increasing the availability of consumer and workplace goods while increasing the number of injuries suffered as a result. She adds to Justice Traynor's critique of the manufacturer–consumer relationship, setting the stage for the use of strict liability, by chronicling its use in workers' compensation and liability for contaminated food. She grounds the need for strict liability on the perils of the increasing use of defective consumer products in the home and other non-workplace contexts. She explores the importance of a no-fault basis of liability in the failed promise of equality of opportunity, for women and people of color. She expands the understanding of the personal impact product failures have on the most vulnerable in our society.

The move toward strict liability in the 1950s and 1960s as the result of the expanding trends in the use of *res ipsa loquitur* has been chronicled.[34] Yet,

[32] For an extended discussion of the pressures of the legal realist movement toward expanded use of public policy to decide cases, and the influence on Justice Traynor's opinion in Escola, see Geistfeld, *supra* note 2, at 243–44.

[33] *See* Critical Race Feminism: A Reader (Adrien Katherine Wing, ed.) (2d ed. 2003).

[34] Graham, *supra* note 2, at 607–08 ("The increasingly aggressive application of res ipsa loquitur in bottle cases meant that by mid-century, many observers understood that some courts were applying negligence in name only in these matters, and justifying this sleight-of-hand on public-policy grounds").

this doctrinal change was built on very few cases. Rather, the scholarly thought leaders of the day, including Professor William Prosser, the reporter for the *Restatement (Second) of Torts*, Fleming James, and others advocated for an expansion of tort liability based, in part, on the widespread adoption of workers' compensation and other broader social forces, as does Professor Fenton.[35] Justice Traynor's influence was certainly present, but the importance of the *Escola* concurrence was largely lost over the ensuing two decades, as many academics and judges did not broadly endorse it until the *Restatement* drafting process began.[36] Professor Fenton goes beyond Traynor and explores the full impact on women and people of color of the liability-limiting doctrines of the day, which fell most harshly on those who were least capable of surviving the harms inflicted by inevitable product failures.

Had Professor Fenton's voice been heard in 1944, it is certainly possible that it would not have taken another twenty years before strict products liability was adopted. Professor Fenton's concurring opinion would have provided a powerful judicial influence, and perhaps given her the opportunity to write the ultimate opinion recognizing strict products liability sooner than 1963. Her withering attack on the underlying economic and social inequities that existed, the link from those inequities to the importance of strict liability as a method of gender and racial equality as well as overall consumer protection, and the analogies to workers' compensation and duties of property owners based on premises liability, provide a robust explanation for the "absolute" liability which Justice Traynor advocated.

For Gladys Escola, $2,900 was "a lot of money" when you only make $18 a week.[37] She lived a life of influence in the town of Merced, California. She became Director of Food Services for Merced High School and Merced Junior College; she was a member and past president of the Merced Business and Professional Women, an advocate for seniors, and a volunteer at the Courthouse Museum. She died in 2006 at the age of 94.[38] She lived a life of influence in the law, too.

[35] *See* Geistfeld, *supra* note 2, at 252.

[36] *See Id.* at 240 (legal academics did not immediately appreciate the *Escola* concurrence, limiting it to food cases; important academic articles did not rely on it until late in the 1950s). Justice Traynor's opportunity to endorse strict products liability for California came in 1963 in *Greenman v. Yuba Power Prod., Inc.*, 377 P.2d 897 (Cal. 1963), at the same time as the *Restatement* drafting process was in full swing.

[37] *See* Moss, *supra* note 5, at 555.

[38] *Obituary of Gladys Escola*, MERCED (CAL.) SUN-STAR, December 20, 2006.

ESCOLA v. COCA-COLA BOTTLING CO. OF FRESNO, 150 P.2D 436 (CAL. 1944)

JUSTICE ZANITA E. FENTON, CONCURRING IN THE JUDGMENT OF THE COURT AND IN THE OPINION OF JUSTICE TRAYNOR

Chief Justice Gibson's opinion for the court and Justice Traynor's concurring opinion provide legitimate alternative theories for addressing product-related injuries under tort law and, together, reveal a crossroad between doctrines. While I endorse Chief Justice Gibson's ratification of *res ipsa loquitur* as an evidentiary doctrine designed to operate in the absence of key evidence available to the claimant, I also join Justice Traynor's progressive concurrence because his reasoning is most in line with my own. Nevertheless, I recognize that it may take time for Justice Traynor's approach to gain traction in state courts and legislatures and I accept the use of *res ipsa loquitur* as an appropriate interim solution.

I write separately to emphasize three interrelated policy imperatives not addressed by either opinion: (1) claimant equality; (2) workplace safety; and (3) consumer protection. These objectives are an outgrowth of rapid social developments produced in large part by our nation's entry into World War II. During this time, we have witnessed the opening of work opportunities for broader segments of the population and have also seen technological advances, promising increased postwar production of consumer goods. Tort law must now respond to these significant changes in a fair and equitable manner.

I FACTS

The accident that led to this case occurred in a restaurant where plaintiff, Gladys Escola, worked as a waitress. At the time of the accident, plaintiff was restocking restaurant inventory from cases of Coca-Cola delivered by defendant-manufacturer's driver. She took bottles, one at a time, from the case with her right hand and put them into the refrigerator.

When a Coca-Cola bottle exploded in her hand Escola sustained a deep 5-inch cut to that hand, severing blood vessels, nerves, and muscles of the thumb and palm. Two jagged pieces of glass from the broken bottle were found to be responsible for the injury. Evidence proffered at trial indicated that plaintiff successfully placed three bottles in the refrigerator, but that the fourth bottle "exploded in [her] hand." *Escola*, 150 P.2d at 438. Plaintiff's account was confirmed by her employer who stated that he "heard the explosion." *Id.* A more detailed account of the accident was provided by a fellow employee who stated that plaintiff "didn't bang either the case or the door or another bottle," that the bottle "popped … [and] sounded just like a fruit jar would blow up," and that the contents of the bottle "flew all over the plaintiff and herself, and the walls," and everything in the vicinity. *Id.* Plaintiff's theory of the case was that Coca-Cola had bottled and delivered a bottled beverage, "which on account of excessive pressure of gas or by reason of some defect in the bottle was dangerous … and likely to explode." *Id.* at 437. Plaintiff received a jury verdict below. The court of appeals reversed. *Escola v. Coca-Cola Bottling Co.*, 140 P.2d 107 (Cal. App. 1942).

II *RES IPSA LOQUITUR*

Today the majority of this court, per Chief Justice Gibson, declares that the primary issues in the case are whether the doctrine of *res ipsa loquitur* applies in the defective product context, and, relatedly, whether the evidence submitted to the jury was sufficient to support the judgment. In the absence of evidence showing specific acts of Coca-Cola's negligence in bottling its beverage, plaintiff's case must rely on the doctrine of *res ipsa loquitur.*

According to the court, *res ipsa loquitur* applies only in cases in which "(1) defendant had exclusive control of the thing causing the injury and (2) the accident is of such a nature that it ordinarily would not occur in the absence of negligence by the defendant." *Escola*, 150 P.2d at 438. In analyzing the "exclusive control" element of the test, Justice Gibson notes that courts have struggled to apply the doctrine in cases involving accidents that occur after a defendant has relinquished physical control of the instrumentality causing the accident. *Id.* at 438–39.

To clarify the application of *res ipsa loquitur* in such cases, Justice Gibson examines a wide range of cases permitting the use of *res ipsa loquitur* as well as those refusing to do so. Indeed, the discussions in those cases, of either stance, demonstrate that there has been widespread confusion and misperceptions concerning the appropriate use of the doctrine. I agree with Justice Gibson's assessment that a plaintiff's only duty in such cases is to present evidence from which the jury can infer that the instrumentality was not changed or damaged from an extraneous force, including handling by the plaintiff. In my view, Justice Gibson puts these cases into proper perspective when he concludes that *res ipsa loquitur*, properly argued and applied, simply invites a jury to use logic and common sense in its assessment of the probabilities from the array of relevant, possible causes of an accident. *Id.* at 439. A court need only assure that the circumstantial evidence presented to the jury is sufficient to support a valid inference.

Justice Gibson then examines whether the jury in this case could properly infer that the manufacturer-defendant's negligence was the cause of the bottle's explosion. *Id.* at 439–40. Here, although the exploding coke bottle was the immediate cause of Escola's injuries, the focus of inquiry should be on the reason that the bottle broke with such force. In *res ipsa* cases such as this, the arguments and proofs are directed toward a process of elimination in an effort to identify the most probable cause of the accident. Here, given the witness testimony regarding the normal handling of the bottle and assurances of no impact preceding the accident, a jury might properly eliminate plaintiff's actions as the cause of the bottle's explosion. More importantly, the testamentary evidence regarding the force of the explosion suggests that it was too great to emanate from routine handling, or even from playful shaking of the bottle. Indeed, if evidence regarding the explosion demonstrates that it was of extraordinary strength, this alone would be sufficient to eliminate regular human handling as the cause. Logically, the only remaining likely causes for this accident were that there was some defect in the glass or that there was overpressurization of the bottle. The circumstantial evidence in this case thus was strong enough for the jury to draw an inference of negligence. *Id.* at 440.

Although application of *res ipsa loquitur* proved capable of achieving what I regard as the correct result in this case, I am not convinced that application of the doctrine can always be counted upon to achieve justice for the parties. My concerns center mainly on the allocation of the burden of proof. To assure procedural fairness to the defendant, generally the initial burden of proof is placed on the plaintiff. Underlying this allocation is the presumption that the plaintiff has access to the necessary information and relevant direct evidence. Yet consumer-plaintiffs do not typically have access to crucial information regarding product construction, handling, or marketing streams. Instead, it is the defendant-manufacturers which usually have the greater access to evidence regarding their own products: they maintain control over the materials used in production, determine the source of any component parts, and select the packagers and distributors. The manufacturer especially maintains control over the design of product, as this is often safeguarded as a valuable corporate secret. *Id.* at 443 (Traynor, J., concurring). Given this asymmetry of information, plaintiff-consumers are generally left with only circumstantial evidence and invocation of the doctrine of *res ipsa loquitur* to prove their case. However unpredictable, relying on *res ipsa loquitur* has often been the only doctrinal avenue available for plaintiff-consumers in defective product litigation.

While I welcome Justice Gibson's clarification of this confusing, albeit useful, evidentiary doctrine, I am now convinced that strict liability theory is preferable for use in defective products cases. As applied by many courts, particularly in exploding bottle cases, *res ipsa loquitur* now approximates strict liability and "[i]mposes what is in reality liability without negligence." *Id.* at 447 (Traynor, J., concurring). But compared to strict liability, application of *res ipsa loquitur* is unpredictable because any given jury may or may not decide to draw an inference of negligence. Adopting a regime of strict liability will produce more consistent results across cases and across similar products and seems the natural progression from *res ipsa loquitur* to govern cases involving dangerous defective products.

III STRICT LIABILITY

In his concurring opinion, Justice Traynor proposes strict liability as the best doctrinal approach to determine liability for product injury. He marshals strong doctrinal and policy arguments in favor of the use of strict liability for product defects and his analysis relies on sound tort-based policies – deterrence and loss-spreading – to place responsibility on the party best positioned to prevent the harms. His opinion also has the virtue of avoiding illusion and legal fictions. On the latter point, I would point out that a properly applied *res ipsa loquitur* doctrine may accomplish the same effect as strict liability, just less directly. Indeed, some legal scholars have discussed *res ipsa loquitur* as one means for accomplishing absolute liability. *See* Lindsey R. Jeanblanc, *Manufacturers' Liability to Persons Other than Their Immediate Vendees*, 24 VA. L. REV. 134, 134–58 (1938); Howard Osterhout, *The Doctrine of* res ipsa loquitur *as Applied to Aviation*, 2 AIR L. REV. 9 (1931); Fowler V. Harper & Fred E. Heckel, *Effect of the Doctrine of* res ipsa loquitur, 22 ILL. L. REV. 724 (1928). To my mind, this point alone suggests that the choice of *res ipsa loquitur* over strict liability has no sound basis in logic.

Justice Traynor believes, as do I, that even without negligence, a manufacturer ought to incur an "absolute liability when an article that he has placed on the market, knowing that it is to be used without inspection, proves to have a defect that causes injury to human beings." *Escola*, 150 P.2d at 440 (Traynor, J. concurring). I agree with Justice Traynor that, especially with advances in technology, "[t]he consumer no longer has means or skill enough to investigate for himself the soundness of a product, even when it is not contained in a sealed package, and his erstwhile vigilance has been lulled by the steady efforts of manufacturers to build up confidence by advertising and marketing devices such as trade-marks." *Id.* at 443 (Traynor J., concurring).

Justice Traynor also proposes strict liability because the manufacturer is in the best position to prevent the harm and thus can most effectively reduce the dangers of their products that reach the market. In addition to minimizing injuries, Justice Traynor sees it as in the public interest to place responsibility on the manufacturer when losses do occur because the manufacturer has the ability to spread the cost of injury among all those who benefit from the production and use of the product. *Id.* at 440–41 (Traynor, J. concurring).

Justice Traynor points out that we already impose criminal liability for adulterated foodstuffs without proof of fault and that such strict criminal liability may extend to containers and bottles as well. *Id.* at 441 (citing Cal. Health & Saf. Code § 26510). Further, refusing to impose strict liability gives manufacturers an advantage over retail sellers who are subject to liability under warranty to consumer-plaintiffs for defects in the products they sell. I agree that we ought to hold manufacturer-defendants directly responsible in tort for dangerously defective products, especially since we no longer require privity in product defect cases. *Id.* at 440 (citing *MacPherson v. Buick Motor Co.*, 217 N.E. 1050 (N.Y. 1916)).

Thus, for the reasons of simplicity, efficient prevention of injury and the associated costs, and in keeping with inevitable technological advances, I join Justice Traynor's concurrence and encourage the use of strict liability for defective product cases.

IV POLICY IMPERATIVES

In addition to the reasons advanced by Justice Traynor in support of strict liability, I write separately to provide some context to the debate over the choice of liability principles and to suggest three additional policy imperatives that ought to guide our judgment. In my view, adoption of strict liability is warranted to assure equality among claimants, enhance workplace safety and guarantee consumer protection, three important social goals that should be promoted through our system of tort compensation. Significant changes in the composition of the workplace, in the development and use of consumer products, and in social and legal attitudes toward the protection of workers and consumers all point to strict liability as our best course of action.

New Workers

Since December 7, 1941, our nation has been engaged in the Second Great War. As such, large numbers of our veterans returning from combat are now physically and emotionally disabled. As of May 11, 1944, there are 76,391 wounded soldiers, in addition to the 46,518 dead. *U.S. Casualties Now 201, 454*, ASSOCIATED PRESS, May 11, 1944. As we know all too well, the casualties of war impose great suffering and hardship not only on the injured service members themselves, but on their families and communities. We should not compound the human and financial toll of this war by adding to these numbers with home-related and workplace accidents and injuries.

It is a sad fact that the workplace has also become a place of danger. Just last year, industrial injuries accounted for 18,400 deaths, 1,700 permanent total disabilities, and 108,000 permanent partial impairments. *Industrial Injuries in 1943*, 58 MONTHLY LAB. REV. 242, 242 (Feb. 1944). Similar numbers were reported in the prior year when the Bureau of Labor Statistics estimated that in 1942 there had been 18,100 work-related fatalities, 1,800 permanent total disabilities, 100,800 permanent partial impairments, and 2,147,000 temporary total disabilities. *Industrial Injuries in the United States during 1942*, 57 MONTHLY LAB. REV. 865, 865 (1943).

We must also recognize that the war has changed the composition of the workplace. It has opened employment opportunities to new segments of the population, including middle-class white women, who might otherwise be engaged exclusively in home-making activities, but have heeded the call in the nation's service to work in the industrial sector. *See* Mary Elizabeth Pidgeon, *A Preview as to Women Workers in Transition from War to Peace*, Women's Bureau SPECIAL BULLETIN NO. 18 (Women's Bureau, Wash.), March 1944 at 9. Notwithstanding the National War Labor Board's call for equal pay for equal work for women, however, there are still significant pay disparities between male and female workers at every skill level. National Women's Trade Union League of America, Life and Labor Bulletin No. 36 (November 1942); Lucy Ogden Norton & Royce H. Knapp, *Professional Women at War*, 21 PI LAMBDA THETA Journal 151 (1943). Aside from the perpetuation of social inequality that stems from income inequality, thinner resources leave such potential plaintiffs ill-equipped to internalize the losses associated with personal injury.

It is also the case that Negro men and women have found more employment options because of war needs. *See* Robert C. Weaver, *The Employment of the Negro in War Industries*, 12 J. OF NEGRO EDUC. 386 (1943); Robert C. Weaver, *Racial Employment Trends in National Defense*, 2 PHYLON 337, 352–56 (1941). Both President Roosevelt's Committee on Fair Employment Practices and his Executive Order banning employment discrimination has greatly facilitated the opening of jobs and opportunities to classes of persons formerly excluded from the workplace. Executive Order No. 8802, 6 FR 3109 (June 27, 1941). However, unfortunately, Negroes have not benefited fairly from these developments. As one scholar concluded, "it can be stated definitely that, until mid-1942, Negroes had not profited from the war boom to the same extent as had white workers." GUNNAR MYRDAL, AN AMERICAN DILEMMA 409 (1944) (demonstrating how prejudice operates to disguise the moral conflict between the American credo and the prevalence of anti-Negro practices). Unfortunately, more entrants to the workforce also means subjecting more individuals to the possibility of workplace injury. In truth, the specter of work-related disability is not new to the disadvantaged Negro. *Id.* at 357–58, 1004–10. Decades of Jim Crow separation make injury more likely for this unfortunate population, perhaps more so at work. *Id.* at 171–75. While domestic support for the Second Great War has opened employment opportunities for a broader swath of the population, the promise of equality has not followed them. There is no dispute that individuals who recently joined to the workforce have not been as well-compensated as the white men who held these same positions prior to their departure to foreign shores. *See* Lloyd H. Bailer, *The Negro Automobile Worker*, 51 J. OF POL. ECON. 415 (1943).

As the workforce and general make-up of the consuming public expands, strict liability has the advantage of placing the focus of litigation on the product rather than on the conduct or identity of the parties; in this way, strict liability discourages bias and subjectivity in juror decision-making and reduces the subjective evaluations more commonplace in negligence analyses. Given that a defective product might hurt *anyone*, avoiding jury bias is important to comply with the dictates of *Plessy v. Ferguson*, 163 U.S. 537 (1896), and ensure equal application of the laws, regardless of the separate social, political, and economic spheres that still exist for different populations, furthered by the various state and local Black Codes and Jim Crow legislation, not to mention laws here in California that support differential treatment of individuals of East Asian origin. *See, e.g.*, Alien Land Laws of 1913 (Deering's Gen. Laws, Act 261, as amended).

More Products

The Second Great War has brought with it increased use of products that facilitate workplace productivity as well as enhanced technology related to war efforts. Milton Gilbert, *Measuring National Income as Affected by the War*, 37 J. AM. STAT. ASS'N 186 (1942). This in turn has led to the development of new consumer products that benefit people in private settings, but also increase the likelihood of consumer-based injury. SIMON KUZNETS, NATIONAL PRODUCT WAR AND PREWAR (Nat'l Bureau of Econ. Research, Occasional Papers No. 17 (1944)). The prospects of and expectations for more widely available sophisticated consumer products dictate that the primary responsibility for product-related harm should not continue to reside solely with the injured party. Whether at home or at work, the consumer or user deserves protection from dangerous product defects. To quote Justice Traynor, "[t]he consumer no longer has means or skill enough to investigate for himself the soundness of a product, even when it is not contained in a sealed package, and his erstwhile vigilance has been lulled by the steady efforts of manufacturers to build up confidence by advertising and marketing devices such as trade-marks." *Escola*, 150 P.2d at 443 (Traynor, J. concurring).

Moreover, as production increases, manufacturers and their associated retailers have continued to invite consumers to purchase and use their products through advertisements to the general public. It is only fair that a manufacturer who invites the public, through advertisements and other means, to choose their products should be responsible for the dangerously defective chattels they produce. By way of analogy, tort law imposes a heightened duty on owners and occupiers of realty in regard to their business invitees, requiring owners make their premises safe from many dangers. William L. Prosser, *Business Visitors and Invitees*, 26 MINN. L. REV. 573 (1942). Such a heightened duty approaches strict liability and suggests that a similar expectation and duty should exist for the sellers of chattel property with respect to their "invited" consumers.

It is now time to impose legal responsibility on the party best able to prevent the harm and who has the ability to spread the cost of accidents among those who benefit from product use. Placing responsibility on the manufacturer will benefit the public by reducing the incidence of disabling injuries from consumer and workplace products. The alternative places too heavy a burden on injured individuals, imposing costs that they, as a class, are ill equipped to bear. We owe more to the women who "stepped up" to fill industrial jobs for the war effort, including those women who are part of the new classes of workers. Whether at work or at home, we should no longer leave them to shoulder the costs of their injuries alone.

Expansion of No-Fault Legal Liability

In response to the growth of workplace injuries, in particular, states have replied by adopting workers' compensation laws, a type of no-fault legal liability. By 1921, forty-six states had enacted workers' compensation legislation. Indeed, California was one of the earliest states in 1913 to adopt a workers' compensation act, also known as the Boynton Act. The Boynton Act was modeled after the compensation scheme in New York, first adopted in 1910.

1910 N.Y. Laws 625. In upholding the New York legislation against a constitutional challenge, the US Supreme Court specifically approved of the imposition of liability without fault, noting its resemblance to longstanding common-law doctrines:

> Much emphasis is laid upon the criticism that the act creates liability without fault . . . but we may add that liability without fault is not a novelty in the law. The common law liability of the carrier, of the inn-keeper, of him who employed fire or other dangerous agency or harbored a mischievous animal, was not dependent altogether upon questions of fault or negligence. Statutes imposing liability without fault have been sustained.
>
> New York Central R.R. v. White, 243 *U.S.* 188, 204 (1917)

Under most state statutes, employers are required to participate in workers' compensation and to make payments to workers for their workplace injuries, regardless of employer fault. Although the laws require proof that an employee's injuries "arise out of and in the course of employment," such a showing does not necessitate proof of a direct connection between defendant's specific acts and plaintiff's harm, and may even include injury precipitated by plaintiff's own actions.

Workers' compensation legislation reflects a public policy of holding corporate actors accountable for causing and perpetuating physical injury. There is no logical reason for limiting this policy to employers. Instead, accountability for accidents and injuries should extend to the full range of corporate actors involved, in a sharing of responsibility for their relevant part. It is an odd and illogical practice to impose no-fault liability on employers for workplace injuries, including those caused by products manufactured by other businesses, but not to hold manufacturers responsible for their dangerous defective products simply because they are used in a separate workplace or in someone's home. Manufacturers of products used in the workplace should have no less responsibility than businesses employing human labor.

To take another industry-related example, manufacturers now have less responsibility for injuries caused by the products they produce than retailers currently have. Under a warranty theory, consumers may recoup their losses against retailers, regardless of the retailer's ability to test the product and regardless of the retailers' lack of involvement in the creation of the defect in a product. Given retailer responsibility for product-based injury and the elimination of the privity requirement, the next logical step is to afford consumer-plaintiffs the right to sue manufacturers directly for dangerously defective products. Just as employers should not bear the entire cost of product-related workplace injuries, retailers should not be solely responsible for product-related injuries.

Finally, the working and consuming public cannot afford to wait for legislative action at the federal or state level. With the exception of the Federal Employers' Liability Act, 45 U.S.C. § 51 et seq. (1908), that provides compensation to injured railroad workers, there are currently no federal standards designed to reduce workplace hazards and related injuries. And while an essential part of the Boynton Act, and similar legislation in other states, requires coverage for permanent disability and permanent partial disability, there are no formal measures, in the state of California nor through national regulation, to ensure continuation of employment or other opportunities for employable individuals with disabilities. Even though the federal Pure Food and Drug Administration Act of 1906 regulates foodstuffs and medical devices, its protections do not extend to general consumer products or to consumer product safety. Ch. 3915, 4 Stat. 768 (codified 21 CFR §§ 1–1499). Given the lack of government leadership in regulating product safety and enacting adequate consumer protection or workplace standards, it falls to private law, including tort law, to place responsibility on those entities best able to prevent loss. Extending liability without fault to cover injurious products is thus a timely and sensible approach.

Workers' compensation legislation represents only the first step in addressing worker safety and assuring the financial security of injured employees. Alone it has proven inadequate to meet the needs of accident victims. Indeed, in this case, Gladys Escola received a meager workers' compensation award of $42.60, an insufficient sum to cover her medical expenses and lost wages. Providing workers and consumers with a viable strict liability tort claim would serve as an important complement to the overall system of compensation. It would give courts a role in providing workplace and product safety incentives for industry actors to ensure product safety and to distribute the costs of product injury directly to all consumers. California has already acknowledged the need for no-fault liability in one subset of product matters, those involving sickness and injuries caused by harmful foodstuffs, where health and safety statutes impose criminal penalties without fault. It is time to extend liability without fault to all dangerously defective products.

For the reasons stated in this opinion, I concur in the judgment of the court and I endorse Justice Traynor's call to adopt strict liability in dangerous defective product cases.

4

Commentary on *Farwell v. Keaton*

E. CHRISTI CUNNINGHAM

INTRODUCTION

The Michigan Supreme Court's decision in *Farwell v. Keaton*[1] held that a teenager owed a duty to aid his teenaged companion when he left him beaten and asleep in the back seat of a car in his grandparents' driveway. *Farwell* is significant to tort law and to feminist theory for two reasons. First, it pushes the boundaries of two exceptions to the general rule that one does not have a duty to render aid. Second, the case and most commentary on the case normalize sexual harassment and stalking behavior, either by ignoring such behaviors completely or by characterizing them in ways that suggest that they are common, acceptable activities. The feminist judgment by Professor Sarah Swan, writing as Justice Swan, offers a welcomed relational-feminist expansion of the common law so that the exceptions envelop the rule and a humanitarian duty to render aid exists whenever failing to render aid would shock the conscience. Her vision falls short, however, in that sexual harassment and stalking behavior remain normalized and do not shock the conscience. As a result, failing to render aid in the face of them does not compromise humanitarian concerns.

THE ORIGINAL OPINION

Richard Farwell's father brought a wrongful death action claiming that David Siegrist was negligent for leaving Farwell in the car without telling anyone. The trial court rejected Siegrist's argument that he had no duty to provide assistance to Farwell as a matter of law and instead accepted a jury determination that Siegrist had a duty.

[1] Farwell v. Keaton, 240 N.W.2d 217 (Mich. 1976).

Typically, a duty arises when a person engages in some affirmative act. A prima facie negligence claim requires plaintiff to prove that the defendant has breached a duty that was a cause in fact and proximate cause of damage. By 1976, when the Michigan Supreme Court decided *Farwell*, the common-law differentiation between misfeasance (acting) and nonfeasance (not acting) had long been settled. Although the line between misfeasance and nonfeasance has not always been clear, in general, when one acts, those actions must conform to the applicable standard of care, but one is not required to act. According to the common-law understanding of the time, a person does not have the duty to act, including aiding or rescuing, unless that person is involved in some way that implies responsibility.

Farwell significantly expanded the contexts in which responsibility could be implied. Exceptions to the common-law understanding that one is not required to help another person included situations where one had voluntarily attempted aid and where there were preexisting relationships among the parties. In general, a duty was implied where action was needed to avoid worsening a situation, where a relationship created some economic benefit to the defendant, or where immediate family members were involved.

The common understanding of a Good Samaritan is someone who has no familial or economic relationship with a person in need, but nevertheless attempts to help. Notably, under the common law, when a Good Samaritan attempts to render aid by taking charge and control of a situation, the Good Samaritan then has a duty to act reasonably and to not worsen the condition of the person in need. The duty only arises, however, if the Good Samaritan voluntarily assumes the responsibility of rendering aid.

The court in *Farwell* considered the circumstances under which actions would constitute voluntarily taking charge and control to offer aid. The common law was clear that a person's actions could not constitute rendering aid if the person did not know that aid was needed, that is, if the defendant "neither knows nor should know of the unreasonable risk, or of the illness or injury."[2] The *Farwell* majority equated Siegrist's knowledge of the circumstances surrounding the fight to knowledge that Farwell needed medical treatment. Thus, the court concluded that Siegrist did not actually have to be aware that help was needed so long as he acted knowing that Farwell had been injured in some way.

The majority's expansion of the context in which responsibility may be implied was significant because many of the facts suggested that neither

[2] William L. Prosser, Law of Torts 343 (4th ed. 1971); *see also Farwell*, 240 N.W.2d at 221–22.

Farwell nor Siegrist knew that Farwell needed medical attention. At Farwell's request, they drove to several restaurants after the fight, and Farwell never mentioned feeling pain and expressed a desire to retaliate against his attackers. The court, however, was persuaded by testimony from Farwell's father of Siegrist's hindsight[3] consolation to him that Farwell "was hurt bad," that Siegrist was scared, and that Siegrist told him that "I know I should have [told someone], I don't know."[4] Thus, the court weighed words of comfort to a grieving father over testimony by an expert that only a qualified physician would have suspected that Farwell needed immediate medical attention.[5]

As a result, the majority accepted the jury's conclusion that Siegrist's effort to wake Farwell was an attempt to aid someone in peril, rather than merely an attempt to wake a teenager who had consumed five beers. So, by attempting to rouse Farwell, Siegrist assumed the duty of a Good Samaritan. The court's interpretation suggested that responsibility may be implied when a defendant has knowledge of any injury, even if the defendant could not have known that the injury required medical treatment.

Another exception at issue in *Farwell* was that arising from special relationships that imply a duty to act. Although the common law permitted bystanders to remain uninvolved, even though someone might be hurt by such inaction, it recognized that some special relationships justified the creation of a duty. These relationships included common carriers to passengers, ships to sailors, employers to employees, shopkeepers and hosts to business and social guests, spouses to each other, and parents to their children. To this list,[6] the court in *Farwell* added "companions on a social venture."[7]

The *Farwell* majority's decision that "companions" constituted a relationship that created a duty to act was an expansion of the common law. Under the common law, being present or in the company of someone in need had not typically been sufficient to establish a duty. For example, an expert swimmer with safety equipment at hand may simply sit and watch a person drown,[8] and a person may do nothing while watching a neighbor's child hammer explosives.[9]

3 *Cf.* Bell & Hudson, P.C. v. Buhl Realty Co., 462 N.W.2d 851, 853 (Mich. 1990) (distinguishing *Farwell* as a plurality decision and noting that retrospective wisdom is not sufficient to establish duty).

4 *Farwell*, 240 N.W.2d at 221.

5 *Id.* at 224 (Fitzgerald, J., dissenting).

6 Prosser described this list as "a limited group of relations, in which custom, public sentiment and views of social policy have led the courts to find a duty of affirmative action." Prosser, *supra* note 2, at 339.

7 240 N.W.2d at 222.

8 Prosser, *supra* note 2, at 341.

9 *Id.*

Why the majority determined that Farwell and Siegrist's relationship warranted elevation to a special relationship is a point of interest. Farwell and Siegrist drove around together, drank together, harassed two teenaged girls, followed them, and fled their pursuers together. After the fight, Siegrist retrieved Farwell from under his car and gave him an ice pack.

The majority described these activities as a "common undertaking" giving rise to an "implicit ... understanding that one will render assistance to the other when he is in peril if he can do so without endangering himself."[10] Something about their common undertaking led the majority to conclude that there was an implicit understanding between them that a physician does not owe to a dying person who could be saved and that neighbors do not owe to each other.

Perhaps the majority saw Farwell and Siegrist as engaging in stereotypical masculine bonding, commonly attributed to college fraternities and locker-room patrons. Against a backdrop in which "the law has persistently refused to recognize the moral obligation of common decency and common humanity,"[11] the majority nevertheless recognized an exception for a "commonly accepted code of social conduct."[12] Perhaps the special relationship that the majority recognized in the common undertaking of Farwell and Siegrist was the male bonding reflected in the colloquialism "bros before hos" and the shared understanding that can be detected in the uproarious laughter that Dr. Christine Blasey Ford described between her drunken attacker and his male companion.[13]

To explain its expansion of the common-law exception for special relationships to "companions on a social venture,"[14] the majority cited cases involving social guests. In *Depue v. Flatau*, the plaintiff became ill while he was an invited guest in the defendants' home. Then, defendants set the plaintiff on

[10] *Farwell*, 240 N.W.2d at 222.

[11] PROSSER, *supra* note 2, at 340.

[12] *Farwell*, 240 N.W.2d at 222.

[13] In the 2018 Senate confirmation hearings of Justice Brett Kavanaugh, Dr. Christine Blasey Ford testified that she had been sexually assaulted by him as a teenager. Then Judge Kavanaugh vehemently denied the allegation. During the hearing Senator Patrick Leahy asked Dr. Ford what she remembered most about the assault. Dr. Ford replied that as she lay fearing for her life, she remembered "the uproarious laughter [between her drunken attacker and his drunken companion] and their having fun at my expense." Marcia Coyle, *"Uproarious Laughter" Haunts Ford from Alleged Kavanaugh Attack*, NAT. L.J. (Sept. 27, 2018), https://www.law.com/nationallawjournal/2018/09/27/uproarious-laughter-haunts-blasey-ford-from-alleged-kavanaugh-attac/?sltreturn=20190007095148; *see also* Hager v. Griesse, No. CA-3143, 1986 WL 3915, at*2 (Ohio Ct. App. Mar. 19, 1986) (describing relationship in *Farwell* as that of "drinking companions").

[14] *Farwell*, 240 N.W.2d at 222.

his wagon in the middle of a January night in Minnesota, placed the reins on his shoulders, and started his horses toward home, moving him from a place of safety in defendants' home to a place of peril in the winter night.[15] In *Hutchinson v. Dickie*, plaintiff was an invited guest on the defendant's boat.[16] The defendant used the vessel even though it was unseaworthy due to a lack of sober and able-bodied crewmembers. In both cases, there was some suggestion, either explicitly or through inference, that the parties were males engaged in excessive drinking.[17]

Farwell's decision to extend the special relationship exception to social companions has had limited application, however. While moral and policy considerations might welcome an expansion of the duty to render aid, subsequent case law citing *Farwell* has not expanded duty to social companions, generally, or drinking buddies, in particular.[18] In addition, courts that have cited *Farwell* have been reluctant to impose a duty on bystanders who are not drinking companions to assist intoxicated people or those who may be harmed by them.[19]

The impact of the *Farwell* decision, then, has come primarily from its affirmation of the common-law nonfeasance rule and the obligation to render

[15] Depue v. Flatau, 111 N.W. 1, 2 (Minn. 1907).

[16] Hutchinson v. Dickie, 162 F.2d 103, 106 (6th Cir. 1947).

[17] In *Hutchinson*, the trial court made explicit findings concerning the parties' status as drinking companions: "I find that in all these places (except Rudd Machine Company) intoxicating liquor was consumed by petitioner, and his guests, including claimant's decedent, and that in all they undoubtedly had five or six of such drinks, all within a period of 4 to 5 hours." 162 F.2d at 105 (quoting trial court Findings of Fact and Conclusions of Law). In *Depue*, the inference is more attenuated. Plaintiff became "sick" after dining with defendants and sitting with them in their sitting room. The facts suggest that at some point he had a fainting spell and "stumbled" against a wall. The court observes that "the evidence is somewhat in doubt as to the cause of plaintiff's condition while in defendants' home." 111 N.W. at 2.

[18] *See, e.g.*, Webstad v. Stortini, 924 P.2d 940, 948 (Wash. Ct. App. 1996) (former employer who had extramarital affair with employee did not have a special relationship implying duty to prevent her suicide as an invited guest in his home); Sierocki v. Hieber, 425 N.W.2d 477, 477 (Mich. Ct. App. 1988) (81-year-old man who lived with aging sister-in-law and observed her deteriorating memory and behavior did not have a special relationship with her that created duty to her or others). *But see* Lindsey v. Miami Dev. Corp., 689 S.W.2d 856, 858 (Tenn. 1985) (host who allegedly told others to wait awhile before calling ambulance had duty to drunken social guest who had hit her head).

[19] *See, e.g.*, McGee In re McGee v. Chalfant, 806 P.2d 980, 985 (Kan. 1991) (describing cases in which there was no duty toward intoxicated people or their victims); Holloway v. Martin Oil Serv., Inc., 262 N.W.2d 858, 862 (Mich. Ct. App. 1977) (gas station did not have duty to refrain from selling gas in container to intoxicated young people); Swartz v. Huffmaster Alarms Sys., Inc., 377 N.W.2d 393, 396 (Mich. Ct. App. 1985) (restaurant did not have duty to prevent intoxicated patron from leaving premises and walking into traffic).

aid reasonably and not worsen the condition of someone in peril.[20] In addition, courts have also relied on its conclusion that a jury may determine the existence of a duty where the issue is a mixed question of law and fact. However, few cases have followed its conclusion that implicit in social companionship is a duty to render aid.

THE FEMINIST JUDGMENT

The feminist judgment of Professor Sarah Swan, writing as Justice Swan, reaches the same conclusion as the majority in *Farwell*, that the jury correctly found that Siegrist had a duty. It does not, however, reach this conclusion by expanding the exceptions to the general rule that one does not have a duty to render aid. Instead, Justice Swan replaces the exceptions with a new rule establishing a duty to rescue. She cites the expansion of the exceptions in many jurisdictions and the court's decision in *Prigden v. Boston Housing Authority* to justify her rationale that the law evolves to reflect changing standards of well-being and rights and duties among members of society.[21] She concludes:

> Once the undue formalism of the categories is removed, the rule that emerges is this: at the heart of the instances where a duty to rescue has been found lies a circumstantial connection between an imperiled person and a potential rescuer such that it would be "shocking to humanitarian considerations and the commonly accepted code of social conduct" to not impose a duty.

The new rule that she announces is the "shock the conscience" test – "[w]here the circumstances are such that it would be shocking to the conscience to not impose a duty to rescue, such a duty will be found."

Justice Swan's approach finds strong representation in the cultural feminist approach to legal analysis. This strand of feminism, emanating from Carol Gilligan's "different voice" theory identifies commonly perceived (perhaps, essential) differences between women and men and approaches law in a manner amplifying women's distinctive nature, perspectives, and contributions.[22] Also called relational feminism, this branch of feminist theory often

[20] *See also* Dan B. Dobbs, Paul T. Hayden & Ellen M. Bublick, Torts and Compensation: Personal Accountability and Social Responsibility for Injury 418 (8th ed. 2016) (questioning whether Farwell would have been better off if Siegrist had left him under the car).

[21] Prigden v. Bos. Hous. Auth., 308 N.E.2d 467 (Mass. 1974).

[22] Mary Becker, *Patriarchy and Inequality: Towards a Substantive Feminism*, 1999 U. Chi. Legal F. 21, 44 (critiquing "our culture's insistence that people are separate and autonomous rather than fundamentally relational").

elevates "human relationships and . . . the positive values of caring, nurturing, empathy, and connection."[23] An example of a relational approach is Lucinda Finley's revelation that limiting damages to pecuniary losses for the negligent death of a child tends to undercompensate women, whose injuries often include emotional losses related to their frequent role as primary caregivers.[24] Robin West has also made the observation that women are "'essentially connected,' not 'essentially separate,' from the rest of human life" by virtue of the physicality of conception and mothering.[25]

Justice Swan continues this tradition by making connectivity the rule rather than the exception. She expands the value of relationship beyond an essentially female experience to advance a rationale of humanitarianism and morality. The framework that she presents is a golden rule of duty: "I have a duty to rescue others, just as they have a duty to rescue me." Although Justice Swan makes passing reference to the common-law misfeasance–nonfeasance distinction, her golden rule jettisons the prerogative to refrain from action in favor of a principle of reciprocity of rescue, which Justice Swan suggests has been present but "obscured" in traditional common-law discourse. Her framing of duty breathes life into feminist theory of relational equality, achieving human happiness through mutual expectation and treatment.[26] In support of a golden rule framework of duty, Justice Swan references states that have statutes indemnifying or immunizing those who render aid. However, these statutes are as much evidence of the traditional common-law distinction as they are of a reciprocity of rescue. Statutory incentives encourage action that is not otherwise required.

Without a doubt, Justice Swan's departure from the common law is a step toward a more connected and holistic vision of human interaction. "Duty is ultimately 'an obligation grounded in the natural responsibilities of social living and human relations.'"[27] If broadly applied, Justice Swan's golden rule of social responsibility would significantly serve feminist advocacy within tort jurisprudence and beyond. If male dominance bent to this duty, for example, many injustices affecting the community of women, men, and transgender people might be ameliorated.

[23] Martha Chamallas, Introduction to Feminist Legal Theory 22 (3d ed. 2013).

[24] *See* Leslie Bender, *An Overview of Feminist Torts Scholarship*, 78 Cornell L. Rev.575, 585 (1993) (discussing Lucinda M. Finley, A *Break in the Silence: Including Women's Issues in a Torts Course*, 1 Yale J.L. & Feminism 41, 50–51 (1989)).

[25] Robin West, *Jurisprudence and Gender*, 55 U. Chi. L. Rev. 1, 3 (1988).

[26] *See* Becker, *supra* note 22, at 48.

[27] *See Wytupek v. Camden*, 136 A.2d 887, 895 (N.J. 1957).

Unfortunately, however, her excellent vision does not seem to extend as far as it could or should, to women and girls in harm's way as a result of unwelcomed heterosexual male sexual advances. Although this fact is often overlooked, the first instance of peril in *Farwell* was to the teenaged girls who endured street harassment by Farwell. The details of what was said are not clear in the opinion of the court, only that it was evening, the girls were walking by, and Farwell (who had consumed several beers) initiated "an unsuccessful attempt to engage them in conversation." That Farwell's advances were unwelcomed may be inferred from the fact that his attempt was "unsuccessful" and reported. Using Justice Swan's definition of reciprocity of rescue, Siegrist's duty arose for the first time when he was aware that the girls were being subjected to harassment.

The second instance of peril arose when Farwell exited his car and began stalking the girls.[28] Justice Swan's opinion indicates that Siegrist followed Farwell as Farwell was following the girls. Therefore, although Siegrist had knowledge that the girls were being pursued by Farwell and could have intervened with little or no risk to himself, he participated in the harmful activity rather than attempt to render aid

In both the majority opinion and Justice Swan's opinion, the interests of the teenaged girls and any duty arising from that danger to them are invisible. Justice Swan describes Farwell and Siegrist's behavior as "mild debauchery" and "carousing." She describes the girls' report of Farwell and Siegrist's behavior toward them as complaining, rather than reporting.[29] The violent reaction of the Keaton brothers to the girls' report suggested that Farwell's behavior was at least offensive and probably intentionally intimidating and threatening. Nevertheless, Justice Swan does not hint that Siegrist had a duty as a bystander[30] with a human connection both to his friend and the girls, nor that Siegrist's failure to intervene at that point "shocks the conscience" in the way that leaving Farwell asleep in the back seat of his car does.

Significantly, Justice Swan recounts the murder of Kitty Genovese and the failure of thirty-eight people who heard her attack to assist her because they

[28] In Michigan, stalking involves "repeated or continuing harassment of another individual that would cause a reasonable person to feel terrorized, frightened, intimidated, threatened, harassed, or molested." Mich. Comp. Laws Ann. § 750.411h (West 1998). Although there is no evidence that Farwell's actions were a continuation of past conduct, his actions could likely be characterized as stalking behavior.

[29] ("When the girls reached a restaurant a short distance down the street, they apparently complained to those present that they were being followed.") *See Farwell*, 240 N.W. 2d at 223 (Fitzgerald, J. dissenting).

[30] *See* Sarah L. Swan, *Bystander Interventions*, 2015 Wis. L. Rev. 975, 1028 (2015).

perceived the violence against her as "a private matter between a man and woman." Yet, the exclusion of the girls in *Farwell* from Justice Swan's reciprocity of rescue is a similar failure and signals an assumption of the girls' sexual availability, according to some tenets of dominance feminism.[31] Neither Siegrist, the majority in *Farwell*, nor Justice Swan perceive a duty to stop Farwell's aggression toward the girls because it is a private matter between a boy and some girls. As a result, Farwell's aggression is normalized as accepted social conduct. In fact, Farwell and Siegrist's debauchery and carousing of the girls provides part of the context for the special relationship that creates Siegrist's duty to rescue Farwell:

> As companions engaged in an evening of carousing around together, they had an implicit understanding that each would render to the other the care that friends generally render to each other, including assisting the other if he is in peril, if he can do so without endangering himself.

Justice Swan's humanitarian considerations do not extend far enough to make the girls' experiences visible; instead, the bonding resulting from aggression toward the girls provides part of the context for Farwell and Siegrist's duty to each other.

Perhaps a duty to the teenaged girls as imperiled persons is omitted from both the majority opinion and Justice Swan's opinion because the girls were neither petitioners nor respondents in the case. Farwell's father sued the Keaton brothers and Siegrist. Nevertheless, if the focus remains on Farwell as the imperiled person, Siegrist also had a duty to intervene in Farwell's oppressive behavior. In considering Siegrist's reciprocal duty to Farwell, both opinions fail to consider Siegrist's first opportunities to rescue Farwell. Siegrist knew that Farwell was engaging in drunken harassment of the girls and stalking behavior toward them. It shocks the conscience that Siegrist did not stop Farwell from engaging in conduct that exposed him to a variety of dangers, including those that ultimately resulted in his death. Just as friends don't let friends drive drunk, friends have a duty to prevent friends from engaging in drunken unwelcomed sexual aggression.

The tragedy of Kitty Genovese, as Justice Swan presents it, makes clear the importance of a duty to rescue those imperiled by the criminal actions of others. Her framework should also recognize the inhumanity of failing to

[31] *See* Bender, *supra* note 24, at 593 (citing Stephanie M. Wildman, *Review Essay: The Power of Women*, 2 Yale J.L. & Feminism 435 (1990)) (describing interpretation of Catharine MacKinnon's Feminist Theory of the State that "the law and the legal system are gendered male and do not take seriously the abuse of women by men").

rescue individuals from their own drunken abuses. Had Siegrist not breached this duty to Farwell, Farwell most likely would not have died.

Justice Swan's reciprocity of rescue, if adopted broadly, would go a long way in advancing a feminist vision of law and relationships by making humane and moral behavior a legal duty. In order to make that vision a reality, however, women and girls must be visible and the duty to humanity must include a duty to them. Instead, Justice Swan's feminist judgment finds a duty to render aid where it was not possible to know that rescue was needed, and finds no duty to render aid where the need is plain, but involves sexual aggression toward teenaged girls. Justice Swan's concurrence is a very important light, but does not shine quite as brightly as it could.

FARWELL v. KEATON, 240 N.W.2D 217 (MICH. 1976)

JUSTICE SARAH L. SWAN DELIVERED THE OPINION OF THE COURT

This case presents two separate but interrelated questions: (1) is there a duty to rescue, and, if so, what is the scope of that duty? (2) Is the question of whether or not a duty to rescue exists always a matter of law to be determined solely by the court?

We hold that when there exists a circumstantial connection between a person in peril and a potential rescuer, such that failing to impose a duty would be shocking to humanitarian considerations, a duty to rescue arises. Because determining whether such a circumstantial connection exists will often involve findings of fact, the question of whether a duty exists may properly be considered by the jury.

I FACTS

The opinion of the court of appeals details the facts as follows.[1]

On August 26, 1966, Richard Murray Farwell, deceased 18-year-old son of the plaintiff, visited the home of his friend, David Siegrist, a 16-year-old. That evening they drove to a trailer rental lot, where Siegrist was returning an automobile he had borrowed from a friend who was employed by the rental agency.

Siegrist and Farwell planned to wait in the car until the friend had finished work and then "drive around," stopping at various restaurants and drive-ins.

[1] Farwell v. Keaton, 215 N.W.2d 753, 754 (Mich. App. 1974).

While they were waiting, Siegrist estimated that they consumed "four or five" beers each.

Shortly before 9 o'clock PM, two teenage girls walked past the car. After an unsuccessful attempt to engage them in conversation, Farwell left the car and followed the girls. Siegrist got out of the car and followed Farwell.

When the girls reached a restaurant a short distance down the street, they apparently complained to those present that they were being followed. Defendants Ingland, Brock, Donald Keaton, Daniel Keaton, and at least two others in the restaurant began to chase Farwell and Siegrist, both of whom ran back to the trailer lot.

Siegrist escaped by ducking into the trailer rental office, where he requested those inside to assist Farwell. They stepped out of the office and were confronted by the group from the restaurant. The two groups faced each other, but no violence ensued, and the two groups scattered.

It was then discovered for the first time that Farwell had been caught and beaten by those who had been pursuing him and Siegrist; Farwell was found underneath his automobile in the lot.

Farwell was taken to the trailer rental office, where Siegrist gave him a plastic bag full of ice for his injuries. Shortly thereafter, Farwell and Siegrist left the rental office, and between 10 o'clock PM and midnight, they visited four different drive-in restaurants. While en route from the third to the fourth restaurant, Farwell stated that he wanted to lie down, climbed into the back seat, and went to sleep. Around midnight, Siegrist drove the car to the home of Farwell's grandparents (where Farwell lived), parked it in the driveway, and attempted to rouse Farwell. When Farwell merely made a sound as if 'in a deep sleep,' Siegrist left with a friend who had followed him to the grandparents' house. The next morning, Farwell was found by his grandparents, apparently taken to a hospital, and died of an epidural hematoma.

At trial, plaintiff contended that if Siegrist had taken Farwell to the hospital, or notified someone of Farwell's condition and whereabouts, Farwell would not have died. A neurosurgeon testified that someone in Farwell's condition who is taken to a doctor either before or within half an hour of a loss of consciousness has an 85 to 88 percent chance of survival. Plaintiff testified that Siegrist told him that he knew Farwell was badly injured and that he should have done something.[2]

[2] Parts of this opinion are taken intact from the original opinion. This paragraph and the following paragraph largely correspond to two paragraphs at *Farwell*, 240 N.W.2d at 219. Part III of this opinion corresponds to *Farwell*, 240 N.W.2d at 219–21 in the original opinion.

The jury returned a verdict for plaintiff and awarded $15,000 in damages. The court of appeals reversed, finding that Siegrist had not assumed the duty of obtaining aid for Farwell and that he neither knew nor should have known of the need for medical treatment. We reverse the court of appeals, for the following reasons.

II THE DUTY TO RESCUE

It is often said, as though it were set in stone, that no matter how easy it may be to do so, there is no general duty to aid another person in peril. *See, e.g.*, Osterlind v. Hill, 160 N.E. 301 (Mass. 1928); Yania v. Bigan, 155 A.2d 343 (Pa. 1959); Handiboe v. McCarthy, 151 S.E.2d 905 (Ga. Ct. App. 1966); Buch v. Armory Mfg. Co., 44 A. 809 (N.H. 1897); Union Pac. Ry. v. Cappier, 72 P.2d 281 (Kan. 1903). However, "no authority on high has immutably fixed" that rule as the eternal scope of the duty. John H. Scheid, *Affirmative Duty to Act in Emergency Situations – The Return of the Good Samaritan*, 3 JOHN MARSHALL J. OF PRAC. & PROC. 1, 12 (1969). Rather, like any duty, it "shifts and readjusts to the exigencies and mores of the times." *Id.* Often, the "political, social and economic changes" of a society "entail the recognition of new rights, and the common law, in its eternal youth, grows to meet th[ose] demands." Samuel D. Warren & Louis D. Brandeis, *The Right to Privacy*, 4 HARV. L. REV. 193, 193 (1893). As "the ever changing concepts of each individual's rights and duties in relation to all other members of our society" evolve, so too does the law come to "reflect[] current standards of concern for the personal safety and well being of each individual." Prigden v. Bos. Hous. Auth., 308 N.E.2d 467, 477 (Mass. 1974). Such has been the case with the duty to rescue.

Many jurisdictions have recognized a duty to rescue in an increasing range of circumstances. *See, e.g.*, Ploof v. Putnam, 71 A. 188 (Vt. 1908) (dock owner owed duty of care to imperiled ship occupants); Kline v. 1500 Mass. Ave. Apartment Corp., 439 F.2d 477 (D.C. Cir. 1970) (landlord owed duty of care to tenant assaulted by a third party in a common hallway); Tubbs v. Argus, 225 N.E.2d 841 (Ind. Ct. App. 1967) (driver of car involved in accident had duty to aid passenger); L.S. Ayres & Co v. Hicks, 40 N.E.2d 334 (Ind. 1942) (store had duty to child injured by escalator); Prigden, 308 N.E.2d at 46 (property owner owed a duty of care to an imperiled trespasser); Middleton v. Whitridge, 108 N.E. 192 (N.Y. 1915) (street car operator owed duty of care to ill passenger).

There are four already acknowledged categories of exceptions to the no-duty-to-rescue rule: (1) a duty imposed by statute or contract; (2) a duty arising from a special relationship; (3) a duty to avoid any affirmative acts which may make a situation worse; and (4) a duty to take reasonable and prudent care that arises from voluntarily lending aid. Many of the cases imposing liability for breaching a duty to rescue do so by expanding and adding to these existing categories of exceptions. With this growth, these "exceptions" have become less and less exceptional, and more and more instead the rule. For instance, within the "special relationship" exception, legislatures have seen fit to hold that a circumstantial connection arising from a car collision is sufficient to trigger a duty, as the "mere happening of an automobile accident creates such a relation among all the parties involved that the healthy must assist the injured." Scheid, *supra* at 8.

Indeed, the exceptions have expanded and evolved to the point where they now reveal their own broader rule. Once the undue formalism of the categories is removed, the rule that emerges is this: at the heart of the instances where a duty to rescue has been found lies a circumstantial connection between an imperiled person and a potential rescuer such that it would be "shocking to humanitarian considerations and the commonly accepted code of social conduct" to not impose a duty. Hutchinson v. Dickie, 162 F.2d 103, 106 (6th Cir. 1947). Where the circumstances are such that it would be shocking to the conscience to not impose a duty to rescue, such a duty will be found. A situation in which an individual realizes another person is in peril of serious bodily injury or death, and has the easily available means to effect a rescue yet fails to do so, will virtually always meet this shocks-the-conscience standard.

This test was clearly articulated in the Sixth Circuit decision. *Id.* at 106. There, the Sixth Circuit held that a host had an affirmative duty to attempt to rescue a guest who had fallen off his yacht. The host controlled the only instrumentality of rescue. The court declared that to ask of the host anything less than that he attempt to rescue his guest would be "so shocking to humanitarian considerations and the commonly accepted code of social conduct that the courts in similar situations have had no difficulty in pronouncing it to be a legal obligation."

Similarly, in the earlier case of *Depue v. Flatau*, 111 N.W. 1 (Minn. 1907), the Supreme Court of Minnesota held that if the defendants knew their dinner guest was ill, it was for the jury to decide whether they were negligent in refusing his request to spend the night and instead propping him up on his wagon with the reins thrown over his shoulder, sending him toward home. Indeed, the Missouri Court of Appeal in *Trout v. Watkins Livery & Undertaking Co.*, 130 S.W. 136, 141 (Mo. Ct. App. 1910), citing, inter alia, *Depue v. Flatau*, acknowledged that "it has been declared by courts of high authority that the precepts of humanity alone, unattended by any other obligation whatever, enjoins the duty of ordinary care upon one knowing the condition of a sick person to look out for the safety and welfare of those who are thus enfeebled." The Supreme Court of Indiana also found that *Depue v. Flateau* supported a rule that "under some circumstances, moral and humanitarian considerations may require one to render assistance to another who has been injured, even though the injury was not due to negligence on his part, and may have been caused by the negligence of the injured person." *Hicks*, 40 N.E.2d at 337.

Duty is ultimately an obligation "grounded in the natural responsibilities of social living and human relations." Wytupek v. Camden, 136 A.2d 887, 893 (N.J. 1957). While some scholars and theorists have enjoyed debating the philosophical issues surrounding rescue obligations, often positing that such a duty is not legally required and is incongruent with certain common-law principles, the fact remains that were it their own child drowning and dying in a small pool of water while an onlooker stood idly by and watched, one could expect their feelings on the matter to change. Philosophical vagaries aside, part of living in a civilized, modern society is "I agree to pluck your drowning child out of a small pool of water, just as you agree to pluck mine." This reciprocity of rescue is a "natural responsibilit[y] of social living and human relations." *Id.*

The reciprocity of rescue is important for the misfeasance–nonfeasance or act–omission distinction that is often raised in discussions of the duty to aid. While the distinction itself is, as many scholars have noted, fundamentally untenable (because many acts can be plausibly characterized as omissions and many omissions can be plausibly characterized as acts), in simplistic terms, it has been said that the law has traditionally been hesitant to involve itself with nonfeasance on the basis that merely refusing to confer a benefit on someone else should not be considered wrongful. However, often obscured in this discussion is that the duty to rescue applies to all: the non-rescuer is being asked only to confer *that which is also conferred upon him*. When viewed as something one owes to the world, the duty to rescue can seem like an unwarranted imposition. However, when viewed as a reciprocal duty which one both performs and *receives*, its rational basis becomes more apparent. I have a duty to rescue others, just as they have a duty to rescue me. Such is the social pact we have entered into, a collective covenant which most of us readily agree to, and to which all of us are bound.

The legal recognition of this social, reciprocal duty is consistent with the state of the law in many of the world's nations. Indeed, fourteen countries on the European continent have formally imposed a duty to rescue. THE GOOD SAMARITAN AND THE LAW 92 (James Radcliffe ed., 1966).

Here in the United States, too, there is a growing recognition that society has a significant interest in motivating citizens to prevent harm to others in peril. For instance, Vermont has statutorily imposed a duty to rescue. Under that law, a person who knows that another is in grave danger has a duty to make reasonable rescue efforts, unless such a rescue would pose a risk to the rescuer. A failure to do so is punished criminally, with a fine not exceeding $100. Vt. Stat. Ann. tit. 12 § 519 (1973). Similarly, many states have been enacting two other kinds of statutes meant to encourage rescue: statutes that indemnify rescuers for any loss that may befall them while rescuing, and statutes immunizing individuals who render aid in an emergency. For instance, "[s]ome states now pay citizens for injuries they sustain in preventing [harms to others]" that occur through crime. Scheid, *supra* at 15. Such rescuing actions are understood as beneficial to the entire public, and thus, it is seen as appropriate for the state to indemnify "any injury . . . or damage" that the rescuer might incur "as a direct consequence of such meritorious action." *See* Cal. Penal Code § 13600 (West 1965). To be clear, the tort *duty* to rescue those who are in peril of serious bodily injury or death in circumstances where a failure to do so would shock the conscience in no way requires a rescuer to risk any sort of injury at all in fulfilling the duty. But, in circumstances where a person has voluntarily opted, duty or not, to engage in a risky activity to prevent criminal harm to others, some states have seen fit to reward such a person with indemnification for any losses that result. Similarly, virtually all states, including Michigan, have enacted statutes specifically immunizing those who offer aid in an emergency. Mich. Comp. Laws Ann. § 691.1501 (1968). A tort duty to rescue aligns with these statutory efforts and the underlying recognized public interest in encouraging rescue and preventing harm to others.

Having concluded that jurisprudence and the orderly development of the common law, as well as the general social contract, the laws of other nations, and recent statutory efforts all support the existence of a duty to rescue, and having determined that such a duty arises when a circumstantial connection between an imperiled person and a rescuer is such that the failure to impose a duty would shock the conscience, the question becomes what one must do to discharge that duty. As with any duty in negligence, the question will come down to whether the rescuer acted reasonably under all the circumstances. As mentioned, the duty does not involve placing oneself in jeopardy. Rather, in circumstances where it would shock the conscience to not impose a duty to rescue, that duty is met by simply exercising the reasonable care of a fellow citizen. The duty does not require that a person engage in any activities or behavior that brings risk to him or herself. No one is expected to jump into a river to save another. But one may be expected to throw in a life-preserver, if one is easily and readily accessible, and one may be required to alert others who would be better equipped to assist.

In fact, technological changes in society also both support the recognition of a general duty to rescue, and offer a path to its easy fulfillment. The recent development and increasing implementation of the 911 telephone emergency system portend that national access to emergency services by simply dialing those three numbers is on the horizon. Currently, approximately seventeen percent of the national population is able to contact emergency services such as police, fire, and ambulance simply by telephoning 911, and such coverage is constantly expanding. Alerting emergency responders to the situation of a person in peril through a 911 telephone call will likely often be a simple way of fulfilling a duty to rescue. And of course, even without 911 in full operation in many areas, the duty to rescue a person in peril of serious bodily injury or death can often be fulfilled by simply telephoning the police or another third party who has the duty or ability to render aid, with no risk at all to the rescuer.

Notably, a motivating force behind the implementation of this growing 911 system was a well-publicized failure to rescue: the shocking murder of Kitty Genovese in New York in 1964. A reported thirty-eight people in the area either saw or heard the brutal stabbing of this young woman, yet did nothing to assist. The thirty-eight people who witnessed the attack on Kitty Genovese, for their part, offered up a number of explanations for their failure to attempt rescue. One reason was that many felt the attack was likely part of a "domestic dispute," and thus a private matter between a man and woman or husband and wife. As the Kitty Genovese case helped bring to light, domestic violence is a significant social problem, and the American public consciousness is slowly becoming more aware of its prevalence. The response of turning a blind eye to it, though perhaps done with a nod to the importance of family privacy, has contributed to the deaths of women like Kitty Genovese. The recognition of a duty to rescue as established in the present case may motivate those who hear and witness such scenarios to take action and alert the relevant authorities.

The large number of witnesses in the Kitty Genovese case also connects to a common objection raised in response to proposals of a robust duty to rescue rule: what should be done in situations of such mass failure? "[W]hich person among fifty who watched the victim drown had the duty to aid? Are all liable for one man's death?" Schied, *supra* at 14. While this is often presented as an intractable problem, the answer is in fact straightforward and simple. If the circumstantial connection between each witness and the imperiled person is such that failing to impose a duty would shock the conscience, each is liable for failing to attempt a rescue. *Id.* The "inhumanity of forty-nine does not excuse that of the fiftieth." *Id.* If the behavior of each would shock the conscience, then the duty to rescue would apply to each.[3] And, it is hoped, once the duty to rescue becomes widely known and develops into a common practice, situations in which multiple individuals fail to fulfill it should be few and far between.

In the case at bar, on the facts as the jury determined them, friends Siegrist and Farwell had agreed to spend the evening together, and were alone in a vehicle late at night when Farwell became unconscious. Siegrist, knowing of the recent violent assault on Farwell and knowing that he was not responding to normal stimuli, nevertheless abandoned him unconscious in the back seat of his car, with the knowledge that it was likely no one would discover him until morning. Under these circumstances, to say that Siegrist had no duty to obtain assistance or to at least notify someone of Farwell's unconscious condition and whereabouts would be "shocking to humanitarian considerations" and fly in the face of "the commonly accepted code of social conduct." Siegrist thus owed a duty of rescue to Farwell.

The traditional categories of exceptions also help to support this conclusion. Though they are by no means required for finding that a duty to rescue exists, the traditional four bases for finding an affirmative duty to rescue can inform the analysis regarding whether the circumstantial circumstances surrounding the imperiled person and the rescuer are such that failing to impose a duty would shock the conscience. Two traditional exceptions, in particular, are relevant to the analysis here. The first relevant exception is that once someone has attempted to give aid, they then have a duty to avoid worsening a situation and adding to the peril. In the case at bar, Siegrist tended to Farwell's injuries immediately following the beating, by bringing and applying ice to his head. Later, though, Siegrist isolated and secluded the plaintiff from any source of potential additional aid, when he left him, unbeknownst to others, unconscious in the backseat of his car. When considering the circumstantial connection between the imperiled person and the rescuer, such facts remain important.

The second traditional category for finding an affirmative duty to rescue that is relevant to this case is that of a "special relationship" between the parties. This traditional exception suggests that a previously existing

[3] Of course, one can also imagine situations in which a would-be rescuer is actually entirely justified in believing that another person will perform the rescue. *See, e.g.*, The Good Samaritan and the Law 103 (James Ratcliffe ed., 1966), describing a Polish criminal statute which exempts liability when "there exists a strong possibility of prompt and effective aid by another person or institution whose duty to render aid is obviously greater, or when the potential rescuer, having good reasons for it, was convinced that such a strong possibility exists."

relationship between the parties may be relevant to determining the existence of a duty. Courts have previously held that there are duties to aid in situations involving common carriers and passengers, innkeepers and guests, businesses and invitees, employers and employees, schools and students, landlords and tenants, jailors and prisoners, and parents and children. RESTATEMENT (SECOND) OF TORTS § 314 (1965). But some courts have taken an overly formalistic view of these categories, as occurred in this court in the case of *People v. Beardsley*, 113 N.W. 1128 (Mich. 1907). In that case, a man whose long-term lover fatally overdosed on morphine in his presence was acquitted of criminal charges flowing from his failure to provide any assistance to her, on the grounds that absent a formal marital relationship, he owed her no duty. A more flexible approach, which does not slavishly defer to the formal status relationship between the parties but instead considers the relationship between the parties as part of the circumstantial connection between then, avoids such a result.

Here, Farwell and Siegrist were close friends. As companions engaged in an evening of carousing around together, they had an implicit understanding that each would render to the other the care that friends generally render to each other, including assisting the other if he is in peril, if he can do so without endangering himself. Siegrist knew that Farwell was in a state of unconsciousness and isolated in the backseat of the car. He could, with little inconvenience, easily have notified Farwell's grandparents, or another adult of Farwell's precarious state. His failure to do so in light of their preexisting relationship and expectation of care further supports the conclusion that there is a circumstantial connection between the parties in this case such that failing to impose a duty would meet the requirements of the shock the conscience test.

III WHETHER THE EXISTENCE OF A DUTY IS A MATTER OF LAW TO BE DETERMINED SOLELY BY A COURT

Having addressed the content of the duty to rescue, the next question that this court must consider is whether the existence of a duty in a particular case is always a matter of law to be determined solely by the court. "A duty, in negligence cases, may be defined as an obligation, to which the law will give recognition and effect, to conform to a particular standard of conduct toward another." WILLIAM PROSSER, TORTS 324 (4th ed. 1971).

The existence of a duty is ordinarily a question of law. However, there are factual circumstances which give rise to a duty. The existence of those facts must be determined by a jury. In *Bonin v. Gralewicz*, 146 N.W.2d 647, 649 (Mich. 1966), this court reversed a directed verdict of no cause of action where the trial court had determined as a matter of law that the proofs were insufficient to establish a duty of care:

> Usually, in negligence cases, whether a duty is owed by the defendant to the plaintiff does not require resolution of fact issues. However, in some cases, as in this one, fact issues arise. When they do, they must be submitted to the jury, our traditional finders of fact, for ultimate resolution, and they must be accompanied by an appropriate conditional instruction regarding defendant's duty, conditioned upon the jury's resolution of the fact dispute.

This same rule was stated more recently in *Davis v. Thornton*: "The trial judge in this case determined the defendant owed the plaintiff no duty. We believe this conclusion could properly be made only by a jury." 180 N.W.2d 11, 13 (Mich. 1970).

In a case such as the one at bar, the jury must determine, after considering all the evidence, whether there existed, on the facts, a circumstantial connection between the imperiled person, such that to not impose a duty would be shocking to humanitarian considerations. If such a circumstantial connection exists, then a duty also exists.

"Before any duty, or any standard of conduct may be set, there must first be proof of facts which give rise to it." PROSSER, *supra*, at 205. Whether those facts have been proved is a question for the jury and thus the jury may play a role in determining the existence of a duty.

> Professor Green argues that it is impossible in the nature of things for the duty problem to be decided by the jury, for if the court sends the issue to the jury this "necessarily operates as a ruling that there is a duty or else he would never have submitted the case to the jury at all." But that is not so. As in the case of any other issue, the judge will leave the question to the jury if it is a debatable one, but the jury may decide that (for example) plaintiff was beyond the apparent scope of danger from defendant's conduct, and so beyond the scope of the duty to perform it carefully, even where they are quite ready to find defendant's conduct clearly below the standard of reasonable care.
>
> 2 HARPER & JAMES, THE LAW OF TORTS 1060 (1956)

There were multiple findings of fact relevant to the determination of whether a circumstantial connection that supports a duty to rescue existed in this case. These facts included the history of the relationship between the parties, whether either party had any characteristics that would make them particularly dependent on the other, whether Siegrist knew that Farwell had been injured or was in need of medical assistance, and what Siegrist believed regarding when Farwell would be discovered. To make these assessments, the jury would be required to weigh the credibility and value of conversational exchanges like the following, in which Farwell's father testified to admissions made to him by Siegrist:

Q. Witness, just before the jury was excused, I asked whether you had any conversation with Mr. Siegrist after this event occurred. You answered, "Yes, the day after in the living room of Mrs. Grenier's (the deceased's mother) home." Then, the jury was excused, and we made a special record, and now I would like to ask you some questions that I asked and that you answered out of the presence of the jury.
A. Yes.
Q. What did Mr. Siegrist say, how did the conversation go?
A. I asked him why he left Ricky (the deceased) in the driveway of his grandfather's home.
Q. What did he say?
A. He said, "Ricky was hurt bad, I was scared." I said, "Why didn't you tell somebody, tell his grandparents?" He said, "I know I should have, I don't know."

The jury in this case found that Siegrist owed a duty to Farwell, that Siegrist did not act reasonably in discharging that duty, and that his negligence was the proximate cause of Farwell's death. The court of appeals, in error, misinterpreted the law governing the duty to rescue and substituted its own judgment for these findings. The verdict of the jury is hereby reinstated, and the court of appeals decision is reversed.

5

Commentary on *Tarasoff v. Regents of University of California*

JAMIE R. ABRAMS

By any account, *Tarasoff v. Regents of University of California* belongs in the canon of critical torts cases.[1] It "reconceptuali[zed] the nature and source of duty and of tort liability" by creating a duty on psychotherapists to protect third parties from the foreseeable criminal acts of their patients.[2] This reconceptualization sent shock waves through the medical community and raised larger questions of just how far affirmative duties of care might extend. The case's reverberations can still be felt more than forty years later as medical and legal communities alike debate the holding's scope and implications.

There is no doubt of the case's sweeping impact in torts. The case raised questions regarding the fundamental rights and responsibilities underlying our most trusted relationships, including doctors and patients, police and communities, intimate partners, siblings, and students and personnel on college campuses. These relationships trigger consideration of our most basic vulnerabilities and dependencies. The original opinions made no explicit mention whatsoever of gender and offered no direct or indirect contributions to feminist thinking or activism contemporaneously. Feminist framings were, however, just below the surface and the feminist judgment successfully explores them richly and thoroughly.

CASE BACKGROUND AND THE ORIGINAL OPINIONS

Reading the original opinions, readers sparsely learn only that a male student (Prosenjit Poddar) murdered a female college student at Berkeley.[3] Upon the

1 551 P.2d 334 (Cal. 1976).

2 Peter F. Lake, *Revisiting Tarasoff*, 58 ALB. L. REV. 97, 98 (1994).

3 *Tarasoff v. Regents of Univ. of California*, 529 P.2d 553 (Cal. 1974) ("*Tarasoff I*"), *reh'g granted, opinion not citable* (Mar. 12, 1975), *vacated*, 551 P.2d 334 (Cal. 1976) ("*Tarasoff II* ").

advice of a friend, Poddar sought mental health counseling before this crime at Berkeley's Cowell Memorial Hospital operated and maintained by the Regents of the University of California.[4] Dr. Moore, the therapist treating Poddar, knew of his threats against the victim (Tatiana Tarasoff) and only informed campus police, but did not warn her directly.[5] The police did detain the assailant, but they released him after concluding that he was "rational."[6]

In their feminist judgment, Justices Sharmila Lodhia and Stephanie Wildman reveal much more about the cultural and social context of what was happening. For example, Poddar grew up in northern India as a member of "the Harijan or 'untouchable' caste," having only attended all-male schools.[7] Even the feminist judgment, however, is understandably restrained in its characterization of the facts, consistent with the likelihood of feminist coverage contemporaneously in the 1970s. In a modern context, the facts might be portrayed even more dramatically as an eerie stalking and predatory pursuit of a woman over months, not the singular criminal act of murder as the original published opinions portrayed.

The premise to understanding *Tarasoff*'s relevance to tort law is that ordinarily individuals do not owe affirmative duties to prevent the criminal acts of third parties. Tarasoff's parents originally sued both the police and the therapists through the Board of Regents on two grounds: defendants' failure to warn plaintiffs of the impending danger and their failure to bring about Poddar's confinement.[8] The initial case theory did not include a "failure to protect" claim.

The court's first holding in 1974 stated that there was a duty on therapists to warn the victim where a specific threat existed. The court allowed the plaintiffs to amend their complaint to state this claim. The court originally reasoned that the psychiatric community's concerns for patient–doctor confidentiality did not justify concealing knowledge of this specific danger.[9]

Two years later, the court reheard the case in an unusual procedural move, vacating its prior decision, after the American Psychiatric Association (APA)

4 *Id.*

5 *Id.* (revealing that Poddar said he would kill "an unnamed girl, readily identifiable as Tatiana Tarasoff, when she returned home to Berkeley from Brazil").

6 551 P.2d at 341.

7 Mark A. Rothstein, *Tarasoff Duties after Newtown*, 42 J. L., Med. & Ethics 104, 104 (2014).

8 *Tarasoff II*, 551 P.2d at 340. Both parties were immune from suits for failure to confine in both *Tarasoff* I and II.

9 Justices Mosk and Clark separately dissented. Because their dissents are similar to their dissents in the 1976 opinion, they are not summarized separately.

sought clarification of the 1974 ruling.[10] The rehearing also followed publication of an influential scholarly article on the topic.[11] It is this second decision, released in July 1976 – eighteen months after the original decision – that sets out the well-known "*Tarasoff* rule."

Generally, one person owes no duty to control the conduct of another unless the defendant is in a "special relationship to either the person whose conduct needs to be controlled or … to the foreseeable victim of that conduct."[12] However, California courts have departed from the general rule by balancing factors such as how foreseeable the harm is, how certain the injury is, how close the defendant is to the injury, the "moral blame attached to the defendant's conduct," the policy rationales for preventing the harm, the burden on the defendant to comply with the duty, and the insurability of risk.[13]

Here, the pleadings had not raised any question as to the failure of defendant therapists to predict that Poddar actually presented a serious danger of violence,[14] although the predictability of violence could be an issue in other cases. The *Tarasoff* rule comes into play once the therapist determines, or should have determined, that there is a serious risk of violence. In the court's words:

> When a psychotherapist determines, or pursuant to the standards of his profession should determine, that his patient presents a serious danger of violence to another, he incurs an obligation to use reasonable care to protect the intended victim against such danger. The discharge of this duty may require the therapist to take one or more of various steps, depending on the nature of the case. Thus it may call for him to warn the intended victim or others likely to apprise the victim of the danger, to notify the police, or to take whatever other steps are reasonably necessary under the circumstances.[15]

The therapist need only exercise "that reasonable degree of skill, knowledge, and care ordinarily possessed and exercised by members of (that professional specialty) under similar circumstances."[16] The court allowed plaintiffs to

10 Brief of Amicus Curiae, Am. Psychiatric Ass'n, *Tarasoff I* (Cal. 1974).

11 John G. Fleming & Bruce Maximov, *The Patient or His Victim: The Therapist's Dilemma*, 62 Cal. L. Rev. 1025 (1974). Notably, the article begins with a vignette about whether a therapist has a duty to warn involving a plan to kill a patient's "former lover." *Id.* at 1025 (insinuating that these were *Tarasoff*'s facts).

12 *Tarasoff II*, 551 P.2d at 343.

13 *Id.* at 342.

14 *Id.* at 344–45.

15 *Id.* at 340.

16 *Id.* at 345.

amend their complaints to state a cause of action against defendant therapists.[17]

The court reached a different holding, however, for police liability. It is this different treatment that leads Justices Lodhia and Wildman to concur with respect to the therapist liability holding and dissent with respect to the police department holding. On the question of police liability, the court held that the police did not have any such special relationship to either the victim or to the perpetrator sufficient to impose upon the police defendants a duty to warn Tarasoff of Poddar's violent intentions.[18]

Justice Mosk issued a partial concurrence and partial dissent. He concurred in the result "only because the complaints allege[d] that defendant therapists did in fact predict that Poddar would kill and were therefore negligent in failing to warn of that danger."[19] He declined to hold therapists liable for failing to predict a patient's violence tendencies under tort standards based on what *other* practitioners would have done.[20] The court's prior decision in *People v. Burnick* had reasoned that psychiatric predictions of violence were not reliable enough for admission into evidence.[21] Although the majority concluded its holding was not inconsistent with *Burnick*, Justice Mosk considered it inconsistent to bar a psychiatrist's testimony because of questions surrounding the profession's ability to predict dangerousness, while imposing liability for failure to predict dangerousness in *Tarasoff*.[22]

Justice Clark also dissented, reasoning that the question of whether to sacrifice confidentiality was for the legislature and that statutory law provided no applicable confidentiality exception.[23] Sacrificing confidentiality, Justice Clark argued, offered virtually no benefit to society, save to "frustrate psychiatric treatment, invade fundamental patient rights and increase violence."[24]

Tarasoff had far-reaching effects. It expanded legal and societal understandings of duties owed and reframed the physician–patient relationship to impose obligations to individuals outside that relationship. Although the APA had sought clarification in *Tarasoff II* out of concern for the profession, the result was arguably worse for psychologists and psychiatrists. The choice originally presented in litigation was between a duty to warn and a duty to confine. The

[17] *Id.* at 340.
[18] *Id.* at 349.
[19] *Id.* at 353 (Mosk, J., dissenting).
[20] *Id.* at 344.
[21] *Id.* at 346 (*citing* People v. Burnick, 535 P.2d 352 (Cal. 1975)).
[22] *Id.* at 354 (Mosk, J., dissenting).
[23] *Id.* at 354–62.
[24] *Id.* at 358.

court instead imposed an ambiguous duty to protect, without clarifying "what steps were legally necessary and sufficient to meet this obligation to protect the public."[25] Critics argued that the holding was "designed to change private behavior without reliable data regarding the practices it was intending to change, the extent of the problem it was trying to remedy, or the costs which the proposed cure would impose."[26] The opinion was criticized generally for its "conclusory reasoning and lack of analysis."[27] It led to legislative limitations in California on monetary liability.[28]

When faced with the vulnerability of an unknowing victim and the vulnerability of a patient struggling with mental illness and seeking medical care, the court chose to place accountability squarely with the medical community and to immunize law enforcement from accountability. One scholar complained that "the court's pious rhetoric about protecting the public as a justification for placing this burden on psychotherapists" was "hypocritical when the police who decided not to confine Poddar were found not to be liable. Can courts claim to be protecting the public when they assign police duties to psychotherapists and absolve the police of those same duties?"[29] Justices Lodhia and Wildman remedy this injustice in their rewritten opinion.

Tarasoff created a national wave of state reforms and debate,[30] even though the holding itself was limited to California. Some courts followed *Tarasoff* requiring affirmative obligations of therapists, others created permissive approaches allowing warnings or interventions, while others explicitly rejected *Tarasoff*.[31] *Tarasoff* prompted efforts to develop better "risk-assessment tools" to "assist mental health professionals in their decision-making, enabling preservation of the integrity of the provider–patient relationship and minimizing the

[25] Alan A. Stone, Law, Psychiatry, and Morality 169 (1984).

[26] Daniel J. Givelber, William J. Bowers, & Carolyn L. Blitch, *Tarasoff, Myth and Reality: An Empirical Study of Private Law in Action*, 1984 Wisc. L. Rev. 443, 444 (1984).

[27] *Id.* at 447.

[28] Calif. Civ. Code § 43.92 (2017) (requiring "reasonable efforts" and limiting liability to cases where the threat has been communicated to the therapist and involves a "serious threat of physical violence against a reasonably identifiable victim or victims").

[29] Stone, *supra* note 25, at 174.

[30] *See* Ahmad Adi & Mohammad Mathbout, *The Duty to Protect: Four Decades after Tarasoff*, Am. J. of Psychiatry Residents' J. (Apr. 2018) (for a state breakdown of the *Tarasoff* implementation across states). *See generally* Givelber, *supra* note 26, at 457–62 (concluding that 96 percent of California psychiatrists and 87 percent of psychiatrists surveyed outside of California knew the case by name or had heard of a similar case).

[31] *See* W. Jonathan Cardi, *A Pluralistic Analysis of the Therapist/Physician Duty to Warn Third Parties*, 44 Wake Forest L. Rev. 877, 881 (2009) (explaining that the Third Restatement is silent on this).

risk of legal liability."[32] Critics of *Tarasoff* argued it was "too great an imposition on one's liberty" and that it "would present courts with intractable line-drawing difficulties."[33] They also expressed worry about the effectiveness of predicting dangerousness because "providers are often unclear about how to accurately prognosticate, both 'prediction and assessment of violent behavior do not yet have reliable, clinically validated paradigms.'"[34]

Secondary scope questions emerged after *Tarasoff* regarding whether the holding extended to physicians in other contexts such as communicable diseases,[35] and attorney liability in cases of domestic violence.[36] Four decades later, "a clear and ubiquitous method for its application has not yet been established. Discrepancies and vagueness between states, as well as between providers, regarding how and when to apply the duty to protect still exist. Such variations affect both therapeutic alliances and providers' risk of legal liability."[37]

THE FEMINIST JUDGMENT

In their feminist judgment, Justices Lodhia and Wildman concur with the *Tarasoff II* opinion, finding a therapist duty to warn a third party of potential criminal harm. They also dissent and would likewise hold the campus police department liable for a similar duty to warn. Their opinion weaves together strands of relational feminism, dominance feminism, and intersectional feminism.

The Justices begin by asking readers to consider the role of the Good Samaritan biblical parable in tort law. This framing reminds us of *Tarasoff*'s modern relevance and looming questions about its scope in law and society. Iconic images, names, and stories exist in popular culture of Good Samaritans, such as the image of the rescuer in the cowboy hat carrying a Boston Marathon bombing terrorist attack victim or concertgoers in Las Vegas carrying injured patrons out of the music festival on metal crowd barriers.[38] For

[32] Adi & Mathbout, *supra* note 30.

[33] Cardi, *supra* note 31, at 882.

[34] Adi & Mathbout, *supra* note 30.

[35] Cardi, *supra* note 31, at 877.

[36] *See e.g.*, Christine A. Picker, *The Intersection of Domestic Violence and Child Abuse: Ethical Considerations and Tort Issues for Attorneys Who Represent Battered Women with Abused Children*, 12 St. Louis U. Pub. L. Rev. 69 (1993).

[37] Adi & Mathbout, *supra* note 30, at 58.

[38] *See* Bonnie D. Ford, *Portrait of a Rescue*, ESPN.com, Oct. 30, 2013; Sheri Fink, *After the Las Vegas Shooting Concertgoers Become Medics*, N.Y. Times, Oct. 15, 2017.

every Good Samaritan story, however, there are questions of who could have and should have done more to stop preventable harms such as school shootings, drug overdoses, sexual assaults, and domestic violence. Justices Lodhia and Wildman frame the question before the court around the merits of the Good Samaritan parable as a doctrinal torts principle. This framing sets up the impact of the opinion and lays the foundation for a dominance feminism analysis of how the state deploys its power and for whom.

Justices Lodhia and Wildman next highlight the case facts and its cultural context. The original opinion wrote the gendered and cultural dimensions out of the case entirely, reminding us of the FEMINIST JUDGMENTS project's power and value. Lodhia and Wildman reveal the story of culture and gender in the case history. Analyzing both the gender and the ethnic identity of the parties moves the court toward an intersectional feminist analysis.

By examining the cultural and social interactions between Tarasoff and Poddar, the feminist judgment also invokes relational feminism. When the law ignores social context, it makes power invisible by leaving unacknowledged the "assumptions and invisible mechanisms through which relational presumptions enter the law."[39] Relational feminism shows how the law acts within a social context by "creating rights defining relationships, and interpreting the meaning of social events."[40] When we simply take for granted commonplace categories, they are normalized as "simply the way things *are*, not a judgment about the way things *should be*."[41] Relational feminists, like Mary Becker, push for substantive reforms that engage feminism in work differentiating good relationships from bad ones.[42]

The authors do just that, leading them directly to their critique of state action. They define new normative relational standards between the state and women and between individuals and potential victims of violence arguing that "bodily integrity" is a "cornerstone of democracy" necessary to "engage in democratic practice." They explain that this right to democratic participation was allowed to "recede from public consciousness" as a right because its absence has been uniquely experienced by women. Their basic claim is that because men experience the need for protection from bodily harm less often and less urgently than women, the law has not adequately taken account of it. For centuries, the doctrine of coverture pretended that women were under the protection of their husbands – rather than the state – which ignored state

39 C. Albiston, T. Brito, & J. E. Larson, *Feminism in Relation*, 17 WIS. WOMEN'S L.J. 1,3 (2002).
40 *Id.* at 4.
41 *Id.*
42 Mary Becker, *Feminists and Care*, 17 WIS. WOMEN'S L.J. 57 (2002).

responsibility to protect women from harm. Although state responsibility to protect the bodily integrity of its citizens has not yet been "widely recognized," Lodhia and Wildman insist that tort law would benefit from its incorporation. Their overarching objective is to assure that tort law aspires to a society in which women's bodily harms are valued equally to men's.

This reasoning answers Catharine MacKinnon's later call to action situated in dominance feminism. Specifically, the feminist authors' analysis calls out the state for devaluing women's lived experiences. It challenges existing norms of state accountability built upon the subordination of women.[43] The authors give concrete voice to MacKinnon's idea of the masculine state built around male experiences and silencing women's experiences.

If the state did not normalize threats of violence against women, it might have disrupted this tragic chain of events by changing norms and behaviors. Using real-time sources, Lodhia and Wildman demonstrate just how much we knew (and have known for a long time) about gendered violence, how it occurs, when it occurs, and why it occurs.[44] They challenge myths that women are most in danger in dark alleys, instead urging for greater interventions within intimate relationships.

The feminist Justices outline a mandate for deeper state accountability. They call us to state action, which allows us to see how adoption of their judgment might have reformed society more systemically and relationally, even before the flowering of feminist legal theory that began in the 1980s. Like the majority, Lodhia and Wildman find a duty arising from the doctor–patient relationship,[45] but they also cite and adopt James Barr Ames's famous proposal made in 1908 that, when no special relationship exists, civil liability should nonetheless attach to bystanders who fail to act when it requires little risk or inconvenience to intervene and such intervention would prevent a grave harm. This move positions *Tarasoff* into the "easy rescue" category. Using the Ames analysis, it also becomes an easy call for campus police to warn Tarasoff as well.

[43] Catharine A. MacKinnon, *Feminism, Marxism, Method, and the State: Toward Feminist Jurisprudence*, 8 Signs 635, 643–44 (1983) ("The question for feminism, for the first time on its own terms is: What is this state, from women's point of view?").

[44] Here the Justices draw upon the subsequent work of Martha R. Mahoney in *Legal Images of Battered Women: Redefining the Issue of Separation*, 90 Mich. L. Rev. 1 (1991) in which Mahoney surveys historic cases describing "separation assault."

[45] A recent 2018 California case has led to further expansions of duties of care consistent with the opinion of the feminist judgments. *Regents v. Superior Ct.*, 413 P.3d 656 (Cal. 2018) (citing *Tarasoff* and holding that universities have a special relationship with their students that requires them to protect students against violence during curricular activities after a student was attacked by another student with a knife in a chemistry lab).

While the feminist Justices see no distinction between the accountability of therapists and campus police, they do limit their analysis to *campus* police liability, distinct from state and municipal police. They reason that universities, by relying on and funding campus police departments, have taken on a duty separate and distinct from state and municipal police departments. It is an interesting thought experiment to consider which direction this analysis might have gone in subsequent cases. The dominance feminism lens suggests a strong stance on state accountability emerging from the holding, but the holding aligns with the narrower facts before it. Might university communities have used this reasoning as a justification to abandon campus police departments entirely, or might its reasoning, while technically limited to campus police, nonetheless have expanded to reforming and transforming the culture of police practices in state and local government as well?

Imagine if law enforcement personnel, for example, were not just begrudgingly compelled to attend occasional domestic violence trainings, but were forced to redesign police practices and interventions around the risk of accountability for failure to act.[46] Arguably, given the highly masculinized field of law enforcement, the gendered dynamics and complexities that come into play when we attempt to hold police accountable for their actions in policing violent crimes against women are *even greater* than those present in the therapist–patient context. Justices Lodhia and Wildman note that it was a male police officer who concluded that a male detainee appeared "rational" before release. Here, might the implicit reason why campus police accepted Poddar's minimization of the events sit in the gendered context of male law enforcement policing male crimes against women?[47]

The tension this feminist analysis creates for feminist theory is how to give voice and substance to these duties without recreating the same hierarchies

[46] *See, e.g.*, Angela R. Gover et al., *Law Enforcement Officers' Attitudes about Domestic Violence*, Violence Against Women 1, 16 (2011) (concluding that many officers do not support more training and have not fully accepted the "causal factors and prevalence rates of domestic violence").

[47] *See, e.g.*, Leigh Goodmark, *Hands Up at Home: Militarized Masculinity and Police Officers Who Commit Intimate Partner Abuse*, 2015 Brigham Young L. Rev. 101, 151 (2016) ("The hypermasculine environment of policing is extremely resistant to change and fosters a climate within which violence against women or against those who are feminized is not only tolerated, but used to assert one's own status as a hegemonic male"); Jamie R. Abrams, *The Collateral Consequences of Masculinizing Violence*, 16 Wm. & Mary J. Women & the Law, 703, 723–27 (2010) ("With this foundational feminist challenge to hegemonic masculinity and the resulting extraction of violence against women from masculine norms came at least two collateral consequences: (1) the entrenchment of binary roles positioning men as potential perpetrators of violence and women as vulnerable to victimization; and (2) the empowerment of the state as the surrogate masculine defender of women and families").

that led to the underlying harm. When we add gender and cultural context into the mix, interesting questions arise as to whether we might actually end up with more misunderstandings. How do we enforce duties of care without exacerbating discriminatory practices and implicit bias in law enforcement?[48] For example, in *Tarasoff*, there were suggestions that Poddar believed his "honor" had been violated. Careful training is necessary to teach police officers and mental health professionals how to intervene to prevent gendered harms without essentializing or stereotyping communities, particularly communities of color.[49] The feminist Justices' intersectional approach suggests their sensitivity to these realities, but would that sensitivity translate effectively to state and private actors?

Justices Lodhia and Wildman close their opinion boldly and accurately, concluding that their revised analysis might have had life-saving consequences for Tarasoff and life-altering consequences for all individuals, allowing us each to realize our central right to bodily integrity from harm. Their view is indeed an empowering one in its theoretical underpinnings. Given the deep entrenchment of violence against women in institutions, society, and cultural norms, however, perhaps even this feminist judgment would not have been enough to actualize the eradication of violence against women.

TARASOFF v. REGENTS OF THE UNIVERSITY OF CALIFORNIA, 551 P.2D 334 (CAL. 1976)

JUSTICES SHARMILA LODHIA AND STEPHANIE M. WILDMAN, CONCURRING AND DISSENTING

This tort lawsuit stems from the homicide committed by Prosenjit Poddar, who killed Tatiana Tarasoff on October 27, 1969. As the majority opinion observes, this civil action comes before us on an appeal filed by the deceased's parents from defendants' successful demurrer. The appeal poses the issue "whether [the second amended] complaint now state[s], or can be amended

[48] *See, e.g.*, United States Department of Justice, *Identifying and Preventing Gender Bias in Law Enforcement Response to Sexual Assault and Domestic Violence*, www.justice.gov/ovw/identifying-and-preventing-gender-bias ("Gender bias in policing practices is a form of discrimination that may result in [law enforcement agencies] providing less protection to certain victims on the basis of gender, failing to respond to crimes that disproportionately harm people of a particular gender or offering reduced or less robust services due to a reliance on gender stereotypes").

[49] *See, e.g.*, Michelle Alexander, The New Jim Crow: Mass Incarceration in the Age of Colorblindness (2010).

to state, causes of action against defendants." *Tarasoff v. Regents*, 551 P.2d 334, 340–41 (Cal. 1976). We are deciding whether, assuming the factual allegations in the complaint can be proven as true, a negligence cause of action can be stated against the defendant campus therapists, the campus police, and thus their employer, the Regents of the University of California.

We concur with the majority in finding that a negligence action can be brought against the campus therapists, but we dissent from the majority's holding that no such action is available against the campus police. The University owed a duty that should have been carried out by its employees to act reasonably to protect Tarasoff from the peril she faced, a peril known to the campus therapists and campus police based on Poddar's explicit threat that he planned to kill her. As the majority pointed out in regard to the therapists, this duty might have been discharged by a simple warning to Tarasoff or her family.

In considering the facts before us, we are reminded of an earlier case involving violence against women which jolted the public conscience. In 1964, Catherine (Kitty) Genovese died after being attacked and stabbed in a well-populated area of Queens, New York. Early reports suggested that bystanders watched or listened but did not respond to her cries for help. The case became a metaphor for the Good Samaritan conundrum in US tort law. In the biblical text (Luke 10:30–39), which presents the parable of the Good Samaritan, the priest and the Levite pass an injured, attacked man; they walk to the other side of the road ignoring his need, but the passing Samaritan comes to the man's aid. Merriam Webster refers to this story in defining the "good Samaritan" as "a person who helps other people and especially strangers" in distress. The parable suggests that the failure of the priest and Levite to act in coming to the aid of another is morally wrong. However, while the failure to act may be immoral, within tort law there has traditionally been no automatic duty to act to come to the aid of another, outside of certain established "special relationships."

Now, a decade later, another woman has died after being attacked and stabbed. Individuals were aware prior to the homicide that her assailant had threatened to kill her, yet they did nothing to warn her of the risk to her life. Does the law need to be so insubstantial as to permit an actor simply to "walk on the other side?" We think not, particularly given the facts of this case, where the required action would have been merely to convey a warning. Had the therapists or the campus police, who knew of the threat, simply warned Tarasoff that Poddar had threatened her life, she might still be alive today.

We believe the factual background, not detailed in the majority opinion, provides significant insight into the cross-cultural and gender realities that bear on understanding why a duty by defendants to warn Tarasoff of her physical peril existed in this case. Therefore, we first set out that background in detail. We then explain some fundamental precepts of the prima facie case for finding tort liability and explore the conundrum of liability for action versus inaction as it relates to the concept of duty toward another. Relying on the work of James Barr Ames, we contend that a workable standard for finding a duty to protect by warning existed here. Further justification for a duty reasonably to warn can be found in a principle of our democracy, which requires protection of the bodily integrity of its citizenry in order to function. Recognizing a duty to warn enables law both to take a moral position and to play a role in supporting and sustaining democracy. We then turn to the cultural and gender context in which the question of duty to protect arises on the basis of these facts. This context strengthens the imperative for finding a duty reasonably to warn of physical danger. The opinion then shifts to consider whether the campus therapists and the campus police owed a duty to warn Tarasoff of her peril. The opinion concludes that each did indeed have such a duty if the plaintiffs can prove the alleged facts.

I FACTUAL BACKGROUND

This homicide case has been before this court prior to the initiation of the civil tort lawsuit that is the focus of this decision. We refer, of course, to Poddar's criminal trial and appeal. That trial resulted in a second-degree murder conviction, which this court reversed on appeal, finding that the trial judge's instructions on diminished capacity were inadequate. Even though the legal grounds for the criminal conviction were not sustainable, we note that the court gained knowledge of some of the facts of this case from the public record in the criminal case. Because this civil case comes to us on appeal prior to a trial of the tort claims, plaintiffs will carry the burden of proving the relevant facts in the remanded case.

Prosenjit Poddar was an international student pursuing graduate studies in naval architecture at the University of California, Berkeley. He had immigrated to the United States from a rural village in Bengal, India in September 1967, and he was a member of the Harijan or "untouchable" caste.[1] Prior to

[1] The caste system in India among Hindus reflects a deeply embedded social hierarchy based on one's work and one's larger spiritual commitment or sense of duty. The four major castes from highest to lowest are Brahmins, Kshatriyas, Vaishyas, and the Shudras (who are sometimes also referred to as "untouchables," Harijans ("Children of God"), or, more recently, Dalits). As Arthur Niehoff writes "although there are rigid class systems known elsewhere, the complexity, elaboration and rigidity of caste in India make it an almost unique system," tied to occupation,

coming to the United States, Poddar had been a successful and accomplished student, graduating from the prestigious Indian Institute of Technology in 1961, a considerable achievement given the social, economic, and educational constraints he labored under due to his position in the lowest rung of India's caste hierarchy. His achievements continued upon his arrival in the United States. He first met Tarasoff in 1968 through a folk-dance group at the International House in Berkeley where he lived. She was also an international student of Russian descent. They cultivated a friendship during their weekly dance group meetings throughout that fall.

The criminal case record indicates that, on New Year's Eve, Tarasoff kissed Poddar and that Poddar interpreted that expression of affection and the conversations between them as signaling a significant relationship between them. However, Tarasoff did not share his interest or interpret their relationship in the same way. Instead, she informed Poddar that she was seeing other people. This rejection prompted a "severe emotional crisis" in Poddar. *People v. Poddar*, 518 P.2d 342, 344 (Cal. 1974). The Supreme Court record indicates he "became depressed and neglected his appearance, his studies and his health." *Id.* He also became obsessive in his behavior towards her, secretly taping several hours of their conversations when they were together and seeking to understand their relationship. His academic work and job performance deteriorated as his desire for a relationship with Tarasoff intensified.

During this time, Poddar also began openly expressing threats to harm Tarasoff to his friends. In May 1969, he told his friend from India, Farrokh Mistree, that he would kill Tarasoff. In the summer of 1969, Tarasoff left on a trip to South America and, during that time, Poddar sought mental health services at Cowell Memorial Hospital. Mistree informed the psychiatrist at Cowell about the threats to Tarasoff, and Poddar began seeing Dr. Lawrence Moore, a psychologist. Dr. Moore saw Poddar for seven clinical sessions. Ultimately, Poddar expressed a threat to kill an unnamed woman, readily identifiable as Tarasoff, when she returned from Brazil. At that point, Dr. Moore contacted campus police officers Everett D. Atkinson and Johnny C. Teel. The doctor said he would be sending a letter describing Poddar's condition so that the police could take him to the Herrick Hospital where Dr. Moore would assign a seventy-two-hour Emergency Psychiatric Detention.

marriage practices, and dietary habits. (Arthur Niehoff, *Caste and Industrial Organization in North India*, ADMINISTRATIVE SCIENCE QUARTERLY, Vol. 3. No. 4, Mar. 1959 at 495). Although the idea of "untouchability" and the tremendous social and political inequalities it produced were forbidden as a matter of law under Article 17 of the Indian Constitution, patterns of discrimination against members of low castes persist (Central Government Act, INDIA CONST., art. 17, 1949).

Other staff at Cowell Memorial Hospital, Stuart Gold MD, who had first examined Poddar at Cowell, and James Yandell MD, the assistant to the director of the department of psychiatry, agreed with the recommendation that Poddar be committed for observation at a mental hospital.

In Dr. Moore's letter to William Beall, chief of campus police, dated August 20, 1969, he explained that Poddar's mental state varied considerably and that "at times he appears quite rational and at other times he appears quite psychotic" (Dr. Moore's letter to William Beall, August 20, 1969). In the letter, he diagnosed Poddar with "paranoid schizophrenic reaction, acute and severe" and suggested that he was "a danger to the welfare of other people and himself." *Id.* He wrote that "he had been threatening to kill an unnamed girl, who he feels has betrayed him and violated his honor" and that "he has told a friend of his (Farrokh Mistree, also of the International House) that he intends to go to San Francisco to buy a gun and that he plans to kill the girl." *Id.*

The campus police did, in fact, take Poddar into custody. He denied having a weapon, and his explanation was that Tarasoff and he had a troubled relationship. Poddar promised to stay away from Tarasoff. The campus police made the determination not to commit him, reasoning that he "appeared rational." *Tarasoff*, 551 P.2d at 338. As the majority notes, "Powelson, director of the department of psychiatry at Cowell Memorial Hospital, then asked the police to return [Dr.] Moore's letter, directed that all copies of the letter and notes that [Dr.] Moore had taken as therapist be destroyed, and 'ordered no action to place Prosenjit Poddar in 72-hour treatment and evaluation facility.'" *Id.* at 341. From that point on, Poddar discontinued his treatment.

In September 1969, Tarasoff returned from her trip to South America and resumed her participation in the folk dancing group. Apparently she talked about a summer relationship she had with another man in front of Poddar. At that point, Poddar sought Tarasoff's brother's help in pursuing a relationship with her. Her brother refused and told Poddar to leave her alone. Poddar began carrying a gun during this period.

Two months elapsed after the recommendation by the treating psychologist to commit Poddar and the campus police's refusal to do so. When the campus police released Poddar from their custody, they did not notify Tarasoff or her parents that she might be in danger. On October 27, 1969, Poddar went to Tarasoff's family home and attempted unsuccessfully to speak with her.

Poddar ended up returning to Tarasoff's home later that day when her family was not there. He took a kitchen knife and a pellet gun with him. Tarasoff told him to leave, and he refused to do so. They fought and she ran out of the house. Poddar shot her with the pellet gun and stabbed her fourteen times with a butcher knife. Tarasoff died near the front door from the knife wounds she sustained. Poddar then called the police, saying he had stabbed someone and wanted to be taken into custody.

The State of California prosecuted Poddar for this crime. This court has previously addressed the issues raised in the criminal case. *Poddar*, 518 P.2d 342.

II POTENTIAL TORT LIABILITY

The present case involves the civil suit brought as a result of Poddar's homicidal action and the conduct of employees of the University of California at Berkeley preceding that event. The University Regents are the named defendants, along with the involved therapists and the campus police. The complaint alleged that two months prior to the homicide, Poddar had "confided his intention to kill [Tarasoff] … to Dr. Lawrence Moore, a psychologist employed by the Cowell Memorial Hospital at the University of California at Berkeley." *Tarasoff*, 551 P.2d at 339. In considering the novel issues raised by this case, we have asked ourselves whether the law ought to impose an obligation on those in a position to prevent such tragic deaths to take steps to avert them. The answer to this compelling question rests in the law of negligence.

Negligence is one of three possible bases for liability in the common-law tort system to address civil "wrongs" or injuries to persons and property, along with intentional torts and strict liability claims. It falls midway on the liability spectrum from intentional wrongdoing to strict liability without fault. In common parlance, an assessment of negligence requires a finding that the tortfeasor has been careless in that he used "less than reasonable care" in conducting his behavior that resulted in harm.

The requisite elements of a negligence case include duty, breach of duty (or lack of reasonable care), actual cause, proximate cause, and damages. All five elements must be proven to establish the cause of action for negligence. Writers often use the word negligence to refer to the first two of these elements – duty and breach together. However, no breach can exist without an antecedent duty. Duty and breach thus combined comprise negligence – the breach of a duty owed.

The critical first element of duty involves considerations of public policy as well as an assessment of the relationship between the parties and involved third parties. In some cases, a duty is clearly established. Thus, on one end of the duty continuum, a car driver clearly owes a duty to drive with reasonable care and follow the rules of the road. Likewise, few would dispute that a parent watching their young child owes a duty to use reasonable care for the child. If the child is hurt, liability is not automatic – that would be strict liability. But if, for example, the child leaves the parent's side to climb into a tiger enclosure at a zoo, most would agree that the parent has an obligation to take reasonable care to protect the child from being injured.

To determine duty, we often ask "does the defendant owe the plaintiff a duty to act as a reasonable prudent person would?" Or to put the question another way, "What are the limitations on the duty to act reasonably?" It should be noted that the existence of duty is not an issue when a party has taken some affirmative action that actively creates a risk of harm to another. In such cases, the person clearly owes a duty to act reasonably. But in situations of "inaction," rather than "action," courts have struggled with whether to impose a duty to act reasonably.

Despite its longevity, the misfeasance–nonfeasance distinction – harm arising from action compared to harm arising from inaction – is not always easy to apply. Consider an actor driving an automobile through a stop sign at an intersection, traveling at high speed without blowing the horn. Is that misfeasance – the negligent operation of the vehicle from which liability follows? Or might the conduct be viewed as nonfeasance – the failure to warn others of danger by negligently omitting to sound the horn, resulting in no liability because the law imposes no duty to act? Although the characterization of an actor's conduct as misfeasance or nonfeasance is a crucial step to determining liability, such conduct could arguably fall under either categorization, and any bright-line distinction is illusory.

In general, Anglo-American jurisprudence posits no duty to come to the aid of or rescue another. Thus, if a stranger claims she would have been saved from harm but for another's inaction, and she sues the other for negligence, the standard response of the defendant is not "I acted reasonably in not saving her," but rather, "I owed no duty to come to her aid." Thus, even an unreasonable failure to act may not give rise to civil liability in the absence of a foundational duty.

Historically, this "no duty to come to the aid of another" doctrine has raised serious philosophical issues. Commentators view it as characteristic of Anglo-American culture, which is described as either "selfishly individualistic" or, alternatively, as "respectful of the autonomy of the individual." These two ways of describing the same doctrine illustrate a tilt in one's political value system. The contrast between "selfishly individualistic" or "respectful of the autonomy of the individual" sits at the heart of many issues in legal theory, and one's political vision may govern the policy choice a decision-maker selects.

Even in nonfeasance cases, however, a duty may arise from a special relationship, as the majority suggests. The majority posits that the relationship between the patient and therapist is strong enough to create a duty on the part of the therapist to warn the patient's potential victim. As discussed more fully below, we agree with that assessment. We write separately, however, because we believe that there is another, more fundamental basis for finding that a duty exists in this case.

III AMES'S DUTY OF "EASY" RESCUE

In his famous article "Law and Morals," James Barr Ames wrestled with the classic issues of the relationship of the law to action, inaction, and liability. James Barr Ames, *Law and Morals*, 22 HARV. L. REV. 97 (1908). Tracing the origins of English law from a formal and amoral beginning to a moral period in which an actor's conduct was assessed to determine whether it was blameworthy, Ames found that an ethical standard of reasonable conduct generally replaced the amoral standard of acting at one's peril. He observed: "On grounds of public policy there are and always will be, on the one hand, many cases in which persons damaged may recover compensation from others whose conduct was morally blameless, and on the other hand, many cases in which persons damaged cannot obtain compensation even from those whose conduct was morally most reprehensible." *Id.* at 109.

In the first category, where liability is imposed on the morally blameless person, he cites the vicarious liability theories that make a master responsible for a servant's actions. Vicarious liability means that the master will be liable even when the master acted reasonably, for example, in selecting the servant with care. Ames explained that results in such cases are "much less disturbing to one's sense of fairness than cases in which innocent victims of the unrighteous are allowed no redress." *Id.* In his view, the law is rightly viewed as utilitarian, existing "for the realization of the reasonable needs of the community." *Id.* at 110. Innocents may suffer when individual interests run counter to community needs, *id.*; but acts that damage another in a manner against "good morals" are unlawful acts. *Id.* at 111.

Ames then turns to the class of "morally reprehensible" cases between unrelated parties having no special relation to one another in which the damage would not have happened but for the willful inaction of another. His examples include the strong swimmer who sees a man drowning, when a rope to toss is easily available, but the swimmer does nothing. He also gives the example of a child on the railroad tracks, unaware of an approaching train, while a bystander, who could easily pull the child to safety, fails to do so. He proposes a workable rule to counter the common-law rule that a bystander has no responsibility to take any action. In terms we endorse today, Ames would impose civil or criminal liability when one "fails to interfere to save another from impending death or great bodily harm, when he might do so with little or no inconvenience to himself, and death or great bodily harm follows as a consequence of his inaction." *Id.* at 113.

In the case at hand, the action required that might have saved Tarasoff from impending death, that could have been done with little or no inconvenience, was a simple warning to Tarasoff. Ames's analysis offers solid grounding for imposing a duty to warn on the University and its agents, the campus therapists and the campus police. The argument that the University and its employees owed a duty to protect Tarasoff by warning is further strengthened when one considers the importance of bodily integrity to the practice of democracy and the cultural and gender aspects of the case, which remain largely unexamined by the majority.

IV DEMOCRACY AND THE DUTY TO WARN

Conceptualizing democracy and the necessary components of a functional democracy has been the work of political philosophers, who have pondered the question of why individuals should give up any of their freedom to organized government. Famously, John Locke recognized that individuals enter into civil society, in part seeking protection from fear of bodily harm in a group. John Locke, Second Treatise on Government (1689).

In our day, the right to call on the state for protection against physical harm, particularly as it relates to domestic violence among intimates and the protection of children, has been vigorously debated. In the debate, we often lose sight of the fact that protection from physical harm and state accountability for that harm is a cornerstone of democracy. A key aspect of life, liberty, and the pursuit of happiness is the ability to be free from physical harm and the provision of this freedom equally to all members of society. One cannot engage in democratic practice without a sense of bodily integrity. Liberal legal theories tout the importance of individual choice and protection of the self. Thus, protection against physical harm logically fits into liberal theory as a precondition to democratic participation.

It may be that the gender-linked nature of violence in our society – the fact that men feel the need for protection from bodily harm less often than women – has colored our conceptualization of freedom from physical harm as a fundamental building block of a democratic community, making it recede from public consciousness. Historically, women, living within patriarchal contexts, were seen as living "under a man's protection." The common-law doctrine of coverture went so far as to mark women as "civilly dead" and to deny her valuable rights. Thus, state responsibility for ensuring protection from physical harm equally to men and women has not been widely recognized. In particular, tort law would benefit from imagining a wider range of harms and risks to which both men and women are subject.

Consider the context of racial injustice. Congress recognized the significance of freedom from fear of bodily harm when it enacted the Ku Klux Klan Act, as part of the Civil Rights Act of 1871 (legislation now codified at 42 U.S.C. § 1985 (3)).The Act provides citizens with a cause of action against persons who conspire to violate their constitutional rights, dispensing with the prerequisite of proving state action. Faced with state governments which were unwilling or unable to enforce their own laws to provide protection from or deterrence of criminal acts, Congress did not stand idly by and watch terror inflicted on black citizens, but instead provided a new legal remedy for their protection and compensation. Laurent B. Frantz, *Congressional Power to Enforce the Fourteenth Amendment Against Private Acts*, 73 YALE L.J. 1353, 1354–56 (1964).

Tort law similarly provides a vehicle for the legal system to recognize a duty to protect others from physical harm. This case involves a duty to protect by warning someone of potential physical harm arising from an explicit threat directed against them. To ensure that tort law, like civil rights law, equally and justly serves all, courts must be attentive to whether claims for harm to women are considered with the same seriousness as harms to men. We should not overlook the specific nature of this violence in this case, perpetrated by a male on a female due to perceived unrequited love. The gender dimension of violence in a society where women continue to fight for equal treatment should not be ignored, for the simple reason that a democratic society owes each of its members equal regard with respect to their physical safety.

V CULTURAL AND GENDER CONTEXT FOR IMPOSING A DUTY TO WARN

Recent case law and anti-violence advocacy by women's rights activists have increased our awareness of patterns of violence with distinctly gender-linked impacts. For example, violence in the context of the marital relationship, now referred to as domestic violence, has led to the development of shelters for women leaving abusive relationships. California opened its first such shelter – La Casa de las Madres – in 1976, just a few months ago. We now recognize that the sphere of the "domestic" is not confined to marriage but includes the realm of intimate relationships more broadly. Whenever wives or intimate partners, real or imagined, are at greater risk, there is a need to exercise reasonable care. Such need to exercise reasonable care is or should be an expectation of professionals, such as therapists and campus police, who must be attuned to this reality of the increased risk of violence to women seeking to leave unsafe or undesired relationships.

More careful scrutiny of the behavior of individuals involved in this case by the therapist and/or police might have revealed the volatility of this particular relationship. Poddar's reaction to the rejection of his advances may well have been compounded by cross-cultural differences. While we seek to avoid stereotypes and do not want to ignore the complexities of Indian culture, the factual record contains at least some evidence that Poddar may have had a different framework for interpreting the significance of cues in their relationship. Poddar had resided in the United States for only one year before meeting Tarasoff. Growing up without a female sibling and attending all-male educational institutions up to that point, he had had very minimal interaction with women. As a foreign student from a rural community and a culture where family members frequently arrange marriages within rigid caste-defined boundaries, Poddar likely had little familiarity with American dating norms. It is possible that he interpreted Tarasoff's acts of friendship and kindness towards him as implying a promise of an intimate relationship and felt a profound and disconcerting rejection when Tarasoff rebuffed his advances. His behavior following her rejection certainly suggests so. His peers and the medical professionals around him witnessed his deterioration within a matter of months and their concern escalated when Poddar began expressing threats openly and spoke of purchasing a weapon. Dr. Moore asserted in his letter to the campus police that one of the causes of Poddar's severe emotional distress was his perception that Tarasoff had violated "his honor." Letter from Dr. Stuart Gold to William Beall, Chief of Police dated August 20, 1964.

The daily news provides examples of violence when women seek to leave intimate relationships, whether assumed or real. This break-up period appears to pose an elevated risk of harm. Many cases involving violence in intimate relationships occur at the time of separation. Indeed, this court has considered several cases in which violent harm befell women at the break-up point in a relationship. *People v. Disbrow*, 545 P.2d 272 (Cal. 1976), came before us on a question of the privilege against self-incrimination guaranteed by the California Constitution. But the facts of the case reveal a double homicide by the defendant whose wife had separated from him. He killed both his wife and the friend in whose home she had sought shelter. In *People v. Wilson*, 462 P.2d 22 (Cal. 1969), the legal issue before us involved a felony-murder instruction, but, again, the facts portrayed a double homicide perpetrated by the defendant. Defendant and his wife had separated; during the separation, defendant sought to reconcile. He killed both his wife and her male friend. The appeal in *People v. Sears*, 465 P.2d 847 (Cal. 1970), also involved issues relating to confession and the felony-murder rule. But the fact pattern similarly involved a homicide by the defendant perpetrated against a family member in conjunction with an attack on his estranged wife and others. These cases show that the perpetration of violence during separation has been before this court in criminal cases. We cannot pretend to be wholly ignorant of the culture of violence against women simply because we are tasked with adjudicating a civil claim in this case.

Though our awareness of violence against women is continually evolving and expanding, we now have an understanding of heightened contexts of risk. This awareness can and should be borne by individuals such as mental health professionals and campus police who are best trained and positioned to determine when a serious risk of violence to a potential victim exists. The duty to exercise reasonable care in this scenario is much like decisions in other jurisdictions finding tort liability when a doctor failed to warn about a contagious disease, *Hofmann v. Blackmon*, 241 So. 2d 752 (Fla. App. 1970), or a government agency allowed a dangerous mental patient to work on a farm without informing the farmer of the patient's condition. *Merchants Nat. Bank & Trust Co. of Fargo v. United States*, 272 F. Supp. 409 (D.N.D. 1967).

Women may fear that they are at greater risk of violence from strangers in dark alleys, a presumption bolstered by popular culture and media representation, but emerging research on violence within the family and the cases above suggest that women are more likely to be harmed by someone they know.[2] Violence against women has been and remains prevalent in our society. This violence takes many forms, from well-recognized violent crimes, such as homicide, battery, and rape to less-acknowledged violent acts, such as violence among intimates and marital rape. This history of gender-related harms serves as an important backdrop to this case. While prevention of harm may not always be possible, warning a potential victim whose identity is known, as it was here to campus psychotherapists and campus police, constitutes a reasonable first step in acknowledging both the heightened risk of violence facing women and in empowering potential subjects of that violence to take steps for their self-protection.

[2] William Goode, in fact, offers a theoretical framework to begin to explore the complexities surrounding violence among intimates. William J. Goode, *Violence among Intimates*, in Crimes of Violence (D. Mulvihill & M. Turnin eds., 1969).

Given these cultural and gender realities, we turn now to consider the specific facts of this case and whether the campus therapists or campus police had a duty to protect Tarasoff by warning her of the danger she faced.

VI THERAPIST'S DUTY TO PROTECT BY WARNING

We concur in the majority opinion's finding that the therapists' failure to warn Tarasoff or others likely to apprise her of the danger she faced "constituted a breach of the therapists' duty to exercise reasonable care to protect Tatiana." *Tarasoff*, 551 P.2d at 340. In finding that defendant therapists breached a duty in negligently failing to warn Tarasoff, the majority explains that the duty issue raises a policy question, asking whether law entitles a particular person to protection from another's careless conduct. *Id.* at 342. The court continues by recognizing, as Justice Peters did in *Rowland v. Christian*, 443 P.2d 561 (Cal. 1968) that:

> liability should be imposed "for an injury occasioned to another by his want of ordinary care or skill" as expressed in section 1714 of the Civil Code. Thus, Justice Peters, quoting from *Heaven v. Pender* (1883) 11 Q.B.D. 503, 509, stated: "whenever one person is by circumstances placed in such a position with regard to another . . . that if he did not use ordinary care and skill in his own conduct . . . he would cause danger of injury to the person or property of the other, a duty arises to use ordinary care and skill to avoid such danger."

Tarasoff, 551 P.2d at 342.

Rowland was a landmark case precisely because of its expansive reading of tort duties. As the majority opinion emphasizes, such an expansive notion of the duty to exercise reasonable care toward others is even more important in "[o]ur current crowded and computerized society [which] compels the interdependence of its members." *Id.* at 347.

As the majority opinion reiterates, we have created an exception to the common-law rule that holds a person generally owes no duty to control the conduct of another or any duty to warn those jeopardized by such conduct. *Id.* at 343. The exception to this "no-duty" rule arises in cases in which the defendant stands in some special relationship to either the person whose conduct needed to be controlled or to the foreseeable victim of that conduct. *Id.*

Applying this exception to the facts as alleged, the majority notes "that a relationship of defendant therapists to either Tatiana or Poddar will suffice to establish a duty of care; as explained in section 315 of the Restatement (Second) of Torts, a duty of care may arise from either '(a) a special relation . . . between the actor and the third person which imposes a duty upon the actor to control the third person's conduct, or (b) a special relation . . . between the actor and the other which gives to the other a right of protection.'" *Id.* The court bases its finding that the campus therapists owed a duty to Tarasoff based on the special relationship between a therapist and patient.

The court provides two similar examples of such affirmative duties, including a hospital which was bound to exercise reasonable care to control the behavior of a patient who might endanger other persons and a doctor who must warn a patient, if the patient's condition or medication will render actions, like driving a car, dangerous to others. *Id.* at 344.

Defendants have argued that patients often threaten violence but do not carry it out. They suggest holding the mental health community to this reasonable care standard has the potential to disrupt the therapeutic relationship. They further argue that psychotherapy demands free and open communication.

The majority acknowledges the public interest in supporting the effective treatment of mental illness and in protecting the rights of patients to privacy. Thus, the court recognizes the significance of safeguarding the confidential nature of psychotherapeutic communication. But against this interest the majority weighs "the public interest in safety from violent assault." *Tarasoff*, 551 P.2d at 346. As the court notes "the public policy favoring protection of the confidential character of patient–psychotherapist communications must yield to the extent to which disclosure is essential to avert danger to others. The protective privilege ends where the public peril begins." *Id.* at 347.

This case is being decided at a moment characterized by a climate of fear of crime and an inability to rein in a sense of peril on the part of the public. Some researchers have urged limiting the role of psychiatrists in predicting dangerousness because they believe such predictions are often unreliable and that warnings about dangers posed by patients will deter some patients from receiving mental health services. Bernard Diamond, *The Psychiatric Prediction of Dangerousness*, 123 U. PA. L. REV. 439 (1974).

However, we agree with the majority that "[w]eighing the uncertain and conjectural character of the alleged damage done the patient by such a warning against the peril to the victim's life, we conclude that professional inaccuracy in predicting violence cannot negate the therapist's duty to protect the threatened victim." *Tarasoff*, 551 P.2d at 346. The concern that therapists cannot accurately predict simply does not hold given the realities of this case. Given the risk of gender-related violence in this case and the explicit threats made by Poddar, the professionals had ample basis to believe that Tarasoff was in danger. Tragically, the only error here was their failure to warn Tarasoff of the imminent threat to her life.

We agree with the majority's rationale that the campus therapists owed a duty reasonably to protect Tarasoff that could have been discharged by a warning. The majority, however, found no similar duty owed by the campus police toward Tarasoff, reasoning that the special relationship rule does not apply to them. We differ from the majority on this aspect of the case and turn to consider why we believe the campus police also owed Tarasoff a duty to warn of physical danger in this case.

VII DUTY OF THE CAMPUS POLICE TO WARN

While we concur in the court's holding that the university therapists had a duty to warn Tarasoff of her peril, we dissent as to the court's holding that the campus police owe no such duty because they, unlike the defendant therapists, have no "special relationship to either Tatiana or to Poddar sufficient to impose upon such defendants a duty to warn respecting Poddar's violent intentions." *Tarasoff*, 551 P.2d at 349. We fail to see a distinction between these two sets of university employees. Each group owed a duty to Tarasoff to warn her that Poddar had threatened to kill her and each group could have given that warning with little inconvenience to itself, the standard that James Barr Ames proposed.

This case can readily be distinguished from the oft-cited *Riss v. City of New York* which addressed "the issue of the liability of a municipality for failure to provide special protection to a member of the public who was repeatedly threatened with personal harm and eventually suffered dire personal injuries for lack of such protection." 240 N.E.2d 860 (N.Y. 1968). The court in *Riss* denied liability, expressing a concern for the budgetary constraints of cities and states and observing: "The amount of protection that may be provided is limited by the resources of the community and by a considered legislative-executive decision as to how those resources may be deployed." *Riss*, 240 N.E.2d at 860. However, the monetary concerns and the facts of *Riss* are a far cry from this case. In that case, Pugach had threatened Riss multiple times and ultimately attacked her by throwing acid in her face. Unlike Tarasoff, however, Riss was aware of the threat posed against her by Pugach. In fact, she was the one who contacted the police. The court's decision to deny liability was based on its concern about depleting municipal resources. Unlike *Riss*, however, this case does not involve the duty of campus police to protect every individual who requests their assistance. Requiring a warning as we do today differs significantly from imposing an absolute duty to protect from all physical violence.

Further, campus police, the body at issue here, and municipal police are differently situated. State and local taxes fund municipal police departments, whereas a university funds its campus police. Universities take on a duty by employing campus police, a line of protection separate from state or local "police" that is far more limited in scope. The duty to protect from violent harm sought in *Riss* was more far-reaching and potentially burdensome than a simple duty to warn of a known, identifiable danger. Here, the campus police had specific information and could easily have warned Tarasoff of her peril. While such a warning does rely on police resources, it constitutes a de minimis burden in comparison to the potential harm to the victim.

In this case, the treating psychiatrist reached out to the campus police for help, referencing the potential danger to Tarasoff in writing and requesting Poddar be confined. The campus police refused to do so. They instead released Poddar from custody after determining that he appeared "rational." The record does not provide the evidence the campus police relied upon to determine that Poddar was "rational" before releasing him, but Dr. Moore's own written description of his condition indicated that Poddar's behavior was highly variable. The campus police appeared to have ignored that critical detail. For many years, women's advocates have urged that violence occurring in the private space of the home be recognized as a public harm to be addressed by police and the criminal justice system. The traditional unwillingness to pierce the sanctity of the domestic sphere has been an obstacle to that recognition. Here, too, we have an example of this problem. The campus police may have been too willing to accept Poddar's word that what was happening was "relationship trouble" and too willing to believe that he would leave Tarasoff alone. Additionally, Poddar identified the potential victim, Tarasoff, by name. He did not, for example, say that he would kill the first person he saw in Berkeley carrying a copy of Simone de Beauvoir's *The Second Sex*. His threat was personal, specific, and easily identifiable. That potential harm could come to Tarasoff in this case, given the knowledge that the police had of Poddar's mental health issues, his expression of a threat, his erratic behavior, and his purchase of a weapon, all indicates that the potential risk to Tarasoff was foreseeable. No one warned Tarasoff of this threat and she remained ignorant of the danger to her until Poddar appeared at her doorstep and killed her.

VIII CONCLUSION

Traditional common law recognized no general duty to act to protect another. But tort law may now provide a new blueprint for social relations, imagining a greater sense of connectedness and societal responsibility in cases where foreseeability of harm can be meaningfully informed by particular attention to elevated contexts of risk. As we noted, the court wrote, "our current crowded and computerized society compels the interdependence of its members." *Tarasoff*, 551 P.2d at 347. We add that we also live in an increasingly violent society and that one significant arena of increased risk of violence occurs in intimate relationships, particularly at the moment of termination of such relationships when one party wishes to break it off. Viewing this case through the lens of widespread gender violence at the time of separation suggests that a duty to warn here could have saved a life. Of course, from Tarasoff's perspective, no relationship existed, so she may not even have realized her peril. From Poddar's view, however, his state of mind about the ending of a "romantic" relationship put his behavior into an "at-risk" category.

We recognize that neither psychiatrists, police, nor judges can predict the future nor can they reasonably be expected to prevent any and all harms to individuals or groups. Yet legal recognition of civil wrongdoing in the failure to warn of known dangers gives the law a moral purpose, allowing it to serve the common good of greater public safety. It further teaches that the moral, humane response is to take action when little or no inconvenience is at stake and death or great bodily harm might ensue. Just as the creation of women's shelters has provided safe haven for women at dangerous points in their lives, holding campus mental health professionals and campus police to a duty to warn victims of danger may in the future save the lives of female students like Tatiana Tarasoff. Both the campus therapists and campus police were in a good position to avert the danger to Tarasoff, when others could not, because these actors knew of the threat and the facts that made it credible. Warning potential victims of their peril, when such a warning is easy, is a small, meaningful step toward building a more just society.

PART III

Intentional Torts

6

Commentary on *Robinson v. Cutchin*

YVONNE LINDGREN

INTRODUCTION

In *Robinson v. Cutchin*,[1] Glenda Robinson sued her obstetrician, Joseph Cutchin, for damages suffered when she was subjected to a tubal ligation during the birth of her sixth child by cesarean section. Robinson, an African-American woman, had consented to the cesarean section but denied that she had consented to the tubal ligation.[2] She claimed that she did not learn that she had been sterilized until two years later when she attempted unsuccessfully to conceive her seventh child. Her suit against Cutchin, who is white, alleged claims for negligence, lack of informed consent, battery, and intentional infliction of emotional distress and sought both compensatory and punitive damages. Cutchin, in response, insisted that Robinson had given consent to the sterilization procedure, though the doctor was unable to provide any written consent form. Instead, Cutchin relied on hospital records and the deposition testimony of hospital staff who asserted that Robinson had consented to the sterilization procedure.

Federal district court judge, Alexander Harvey, II, granted summary judgment for the defendant on Robinson's intentional tort claims of battery and intentional infliction of emotional distress.[3] The court concluded that the forced sterilization did not rise to the level of a battery, which requires that the touching must be harmful or offensive, because "it did not cause any

[1] 140 F. Supp. 2d 488 (D. Md. 2001).

[2] *Id.* at 490–91. A tubal libation is an irreversible sterilization process of closing a woman's fallopian tubes to prevent further pregnancies. *See Tubal Ligation*, U.S. NAT'L LIBRARY OF MEDICINE, NAT'S INST. OF HEALTH: MEDLINE PLUS (Oct. 9, 2014).

[3] The surviving negligence claim arising from the lack of informed consent resulted in a settlement agreement and therefore the published opinion only addresses the intentional tort actions for battery and intentional infliction of emotional distress.

additional physical pain, injury or illness other than that occasioned by the C-Section procedure."[4] The court also held that the procedure was not offensive because "the fact that [Robinson] was not able to have a seventh child after previously giving birth to six children is hardly something which would offend her reasonable sense of personal dignity."[5] Departing from traditional tort principles by conflating battery claims with negligence claims, the court held that the fact that the tubal ligation occurred in the context of a medical procedure that was more extensive than agreed upon presented only a violation of the duty to obtain informed consent, which is a tort action in negligence, not battery.[6] In granting summary judgment on the intentional infliction of emotional distress claim, the court concluded that Robinson had failed to provide adequate evidence of "severe emotional distress" and "mental anguish" and that the doctor had not acted "outrageously" because there was no evidence that he had acted with intent or malice purposefully to deprive Robinson of her reproductive capacity.[7] Because the court decided that Robinson had no valid intentional tort claims, it also summarily rejected her claim for punitive damages.

Although the opinion never mentioned Robinson's race, it is rife with implicit racialized judgments about Robinson's reproductive history and responsibility. The opinion noted that Robinson had three children "out of wedlock" with other men before marrying and having another three children with her husband, a co-plaintiff in the lawsuit. Indeed, not only did the judge take note that Robinson's reproduction was nonmarital, but he made five references to the fact that this was Robinson's sixth child, presumably signaling that her reproduction was not only deviant but excessive.[8] The court's conclusion that her dignity was not offended by being unable to have the seventh child that she and her husband very much wanted certainly suggests a value judgment that six children was more than enough for this African-American woman.

The *Robinson* case has been criticized as an example of how tort law's overemphasis on *physical* injury disadvantages women by failing to adequately compensate for emotional and relational harms disproportionately experienced by women.[9] In denying Robinson's battery claim the court adopted a

[4] *Robinson*, 140 F. Supp.2d at 493.

[5] *Id.*

[6] *Id.* at 492.

[7] *Id.* at 494–95.

[8] *Id.* at 489, 490, 491, 493.

[9] Martha Chamallas with Linda K. Kerber, *Women, Mothers, and the Law of Fright: A History*, 88 MICH. L. REV. 814, 814 (1990); MARTHA CHAMALLAS & JENNIFER B. WRIGGINS, THE

constrained view of harm as *physical* injury or pain, and then ignored the physical harm of permanently severed fallopian tubes, and also failed to adequately recognize the emotional and relational harms that Robinson experienced as the result of the loss of her reproductive capacity. The case highlights how, when faced with women's claims of reproductive harm, tort law simultaneously diminishes both the physical nature of what has happened to a woman's body and the devastating emotional and relational impact.[10]

The opinion has also been criticized for the way it trivialized Robinson's emotional distress, particularly because of the court's unwillingness to acknowledge that forced sterilization is deeply tied to an individual's sense of personal dignity. For example, relying on constitutional law principles that recognize a fundamental right of reproductive autonomy and liberty in intimate family relationships, Professor Martha Chamallas argues that tort law should similarly recognize that medical personnel owe patients a heightened duty of care with respect to harms to reproductive capacity and choice when it results in either emotional or physical harm.[11] Citing *Robinson*, Professor Chamallas argues that such a rule would recognize that when private actors strip someone of their reproductive capacity, they do serious damage to important personal interests involving intimate human relationships and well-being central to a plaintiff's identity as a woman, mother, or family member.[12]

THE FEMINIST JUDGMENT

The rewritten opinion by Professor Alena Allen, writing as the district judge, takes up Professor Chamallas's critique by identifying a fundamental right to procreate and by respecting the profound harm experienced by Robinson at involuntarily losing her reproductive capacity. Allen's opinion recognizes the power of tort law and punitive damage awards to vindicate reproductive harms inflicted by private medical providers. It does more than this, however; it also

MEASURE OF INJURY: RACE, GENDER, AND TORT LAW (2010); Martha Chamallas, *Unpacking Emotional Distress: Sexual Exploitation, Reproductive Harm, and Fundamental Rights*, 44 WAKE FOREST L. REV. 1109 (2009).

[10] CHAMALLAS & WRIGGINS, *supra* note 9, at 2. I use the term "women" but want to acknowledge that transmen and other gender-non-conforming people may also have even more difficulty accessing reproductive healthcare, and having their physical and emotional harm recognized, than ciswomen. *See, e.g.*, Robin Marantz Henig, *Transgender Men Who Become Pregnant Face Social, Health Challenges*, NPR (Nov. 7, 2014); *see also* Katha Pollitt, *Who Has Abortions?*, THE NATION (Mar. 13, 2015).

[11] Chamallas, *supra* note 9, at 1109, 1127–30.

[12] *Id.* at 1114.

resituates Robinson as a childbearing woman with decision-making autonomy and bodily integrity, pushing back against long-standing paternalism, deference to doctors, and erasure of women's harm through emphasis on the "healthy child." And it brings race rightly into the story by situating Robinson's experience within the historical and social context of sterilization abuse of women of color at the hands of white doctors. In so doing, Judge Allen draws upon critical race theory and reproductive justice scholarship that considers the intersection of race, gender, and class in cases of reproductive oppression.

In the rewritten opinion, Allen immediately identifies the plaintiff as "Glenda Ann Robinson, an African-American woman," thereby foregrounding the salient aspect that race played in this case, an issue never acknowledged in the original opinion. At the outset Allen states that the case raises "fundamental issues of the right to procreate and racial and gender equality." Allen contextualizes Robinson's harm within the larger social and historical experience of devaluing and pathologizing African-American women's reproduction. As Professor Dorothy Roberts has observed, controlling black women's reproduction has been a critical means of racial oppression throughout US history.[13] The turn of the twenty-first century has given rise to policy initiatives – from welfare rules cutting off support for additional children to prosecutions of pregnant women for using drugs – that regulate and punish poor and minority women's reproduction[14] based on stereotypes of black female sexual and reproductive irresponsibility, symbolized by the trope of the "Welfare Queen."[15]

While masking the relevance of Robinson's race, the original opinion's repeated mention of her reproductive history reveals normative values about deviant and hyper-fertile African-American reproduction that have

[13] *See generally* Dorothy Roberts, Killing the Black Body: Race, Reproduction, and the Meaning of Liberty (2014).

[14] A rich body of scholarship has highlighted the intersection of reproductive oppression and racial control in a variety of contexts including forced sterilization, family caps on public support, lack of access to culturally sensitive birth control, and criminalizing women for negative birth and pregnancy outcomes. *See, e.g.*, *id.*; Jael, Silliman et al., Undivided Rights: Women of Color Organize for Reproductive Justice 127 (2004); Rebekah J. Smith, *Family Caps in Welfare Reform: Their Coercive Effects and Damaging Consequences*, 29 Harv. J.L. & Gender 151, 152–54 (2006).

[15] By identifying African-American procreation as the cause of poverty and social decay, welfare reform has been transformed from a system of aid to a system of behavior modification that regulates the sexual, marital, and childbearing decisions of poor women by placing conditions on the receipt of assistance that directly targets their reproduction. *See* Dorothy E. Roberts, *Privatization and Punishment in the New Age of Reprogenetics*, 54 Emory L.J. 1343 (2005).

undergirded systemic reproductive oppression, including sterilization abuse.[16] Allen's rewritten opinion reclaims Robinson's reproductive autonomy, asserting that "[i]t is not for Dr. Cutchin, or this court, or a jury to decide whether six children were enough for Robinson. Whether Robinson had one child, no children, or twenty, Dr. Cutchin's decision to perform a sterilization procedure was a harmful violation of her bodily integrity."

Allen's opinion recognizes that it is essential to maintain battery, with its focus on whether a patient in fact consented, as an independent tort claim distinct from the negligence-based informed consent claim, which inquires whether the physician acted reasonably in providing sufficient material information to the patient. Allen notes that the battery claim is especially critical for female patients in light of the history of medical paternalism in maternity care. Medical paternalism reflects views of male physicians who declared themselves reproductive experts, and characterized women as weak and uninformed, and thus medicalized childbirth, moving it from the home where midwives and female relatives attended laboring women,[17] and into hospitals where male physicians were the ultimate decision makers.[18] Allen's opinion places claims for unconsented-to medical treatment within this context, noting "the long history of the largely male medical profession disregarding women's agency, especially in the context of women's reproductive decision-making." Under the paternalistic view, it was not important for a doctor to obtain a woman's consent to medical treatment, because the physician knew better what was in her best interest. While the medical profession has replaced paternalism with a shared decision-making model, enduringly stubborn social values of maternal self-sacrifice and medicalization of childbirth mean that courts, as in *Robinson*, are more willing to defer to doctors and fail to recognize the dignitary harms that flow from a physician violating a laboring woman's bodily autonomy and

[16] *See* Maya Manian, Coerced Sterilization of Mexican-American Women: The Story of *Madrigal v. Quilligan*, *in* Reproductive Rights and Justice Stories 97, 112 (2019); Rebecca Kluchin, Fit to be Tied: Sterilization and Reproductive Rights in America, 1950–1980, 160–61, 171–72 (2009).

[17] Elizabeth Kukura, *Contested Care: The Limitations of Evidence-Based Maternity Care Reform*, 31 Berkeley J. Gender L. & Just. 241, 256–58 (2016); Jennifer Block, Pushed: The Painful Truth About Childbirth and Modern Maternity Care (2007) (describing the social norms and forces that shaped modern maternity care).

[18] *See* Kukura, *supra* note 17, at 258 n.120 (discussing the history of obstetricians who introduced interventions on the assumption that female weakness required male physician interference with the body's natural process); Julie Gantz, *State Statutory Preclusion of Wrongful Birth Relief: A Troubling Re-Writing of a Woman's Right to Choose and the Doctor–Patient Relationship*, 4 Va. J. Soc. Pol'y & L. 795, 798 (1997) (noting that the paternalistic medical model was most pronounced in maternity care and was characterized by the "all-knowing, all-powerful, father-figure doctor and the uninformed, blindly trusting, child-like patient").

decision-making in the form of informed consent violations.[19] By contrast, Allen's opinion recognizes the importance of maintaining a battery claim for unconsented medical treatment that is separate from medical negligence because "the battery claim more fundamentally vindicates the underlying autonomy and self-determination interests at stake."

Crucially, Judge Allen's opinion reclaims consent in the medical context from the negligence inquiry about a doctor's "good faith" or "reasonableness," to a patient-centered model designed to protect patients who are vulnerable to reproductive oppression. Allen's opinion highlights that instead of the "reasonable medical practitioner" standard that a majority of jurisdictions apply in negligence-based informed consent cases, the battery claim is a patient-centered model where "[a]ll that a patient has to prove is that she did not consent. She does not have to prove what the prevailing medical standard of care is, or whether the doctor reasonably or unreasonably deviated from it." Allen's patient-centered model is attentive to the individual patient's preferences and needs rather than the doctor's good faith, and shifts the burden to the healthcare provider to obtain actual and effective consent, a goal that is especially critical in sterilization cases in which the fundamental right to procreate is at stake. By contrast, the judge in the original case viewed informed consent as a shield for doctor liability rather than as a tool for protecting patient autonomy. Allen's opinion corrects this inversion of the role of consent and prioritizes protecting Robinson's reproductive desires and goals rather than the doctor's "good faith" paternalistic notions of whether she should have more than six children.

Allen identifies plaintiff's injury by addressing the nature of what Professor Chamallas has described as its impact on intimate human relationships.[20] In contrast to the original opinion, which diminished Robinson's injury by focusing only on whether the sterilization procedure imposed any pain beyond that of the simultaneous C-section, Judge Allen concludes that, "Robinson was subjected to one of the most profound losses that a human being can experience, one that alters a fundamental aspect of her identity. She is no longer a fertile woman who can exercise her constitutionally protected right to make her own procreative decisions." Allen further recognizes the relational harm within Robinson's marriage that resulted from the involuntary

[19] *See* Farah Diaz-Tello, *Invisible Wounds: Obstetric Violence in the United States*, 24 Reprod. Health Matters 56, 61 (2016) (discussing the barriers to tort recovery due to the societal expectation that women "sacrifice their health and dignity, and even potentially their lives, in the name of having a healthy baby").

[20] Chamallas, *supra* note 9, at 1114.

sterilization. Situating her experience of harm within the broader history of sterilization abuse of African-American women, she notes that there is an even more "degrading impact on a woman from the sense that her humanity and rights do not matter." Allen's opinion acknowledges that the defendant's decision to sterilize plaintiff had lasting harm to a myriad of relationships: to the relationship with herself in terms of her self-identity, to her relationship with her husband, and to her relationship to a larger community as an African-American woman subjected to sterilization in the context of a history of racially motivated sterilization abuse.

Allen also shifts the focus of the battery inquiry from the outcome of the birth of a healthy baby and the doctor's good faith decision-making, to the plaintiff's bodily integrity and autonomy. The original opinion validated the doctor's decision to perform an emergency cesarean and then concluded, "a healthy baby boy was later delivered."[21] Commentators have noted that judges often fail to recognize harms to laboring women when the outcome is the birth of a healthy child.[22] In so doing, the original opinion reflects normative values about women's bodies being in service to children, selfless in the context of reproduction. Allen's rewritten opinion, in contrast, recognizes that a plaintiff may still successfully assert a claim for battery when the outcome was successful, because a person's first and greatest right is "the right to the inviolability of his person," and this right forbids a physician "however skilled or eminent" to violate the right without permission.

The rewritten opinion also corrects the oversight of the original by situating Robinson's battery claim for unconsented sterilization within the context of the reproductive oppression of African-American women, describing the nation's "long and sordid history of largely white and male doctors sterilizing women of color and other marginalized women, such as disabled or impoverished women, without their consent." Allen cites *Relf v. Weinberger*,[23] a case from the 1970s in which two African-American sisters, Mary Alice and Minnie, who were only 12 and 14 at the time, were sterilized without consent at a federally funded clinic in Alabama. The trial judge in *Relf* concluded that sterilization abuse often occurred when poor African-American patients

[21] 140 F. Supp. 2d at 490.

[22] Jamie R. Abrams, *Distorted and Diminished Tort Claims for Women*, 34 CARDOZO L. REV. 1955, 1980 (2013) (concluding that tort law elevates fetal harms and subordinates women's harms during childbirth); Elizabeth Kukura, *Obstetric Violence*, 106 GEO. L.J. 721, 785–86 (2018) (discussing lack of available tort remedies for a broad range of obstetrical misconduct); Diaz-Tello, *supra* note 19, at 61 (societal expectation that women sacrifice their health and dignity in the name of having a healthy baby poses barriers to tort recovery).

[23] 372 F. Supp. 1196 (D.D.C. 1974).

sought medical treatment for childbirth, and noted that "an indefinite number of poor people have been improperly coerced into accepting a sterilization operation."[24] The revelations in *Relf* led to public outcry, congressional hearings, and regulatory reform.[25] Allen uses the widespread condemnation of the conduct challenged in *Relf* to conclude that a jury could find that punitive damages are appropriate in Robinson's case. Situating the case as Allen does within the historic context of widespread sterilization abuse reveals how the battery claim, with its potential for punitive damages, is important to punish and deter wrongful conduct and to warn others contemplating similar conduct of the serious risk of monetary liability.

Turning to the claim for intentional infliction of emotional distress, Allen's opinion again shifts the inquiry to the nature of plaintiff's harm rather than the good faith of the doctor. The original opinion concluded the doctor had not acted "outrageously" because there was no evidence that he had acted with intent or malice to deprive Robinson of her reproductive capacity. In contrast, Allen's opinion is more true to traditional tort standards, noting that this tort can also be established by reckless conduct. She reasons that because the result of tubal ligation is permanent sterilization, a jury could reasonably find that "it is at least extremely reckless for a physician to perform the procedure without tangible evidence of freely given consent from the patient." Allen also notes that because the ability to bear children can be a defining aspect of a person's life, a jury could reasonably conclude, even without expert testimony, that losing the ability to procreate by being sterilized against one's will could cause severe emotional distress. Analyzing whether Cutchin's conduct could be characterized as outrageous, Allen again draws on the history of sterilization abuse of women of color because of judgments about their fitness to produce additional children. Noting the outcry after *Relf*, she concludes that a jury could readily find such conduct to be inherently outrageous, and likely to produce an even more devastating and degrading impact on a woman of color because it signals that her humanity and rights do not matter.

The shift away from deference to the good faith of doctors to consider the outrageousness of the doctor's conduct within the context of reproductive oppression, is an important one, especially in light of the history of plaintiffs' inability to successfully prosecute tort claims for sterilization abuse. For example, the case of *Madrigal v. Quilligan* revealed rampant sterilization abuse

[24] *Id.* at 1199 (noting that one patient was refused medical treatment by her physician unless she submitted to tubal ligation after birth.)

[25] *See*, Lisa C. Ikemoto, *Infertile by Force and Federal Complicity: The Story of* Relf v. Weinberger, *in* Women And The Law Stories 179 (Stephanie Wildman & Elizabeth Schneider eds., 2010).

of Mexican-American women in the 1970s at a Los Angeles public hospital. As Professor Maya Manian describes in a chapter telling the story of this case, sterilization abuse of minority women was driven by concerns about population control, immigration, and welfare costs, and medical personnel would often coerce laboring women to sign consent forms under duress.[26] And like the *Robinson* case, while the court recognized that the plaintiffs had been sterilized without proper informed consent, the white male judge refused to award monetary damages to the plaintiffs, instead concluding that in each case the attending physician had a "bona fide" or "good faith" belief that the patient had consented. The *Madrigal* judge opined that it was reasonable for a doctor to persuade a woman not to have a large family, and he rejected testimony from plaintiffs' witnesses that there was a "concerted plan by hospital attendants and doctors to push them, as members of a low socio-economic group . . . to consent to sterilization in order to accomplish some sinister, invidious, social purpose."[27]

IMPLICATIONS

Allen's opinion harnesses the power of critical race scholarship and feminist legal theory to improve tort law's ability to recognize dignitary harms and violations of laboring women's bodily integrity by situating those harms within the context of racial oppression. Based on the history of reproductive oppression of women of color, Allen's opinion recognizes how essential it is to maintain battery as a tort claim distinct from the negligence-based informed consent claim. Given the lack of compensatory damages recovery under the informed consent theory for victims of coercive sterilization, as documented in *Madrigal*, and the limited recovery for women plaintiffs in general who claim "emotional" harm from reproductive loss, Allen's opinion reinvigorating intentional tort theories is a significant contribution. In light of this history, the rewritten opinion's recognition of a claim for punitive damages is vital for meaningful recovery and deterrence against more widespread sterilization abuse of women of color. The rewritten opinion also offers the potential for tort law to protect people across a broad range of sexual and reproductive harms such as forced medical treatment for pregnant women,[28] including

[26] Dr. Quilligan stated that his goal was to cut the birth rate of the "Negro and Mexican population" in Los Angeles County. All of the "Madrigal Ten" were in active labor when they were asked to sign the consent form, were Spanish speakers but were asked to sign a consent form written in English, and many were threatened with withholding pain medication or medical care unless the consent form was signed. Manian, *supra* note 16, at 97, 101–03, 108.

[27] *Id.* at 109–10.

[28] *See* Melissa Murray & Kristin Luker, Cases on Reproductive Rights and Justice 198–210 (2015) (describing ways in which pregnant women are forced to submit to unwanted

court-ordered involuntary cesarean sections,[29] forced ultrasounds,[30] obstetric violence,[31] and the harms and indignities suffered by trans and gender-nonconforming people seeking reproductive healthcare.[32]

Recognizing the critical role of race in medical cases involving reproductive oppression may also offer greater protections for African-American women who are dying in labor in significant and disproportionate numbers.[33] Recent research and scholarship has challenged the prevailing view that black women's negative birthing outcomes are attributed solely to poverty and a lack of access to care.[34] While structural racism contributes to increased black maternal mortality,[35] research has revealed that implicit bias may cause doctors to spend less time with black patients, underestimate black patients' complaints of pain, and ignore symptoms.[36] Allen's opinion draws explicit connection between Robinson's birthing experience within the context of racial oppression and medical paternalism in finding that the defendant

medical treatment deemed necessary by their obstetricians, including detention in the hospital for enforced bed rest, administration of intravenous medications, and surgical delivery of the fetus); Nancy Erenreich, *The Colonization of the Womb*, 43 DUKE L.J. 492 (1993).

29 *See, e.g.*, In re Madyun, 114 Daily Wash. L. Rep. 2233 (D.C. Super. Ct. July 26, 1986); In re A.C., 533 A.2d 611 (D.C. 1987).

30 *See* Maya Manian, *Perverting Informed Consent: The South Dakota Court Decision*, REWIRE NEWS (Aug. 1, 2012), https://rewire.news/article/2012/08/01/perverting-informed-consent-south-dakota (noting that mandatory ultrasound laws impose a medical procedure in violation of a patient's right to refuse medical treatment protected by informed consent law).

31 Kukura, *supra* note 22; Diaz-Tello, *supra* note 19.

32 *See, e.g.*, Courtney Sirwatha, Note, *Unlikely Partners: Tort Law as a Tool for Trans Activism*, 20 CARDOZO J.L. & GENDER 111 (2013) (expanding intentional torts and emotional distress claims for sexual harms would help transpeople to recover for harms inflicted by healthcare providers).

33 The risk of dying in childbirth for black women is three to four times higher than that of white women. *Meeting the Challenges of Measuring and Preventing Maternal Mortality in the United States*, CENTER FOR DISEASE CONTROL AND PREVENTION (Nov. 14, 2017), https://www.cdc.gov/grand-rounds/pp/2017/20171114-maternal-mortality.html; Myra J. Tucker et al., *The Black–White Disparity in Pregnancy-related Mortality from 5 Conditions: Differences in Prevalence and Case-fatality Rates*, AM. J. PUB. HEALTH (Feb. 2007), https://www.ncbi.nlm.nih.gov/pmc/articles/PMC1781382.

34 *See, e.g.*, *Maternal Health in the United States*, MATERNAL HEALTH TASK FORCE, https://www.mhtf.org/topics/maternal-health-in-the-united-states.

35 Zinzi D. Bailey et al., *Structural Racism and Health Inequities in the USA: Evidence and Interventions* (Apr. 8, 2017), THE LANCET, https://www.thelancet.com/action/showPdf?pii=S0140-6736%2817%2930569-X; Theresa Chalhoub & Kelly Rimar, *The Health Care System and Racial Disparities in Maternal Mortality* (May 10, 2018), CENTER FOR AMERICAN PROGRESS, https://www.americanprogress.org/issues/women/reports/2018/05/10/450577/health-care-system-racial-disparities-maternal-mortality.

36 MiQuel Davies, *Racism in Health Care – For Black Women Who Become Pregnant, It's a Matter of Life and Death*, NATIONAL WOMEN'S LAW CENTER (Apr. 13, 2018), https://nwlc.org/blog/racism-in-health-care-for-black-women-who-become-pregnant-its-a-matter-of-life-and-death.

doctor can be liable for battery and intentional infliction of emotional distress claims as well as punitive damages. The availability of these tort remedies for violations of the bodily integrity and autonomy of laboring women may result in important shifts in the medical profession's response to African-American women's childbirth experiences by recognizing the connection between maternal mortality rates and racial and gender oppression.

ROBINSON v. CUTCHIN, 140 F. SUPP. 2D 488 (D. MD. 2001)

ALENA ALLEN, DISTRICT JUDGE

In this civil action, plaintiff Glenda Ann Robinson, an African-American woman, and her husband are seeking compensatory and punitive damages from Dr. Joseph H. Cutchin, Jr. and Peninsula Regional Medical Center for an allegedly unconsented-to bilateral tubal ligation which resulted in permanent sterilization. Although on its face this case may seem to be a routine medical malpractice case, it raises fundamental issues of the right to procreation and racial and gender equity.

The complaint contains four counts. In Count I, plaintiff alleges that Dr. Cutchin negligently failed to obtain her informed consent for the sterilization procedure and that the defendant's negligence was the proximate cause of damages suffered by her and her husband. Count II alleges that Dr. Cutchin committed a battery by performing the sterilization procedure without her consent. In Count III, plaintiff seeks a recovery for intentional infliction of emotional distress, and in Count IV, Robinson and her husband jointly seek damages for loss of consortium. Diversity jurisdiction exists under 28 U.S.C. § 1332, and Maryland law is controlling.

Discovery has now been completed, and a trial date has been set. Presently pending in the case is defendants' motion *in limine*. By way of that motion, defendants seek to preclude Robinson from asserting a claim for battery and a claim for intentional infliction of emotional distress. Defendants also argue that plaintiff is not entitled to recover punitive damages.

Since defendant's pending motion asks the court to enter judgment as a matter of law on some of plaintiffs' claims, the motion will be treated as a motion for summary judgment. In support of defendants' motion, defendants have submitted memoranda of law and exhibits, including the deposition testimony of Robinson and Dr. Cutchin. Plaintiffs, in turn, have filed an opposition to defendants' motion for summary judgment, together with exhibits.

After reviewing the pleadings, memoranda and exhibits, this court has concluded that no hearing is necessary for a decision on the pending motion. *See* Local Rule 105.6. For the reasons stated herein, defendants' motion *in limine*, treated as a motion for summary judgment, will be denied because the complaint states a valid claim for battery and for intentional infliction emotional distress.

I BACKGROUND FACTS

On the morning of September 17, 1997, Robinson, an African-American woman, was admitted to the Peninsula Regional Medical Center in Salisbury, Maryland, for the birth of her sixth child. Robinson anticipated having a vaginal delivery. At some point, Robinson's labor was augmented with drugs to aid the progression of her labor, but her labor still did not progress. As a result, Robinson was scheduled for emergency cesarean section.

Dr. Cutchin delivered a healthy baby boy by way of the cesarean procedure. However, during the delivery of her son, Dr. Cutchin also performed a bilateral tubal ligation on Robinson. A tubal ligation is a permanent sterilization procedure consisting of surgical removal of a portion of the fallopian tube, followed by closure of the end with an absorbable suture or ligature.

Robinson alleges that she did not learn that this procedure had been performed until June of 1999 when she approached Dr. Cutchin and the hospital and asked to see records pertaining to the operation. Robinson alleges that Dr. Cutchin did not obtain her consent for the tubal ligation. In response, defendants assert that the sterilization procedure was performed with plaintiff's prior knowledge and consent. Hospital records and the testimony of several nurses indicate that plaintiff had expressed a willingness to have the tubal ligation procedure, if it became necessary that her son be delivered by way of a cesarean section. However, the defendants were not able to produce a consent form signed by Robinson for the sterilization procedure.

Robinson contends that she and her husband were planning on having an additional child and that she has sustained severe emotional damages as a result of being permanently sterilized. Robison seeks compensatory and punitive damages.

II SUMMARY JUDGMENT STANDARD

In granting a motion for summary judgment, the trial judge may not resolve factual disputes, but instead is limited to ruling on matters of law. Pittman v. Atlantic Realty Co., 754 A.2d 1030, 1043 (Md. 2000); Sheets v. The Brethren

Mut. Ins. Co., 679 A.2d 540, 542 (Md. 1996). Summary judgment is generally inappropriate when matters such as knowledge, intent, and motive are at issue. Brown v. Dermer, 744 A.2d 47, 53 (Md. 2000). Credibility is not an issue to be determined on summary judgment. Coffey v. Derby Steel Co., 434 A.2d 564, 571 (Md. App. 1981). If any inferences may be drawn from the well-plead facts, the trial court must construe those inferences in the light most favorable to the non-moving party. Ashton v. Brown, 660 A.2d 447, 452 (Md. 1995).

III BATTERY

The tort of battery, which consists of an intentional harmful or offensive contact with another without that person's consent, see RESTATEMENT (SECOND) OF TORTS § 13 cmt. d (Am. Law Inst. 1979), has long played a significant role in the medical context. When a physician treating a mentally competent adult performs surgery or administers other therapy without the prior consent of his patient, the physician commits a medical battery. McClees v. Cohen, 148 A. 124 (Md. 1930). The requirement that a patient must freely and willingly consent to medical care is based on bedrock principles of individual autonomy and self-determination. A patient has a fundamental right to exercise control over her own body, at least when undergoing elective surgery, by deciding for herself whether or not to submit to the particular therapy. As Judge Cardozo said for the New York Court of Appeals in *Schloendorff v. Society of N.Y. Hospital*, 105 N.E. 92, 93 (N.Y. 1914), "[e]very human being of adult years and sound mind has a right to determine what shall be done with his own body."

Consent to medical treatment as a legal concept developed within the framework of the law of trespass. Two of the earliest cases to discuss the notion of consent and medical treatment involved female patients – perhaps not coincidental given the long history of the largely male medical profession disregarding women's agency, especially in the context of women's reproductive decision-making. *See, e.g.*, SUE FISHER, IN THE PATIENT'S BEST INTEREST – WOMEN AND THE POLITICS OF MEDICAL DECISIONS 30–31 (1986); Lisa C. Ikemoto, *Furthering the Inquiry: Race, Class, and Culture in the Forced Medical Treatment of Pregnant Women*, 59 TENN. L. REV. 487 (1992) (investigating how doctors often force unwanted treatment on pregnant women without their consent). In *Mohr v. Williams*, 104 N.W. 12 (Minn. 1905), Anna Mohr sued her doctor for performing an operation without her consent. The physician had obtained consent to operate on her right ear. While Mohr was under anesthesia, Dr. Williams unilaterally decided to operate on her left ear because it looked more diseased.

Mohr sued Dr. Williams for battery, and Williams argued that he should not be held liable because "plaintiff's left ear was in fact diseased, in a condition dangerous and threatening to her health, [and] the operation was necessary." *Id.* at 15.

In *Pratt v. Davis*, which was also decided in 1905, Davis, on behalf of his wife, sued Dr. Pratt for performing a hysterectomy on Davis without consent. 118 Ill. App. 161, 166 (1905), aff'd, 79 N.E. 562 (1906). Davis hired Dr. Pratt to treat his wife for epilepsy and placed her in a sanitarium under Dr. Pratt's care. Dr. Pratt deemed a hysterectomy to be an appropriate treatment for Davis's condition and performed the procedure without informing or obtaining consent from either Davis or her husband. 118 Ill. App. at 171–72. At trial, Dr. Pratt did not argue that he obtained consent. In fact, he readily admitted that he did not obtain consent from Davis. He stated, "I worked her deliberately, systematically, taking chances which she did not realize the full aspect of, deliberately and calmly deceived the woman. That is, I did not tell her the whole truth." *Id.* at 170. Instead, Dr. Pratt argued that it would be an injustice to hold him liable because he used his best efforts to heal Davis. Dr. Pratt stated that, in his opinion, the surgery was "proper and essential to her welfare" and that "the employment of the physician or surgeon gives him implied license to do whatever in the exercise of his judgment may be necessary." *Id.* at 166. He further argued that when a patient places herself under the care of a physician for treatment that "upon his authority, she thereby in law consents that he may perform such operation as in his best judgment is proper and essential to her welfare." *Id.*

In both *Pratt* and *Williams*, the physicians maintained that they acted for the sole benefit of their patient. They approached patient care with the commonly held belief that "patients are neither emotionally nor intellectually equipped to play a significant role in decisions affecting their medical fate." Jay Katz, *Informed Consent – A Fairy Tale? Law's Vision*, 39 U. PITT. L. REV. 137, 148 (1977). However, in both cases, the courts rejected the defendants' arguments and upheld the right of patients, particularly female patients, to exercise autonomy over medical decision-making. The court in *Pratt* provided a compelling analysis of the fundamental and inviolable nature of the rights underlying the consent requirement:

> [U]nder a free government at least, the free citizen's first and greatest right, which underlies all others – the right to the inviolability of his person, in other words, his right to himself – is the subject of universal acquiescence, and this right necessarily forbids a physician or surgeon, however skillful or eminent ... to violate without permission the bodily integrity of his patient by ... operating on him without his consent or knowledge.
>
> 118 Ill. App. at 166

As the tort of battery for performing medical treatment without a patient's consent evolved, cases were brought where the claim was that the patient's consent, although voluntarily given, was nullified because the physician had not fully explained the risks of the medical procedure. Courts realized that the crux of these claims was whether the patient's consent was in fact effective and fully informed. The evolving caselaw reasoned that the same interests in self-determination and autonomy that require consent to medical treatment also demand that the consent be based on material information about the patient's condition, the treatment alternatives, risks, and benefits. *See, e.g.*, Canterbury v. Spence, 464 F.2d 772, 788–89 (D.C. Cir. 1972), cert. denied, 409 U.S. 1064 (1972). The tort of battery, which rests on the notion of intent to harm or offend, did not seem well suited to cases where the issue was whether the physician had disclosed sufficient information to enable the patient to make an informed decision about their medical care. Thus, courts determined that cases involving insufficient disclosure of information should be brought as medical negligence claims for breach of the duty to obtain informed consent, rather than as medical battery claims. *See, e.g.*, Salgo v. Leland Stanford Jr. Univ. Bd. of Trustees, 317 P.2d 170 (Cal. Ct. App. 1957).

The development of the informed consent negligence claim, however, did not fully replace medical battery claims. Battery remains the appropriate tort claim when a patient alleges that medical treatment was performed without her consent. As the California Supreme Court more recently explained:

> [T]he battery theory should be reserved for those circumstances when a doctor performs an operation to which the patient has not consented. When the patient gives permission to perform one type of treatment and the doctor performs another, the requisite element of deliberate intent to deviate from the consent given is present. However, when the patient consents to certain treatment and the doctor performs that treatment but an undisclosed inherent complication with a low probability occurs, no intentional deviation from the consent given appears; rather, the doctor in obtaining consent may have failed to meet his duty of due care to disclose pertinent information. In that situation the action should be pleaded in negligence.
>
> *Cobbs v. Grant*, 502 P.2d 1, 8 (Cal. 1972)

There are compelling reasons to maintain battery as a claim for unconsented-to medical treatment, instead of folding it all into the negligence-based informed consent claim. The battery claim more fundamentally vindicates the underlying autonomy and self-determination interests at stake, since its essence is whether or not the patient actually consented to what was done to her body. All that a plaintiff has to prove is that she did not consent. She does not have to prove what the prevailing medical standard of care is, or whether the doctor reasonably or unreasonably deviated from it. She does not have to prove what information she was given about risks and what was withheld, nor does she have to prove the materiality of any of the information – which may sometimes require expensive expert testimony. Further, she does not have to prove any causal connection between a lack of fully informed consent and ensuing harm – the unconsented-to medical treatment is the harm. Nor does she have to prove actual damages, and punitive damages are available. *See* Lisa Napoli, *The Doctrine of Informed Consent and Women: The Achievement of Equal Value and Equal Exercise of Autonomy*, 4 AM. U. J. GENDER & L. 335, 343–44 (1996)

Despite these important reasons for preserving the battery claim for medical treatment performed without consent, defendants contend that Maryland law has eroded the distinction between battery claims and negligence claims in the context of medical consent. Defendants contend that cases such as Robinson's where the plaintiff alleges that a physician performed an additional procedure during an initially consented to surgery, must be brought only as informed consent negligence claims. They rely for this proposition on *Lipscomb v. Memorial Hospital*, 733 F.2d 332 (4th Cir. 1984), a case that analyzed the proper classification of the type of tort claim in order to determine the appropriate statute of limitations. In *Lipscomb*, the patient had consented to gall bladder surgery, but during the operation, her doctor additionally repaired her hiatal hernia while she was under anesthesia. The district court, applying Maryland law, ruled that the claim was appropriately brought as a negligence claim for failure to obtain fully informed consent, and not a battery claim for failing to obtain any consent at all to the additional hernia surgery, and the Fourth Circuit affirmed. But defendants' contention that *Lipscomb* abolished battery claims in the context of additional procedures added on to an initially consented to surgery misreads the facts and the holding in that case. In *Lipscomb*, the physician and patient had extensive discussions about whether her digestive issues could be alleviated by gall bladder surgery alone, or whether her hiatal hernia that was contributing to the problems had to be repaired surgically or could be treated less aggressively. The doctor advised her that he thought the hernia could be dealt with by nonsurgical means, unless it turned out to be larger than he thought, so Lipscomb agreed that they would do only the gall bladder surgery the next day. But she signed a consent form that not only authorized the gall bladder removal, but also explicitly consented to any additional surgery the surgeon or his associates may "judge necessary or desirable to correct the existing condition or any unhealthy condition which they may discover." *Id.* at 334. The court ruled that this additional language was sufficient to constitute consent to the hernia surgery that the doctor performed during the gall bladder procedure when he saw that the hiatal hernia was indeed much larger than he had thought, and was of such size that it could only be repaired surgically. The court then analyzed whether she had been fully informed of the risks of the hiatal hernia surgery, in particular the risk of the chronic complication that she developed. Such a claim is one for informed consent, rather than for battery.

In the present case, Robinson did not sign a consent form that authorized the physician to perform additional procedures to correct the "existing condition or any other unhealthy condition" that he might discover. Nor was the tubal ligation correcting an "unhealthy condition" – her ovaries and fallopian tubes were quite healthy and functioned well, and Robinson alleges that preserving their functionality was important to her. She does not allege that she was not fully informed about the risks or benefits of a tubal ligation. The plaintiff simply and straightforwardly alleges that the defendant performed a medical procedure without her consent, a claim that sounds in battery. Specifically, Robinson alleges that during a consented-to emergency cesarean, Dr. Cutchin performed an unconsented-to bilateral tubal ligation, which resulted in permanent sterilization. Although hospital staff allege that Robinson did consent to the tubal ligation, the hospital was not able to produce a signed consent form. This crucially important dispute of material fact – whether or not Robinson consented to the tubal ligation – precludes granting summary judgment on the battery claim.

The battery claim, with its sharp focus on actual consent, and with its notion that unconsented-to medical treatment is in and of itself a harm that can lead to punitive damages, is especially important to preserve in the context of this case, where an African-American woman alleges that a white male physician sterilized her without her consent, arguably because he thought that six children was enough for her. The United States unfortunately presents a long and sordid history of largely white and male doctors sterilizing women of color and other marginalized women, such as disabled or impoverished women, without their consent. *See* DOROTHY ROBERTS, KILLING THE BLACK BODY 89–98 (1997). In the south, throughout the 1950s through 1980s, unnecessary hysterectomies performed without consent on poor black patients in teaching hospitals were so prevalent that they became known as "Mississippi appendectomies." *Id.* at 90. Involuntary sterilization of black women was widely practiced in South and North Carolina in the post–World War II years through the 1970s. PHILLIP REILLY, THE SURGICAL

SOLUTION: A HISTORY OF INVOLUNTARY STERILIZATION IN THE UNITED STATES 111–27 (1991).[1] Press exposés and reports by hospital-affiliated physicians in the mid-1970s in Boston, New York, and Los Angeles revealed that involuntary sterilization of poor black and Puerto Rican women was prevalent simply to train medical residents. ROBERTS, *supra* at 91. In Baltimore, Maryland, not far from Salisbury where plaintiff was sterilized, a study followed poor African-American women who had given birth as teenagers for an eighteen-year period during the 1970s and 1980s. This study found that 56 percent of the women had been sterilized, often when relatively young, and in many instances without full consent. FRANK FURSTENBERG, ADOLESCENT MOTHERS IN LATER LIFE (1987).

The case of *Relf v. Weinberger*, 372 F. Supp. 1196 (D.D.C. 1974), brought great public attention to the extent of the problem of involuntary or coerced sterilization. The case was a class action challenging the statutory authority and constitutionality of federal family-planning regulations, contending that the regulations improperly incentivized or coerced sterilization. Minnie and Mary Alice Relf were African-American women who had been sterilized when they were 14 and 12. Their illiterate mother had signed an X on a consent form, thinking that she was authorizing her daughters to receive birth control shots. The district court found that in the few years prior to its decision, an estimated 100,000 to 150,000 poor women had been sterilized annually using federal family-planning funds, nearly half of whom were black, and many of whom did not give actual or informed consent. *Id.* at 1199. The court found that "uncontroverted evidence in the record [shows] that minors and other incompetents have been sterilized with federal funds and that an indefinite number of poor people have been improperly coerced into accepting a sterilization operation under the threat that various federally supported welfare benefits would be withdrawn unless they submitted to irreversible sterilization. Patients receiving Medicaid assistance at childbirth are evidently the most frequent targets of this pressure." *Id.* The court prohibited the use of federal dollars for involuntary sterilizations, for sterilizations of minors or incompetent people, and also prohibited the practice of threatening women on welfare with the loss of their benefits if they refused to agree to be sterilized. The litigation led the federal government to adopt new regulations, which require written signed consent forms and a waiting period before any federal funds can be used for a sterilization procedure. *See* Provision of Sterilization in Federally Assisted

[1] It may be merely coincidental, but Defendant Dr. Cutchin did his medical training at the University of South Carolina in the 1950s, during the time when university teaching hospitals in that state engaged in the practice of involuntarily sterilizing black women. REILLY at 111–27.

Programs of the Public Health Service, 43 Fed. Reg. 52, 146–65 (Nov. 8, 1978) (codified at 42 C.F.R. pt. 50).[2]

In the aftermath of *Relf*, studies revealed that many hospitals ignored the regulatory requirements. ROBERTS, *supra* at 97. Moreover, the regulations do not address the allegations in this case, where federal funds are not involved, and an individual physician performed a sterilization on a woman deemed to already have "enough" children. A battery claim, with its potential for punitive damages, remains an important vehicle for deterring sterilization abuse and for vindicating the fundamental individual interest in reproductive autonomy. Defendants' contention that as a matter of law this case does not present a battery claim is rejected.

We now turn to defendants' other objection to permitting plaintiff's battery cause of action to proceed. Defendants contend that there is no proof that Dr. Cutchin acted "intending to cause a harmful or offensive contact." Nelson v. Carroll, 735 A.2d 1096, 1100 (Md. 1999) (quoting RESTATEMENT (SECOND) OF TORTS § 13 (1965)). They argue that the touching by Dr. Cutchin was not harmful because it did not cause any additional physical pain, injury, or illness other than that occasioned by the C-section procedure. They further contend that what occurred here did not offend Robinson's reasonable sense of personal dignity because not being able to have a seventh child after previously giving birth to six children is hardly something which would offend her reasonable sense of personal dignity.

This argument fails for several reasons. It incorrectly states the law of intent for a battery claim, and it egregiously – indeed insultingly – diminishes the inherently harmful and offensive nature of an allegedly involuntary sterilization. Intent to do harm is not essential to a battery. Ghassemieh v. Schafer, 447 A.2d 84, 88 (Md. Ct. Spec. App. 1982). A viable claim for battery does not require hostile intent on the part of the defendant. The absence of consent to the contact on the plaintiff's part is sufficient. WILLIAM L. PROSSER, LAW OF TORTS 36 (4th ed. 1971). The many physicians over the years who involuntarily sterilized women did not "intend" to harm them; they acted out of a misguided sense that they were doing what was in the patient's or society's best interest. But as *Pratt v. Davis* eloquently stated over a century ago, the misguided intentions do not salvage what is a profound violation of the bodily integrity of the patient. 118 Ill. App. at 161.

[2] Considering that the federal government requires a written signed consent form for any sterilization supported by federal funds, a best practices standard that should apply to any sterilization given the history of abuse outlined above, a jury may consider it highly relevant to credibility that the defendants in this case cannot produce a signed consent form.

Viewing the facts in the light most favorable to Robinson, the nonmoving party, a reasonable jury could credit her testimony and that of her husband, and find that Dr. Cutchin intentionally and impermissibly touched and irreversibly severed Robinson's fallopian tubes without her consent, which caused her severe harm. She has undoubtedly suffered a physical injury – the mutilation of a body part. Her previously healthy and fully functioning fallopian tubes were cut and tied off, and no longer can perform their biological function. Robinson is now sterile. In cases in which men have been sterilized as a result of medical treatment, courts have never questioned the obvious fact that the man has suffered a profound injury. *Cf.* Bang v. Charles T. Miller Hosp., 88 N.W.2d 186 (Minn. 1958) (man's spermatic cords were severed during surgery for urinary problems).

Even if severed fallopian tubes were not a serious physical injury, Robinson still has suffered a devastating loss – namely the ability to procreate in the future. She has lost her right to decide whether to have additional biological children and has alleged that she desired to have more children. Losing control of the deeply personal decision of whether to have a child would offend the reasonable sense of dignity of any woman. At the heart of liberty "is the right to define one's own concept of existence, of meaning, of the universe, and of the mystery of human life." Planned Parenthood of S.E. Pa. v. Casey, 505 U.S. 833, 851 (1992). The Supreme Court has recognized that the right to personal autonomy includes decisions relating to childbearing. Carey v. Population Servs. Int'l, 431 U.S. 678, 685 (1977) ("The decision whether or not to beget or bear a child is at the very heart of this cluster of constitutionally protected choices"); Roe v. Wade, 410 U.S. 113 (1973) (invalidating a Texas law that prohibited abortions on the basis that a woman has a due process right to make fundamental decisions affecting her body). Thus, the gravity of the loss that Robinson suffered cannot be overstated. The fact that Robinson already has six children does not make sterilization any less harmful or offensive. Robinson was entitled to have as many children as she and her husband desired. Children have the potential to enrich their parents' lives in countless ways: companionship, love and affection, pride in watching them grow and develop, and potential caregiving in old age.

While the decision to have a child is undoubtedly a large responsibility, it is a decision that the law places with parents, not with legislatures, judges, or physicians. Griswold v. Connecticut, 381 U.S. 479 (1965); *Roe v. Wade, supra.* In light of the important decisional autonomy interests involved, courts widely recognize that there is a cause of action in tort based in negligence for ineffective performance of a sterilization procedure. *See* Gregory G. Sarno, Annotation, *Tort Liability for Wrongfully Causing One to Be Born*, 83

A.L.R.3d 15 (1978). Maryland law is in accord. *See* Sard v. Hardy, 379 A.2d 1014 (Md. 1977). While courts are split as to whether it is appropriate to award damages for the cost of rearing a healthy child, courts uniformly recognize that the decision to procreate is a deeply personal decision with lifelong consequences, and that wrongful interferences with that decision constitute a harm. Thus, courts have shown a willingness to compensate parents when a doctor's actions interfere with their ability to make a deliberate and informed choice with respect to procreation.

It is not for Dr. Cutchin, or this court, or a jury to decide whether six children were enough for Robinson. Whether Robinson had one child, no children, or twenty, Dr. Cutchin's decision to perform a sterilization procedure was a harmful violation of her bodily integrity. Battery protects the right to be free from intentional invasions of the body. If Robinson's allegations are true, her right to bodily integrity was clearly violated when Dr. Cutchin performed the tubal ligation without consent. She suffered lasting harm. It is for the jury to assess credibility and decide whether Robinson's allegations of lack of consent are true. Thus, summary judgment on the claim of battery is denied.

IV INTENTIONAL INFLICTION OF EMOTIONAL DISTRESS

In Count III of the complaint, plaintiffs seek a recovery for intentional infliction of emotional distress. It is alleged that the actions of Dr. Cutchin were intentional, reckless, extreme, and outrageous and that they caused severe emotional distress to Robinson.

The tort of intentional infliction of emotional distress has four elements: (1) the conduct must be intentional or reckless; (2) the conduct must be extreme and outrageous; (3) there must be a causal connection between the wrongful conduct and the emotional distress; and (4) the emotional distress must be severe. All four elements must be proven. Hamilton v. Ford Motor Credit Co., 502 A.2d 1057, 1063 (Md. 1986). Previous opinions have acknowledged that "[i]n developing the tort of intentional infliction of emotional distress, whatever the relationship between the parties, recovery will be meted out sparingly, its balm reserved for those wounds that are truly severe and incapable of healing themselves." Figueiredo-Torres v. Nickel, 584 A.2d 69, 75 (Md. 1991) (*quoting Hamilton*, 502 A.2d at 1065).

In 1977, the court of special appeals, in a case of first impression, first recognized the tort of intentional infliction of emotional distress in Maryland. Jones v. Harris, 371 A.2d 1104 (Md. Ct. Spec. App. 1977). Since being recognized in Maryland, such claims have been upheld on appeal against a physician three times. *See* Faya v. Almaraz, 620 A.2d 327 (Md. 1993) (reversing dismissal when HIV-positive surgeon operated on the appellants without their knowledge of his disease); *Figeuiredo-Torres, supra* (reversing dismissal where plaintiff alleged psychologist engaged in sexual relations with plaintiff's wife during the time he was counseling the couple); B.N. v. K.K., 538 A.2d 1175 (Md. 1988) (holding that a cognizable cause of action could exist when physician had sex with nurse without informing her he had herpes and infected her with the disease).

Here, Robinson has alleged that Dr. Cutchin intentionally or recklessly performed the tubal ligation procedure without her consent. Based on case law, even if Dr. Cutchin did not actually intend to inflict severe emotional distress, it is enough if "he [knew] that such distress [was] certain, or substantially certain, to result from his conduct; or where [he acted] recklessly in deliberate disregard of a high degree of probability that the emotional distress [would] follow." Harris v. Jones, 380 A.2d 611, 614 (Md. 1977). A reasonable jury could conclude that given that the result of tubal ligation is permanent sterilization, it is at least extremely reckless for a physician to perform the procedure without tangible evidence of freely given consent from the patient.

For conduct to meet the test of "outrageousness," it must be "so extreme in degree, as to go beyond all possible bounds of decency, and to be regarded as atrocious, and utterly intolerable in a civilized community." *Id.* (quoting RESTATEMENT (SECOND) OF TORTS § 46 cmt. d (1965)). Whether the conduct complained of meets this test is, in the first instance, for the court to determine; in addressing that question, the court must consider not only the conduct itself but also the "personality of the individual to whom the misconduct is directed." *Harris*, 380 A.2d at 615. This high standard of culpability exists to screen out claims amounting to "mere insults, indignities, threats, annoyances, petty oppressions, or other trivialities" that simply must be endured as part of life. *Id.* at 614 (quoting RESTATEMENT (SECOND) OF TORTS § 46, cmt. d (1965)). With these qualifications firmly in mind, we consider the defendants' argument that the evidence is insufficient to prove the element of extreme and outrageous conduct on their part.

"Where reasonable men may differ, it is for the jury to determine whether, in the particular case, the conduct has been sufficiently extreme and outrageous to result in liability." *Id.* at 615. Viewing the facts in the light most favorable to Robinson, the nonmoving party, the facts easily meet the standard of "extreme and outrageous" conduct. Robinson was not subjected to "mere insults, indignities, threats, annoyances, petty oppressions, or other trivialities." *Id.* at 614. Nor was this a case of mere rudeness and annoying debt collection efforts that were found not outrageous in Dick v. Mercantile-Safe Dep. & Trust,

492 A.2d 674, 677 (Md. Ct. Spec. App. 1985), or the "bad taste and poor judgment" that did not suffice in *Hamilton*, 502 A.2d at 1064. Robinson was subjected to one of the most profound losses that a human being can experience, one that alters a fundamental aspect of her identity. She is no longer a fertile woman who can exercise her constitutionally protected right to make her own procreative decisions.

The widespread public outcry over the extent of abusive and coercive sterilization in the United States revealed by the *Relf* case and the media attention it received, demonstrates that our society has come to understand that being sterilized without consent is indeed extreme and outrageous. The revelations from the *Relf* litigation prompted congressional hearings, the formation of advocacy organizations dedicated to preventing sterilization abuse, and new federal regulations intended to protect the fundamental right not to be sterilized without consent. ROBERTS, *supra* at pp. 95–97. As we enter the twenty-first century, we recognize that no civilized society should tolerate coerced or involuntary sterilization.

The causal connection between the wrongful conduct and the emotional distress is apparent, if a jury believes Robinson's allegations. Thus, the remaining element to consider is the requirement that the emotional distress be severe. To prove her claim of emotional distress, plaintiff does not intend to call a psychiatrist or psychologist as an expert witness. There is no indication in the record here that Robinson was ever treated by a physician for her mental anguish. To support her pleading of emotional distress and anguish Robinson offers counseling sessions with her sister-in-law as evidence of severe emotional distress. Defendants contend that these pleadings cannot, as a matter of law, demonstrate the required level of severity of emotional distress, so that summary judgment should be granted on this claim.

While this element of the tort requires the plaintiff to show that she suffered a severely disabling emotional response to the defendant's conduct, *Harris*, 380 A.2d at 616, the *Harris* court emphasized that "in many cases the extreme and outrageous character of the defendant's conduct is in itself important evidence that the distress has existed ... It is for the court to determine whether on the evidence severe emotional distress can be found; it is for the jury to determine whether, on the evidence, it has in fact existed." *Id.* Moreover, in *B.N. v. K.K.*, the court of appeals held that severe emotional distress can be proven based largely on the extreme and outrageous conduct of the defendant. *B.N.*, 538 A.2d at 1181–82. That is, if "the acts of the defendant are so horrible, so atrocious and so barbaric that no civilized person could be expected to endure them without suffering mental distress, [a] jury may find as a matter of fact that 'severe' emotional distress resulted." *Id.* at 1182, *citing*

Reagan v. Rider, 521 A.2d 1246, 1251 (Md. Ct. Spec. App. 1987). In *B.N. v. K.K.*, the court held that the defendant's conduct of knowingly transmitting genital herpes to the plaintiff during consensual sexual intercourse without informing her that he was in the active, highly contagious stage of a sexually transmitted disease, was sufficiently outrageous conduct to permit a jury to infer that any reasonable plaintiff would suffer severe emotional distress from having contracted the disease. Drawing on research about the emotional and physical effects of genital herpes on women, the court noted that genital herpes is irreversible, and causes many women to suffer from a sense of being "damaged goods" in the sexual or reproductive sense. The court also noted that genital herpes can impair a woman's reproductive health, increasing the risk of miscarriage, and presenting a high risk of transmitting the disease to one's newborn child during vaginal delivery. *Id.* at 1180. These effects, the court held, went well beyond the sort of minor humiliations and indignities that did not amount to severe emotional distress.

We hold that sterilizing a woman without her consent is the type of atrocious conduct that will permit a jury to find severe distress from the nature of the defendant's conduct. As the U.S. Supreme Court noted in *Skinner v. Oklahoma*, 316 U.S. 535, 541 (1942), in striking down a discriminatory sterilization law, sterilization "involves one of the basic civil rights of man ... [P]rocreation [is] fundamental to the very existence and survival of the race." The birth of a child and the joy and pride in rearing that child is not only the basis of a civilization, but it can also be a defining aspect of a person's life. It is not hard to fathom how losing the ability to procreate could cause severe emotional distress. The impact of involuntary sterilization is even more profoundly devastating than the severe impact of having been infected with genital herpes. Sterilization is equally irreversible, and while a woman who suffers from herpes can still procreate, albeit having to be managed as a high-risk pregnancy, a woman who has been sterilized has been permanently deprived of her fundamental human and constitutional right to decide whether to procreate. A couple like the Robinsons, who had wanted to have more biological children, have been permanently deprived of the ability to do so. When a physician sterilizes a woman without obtaining her well informed, clear, and unequivocal consent, that physician evinces an extreme disregard for her autonomy and human rights. When, as in this case, there are overtones of our nation's shameful history of physicians sterilizing African-American woman without their consent because of judgments about their fitness to produce additional children, the outrageous conduct is likely to produce an even more devastating and degrading impact on a woman from the sense that her humanity and rights do not matter. Any reasonable woman would clearly suffer extreme anguish and have trouble enduring the pain of being sterilized against her will.

While Robinson has not offered medical testimony to support her claims of emotional distress, she has alleged that she was sterilized without her consent that she and her husband planned to have more children, that she suffered severe emotional distress, and that she sought counseling from her sister-in-law. Based on these allegations, a reasonable jury could find that Robinson suffered severe emotional distress. Robinson deserves the opportunity at trial to tell the jury, in her own words, of the impact on her psyche and her life, of being sterilized without her consent. Therefore, the defendant's motion for summary judgment on the claim for intentional infliction of emotional distress is denied.

V PUNITIVE DAMAGES

Robinson has asserted a claim for punitive damages. "[T]he purposes of punitive damages relate entirely to the nature of the defendant's conduct." Schaefer v. Miller, 587 A.2d 491, 503 (Md. 1991). "Awarding punitive damages based upon the heinous nature of the defendant's tortious conduct furthers the historical purposes of punitive damages – punishment and deterrence. Thus, punitive damages are awarded in an attempt to punish a defendant whose conduct is characterized by evil motive, intent to injure, or fraud, and to warn others contemplating similar conduct of the serious risk of monetary liability." Owens-Illinois v. Zenobia, 601 A.2d 633, 650 (Md. 1992).

"In a tort case where punitive damages are permitted, in order to obtain such an award a plaintiff must prove actual malice or its legal equivalent." Siegman v. Equitable Trust Co., 297 A.2d 758, 761 (Md. 1972). Implied or legal malice "may be defined as conduct of an extraordinary nature characterized by a wanton or reckless disregard for the rights of others." Wedeman v. City Chevrolet Co., 366 A.2d 7, 13 (Md. 1976).

Whether Dr. Cutchin acted with malice is a question of fact for the jury to decide at trial. Robinson has alleged that Dr. Cutchin recklessly performed a permanent sterilization without her consent during the course of an emergency cesarean section. As we have noted, this act can be considered outrageous, and violative of Robinson's fundamental human rights and dignity. If a jury finds these allegations to be true, then an award of punitive damages would be appropriate, and would send an essential message that no person should be sterilized without their well-informed, clear, and unequivocal consent. Accordingly, plaintiffs will be permitted to request punitive damages at trial.

VI CONCLUSION

For all the reasons stated, this court concludes that plaintiff will be permitted to present to the jury her claim for battery and her claim for the intentional infliction of emotional distress. Moreover, plaintiff may seek punitive damages.

Accordingly, for all the reasons stated, it is this 18th day of April, 2001 by the United States District Court for the District of Maryland

ORDERED:

1. That defendants' motion *in limine*, treated herein as a motion for summary judgment, is hereby denied;
2. That plaintiffs are entitled to seek punitive damages in this case.

7

Commentary on *Guthrie v. Conroy*

L. CAMILLE HÉBERT

INTRODUCTION

Guthrie v. Conroy[1] is not an unusual case. Instead, it is a fairly common example of cases at the state and federal levels in which courts have found that sexual harassment occurring in the workplace is not the type of tortious conduct that constitutes the "extreme" and "outrageous" conduct required to state a claim for intentional infliction of emotional distress. Some of those cases go so far as to hold that "as a general rule, sexual harassment alone does not rise to the level of outrageousness necessary to make out a cause of action for intentional infliction of emotional distress."[2] Most of the cases instead recognize the theoretical possibility that sexual harassment can rise to that level, but simply find that the particular conduct, which is often quite serious, does not.[3]

This divergence between sexual harassment claims and claims for intentional infliction of emotional distress may not be altogether surprising, at least in part because of the origins of the two types of claims. Sexual harassment claims were recognized under Title VII of the Civil Rights Act of 1964 as a form of discrimination on the basis of sex, largely as a result of the efforts of feminist scholars who challenged the idea that sexual harassment resulted from sexual desire, instead demonstrating the ways in which inequality

1 Guthrie v. Conroy, 567 S.E.2d 403 (N.C. Ct. App. 2002).

2 Andrews v. City of Philadelphia, 895 F.2d 1469, 1487 (3d Cir. 1990) (applying Pennsylvania law).

3 *See, e.g.*, Pucci v. USAIR, 940 F. Supp. 305, 307–09 (M.D. Fla. 1996) (no liability for intentional infliction of emotional distress when sole female employee in maintenance department had pornographic pictures placed on her desk and received a card soliciting sex, and sexual comments made about her, because although the behavior was not "civilized," it was not sufficiently outrageous).

between men and women in the workplace both caused and resulted from sexually harassing behaviors.[4] The tort of intentional infliction of emotional distress, on the other hand, had a much different genesis. Although the tort owes much of its development to scholars and was influenced by cultural attitudes about gender, the interest of women sought to be protected by the tort was not their equality, but rather their honor and presumed delicacy as compared to men. And the early academic champions of the tort found its requirements generally not to be satisfied by solicitations of sexual conduct, seeming to trivialize those solicitations with the indication that there "is no harm in asking."[5]

This divergence, however, is not inevitable. The legal standard for the tort of intentional infliction of emotional distress requires "extreme and outrageous" conduct; that standard is satisfied "when a defendant's conduct exceeds all bounds usually tolerated by decent society"[6] and when it is "so outrageous in character, and so extreme in degree, as to go beyond all possible bounds of decency, and to be regarded as atrocious, and utterly intolerable in a civilized community."[7] The MeToo movement, which has resulted in millions of women coming forward with their stories of sexual harassment and sexual assault, has raised awareness of not only the prevalence of this conduct but also the harms that it imposes. It would not be at all surprising for litigants to argue and for courts to agree that sexual harassment is indecent conduct that is in fact intolerable in any civilized society. In fact, it would seem quite odd for members of a civilized society to argue that women should be required to tolerate such degrading and abusive conduct.[8]

4 *See generally* Catharine A. MacKinnon, Sexual Harassment of Working Women: A Case of Sex Discrimination 143–221 (1979) (explaining how sexual harassment constitutes a form of sex discrimination under inequality and difference approaches to the law).

5 *See* Martha Chamallas, *Discrimination and Outrage: The Migration from Civil Rights to Tort Law*, 48 Wm. & Mary L. Rev. 2115, 2155–61 (2007) (discussing origins of tort of intentional infliction of emotional distress and the role played by professors William Prosser and Calvert Magruder).

6 *Guthrie*, 567 S.E.2d at 408 (*quoting* Watson v. Dixon, 502 S.E.2d 15, 19–20 (1998), aff'd, 532 S.E.2d 175 (N.C. 2000)).

7 *Id.* at 408–09 (*quoting* Briggs v. Rosenthal, 327 S.E.2d 308, 311, cert. denied, 332 S.E.2d 479 (N.C. App.1985)).

8 *See generally* L. Camille Hébert, *Conceptualizing Sexual Harassment in the Workplace as a Dignitary Tort*, 75 Ohio State L.J. 1345 (2014) (explaining how sexual harassment claims can satisfy the requirements of the tort of intentional infliction of emotional distress); Chamallas, *supra* note 5, at 2171–76 (arguing for the migration of features of anti-discrimination law to the tort of intentional infliction of emotional distress).

THE ORIGINAL OPINION

In *Guthrie v. Conroy*, the Court of Appeals of North Carolina considered whether a former employee, Linda Guthrie, had established a claim of intentional infliction of emotional distress against her former employer, Clegg's Termite and Pest Control, Inc., and coworker, Raymond Conroy, based on extensive sexual harassment by the coworker and the employer's inaction in responding to Guthrie's complaints about the harassment. The court of appeals took pains to distinguish claims of sexual harassment from claims of intentional infliction of emotional distress, noting that tort claims "do not involve a generalized assessment of acceptable workplace behavior, nor an analysis of the 'workplace environment.'" The court failed to explain, however, why an assessment of acceptable or unacceptable workplace behavior and the environment of the workplace was deemed irrelevant to Guthrie's claim.

The court concluded that Guthrie's allegations did not meet the standard of outrageousness by trivializing the conduct contained in those allegations as "mere insults," "rough language," and "inconsiderate and unkind," and by giving examples of how much worse conduct Guthrie might have faced. The court ignored or mischaracterized the nature of Guthrie's allegations to find that the conduct was only "annoyingly juvenile, obnoxious, and offensive." While professing not to "condone defendant's behavior," the court did precisely that, effectively concluding that the conduct that Guthrie was forced to endure was within the bounds of decency and tolerable in a civilized community. It then concluded that a claim of intentional infliction of emotional distress could be made against the employer only as a matter of vicarious liability, completely ignoring the possibility that the employer might have been liable for its own tortious action in allowing the harassment of Guthrie to continue unabated.

The court next rejected Guthrie's claim of negligent infliction of emotional distress. While acknowledging that the claim does not require outrageous and extreme conduct, the court held that a showing of negligence could not be made without proof of the existence of a duty owed by the coworker to the plaintiff and breach of that duty, which the court summarily concluded had not been established. The court also rejected any possibility that the employer could be liable for negligent infliction of emotional distress based on its own negligence, instead concluding that the employer's liability had to be derivative of the coworker's tortious acts.[9]

[9] The court also summarily rejected Guthrie's claim of negligent retention and supervision, but did hold that district court had erred in granting summary judgment on her claim that the

The *Guthrie* court was able to reach the result that it did not only by erasing particular allegations of this plaintiff, but also by erasing generally the experiences of women who face workplace sexual harassment. The court also erased any obligation on the part of coworkers or employers to avoid creating or to remedy a working environment hostile to women.[10] The feminist judgment recognizes these shortcomings.

THE FEMINIST JUDGMENT

The feminist judgment by Professor Sandra Sperino, writing as Judge Sperino, takes the form of an opinion concurring in part and dissenting in part from the original opinion, although on the issue of whether the plaintiff has stated a claim of intentional or negligent infliction of emotional distress, Judge Sperino writes in dissent. Fully grounded in the particulars of the case, the feminist judgment also brings important aspects of feminist legal theory to its resolution of the issues.

Incorporation of Feminist Legal Theory

1 Recognition of Women's Experiences and Perspectives

An important hallmark of feminist approaches to the law is the recognition of women's realities, which are often discounted or ignored by traditional approaches to the law. In addressing whether the plaintiff's allegations were sufficient to avoid summary judgment on her claim of intentional infliction of emotional distress, the feminist judgment notes the ways in which the original opinion ignored, misstated, and minimized the actual allegations and evidence that the plaintiff offered in support of her claim. The feminist judgment cautions judges to be skeptical of their ability to evaluate the severity of conduct because their current life experience may blind them to the dynamics of most workplaces. It also shows that the actual allegations and evidence in the case, not just those acknowledged by the court in the original opinion,

employer had ratified the civil assault by the coworker, based on its alleged failure to take disciplinary action against the coworker or otherwise to remedy the situation.

10 In the part of the original opinion dealing with Guthrie's claim that the employer had ratified her assault by her coworker, the court cited the actions of the employer in remodeling the office "to place a privacy wall around the plaintiff's desk." The court seemed to treat that action as part of the employer's actions to remedy the harassment, while the action might just as well have been thought of as part of the creation of a hostile environment, by taking action to isolate Guthrie rather than discipline her harasser.

indicate that a question of fact existed as to whether the conduct to which the plaintiff was subjected was extreme and outrageous, a question which the jury, not the court, was required to decide.

Perhaps the most striking feature of Sperino's opinion is its demonstration that the allegations and evidence presented by the plaintiff were much more extensive than the seemingly isolated incidents described by the original opinion. Although the court in the original opinion purported to be describing the evidence "in the light most favorable to the plaintiff," in reality it refused to consider the evidence from Guthrie's perspective. Instead, the court discounted the allegations and evidence that Guthrie's coworker repeatedly touched her inappropriately, held her while she pushed him away, and pulled open her blouse to drop items down its front. Even with respect to the allegations and evidence that the original opinion acknowledged, Sperino's opinion demonstrates that the conduct was not isolated but repeated.

2 The Influence of Dominance or Anti-Subordination Feminism

When the feminist judgment notes the way in which the original opinion erases and minimizes the experiences of the female plaintiff and women generally, it invokes the concept of anti-subordination or dominance feminism, as famously articulated by Catharine MacKinnon in her books, *Sexual Harassment of Working Women*[11] and *Feminism Unmodified.*[12] Men sexually harass women in the workplace not because of sexual attraction, but because of social or workplace power or both. Anti-subordination feminists have asserted that men feel entitled to treat women any way they want because of that power and often touch, grab, or hold women against their wishes and protests to remind women that they do not have the power to effectively prevent that behavior. Because of their subordinate position, women may not even have the power to have their experience of this abuse taken seriously.

Anti-subordination feminism underscores the importance of perspective. The way in which women are oppressed by men, and the way in which women experience that oppression, is seen as trivial and juvenile behavior

[11] *See* MacKinnon, *supra* note 4 (demonstrating that sexual harassment is a form of sex discrimination in that it is used to perpetuate women's inferior status in the workplace).

[12] *Sexual Harassment: Its First Decade in Court* (1986) in Catharine A. MacKinnon, Feminism Unmodified: Discourses on Life and Law 108–09 (1987) (discussing ways in which claims of sexual harassment have been regarded as concerns of "oversensitive" women, claiming harm from men who were being "affectionate or friendly or fun," as viewed from the harasser's viewpoint).

because it is viewed from the point of view of men.[13] Just as courts often accept harassing men's protestations that they were "only joking," the *Guthrie* court viewed the behavior as merely offensive because of the presumed intent of the harasser. That the behavior had a severe enough effect on Guthrie that she felt forced to quit her job was discounted or ignored. The court seemed to have believed that the conduct could not be "outrageous" when the harasser presumably did not intend it that way – and Guthrie's male supervisor thought it so unimportant that he did not even reprimand the harasser for the conduct, but instead accused Guthrie of "making his life 'hell'" because of her harassment complaints.

3 Judicial Techniques to Exclude Feminist Perspectives

The feminist judgment not only invokes principles of anti-subordination feminist legal theory to reach a different result than the original opinion, but also reveals a number of judicial techniques that have been used to exclude feminist perspectives from the resolution of cases.

(a) Use of Summary Judgment to Exclude Women's Narratives

Feminist scholars have argued that the device of summary judgment has been used to deprive women of the opportunity to provide their perspectives on workplace conditions, including with respect to sexual harassment.[14] The feminist judgment highlights the way that the original opinion framed the requirements of a claim of intentional infliction of emotional distress involving sexually harassing conduct so as to support its conclusion that the plaintiff's allegations and evidence were insufficient to survive summary judgment. The original opinion listed criteria that successful claims of intentional infliction of emotional distress have satisfied – all criteria that Guthrie did not meet – while ignoring criteria that other successful claims have involved – criteria that Guthrie's allegations and evidence did meet.

[13] Interestingly, in a case in which the target of harassment was a man, a court had no trouble concluding that the conduct in that case, which involved unwanted touching of the plaintiff's buttocks, use of "lewd" name calling, and "multiple unsolicited and unwanted requests for homosexual sex," was "one in which the recitation of the facts to an average member of the community would arouse his resentment against the actor, and lead him to exclaim, 'Outrageous!'" Brewer v. Hillard, 15 S.W.3d 1, 7 (Ky. Ct. App. 1999).

[14] *See* Elizabeth M. Schneider, *The Dangers of Summary Judgment: Gender and Federal Court Litigation*, 59 RUTGERS L. REV. 705 (2007) (describing the use of summary judgment in cases with female plaintiffs, including employment discrimination and tort claims).

The feminist judgment also disagrees with the cursory way in which the original opinion deals with the negligent infliction of emotional distress claim. The original opinion asserts – inaccurately – that the "plaintiff alleges no duty that Conroy owed plaintiff, and no evidence was presented of a breach of any duty of care owed by Conroy to plaintiff." Guthrie's complaint, however, does contain such an allegation, when it asserts that "Defendants owed Plaintiff a duty of care to maintain a safe and secure work environment, free from sexual discrimination, sexual harassment, retaliation, misconduct, embarrassment and humiliation" and that "Conroy was negligent in continuing to harass and intimidate the Plaintiff after Plaintiff had specifically told him to leave her alone."[15] The feminist judgment appropriately faults the original opinion for failing to seriously address the issues of whether such a duty existed and was breached, particularly in light of the court's recognition that it is the public policy of the state of North Carolina to prohibit sex discrimination including, presumably, sexual harassment.

(b) *"Slicing and Dicing" the Plaintiff's Claims and Evidence*

Another judicial device that has been used to exclude feminist perspectives from the resolution of claims has been to "slice and dice" the plaintiff's allegations and evidence to consider only certain allegations to support certain claims, effectively limiting the ability of plaintiffs like Guthrie to present a complete picture of their experiences and the hostility of the workplace environment.[16] Sperino writes that by failing to consider the plaintiff's evidence of intentional infliction of emotional distress in its totality, the original opinion excluded consideration of both the coworker's threatened acts of retaliation and the reaction of her supervisor and other management employees to her complaints. By chopping up the evidence in this way, the court failed to appreciate the effect of the actions of the supervisor, who largely ignored plaintiff's complaints of harassment, called her "a damned liar," and documented anything he believed Guthrie did that was wrong in response to her complaints of harassment.

Additionally, the feminist judgment criticizes the original opinion for focusing only on whether the employer could be vicariously liable for the actions of the coworker and completely ignoring Guthrie's claim that the employer might be liable for its own negligence in failing to stop the

[15] Guthrie v. Conroy and Clegg's Termite and Pest Control, Inc., Complaint, Jury Trial Demanded, 1999 WL 34988354 (N.C. Super. October 5, 1999), paras. 46, 48(B).

[16] *See* Sandra F. Sperino & Suja A. Thomas, Unequal: How America's Courts Undermine Discrimination Law 152–55 (2017) (describing how courts use a number of devices, including "slicing and dicing" claims, to prevent full consideration of evidence of discrimination as a whole).

harassment and for the retaliatory behavior directed against Guthrie by supervisory and other employees. Sperino's more holistic approach recognizes that the employer might be liable for its own actions or inactions and that the employer's actions should also be considered in determining whether Guthrie suffered intentional or negligent infliction of emotional distress.

(c) Emphasizing the Sexual over Gender-Based Hostility

Sperino's dissent also reflects feminist criticism of the tendency of courts in sexual harassment cases to focus on sexual conduct to the exclusion of nonsexual, but gender-based, conduct, generally finding only conduct of a sexual nature to be actionable.[17] She faults the original opinion for focusing only on whether the conduct alleged by Guthrie was sexual, seeming to suggest that while sexual advances might be considered outrageous activity, the nonsexual, but nevertheless denigrating, actions of Guthrie's coworker could not be. At the same time, the feminist judgment notes the way in which the original opinion refused to see that much of the behavior aimed at Guthrie by her coworker was in fact sexually charged.

(d) Separating Tort Law from Sexual Harassment Law

Finally, the feminist judgment addresses the relationship between tort claims and sexual harassment claims, faulting the court's willingness to dismiss Guthrie's tort claims with the suggestion that she should have instead asserted a sexual harassment claim under Title VII of the Civil Rights Act of 1964 or under state anti-discrimination law. Sperino challenges any suggestion that Guthrie would necessarily have been afforded an adequate remedy under Title VII, noting the many restrictions, both procedural and substantive, that apply to such claims.

The feminist judgment is also important for the way that the opinion insists that tort law has a role to play in the resolution of sexual harassment claims. While the original opinion suggested that this claim would have been better asserted under the anti-discrimination laws, the feminist judgment indicates that there is no reason that claims of sexual harassment are not also actionable as a matter of tort. As the feminist judgment notes, "tort law should not stop at the front door of a workplace."

[17] *See* Ruth Colker, *Whores, Fags, Dumb-Ass Women, Surly Blacks, and Competent Heterosexual White Men: The Sexual and Racial Morality Underlying Anti-Discrimination Doctrine*, 7 YALE J.L. & FEMINISM 195, 199, 209–10 (1995) (noting the way that successful sexual harassment plaintiffs have been required to demonstrate that they were treated in a sexual way).

Indeed, there is reason to believe that Guthrie's ability to state a claim for sexual harassment under Title VII should have increased, not decreased, the odds of her stating a viable claim for intentional infliction of emotional distress. As the original opinion recognized, the standard of outrageousness is that the defendant's conduct "go beyond all possible bounds of decency" and be "utterly intolerable in a civilized community." Each of these prongs appears to have been satisfied in this case. The court, which purported not to condone the conduct directed at Guthrie and called it offensive, seemed not to view the conduct as decent. And the proposition that sexual harassment is not tolerated by our civilized society is amply demonstrated by the fact that Congress and state legislatures, including the North Carolina legislature, have declared sex discrimination and sexual harassment to be unlawful and contrary to public policy.

Other courts have been willing to see the close connection between sexual harassment and outrageous behavior:

> It is worth stating forcefully that any other conclusion would amount to an intolerable refusal to recognize that our society has ceased seeing sexual harassment in the work place as a playful inevitability that should be taken in good spirits and has awakened to the fact that sexual harassment has a corrosive effect on those who engage in it as well as those who are subjected to it and that such harassment has far more to do with the abusive exercise of one person's power over another than it does with sex.[18]

The recognition that "sexual harassment is simply unacceptable in today's society"[19] also demonstrates the original opinion's error in looking to past cases to determine what the courts have found to be sufficiently egregious behavior, rather than undertaking an analysis of what society would find intolerable, atrocious, and indecent in 2002, when the *Guthrie* case was decided.

CONCLUSION

Sperino's feminist judgment makes clear the effect that an explicitly feminist perspective – one that expressly takes into account the experiences of women as women, and takes those experiences seriously, rather than trivializing them – could have on the development of tort law. Interestingly, the original opinion in *Guthrie* was not written in another era by a man out of touch with

[18] Retherfold v. AT&T Commc'ns of Mountain States, Inc., 844 P.2d 949, 978 (Utah 1992). The court went on to note that one of the leading authorities on torts has declared that sexual harassment on the job is "'undoubtedly an intentional infliction of emotional distress." *Id.* (*quoting* W. Page Keeton et al., Prosser & Keeton on the Law of Torts § 12 18 (1988)).

[19] *Retherfold*, 844 P.2d at 978.

the challenges and requirements of a modern workplace. Instead, the opinion was written by a female judge who is a woman of color and who would go on to be the first black woman to be appointed to a federal court in North Carolina.[20] But she was deciding the case in the context of a body of tort law created and applied with the interests of men in mind, deciding what types of conduct that men believe should be tolerated.

The *Guthrie* decision has been widely cited by other courts in determining whether workplace conduct is sufficiently harmful to be actionable in tort. Along with other similar decisions, it has encouraged courts to conclude that insulting and degrading conduct directed at women is tolerable, merely because the conduct could have been worse. Presumably because holding and rubbing a woman's neck and shoulders against her will and pulling open her blouse to drop items on her breasts is not as bad as touching her genitals, that conduct is labeled as merely "obnoxious" and is viewed as conduct that women should expect in the workplace. As a result, women who feel compelled to quit their jobs to escape harassment and the retaliation that comes from reporting such behavior are criticized for being overly sensitive and unreasonable. Viewing these cases from a feminist perspective, as the feminist judgment does, could, however, change this dynamic and provide support for the conclusion that sexual harassment of women in the workplace has become – and always was – "utterly intolerable in a civilized society."

GUTHRIE *v.* CONROY, 567 S.E.2D 403 (N.C. CT. APP. 2002)

JUDGE SANDRA F. SPERINO, CONCURRING IN PART AND DISSENTING IN PART

I

Linda Guthrie sued her former coworker, Raymond Conroy, and her former employer, Clegg's Termite and Pest Control, Inc. for injuries arising from their hostile treatment of her at the workplace. The trial court granted summary judgment on several of Guthrie's claims against both defendants, and this court largely affirms those dismissals. The majority reasons that the

[20] The author of the original opinion is Loretta Copeland Biggs, who served on the North Carolina Court of Appeals from 2001 to 2002 and who was appointed to the United States District Court for the Middle District of North Carolina in 2015. *See* Erin Mizelle, *Loretta Biggs Becomes U.S. Judge*, The Chronicle (Mar. 12, 2015), http://www.wschronicle.com/2015/03/loretta-biggs-becomes-u-s-judge.

plaintiff has not presented sufficient evidence that defendant Conroy's conduct met either the elements of intentional infliction of emotional distress (IIED) or negligent infliction of emotional distress (NIED). Since the IIED and NIED claims against Conroy do not survive, the majority concludes that the employer cannot face derivative liability for these claims.

I write largely in dissent. In my view, the trial court improperly granted summary judgment in favor of both defendants on plaintiff's IIED claims. And, to the extent that the plaintiff's negligent supervision and retention claim against her former employer is linked to the survival of her IIED claim, summary judgment on that claim was improper. I would remand the case for further briefing on the existence of a duty regarding NIED and additional briefing on the facts of the case supporting that claim. I concur with the majority that the trial court committed error in granting summary judgment on plaintiff's claim against her employer for ratification of civil assault.[1] Given the importance of the IIED issues in this case, this dissent focuses mainly on the IIED claims.

Unfortunately, the majority opinion erases or minimizes most of Guthrie's evidence and experiences from the facts it chooses to recount. *See* Martha Chamallas, *Writing about Sexual Harassment: A Guide to the Literature*, 4 UCLA Women's L.J. 37, 46 (1993) (discussing literature on how women's accounts of workplace conduct are often undermined). As discussed below, the plaintiff's evidence as a whole paints a very different picture than the one stated by the majority.

The majority also focuses solely on Conroy as the tortfeasor and only considers management's actions through the lens of vicarious or derivative liability. However, as discussed below, a different story emerges if we consider Guthrie's evidence that her manager ignored Conroy's conduct and her allegations that she was threatened with retaliation after she enlisted the help of the central office in stopping the conduct. All of this conduct should be considered together in determining whether Clegg's Termite and Pest Control is liable for IIED and NIED. Employer liability must be viewed through two lenses: the employer's direct liability for its own actions and its vicarious or derivative liability for the actions of its employees.

I do not know what happened at Clegg's Termite and Pest Control. Importantly, the majority also does not know what happened. The facts are

[1] The civil assault claim is contained in plaintiff's allegation that Conroy held her from behind and touched her neck and shoulders, placed a lampshade on her head, threw potting soil in her hair and threw water at her, remarking that he wanted to see her in a wet T-shirt. The majority notes that her supervisor knew about this conduct and did not effectively intervene, even when higher levels of management indicated that the local office should take care of the issues.

contested. Fortunately, it is not our job as judges to resolve these fact disputes. Instead, the governing rules of procedure determine who gets to make those decisions: a jury.

II

When a jury trial is properly available, the rules of civil procedure constrain when judges may dismiss cases before they reach the jury. The summary judgment standard is not something that judges may or should choose to ignore. That standard is important to maintain the proper allocation of power between judge and jury. Additionally, especially in cases of alleged workplace misconduct, judges should be skeptical of their abilities to appreciate and evaluate the severity of conduct. As federal judge Jack Weinstein has noted:

> The factual issues in this case cannot be effectively settled by a decision of . . . [a] judge on summary judgment. Whatever the early life of a . . . judge, she or he usually lives in a narrow segment of the enormously broad American socio-economic spectrum, generally lacking the current real-life experience required in interpreting subtle . . . dynamics of the workplace based on nuances, perceptions, and implicit communications.
>
> *Gallagher v. Delaney*, 139 F.3d 338, 342 (2d Cir. 1998)

Summary judgment is proper only when "the pleadings, depositions, answers to interrogatories, and admissions on file, together with the affidavits, if any, show that there is no genuine issue as to any material fact and that any party is entitled to a judgment as a matter of law." N.C. Gen. Stat. § 1A–1, 56(c) (2001). In ruling on a motion for summary judgment, "the evidence presented by the parties must be viewed in the light most favorable to the non-movant." *Bruce–Terminix Co. v. Zurich Ins. Co.*, 504 S.E.2d 574, 577 (N.C. Ct. App. 1998).

The non-moving party in this case is Guthrie, the plaintiff. To give a full picture of the facts, I will review the set of facts as stated by the majority, but also juxtapose this set of the facts with the additional evidence the plaintiff submitted. This full picture of the evidence shows that the lower court improperly granted summary judgment on her IIED claims.

III

A *The IIED Claims*

I start with plaintiff's claim of IIED against Conroy and Clegg's Termite. To make out a claim, plaintiff must establish the elements of IIED: "(1) extreme and outrageous conduct by the defendant (2) which is intended to and does in fact cause (3) severe emotional distress." Waddle v. Sparks, 414 S.E.2d 22, 27 (N.C. 1992) (citation omitted). It is settled law that it "is a question of law for the court to determine, from the materials before it, whether the conduct complained of may reasonably be found to be sufficiently outrageous as to permit recovery." Brown v. Burlington Indus., Inc., 378 S.E.2d 232, 235 (N.C. Ct. App. 1989). However, the jury also plays a role in the determination of outrageous conduct because "once conduct is shown which may be reasonably regarded as extreme and outrageous, it is for the jury to determine, upon proper instructions, whether the conduct complained of is, in fact, sufficiently extreme and outrageous to result in liability." *Id.* In this case, a question of fact remains about whether the defendants' conduct was extreme and outrageous.

The majority opinion tells us that plaintiff began working for Clegg's Termite and Pest Control in 1998 as a secretary. Defendant Conroy was Clegg's coworker, employed as a salesman and pesticide technician. In May of 1999, she resigned her position, stating that she was "quitting in order to escape sexual harassment by defendant Conroy." *Guthrie*, 567 S.E.2d at 405.

Based on its evaluation of the evidence, the majority determined that the plaintiff could not meet the first element of IIED that requires "extreme and outrageous conduct by the defendant." *Waddle*, 414 S.E.2d at 27. Here is how the majority summarizes the plaintiff's evidence.

> In contrast, the evidence in the case *sub judice*, taken in the light most favorable to the plaintiff, tends to show that defendant Conroy engaged in the following behavior: (1) held plaintiff from behind, and touched or rubbed her neck and shoulders; (2) "irritated" her by placing a lampshade on her head when [she] fell asleep with her head on her desk; (3) threw potting soil and water on plaintiff while she was planting flowers at work, remarking when he threw a cup of water on plaintiff that he'd "always wanted to see [her] in a wet T shirt"; and (4) placed a Styrofoam "peanut" and other small objects between the legs of a "naked man" statuette that plaintiff displayed on her windowsill at work and asked her "how she liked it" with the addition.
>
> *Guthrie*, 567 S.E.2d at 410

The numbering above suggests that Conroy engaged in four, isolated incidents and that her claim must rise or fall on an assessment of those discrete events. However, this is not what the plaintiff's evidence suggests. Rather, the plaintiff stated during her deposition, "He would touch me and I'd tell him to stop. He put his hand on my neck, on my shoulder. He would hold me and I'd push him away." (Deposition Testimony presented in Defendant's Brief in Support of Its Motion for Summary Judgment.) In her Statement of Facts in

Opposition to Defendant's Motion for Summary Judgment, the plaintiff stated the following:

> Beginning in August 1998, Mr. Conroy started touching Ms. Guthrie, putting his hands on her, grabbing her from behind and holding her against her will, rubbing her neck, and pulling open her shirt to drop items down the front of her blouse. (L. Guthrie Dep. 26–27; Int. No. 5; Conroy Dep. 33; W. Guthrie Dep. 27.) Ms. Guthrie repeatedly asked Mr. Conroy to stop and leave her alone. (L. Guthrie Dep. 26–27; Conroy Dep. 63.) He would hold her and Ms. Guthrie would attempt to push him away. (L Guthrie Dep. 27.) Mr. Conroy simply laughed. *Id.* Ms. Guthrie went to the Branch Manager, Joseph Joy, to complain about what Mr. Conroy was doing, but Mr. Conroy continued his conduct. (L. Guthrie Dep. 34, 56–57.)
>
> Plaintiff's Memorandum of Law in Response to Defendant's Motion for Summary Judgment, Statement of Facts

The plaintiff provided this further evidence about Conroy's conduct:

> In addition to touching her inappropriately, Mr. Conroy began to play suggestively with a figurine. A four-year-old son of a technician had given her a four-inch figurine shaped like a super hero, but wearing no clothes. (L. Guthrie Dep. 27, 28; Henry Dep. 17–19.) The little boy called the child's figurine "Naked Man." (L. Guthrie Dep. 28.) Ms. Guthrie put the present on her windowsill where she kept her knick-knacks, including a picture of her son, her grandson, and her granddaughter, a frog, and two little boats. *Id.* Mr. Conroy picked up the figurine and put a styrofoam shipping "peanut" between the figurine's legs and asked Ms. Guthrie how she liked it. (L. Guthrie Dep. 28; Conroy Dep. 22; Henry Dep. 19, 21.) When Ms. Guthrie took the peanut and threw it in the trash, Mr. Conroy then inserted the cap of a pen and asked whether she liked that one better. (L. Guthrie Dep. 29.) Ms. Guthrie reported the incident to Mr. Joy who simply responded that he had not seen anything happen. As a result, Mr. Conroy continued to place pencils and ink pen caps between the figurine's legs. (L. Guthrie Dep. 29; Int. No. 5; Henry Dep. 23–24.)
>
> Plaintiff's Memorandum of Law in Response to Defendant's Motion for Summary Judgment, Statement of Facts

B *Viewing IIED Evidence in Its Totality*

I find the majority diminishes the plaintiff's evidence by potentially downplaying both the quantity and the severity of Conroy's actions toward the plaintiff. The majority slices and dices plaintiff's evidence, attaching certain pieces of evidence only to specific claims and failing to see the evidence as a whole. In contrast to the majority's analysis, the tort of IIED allows a plaintiff to allege a course of conduct over time and does not require her to focus on a single event or small set of events. Given the evidence before us and reading all inferences in favor of the plaintiff, a jury must determine what acts occurred and their severity. In doing so, I am not stating who should prevail on the underlying IIED claim, only that this is properly the decision of a jury and not this court.

In finding that the behavior the plaintiff faced was not "extreme and outrageous," the majority made additional errors. The majority failed to discuss the alleged acts of retaliation when considering whether the conduct was outrageous. The majority also erred by focusing on Conroy's conduct only and not the combined effect of the actions taken by both Conroy and Joseph Joy, the manager of the branch location where plaintiff worked. In determining the employer's liability for IIED, this court must consider the combined effects of Conroy and Joy's conduct, as well as other managers' conduct. *Coates v. Wal-Mart Stores, Inc.*, 976 P.2d 999, 1009 (N.M. 1999) (noting that outrageous conduct can include the cumulative actions and nonactions of multiple employees).

The plaintiff did not experience her workplace as a series of isolated incidents committed by separate individuals under the heading of separate tort causes of action. Rather, reading the evidence in the light most favorable to the plaintiff, she experienced multiple unwanted touchings at work from a male coworker, reported that conduct to higher-ups, and then faced retaliation. Even though these facts are contested, at the summary judgment stage, we must view the facts in the light most favorable to the plaintiff.

Here is additional evidence missing from the majority's account relating to Joy's conduct toward the plaintiff. Again, I quote the evidence submitted by the plaintiff in response to the defendant's motion for summary judgment.

> During the fall, Ms. Guthrie reviewed the Clegg's sexual harassment policy several times. She made a copy of the policy and posted it on the office bulletin board. (L. Guthrie Dep. 44.) Mr. Joy, however, took it down. (L. Guthrie Dep. 44; Interrogatory No. 12; Henry Dep. 31.)
>
> Mr. Joy's office was across from Ms. Guthrie's desk, his door was always open, and he should have been able to observe Mr. Conroy's behavior. (Int. No. 12; Joy Dep. 14.) On more than one occasion, Ms. Guthrie asked him, "Joe, you have got to do something with Ray. I can't take this anymore. He won't keep his hands off of me. You sit right there and look at me and you see what he's

> doing to me." (Int. No. 12.) Mr. Joy would simply claim that he had not seen anything. *Id.*
>
> Plaintiff's Memorandum of Law in Response to Defendant's Motion for Summary Judgment, Statement of Facts

The plaintiff continues by recalling that when she called an employee at the head office to complain, she was told that Joy should handle the problem because he was the manager at the local office. The plaintiff testified that the problems continued after the complaint. *Id.*

One additional incident deserves special mention: an incident in which plaintiff alleges that Conroy threw water and soil at her while they were planting flowers outside the office.

> In early April 1999, Ms. Guthrie was planting pansies outside of the office. When Mr. Conroy joined her and offered to help, she told him that she wanted to do it by herself. While she was placing the pansies in the ground, he covered the pansies with potting soil and threw soil in her hair. He then proceeded to water the pansies with a hose, but also sprayed water on Ms. Guthrie. He announced that he had always wanted to see her in a wet T-shirt. (L. Guthrie Dep. 50; Int. No. 5; Henry Dep. 29.) Ms. Henry, who was inside the office, could hear Ms. Guthrie yelling at Mr. Conroy to leave her alone. Ms. Henry turned to Mr. Joy, who was watching what was happening, and said, "If he doesn't leave her alone, she's going to end up killing him today." (Henry Dep. 28.) Mr. Joy simply turned and went back into his office. *Id.* Mr. Conroy returned inside, took Mr. Joy's coffee cup, filled it with water, opened the door, and threw cold water in Ms. Guthrie's face. (L. Guthrie Dep. 50–51.)
>
> Plaintiff's Memorandum of Law in Response to Defendant's Motion for Summary Judgment, Statement of Facts

The plaintiff presented evidence that Joy did not speak to Conroy about Guthrie's concerns until seven months after the problems started. *Id.* When Joy gave Conroy a written memo documenting an oral reprimand, it simply stated, "from this day forward, any and all discussions to employees will be of a business nature." *Id.* From the record before the court, it does not appear the reprimand discussed unwanted touching or any other actions toward Guthrie.

The plaintiff's response to summary judgment also provides evidence of a retaliatory threat by Conroy. Again, quoting from the plaintiff's submission:

> [Mr. Conroy] said that if she did not drop her complaints about sexual harassment, he was going to tell everyone falsely that she had gone to work high on Valium. (L. Guthrie Dep. 49.) Ms. Guthrie informed the main office of Mr. Conroy's remark. (Smith Dep. 63.) On April 27, Mr. Joy wrote a

> reprimand to Mr. Conroy regarding this comment and indicated on the handwritten note that Mr. Conroy had seen it and refused to sign it. (Ex. 3.) In fact, Mr. Joy never showed the reprimand to Mr. Conroy. (Conroy Dep. 48.)
>
> Plaintiff's Memorandum of Law in Response to Defendant's Motion for Summary Judgment, Statement of Facts

It was only when Guthrie complained to a manager from another office, Lynn Edwards, that Edwards gave Conroy a written reprimand for "harassment of secretaries, touching, remarks, repeated warnings." *Id.* The company then erected a wall around the plaintiff's desk. Guthrie testified that when she asked Edwards why a wall "was being built around her desk, he explained that it was because the 'ladies could not keep the men away from [them].'" *Id.*

Guthrie presented evidence that after she reported another incident to the main office, Joy told her "I am sick and damn tired of every time I leave this office you are on the phone to Phil Clegg about something I've done and you are a damn liar." (Plaintiff's Memorandum of Law in Response to Defendant's Motion for Summary Judgment, Statement of Facts.)

The plaintiff further submitted the following evidence:

> Mr. Joy admitted that "[b]ecause [he] kept getting calls from Mr. Clegg and Lynn Edwards, stating that Linda Guthrie has been calling them and telling them that Raymond Conroy has been saying or doing things to her that were inappropriate," he began writing down anything that Ms. Guthrie did that he felt was inappropriate. (Joy Dep. 72.) He never, however, made any notes of what Mr. Conroy did. (Joy Dep. 80, 81.) He complained instead that Ms. Guthrie was, during the first weeks of May, making his life "hell." (Joy Dep. 83.)
>
> Plaintiff's Memorandum of Law in Response to Defendant's Motion for Summary Judgment, Statement of Facts

The plaintiff also submitted the defendant's sexual harassment policy, which states that harassed employees should report problems to any member of management and that "[m]anagement will investigate all such claims and take appropriate, corrective action." (Ex. 5 at p. 10.) The policy further provides: "Employees who utilize the complaint procedure outlined in this manual will not be retaliated against and will not have their employment adversely affected by making such a complaint." *Id.*

Indeed, the majority recognizes many of the facts related to Joy's conduct, but discusses them only in the context of whether there was sufficient evidence to allow plaintiff's claim that the company ratified the assault to proceed. *Guthrie*, 567 S.E.2d at 412. While the majority views this conduct as relevant to ratification, it omits this evidence when it considers whether the defendants engaged in an outrageous course of conduct.

The majority opinion does not present the facts in the light most favorable to the plaintiff both because it omits many facts supporting her case and because it fails to consider alleged acts of retaliation and acts by her manager as part of the outrageous course of conduct. By doing so, the majority has distorted the totality-of-the-circumstances approach that must guide courts' judgment about whether a claim of IIED should be submitted to a jury.

C *Improper Limits on the IIED Claims*

Additionally, the way the majority has framed the legal standard related to IIED is problematic. The majority appropriately recognizes that conduct that constitutes sexual harassment under statutory civil rights claims may also meet the elements of IIED. Nonetheless, the majority concludes that the two claims do not always overlap and then places arbitrary limits on when conduct amounting to sexual harassment will qualify as outrageous conduct. The majority provides a list of factors taken from prior cases decided in our state courts, each of which it claims militate against finding extreme and outrageous conduct in the plaintiff's case. The majority reasons as follows:

> [O]ur review of the relevant case law indicates that claims of IIED based upon allegations of sexual harassment generally have included one or more of the following: an unfair power relationship between defendant and plaintiff; explicitly obscene or "X rated" language; sexual advances towards plaintiff; statements expressing desire to engage in sexual relations with plaintiff, or; defendant either touching plaintiff's private areas or touching any part of the plaintiff's body with his private parts ...
>
> We note that Conroy was not plaintiff's supervisor or workplace superior; that he did not swear or employ obscene language; that he referred to nothing more vulgar than a "wet T shirt"; that although he gave plaintiff a "shoulder rub" against her wishes, he never expressed any interest in sexual activity with plaintiff; and that, notwithstanding allegations in plaintiff's complaint that defendant dropped items down the front of her blouse, the only specific instance of this behavior she described was his throwing potting soil at her while she planted flowers.
>
> *Id.* at 410

There are, however, several important problems with the majority's list and the cases cited to support this list. First, none of the cases cited by the majority in its string of parentheticals purports to define the minimum threshold for conduct to be considered outrageous. Yet the question before this court, given the procedural posture of summary judgment, is whether the plaintiff's facts surpass the minimum threshold for outrageous conduct. It is noteworthy that many of the cases cited by the majority are unrelated to that question. *See* Poole v. Copland, Inc., 498 S.E.2d 602 (N.C. 1998) (focusing on jury instruction related to thin skull rule); Waddle, 414 S.E.2d 22 (focusing on whether a plaintiff suffered requisite degree of distress and on statute of limitations); Ruff v. Reeves Bros., Inc., 468 S.E.2d 592 (N.C. Ct. App. 1996) (largely discussing statute of limitations issue); Bryant v. Thalhimer Bros., Inc., 437 S.E.2d 519 (N.C. Ct. App. 1993) (same).

Second, it is impossible to create a comprehensive list of factors that support a finding of outrageous conduct. The determination of the outrageous nature of a course of conduct is highly contextual, making it impossible to describe in advance just what combination of incidents and behavior will qualify as actionable conduct. Indeed, missing from the list created by the majority are several factors that would militate in favor of the plaintiff. For example, conduct may also be considered outrageous when it (1) harms a person known to be vulnerable; (2) when there is a pattern of repeated conduct; and (3) where the defendant's conduct threatens serious economic harm to a person.

Importantly, several of the cases cited by the majority point to other factors that might be relevant to a determination of outrageousness, yet the majority fails to mention them. For example, several of the cases list the fact that managers did not stop the conduct. *See* Poole, 498 S.E.2d at 603; Ruff, 468 S.E.2d at 594; Bryant, 437 S.E.2d at 525; Brown v. Burlington Industries, 378 S.E.2d 232 (N.C. Ct. App. 1989). Moreover, in *Bryant*, the court mentioned retaliatory conduct in detailing defendant's outrageous conduct, as well as evidence showing that the plaintiff quit in response to the conduct. *Bryant*, 437 S.E.2d at 524–25. While such evidence is relevant to whether the employer ratified the individual defendant's actions in connection with her civil assault claim, it is also potentially relevant to determining whether the underlying conduct by either the individual defendant or the employer was outrageous. For example, the jury might find that a supervisor and an individual defendant who is not a supervisor were acting in concert, such that a reasonable person in plaintiff's position might conclude that she was facing conduct not only from the individual defendant, but from her supervisor as well. Additionally, an employer's failure to intervene may embolden repeated conduct by harassing individuals or increase the plaintiff's fear that she might face retaliation. In some cases, the failure to intervene may also increase the likelihood that such retaliation would actually occur. And, when retaliatory conduct does happen, such conduct must be included in determining whether the plaintiff can establish outrageousness.

D IIED Does Not Require Sexual Conduct

One of the biggest flaws with the majority's list is that the list focuses on conduct that is largely sexual in nature. However, the courts have long recognized that harassment does not need to be sexual in nature to constitute sex-based harassment. Williams v. Gen. Motors Corp., 187 F.3d 553, 564–65 (6th Cir. 1999) (recognizing that sex-based conduct is detrimental); Hall v. Gus Constr. Co., 842 F.2d 1010, 1014 (8th Cir. 1988) ("Intimidation and hostility toward women because they are women can obviously result from conduct other than explicit sexual advances"); *see also* Vicki Schultz, *Reconceptualizing Sexual Harassment*, 107 YALE L.J. 1683, 1692 (1998) (discussing the incompleteness of the sexual desire paradigm); Martha Chamallas, *Structuralist and Cultural Domination Theories Meet Title VII: Some Contemporary Influences*, 92 MICH. L. REV. 2370, 2382 (1994) (discussing sexual and sex-based harassment).

Specifically, the tort of IIED does not require conduct of a sexual nature, or even sex-based conduct, to be actionable and it is unclear why the majority places such a limit here. Simply put, conduct need not be sexual to be outrageous, whether that conduct occurs inside or outside the workplace. RESTATEMENT (SECOND) OF TORTS, § 46, Illus. 1 (Am. Law Inst., 1977) (noting that falsely telling a wife that her husband is injured in hospital with both legs broken is outrageous conduct).

If the majority finds that the conduct alleged by the plaintiff is not sexual in nature, it should compare that conduct to other nonsexual IIED cases and judge her claim against that standard. Instead, I fear that this case will be cited in future cases as standing for the proposition that all plaintiffs alleging IIED in the workplace must allege sexual conduct. This would be a regrettable mistake. Holloway v. Wachovia Bank & Tr. Co., 452 S.E.2d 233, 241 (N.C. 1994) (holding that elements of IIED claim remain the same no matter the factual context under which they arise).

It also is unclear why the facts alleged by the plaintiff do not meet the sexual criteria espoused by the majority. Engaging in multiple instances of sexual innuendo with the action figure, asking whether the plaintiff liked it, and getting the plaintiff's shirt wet and referencing a wet T-shirt contest, could certainly be determined to be sexual in nature. And, given that secretaries often perform work for multiple people in an office environment, it is certainly possible that, even though he was not her supervisor, Conroy did at least oversee some of the plaintiff's work. Again, I do not know exactly what happened at this workplace, but there is enough evidence presented here to go before a jury.

E *Improper Use of Parenthetical Citations*

Additionally, the majority's use of parenthetical cites to determine what is and what is not sufficient to meet the minimal standard for "extreme and outrageous" conduct is problematic and at odds with the holistic approach that courts have historically taken in IIED cases. As I have shown, the majority in this case has ignored much of the plaintiff's underlying evidence. My concern is that its reliance on parenthetical, barebones descriptions of prior cases has severely hampered its ability to understand the facts and reasoning in those earlier cases. As a result, it has reduced its analysis of this case to a rote sorting process whereby it first compiles a list of conduct that purportedly does and does not constitute outrageous behavior in prior cases and then compares the conduct alleged in this case against that list. However, as described, the conduct chosen provides only the barest glimpse about the actual conduct alleged in those prior cases. Indeed, I fear that this case too will eventually be boiled down to its bare allegations and then used as a parenthetical in future cases to justify summary judgment.

What is missing from the parentheticals is the context. And, context is especially important in cases like this one. The United States Supreme Court has affirmed the importance of the "social context in which particular behavior occurs and is experienced by its target." Oncale v. Sundowner Offshore Servs., Inc., 523 U.S. 75, 81 (1998). The Court explained its contextual approach using the following examples:

> A professional football player's working environment is not severely or pervasively abusive, for example, if the coach smacks him on the buttocks as he heads onto the field – even if the same behavior would reasonably be experienced as abusive by the coach's secretary (male or female) back at the office. The real social impact of workplace behavior often depends on a constellation of surrounding circumstances, expectations, and relationships which are not fully captured by a simple recitation of the words used or the physical acts performed. Common sense, and an appropriate sensitivity to social context, will enable courts and juries to distinguish between simple teasing or roughhousing … and conduct which a reasonable person in the plaintiff's position would find severely hostile or abusive.
>
> *Id.* at 81–82

This same reasoning applies equally to the case before us. Rather than acknowledging that all of the complexities of workplace conduct and how it is experienced by employees make it difficult for courts to hold conduct insufficient as a matter of law, the majority is content to draw a sharp line in this case and simply repeats the mantra that there is a difference between outrageous conduct and the conduct alleged here. The majority's conclusion that Conroy's alleged behavior, "while annoyingly juvenile, obnoxious, and offensive, does not rise to the level of 'outrageous and extreme' conduct as the term has been interpreted and applied in tort actions alleging IIED" (*Guthrie*, 567 S.E.2d at 410), is unconvincing and unilluminating.

I am especially troubled by the majority's parenthetical cite to *Wilson v. Bellamy*, 414 S.E.2d 347, 359 (N.C. Ct. App. 1992), as an example of when conduct is not extreme and outrageous enough to constitute IIED. The parenthetical states that in that case there was no viable IIED claim where "defendants engaged in kissing and heavy petting with the plaintiff in the presence of others while plaintiff was intoxicated to the point of unconsciousness." Under any fair interpretation of the IIED tort, that case was wrongly decided. The conduct in *Wilson* was extreme and outrageous conduct. Even if it were debatable whether sexually groping a person who is so severely intoxicated that they are incapable of giving consent was not outrageous in 1992, it is indisputably outrageous today. To continue to cite this wrongly decided and outmoded case for the proposition that such conduct is not outrageous as matter of law entrenches repudiated and gender biased societal judgments into an area of law that is supposed to reflect contemporary societal standards of what is unacceptable and outrageous.

F *Improper Focus on Employer's Derivative Liability*

In addition to its flawed assessment of the quality of Conroy's and other employees' behavior toward Guthrie, I write in dissent to emphasize that the majority has misstated the potential legal bases on which the employer may be held liable for IIED. The majority addresses only the possibility that the employer is derivatively liable for the acts of Conroy. It then dismisses the IIED and NIED claims against the company, finding that Conroy's actions did not meet the elements of either of those torts.

As discussed earlier, the facts must be expanded to consider the conduct of all of the employees that work for the defendant employer. This is because the employer faces two kinds of potential liability. First, the employer may be liable derivatively for the acts of its employees. However, the employer may also face liability for its own actions or failures to act.

Indeed, courts have found employers liable for IIED based on the employer's own actions. As the Supreme Court of Arizona noted, "We recognize that where there is independent negligence on the part of the master, the master may be liable, apart from his derivative liability for his servant's wrongful acts." Ford v. Revlon, Inc., 734 P.2d 580, 584 (Ariz. 1987) (*citing* Siebrand

v. Gossnell, 234 F.2d 81 (9th Cir. 1956)); First National Bank v. Otis Elevator Co., 406 P.2d 430 (Ariz. 1965), opinion on rehearing, 411 P.2d 34 (Ariz. 1966)).

The Arizona Supreme Court recognized that a company may be liable for IIED when an employee repeatedly complains about workplace harassment, and the company ignores those complaints, leaving the plaintiff without redress. *Ford*, 734 P.2d at 584. The court noted that the company may be held liable either through a showing of intent or reckless disregard. *Id.* at 585. The court also noted that if a company has a complaint procedure, but recklessly disregards that procedure, this fact can support an IIED claim. *Id.* at 586.

The majority ignores that the employer may be liable for its own actions and inactions, not just derivatively liable for the actions of its employees. Thus, it fails to properly consider the full impact of the employer's conduct on potential liability.

IV THE NIED CLAIMS

Without much discussion, the majority affirms the grant of summary judgment on plaintiff's NIED claim by noting that there is no duty owed by Conroy to the plaintiff. *Guthrie*, 567 S.E.2d at 410. It also claims that Guthrie's employer can only be derivatively liable for NIED. *Id.* at 411. Again, I find the majority's cursory reasoning problematic.

While I am uncertain whether a duty is owed in cases such as this, I do not believe that this court should dismiss the claim without considering the question more deeply. Indeed, the majority recognizes that it is the policy of the state of North Carolina to prohibit sex discrimination. N.C. Gen. Stat. Ann. § 143–422.2; *See also* Phelps v. Vassey, 437 S.E.2d 692, 695 (N.C. Ct. App. 1993) ("[t]he public policy of North Carolina must be to stop sexual harassment in the work place"). And it is well recognized that duties in negligence cases often arise from articulated state statutes and public policy. Unfortunately, because this issue has not been sufficiently briefed, we are not in a position to decide it today.

Whether sexual harassment claimants should be permitted to bring NIED claims, in addition to claims for IIED, is an important issue that deserves more thorough treatment than the majority gives it.

V RELATIONSHIP BETWEEN TORT LAW AND ANTI-DISCRIMINATION CLAIMS

Finally, I write in dissent to express my concern that the majority misunderstands the relationship between state tort claims and statutory anti-discrimination claims. Specifically, I am worried that this court is content to dismiss plaintiff's claims for IIED and NIED primarily because they occurred within the workplace and because the court assumes that the plaintiff should have brought her claims under Title VII, the federal statute that addresses workplace harassment and discrimination, or under our state statutes that prohibit sexual harassment in the workplace. However, the majority's view of the proper domains of tort and anti-discrimination law is mistaken. In my view, tort law should not stop at the front door of a workplace.

Part of the majority's reluctance to allow plaintiff's IIED and NIED claims to proceed appears to stem from its intuition that plaintiff's claims are *really* sexual harassment claims. I do not dispute that plaintiff's tort claims and the federal discrimination statutes require proof of different elements and must be analyzed separately. However, I want to caution against any notion that federal anti-discrimination law provides a comprehensive and adequate remedy for sexual harassment.

Unfortunately, Title VII does not provide a comprehensive remedy for plaintiffs. In fact, there are many instances where workers suffer sexual harassment, yet are unable to obtain relief under Title VII. Title VII imposes very tight time limitations on when a plaintiff must act to maintain her claim and it also imposes an onerous administrative exhaustion requirement. 42 U.S.C.S. § 2000e-5(e) (1), (f)(1). Additionally, if the plaintiff does not properly describe her claim to the Equal Employment Opportunity Commission or the state administrative agency, a court can dismiss that claim.

Likewise, the remedies for sexual harassment under Title VII are not comprehensive. If the harassment does not result in a tangible employment action (or a constructive discharge), the plaintiff's only remedy is to seek compensatory damages and punitive damages under federal law. However, the federal statute places caps on the total combined compensatory and punitive damages that a plaintiff may recover under Title VII based on the number of employees employed by the defendant. 42 U.S.C. § 1981a(b)(3). The highest cap, which applies to employers with more than 500 employees, is $300,000. The Title VII damages cap is fixed. It is not adjusted upward if the employer engaged in especially egregious discrimination. Moreover, the cap has not changed since 1991, when it was enacted, and it is not adjusted for inflation.

Additionally, federal sexual harassment claims are subject to their own distinctive vicarious liability structure that is not coterminous with vicarious liability under the common law. Most significantly, if a coworker commits the harassment, the employer is only liable for that harassment if it knew or should have known of the harassment and failed to prevent it. Faragher v. City of Boca Raton, 524 U.S. 775 (1998); Burlington Indus. Inc. v. Ellerth, 524 U.S. 742 (1998).

Importantly, this vicarious liability structure means that there are many cases in which an employee is subjected to clear-cut harassment in the workplace, yet federal law will not provide any remedy. This is the case even though common-law standards of vicarious liability would allow for other, more flexible ways to prove employer liability.[2]

VI

For the reasons stated above, I would reverse the trial court's grant of summary judgment in favor of defendants on plaintiff's IIED claims. As noted, the trial court did not consider all of the evidence submitted by the plaintiff and it did not consider that evidence in the light most favorable to the non-moving party, i.e., the plaintiff. Nor did the trial court consider whether the combined acts of plaintiff's coworker and the employer's other agents were sufficient to meet the elements of IIED. To the extent that the plaintiff's negligent supervision and retention claim is linked to the survival of her IIED claim, summary judgment was improper.

I would remand the case for further briefing on the existence of a duty regarding NIED and additional briefing on the facts of the case supporting that claim.

I concur with the majority that the trial court committed error in granting summary judgment on plaintiff's claim against her employer for ratification of civil assault. The same evidence that allows plaintiff's ratification claim on assault to proceed applies with equal force to the underlying IIED claim. Because I find that it was error for the trial court to grant summary judgment on the IIED claim, I would also allow plaintiff's ratification claim against her employer to proceed based on the IIED claim.

2 Courts in the State of North Carolina have refused to recognize a separate cause of action for sexual harassment or wrongful discharge based on the state's public policy. *See, e.g.*, Smith v. First Union Nat. Bank, 202 F.3d 234, 247 (4th Cir. 2000) (citing cases).

8

Commentary on *Lyman v. Huber*

CAROLINE FORELL

INTRODUCTION

Lyman v. Huber[1] is a 2010 Supreme Judicial Court of Maine[2] decision reviewing the trial court's application of the test for intentional infliction of emotional distress (IIED). The case involved a man who engaged in a pattern of serious verbal and emotional abuse against his female domestic partner over the course of fifteen years. Although the trial court found that the plaintiff Elizabeth Lyman had suffered severe emotional distress from the abusive conduct, on appeal the highest court in Maine ruled that her distress was not more severe than what an objective reasonable person should be expected to endure. The rewritten feminist opinion addresses how setting such a high bar to recovery deviates from traditional tort principles that focus on the victim's actual harm, and presents an unwarranted barrier to the ability of domestic abuse victims to recover for IIED.

In reversing the trial court's finding that the test for IIED had been satisfied, the appellate court found that all the elements[3] of the IIED tort were met

[1] 10 A.3d 707 (Me. 2010).

[2] The Supreme Judicial Court is Maine's only state appellate court.

[3] The Maine appellate court's test for IIED was similar to the RESTATEMENT (SECOND) OF TORTS, § 46. The elements of its test are:

> (1) the defendant intentionally or recklessly inflicted severe emotional distress or was certain or substantially certain that such distress would result from [the defendant's] conduct;
> (2) the conduct was so extreme and outrageous as to exceed all possible bounds of decency and must be regarded as atrocious, utterly intolerable in a civilized community;
> (3) the actions of the defendant caused the plaintiff's emotional distress; and
> (4) the emotional distress suffered by the plaintiff was so severe that no reasonable person could be expected to endure it.
>
> *Id.* at 711

except for legally adequate proof that the plaintiff suffered sufficiently severe emotional distress. The test the court applied for whether the emotional distress was sufficiently severe was whether the "emotional distress was so severe that no reasonable person could be expected to endure it."[4] The source of this test was comment j of the *Restatement (Second) of Torts*, § 46.

Until the mid-twentieth century, IIED was rarely allowed in the United States.[5] For example, the 1934 *Restatement of the Law of Torts* stated that no recovery for emotional injury was permitted, even if it was intentionally inflicted and even if it resulted in physical harm or consequences, unless the defendant's conduct otherwise amounted to a tort.[6]

Intentional infliction of emotional distress as a stand-alone tort was first recognized by the American Law Institute in the 1948 *Supplement to the Restatement of Torts*.[7] Today the *Restatement (Second) of Torts*, § 46[8] supplies the test for IIED used in most American jurisdictions including Maine. It states that "[o]ne who by extreme and outrageous conduct intentionally or recklessly[9] causes severe emotional distress to another is subject to liability for such emotional distress." Under this test, proof of "extreme and outrageous conduct," rather than proof of either resulting physical harm or that the emotional distress was severe, is viewed as critical in most cases.[10] Nevertheless, in *Lyman*, even though the defendant's conduct was found to be extreme and outrageous, the appellate court held that plaintiff's emotional harm from this conduct was not sufficiently severe.

The *Restatement*'s objective test for severe emotional harm was first published in 1965 and fails to adequately account for the serious emotional abuse

4 *Id.*

5 Unlike other intentional torts for emotional or dignitary harm (assault, offensive battery, false imprisonment) which are of ancient origin, IIED is quite new and still evolving. The first reported stand-alone case for IIED was decided in England at the end of the nineteenth century. Wilkinson v. Downton, 2 Q.B. 57 (1897).

6 Restatement of Torts § 46 (Am. Law Inst. 1936).

7 "One who, without a privilege to do so, intentionally causes severe emotional distress to another is liable (a) for such emotional distress, and (b) for bodily harm resulting from it." Restatement in the Courts, 1948 Supplement 612 Torts § 46 (Am. Law Inst. 1949).

8 The Restatement (2d) of Torts' test for IIED was adopted verbatim by the 2012 Restatement (3d) of Torts.

9 While intentional infliction of emotional distress continues to be described today as an intentional tort, for § 46 proof of reckless conduct is sufficient. The justification for the lower conduct requirement for this tort than for battery or assault is that, unlike those torts, the conduct must be extreme and outrageous.

10 Daniel Givelber, *The Right to Minimum Social Decency and the Limits of Evenhandedness: Intentional Infliction of Emotional Distress by Outrageous Conduct*, 82 Colum. L. Rev. 42, 46 (1982).

experienced in domestic partner settings where women are more often the victims and men are more often the abusers. At that time, the women's movement was in its infancy and the perspective for determining whether conduct was tortious was that of the reasonable man.[11] Even severe physical domestic violence was still not treated as real violence. Domestic violence was something that women should forgive and forget.[12] Only recently has emotional abuse without accompanying physical violence even been considered as domestic violence. For serious emotional abuse suffered by women in the domestic sphere, the *Restatement*'s test for severe emotional distress is inadequate and unfair. It is this problem that the rewritten *Lyman* opinion addresses.

THE ACTUAL CASE

The feminist judgment includes the factual background of this case and its discussion of intentional and reckless acts verbatim from the original opinion. Only the part of the opinion that addressed severe emotional distress is rewritten.

Elizabeth Lyman and Luke Huber were domestic partners from 1991 to 2006. In 1994, they purchased a rural property as tenants in common where Lyman planned to operate a horse-riding and breeding business. She lived there from 1994 to 2006 while Huber only lived there full-time from 2002 or 2003.

Huber began to be abusive in 1995 with his behavior escalating over time. The appellate court described the abuse as having "a substantial emotional impact on Lyman."[13] While Huber was never physically violent, "he was commanding and intimidating to the point that [Lyman] feared him and his anger … [which] made Lyman feel inadequate and withdrawn."[14] She left Huber and the property with her horses in 2006. She subsequently sued Huber

[11] The distress must be "so severe that no reasonable man could be expected to endure it." Restatement (Second) of Torts § 46, cmt. j (Am. Law Inst. 1977); *see also* Caroline Forell & Donna Matthews, A Law of Her Own: The Reasonable Woman as a Measure of Man 6 (2000).

[12] Abbott v. Abbott, 67 Me. 304, 307 (1877). In *Abbott*, the Supreme Judicial Court of Maine reasoned that "it is better to draw the curtain, shut out the public gaze, and leave the parties [translate: women] to forget and forgive." This reasoning was finally rejected in 1993 in *Henricksen v. Cameron*, 622 A.2d 1135 (Me. 1993).

[13] *Lyman*, 10 A.3d at 710.

[14] *Id.*

for IIED, and also claimed that her forced abandonment of her equestrian business amounted to an "ouster."[15]

The trial court found that Lyman had proved all the elements of IIED and awarded her damages of $106,000. The trial court noted that Maine did not allow a separate claim for ouster; instead, it included $31,000 for loss of her business opportunity in the damages for intentional infliction of emotional distress.

Of the elements of intentional emotional distress, Huber only appealed the trial court's findings that his conduct was intentional or reckless and that Lyman suffered severe emotional distress.[16] The appellate court, in vacating Lyman's judgment for damages for IIED, found sufficient evidence of intent or recklessness[17] but insufficient evidence of severe emotional distress.[18]

In addressing the issue of whether there was sufficient evidence that Lyman suffered severe enough emotional distress, the court followed the *Restatement (Second) of Torts* § 46, comment j[19] and its own precedent[20] in requiring an objective test. As the court noted, the fourth element of Maine's test for intentional infliction of emotional distress is that the distress "was so severe that no reasonable person could be expected to endure it."

The appellate court stated that for emotional distress to be objectively severe it usually has to result in bodily harm or consequences.[21] However, it acknowledged that under both the *Restatement* and Maine tests,[22] bodily harm or consequences (described in Maine law as "objective symptomology") was "not an absolute prerequisite."[23] Instead, in egregious cases, severity could be "inferred from the 'extreme and outrageous' nature of defendant's conduct alone."[24] It also noted that expert medical testimony was not necessarily required.[25] Finally, it acknowledged that in domestic abuse situations,

[15] "Ouster refers to the wrongful dispossession of a rightful owner or tenant of real property, which forces the dispossessed party to bring a lawsuit to regain possession. This often occurs between partners in an enterprise or roommates, when one co-owner or co-tenant forces out the other, changes locks or makes the premises inhabitable." Definition of ouster (U.S. LEGAL), https://definitions.uslegal.com/o/ouster.

[16] The appellate court did not review the trial court's finding that there was extreme and outrageous conduct and causation. *Lyman*, 10 A.3d at 711.

[17] *Id.* at 711–12.

[18] *Id.* at 713–14.

[19] *Id.* at 713.

[20] *Id.* at 713 (*citing* Vicnire v. Ford Motor Credit Co., 401 A.2d 148, 154 (Me. 1979)).

[21] *Id.*

[22] *Id.* (*citing* Latremore v. Latremore, 584 A.2d 626, 632–33 (Me. 1990)).

[23] *Id.*

[24] *Id.*

[25] *Id.* (*citing* Feltmeier v. Feltmeier, 798 N.E.2d 75, 84 (Ill. 2003) (allowing a wife to recover for purely emotional harm against her former husband without expert evidence).

cumulative acts over an extended time could suffice to prove objectively severe emotional distress.[26] Thus, it was legally possible to prove objectively severe emotional distress in a case where there was no bodily harm or consequences, no expert medical testimony was provided, and the harm became sufficiently severe as a result of cumulative abuse over time.

The court then explained why, in this case, as a matter of law Lyman did not show she "suffered emotional distress so severe that no reasonable person could be expected to endure it."[27] The court said Lyman's feelings of inadequacy, social paralysis, fear, and intimidation simply were not objectively severe enough, pointing out that she was able to manage her business and daily life for fifteen years and failed to seek help from public officials or medical or mental health providers.[28] The court went further, saying that under the facts found by the trial court, even if Lyman actually suffered from a "recognized medical or psychological diagnosis," the objective test would not have been met.[29]

The most problematic, but not unusual,[30] rationale for holding that the objective test for severity of harm had not been met was that this was a case involving domestic partner abuse. The court said:

> [O]ur application and development of this civil action in the context of domestic relationships must also account for the sad reality that dysfunctional domestic relationships are not uncommon in modern society. If the elements of proof governing actions for intentional infliction of emotional distress are left vague or set too low, we risk elevating all dysfunctional domestic relationships into potential damages actions.[31]

By drawing a distinction between how to "objectively" assess the impact of domestic partner abuse more stringently than other forms of infliction of emotional distress, the court relegates a type of injury suffered by far more women than men to a lesser harm. In contrast, the feminist judgment's test for severe emotional distress seeks to treat the harms women suffer as just as deserving as other harms.

[26] *Id.*

[27] *Id.* at 714.

[28] *Id.*

[29] *Id.*

[30] Martha Chamallas & Jennifer B. Wriggins, The Measure of Injury: Race, Gender and Tort Law 75 (2010); *see also* Ira Mark Ellman & Stephen D. Sugarman, *Spousal Emotional Abuse as a Tort?*, 55 Md. L. Rev. 1268, 1294 (1996).

[31] *Lyman*, 10 A.3d at 714.

The appellate court concluded its opinion by agreeing with the trial court that Maine does not recognize a separate tort of ouster. It refused to recognize one in this case, and, as a result, the loss of business opportunity damages flowing from the IIED claim were denied along with the rest of Lyman's damages.

THE FEMINIST JUDGMENT

In their feminist judgment, Professor Jeffrey Thomas and Leah Thomas address the appellate court's sole basis for reversing the trial court – that, as a matter of law, the harm plaintiff suffered was not sufficiently severe – and instead affirm the trial court decision. In upholding the lower court, their feminist judgment overrules Maine's normatively male reasonable person test[32] for assessing severity, and replaces it with a subjective test which acknowledges the plaintiff's actual experience of severe emotional distress. The feminist judgment's test more fully takes into account the different perspectives and experiences of those who are abused or exploited in our society. It thereby recognizes the disparities of power that exist and allows those who are disempowered to recover for emotional harms that they experience as severe.

The feminist judgment notes that the purported source of the reasonable person test for severity, the *Restatement (Second) of Torts*, § 46, does not actually set out such a test. The *Restatement (Second)*'s black-letter law simply says "severe emotional distress" must be shown. Instead, the objective test is set out in the *Restatement*'s comment j.[33] The change the feminist judgment makes still allows for a distinction between severe emotional distress and "transient and trivial emotional distress," which is the concern of comment j, because it requires proof of harm that is "so severe that plaintiff should not be expected to endure it."

In justifying its overruling of the objective "severity" test, the feminist judgment highlights the previous test's male bias. Even though, unlike the reasonable man test set out in the *Restatement (Second)*, comment j, Maine's reasonable person test no longer expressly used a male perspective, the

[32] While Maine first adopted the reasonable person test for severity in *Vicnire*, 401 A.2d at 154, the feminist judgment finds that it had not been sufficiently analyzed and is an inappropriate test for the twenty-first century.

[33] The RESTATEMENT (THIRD) OF TORTS was published in 2012. It retains the exact wording of the black-letter law of the RESTATEMENT (SECOND) § 46 and says, referring to comment j, that its severity element requires a showing that "a person of ordinary sensitivities in the same circumstances would suffer severe harm."

feminist judgment finds that it was still insufficient to protect the less powerful in our society. While it considered the reasonable woman standard as an alternative, the feminist judgment chose a subjective test that takes into account the plaintiff's actual experience of harm.

The feminist judgment also justifies its subjective test by noting that Maine's claim for intentional emotional distress employs other means of assuring that claims are limited to situations of severe conduct and distress. Notably, intent or recklessness must be shown instead of mere negligence. In addition, an IIED claim frequently relies on evidence of objective symptomology to prove sufficient severity of emotional harm and always requires proof that the defendant's conduct was "extreme and outrageous."

The Maine appellate court originally introduced objective symptomology as a requirement for sufficient emotional harm to recover for negligent infliction of emotional distress.[34] When the appellate court first recognized intentional infliction of emotional distress as a stand-alone claim in 1979, it also adopted objective symptomology as the physical indicia that is usually, but not always, required for a viable claim for IIED.[35] The feminist judgment finds that Lyman provided sufficient evidence of objective symptomology in this case. It also emphasizes that even without proof of objective symptomology, under Maine law the finding of extreme and outrageous conduct may suffice to assure that the emotional harm suffered was sufficiently severe.[36] The feminist judgment then finds that under its subjective test, Huber's extreme and outrageous conduct did suffice without proof of objective symptomology.

Another justification the feminist judgment gives for applying a subjective test is that it treats damages for serious emotional harm, which women are often more likely to suffer,[37] as on par with physical harm where the test requires that the defendant "takes [the plaintiff] as he finds him."[38] When a defendant commits a tort that causes physical injury, the defendant is responsible for the full extent of harm suffered by someone who is susceptible to

[34] Wallace v. Coco-Cola Bottling Plants, Inc., 269 A.2d 117, 121 (Me. 1970).

[35] *Vicnire*, 401 A.2d at 154. Instead of "objective symptomology," RESTATEMENT (THIRD) § 46, comment l, refers to illness or other bodily harm that accompanies severe emotional distress.

[36] It is especially appropriate that objective symptomology is not a requirement to prove severe emotional distress because Maine's test for IIED requires conduct that exceeds "all possible bounds of decency and must be regarded as atrocious, utterly intolerable in a civilized society." *Lyman*, 10 A.3d at 711. If such egregious conduct is shown to have been inflicted intentionally or recklessly, such conduct should be expected to cause severe emotional distress.

[37] CHAMALLAS & WRIGGINS, *supra* note 30, at 91–92.

[38] RESTATEMENT (THIRD) OF TORTS: LIABILITY FOR PHYSICAL HARM § 31, cmt. a (Am. Law Institute 2005).

greater harm than would ordinarily be expected.[39] The feminist judgment asserts that compensation should similarly be available in cases where, by extreme and outrageous conduct, a defendant intentionally or recklessly inflicts and the plaintiff subjectively experiences severe emotional distress.

Having held that the claim for IIED should be affirmed, the feminist judgment then addresses whether to allow loss of business opportunity damages as part of the award for this claim; it concludes that such damages should be allowed. By allowing these additional damages the feminist judgment makes IIED recovery more like damages for physical injury, where damages for diminished economic opportunity can be recovered, instead of requiring some additional tort such as ouster from co-owned property.

IMPLICATIONS

The feminist judgment's substitution of a subjective test for the reasonable person test for determining whether the severity of emotional harm is sufficient may seem at first glance like a relatively minor change. Nevertheless, it has significant implications, and makes it more likely that women and other disempowered groups will be able to make out their intentional infliction of emotional distress claims for the severe emotional distress they in fact suffer. The subjective standard credits and validates that actual distress experienced by the abuse victim. If her distress is severe, under the subjective "victim's actual harm" test, it is legally irrelevant if other people might not have suffered so severely from a similar pattern of abuse in other contexts.

This is especially important for survivors of domestic violence who, for various reasons, rarely bring successful lawsuits for tort damages.[40] Until recently, spousal immunity was a complete bar to tort actions between spouses. In Maine, it wasn't until 1993 that the appellate court expressly held that spousal immunity did not bar torts for domestic violence.[41] This now-abandoned immunity still haunts tort claims in the domestic setting. In fact, the appellate opinion in this case elaborated on the special concerns that arise "in the context of domestic relationships" as a reason for requiring that its

39 *Id.*

40 Chamallas & Wriggins, *supra* note 30, at 67.

41 Henricksen v. Cameron, 622 A.2d 1135, 1140 (Me. 1993). ("No valid public policy suggests making the intentional infliction of emotional distress through physical violence and accompanying verbal abuse during the marriage privileged conduct . . . We hold, therefore, that such an action between spouses is not barred by interspousal immunity.")

objective test be especially rigorous for claims of intentional infliction of emotional distress for domestic abuse.[42]

The biggest hurdle for domestic violence survivors seeking money damages today is the exclusion of intentional torts from liability insurance coverage. This omission means that very few tort cases are brought against perpetrators for any form of domestic violence.[43] Allowing a plaintiff to recover when she credibly claims that she suffered severe emotional distress due to extreme and outrageous conduct intentionally or recklessly inflicted by her partner or former partner at least means that those survivors whose abusers have resources will have a better chance to recover.

The feminist judgment's allowance of damages for the economic loss Lyman suffered due to the abuse also would have significant benefits for domestic violence survivors, by treating them more like other tort victims. Where a defendant has sufficient resources, the additional damages for economic harm would also make it more likely that it would be worthwhile for an attorney to take the case.

The crux of the tort of intentional infliction of emotional distress is outrageousness.[44] In fact it is sometimes called the tort of outrage.[45] Extreme and outrageous conduct is what justifies recovery for this claim, and the feminist judgment recognizes that such conduct should speak for itself. It is bound to lead to severe emotional distress and plaintiff's credible claim that it did should suffice. I would go further in this regard to reshape the tort. As the appellate court, I would expressly say existence of "severe emotional distress" is determined from the plaintiff's perspective. If the conduct is proved to be intentional or reckless and outrageous, and the plaintiff provides credible evidence that she experienced severe emotional distress, the elements of the tort should be satisfied. In other words, the law should allow the outrageousness and testimony of the victim to speak for themselves.

Believing victims is the essence of feminist practice and therefore I would not set out any test for severity of the emotional distress beyond the plaintiff credibly showing that she experienced it as severe. The feminist judgment, however, appears to suggest that there could be cases where the plaintiff

[42] *Lyman*, 10 A.3d at 714. New York goes further by expressly retaining spousal immunity to bar recovery for intentional infliction of emotional distress when it involves spouses or domestic partners. Weicker v. Weicker, 237 N.E.2d 876 (N.Y. 1968). *See generally*, Camille Carey, *Domestic Violence Torts: Righting a Civil Wrong*, 62 U. Kan. L. Rev. 695, 725–28 (2014).

[43] Chamallas & Wriggins, *supra* note 30, at 70–71.

[44] Givelber, *supra* note 10, at 42–43. *See also* Restatement (Third) of Torts, § 46, Scope and History.

[45] Ellman & Sugarman, *supra* note 30, at 1269.

credibly claims that she experienced severe distress when in the view of the court she ought not to have suffered such distress. The feminist judgment's proposed test is that "the emotional distress suffered by the plaintiff was so severe that the plaintiff should not be expected to endure it." This "should" standard could potentially leave the door open for value judgments about what women in dysfunctional domestic relationships "should" endure – the very sort of attitude that led the actual appellate court to downplay Lyman's harm and demand a higher level of proof of severity for domestic abuse victims.

Another change I would recommend is to abandon Maine's use of its objective symptomology test for physical manifestations that result from the severe emotional distress. I would instead return to the *Restatement*'s physical harm or consequences test that is more easily understood. In Lyman's case, unlike the feminist judgment, I would also not conclude that there was sufficient evidence of physical harm or consequences. Arguably, the facts in this may not strongly support such a finding.

Finally, I would also hold that claims of intentional infliction of emotional distress between domestic partners or former domestic partners will not be assessed differently than claims between other parties. The appellate court opined that in doing this it was not "in any way minimizing the seriousness of the emotional harm suffered by Lyman as a result of her relationship with Huber"[46] when it did exactly that. I would hold that the same assessment of "severity" applies for all claims of IIED.

Either the feminist judgment or my recommendations would make a significant difference for women and other oppressed groups. They would be able to recover damages more often and would be allowed to recover greater damages. These changes would make tort law fairer to people who have traditionally been disempowered and are vulnerable to emotional abuse by those who wield power over them.

LYMAN *v.* HUBER, 10 A.3D 707 (ME. 2010)

JUSTICES JEFFREY E. THOMAS AND LEAH THOMAS DELIVERED THE OPINION OF THE COURT

Luke D. Huber appeals from a judgment entered in the Superior Court (Cumberland County, Delahanty, J.) following a bench trial, awarding Elizabeth E. Lyman damages totaling $106,000 for intentional infliction of

46 *Lyman*, 10 A.3d at 714.

emotional distress. Huber argues that the evidence was insufficient to establish two of the elements for intentional infliction of emotional distress. He also asserts that the court erred by including damages for Lyman's loss of business opportunity. Because we conclude that Lyman submitted sufficient evidence to prove the elements of intentional infliction of emotional distress, and that the loss of business opportunity was a permissible element of damages for her intentional infliction of emotional distress claim, we affirm the judgment.[1]

I BACKGROUND

We view the record in the light most favorable to Lyman as the prevailing party. *See* Camden Nat'l Bank v. S.S. Navigation Co., 991 A.2d 800, 801 (Me. 2010).

Luke Huber and Elizabeth Lyman began a romantic relationship in 1991 that lasted until 2006. By the middle of 1994, the parties purchased property in Cape Elizabeth that they held as tenants in common. Prior to purchasing the property, Lyman had boarded three horses at the property. The property consisted of 3.5 acres and contained a barn, paddock, riding arena, trails, and a house. Lyman intended to open a horse farm where she could teach riding classes and breed horses. Lyman lived on the property full-time from the fall of 1994 until she moved out in April 2006. Huber, however, did not reside at the property full-time until late 2002 or 2003.

In 1995, Huber began behaving strangely, and he became more controlling and authoritative. He accumulated piles of papers, boxes, newspapers, and trash and left them throughout the house to the point that there were only paths to get from one room to another. Despite these piles, he commanded Lyman to neither touch his things nor move his mail, and he got angry with her when she did. He would regularly yell, scream, and swear during his morning shower and stomp and kick the walls. He went on tirades toward Lyman over matters ranging from her using the telephone to a piece of horse manure in the driveway. He made degrading comments to her regarding her body when they were being sexually intimate.

Huber's behavior continued over time and escalated. He also became obsessive about taking showers, and he constantly washed his hands. He would inspect his bed and sheets with a flashlight before getting in. Moreover, sex became "dirty" to him, and he would recoil from a mere hug.

[1] Much of the description of the facts of the case and the governing law is taken verbatim from the original opinion.

Huber also became increasingly demanding of Lyman's time. He would insist that she be available when he was home. Out of fear and intimidation, she cleared her schedule of social engagements and canceled riding lessons and appointments. Lyman believed that Huber's outbursts would lead to violence if she did not comply with his increasingly irrational demands. She eventually had to give up her horse business, which had eighty-five clients. His actions socially paralyzed her and withdrew her from her friends. Moreover, her family visited less often and when they did, because of her fear she asked them not to touch Huber's things or sit in his chair. When Lyman's mother put something on Huber's things, he became very upset.

In February 2004, Lyman broke her ankle. Although Huber took her to a doctor, he left her there, and she was forced to call a friend to take her to the hospital. During her recuperation, Huber did not care for Lyman, even though she could not help herself.

Huber's actions were severely damaging to Lyman emotionally. Huber was commanding and intimidating to the point that she feared him and his anger. Huber's actions made Lyman feel inadequate and withdrawn. One friend observed that she looked exhausted and stressed, with dark circles under her eyes. Family members and friends described her as "guarded, jumpy, and withdrawn," "shaken," and "tense, afraid and on edge." Lyman v. Huber, Civil Action No. CV-06–145 at 8 (Me. Super. Ct., Jul. 24, 2009) [hereinafter "Trial Court Opinion"]. In April 2006, Lyman ended the relationship and left the Cape Elizabeth property with her horses.

Lyman filed an eight-count complaint for equitable partition (Count I), waste or trespass (Count II), ouster (Count III), unjust enrichment (Count IV), quantum meruit (Count V), negligent infliction of emotional distress (Count VI), intentional infliction of emotional distress (Count VII), and punitive damages (Count VIII). Huber later moved for entry of summary judgment, and the court granted his motion in part as to Lyman's claims for unjust enrichment (Count IV), quantum meruit (Count V), and negligent infliction of emotional distress (Count VI).

A three-day bench trial was held in May 2008. After Lyman rested, Huber moved for a judgment as a matter of law on the claims for trespass, intentional infliction of emotional distress, and punitive damages. The court reserved judgment on the trespass claim, denied the motion as to the intentional infliction of emotional distress claim and the punitive damages claim.

The trial court's judgment equitably partitioned the property and found for Huber on Lyman's claims for waste and trespass. It entered judgment in favor of Lyman in the amount of $31,000 for ouster, treating the claim as constituting part of Lyman's separate intentional infliction of emotional distress claim.

Although the court acknowledged that ouster was not recognized as an independent tort in Maine, it concluded that Huber's intentional conduct caused Lyman emotional distress and led to her loss of business opportunity and earning capacity:

The court also awarded Lyman $75,000 in damages on her claim for the intentional infliction of emotional distress. It found that "Huber's behavior toward Lyman constituted a pattern of cruelty and intimidation over a prolonged period so that the court can only conclude that it is extreme and outrageous." *Id.* at 9. In addition, the court found that "Huber's behavior was, in fact, bizarre and escalated over time so that it eventually became extreme and outrageous, if not for any particular incident, certainly for his cumulative conduct." *Id.* Although it could not identify a specific date for the onset of Lyman's severe emotional distress, the court found that it developed "over a period of more than several years" and that Lyman was "entitled to damages." *Id.*

Huber moved for reconsideration and to alter or amend the judgment pursuant to M.R. Civ. P. 59(e). Among other arguments, Huber claimed that Lyman was not entitled to a damages award for ouster because such "a theory ... is not a recognized cause of action." The court denied Huber's motion. Neither party moved for additional findings of fact pursuant to M.R. Civ. P. 52. Huber's appeal followed.

II DISCUSSION

Huber's appeal presents two questions: whether the court erred in awarding Lyman damages for (1) the intentional infliction of emotional distress and (2) loss of business opportunity.

A *Intentional Infliction of Emotional Distress*

A plaintiff must satisfy four elements to recover on a claim of intentional infliction of emotional distress. We state the four elements based on prior case law, except that we modify the fourth element for reasons explained in more detail below. The four elements are:

(1) the defendant intentionally or recklessly inflicted severe emotional distress or was certain or substantially certain that such distress would result from [the defendant's] conduct;

(2) the conduct was so extreme and outrageous as to exceed all possible bounds of decency and must be regarded as atrocious, utterly intolerable in a civilized community;

(3) the actions of the defendant caused the plaintiff's emotional distress; and
(4) the emotional distress suffered by the plaintiff was so severe that the plaintiff should not be expected to endure it.

See Curtis v. Porter, 784 A.2d 18, 22–23 (2001). For the fourth element, we have substituted "plaintiff" for "reasonable person," changing this element from an objective to a subjective test.[2] Here, Huber assigns error to the court's findings as they relate to the first and fourth elements.[3]

1 Intentional or Reckless Acts

Huber argues that the court failed to analyze whether his conduct was intentional or reckless and that the evidence was insufficient to establish that Huber intentionally or recklessly caused Lyman's emotional distress. He further argues that his self-directed outbursts and the physical condition of the house do not constitute intentional or reckless conduct and that such conduct was the product of certain "compulsions."

"[A] person acts intentionally if [the person] subjectively wants or subjectively foresees that harm to another will almost certainly result from [the person's] actions." *Curtis*, 784 A.2d at 23 (quotation marks omitted). "A person acts recklessly if [the person] knows or should know that [the person's] conduct creates an unreasonable risk of harm to another person and the unreasonableness of [the person's] actions exceeds negligence." *Id.*

Here, because neither party filed a motion for additional findings of fact pursuant to M.R. Civ. P. 52, we infer that the trial court found that Huber's conduct was intentional or reckless.[4] The record contains evidence of Huber's

[2] Although the court's reasoning will be explained more below, at this point we wish to note that the original phrase in the fourth element was that "no reasonable *man* could be expected to endure" the distress. *See, e.g.*, Finn v. Lipman, 526 A.2d 1380, 1382 (Me. 1987) (*citing* Vicnire v. Ford Motor Credit Co., 401 A.2d 148, 154 (Me. 1978)); Restatement (Second) of Torts § 46 (1977) (emphasis supplied). In recognition of the sexist connotation of "reasonable man," in 1999 this court simply substituted "reasonable person" for "reasonable man" without comment or analysis. Loe v. Thomaston, 600 A.2d 1090, 1093 (Me. 1991). As explained below, this was not sufficient to correct the problem.

[3] Although Huber's argument may be construed as challenging the third element of the intentional infliction of emotional distress claim, we find this argument unpersuasive. The court's findings support the conclusion that Huber's conduct caused Lyman emotional distress.

[4] We review the court's factual findings for clear error and its legal conclusions de novo. Windham Land Trust v. Jeffords, 967 A.2d 690, 702 (Me. 2009). In the absence of a motion for additional findings of fact, we will infer that the court found all the facts necessary to support its decision, and we will inquire whether such inferred findings are supported by the record. Weeks v. Krysa, 955 A.2d 234, 237 (Me. 2008).

tirades, hurtful comments, and efforts to control Lyman's activities and to limit her contact with others, all of which may be consistent with intentional conduct. Although some of Huber's behavior was self-directed, many of his actions were directed toward Lyman with the objective of manipulating her behavior. Thus, this evidence supports the trial court's inferred finding that Huber's conduct was intentional or reckless.

2 Severe Emotional Distress

Huber argues that the court erred in finding severe emotional distress because the court's findings did not meet the "high threshold of establishing that the emotional distress suffered was so severe that no reasonable person could be expected to endure it." Huber further argues that Lyman experienced emotional upset more akin to common stress and anxiety caused by everyday events. The breakdown of romantic relationships, he contends, "is an area of emotional injury which does not and should not involve lawsuits and courts."

The fourth element of the tort of intentional infliction of emotional distress has been characterized as one that imposes an objective standard of proof. According to that standard, a plaintiff must do more than prove that the emotional distress he or she suffered was serious; a plaintiff must prove that her emotional distress was "so severe that no reasonable [person] could be expected to endure it." *Curtis*, 784 A.2d at 23 (brackets in original) (*quoting* Champagne v. Mid-Maine Med. Ctr., 711 A.2d 842, 847 (Me. 1998) (*quoting* Loe v. Town of Thomaston, 600 A.2d 190, 193 (Me. 1991)).

This "no reasonable person" requirement[5] was adopted by this court in 1979 based on language of comment j to section 46 of the RESTATEMENT (SECOND) OF TORTS. *See* Vicnire v. Ford Motor Credit Co., 401 A.2d 148, 154 (Me. 1979). However, while it has been oft-repeated, it has not been analyzed to determine if it is appropriate. We find that it is not appropriate, and therefore omit it from the required elements for the tort of intentional infliction of emotional distress. We believe the proper standard is whether the emotional distress suffered by the plaintiff was so severe that the plaintiff should not be expected to endure it.

Although the "no reasonable person" requirement can be traced back to the RESTATEMENT (SECOND) OF TORTS, that phrase was used in the comments, not in the black-letter articulation of the tort of intentional infliction of

[5] As noted above, the original term was "reasonable man" which this court changed to "reasonable person" in 1999. *See supra* note 2.

emotional distress. The black-letter statement of the tort of intentional infliction of emotional distress is as follows:

> One who by extreme and outrageous conduct intentionally or recklessly causes severe emotional distress to another is subject to liability for such emotional distress, and if bodily harm to the other results from it, for such bodily harm.
>
> RESTATEMENT (SECOND) OF TORTS § 46 (1) (1977)

This articulation of the tort is consistent with the elements outlined above. It requires "severe emotional distress," but does not evaluate the severity of such distress by comparison to the reasonable person. The reasonable person reference comes from comment j to section 46, which distinguishes severe distress from "transient and trivial emotional distress" that is part of life. It then states: "The law intervenes only where the distress inflicted is so severe that no reasonable man could be expected to endure it." *Id.*, comment j.

In the context of a case being decided in the twenty-first century, it is widely understood that imposing a "reasonable man" requirement on a claim of emotional distress brought by a woman against her former romantic male partner would be sexist. That is why nearly twenty years ago this court substituted "reasonable person" for "reasonable man." *See* Loe v. Thomaston, 600 A.2d 1090, 1093 (Me. 1991). The fact that a hypothetical reasonable man would be willing to endure the emotional distress suffered by Lyman does not demonstrate that her distress was not severe or that it should not be compensated. Men have been in a position of dominance in our society for a very long time. Applying a "reasonable man" standard perpetuates male dominance by limiting compensation to those instances where the emotional distress is "severe" from a male perspective. One of the purposes of tort law is to protect the disempowered, and to provide compensation for wrongs perpetrated by the powerful. Women are far more likely to be victims of domestic abuse, see MARTHA CHAMALLAS & JENNIFER B. WRIGGINS, THE MEASURE OF INJURY: RACE, GENDER AND TORT LAW 65 (2010), and male partners can use "physical and economic advantage to heighten the disparity of power" with their partners "to intensify the feeling of helplessness on the part of the victim." *Id.* at 67. The tort of intentional infliction of emotional distress must protect women as well as men and cannot be limited to circumstances in which a man would suffer severe distress.

The replacement of the overtly gendered term "reasonable man" with the ostensibly neutral "reasonable person" does not remedy this problem. Because of the pervasiveness of the male perspective in our culture and the weight of male influence over so many of our institutions, the reasonable person perspective is not sufficient to protect the disempowered.[6] Current research shows that when used by the law, the "reasonable person" is "most often the common or ordinary man," which "tends to reinforce the privilege of the powerful while simultaneously exacerbating the plight of those who are disadvantaged." Mayo Moran, *The Reasonable Person: A Conceptual Biography in Comparative Perspective*, 14 LEWIS & CLARK L. REV. 1233, 1236 (2010). The tort of intentional infliction of emotional distress is meant to protect against emotional abuse, particularly in situations involving an abuse of power or exploitations of vulnerability. Requiring a victim to prove emotional distress so severe that "no reasonable person could be expected to endure it" perpetuates a power structure and hierarchy in favor of abusers.

To protect victims, we believe that a subjective standard, focused solely on the degree of actual distress suffered by the plaintiff, is appropriate. Where a person intentionally or recklessly causes severe emotional distress, that person should be liable for the harm caused even if a "reasonable person" would not have experienced severe emotional distress. A subjective standard will better accommodate the wide variety of perspectives present in our pluralistic society. See CHAMALLAS & WRIGGINS, *supra*, at 86 (arguing that multiple perspectives and recognition of subjective vulnerability will better protect those who are targeted). At the same time, the tort is still limited by the requirement of severe distress. The experience of emotional distress alone is not sufficient to satisfy the requirement; the distress, while subjective, must still be severe. It will be up to the finder of fact to determine whether the distress is severe or not, but in so doing, a subjective standard should be used.

The tort remedy is also limited by the requirement that the misconduct be "intentionally or recklessly inflicted" and "so extreme and outrageous as to

[6] One proposed solution for this problem has been the reasonable woman standard in cases involving female victims. We do not choose to go in this direction for several reasons. First, we believe a binary, male/female framework does not accurately reflect the plurality of interests and perspectives in our society. *See* Nancy S. Ehrenreich, *Pluralist Myths and Powerless Men: The Ideology of Reasonableness in Sexual Harassment Law*, 99 YALE L.J. 1177, 1216–18 (1990). Second, while in some circumstances a woman's perspective might be appropriate, we are concerned that using such a perspective may tend to reinforce stereotypes. *See* Jolynn Childers, Note, *Is There a Place for a Reasonable Woman in the Law? A Discussion of Recent Developments in Hostile Environment Sexual Harassment*, 42 DUKE L.J. 854, 895–96 (1993). Third, the reasonable woman standard has only been proposed or adopted in connection with sexual harassment and discrimination, *see, e.g.*, Ellison v. Brady, 924 F.2d 872, 879 (9th Cir. 1991), which is invariably a more gendered setting than the multiple circumstances giving rise to emotional distress claims. For a thorough analysis of the reasonable woman standard, and a proposal that it be used for injuries that tend to be gendered (such as stalking, sexual harassment, rape, and domestic homicide), see CAROLINE FORELL & DONNA MATTHEWS, A LAW OF HER OWN: THE REASONABLE WOMAN AS A MEASURE OF MAN (2000).

exceed all possible bounds of decency." Because the misconduct is intentional or reckless, the tortfeasor is more culpable than a person who is merely negligent, so the law makes it easier for the plaintiff to state a claim. For example, the law recognizes that the mere offensive touching of another, if done intentionally, is enough to constitute battery. *See* JACK H. SIMMONS, DAVID D. GREGORY & DONAL N. ZILLMAN, MAINE TORT LAW § 1.01 (2001). In the case of intentional infliction of emotional distress, the misconduct must be intentional or reckless,[7] but *in addition* the plaintiff must prove that defendant's conduct was extreme and outrageous, and that the plaintiff suffered severe distress. To require proof that the distress is "so severe that no reasonable person would be expected to endure it" goes too far. The victim of intentional or reckless misconduct that reaches the level of being outrageous and causes severe distress is entitled to compensation whether a hypothetical reasonable person would have suffered that distress or not.

Eliminating the reasonable person component of the severe distress element of the tort will help to move closer to parity between physical and emotional torts. The current structure of tort law gives a strong preference to physical injuries over emotional ones, which "tends to place women at a disadvantage because important and recurring injuries in women's lives are more often classified as lower-ranked emotional or relational harm." CHAMALLAS & WRIGGINS, *supra*, at 91–92. While eliminating the "reasonable person" requirement will not put claims for emotional harms on a par with claims for physical harms – because the emotional distress tort requires outrageousness and severe distress – at least it is a step toward parity. In cases of physical harm, the tortfeasor "takes his victim as he finds him." This means that if the victim suffers a greater extent of harm than others might have incurred, due to some physical or mental condition particular to the plaintiff, the negligent tortfeasor is still responsible for the full extent of the harm he caused. There is no "reduction" to only that degree of harm that a "reasonable person" would have suffered. This principle of full compensation is equally, if not more, important in the case of intentional infliction of emotional distress, where the defendant intentionally inflicts harm.

We find that the evidence relied on by the trial court meets the standard of severe distress. Emotional distress that is "severe" is that which is "extremely intense." See AMERICAN HERITAGE DICTIONARY 1123 (2d ed. 1982). While this is a somewhat amorphous standard, additional insight into its intended

[7] Although battery cannot be proven by evidence of recklessness, the more liberal intent requirement for a claim of intentional infliction of emotion distress is more than offset by the requirements that the tortfeasor's actions be outrageous and that it result in severe distress.

meaning is provided by the RESTATEMENT (SECOND) OF TORTS. As comment k to section 46 of the RESTATEMENT (SECOND) OF TORTS recognizes, a plaintiff's emotional suffering normally causes "shock, illness or other bodily harm," which shows that the distress is severe. But even without such manifestation, the severity of the distress can be inferred from the outrageousness of the behavior. Comment k provides:

> *k. Bodily harm* ... The rule stated is not, however, limited to cases where there has been bodily harm; and if the conduct is sufficiently extreme and outrageous there may be liability for the emotional distress alone, without such harm. In such cases the courts may perhaps tend to look for more in the way of outrage as a guarantee that the claim is genuine; but if the enormity of the outrage carries conviction that there has in fact been severe emotional distress, bodily harm is not required.[8]
>
> RESTATEMENT (SECOND) OF TORTS § 46 cmt. k (1965)

Our decisions have employed the term "objective symptomatology" in place of "bodily harm," but follow the RESTATEMENT (SECOND) OF TORTS' approach by recognizing that the fourth element may be satisfied without proof of objective symptomatology if the defendant's conduct was so extreme and outrageous that it can be inferred that it would generate a severe emotional response. Thus, in *Vicnire v. Ford Motor Credit Co.*, we observed:

> Although "severe" emotional distress is usually manifested by "shock, illness or other bodily harm," such objective symptomatology is not an absolute

[8] The two illustrations that accompany comment k both emphasize that proof of physical manifestations of the plaintiff's emotional distress, in instances where the plaintiff did not suffer direct physical harm as a result of the defendant's conduct, should not be required where the intentional act that gave rise to the emotional harm was unquestionably outrageous:

> Illustrations:
>
> 19. A, a police officer, arrests B on a criminal charge. In order to extort a confession, A falsely tells B that her child has been injured in an accident and is dying in a hospital, and that she cannot be released to go to the hospital until she confesses. B suffers severe emotional distress but no physical consequences. A is subject to liability to B.
>
> 20. A organizes a mob, and brings it to B's door at night. A tells B that unless he leaves town within ten days the mob will return and lynch him. B suffers severe emotional distress, but no physical consequences. A is subject to liability to B.
>
> RESTATEMENT (SECOND) TORTS § 46 cmt. k (1965)

See also Reagan v. Rider, 521 A.2d 1246, 1251 (Md. Ct. Spec. App. 1987) (stating that "the very nature of the outrageous conduct – sexual molestation of a child by a person in a position of authority and trust during six of her more critical formative years" could permit a jury to find that the plaintiff suffered severe emotional distress).

> prerequisite for recovery of damages for intentional, as opposed to negligent, infliction of emotional distress. Restatement (Second) of Torts § 46, Comment k. In appropriate cases, "severe" emotional distress may be inferred from the "extreme and outrageous" nature of the defendant's conduct alone.
> 401 A.2d 148, 154 (Me. 1979)

Here, the court's factual findings, and all reasonable inferences that may be drawn from the record to support those findings, demonstrate that Lyman suffered severe emotional distress. Lyman described feeling inadequate and withdrawn, socially paralyzed, and fearful and intimidated by Huber's controlling and compulsive behavior. Her friends described her as being, at times, "guarded, jumpy, and withdrawn," "shaken," and "tense, afraid and on edge." This evidence was sufficient to support the trial court's finding of severe emotional distress. These injuries were more than transient or trivial emotional distress. The testimony showed objective symptomatology of "shock, illness or other bodily harm" even though plaintiff did not submit expert testimony. See, e.g., *Latremore*, 584 A.2d at 632 (husband's testimony of "physical symptom[s] including nervousness, shaking and a worsening speech impediment" were sufficient, without expert testimony, to support a jury's finding of severe distress). See also Feltmeier v. Feltmeier, 798 N.E.2d 75, 84 (Ill. 2003) (holding that a wife's alleged severe mental distress, described as a loss of self-esteem, difficulty forming relationships, post-traumatic stress disorder, and depression was sufficient to state a claim for intentional infliction of emotional distress against her former husband). Moreover, the evidence showed that Lyman endured the distress over the course of her fifteen-year relationship with Huber. In the context of this kind of domestic relationship, recovery may be available in cases involving cumulative acts over an extended period that are in the nature of "coercive, controlling behavior that invades important individual rights of the abused party." Chamallas & Wriggins, *supra*, at 75.

Even if Lyman's condition did not amount to "shock, illness or other bodily harm," the trial court's decision is supported by an inference of severe distress based on the extreme and outrageous nature of defendant's conduct. The evidence supported the trial court's finding "that Huber's behavior toward Lyman constituted a pattern of cruelty and intimidation over a prolonged period so that the court can only conclude that it is extreme and outrageous." Trial court opinion at 9.

Although there are other remedies for the victims of such conduct, including a statutory action for protection from abuse, see 19-A M.R.S. §§ 4001–14 (2009), we recognize a civil action for intentional infliction of emotional distress may also be available to some victims, as it is here.

B *Damages for Loss of Business Opportunity*

Huber also contends that the lower court erred in awarding Lyman money damages for her loss of business opportunity based on her claim of ouster because ouster is not recognized as an actionable tort in Maine. He further asserts that even if we recognize such a tort, the trial court erred because there was no evidence that Lyman was ousted from the Cape Elizabeth property; rather, he contends, she left the property voluntarily.

Ouster has not previously been recognized as an actionable tort in Maine. *See* Porter v. Hooper, 13 Me. 25, 29 (1836) (stating that a tenant in common may occupy property to the exclusion of a cotenant without committing a trespass); Davis v. Poland, 66 A. 380, 382 (Me. 1906) (stating that a tenant-in-common's destruction of common property or practical destruction of a cotenant's property interest constitutes a trespass); see generally SIMMONS, ZILLMAN & GREGORY, MAINE TORT LAW (2004 ed. & Supp. 2009) (not addressing the tort of ouster, but discussing, at § 5.05, that a cotenant's exclusion of another cotenant is not a trespass). The lower court recognized this and, instead of awarding Lyman damages on her ouster claim, it included those damages, measured by her loss of business opportunity, in her damages for intentional infliction of emotional distress.

We decline to recognize the tort of ouster at this time, but we find that Lyman's lost business opportunity is a permissible element of damages for her intentional infliction of emotional distress claim. *See* Snow v. Villacci, 754 A.2d 360 (Me. 2000) (recognizing lost business opportunity as an element of damages). Lyman is entitled to compensation for damages caused by Huber's intentional infliction of emotional distress. The trial court found that Huber's cruelty and intimidation "forced [Lyman] to give up her horse business and that she never had the opportunity to build it into an on-going enterprise." Trial court opinion at 6. Huber's controlling and deliberate behavior is typical of too many instances of abusive domestic relationships. Domestic abusers often act out of a desire to control their victim by keeping her economically and socially dependent. To deny domestic violence victims compensation for their economic loss from diminished professional achievement or opportunities caused by the severe emotional distress intentionally inflicted on them would compound the harm and fail to make them whole.

The trial court's award of $31,000 of damages for this lost opportunity is supported by the evidence and does not constitute clear error. Although Lyman's business had not yet turned a profit, the gross revenue had increased, and she expected the business to become profitable. Huber's behavior forced Lyman to give up eighty-five clients and a uniquely favorable property for the business. In addition, she was forced to give up her horses, valued at $22,000 to $23,000, at "fire sale" prices of $2,500. *Id.* at 7. While this court might have arrived at a different amount of damages than the trial court, this difference does not amount to clear error to warrant reversal. Because we have already concluded that Lyman was entitled to relief for her claim of intentional infliction of emotional distress, we affirm the trial court's award of damages to Lyman for her loss of business opportunity as an element of her damages.

The Judgment is affirmed.

9

Commentary on *Sipple v. Chronicle Publishing Co.*

ANNA LAUREN HOFFMANN

INTRODUCTION

On September 22, 1975, Oliver "Billy" Sipple stood outside of San Francisco's St. Francis Hotel, part of a crowd waiting to catch a glimpse of then President Gerald Ford as he passed from the hotel to the limousine idling on the street.[1] Around 3:30 PM, Ford emerged, pausing to wave to the crowd before getting into his vehicle. Suddenly, a nearby woman raised a handgun and fired two shots at the president. The first shot missed entirely; the second was deflected, as Sipple – a former marine – lunged and grabbed the woman's shooting arm. Following this incident, the San Francisco Police Department and the president's Secret Service commended Sipple for his actions. President Ford followed up with a thank-you letter. The press called him a hero.

Little did Billy know at the time that he'd suffer the consequences of his heroism for the rest of his life.

Days later, *San Francisco Chronicle* columnist Herb Caen would add additional color to Billy's story, most notably by "outing" him as gay and reporting on his connections in San Francisco's gay community.[2] Caen noted that Sipple "was the center of midnight attention at the Red Lantern, a Golden Gate Ave. bar he favors" before quoting gay political figures Rev. Ray Broshears and Harvey Milk as "Sipple's close friends" eager to see the image of a heroic gay ex-marine "break the stereotype" of gay men as weak, effeminate, or deviant. A number of other newspapers picked up on Caen's details – including the *Los Angeles Times* – and effectively broadcast Sipple's sexuality nationally.

[1] Edward Epstein, *Ford Escaped 2 Assassination Attempts/Both Happened in California – One in Capital, Other in* S.F., S.F. GATE (Dec. 27, 2006), https://www.sfgate.com/news/article/Ford-escaped-2-assassination-attempts-Both-2481771.php

[2] Herb Caen, SAN FRANCISCO CHRONICLE, Sept. 24, 1975.

Billy sued the *Chronicle* and several other publications for invasion of privacy. He argued that the newspapers broadcasted what was an ostensibly private fact that lacked newsworthiness relative to his celebrated actions in Union Square. Moreover, he insisted that outing him was not only offensive, but harmful. It opened him up to ridicule and threatened his livelihood. Worse, his family – far removed from San Francisco and until then unaware of Billy's sexual orientation – abandoned him as a result.

In response, the defendants moved that Sipple's privacy claim be dismissed. They did not challenge the harms he may have suffered, but – rather – argued that his sexuality was not wholly private (indeed, it was well known within San Francisco's gay community) and was, at any rate, newsworthy. The trial court agreed and granted the motions. Billy appealed, but the appeals court again sided with the defendants.

Ultimately, Billy lost the case.

BACKGROUND AND CONTEXT

Tort law recognizes a right to privacy. Descended, in part, from the paradigmatic "right to be let alone" detailed by Samuel D. Warren and Louis D. Brandeis in their classic 1890 article, *The Right to Privacy*,[3] the law in this area seeks to defend individuals against unwarranted intrusions into, among other things, their domestic lives and private affairs. In so doing, it echoes, as Julie Cohen notes, liberal political theory's broader commitment to preserving an imagined liberal self by preserving individuals' inviolate personality.[4]

In his influential 1960 article *Privacy*, William Prosser reviewed the landscape of privacy decisions post-1890 and sorted them into a four-part taxonomy: (1) intrusion, including both physical trespass into private domains and nonphysical trespass such as wiretapping and harassing phone calls; (2) public disclosure of private facts, namely by means of publicizing the private matters of another; (3) false light in the public eye, as with the circulation of inaccurate or misleading information; and (4) appropriation, especially nonconsensual use of another's name or likeness.[5] As a reporter for the *Restatement (Second) of Torts*, Prosser later incorporated his taxonomy into a *Restatement* provision, the impact of which is difficult to overestimate. As Anita Allen notes, it has both influenced scholarly understanding of

[3] Samuel D. Warren & Louis D. Brandeis, *The Right to Privacy*, 4 Harv. L. Rev. 193, 193 (1890).

[4] Julie E. Cohen, *What Privacy Is For*, 126 Harv. L. Rev. 1904, 1905 (2013).

[5] William L. Prosser, *Privacy*, 48 Cal. L. Rev. 383, 389 (1960).

the origins of the privacy tort and shaped its doctrinal development in the courts.[6]

Of present concern is the "public disclosure of private facts" claim in *Sipple v. Chronicle Publishing Co.* From the appeals court opinion:

> The complaint was predicated upon the theory of invasion of privacy and alleged in essence that defendants without authorization and consent published private facts about plaintiff's life by disclosing that plaintiff was homosexual in his personal and private sexual orientation; that said publications were highly offensive to plaintiff inasmuch as his parents, brothers and sisters learned for the first time of his homosexual orientation; and that as a consequence of disclosure of private facts about his life plaintiff was abandoned by his family, exposed to contempt and ridicule causing him great mental anguish, embarrassment and humiliation. Plaintiff finally alleged that defendants' conduct amounted to malice and oppression calling for both compensatory and punitive damages.[7]

In deciding the case, the court emphasized three elements of the public disclosure tort originally articulated by Prosser: the first element states that the disclosure in question must be a public disclosure – that is, it must be broadcast to more than a few people; the second states that the facts disclosed must be private facts and not public ones; and, third, the matter made public must be one which would be objectionable to a reasonable person of ordinary sensibilities. As the court also noted, these elements are further constrained by certain constitutional protections – namely, freedom of the press, which exempts the press from liability if a disclosure is deemed newsworthy.[8]

Given the above, the appeals court upheld the original summary judgment against Sipple on two grounds. First, the court argued that Sipple's sexuality was not private "within the meaning of the law" as his "homosexual orientation and participation in gay community activities had been known by hundreds of people in a variety of cities."[9] The court cited as further proof Sipple's time spent in "well-known gay sections of San Francisco" like the Tenderloin and the Castro, as well as his involvement in gay political causes. In this case, it did not matter that Sipple's disclosures were strategically confined to places and activities unlikely to attract any widespread – let alone national – attention. For the court, there was no difference between a widespread general public and San Francisco's narrower gay communities.

6 Anita L. Allen, *Privacy Torts: Unreliable Remedies for LGBT Plaintiffs*, 98 Cal. L. Rev. 1711, 1719 (2010).

7 Sipple v. Chronicle Publ'g Co., 201 Cal. Rptr. 665, 667 (Cal. Ct. App. 1984).

8 *Id.* at 667–68.

9 *Id.* at 668–69.

Second, the court asserted that the disclosures were newsworthy and not motivated by sensational prying into Sipple's private affairs. Rather, they "were prompted by legitimate political considerations, i.e., to dispel the false public opinion that gays were timid, weak and unheroic figures and to raise the equally important political question whether the President of the United States entertained a discriminatory attitude or bias against a minority group such as homosexuals" by, for example, only sending a letter to Sipple and not extending an invitation to the White House.[10] Despite Sipple's involuntary fame, the facts of his disclosures and the questions broached by the press were sufficient to shield the defendants from liability.

Responses to *Sipple* in subsequent academic literature have ranged from ambivalent to sharply critical. Some cite the enduring challenges of selective disclosure for the law, while also falling short of condemning the decision entirely. Allen, for example, notes that "courts are unreceptive to the notion that a person should be legally entitled to disclose selectively – that is, disclose in some contexts to some persons but not others" and viewed Sipple's loss as "understandable."[11]

Others have been more pointed in their criticisms. Kenji Yoshino has criticized the court for failing to understand the social dynamics of "the closet" that inform the lives of many lesbian, gay, bisexual, transgender, queer, and intersex people – in particular, gay men.[12] He argues that "a court that regards the 'public' as monolithic, such that a single disclosure by a gay person of his or her homosexuality can be seen as potentially leaving that person's homosexual identity open to all, puts additional pressure on gays to keep their identities totally secret."[13] Similarly, in his prior work, Skinner-Thompson, the author of the feminist judgment, has criticized the court for "ignoring that information such as one's minority sexual orientation can be extremely sensitive and damaging depending on the context in which it is shared."[14]

More broadly, privacy torts have – despite being "theoretically promising" – generally proven "unreliable remedies" for LGBTQI plaintiffs.[15] On a more critical read, the law may actually be actively biased in favor of prominent or privileged persons at the expense of marginalized groups.[16] Perversely, the

[10] *Id.* at 670.
[11] Allen, *supra* note 6, at 1716, 1748.
[12] Kenji Yoshino, *Suspect Symbols: The Literary Argument for Heightened Scrutiny for Gays*, 96 Colum. L. Rev. 1753, 1794 (1996).
[13] *Id.* at 1814.
[14] Scott Skinner-Thompson, *Privacy's Double Standards*, 93 Wash. L. Rev. 2051, 2073 (2018).
[15] Allen, *supra* note 6, at 1711.
[16] Skinner-Thompson, *supra* note 14, at 2074–80.

public disclosure tort has been leveraged more successfully by celebrities and other public figures that should, in theory, have less claim to its protection.[17] While the judge in *Sipple* reasoned that there was no meaningful difference between voluntary and involuntary public figures when it came to judging the newsworthiness of Sipple's sexual orientation, celebrities such as professional wrestler and reality television star Hulk Hogan have had a right to privacy in information about their sex lives affirmed under the law.

THE FEMINIST JUDGMENT

Scott Skinner-Thompson's rewritten opinion takes aim at the original decision's reductive and limiting conception of privacy. He is keen to acknowledge that individual development – especially for members of stigmatized or otherwise marginalized groups – requires a certain level of autonomy over how information about oneself is communicated. In this way he takes seriously what Allen refers to as LGBTQI persons' "selective disclosure rights,"[18] rights that allow people to navigate social life on their own terms, rather than terms oppressively dictated by dominant or hegemonic norms. In doing so, Skinner-Thompson provides one response to Yoshino's call to take into account "the closet" and its mediating role in queer life.

For Skinner-Thompson, taking selective disclosure rights seriously requires that an analysis of the public disclosure tort's requirements not be conducted in a vacuum. Rather, the analysis must actively consider context and the ways a public disclosure "impacted or harmed the individual plaintiff in the context of their everyday life." It is clear that, by broadcasting Sipple's identity to a national audience, the *Chronicle* and other publications caused Sipple harm.

The publication triggered a rupture in his family that took many years to repair and it exposed him to undue prejudice and ridicule. As Skinner-Thompson notes, "there can be little doubt – and defendants do not seriously contest – that disclosing someone's gay orientation without their consent after they have intervened heroically to prevent an assassination of the president, would be objectionable to a reasonable person of ordinary sensibilities." In this way, the rewritten decision is able to overcome the original's insensitivity to the lived experience of LGBTQI people under biased and often oppressive conditions.

Further, Skinner-Thompson's rewrite reveals the impossible bind generated by the original decision. "If we were to impose a requirement of complete

[17] *Id.* at 2077–79.

[18] Allen, *supra* note 6, at 1746.

secrecy," he argues, "the public disclosure of private facts tort would, in effect, be rendered a null set, particularly as it pertains to some of the information deemed most sensitive by society – information relating to our personal relations." In other words, the conception of "private" in "public disclosure private facts" should not be so narrow as to render the tort irrelevant. The failure to acknowledge the social nature of privacy would have disproportionately damaging effects on LGBTQI people in particular, since "to require complete secrecy in order to state a public disclosure claim would force anyone with information that may be highly stigmatized deeper into a chamber of secrets." Against this, Skinner-Thompson eloquently notes that the public disclosure tort should not "lock the door to the closet from the outside."

Last, Skinner-Thompson injects into *Sipple* attention to a broader range of constitutional considerations that might inform our understanding of the privacy torts. Whereas the original decision limited its analysis to First Amendment considerations around freedom of the press and "newsworthiness," Skinner-Thompson demonstrates how principles of equal protection might be similarly instructive. First, the rewritten decision recasts the public disclosure tort as a safeguard for "the opportunity to test the waters and explore our identities with others. In this way, we as individuals (and collectively, as a society), are able to evolve and incubate our personal (and political) identities within the protected confines of limited circles." Second, Skinner-Thompson's more nuanced understanding of privacy "[permits] people to explore their identity within limited confines and develop strategies for combating societal discrimination." Our interest in equality, then, provides a basis for Skinner-Thompson's contextual approach to the public disclosure tort as it centers "the social values that might be served by privacy protection over the information at issue, taking into account the individual plaintiff's unique social status."

REFLECTION AND LIMITS

Skinner-Thompson's rewrite is both illustrative and indicative. In its break from the original opinion, it illustrates that moving beyond a reductive public/private binary can open up opportunities for the marginalized or oppressed to pursue justice under privacy law. It is also indicative of broader struggles, insofar as his empathetic recounting of Sipple's story brings to mind countless other lesbian, gay, bisexual, transgender, queer, and intersex lives that have been upended or cut short as a consequence of bigotry and violence. It reminds us that LGBTQI individuals are regularly exposed by and through spaces otherwise respected as private for straight and cisgender people.

For example, bathrooms – sites of relative privacy for straight and cisgender people – have long been targets for anti-LGBTQI policies and sentiments. From undercover law enforcement agents leveraging such spaces to "catch" and punish gay men to efforts to legally bar transgender people – and, in particular, transgender women – from using facilities that correspond with their gender, LGBTQI experiences expose the biased norms that underwrite many contemporary and historical conceptions of privacy.

Whether the privacy torts are intrinsically anti-LGBTQI or not, interpretations of them have privileged certain hegemonic forms of identity and community. It is worth noting the law's longer history of homophobia and anti-gay bias as background. For example, the fourth edition of Prosser's famous treatise *The Law of Torts* notes that "the imputation of homosexuality" represents a category of slander – "actionable without proof of damage" – a suggestion that was dropped in subsequent editions.[19] Though some would claim that the law is no longer intrinsically biased against LGBTQI individuals,[20] privacy law – and, in particular, the public disclosure tort – has yet to recognize that for mutual support and survival, particular minority groups need to share and circulate information within their communities, outside of the gaze of dominant groups. Consequently, courts still situate individuals like Sipple as "the most irrational of actors – the politically active figure who is afraid that someone will tell his mother on him."[21]

Skinner-Thompson's reconsideration of *Sipple* is undoubtedly more nuanced, progressive, and humane than the original opinion. It is also arguably feminist in a broadly liberal sense, in that it attends to liberal feminists' concerns with equal social, economic, and legal opportunities for certain marginalized groups. Among the insights Skinner-Thompson's rewrite affords is a recognition that privacy interests have never existed apart or separate from social and political dynamics of power. He employs the language of liberal rights in a way that embraces privacy's role in promoting individual development by sheltering people from outside forces that would seek to unfairly interrogate, intimidate, or exploit them. His opinion would afford individuals

[19] William L. Prosser, Handbook of the Law of Torts 760 (4th ed. 1971); Allison Bailey, *From the Closet to the House-Tops: The Law and Ethics of Media "Outing,"* 33 (1996). https://digitalrepository.unm.edu/law_studentscholarship/54. Notably, the notion that accusations of homosexuality constitute defamation per se arguably persisted despite this change. It was not until 2012 that the idea was directly repudiated in the courts. *Cf.* Yonaty v. Mincolla, 945 N.Y. 2d 774 (App. Div. 2012).

[20] *See, e.g.*, Allen, *supra* note 6, at 1762–64.

[21] Yoshino, *supra* note 12, at 1812.

the freedom to experiment with identities and ideas away from the gaze of potentially hostile others.

In its embrace of the language of liberal rights and norms, however, Skinner-Thompson's progressive reconsideration of the public disclosure tort necessarily falls short of a robust confrontation with foundational norms and structures that generate conditions of oppression in the first place. This is, of course, partly a limit of the genre – judicial opinions are constrained by available precedent and by the facts as presented at the time. Nevertheless, it is also worth noting the ways judicial opinions risk erasing important differences within and across LGBTQI people, especially across lines of race, ethnicity, class, and gender. In many ways, the law often confines itself to – in the words of intersectional theorist and scholar of race Vivian May – a "'special case' closed logic" that prioritizes monolithic group categories at the expense of relevant intragroup differences.[22]

If we foreground the sort of intersecting oppressions with which May is concerned, Skinner-Thompson's rewrite of *Sipple* helps point us toward even deeper tensions between legal reform, feminism, and the liberation of marginalized or stigmatized groups. For example, further feminist engagements with privacy might point to instances of misogyny or classism in the law that may complicate matters for women who are lesbian, bisexual, or transgender. Indeed, Prosser's famous taxonomy contains examples and asides that are, at best, belittling of women or, worse, evidence of an active and hostile misogyny. For example, he illustrated his concern that the privacy torts would allow trivial lawsuits to proliferate by pointing to the hypothetical case of "a lady who insists upon sun-bathing in the nude in her own back yard," thus inviting "neighbors [to] examine her with appreciation and binoculars."[23] In terms of class, a critical analysis of Warren and Brandeis's foundational article on privacy and the "right to be let alone" might point out that the ability to realize this "right" is obviously skewed toward those who, like Warren and Brandeis, had reliable access to the means by which to isolate and exclude oneself – means not readily available to women of lower socioeconomic standing for whom secure and uncrowded housing is difficult to access.

Further, adopting an approach that highlights the relationship between privacy and gender as well as race, religion, and ethnicity can pose a challenge to white supremacist norms that mark a number of legal debates.[24] For

[22] Vivian M. May, Pursuing intersectionality, unsettling dominant imaginaries 26 (2015).

[23] Prosser, *supra* note 5, at 422.

[24] *See* Jennifer C. Nash, *From Lavender to Purple: Privacy, Black Women, and Feminist Legal Theory*, 11 Cardozo Women's L.J. 303, 310 (2005).

example, scholars embracing transnational and decolonial feminist perspectives have shed light on laws that attempt to strike a balance between "privacy" and "security," but in the process inflict harm on women from cultural or religious minorities, as with "Western" laws banning Muslim women from wearing burkas, hijabs, or other types of veils in particular venues.[25] Each of these cases makes clear that while privacy's abstract aim may be to promote "the protection of the person," such protection is rarely articulated in terms that can account for a wide range of gendered, racialized, cultural, or classed experiences.

Finally, even within Sipple's story, there are additional dynamics of oppression left beyond the law's reach. The particular brand of gay progressivism espoused by Sipple's San Francisco community – and, in particular, his friend Harvey Milk – was itself steeped in a kind of misogyny, as it sought mainstream acceptance through conformity to certain masculine expectations. This attitude was evident in the composite quote from Milk and others included in Caen's original article; they specifically singled out Sipple's masculine appearance and history as an ex-marine in hopes that this would help "break the stereotype." Left behind were the transwomen, drag queens, and others who – through their activism and community-building – were instrumental in making Milk's historical moment possible. Instead, it was square-jawed military men like Sipple who found themselves thrust into the spotlight, unwitting victims of a narrow kind of liberation.

CONCLUSION

Billy Sipple was never able to shake the fallout from that day in San Francisco's Union Square, just a few blocks away from the Tenderloin district he once thought of as a refuge. His time spent cultivating meaningful friendships and intimate relationships there, in the Castro, and elsewhere betrayed him. The press exposed him. His friends took advantage of his masculine good looks and military background for political gain. His family was taunted and harassed.

And when he sought restitution, the courts did not defend him.

In the years that followed, Billy began drinking heavily ("I have a lot of stress and I take it out on booze," he once noted in a deposition). Lingering mental and physical health problems from his stint in Vietnam began to worsen. He gained weight, washing out the very looks gay politicos once sought to exploit.

[25] *See* Saba Mahmood, Politics of Piety: The Islamic Revival and the Feminist Subject (2005).

"There were a lot of times he wished he had never saved the president's life, for all the anguish it caused him," his older brother George told the *Washington Post* in 2006. "He only said it when he was drinking. He said life would have been so much simpler if he hadn't done it."[26]

Nonetheless, Billy's community rallied around him as his health continued to deteriorate. He'd buy his friends drinks and they'd make sure he had a ride home from the bar. As a former San Francisco police commissioner recounted to the *Post*, "People really liked the guy and not only because he spent a lot of money on drinks. But after the incident, and after his family disowned him, there were people . . . who would always make sure he had a place to go on a holiday."[27] Eventually, he reconnected with his family – though they never fully accepted him.

As reported by the *Los Angeles Times*, sometime in the early days of 1989, Billy Sipple went to sleep and never woke up. His body was discovered two weeks later when a friend – acting on request of a concerned bartender at one of Billy's regular haunts – went to check up on him. "People shouldn't die like that, alone," his friend said.[28]

Later, his brother would visit San Francisco to clean out Billy's run-down apartment. Speaking with the *Times*, George recalled him once noting that someday, after he died, "somebody will pick up a book and see Oliver Sipple saved President Ford's life."[29]

SIPPLE v. CHRONICLE PUBLISHING CO., 201 CAL. RPTR. 665 (CAL. CT. APP. 1984)

SCOTT SKINNER-THOMPSON, PRESIDING JUDGE

Privacy is not all or nothing. And yet, sometimes, it is everything. The forced "outing" of an individual can be one such time, as the facts of this case illustrate.

On September 22, 1975, President Gerald Ford visited San Francisco, California. While in Union Square, Sara Jane Moore attempted to assassinate

[26] Lynne Duke, *Caught in Fate's Trajectory, Along with Gerald Ford*, WASH. POST (Dec. 31, 2006), http://www.washingtonpost.com/wp-dyn/content/article/2006/12/30/AR2006123000160.html

[27] *Id.*

[28] Dan Moran, *Sorrow Trailed a Veteran Who Saved a President and Then Was Cast in an Unwanted Spotlight*, L.A. TIMES (Feb. 13, 1989), https://www.latimes.com/archives/la-xpm-1989-02-13-vw-1568-story.html

[29] *Id.*

President Ford by shooting him. Just as Moore was about to fire the gun at the president, plaintiff Oliver Sipple, who was in the crowd near Moore, intervened and struck Moore's arm. While no one can be certain whether Sipple actually saved the president's life, the assassination attempt failed and Sipple was rightly considered a hero for his valiant actions.

In the days that followed, several newspaper articles were published about the incident. In one piece, written by Herb Caen in the *San Francisco Chronicle* on September 24, 1975, Sipple was outed without his consent as a gay man. Specifically, according to the article:

> One of the heroes of the day, Oliver "Bill" Sipple, the ex-Marine who grabbed Sara Jane Moore's arm just as her gun was fired and thereby may have saved the President's life, was the center of midnight attention at the Red Lantern, a Golden Gate Ave. bar he favors. The Rev. Ray Broshears, head of Helping Hands, and Gay Politico, Harvey Milk who claim to be among Sipple's close friends, describe themselves as "proud – maybe this will help break the stereotype." Sipple is among the workers in Milk's campaign for Supervisor.

Thereafter, several other newspapers published articles referring to the *Chronicle* article and further disclosing that Sipple was gay. Some of those articles speculated that President Ford failed to immediately thank Sipple because he was gay.

As it happens, the facts suggest that even before the assassination attempt on President Ford and subsequent publicity, Sipple was not completely closeted – the door was a bit ajar. Instead, Sipple spent time in the "Tenderloin" and the "Castro," traditionally gay sections of San Francisco, frequented gay bars, marched in gay pride parades, and was friends with Harvey Milk, a prominent gay politician who has, since the events in question, been tragically assassinated. Sipple is proud of his sexual orientation and, if confronted by others, would not deny his orientation.

Nevertheless, believing that the articles publicly disclosed his private information, on September 30, 1975, Sipple promptly filed suit against the Chronicle Publishing Company, other newspapers that had published his sexuality, and entities and individuals related to the various newspapers. In principal part, the complaint alleges that the defendants published private facts about plaintiff's life – that he was gay – without his permission or consent. As a result, Sipple's parents, brothers, and sisters learned that he was gay for the first time and subsequently abandoned him, subjecting him to contempt, ridicule, mental anguish, and humiliation.

The out-of-state defendants successfully quashed the service of process against them for lack of personal jurisdiction, which was upheld on appeal.

Plaintiff Sipple and the remaining California defendants conducted discovery, including depositions of Sipple, two *Sentinel* reporters, and *Chronicle* writer Caen. Based on this evidence, the California defendants renewed their prior motions for summary judgment arguing that Sipple's invasion of privacy claim based on public disclosure of private facts must be dismissed as a matter of law because: (1) the information disclosed in the articles – Sipple's gay sexual orientation – was already public; and (2) in any event, the information was newsworthy. The trial court granted the motions and Sipple appealed.

On appeal, Sipple argues that sufficient facts exist to satisfy all of the elements of the tort of invasion of privacy for public disclosure of private facts and that, contrary to established law, the trial court erroneously and narrowly interpreted the elements of the tort. Sipple requests that the order of summary judgment in favor of the defendants be reversed and the case remanded for trial.

The tort of public disclosure of private facts is a well-established part of the common law and one of several torts designed to provide privacy protections across a variety of contexts. The tort includes four elements: (1) the disclosure must be "public"; (2) the disclosed facts must be private ones, not previously shared with the public at large; (3) the publication must be offensive to a reasonable person; and (4) the information must not be newsworthy or concerning a matter of legitimate public concern. RESTATEMENT (SECOND) OF TORTS § 652 A (Am. Law Inst. 1977). While each element must be satisfied, courts should not assess whether there has been an actionable privacy invasion in a vacuum. Context is critical, and the tort nimble. A contextual analysis of whether these four elements are satisfied requires the factfinder to assess how the disclosure impacted or harmed the individual plaintiff in the context of their everyday life.

For instance, while the tort requires the disclosure of private facts to be a *public* disclosure, and will often involve disclosures to the public at large, sometimes even more circumscribed disclosures may be actionable. In certain instances, limited disclosures can be just as devastating. This is particularly true if the disclosure is to a person or people with the ability to materially affect the plaintiff's life and livelihood. For example, disclosure of a stigmatized characteristic, such as the fact that one has AIDS to a potential employer, can subject an individual to employment discrimination and lost career opportunities even though the disclosure was publicized to a more limited degree. Similarly, disclosure to a landlord of the fact that one has exercised their right to reproductive choice and had an abortion, could negatively impact someone's ability to find affordable housing. RESTATEMENT (SECOND) OF TORTS § 652D cmt. h (Am. Law Inst. 1977) (noting that an actionable privacy violation is more likely to be found where "harm ... will be done to [the plaintiff] by the exposure"). And, of course, given widespread misunderstanding and social antipathy toward lesbian, gay, bisexual, and transgender people, disclosures of one's minority sexual orientation or gender identity may likewise subject someone to discrimination in a variety of contexts.

The unassailability of the premise that even limited disclosures of certain information can exact devastating consequences is evident from the fact that some of the most (unjustly) reviled characteristics in our society (gay sexual orientation, living with AIDS, and exercising reproductive choice, for example) lack explicit anti-discrimination protections in many contexts. In this way, privacy over those characteristics serves an important liminal or transitional right until such time as anti-discrimination protections are achieved. *Cf.* Griswold v. Connecticut, 381 U.S. 479 (1965) (advancing sex equality goals by protecting right to privacy over decision to use contraception).

More to the point, people who are not public figures – not politicians or celebrities – are less likely to have information about them disclosed broadly (for example, in a newspaper or magazine) in the first instance, for the simple reason that the information is of little interest to the general public. Therefore, if the public disclosure tort is going to apply to those other than the rich and famous, it must extend, in certain situations, to more limited disclosures. And to the extent people from marginalized communities are less able to absorb the social costs that come with unwanted disclosure of stigmatized information, the limited disclosures that are more likely to pertain to the non-privileged must be protected.

In short, the disclosure of sensitive information within limited confines may, as discussed above, be no less damaging than widespread disclosure, particularly to members of marginalized communities. Therefore, to state a claim, the public disclosure tort does not necessarily require that the disclosure be made to the world at large. Consistent with the tort's sensitivity to social context, and depending on the nature of the information at issue, a narrower, more limited disclosure may be actionable.

Bearing in mind the contextually sensitive contours of the tort, we now analyze whether each of the tort's elements is satisfied in this case.

First, as just described, while in certain instances limited disclosure may be actionable, here, given that the defendants widely published Sipple's gay sexual orientation in their periodicals, the public disclosure requirement is easily satisfied.

Second, the facts disclosed must, in fact, be private facts, and not ones that have already been shared with the public at large. Cox Broad. Corp. v. Cohn,

420 U.S. 469, 491–95 (1975) (consistent with the First Amendment's protections for freedom of the press, no tort liability for publishing information already contained in public records). Critically, in order to be deemed "private" information subject to the tort's protection, the information need not have been kept completely secret by the plaintiff beforehand. Indeed, on a practical level, complete secrecy is impossible. RESTATEMENT (SECOND) OF TORTS § 652D cmt. c (Am. Law Inst. 1977) ("Complete privacy does not exist in this world except in a desert[]"). In our increasingly connected and mobile world, information about each of us is more readily accessible than ever before. As Samuel Warren and Louis Brandeis recognized when they wrote their foundational article almost a century ago, technological advances, such as "instantaneous photographs," threatened to erode "the sacred precincts of private and domestic life; and numerous mechanical devices threaten to make good the prediction that 'what is whispered in the closet shall be proclaimed from the house-tops.'" Samuel D. Warren & Louis D. Brandeis, *The Right to Privacy*, 4 HARV. L. REV. 193, 195 (1890). If this was true then, it is even truer today, when technology makes it easier to both obtain and then disseminate information. Put differently, we reject the notion that there is a crystal-clear dividing line between what ought to be considered properly "private" and that which is considered within the "public" realm. And certain kinds of information are entitled to privacy protections even if they have been shared "publicly" previously. Public privacy is not a contradiction in terms.

Moreover, and again as acknowledged by Warren and Brandeis, often the most intimate and precious information we have is information about our relationships – information that is never truly secret and that is, at the very least, shared with an intimate partner. *Id.* at 195–96 (expressing concern over the privacy of "domestic life" and "sexual relations"); *id.* at 201 (explaining that the contents of private letters should be protected). The RESTATEMENT (SECOND) OF TORTS also confirms that "[s]exual relations . . . are normally entirely private matters." RESTATEMENT (SECOND) OF TORTS § 652D cmt. b. If we were to impose a requirement of complete secrecy, the public disclosure of private facts tort would, in effect, be rendered a null set, particularly as it pertains to some of the information deemed most sensitive by society – information relating to our personal relations.

Perhaps even more significantly, to require complete secrecy in order to state a public disclosure claim would force anyone with information that may be highly stigmatized deeper into a chamber of secrets. It would compound their alienation and suggest that in order to have any legal protection over the information, the plaintiff must not share the information with anyone. The tort of public disclosure of private facts is not designed to reinforce taboos. It is not intended to lock the door to the closet from the outside.

Rather, to the extent the tort protects privacy over sensitive, intimate information, it gives us each the power to exercise some measure of control over when, to whom, and under what circumstances the information is disclosed. *Cf.* RESTATEMENT (SECOND) OF TORTS § 652D illus. 11 (fact that pregnant individual gives permission to film their caesarian section for exhibition to medical students does not prevent privacy claim if film is shared to broader audiences). And it gives us the opportunity to test the waters and explore our identities with others. In this way, we as individuals (and collectively, as a society), are able to evolve and incubate our personal (and political) identities within the protected confines of limited circles. *Cf.* Talley v. California, 362 U.S. 60, 64 (1960) (observing the important role of privacy in facilitating speech and, in turn, the progress of humanity).

This principle finds support in constitutional law, including the First Amendment's freedom of association. As the Supreme Court held in *NAACP v. Ala. ex rel Patterson*, the freedom of association includes the ability to refuse state-compelled disclosure of an organization's private membership list. 357 U.S. 449, 463–66 (1958). According to the court, "[e]ffective advocacy of both public and private points of view, particularly controversial ones, is undeniably enhanced by group association," and "[i]t is beyond debate that freedom to engage in association for the advancement of beliefs and ideas is an inseparable aspect of the 'liberty' assured by the Due Process Clause." *Id.* at 460. Put differently, there is a "vital relationship between freedom to associate and privacy in one's associations." *Id.* at 462.

If political affiliations – even when shared within certain confines (that is, with the other members of the organization) – are entitled to constitutional protection, then our most personal of affiliations – even when shared within certain confines (that is, with our intimate partners or in spaces developed to cultivate particular identity characteristics) – ought not be foreclosed from similar common law protection. Complete secrecy is not required to state a claim for public disclosure of private facts.

In this case, the defendants argue that because Sipple participated in gay community activities, including by exercising his freedom of association by attending gay bars and supporting gay politicians, he surrendered any right to privacy. Defendants attempt to use Sipple's pride in his identity against him. In essence, the defendants argue that by embracing his gay identity within certain contexts, everyone had the right to know and publicize that identity to the public. As the defendants would have it, to live as gay (that is, to be gay) is to permit anyone the right to know that information. If accepted, this would force gay people (and others with socially stigmatized characteristics) to choose between life in the closet or potentially having the stigmatized component of their identity broadcast nationwide. That is no right to privacy at all. Instead, it is a catch-22 that leaves a person either imprisoned in self-doubt or publicly shamed. As outlined above, the right to privacy entitles us each some measure of control over our most intimate information and gives us each the reins to decide, for ourselves, who is entitled to that information. The fact that Oliver Sipple refused to deny his identity does not erase his right to privacy. *See* Briscoe v. Reader's Digest Ass'n, 483 P.2d 34, 37 (Cal. 1971) ("The claim is not so much one of total secrecy as it is of the right to *define* one's circle of intimacy – to choose who shall see beneath the quotidian mask. Loss of control over which 'face' one puts on may result in literal loss of self-identity, and is humiliating beneath the gaze of those whose curiosity treats a human being as an object") (citations omitted). He was entitled to embrace and explore that identity – which directly pertains to his intimate, sexual life – with kindred associates and even to advocate for gay rights without trading his right to determine when and where to disclose that identity to those who may be hostile (in this instance, heartbreakingly, his family). *Cf.* Gay Lib v. Univ. of Mo., 558 F.2d 848, 854–55 (8th Cir. 1977) (protecting right of gay students to associate and organize under the First Amendment).

Third, the publication of the subject matter must be one that would be offensive to a reasonable person. Importantly, it is the unauthorized disclosure that must offend, and there is no requirement that the plaintiff ought to be embarrassed or ashamed by the information at issue. The offensiveness requirement is not intended to reinforce societal stigma, but instead is intended to evaluate whether a reasonable person would object to an unauthorized disclosure of the information at issue. Here, there can be little doubt – and defendants do not seriously contest – that disclosing someone's gay orientation without their consent after they have intervened heroically to prevent an assassination of the president, would be objectionable to a reasonable person of ordinary sensibilities.

Fourth and finally, the tort is subject to some limitations imposed by the First Amendment's protections for freedom of speech and freedom of press. If the information at issue is newsworthy and a matter of legitimate public concern, then there is no liability for invasion of privacy. Generally, the criteria for determining newsworthiness are (a) the social value of the information, (b) the depth of the intrusion into private matters, and (c) the extent to which the plaintiff voluntarily accepted a position of public notoriety. *Briscoe*, 483 P.2d at 43.

Under established law, even if a person is not generally a public figure (for example, a politician or an actor), but nevertheless becomes involved in a newsworthy event, their identity and involvement with that event may properly constitute "news" subject to public disclosure. But the definition of newsworthiness cannot become a cyclical tautology – something is not newsworthy just because a newspaper publishes it. There are limits to what counts as "news." Even as to voluntary public figures, certain details of their private lives, including their sexual relations, are off limits. RESTATEMENT (SECOND) OF TORTS § 652D cmt. h. And while the newsworthiness exception protects information of "legitimate" public interest, "morbid and sensational prying into private lives for its own sake" is of no social value and no legitimate public concern. *Id.*

This is particularly true for involuntary public figures, such as victims of crimes or those who attempt to stop crimes. Warren & Brandeis, 4 HARV. L. REV. at 215 ("[T]he propriety of publishing the very same facts may depend wholly upon the person concerning whom they are published, no fixed formula can be used to prohibit obnoxious publications"). If, by virtue of being a victim of a crime or helping to stop a crime, a person's entire life became open to public inspection, the victim's injury would be compounded and the would-be heroine would have no incentive to intervene. Instead, people would be discouraged from entering the public square and enriching public life. For example, in reporting on an automobile accident, it may be an invasion of privacy to disclose that the victim is living with a person who is not the victim's spouse. RESTATEMENT (SECOND) OF TORTS § 652D illus. 20; see also *Sidis v. F-R Publ'g Corp.*, 113 F.2d 806, 809 (2d Cir. 1940) ("Revelations may be so intimate and so unwarranted *in view of the victim's position* as to outrage the community's notions of decency") (emphasis added). The person's living situation simply has no relevance or bearing on the reason why they have become, for a limited purpose, "newsworthy" – the automobile accident. To avoid constituting an invasion of privacy, there must be some relationship or relevance connecting the disclosed (allegedly private) fact and the reason the person is in the news in the first instance. *Cf.* RESTATEMENT (SECOND) OF TORTS § 652D cmt. f (explaining that the publicity authorized for involuntary public figures "is not limited to the event that itself arouses the public interest," but includes additional "*reasonable*" facts) (emphasis added).

What is more, just as First Amendment values may be served by limitations on the tort of public disclosure, so, too, are First Amendment values served by the protection of private information. First Amendment values are implicated on both sides of the ledger. First, as noted, informational privacy can serve as a kind of intellectual and identity incubator, permitting people to explore tentatively developed ideas for subsequent sharing within the public sphere. See, e.g., Warren & Brandeis, 4 HARV. L. REV. at 198 ("The common law secures to each individual the right of determining, ordinarily, to what extent [their] thoughts, sentiments, and emotions shall be communicated to others").

Second, the right to privacy secures intellectual space not only for those who attempt to guard their nascent thoughts, but also prevents public discourse from being polluted and crowded with the banal and trivial. As Warren and Brandeis foresaw: "Even gossip apparently harmless, when widely and persistently circulated is potent for evil. It both belittles and perverts. It belittles by inverting the relative importance of things, thus dwarfing the thoughts and aspirations of a people. When personal gossip attains the dignity of print, [it] crowds the space available for matters of real interest to the community … [T]riviality destroys at once robustness of thought and delicacy of feeling." *Id.* at 196. Embracing this principle does not transform the modest public disclosure tort into a potent vehicle for content-based censorship of speech. Instead, it serves merely to recognize the unremarkable proposition that there are compelling First Amendment reasons for permitting limited regulation of privacy-invading speech of non-public figures.

Third, privacy over one's identity or affiliation with a particular social or political group, can help facilitate the freedom of association and help stigmatized groups formulate means of combating social stigma and discrimination. *Cf.* Gay All. of Students v. Matthews, 544 F.2d 162, 164 (4th Cir. 1976) (holding that the First Amendment protects the ability of a gay student organization to mobilize for the purpose of "advocating a liberalization of legal restrictions against the practice of homosexuality"); Gay Students Org. of Univ. of N.H. v. Bonner, 509 F.2d 652, 660 (1st Cir. 1974) (gay student organization's "efforts to organize the homosexual minority, 'educate' the public as to its plight, and obtain for it better treatment from individuals and from the government thus represent but another example of the associational activity unequivocally singled out for protection in the very 'core' of association cases decided by the Supreme Court").

And, finally, efforts to maintain privacy over certain identity characteristics can serve as a form of expressive or performative statement of resistance themselves. Those who take practical – sometimes visible – measures to protect their privacy even while navigating public space communicate a critique of our increasingly transparent society, and offer reimagined ways of being present in public. Therefore, while the First Amendment may necessitate certain limits on common law efforts to protect privacy over newsworthy information, the common law's protection for informational privacy also advances competing First Amendment values. In short, the First Amendment does not in any way vitiate the public disclosure tort.

Nor is the First Amendment the only constitutional provision that influences the substantive contours of the common law. *See* New York Times Co. v. Sullivan, 376 U.S. 254, 265 (1964) (the Constitution applies in "a civil lawsuit between private parties" because in adjudicating the suit, "courts have applied a state rule of law ... [i]t matters not that that law has been applied in a civil action and that it is common law only"). To the extent the common law of torts is judge-made law imbued with state action, other constitutional rights also bear on the reach of tort law. *See, e.g.*, Shelley v. Kraemer, 334 U.S. 1, 19 (1948) (applying Equal Protection clause to the enforcement of a racially restrictive covenant); Lugar v. Edmondson Oil Co., 457 U.S. 922, 940–41 (1982) (applying Due Process Clause to use of prejudgment enforcement in civil lawsuit). As noted above, nonpublic figures are not likely to have their information broadcast widely and, yet, disclosure within limited confines can be no less devastating to their lives. And, as discussed, privacy over marginalized characteristics can serve important equality principles, permitting people to explore their identity within limited confines and develop strategies for combating societal discrimination. If we are to prevent public shaming of certain characteristics from discouraging marginalized groups from participating in public life, there must be space for the public disclosure tort to hold those responsible for "outing" to account. In this way, the public disclosure tort can help prevent the homogenization of public space by giving each individual the ability to control the terms of their own public expression and appearance.

Therefore, constitutional equality principles, as applied to the common law, suggest that the public disclosure tort be interpreted so as to permit privacy over potentially stigmatized characteristics that might be known within limited confines and do not pertain to the reason the involuntary public figure is in the news in the first instance. Put differently, equality principles militate in favor of a contextual approach to the public disclosure tort, one that considers the social values that might be served by privacy protection over the information at issue, taking into account the individual plaintiff's unique social status. Warren & Brandeis, 4 HARV. L. REV. at 215 ("Any rule of liability adopted must have in it an elasticity which shall take account of the varying circumstances of each case").

In this case, while it may properly be considered First Amendment protected "news" for the defendants to have identified Oliver Sipple as the person who intervened to stop the would-be assassin, Sipple's sexual orientation was not "news." Sipple was an involuntary public figure, thrust into limelight as a result of his heroic deeds. Through his heroism, Sipple did not open up his entire life to scrutiny. The societal value of publishing his sexual orientation was minimal. While disclosure of his orientation arguably could have helped place gay people in a positive light and may have helped explain President Ford's initial reluctance to thank Sipple, forced outing is not the method for achieving those objectives. Moreover, as discussed above, the depth of the intrusion here is significant – in today's society, disclosure of one's gay sexual orientation can subject someone to ridicule, discrimination, and even violence. As the facts of this case demonstrate, it can also lead to estrangement from one's family. Finally, Sipple, by attempting to save the president, was not seeking notoriety – he spontaneously reacted to the brandishing of an assassin's gun.

While involuntary public figures, such as Sipple, do surrender certain privacy rights, particularly those pertaining to the underlying "news" event (in this case, the assassination attempt), they do not surrender their privacy over the most intimate of information, including their minority sexual orientation. Nothing in the First Amendment requires that information so attenuated from the relevant news event be protected. And, indeed, several important First Amendment and Equal Protection values – including the ability to explore and develop one's sexual orientation – are served by protecting Sipple's right not to have his gay orientation disclosed.

In short, today we reaffirm that privacy has a place in our society, and a place in our common law. Rather than eroding individual freedoms and public discourse, the right to privacy enhances individual liberty and enriches our social fabric by protecting some of our most marginalized community members. The application of the facts of this case to the law illustrate that the trial court erred in granting judgment to the defendants. The judgment is reversed, and the case is remanded for proceedings consistent with this opinion.

PART IV

Negligence and Vicarious Liability

10

Commentary on *Sharon P. v. Arman, Ltd.*

JESSICA HYNES

INTRODUCTION

In *Sharon P. v. Arman, Ltd.*,[1] the California Supreme Court was called upon to consider a negligence claim brought by a plaintiff who was sexually assaulted at gunpoint in an underground parking garage. At the time *Sharon P.* was decided, third-party criminal attack cases were on the rise.[2] Unlike battery and assault cases brought against individual perpetrators of the sexual assaults, such third-party tort claims are negligence cases and center around an institutional defendant's failure to exercise reasonable care to prevent a rape or violent attack on premises under its control.[3] The rise of such claims in the 1990s was likely attributable not only to the benefit of reaching the deeper pockets of third-party defendants, but also to a shift in cultural attitudes that made it seem appropriate that "private parties should play a role in curtailing sexual assault."[4] Key to the analysis in this special brand of negligence cases is whether the risk of an attack was reasonably foreseeable to the defendant and, in particular, whether there have been prior similar crimes on the premises. In third-party rape and criminal attack cases, the question for courts most often centers on the element of duty, specifically whether owners of premises on which criminal acts occur must exercise reasonable care in a way that makes their property equally safe for men and women.

Despite the rise in the number of third-party criminal attack cases, the legal landscape in California and elsewhere is far from settled. The only thing

[1] Sharon P. v. Arman, Ltd., 989 P.2d 121 (Cal. 1999).

[2] *See* Ellen M. Bublick, *Tort Suits Filed by Rape and Sexual Assault Victims in Civil Courts: Lessons for Courts, Classrooms, and Constituencies*, 59 S.M.U. L. Rev. 55, 61 (2006).

[3] *See* Martha Chamallas, *Gaining Some Perspective in Tort Law: A New Take on Third-Party Criminal Attack Cases*, 14 Lewis & Clark L. Rev. 1351, 1372–80 (2010).

[4] Bublick, *supra* note 2, at 62.

courts seem to agree on is that the question of duty depends to some degree upon whether the criminal assault was reasonably foreseeable. However, in application, this analysis seems entirely dependent upon what particular test of foreseeability the court chooses to apply, a choice which often is driven more by policy judgments than by objective legal theories.[5]

The most liberal approach to duty is the "totality of the circumstances" approach. Courts taking this approach do not require a finding of prior similar crimes but instead look to all of the facts and circumstances of the case, including the nature, condition, and location of the defendant's premises as well as any other factor that bears on foreseeability.[6] This approach has led many courts around the country to impose a duty of reasonable care on landlords for third-party rapes in cases in which there was no proof of prior rapes or sexual assaults on the property. These courts typically look more broadly to all prior criminal activity in the general area as well as considering the location and physical attributes of the property which may "present[] an easy target for criminal activity."[7] Moreover, some courts consider the special risks that unsafe premises conditions pose to women in their analysis of whether a defendant should have foreseen a third-party attack.[8]

Before 1993, California applied the totality of the circumstances test and considered foreseeability "but one factor to be weighed in determining whether a landowner owes a duty in a particular case."[9] The governing precedent held that while proof of prior similar incidents on the premises was helpful, it was not necessary to a finding of duty.[10] In one important case, for example, the application of this more flexible test led the court to hold a defendant hospital

5 As Professor Chamallas notes, decisions regarding whether to impose a duty on landlords to keep tenants safe from third- party criminal attacks may be "framed in abstract, neutral terms," but in fact have a significant impact on victims and the likelihood that their cases will be heard by juries- who may be more likely to consider the facts of the case from the victim's perspective. Chamallas, *supra* note 3, at 1372.

6 *See, e.g.*, Walker v. Aderhold Props., 694 S.E.2d 119, 122 (Ga. App. 2010); Monk v. Temple George Assocs.,869 A.2d 179, 188 (Conn. 2005); L.A.C. v. Ward Parkway Shopping Ctr., 75 S.W.3d 247, 257–59 (Mo. 2002); Posecai v. Wal-Mart Stores, Inc., 752 So.2d 762, 766–67 (La. 1999); Delta Tau Delta v. Johnson, 712 N.E.2d 968, 971–73 (Ind. 1999); Krier v. Safeway Stores, 46, Inc., 943 P.2d 405, 413–15 (Wyo. 1997); Gans v. Parkview Plaza P'ship, 571 N.W.2d 261, 264 (Neb. 1997); *see also* Doe v. Dominion Bank of Wash., N.A., 963 F.2d 1552, 1554 (D.C. Cir. 1992).

7 *Gans*, 571 N.W.2d at 269.

8 *Id.*; *See also* L.A.C., 75 S.W.3d at 257–59.

9 Isaacs v. Huntington Memorial Hospital, 695 P.2d 653, 658 (Cal. 1985).

10 *Id.* at 659.

liable for a third-party attack on a doctor in a hospital parking lot located in a high-crime area with poor lighting and no security guards, despite the lack of evidence of prior crimes occurring in the parking lot.[11]

The court changed its approach in 1993 in *Ann M. v. Pacific Shopping Center*,[12] another third-party rape case. Denying recovery to a woman who had been raped in a photo store in a shopping center, the court adopted a more restrictive balancing approach to duty that balances the cost of additional security measures against the foreseeability of harm.[13] It was this balancing test that the court later applied in *Sharon P.* to deny recovery. As interpreted by the court, the balancing test provides that when the cost of preventing future harm is great (e.g., requires the provision of security guards), a high degree of foreseeability must be proven. Perhaps most importantly, both *Ann M.* and *Sharon P.* instructed that "the requisite degree of foreseeability rarely, if ever, can be proven in the absence of prior similar incidents of violent crime on the landowner's premises."[14]

ORIGINAL OPINION

After a masked assailant surprised her from behind, held her at gunpoint, and forced her into her car where he sexually assaulted her, the plaintiff in *Sharon P.* sued the owner and operator of the parking garage in which she rented space.[15] The trial court entered summary judgment for the defendant and ruled that the attack on the plaintiff was not reasonably foreseeable, relying almost exclusively on the absence of prior similar crimes occurring within the parking garage. The intermediate appellate court reversed and distinguished *Ann M.*, reasoning that "commercial parking structures such as the one here are 'inherently dangerous' and, by their very nature, facilitate the commission of crime and increase its likelihood."[16]

On defendant's petition, the California Supreme Court reversed the court of appeals, emphasizing that a landlord's "duty to take affirmative action to control the wrongful acts of a third party will be imposed only where such conduct can be reasonably anticipated."[17] The court focused almost exclusively on the question of whether the sexual assault on the plaintiff was

[11] *Id.* at 661–62.

[12] Ann M. v. Pacific Plaza Shopping Ctr., 863 P.2d 207 (Cal. 1993)

[13] *Id.* at 214–16; McClung v. Delta Square Ltd. Partnership, 937 S.W.2d 891, 895–96 (Tenn. 1996).

[14] *Ann M.*, 863 P.2d at 215; *Sharon P.*, 989 P.2d at 126.

[15] *Sharon P.*, 989 P.2d at 123.

[16] *Id.* at 124.

[17] *Ann M.*, 863 P.2d at 213.

sufficiently foreseeable so as to impose a duty on defendants to hire security guards, despite the plaintiff's assertion that she was not asking specifically for security guards, but rather only for "[s]imple things like a clean, brightly lit garage, with working security cameras, and periodic walk throughs [by existing personnel] [which] all give the appearance that someone cares about this garage and sends a message to any potential criminal to go elsewhere."[18] However, the court's focus on the provision of security guards led it to apply the "high degree of foreseeability" standard, which the plaintiff could not meet, given the absence of similar sexual assaults on the property in the previous ten years. The court was unpersuaded by evidence of prior robberies that had occurred at the bank adjacent to the parking garage, as well as the statistical evidence of a high crime rate in the surrounding fifty-block area. It concluded that such events were not sufficiently similar to violent, sexual attacks to make the plaintiff's rape foreseeable.[19]

The court further rejected the appellate court's decision to treat underground parking structures differently from other premises because "rapists and robbers are more likely to lie in wait in underground parking structures than elsewhere."[20] Instead, it weighed the social and economic costs of requiring landlords to provide increased security against the benefit of the measures that the court deemed to be of questionable effectiveness in protecting patrons against violent assaults. It expressed the view that many businesses, such as parking garages, "are economically viable precisely because they do not require any on-site labor."[21] In striking this balance, the court chose to prioritize "the economic interests of shopkeepers and other business entities" over "the safety and compensation interests of local consumers and residents."[22] Concerned that landlords not become "insurers of public safety," the court concluded that "absent any prior similar incidents or other indications of a reasonably foreseeable risk of violent criminal assaults in [the garage], we cannot conclude defendants were required to secure the area against such crime."[23]

[18] *Sharon P.*, 989 P.2d at 125.

[19] *Id.* at 127.

[20] The court was unpersuaded by the plaintiff's reliance on a footnote in the *Ann M.* case in which the court commented: "Ann M. offered no evidence to show that, like a parking garage or all-night convenience store, a retail store located in a shopping center creates 'an especial temptation and opportunity for criminal misconduct.'" *Id.* at 127.

[21] *Id.* at 129.

[22] Chamallas, *supra* note 3, at 1392.

[23] *Sharon P.*, 989 P.2d at 133.

THE FEMINIST JUDGMENT

Writing as Justice Bitton, Professor Yifat Bitton delivers a majority opinion affirming the appellate court and remanding the case to the trial court, with directions to send the case to the jury to determine the issues of breach of duty and causation. Central to the feminist judgment is Bitton's decision to apply the totality of circumstances test of foreseeability, rather than the balancing test applied in the original opinion.

As noted earlier, the original opinion had framed the question as whether the landowner had a duty to provide security guards within the garage and had required the plaintiff to establish a "high degree of foreseeability" of violent crime, which rarely if ever could be met absent proof of prior similar incidents of violent crime on the property. Prior to *Sharon P.*, feminist scholars had argued that such a "site-specific, prior incidents" requirement reflects tort law's implicit male bias because it adopts a male perspective that rape is only foreseeable if a rape has already occurred in that exact location.[24] Leslie Bender, for example, claimed that in order to adopt a world view that rape is not reasonably foreseeable in circumstances such as those present in *Sharon P.*, "the viewer would have to be someone who does not think or worry about the possibility of rape on a regular basis ... [and] would also have to be ignorant of all the literature and reporting about the pervasiveness of rape, while buying into culturally based rape myths."[25]

The feminist judgment starts from the proposition that the foreseeability test, as applied by the original opinion, is based on what is foreseeable to men as judged by male experiences. Bitton appreciates that it is plausible that men, who live their lives free from the constant fear of sexual violence, would not foresee the dangers of a rape occurring in a poorly lit, run-down, deserted underground parking garage. She explains, however, that a finding that rape is not foreseeable in such situations ignores the systemic vulnerability of women and allows tort law to ignore and devalue the real-life experiences of women.

In her feminist opinion, Bitton reframes and simplifies the foreseeability question asking "whether a sexual assault by a third party in the tenant garage was sufficiently foreseeable to support a requirement that defendants take reasonable measures to secure that area against such crime." Rather than focusing only on the provision of security guards, she considers the plaintiff's request for less burdensome precautions that could have prevented the assault.

[24] *See* Leslie Bender, *Is Tort Law Male?: Foreseeability Analysis and Property Managers' Liability for Third Party Rapes of Residents*, 69 CHI.-KENT L. REV. 313 (1993).

[25] *Id.* at 319.

Her broader and more flexible legal test is designed to be more inclusive of female perspectives and to spread the collective responsibility to prevent rape among the members of society in the best position to avoid it, rather than burdening women with the entire responsibility of avoiding rape. Bitton justifies imposing a duty in *Sharon P.* by emphasizing the relatively moderate precautions at stake in the case and citing dicta from *Ann M.* to the effect that: "[I]n cases where the burden of preventing future harm is great, a high degree of foreseeability may be required. On the other hand, in cases where there are strong policy reasons for preventing the harm, or the harm can be prevented by simple means, a lesser degree of foreseeability may be required."[26]

Applying a broader conception of foreseeability, Bitton is able to ground the foreseeability inquiry in women's experiences, a classically feminist perspective. Her opinion is guided by "fundamental observations about rape," including the prevalence of rape and the ubiquitous fear of rape and its deleterious impact on women's autonomy. For Bitton, "[w]hether rape is reasonably foreseeable thus must be based on the experiences of all members of society – women and men alike." By considering the gender implications of the facially neutral legal concept of foreseeability, Bitton implicitly asks "the woman question," "placing women at the center of the inquiry, even when the rule or practice in question appears to have little to do with gender."[27] The feminist opinion concludes that rape is objectively foreseeable to women, instilling them with a persistent "female fear" and rendering them "systemic victims." Its reliance on empirical data and sociological scholarship concerning the prevalence of rape and its impact on women's lives marks it as feminist and sets it apart from the original opinion

Before finally concluding that a duty of care is owed to the plaintiff, Bitton weighs four policy factors which must be considered along with foreseeability: moral blame; availability, cost, and prevalence of insurance; the policy of preventing future harm; and the extent of the burden on the defendant. In each of these factors, the feminist judgment spreads the responsibility for preventing rape among all citizens, placing a particular duty upon those in society who, like commercial landlords, have the greatest knowledge of the risk as well as the greatest ability to protect against such harms by spreading the cost among those with whom they do business. Bitton regards it as in the public interest to recognize a duty in tort law to protect women against violent sexual assaults in situations such as that present in the instant case to ensure that "women are not the sole bearers of the burden of the fear of sexual

[26] *Ann M.*, 863 P.2d at 215.

[27] Martha Chamallas, Introduction to Feminist Legal Theory 8 (3d ed. 2013).

assaults, the main targets of rape, nor the subjects of a de facto 'first free rape' regime as a result of a narrow and inaccurate judicial conception of foreseeability."

IMPLICATIONS

In the years since the *Sharon P.* case was decided, its impact on California law has been clear: it has given rise to a decidedly androcentric interpretation of the foreseeability requirement in landowner liability, solidly grounded in male norms. Cases decided after *Sharon P.* continue to apply the site-specific notice of prior criminal activities requirement, rarely finding enough similarity between prior crimes and the plaintiff's rape or other violent assault to impose a duty on landlords.[28] Lower courts have been convinced to impose a duty and declare that the rape is foreseeable only when several very similar, violent assaults have previously occurred on the defendant's premises.[29] Moreover, not a single case appears to take into consideration the prevalence of rape or the impact that fear of rape has on women's lives or autonomy.

If the court had adopted the feminist judgment, viewing foreseeability of rape from the eyes of a reasonable woman, landowner liability to victims of third-party rape would have been expanded and it is likely that landowners would have conformed their behavior to that standard. As Sarah Swan persuasively argues, "third party decisions regarding safeguards, security protocols, and procedural responses when sexual harms do occur affect whether sexual harms continue to happen."[30] Increasing third-party liability incentivizes landowners to take reasonable precautions and sends a message that the safety and security of women will not be subordinated to the economic interests of business owners.[31] Bitton's feminist opinion sought to spread the responsibility for rape prevention to all members and institutions in our society and required property owners to make their premises equally safe for men and women. Adopting such an approach would be no small matter for women or for tort law. As Martha Chamallas has explained, "[i]ncluding gender-related injuries

[28] *See, e.g.*, Vasquez v. Residential Investments, Inc., 12 Cal. Rptr. 3d 846 (2013).

[29] *See, e.g.*, Tan v. Arnel Mgmt. Co., 88 Cal. Rptr. 3d 754 (2009).

[30] Sarah Swan, *Triangulating Rape*, 37 N.Y.U. Rev. L. & Soc. Change 403, 407 (2013).

[31] As Swan notes, "Compensation as a remedy has multiple expressive and practical functions and benefits. It 'constitutes recognition of the violation of the victim's bodily autonomy and dignity,' compensates for 'tangible and intangible harms,' and 'serves punitive and deterrence purposes.'" *Id.* at 428, citing, Elizabeth Adjin-Tettey, *Protecting the Dignity and Autonomy of Women: Rethinking the Place of Constructive Consent in the Tort of Sexual Battery*, 39 U.B.C. L. Rev. 3, 8 (2006).

in the calculus of due care is important because it begins to counter some of the gender bias in one of the basic elements of negligence law."[32]

One limitation of Bitton's feminist judgment, however, is its narrow holding that leaves open the possibility that courts will continue to apply tests of foreseeability that allow male bias to disguise itself as neutrality. Although Bitton adopts the totality of circumstances test for cases in which the harm "arguably could have been prevented by simple means," her opinion retains the balancing test requiring a "high degree of foreseeability" for cases in which more than simple measures are at issue. *Ann M.*'s more restrictive balancing approach to duty reflects a policy judgment that random acts of violent crime are endemic and unforeseeable, and that institutional actors should not be held liable for rape and sexual assaults unless prevention efforts are simple and low cost.[33] The history of third-party rape litigation demonstrates that courts applying the more restrictive approach often ignore significant indicators of danger and are extremely reluctant to impose duty absent evidence of nearly identical crimes on the property. To accomplish the ambitious objectives of the feminist judgment, it would have been better to simply overrule *Ann M.* and return to the totality of circumstances test for all future cases. Additionally, in my view, there is not sufficient reason to limit the feminist ruling to situations in which the plaintiff and defendant share a contractual, landlord–tenant relationship. Such a limitation does not protect guests or general members of the public, whose rapes may be equally foreseeable, depending upon the type of property and circumstances of the case.

In this respect, the feminist judgment missed an opportunity to construct a more progressive tort doctrine that would provide greater protection to sexual assault victims. The *Restatement (Third)*, for instance, has recently criticized courts' reliance on foreseeability as grounds for determining duty in physical harm cases and has instead created a default duty of reasonable care in most cases of misfeasance and nonfeasance, including third-party criminal attack cases.[34] While it is unclear whether courts will be willing to adopt the default duty rule proposed by the *Restatement*, at the very least, a clear requirement that courts consider the totality of circumstances in all third-party liability cases would have the benefit of sending more cases to the jury and permitting juries to enact a measure of gender equity.

[32] Martha Chamallas, *Feminist Legal Theory and Tort Law* in Research Handbook on Feminist Jurisprudence 399 (Robin West & Cynthia Grant Bowman, eds. 2019).

[33] *See* Chamallas, *supra* note 3, at 1378–79.

[34] Restatement (Third) of Torts § 7(a) (Am. Law Inst. 2012). *See also* Chamallas, *supra* note 3, at 1379–80.

SHARON P. v. ARMAN, LTD., 989 P.2D 121 (CAL. 1999)

JUSTICE YIFAT BITTON DELIVERED THE OPINION OF THE COURT

In this case, an unknown assailant sexually assaulted plaintiff at gunpoint in a commercial parking garage owned and operated by defendants. The question before us is whether and to what extent defendants owed a duty of care to their tenants to provide security measures in the garage. For purposes of our analysis today, we distinguish this question of duty, a question of law for the court, from the questions of whether the defendants breached their duty, and whether their breach was a proximate cause of the plaintiff's injury, elements to be left to the jury to answer.

In *Ann M. v. Pacific Plaza Shopping Center*, 863 P.2d 207 (Cal. 1993), we discussed the scope of a commercial landlord's duty of care and affirmed that it includes the taking of "reasonable steps to secure common areas against foreseeable criminal acts of third parties that are likely to occur in the absence of such precautionary measures." Our conclusion in the case before us is that the defendants, as landlords, owe the tenant plaintiff a duty to take reasonable measures to secure areas under the landlord's control against foreseeable criminal acts of third parties, including sexual assault. We therefore affirm the judgment of the court of appeals and remand the matter to the trial court, with directions to send the case to the jury to determine the issues of the breach of that duty and causation.

I BACKGROUND

A *Facts and Procedure*

Plaintiff Sharon P. conducted an accounting business in a Los Angeles office building. She paid a monthly fee to park in an assigned space in the underground parking garage reserved for tenants of the office building. On Thursday, April 8, 1993, at approximately 11:00 AM, plaintiff parked in her assigned space. As she was preparing to leave her car, an assailant wearing a ski mask approached her from behind. He held a gun to her head and forced her back into her car, where he sexually assaulted her.

Plaintiff sued defendant Arman, Ltd. (Arman), the owner of the premises, and defendant Apcoa, Inc., doing business as Parking Services, Inc. (Apcoa), which provided parking services for Arman. The complaint alleged, among other things, that defendants' failure to provide adequate security for users of the parking garage resulted in the attack upon plaintiff. Plaintiff sought compensatory damages for pain and suffering, severe emotional distress, medical expenses, and loss of income.

Following discovery, defendants moved for summary judgment on the basis that neither of them owed a duty to plaintiff to make the garage more secure, because the attack on her was not reasonably foreseeable. The following evidence was submitted in support of and in opposition to defendants' motion.

Arman purchased the office building and parking garage in 1982. There is a bank on the ground floor of the building. Records indicate that between 1991 and 1994, nine robberies of the bank have occurred, including one armed robbery. A driveway on the east side of the building leads to a one-level subterranean parking garage reserved for building tenants. The tenant garage is approximately 200 feet by 225 feet and contains seventy-nine marked parking stalls. Apcoa's parking attendant operates from a booth at the northwest corner of the visitors' lot, several hundred feet from the driveway entrance to the tenant garage. Both sides presented reports indicating the level of crime in the vicinity. There was no evidence that any sexual assaults had occurred nearby.

Plaintiff submitted a declaration asserting that the overall condition of the tenant garage had deteriorated during the several months preceding her attack. It was not unusual for several lights to be out, which would leave the garage darkened in several places. On the day of her attack, the garage "had several darkened areas that provided vantage points from which someone lying in wait until after the morning influx of tenants could observe a lone woman arriving in her car as easy prey." Several darkened storage areas provided a place to hide. Plaintiff smelled urine at various times as she walked to and from the garage. She never saw defendants' employees monitor or inspect the garage, and in her view, the garage was not clean, well lit, safe, or secure. After the attack, she learned that the security camera in the garage had not been working for several months.

Defendants submitted a declaration from a private security consultant who inspected the garage seventeen months after plaintiff's assault. Although he found the lighting in the garage at that time to be sufficient, because of the lapse of time, his findings are of little value. He conceded in his deposition that underground parking facilities are potential places for criminals to lie in wait, and stated that covered parking structures present a more difficult security problem than surface lots, because of visibility and opportunity problems. Regarding the specific measure of employing a security guard, he believed that posting such guard would pose an unreasonable burden on the defendants because of the garage's small size, the minimal criminal activity in the vicinity, the relatively unobstructed view throughout the garage, and the presence of drivers entering and leaving. He also claimed it would be unreasonable to require the operation of a closed-circuit television and to require someone to monitor and investigate anything that looked suspicious.

The trial court granted the defendants' motions based upon the foreseeability analysis articulated in *Ann M.*, 863 P.2d at 211. The court of appeal reversed by a divided vote. Defendants appeal is before us.

II DISCUSSION

A *Standard of Review*

To prevail in her negligence action, plaintiff must show that defendants owed her a legal duty, that they breached the duty, and that the breach was a proximate or legal cause of her injuries. *Ann M.*, 863 P.2d at 211. Since defendants obtained summary judgment in their favor, "we review the record de novo to determine whether [they have] conclusively negated a necessary element of the plaintiff's case or demonstrated that under no hypothesis is there a material issue of fact that requires the process of trial." *Id.* In so doing, we must draw inferences from the facts in a light most favorable to the plaintiff. *See* Unjian v. Berman, 256 Cal. Rptr. 478, 479 (1989); Hooks v. Southern Cal. Permanente Medical Group, 165 Cal. Rptr. 741, 744 (1980); Hirsch v. Blish, 142 Cal. Rptr. 646, 648 (1977).

B *Guiding Principles Regarding the Duty of Care*

The existence of a duty is a question of law for the court. (Ky. Fried Chicken of Cal., Inc. v. Superior Court, 927 P.2d 1260, 1263 (Cal. 1997) [hereinafter *Kentucky 1*]; *Ann M.*, 863 P.2d at 212. Likewise, "[f]oreseeability, when analyzed to determine the existence or scope of a duty, is a question of law to be decided by the court." *Ann M.*, 6 Cal. 4th at 678. Other questions of foreseeability within negligence law, however, are matters of fact to be answered by the jury. Thus, "[t]he jury considers foreseeability in two more focused, fact-specific settings: likelihood or foreseeability of injury in deciding whether defendant's conduct was negligent in the first place, and whether the negligence was a proximate or legal cause of plaintiff's injury." Brewer v. Teano, 47 Cal. Rptr. 2d 348, 351 (Cal. 1995). The duty-related foreseeability issue in this case is whether a sexual assault by a third party in the tenant garage was sufficiently foreseeable to support a requirement that defendants take reasonable measures to secure that area against such crime.

1 *Ann M.* and Security Guards

By now it is well established that landowners must maintain their premises in a reasonably safe condition (Civ. Code, § 1714), and that in the case of a landlord, the general duty of maintenance includes "the duty to take reasonable steps to secure common areas against *foreseeable* criminal acts of third parties that are likely to occur in the absence of such precautionary measures." (*Ann M.*, 863 P.2d at 212 (emphasis added.) In *Ann M.*, however, we held that, under the facts of that case, the defendant landlord had no duty to post security guards to prevent the risk of a criminal attack, including the risk of rape. It is important, however, to recognize the limits of the *Ann M* ruling.

In *Ann M.*, the plaintiff was raped while working at a photo store in a secluded area of the defendants' shopping center. *Id.* at 209–10. In contrast to the case before us, the court framed the issue as whether there was "a duty to take affirmative action [of posting a security guard] to control the wrongful acts of a third party." *Id.* at 213. Still within this context, *Ann M.* proceeded to declare that in light of the vagueness of the obligation to provide security patrols adequate to deter crime and the significant monetary and social costs entailed, such an obligation would be imposed only in cases in which there is a "high degree of foreseeability" of violent crime by third parties, *id.* at 215, and that such a high degree of foreseeability "rarely, if ever, can be proven in the absence of prior similar incidents of violent crime on the landowner's premises." *Id.*

However, we were careful in *Ann M.* to point out that such a "high degree of foreseeability" is not to be imposed in all cases of criminal attacks or rapes. Instead, "in cases where the burden of preventing future harm is great, a high degree of foreseeability may be required. On the other hand, in cases where there are strong policy reasons for preventing the harm, or the harm can be prevented by simple means, a lesser degree of foreseeability may be required." *Id.* (*quoting* Isaacs v. Huntington Mem'l Hosp., 695 P.2d 653, 658 (Cal. 1985)). The case before us falls into the latter category involving a harm that arguably could have been prevented by simple means.

Unlike *Ann M.*, where the court's scope of liability analysis was tailored to address the landowners' specific duty to provide security guards, the plaintiff in this case does not rest her case on the lack of security guards. In her statement, plaintiff claims she "is not asking for security guards," and contends instead that "[s]imple things like a clean, brightly lit garage, with working security cameras, and periodic walk throughs [by existing personnel], all give the appearance that someone cares about this garage and sends a message to any potential criminal to go elsewhere." Plaintiff has thus pointed to several other less burdensome precautions that could have prevented the assault against her.

Our decision today adheres to the conclusion in *Isaacs v. Huntington Memorial Hospital* that foreseeability of harm ordinarily should be determined upon consideration of "what is reasonable in light of all the circumstances" and that the absence of prior similar incidents of crime does not negate the existence of a duty as such. *Isaacs*, 695 P.2d at 665. Under *Isaacs*, the occurrence of prior similar incidents was deemed "helpful" to determine foreseeability, but "not required to establish it." *Id.* at 661. Given its compelling logic, *Isaacs* has been adopted by other jurisdictions that allow plaintiffs in premises liability cases to base the foreseeability requirement on "an examination of all the circumstances." Daryl J. Lapp & Maria A. Patrizio, *Premises Liability in Massachusetts: The Evolution of Foreseeability*, 29 NEW ENG. L. REV 33, 35 (1994).

2 Relevant Factors for Establishing Duty

As discussed above, foreseeability is a key factor in determining whether a defendant owes a duty to exercise reasonable care. Thus, whether plaintiff's rape was reasonably foreseeable is central to determining whether defendant owed her a duty. However, "[]foreseeability alone is not sufficient to create an independent tort duty ... [The] existence [of a duty] depends upon the foreseeability of the risk and a weighing of policy considerations for and against imposition of liability." Erlich v. Menezes, 981 P.2d 978, 983 (Cal. 1999). These policy considerations include the moral blame attached to the defendant's conduct, the availability, cost, and prevalence of insurance for the risk involved, and the extent of the burden on the defendant. Rowland v. Christian, 443 P.2d 561, 564 (Cal. 1968) (*Rowland*). For the reasons stated below, a weighing of all these relevant factors support a finding of duty in this case.

(a) Foreseeability

The plaintiff argues that her injury was foreseeable, regardless of the absence of prior sexual attacks on the premises. We agree with the plaintiff's central contention that the crime of rape is by its nature a foreseeable harm, even in cases when no prior rapes have occurred. As a general matter, "The mere fact that a particular kind of an accident has not happened before does not ... show that such accident is one which might not reasonably have been anticipated." Weirum v. RKO Gen., 539 P.2d 36, 40 (Cal. 1975). This is because "foreseeability is not to be measured by what is more probable than not but includes whatever is likely enough in the setting of modern life that a reasonably thoughtful [person] would take account of it in guiding practical conduct." Bigbee v. Pacific Tel. & Tel. Co., 665 P.2d 947, 952 (Cal. 1983) (citing Fowler L. Harper & Fleming James, Jr., LAW OF TORTS 1020 (1956)). As will be detailed below, the risk of rape should not be dismissed as unforeseeable both because the risk of rape is pervasive and because women rightfully perceive the risk of being raped as something to take into account in guiding their practical conduct.

We start our analysis with a few fundamental observations about the crime of rape. Although not gender-specific, rape is a gender-related harm for the simple reason that women are much more likely to become the victims of rape than men. Kenneth F. Ferraro, *Women's Fear of Victimization: Shadow of Sexual Assault?*, 75 SOC. F. 667–90 (1996). Indeed, the fear of rape is a ubiquitous feature in women's lives and the risk of rape guides the everyday behavior of women. Describing the 1970s anti-rape movement in the United States, Carol Vance noted that "beyond the actual physical or psychological harm done to victims of sexual violence, the threat of sexual attack served as a powerful reminder of male privilege, constraining women's movement and behavior." CAROL VANCE, PLEASURE & DANGER: EXPLORING FEMALE SEXUALITY 3 (1984). She further argued that "The horrific effects of gender inequality may include not only brute violence, but the internalized control of women's impulses, poisoning desire at its very root with self-doubt and anxiety." *Id.* at 4. Thus, we recognize that women both consciously and subconsciously alter their everyday lives and behavior in ways which are intended to help them avoid the omnipresent threat of sexual assault, of which they are constantly apprehensive.

Affected by the physical and emotional harms of rape, as well as by the fear of rape, women are seriously limited in the exercise of their autonomy. We believe that the public interest mandates taking these life experiences into consideration in establishing a duty of landlords, in order to advance the collective responsibility we share to insure that the risk of rape is diminished in the future. *See* Leslie Bender, *Is Tort Law Male? Foreseeability Analysis and Property Managers' Liability for Third Party Rapes of Residents*, 69 CHI-KENT L. REV. 313, 325–26 (1993) (Bender, *Tort*). A reluctance to allow such policy considerations to affect our assessment of tort duties would only serve to perpetuate the male centeredness of tort law, thereby weakening public confidence in the equal application of the law. See generally, Martha Chamallas, *The Architecture of Bias: Deep Structures in Tort Law*, 146

U. Pa. L. Rev. 463 (1998) (Chamallas, *Architecture*); Lucinda M. Finley, *Tort Reform: An Important Issue for Women*, 2 Buff. Women's. J.L. & Soc. Pol. 10 (1993).

Whether rape is reasonably foreseeable thus must be based on the experiences of all members of society – women and men alike. To be clear, we have no quarrel with the idea that the "reasonable person" standard in negligence law is an objective standard and is not based on the subjective perspective of the victim. However, we are also aware that the reasonable person standard has been misapplied to evaluate reasonableness largely from a male perspective. Leslie Bender, *A Lawyer's Primer on Feminist Theory and Tort*, 38 J. Leg. Educ. 3, 23 (1988); Dolores A. Donovan & Stephanie M. Wildman, *Is the Reasonable Man Obsolete? A Critical Perspective on Self-Defense and Provocation*, 14 Loy. L.A. L. Rev. 435, 436 (1980). To gauge the foreseeability of rape, therefore, we turn to examine women's experiences regarding rape. The reality of the troubling yet inextricable link between women and rape was recently presented by Professor Leslie Bender. Bender, *Tort* at 321–22. Relying on numerous and varied sources, she explains the reality of rape in today's society:

> How foreseeable is rape? Experts estimate that a woman has between a 1 in 5 and a 1 in 8 chance of being raped in her lifetime. Dr. Mary Koss et al.'s study of sexual violence against women determined that 1 in 4 college women will be attacked by a rapist. The Senate Judiciary Committee that year [1990] reported that every hour sixteen women confront rapists and a woman is raped every six minutes. The Bureau of Justice, which uses a very narrow definition of rape, recites the number of reported rapes exceeded one hundred thousand for the first time in 1990. This figure represents a 6.3% increase in rapes in one year, which was nearly three times greater than the yearly increase of 2.2% in 1989. Even if we use the conservative estimate by the Justice Department that almost half of rapes are reported, that still would mean over two hundred thousand rapes a year. Feminist scholars estimate much higher numbers and rates. They would predict between 683,000 and well over two million rapes of women in the U.S. each year, based on studies that reveal that only between 7% to 16% of rapes and attempted rapes are even reported. That means that at least eighty-four percent are never reported and not included in any of the police or government data.

This reality renders rape objectively foreseeable to women. The foreseeability of rape is so dominant in women's lives that it instills in them a persistent fear, urging them to take precautionary measures to protect themselves against the occurrence of a sexual assault. This fear – also known as "female fear" – has been identified in the sociological scholarship. Attempting to describe women's lives and gender-based experiences, sociologists label the dread of being sexually harassed, coerced or raped an "existential fear" that is common to women of different origins, social statuses, and ages. GORDON & RIGER, THE FEMALE FEAR: THE SOCIAL COST OF RAPE (1989); DIANA E. H. RUSSELL, THE POLITICS OF RAPE (1975). Moreover, our society too often compounds the problem by imposing on women alone the responsibility to shield themselves against such dangers. ESTHER MADRIZ, NOTHING BAD HAPPENS TO GOOD GIRLS: FEAR OF CRIME IN WOMEN'S LIVES 1–2 (1997)).

Because women are statistically more likely to be raped and must endure the persistent fear of rape, they may appropriately be regarded as systemic victims, as members of a group who, when they enter tort law, claim compensation for suffering that is typical of the life experiences of their group. Employing the notion of the systemic victim in tort law furthers two goals. First, it affords recognition to harms, affecting a substantial segment of victims, whose injuries have not traditionally been acknowledged by tort law, and, second, it challenges traditional, commonly held beliefs concerning fundamental tort elements such as "duty" and "foreseeability." Systemic victims are people victimized at least twice: first, before the commission of a tort against them, and subsequently, upon the commission of the tort. The first victimization occurs when these victims are placed within a sociopolitical power relationship that constantly threatens to turn them into victims, in part because the society, including the law, does little to prevent or ameliorate the threat of harm faced by their group. The second victimization comes into play when the threat materializes, transforming them from "systematically potential victims" into "realized tort victims." Thus, it may be said that systemic victims ultimately become actual tort victims in part due to their susceptibility and vulnerability to harm.

Determining that rape is not reasonably foreseeable in this case would mean ignoring the systemic vulnerability of women plaintiffs and would allow gender biases to infiltrate tort law, by devaluing women's life experiences and the risks they entail. Patricia Cain, *Feminist Jurisprudence: Grounding the Theories*, 4 BERKELEY WOMEN'S L.J.191 (1989); Martha Chamallas, *Architecture*, at 470–71. Adhering to "the prior similar incidents" test, mentioned before, to establish foreseeability reflects too narrow a concept of foreseeability, one that is oblivious to injuries systemically endured by women and the non-accidental way in which they unfold. Moreover, the disparate impact of the prior similar incidents test on female systemic victims' tort-based rights reveals its false neutrality. Applying such as restriction here would not only make systemic victims more susceptible to gender-related harms, but would perpetuate tort law's blindness to their uniquely vulnerable position.[1]

We stress that our decision today does not undo or substantially alter existing tort doctrine. Rather, we hope that our gender-inclusive application of basic principles will serve to strengthen foreseeability as a doctrine, making it more useful and fairer for all members of society.

To sum up, the logic of foreseeability as ordained by tort law applies here in much the same way as it applies in other premises liability cases, with the important qualification that, for sexual assault cases, where there is no demand for the provision of security guards, there is also no requirement of proof of prior similar criminal incidents. Given the circumstances of this case, we conclude that the risk of rape should have been deemed reasonably foreseeable. To decide otherwise would be to allow "one free rape" for every landowner or business owner, an intolerable interpretation of this state's tort law. *Isaacs*, 695 P.2d at 658; Sharp v. W.H. Moore, 796 P.2d 505, 506 (Idaho 1990).

Before concluding that a duty is owed to the plaintiff, however, we must also weigh additional policy factors, in addition to foreseeability, that are relevant to determining the existence and extent of the duty imposed upon the defendant. We examine four such factors below.

(b) Moral Blame

To be sure, the moral blame factor can be difficult to assess in the absence of a factual record. *See* Randi W. v. Muroc Joint Unified Sch. Dist., 929 P.2d 582, 589 (Cal. 1997). However, this court has previously assigned moral blame, and relied in part on that assessment in finding a duty, in instances where the plaintiffs are powerless or unsophisticated compared to the defendants or where the defendants exercised greater control over the risks at issue. Peterson v. San Francisco Community College Dist., 685 P.2d 1193, 1202 (Cal. 1984) (failure to take intervening action to improve safety of facilities "if established, also indicate[s] that there is moral blame attached to the defendants' failure to take steps to avert the foreseeable harm"). Similar considerations apply here. As commercial owners and operators of the garage, the defendants benefited financially from leasing the garage to tenants and

[1] For critiques of gender bias in tort law, *see* Lucinda Finley, A *Break in the Silence: Including Women's Issues in a Torts Course*, 1 YALE J.L. & FEMINISM 41 (1989); Martha Chamallas with Linda K. Kerber, *Women, Mothers, and the Law of Fright*: A *History*, 88 MICH. L. REV. 814 (1990); Elizabeth Handsley, *Mental Injury Occasioned by Harm to Another: A Feminist Critique*, 14 LAW & INEQ. 391 (1996); Nancy Levit, *Ethereal Torts*, 61 GEO. WASH. L. REV. 136 (1992).

had greater information and control over potential hazards therein than the plaintiff. Thus, this factor weighs in favor of finding a duty.

(c) Availability, Cost, and Prevalence of Insurance

We also reject defendants' argument that a finding of duty here will result in increased insurance costs and tort damages and ultimately impose a burden on consumers and the community. To the contrary, our tort system is designed so that the cost of an injury, instead of amounting to a "needless" and "overwhelming misfortune to the person injured," will instead "be insured by the [defendant] and distributed among the public as a cost of doing business." Escola v. Coca Cola Bottling Co., 150 P.2d 436, 441 (Cal. 1944) (Traynor, J., concurring). Such allocation of costs serves to ensure that those best situated to efficiently prevent such injuries – identified as cheapest cost avoiders – are incentivized to do so. *Id.*; *see generally*, GUIDO CALABRESI, THE COST OF ACCIDENTS: A LEGAL AND ECONOMIC ANALYSIS (1970). In this case, the cheapest cost avoiders are admittedly the defendants, who have the greatest knowledge of the risk and can easily insure against it. This factor weighs in favor of the plaintiff because insurance is available in the course of defendants' business and they are able to allocate the insurance's costs to their tenants, through a relatively marginal addition to the rent.

(d) Policy of Preventing Future Harm

Given women's vulnerable position regarding sexual assaults, and in light of the need to fulfill the public interest in extending a duty of care, we hold that the public interest would be significantly served by recognizing a duty to women under the circumstances hereto specified. As formerly analyzed, public policy mandates that tort law be designed to assure that women are not the sole bearers of the burden of the fear of sexual assaults, the main targets of rape, nor subjects of a de facto "first free rape" regime as a result of a narrow and inaccurate judicial conception of foreseeability.

(e) Extent of the Burden on the Defendant

The final policy factor – which weighs the extent of the burden on the defendant – gives us pause. Because we have concluded that the crime of rape is always foreseeable, we recognize that every landlord is potentially saddled with the responsibility to prevent this serious crime, even in situations in which there have been no prior incidents and it is difficult to predict when or where such a crime may occur. Moreover, we have repeatedly declared that landowners should not be forced to become insurers of public safety and should not be held liable for every crime that occurs on their property, no matter how random. A line must be drawn somewhere, even if the limits of liability are somewhat arbitrary. Therefore, to strike a judicious balance, in which the risk of rape is shared by victims and landowners alike, we limit our ruling today to the situation presented in this case, in which the plaintiff and defendant share a preexisting contractual relationship of landlord and tenant. We leave to future cases the determination of what other relationships or factual circumstances might also warrant the imposition of duty to prevent rape in different contexts.

The tenant–landlord relationship is important because California law has long recognized special duties to customers and other business invitees with respect to risks that occurs on defendants' premises. In *Rowland*, we departed from the English legal tripartite system concerning premises liability and imposed liability based on "ideas of humanistic justice and departure from feudal privileges, with the safety of people becoming the main concern for negligence law, generally perceived, as well as for premises liability." Clearly, imposing a duty in such cases is fair because landowners are more proximate to people whose relation to their land is premised on a commercial contractual obligation. This is the case here, as the plaintiff rented from the defendants an assigned parking space in the subterranean parking garage.

Our cases have also held that, although not determinative, the purpose of plaintiff's presence on the land properly has some bearing upon liability. *Rowland*, 443 P.2d at 568. In the case before us, the plaintiff's status as a business invitee weighs in favor of the imposition of a duty on the landowner. The plaintiff's contractual relationship with the defendants created a classic special relationship, giving rise to a "duty to take affirmative action to control the wrongful acts of third persons which threaten invitees where the occupant has reasonable cause to anticipate such acts and the probability of injury resulting therefrom." Taylor v. Centennial Bowl, Inc., 416 P.2d 793, 797 (Cal. 1966); Ky. Fried Chicken of Cal., Inc. v. Superior Court, 927 P.2d 1260 (Cal. 1997). Although we recognized in *Taylor* that a business proprietor is not an insurer of an invitee's safety, we nevertheless stressed that reasonable care be taken for their safety, and liability exists for injuries resulting from a breach of that duty of reasonable care. 416 P.2d at 797.

In concluding, we emphasize that the imposition of a duty upon defendants carries with it only the duty to exercise reasonable care under the circumstances. Once a defendant takes reasonable precautions, its duty is fulfilled, even if such measures are not adequate to prevent a crime. So "[d]istinguishing between 'reasonable' and 'adequate' security measures … reduces the threat of unlimited landowner liability." Laura DiCola

Kulwicki, A *Landowner's Duty to Guard against Criminal Attack: Foreseeability and the Prior Similar Incidents Rule*, 48 OHIO ST. L.J. 247, 270 (1987). Allowing dilapidated conditions, for instance, may fail to satisfy the reasonable care requirement because such conditions have a tendency to attract criminal activity to the location. The indications of such conditions here were numerous, including the reoccurring smell of urine on the premises, the scarce lighting, the broken surveillance cameras, the lack of walk-throughs, and inadequate upkeep or maintenance. Given that even eighteen months after the crime was committed, the garage was left in almost the same poor condition as prior to the rape, suggests the negligent quality of the defendant's behavior and their disregard of the risk of rapes on their property.

According to plaintiff, defendants were under a "minimal obligation" to keep the tenant garage brightly lit and clean, to hook up a previously installed security camera located over the elevator of the garage, and to require existing personnel to periodically walk through the garage. We agree with the plaintiff that a reasonable jury could conclude that the deteriorated state of the garage under the control of the defendants contributed to the creation of conditions ideal for a rape and therefore increased the ability to foresee such a crime. *Ann M.*, 863 P.2d at 214. This contention is supported by the National Crime Prevention Institute which specifically states that increasing lighting, surveillance, and eliminating obstacles to visibility of dark parking lots acts as a deterrent to crime. National Crime Prevention Institute, Understanding Crime Prevention 3–5 1986. Unlike the open space in *Ann M.*, which could be regarded as hard to control, the case at hand involved an enclosed underground garage that is easier to protect and to be kept in reasonably safe condition.

III CONCLUSION

We conclude that the plaintiff's injury in this case was reasonably foreseeable and that the defendants owed her a duty to exercise reasonable care to maintain their property to prevent or lessen the risk of criminal activity. The case should be remanded for the jury to decide whether the manner in which the defendants operated and maintained the parking garage constituted a breach of the defendants' duty and, if so, whether such breach was the cause in fact and proximate cause of the damages suffered by plaintiff.

11

Commentary on *Broadnax v. Gonzalez*

ELIZABETH KUKURA

INTRODUCTION

Courts have long struggled with questions about the tort concepts of duty and harm in cases alleging medical malpractice that causes a miscarriage or stillbirth. Does the physician owe a duty of care to the pregnant patient to protect her[1] from fetal loss, or is the duty owed only to the fetus? Has the pregnant patient suffered an independent harm when her fetus dies due to malpractice, or is the harm solely to the fetus? If the pregnant patient has been harmed, is her harm purely emotional or is it also physical in nature? If her harm is emotional, what type of "negligent infliction of emotional distress" (NIED) claim is presented – that of a "direct victim" of the physician's negligence, or a derivative claim as a "bystander" who observed harm to the fetus? Overturning long-standing precedent, the New York Court of Appeals in *Broadnax v. Gonzalez*[2] addressed these questions and held that the harm is emotional in nature, and that the physician owes a duty of care to the pregnant patient to protect against this harm.

[1] Like the rewritten opinion, I refer to the default pregnant patient here as female, but it is important to recognize that transgender men are capable of pregnancy and, indeed, are choosing to become pregnant and give birth in growing numbers and visibility. *See* Juno Obedin-Maliver & Harvey J. Makadon, *Transgender Men and Pregnancy*, 9(1):4–8 OBSTETRIC MED. 4, 4 (2016). Feminist theorists and advocates have called for changes in language to reflect the reproductive healthcare experiences of transgender people – including those who become pregnant and give birth. *See, e.g.*, Sally Hines, *The Feminist Frontier: On Trans and Feminism*, 28(2) J. GENDER STUD. 145, 145–57 (2017); S.E. Smith, *Women Are Not the Only Ones Who Get Abortions*, REWIRE (Mar. 1, 2019), https://rewire.news/article/2019/03/01/women-are-not-the-only-ones-who-get-abortions/. It may not be long before the courts confront a transman who has suffered a pregnancy loss due to provider negligence and must apply an appropriate duty and harm framework to a male plaintiff.

[2] 809 N.E.2d 645 (N.Y. 2004).

How courts answer these questions determines whether patients who suffer pregnancy loss due to medical malpractice will have viable tort claims. Only one state high court has unequivocally characterized the patient's harm as a physical injury to her, reasoning that the fetus is a part of her body.[3] Under this view, a negligently caused pregnancy loss presents a straightforward medical malpractice claim, where the doctor owes a duty to the patient and the plaintiff can recover for emotional distress flowing from her physical harm. Other courts assume, without analysis, that the patient's harm is purely emotional in nature and thus analyze the claims under NIED doctrine. Most of these courts have concluded that the pregnant patient has a valid NIED claim as a "direct victim" and that the physician owes her a duty of care arising out of their doctor–patient relationship.[4]

A notable exception to this trend was *Tebbutt v. Virostek*,[5] in which the New York Court of Appeals, that state's highest court, held in 1985 that a pregnant patient whose fetus dies due to malpractice has an emotional distress claim only as a "bystander" to the fetus, unless she can prove that she suffered a physical injury independent and distinct from the fetal harm. In this case, Marta Tebbutt's doctor negligently failed to use ultrasound guidance when inserting an amniocentesis needle into her abdomen to sample amniotic fluid and assess the health of her fetus, ultimately causing fetal injuries that resulted in a stillbirth. Under New York law, a "bystander" can recover for emotional distress only by proving that the bystander was in the zone of physical danger from the tortious conduct and was contemporaneously aware of the risk. The *Tebbutt* court reasoned that Marta Tebbutt did not meet these requirements because she was anaesthetized and unaware during the amniocentesis procedure. Consequently, her doctor owed her no duty of care.

For nearly twenty years *Tebbutt* blocked women from recovering for emotional harm resulting from negligently caused miscarriages or stillbirths in cases where they had not suffered an independent physical injury. New York law held that a child who was injured *in utero* but survived could sue for malpractice after birth,[6] and a pregnant woman had a cause of action for her own independent physical injuries caused by a negligent provider. But under

[3] Modaber v. Kelley, 348 S.E.2d 233, 237 (Va. 1986).

[4] *See, e.g.*, Burgess v. Superior Court, 831 P.2d 1197 (Cal. 1992); Carey v. Lovett, 622 A.2d 1279 (N.J. 1993).

[5] 483 N.E.2d 1142 (N.Y. 1985).

[6] Woods v. Lancet, 102 N.E.2d 691 (N.Y. 1951).

Tebbutt, when medical negligence caused a miscarriage or stillbirth, there was no mechanism for holding the provider liable.[7]

BROADNAX V. GONZALEZ

In 2004, the New York Court of Appeals overruled *Tebbutt*, holding in *Broadnax v. Gonzalez*[8] that a physician owes a duty of care to his pregnant patient, which entitles her to bring a claim as a "direct victim" for emotional distress resulting from a miscarriage or stillbirth. The fairly brief opinion addressed appeals in two separate malpractice actions brought by women who had experienced negligent medical care resulting in fetal death. In these cases, Karen Broadnax and Debra Ann Fahey each reported to their health-care providers symptoms associated with pregnancy complications, and these symptoms were ignored, misinterpreted, or not taken seriously enough until it was too late. Broadnax suffered a placental abruption that resulted in stillbirth, and Fahey delivered her twins prematurely at eighteen weeks due to an undiagnosed "incompetent cervix,"[9] losing them both shortly after delivery.

In overruling *Tebbutt*, the court focused on the fetus's state of "juridical limbo," noting the unfairness inherent in the fact that medical providers faced liability exposure for *in utero* harm when the fetus survived but not if their malpractice caused fetal demise.[10] The court rejected defendants' position that these pregnancy malpractice cases do not involve the violation of a duty to the pregnant woman, finding instead that "medical malpractice resulting in miscarriage or stillbirth should be construed as a violation of a duty of care to the expectant mother, entitling her to damages for emotional distress."[11] But the court engaged in inverted reasoning, starting with a statement about the physician's duty to the fetus and then extrapolating from this duty to recognize

[7] Other New York case law held that parents do not have a cause of action for wrongful death after miscarriage or stillbirth, which might otherwise have provided an avenue for recovery for women who suffer pregnancy loss due to provider negligence. *See* Endresz v. Friedberg, 248 N.E.2d 901 (N.Y. 1969).

[8] 809 N.E.2d 645 (N.Y. 2004).

[9] Feminist scholars have noted that the diagnosis of "incompetent cervix" suggests that the pregnant woman herself bears fault for having a shortened cervix that cannot on its own sustain the weight of the growing pregnancy, conveying societal judgment about any resulting pregnancy loss. *See, e.g.*, "Infertility," Encyclopedia of Motherhood 565 (Andrea O'Reilly ed. 2010); Madeleine R. Michalik, *The "Incompetent" Cervix and the "Good" Mother* (2019) (master's thesis, ProQuest Number 13865793), available at https://search.proquest.com/openview/545a14b335b7eb47f818354847e617ff/1.pdf?pq-origsite=gscholar&cbl=18750&diss=y.

[10] 809 N.E.2d at 648.

[11] *Id.* at 649.

an additional duty to the pregnant woman. It never identified the basis of any supposed duty to the fetus or justified it as the logical starting place for the analysis. Nor did the court engage in any meaningful analysis of the nature of the harm to the pregnant women; it uncritically accepted the characterization of their experiences as lacking physical harm.

THE FEMINIST JUDGMENT

Broadnax marked a significant turning point in New York law – and in legal theorizing about malpractice toward pregnant patients – and yet the court of appeals missed several opportunities to explain its reasoning and provide a clear legal basis for subsequent analysis of childbirth-related malpractice claims. Professors Eileen Kaufman and Laura Dooley, writing as judges for the majority, seize this opportunity to identify the duty of care clearly and explain why the law should recognize the harms suffered by women in Broadnax and Fahey's position – providing a compelling example of legal reasoning grounded in women's experiences that resists gendered assumptions as a foundation for legal analysis of pregnancy-related claims.

Kaufman and Dooley do not start their analysis with the "juridical limbo" of the fetus. They focus instead on the woman as the patient to whom the doctor owes a duty, directly addressing the patient's experience of receiving negligent care that ultimately precludes her from becoming a parent as intended. With this judicial attention to the woman herself, the authors of the rewritten opinion reach the same legal result as the New York Court of Appeals did in 2004 but do so with stronger reasoning grounded in the lived experiences of pregnant women who suffer a loss. In doing so, the authors reveal how gendered understandings of pregnancy and childbirth had previously distorted judicial analysis of both duty and harm in tort cases involving negligent prenatal care. Ultimately, the rewritten *Broadnax* opinion offers a clearer articulation of the legal principles that apply to malpractice in maternity care, with important implications for the subsequent development of tort law related to pregnancy and broader attempts to recognize fetal personhood in US law and policy.

A *Gender Stereotypes and the Duty Analysis*

The *Tebbutt* court's focus on a duty to the fetus reflects a concept in obstetrics called the two-patient model of care, which has shaped maternity care in the ultrasound era. As new technology enabled physicians to visualize the fetus (and diagnose or treat certain conditions affecting the fetus), some physicians began to understand themselves as treating two separate patients during pregnancy and childbirth.[12] As legal scholar Michelle Oberman observes, the two-patient model of care reflects flawed legal reasoning in that a doctor–patient relationship can only be initiated when the patient seeks care, and there is no mechanism for a fetus to initiate such a treatment relationship with a physician.[13] Rather, the pregnant woman is responsible for seeking medical care to benefit herself and the fetus, which appropriately places the focus on the woman as the party with whom the physician has a legal relationship.

The authors of the rewritten opinion recognize the centrality of the woman in the duty analysis; their reasoning begins (and ends) with her. She is the patient, she is the one whose symptoms were ignored or disregarded, and she is the one who suffers an injury when malpractice causes a miscarriage or stillbirth. The *Broadnax* dissent characterized the original majority opinion as "redefining the duty of care owed to a pregnant woman,"[14] but this statement reflects a basic misunderstanding of pregnancy, as well as the rights of patients receiving medical care. In fact, the pregnant woman is the patient receiving care from the physician and thus is the one to whom the duty of care flows.

Unlike the actual *Broadnax* decision, the rewritten opinion explains in detail why *Tebbutt*'s duty of care reasoning is flawed. The rewritten opinion begins with discussion of the muddled way New York courts have understood claims brought by women who suffer negligently caused fetal harm, highlighting a confusing incoherence in the case law – where some claims were characterized as involving physical harm accompanied by emotional distress, some involved only emotional harm with the patient deemed a "direct victim," and others were analyzed as only emotional harm experienced by the woman as a bystander. Kaufman and Dooley recognize that *Tebbutt*'s bystander framework is an inappropriate model for evaluating women's emotional damages claims because "women are not bystanders to their own bodies." The ability to recover after a negligently caused pregnancy loss should not depend on whether the woman was under anesthesia or was otherwise aware of the harm at the moment it occurred.

In addition to rejecting the bystander framework for pregnancy malpractice emotional distress claims, the rewritten opinion also rejects the logic of the

[12] *See* Jack A. Pritchard & Paul C. MacDonald, Williams Obstetrics vii (16th ed. 1980) ("Happily, we have entered an era in which the fetus can be rightfully considered and treated as our second patient").

[13] Michelle Oberman, *Mothers and Doctors' Orders: Unmasking the Doctor's Fiduciary Role in Maternal-Fetal Conflicts*, 94 Nw. U. L. Rev. 451, 472 (2000).

[14] *Broadnax*, 809 N.E.2d at 650.

two-patient model of care inherent in *Tebbutt*'s reasoning. Kaufman and Dooley note that in *Tebbutt*, the court "appeared to view the case as one where there were two completely separate patients" – with the fetus suffering direct harm due to physician's malpractice, while the woman suffered only "indirect" distress. By critiquing this conception of pregnancy-related medical care, the authors highlight how perceiving the fetus as a second patient diverts attention away from the woman as patient. In its most extreme form, this artificial distinction between the fetus and the person whose pregnant body is growing and nourishing it can justify medical or legal intervention in the name of fetal well-being even when such actions override or conflict with the wishes, health, and liberty of the pregnant patient.[15]

In addition to revealing flawed legal and medical thinking, recognizing a duty to the fetus also reflects traditional stereotypes about gender and maternity that assume pregnant women are fulfilling their natural function as child bearers, and that an essential quality of being a woman is not satisfied until one has given birth. Feminist writers have criticized patriarchal attitudes about women and childbirth for reducing women to vessels for producing a healthy baby, as if the reproductive function defines women's individual and collective value in society. Contemporary attitudes about childbirth continue to perpetuate these stereotypes, especially in the context of expectations that in order to be a "good" mother, women must be willing to sacrifice their own body, health, and well-being for the sake of their babies. Prioritizing the fetus over the woman – whether legally or socially – can lead to a variety of negative consequences, including inattention to women's postpartum mental and physical health complications, lack of recourse for birth injuries suffered due to provider negligence or mistreatment, and restrictions on abortion and contraception availability.

It is certainly not necessary for courts to weigh in on a physician's duty to the fetus in order to recognize women's injuries that result from malpractice-induced pregnancy loss. In fact, recognizing a legal duty to the fetus in this context is problematic in that it both obscures the nature of the harm suffered by the woman and may invite claims of fetal rights and fetal personhood. The rewritten opinion's silence on a duty to the fetus closes the door to gendered assumptions about maternity and makes its reasoning about the physician's duty to the woman, as well as the analysis of the harm she suffered, stronger and more convincing.

[15] *See, e.g.*, Lynn M. Paltrow & Jeanne Flavin, *Arrests of and Forced Interventions on Pregnant Women in the United States, 1973–2005: Implications for Women's Legal Status and Public Health*, 38 J. HEALTH POL., POL'Y & L. 299 (2013).

B *Harm and the Lived Experience of Pregnant Patients*

The authors of the rewritten *Broadnax* decision reach two important conclusions about harm, both of which reflect the lived experiences of women who suffer negligently caused pregnancy loss. First, Kaufman and Dooley recognize that emotional harm is real harm, and not superficial or less serious simply because it does not leave visible marks on the body. Second, the woman's harm is also physical because it was her body upon which the malpractice was committed. The rewritten opinion recognizes that the woman and the fetus she carries are intertwined: "the fetus is a physical part of the woman's body inextricably connected to and totally dependent on her physical and emotional well-being." This makes the physician's malpractice "fundamentally an injury to her body, and not just an emotional injury." Consequences such as severe bleeding, cramping, nausea, and surgery further confirm the physical nature of the harm. One significant contribution of the feminist rewrite is that it better reflects how many women experience pregnancy and pregnancy loss. One crucial insight of feminist legal theory is that people's lived experiences are central to understanding how the law functions or for advancing a vision of how the law should operate.[16] In this way, lived experience is a source of both knowledge and power for feminist theorizing and advocacy.

When Kaufman and Dooley write that the physician's duty of care "encompasses both the patient's physical and emotional well-being," they recognize the significance of emotional harm as an injury that may accompany physical injury, or may exist independently but be no less serious than physical harm. The opinion's language accords with how people experience health and illness, often with strong connections between physical, emotional, and psychological well-being. Permitting claims for emotional damages in situations like those of Karen Broadnax and Debra Ann Fahey reflects sound legal reasoning not only because such plaintiffs are otherwise left without recourse, but also because recognizing the significance of emotional harm better aligns the law with how real people perceive the adverse impact of negligently provided medical care on both their physical bodies and their psyches.

The second component of the rewritten opinion's harm analysis similarly reflects the reality of how women experience pregnancy and, in particular, the relationship of a woman to the fetus she carries. By reasoning that negligently caused harm to the fetus is a physical injury to the woman, Kaufman and

[16] *See* Patricia A. Cain, *Feminist Legal Scholarship*, 77 IOWA L. REV. 19, 20 (1991).

Dooley acknowledge that the fetus is part of the woman and it makes no sense to consider fetal harms divorced from the body that sustains and nourishes fetal development. Under the two-patient model of care, discussion about physician duties in pregnancy often loses sight of the fundamental interconnectedness of pregnancy. The woman and fetus are intertwined; an action that harms the fetus is an action that is done to the woman's body, and a failure to act that causes fetal harm also involves the woman's body.[17] Accordingly, the rewritten opinion addresses the harm suffered as "relational" in part, noting that the emotional and relational quality of the harm "does not mean that it is not significant – it is among the most genuine harms that can be sustained."

In general, women's harms suffered during childbirth are under-theorized and under-appreciated as a matter of both medicine and law. Due in part to gendered expectations of maternal self-sacrifice, women sometimes find their needs sublimated during childbirth or are deprived of the ability to make decisions about their medical care due to provider coercion or lack of truly informed consent.[18] When women are not listened to or are denied the ability to make informed decisions, their agency and dignity are diminished. Sometimes this results in physical harm, like when a woman reports symptoms that are dismissed and she later suffers an eclamptic seizure due to undetected high blood pressure, and sometimes it results in emotional or psychological harm. In fact, research shows that an increasing number of women report symptoms of post-traumatic stress syndrome after giving birth, and experiencing birth trauma is most closely associated with a woman feeling coerced to accept an unwanted intervention or being denied the ability to make decisions about her care.[19] The law must not overlook women as central to the childbearing enterprise; women are not simply vehicles for ensuring healthy babies.

[17] The failure to diagnose Karen Broadnax's placental abruption meant that she had to undergo major abdominal surgery in the form of a cesarean to remove the stillborn infant. Although cesareans in other circumstances may be lifesaving, in this instance, Broadnax's surgery – made necessary by provider malpractice – required significant physical intrusion in her body and may also be properly understood as a physical injury resulting from provider negligence.

[18] *See* Elizabeth Kukura, *Obstetric Violence*, 106 Geo. L.J. 721, 738–52 (2018) (describing forms of coercion to consent to medical treatment some women experience while giving birth); Eugene R. Declerq, et al., Listening to Mothers III: Report of the Third National U.S. Survey of Women's Childbearing Experiences 21 (2013) (finding that 63 percent of women giving birth for the first time who gave birth by cesarean reported their doctor, not the patient, made the ultimate decision regarding the cesarean).

[19] Cristen Pascucci, *Caught on Video: Improving Birth Breaks Silence on Abuse of Women in Maternity Care*, Improving Birth (Aug. 28, 2014), http://improvingbirth.org/2014/08/vid/; *see also* Jennifer Jamison Griebenow, *Healing the Trauma: Entering Motherhood with Posttraumatic Stress Disorder (PTSD)*, Midwifery Today (Winter 2006), https://midwiferytoday.com/mt-articles/healing-the-trauma/.

Kaufman and Dooley provide a well-reasoned example of what it means for courts to take women's childbirth experiences – and any harms suffered – seriously.

One final contribution the rewritten *Broadnax* makes to the case law on recovery for negligently caused pregnancy loss rests in an observation the authors make about a pre-*Broadnax* trend in New York cases where judges seemed more comfortable allowing negligence claims for emotional distress when a woman's fetus died from an abortion (even when voluntarily sought, as in *Martinez v. Long Island Jewish Hillside Medical Center)*[20] than when a fetus was lost due to provider malpractice that ended a wanted pregnancy. This trend suggests the bias of judicial decision makers who are more easily convinced that abortion involves exceptional emotional harm, worthy of compensation, while other forms of pregnancy loss, including those where the woman wanted to carry to term and become a parent, do not entail emotional harm that rises to a legally cognizable level.

This bias reflects judgment about the moral status of abortion and the presumed emotional state of people who choose abortion – judgment which, even if implicit, exacerbates stigma around a woman's decision to terminate her pregnancy. Such judgment has been incorporated into the US Supreme Court's abortion jurisprudence, most notably in Justice Anthony Kennedy's decision in *Gonzales v. Carhart*, where he echoed anti-abortion arguments that abortion restrictions are necessary to protect women from regret and other harms that may flow from terminating a pregnancy.[21] Feminist legal theorists have criticized Kennedy's reasoning for its paternalism, and for ignoring the possibility of significant harm to women when abortion is restricted.[22] By applying a feminist lens to *Broadnax*, Kaufman and Dooley have identified a tendency among the New York courts to view abortion-related loss more sympathetically than miscarriage or stillbirth, and thus provide a reasoned basis for rejecting judicial biases regarding the circumstances of pregnancy termination or loss.

C Broadnax *Reimagined and the Future of Fetal Rights*

The legal reasoning in *Tebbutt* and in the original *Broadnax* conceiving of the fetus as a separate entity to whom the physician owes an independent duty

[20] 512 N.E.2d 538 (N.Y. 1987).
[21] 550 U.S. 124, 159 (2007).
[22] *See, e.g.*, Maya Manian, *The Irrational Woman: Informed Consent and Abortion Decision-Making*, 16 Duke J. Gender L. & Pol'y 223 (2009).

could bolster claims for fetal rights and personhood. One consequence of enhanced fetal rights is often a more cramped understanding of the autonomy rights of the people carrying those pregnancies. Scholars have observed that recognizing fetal rights enables prosecutors and courts to hold women responsible for the outcomes of their pregnancies in a manner that is both unfair and defies medical evidence that certain pregnancy losses are unavoidable or result from unknown causes. Lawyer and commentator Lynn Paltrow argues that a logical conclusion of recognizing fetal rights claims is that pregnant women have diminished civil and constitutional rights simply by virtue of the fact that they become pregnant.[23]

Indeed, the issue of fetal rights was in the public consciousness when *Broadnax* was decided. In the year leading up to the court of appeal's decision, Congress had been debating the Unborn Victims of Violence Act, which recognizes an embryo or fetus *in utero* as a legal victim if injured during the commission of various federal crimes of violence.[24] Congress ultimately approved this legislation, and it was signed into law on April 1, 2004, the very same day that the court of appeals issued its decision in *Broadnax*.[25]

Because Kaufmann and Dooley's rewritten *Broadnax* opinion focuses solely on harm to the woman and the physician's duty to the woman, it does not implicate the legal recognition of fetal rights. The feminist judgment, grounded firmly in the rights of pregnant women as patients to whom the physician owes a duty, rejects the invitation to engage in legal reasoning that bolsters fetal personhood claims. Rather, it closes the door to enhanced status for the fetus in the legal imagination without denying the very real harm experienced by pregnant women who experience miscarriage or stillbirth due to provider negligence. If the rewritten version of the opinion had been issued in 2004 in the midst of debate about the Unborn Victims of Violence Act, it would have provided a model of legal reasoning that recognizes the tragedy of pregnancy loss – and the very real harms of those who suffer such loss – without endowing the fetus with rights separate from the woman. While a single New York Court of Appeals opinion is unlikely to have stopped the subsequent wave of state legislative action in the name of the fetus, a clear

[23] Lynn M. Paltrow & Jeanne Flavin, *Pregnant, and No Civil Rights*, N.Y. Times (Nov. 7, 2014), https://www.nytimes.com/2014/11/08/opinion/pregnant-and-no-civil-rights.html.

[24] Unborn Victims of Violence Act, Pub. L. 108–212, 18 U.S.C. § 1841, 10 U.S.C. § 919a, et seq. (2004).

[25] In subsequent years, a majority of states have enacted laws penalizing fetal assault or homicide, and the movement to recognize fetal personhood has gained political momentum in several states. *See* ProPublica, *The Personhood Movement*, https://www.propublica.org/article/the-personhood-movement-timeline.

declaration about the centrality of women in pregnancy-related legal analysis would have been welcome to those fighting to articulate a different vision.

BROADNAX *v.* GONZALEZ, 809 N.E.2D 645 (N.Y. 2004)

JUDGES EILEEN KAUFMAN AND LAURA DOOLEY DELIVERED THE OPINION OF THE COURT

This appeal involves two consolidated cases – *Broadnax v. Gonzalez* and *Fahey v. Canino* – that both involve medical malpractice committed on pregnant women that led to the death of their fetuses. These combined cases require us to revisit *Tebbutt v. Virostek*, 483 NE2d 1142 (NY 1985), which held that a woman could not recover damages for emotional distress resulting from medical malpractice that causes a stillbirth or miscarriage, absent some physical injury to her independent of the harm to the fetus. Because *Tebbutt* undervalued and misapprehended the harm, failed to recognize the nature of the duty that a physician owes a pregnant patient, and comported with neither reality nor fundamental fairness, we overrule it. We hold that a pregnant woman is owed a duty of care by her healthcare providers who are providing prenatal and obstetrical delivery care, and that she undoubtedly is physically impacted by medical malpractice in the treatment of her pregnancy that harms her fetus. Consequently, a woman may state a claim against the doctor whose malpractice caused the death of the fetus for all of her harm that proximately flows from the malpractice, including emotional harm connected to the loss of the fetus.

I FACTS

A *Broadnax*

Karen Broadnax, then nine months pregnant, contacted her nurse-midwife at 1:45 AM to report that her water had broken and that she had expelled a large amount of blood. The midwife, defendant Georgia Rose, advised plaintiff and her husband to come to the Westchester Birthing Center. When she arrived at 3 AM, Broadnax experienced vaginal bleeding and she asked Rose whether she should seek immediate treatment at the hospital across the street. The midwife then called defendant Dr. Frederick Gonzalez, the obstetrician supervising Broadnax's care, who advised the midwife to transport his patient to Columbia Presbyterian Hospital in Manhattan. Accompanied by Rose, Broadnax and her husband arrived at the Manhattan hospital at 3:45 AM but Dr. Gonzalez had not yet arrived. Rose did not contact the physician on call. At 4:30 AM, Dr. Gonzalez arrived, examined the plaintiff, and detected fetal heart decelerations. Dr. Gonzalez chose not to perform an immediate emergency cesarean section but instead conducted a vaginal and pelvic examination followed by a sonogram, which failed to detect a fetal heartbeat. Thirty minutes later, at 5:15 AM, Dr. Gonzalez performed a cesarean section, delivering a full-term stillborn girl. An autopsy showed that a placental abruption caused the death of the fetus prior to delivery.

Broadnax and her husband sued for medical malpractice, consisting of the doctor's failure to recognize and properly or promptly treat plaintiff's placental abruption. On the basis of our ruling in *Tebbutt*, the trial court dismissed the claim as a matter of law because Broadnax showed no evidence of having suffered a physical injury distinct from the harm to the fetus.

B *Fahey*

In the second case, Debra Ann Fahey, pregnant with twins, was an obstetrical patient of defendant Dr. Anthony C. Canino and his practice OBGYN Health Care Associates, PC. On October 28, 1999, during a prenatal checkup during her eighteenth week of pregnancy with Dr. Canino's partner, defendant Dr. Patrick F. Ruggiero, Fahey complained of abdominal pains and cramping. Dr. Ruggiero performed an ultrasound and concluded that one twin was pressing against Fahey's sciatic nerve. Two days later, when plaintiff's pain became increasingly intense and was accompanied with nausea, she called Dr. Canino. Relying on Dr. Ruggiero's examination, he told her to lie down and said that the pain was likely connected to her sciatic nerve and the nausea was probably due to something she ate for lunch. Two hours later, while sitting on the toilet, Fahey gave birth to one of the twins. With that twin still connected by the umbilical cord, she was transported by ambulance to the hospital where her second twin was delivered. Both twins died.

Other doctors subsequently diagnosed plaintiff as having an incompetent cervix, a condition that means the cervix is not capable of holding in a pregnancy to full term, causing premature expulsion of the fetus. During a subsequent pregnancy, the other doctors did a procedure to stitch her cervix so that she was able to carry that subsequent pregnancy and to give birth successfully.

Fahey's and her husband's claim of medical malpractice, consisting of the doctor's failure to diagnose and treat plaintiff's cervical condition, was dismissed as a matter of law on the basis of our ruling in *Tebbutt*, on the ground that Fahey did not suffer any independent physical injury.

II OUR DECISION IN *TEBBUTT V. VIROSTEK*

The cases at bar require us to reconsider the approach we set out in *Tebbutt v. Virostek*, another negligence case involving a stillbirth. In *Tebbutt*, Dr. Robert Virostek advised Marta Tebbutt to undergo amniocentesis to ascertain the health of her fetus. Amniocentesis is a procedure that involves extracting amniotic fluid by inserting a needle into and through the abdomen of the pregnant woman, and then into her womb. It is standard procedure for an ultrasound to be conducted when performing an amniocentesis because it reveals the position of the fetus and thus where the needle can safely be inserted without puncturing the fetus. Prior to the performance of the amniocentesis on Tebbutt, the fetal heart monitor indicated that the fetus was viable and normal in size for a sixteen-week gestation. Without performing an ultrasound, Dr. Virostek inserted a syringe into Marta Tebbutt's abdomen approximately four and a half inches below her navel. Because he was unable to extract any fluid, Dr. Virostek reinserted the needle two more times. Each time, the needle was withdrawn without amniotic fluid, but with blood. Dr. Virostek did not inform his patient about his difficulty in extracting the amniotic fluid or of the ominous significance of blood in the needle.

A few weeks later Marta Tebbutt began experiencing severe cramps, pain, and hemorrhaging. Dr. Virostek examined her with a fetal heart monitor, which detected no fetal heartbeat. The next day Tebbutt went to a different hospital, where they took a sonogram which revealed that her baby was dead. The doctors induced labor and delivered a stillborn male 20-week-old fetus. Her husband demanded an autopsy, which revealed three hemorrhagic blisters in the fetal torso, consistent with Dr. Virostek's three clumsy attempts to insert the amniocentesis syringe. The physician who delivered the stillborn fetus opined that there was a probable causal connection between the blisters, the blood extracted during the amniocentesis, and the fetus's demise. *Tebbutt*, 483 N.E.2d at 1144–45.

Marta Tebbutt sued Dr. Virostek for medical malpractice in negligently performing the amniocentesis procedure, causing the death of her fetus. She sought compensation for her "pain, severe disappointment, anxiety, despondency, bitterness, and suffering." *Id.* at 1145. We dismissed that claim, holding that a doctor who negligently performs an amniocentesis on a pregnant woman and thereby kills her unborn child and causes her emotional injury owes her no duty of care. The majority never fully analyzed or explained why the well-established duty of care physicians owe to their patients did not apply to Marta Tebbutt. Instead, the majority ignored the fact that the improper amniocentesis was performed on Marta, and appeared to view the case as one where there were two completely separate patients, the pregnant woman and the fetus, with the latter directly physically harmed by the malpractice, and the other, the woman, physically unscathed but complaining of "indirect" distress due solely to the emotional impact on her of harm to the fetus.

Under this view, the case was placed into the doctrinal framework of claims for "bystander" emotional distress, where plaintiffs who are in the "zone of physical danger" from tortious conduct but are physically uninjured seek compensation for the emotional distress of witnessing serious injury to a close family member. Bovsun v. Sanpieri, 461 N.E.2d 843, 846–50 (N.Y. 1984). The *Tebbutt* majority ruled that Tebbutt could not recover as a bystander, reasoning that she was not within the zone of danger since she was anesthetized and thus unaware at the time of the procedure that any harm had occurred. 483 N.E.2d. at 1143.

The majority opinion sparked two strong dissents. Judge Matthew Jasen criticized the use of the bystander emotional distress framework, noting that "the majority renders the mother a bystander to medical procedures performed upon her own body." *Id.* at 1148 (Jasen, J. dissenting). He reasoned that the case fell squarely within the tort duty that a physician owes to his patient, who was the pregnant woman: "At the time of the commission of the tortious act, there was but one patient to whom defendant owed an absolute duty of care pursuant to a professional relationship: Marta Tebbutt." *Id.* at 1146 (Jasen, J. dissenting).

Given the physician's duty of care, he asserted that the case aligned squarely with numerous precedents that permitted plaintiffs to claim that a defendant's breach of a duty of care owed to them caused emotional distress, including when that distress resulted from pregnancy loss. *See Endresz v. Friedberg*, 248 N.E.2d 901 (N.Y. 1969) (pregnant victim of car crash may sue for any injury which she sustained in her own person, including her suffering as a result of the stillbirth.)

While recognizing the mother's tort claim for her own injuries, *Endresz* did not permit parents to bring a wrongful death claim on behalf of stillborn fetuses. If a child were born alive but injured due to pre-natal negligence, a tort action could be brought for the child's injuries. *Woods v. Lancet*, 102 N.E.2d 691 (N.Y. 1951). Judge Jasen's dissent in *Tebbutt* noted that the combination of the holdings in *Endresz, Woods*, and *Tebbutt* perversely insulated defendants from any liability for tortious acts toward pregnant women that lead to fetal death:

> Denial of recovery for emotional distress creates an anomalous situation, to wit: liability is imposed where defendant's negligence caused mere injury to

> the subsequently born child (*Woods v. Lancet*, 102 N.E.2d 691), while all liability evaporates when the negligence has had fatal effect. This, I submit, is unjust and unwise.
>
> 483 N.E.2d at 1148 (Jasen, J. dissenting)

Judge Judith Kaye also dissented, joining Judge Jasen's criticism of the majority for freeing the physician from all legal responsibility for his fatal negligence. She succinctly reasoned that Marta Tebbutt should have a claim because the defendant owed a duty to a patient in his care, performed the negligent acts on her, and the injury was done to the mother. *Id.* at 1149 (Kaye, J. dissenting).

III ANALYSIS

Broadnax's and Fahey's cases, like *Tebbutt*, require us to revisit the notion of duty in tort law in the specific context of medical malpractice toward a pregnant woman that results in fetal harm. Duty, as an essential element of a tort claim, is a legal concept defined by judges in particular cases and is the threshold issue in establishing liability. We determine whether a duty is owed "by balancing factors, including the reasonable expectations of parties and society generally, the proliferation of claims, the likelihood of unlimited or insurer-like liability, disproportionate risk and reparation allocation, and public policies affecting the expansion or limitation of new channels of liability." *Hamilton v. Beretta U.S.A. Corp.*, 750 N.E.2d 1055, 1060 (N.Y. 2001). We have often noted our reluctance to extend the duty of care, imposing such duty only where the defendant's relationship with the plaintiff "places the defendant in the best position to protect against the risk of harm" and "the specter of limitless liability is not present because the class of potential plaintiffs to whom the duty is owed is circumscribed by the relationship." *Id.* at 1061.

The essence of *Tebbutt* was that a physician owes no duty of care to a pregnant woman patient when the fetus dies *in utero* as a result of the physician's malpractice, in the absence of any physical injury to the woman independent of the injury to the fetus. We now believe our duty analysis in *Tebbutt* was in error for several reasons. We start with the recognition that a doctor's duty of care to patients encompasses both the patient's physical and emotional well-being, and this duty can be violated without causing any direct physical injury to the patient. *See, e.g.*, Perry-Rogers v. Obasaju, 723 N.Y.S.2d 28 (N.Y. App. Div. 2001) (inadvertently implanting embryo into wrong patient caused foreseeable emotional harm due to lost opportunity of experiencing pregnancy); Molien v. Kaiser Hosp. Found., 616 P.2d 813 (Cal. 1980) (claim for emotional distress due to erroneous diagnosis of sexually transmitted disease). Recognizing the doctor–patient relationship as the type of relationship that encompasses a duty to protect a patient from foreseeable mental harm fully comports with the policies expressed in *Hamilton*, 750 N.E.2d 1055. The physician–patient relationship is a fiduciary relationship based on trust and the physician's ethical obligation to prioritize the patient's welfare and overall well-being. *Code of Medical Ethics* Ch. 1.1.1 (Am. Med. Ass'n). Patients reasonably expect that their healthcare providers will meet professional standards to protect their overall well-being, both physical and mental. Unquestionably the doctor is in the best position to protect against the risk of harm. Furthermore, imposing liability when the doctor's malpractice causes harm to the fetus does not invite limitless liability because the duty is circumscribed by the doctor–patient relationship.

A *Direct Victim Analysis*

A primary reason why our duty analysis in *Tebbutt* was erroneous is that it framed Marta Tebbutt's claim as one where her distress resulted not from being a direct victim of the defendant's malpractice, but from being a mere bystander to the harm inflicted on the 18-week-old fetus in her body. Judge Jasen's dissent pointed out the absurdity of considering a woman a mere bystander to a medical procedure performed on her own body. We now hold that pregnant women are not bystanders to their own bodies – they are a wholly embodied patient owed a duty of care by their physician, and they are directly injured when that duty is breached.

To fully understand why the bystander emotional distress lens is not appropriate for claims of emotional distress due to harm to a fetus, we first survey the varying ways that New York courts have characterized pregnant women's claims.

Under New York law, there are three routes by which a plaintiff might recover for emotional distress. First, there is the traditional tort rule that if a defendant's breach of duty to the plaintiff causes the plaintiff physical injury, then the plaintiff may recover for any pain, suffering, and mental anguish that flows from that physical injury. In these cases, the emotional harm is considered derivative of the physical harm, and the cases are not even classified as ones for negligent infliction of emotional distress, even if the physical harm is temporary and slight, and the emotional harm is serious and enduring. Second, if the defendant owes a duty of care to protect the plaintiff from physical harm, and breaches that duty to them with resulting emotional harm, even though unaccompanied by any physical harm, the plaintiff may sue as a direct victim of the defendant's negligence and is entitled to prove that the emotional harm was proximately caused by the negligence even if no physical harm resulted. Battala v. State of New York, 176 N.E.2d 729, 731–32 (N.Y. 1961). Third, if the plaintiff claims emotional injury not from the breach of a duty owed directly to her, but due to the breach of a duty to a close family member, then she may seek compensation for her emotional distress over the family member's injury so long as she was a "bystander" within the zone of physical danger created by the defendant's negligence and contemporaneously experienced the injury to her family member. *Bovsun*, 461 N.E.2d at 850.

New York courts have been inconsistent in how they have used these frameworks to categorize claims brought by pregnant women for emotional distress due to medical malpractice by their doctors that results in harm to their fetuses. Some cases have been treated as involving physical harm to the woman accompanied by emotional distress, whereas others have been analyzed as a case where the woman is a direct victim of a doctor's duty to avoid malpractice that causes only emotional harm, while in other cases courts uncomfortably try to pigeonhole a pregnant woman's claim into the bystander emotional distress category.

In addition to *Tebbutt*, cases in which this court evaluated a woman's claim under the bystander emotional distress doctrinal framework include *Howard v. Lecher*, 366 N.E.2d 64 (N.Y. 1977), and *Vaccaro v. Squibb Corp.*, 418 N.E.2d 809 (N.Y. 1980). *Howard* involved a woman who was at high risk of passing on to her fetus Tay–Sachs disease, a progressive degenerative genetic disorder of the nervous system. She claimed that the doctor negligently never advised her of the risk nor tested her to determine whether her fetus was afflicted. She claimed that she would have chosen to abort if she knew that her child would have this disease. Her daughter was born with Tay–Sachs, and she and her husband claimed emotional distress for watching her suffer and die. The court never considered that the woman's own right of reproductive autonomy, which includes the right to make fully informed choices about whether or not to terminate a pregnancy, was violated by her physician's failure to test and diagnose her condition. Instead, the court saw the case as involving only compensation for the harm done to her child and denied the claim.

In *Vaccaro*, a pregnant woman was prescribed a drug that caused her child to be born with limb deformities and other congenital defects. She brought a medical malpractice and products liability claim for her own physical injuries and for her emotional distress at having a severely deformed child. Ignoring her allegations that the drug caused her dizziness, nausea, vomiting, and nervous system injuries, the court focused solely on her allegations of emotional distress. We held that because she was claiming distress due to harm to another person, her case had to be analyzed under the bystander framework, and we denied her claim because she was not in the zone of danger. The dissent argued that the case should have been analyzed as a straightforward medical malpractice and products liability case involving physical harm to the woman from the drug, with accompanying emotional harm.

However, we have not invariably used the bystander approach in malpractice cases involving childbirth. Thus, in *Martinez v. Long Island Jewish Hillside Medical Center*, 512 N.E.2d 538 (N.Y. 1987), a case with some factual resonances with both *Howard* and *Vaccaro*, we rejected the bystander framework and invoked the direct victim approach. Martinez was taking medication while pregnant, and she sought medical advice from defendants to determine if the drug might affect her fetus. Defendants erroneously told her that the drug would cause severe congenital defects and advised an abortion. Although abortion was against her strongly held religious beliefs, Martinez chose to have one in order to avoid the harm to her child. An examination of the fetal remains after the abortion revealed that the fetus was normal, and thus the abortion was unnecessary. Martinez brought a claim for her emotional distress. We held that her mental anguish was a direct result of defendant's breach of a duty owed directly to her to provide nonnegligent medical advice and diagnosis. We also reasoned that her anguish was due not to the needless death of her fetus, but rather from being led into deviating from her religious beliefs.

Further, in *Ferrara v. Bernstein*, 613 N.E.2d 542 (N.Y. 1993), a case that involved an incomplete abortion and subsequent miscarriage, we allowed the woman's claim for emotional distress because we categorized her as having been directly physically injured by the defendant's negligence in not properly performing the abortion and in not informing her of pathology results that showed she was still pregnant. The plaintiff claimed that if the doctor's office had promptly informed her that the abortion had failed, she would have quickly scheduled another abortion and would not have delayed her follow-up appointment. While awaiting her follow-up appointment, she had severe cramps and bleeding, and miscarried the fetus into a toilet. We listed her physical injuries as pain from cramps, bleeding, and the miscarriage of the fetus after the incomplete abortion. We considered her distress as emanating from her own physical injuries, and not from witnessing the miscarriage, and we held that the doctor breached a duty owed directly to the plaintiff leading to emotional distress.

These conflicting analyses present the disturbing picture that we have been much more likely to permit a woman to bring a negligence claim for emotional distress when her fetus dies from an abortion, even when she voluntarily sought the abortion, than when a woman seeks compensation for malpractice that harms a fetus that she desperately hoped would be born healthy. Yet a woman's right to reproductive health and autonomy is equally harmed regardless of whether malpractice causes death or harm to a wanted fetus, or whether she is erroneously led into having an abortion that she otherwise would not have chosen, or whether an abortion that she did want was negligently performed. In none of these instances is she a bystander to her own body; in each instance her physician owes her a direct duty of care; in each instance her body and her rights have been adversely affected.

It is now clear to us that a woman's claim for emotional distress arising from a doctor's malpractice that causes the death of her fetus is properly analyzed as a direct victim claim for the breach of a duty owed directly to her, and not as a bystander claim. Analytically, it defies the reality of pregnancy to conclude that a pregnant woman being treated by the doctor managing her pregnancy is a mere bystander to her own body. Given that it was Marta Tebbutt's abdomen through which the amniocentesis needle passed, that bystander analysis was inapt. Moreover, the *Tebbutt* court's concern about unduly broadening the scope of liability was cramped and unrealistic. The potential plaintiffs in cases like the ones we confront today are not only physically present at the time of the doctors' negligence, but also enormously invested, both physically and emotionally, in the procedures being performed. In recognition of this reality, we hold that pregnant women may recover directly for medical malpractice during pregnancy that results in the death of or harm to the fetus.

Accordingly, we firmly reject treating the expectant mother as a bystander and instead join those jurisdictions that have properly analyzed the claim as one asserted by a direct victim seeking redress for the breach of a duty owed to her.[1] To conclude, as we did in *Tebbutt*, that a doctor owes no duty to a pregnant woman simply ignores the fact that it is the pregnant woman who is the doctor's patient.

Our holding today is consistent with our holding in *Ferrara*, 613 N.E.2d 542. Although defendants argue that *Ferrara* is distinguishable because here the doctor's malpractice only injured the fetus and not the mother, that view

[1] *See, e.g.*, Johnson v. Superior Court, 177 Cal. Rptr. 63 (Cal.Ct. App.1981); Bourquin v. Melsunger, 1990 WL 290127 at *2 (Conn. Superior Ct. Sept. 4, 1990) ("To infer that a mother is a bystander at the birth of her infant manifests a basic misunderstanding of the duty owed a patient by a physician"); Carey v. Lovett, 622 A.2d 1279 (N.J. 1993); Fortes v. Ramos, 2001 WL 1685601 (R.I. Super. Ct., Dec. 19, 2001) (holding that the mother can recover as a direct victim and that Rhode Island's rule requiring physical symptomatology in order to ensure the genuineness of the claim should not apply).

ignores the fact that the *pregnant woman* is the doctor's patient, and any treatment of her pregnancy has physical effects on her. Acknowledging the duty of care owed by a doctor to his pregnant patient is not controversial and comports with the common understanding of the doctor–patient relationship during pregnancy.

Other jurisdictions that have reached this result persuasively explain that "the obstetrician and the pregnant woman [who] enter into a physician-patient relationship ... understand that the physician owes a duty to the pregnant woman with respect to the medical treatment provided to her fetus," and "[a]ny negligence during delivery which causes injury to the fetus and resultant emotional anguish to the mother, therefore, breaches a duty owed directly to the mother." Burgess v. Superior Court, 831 P.2d 1197, 1203 (Cal. 1992). That court noted that "[d]uring pregnancy the mother and child are a unique physical unit and the welfare of each is intertwined and inseparable." *Id.* at 1206. Thus, "it is ... patently clear that a mother forms a sufficiently close relationship with her fetus during pregnancy so that its stillbirth will foreseeably cause her severe emotional distress. Where the stillbirth results from medical malpractice rather than from natural and unavoidable causes the loss is all the more poignant and should be legally redressable." *Id.* at 1080 (*quoting* Johnson v. Superior Court, 177 Cal. Rptr. 63 (Cal. Ct. App. 1981)).

Moreover, our decision to analyze a pregnant woman's claim as a direct victim claim rather than a bystander claim does not raise any specter of limitless liability. In a complicated world in which careless behavior can have ripple effects infinitely more far-reaching than its immediate consequence, the concept of duty (along with its sister concept of proximate cause, typically decided by juries) provides the courts a vehicle to rein in potentially unlimited liability. Our decision here, however, does not evoke Palsgrafian concerns about tort responsibility run amuck. A pregnant woman whose fetus dies or is harmed *in utero* or during childbirth due to a physician's medical malpractice is not a far-fetched, unforeseeable plaintiff. Indeed, the pregnant woman is the defendant obstetrician's immediate patient throughout her pregnancy and childbirth. It will come as no surprise to any reasonable obstetrician that harm will befall that patient if his or her malpractice results in harm to the fetus. And the fact that the majority of the woman's harm suffered is emotional distress, rather than long-lasting physical injury with pecuniary costs, should not and does not bar recovery. The fact that the harm is primarily emotional and relational does not mean that it is not significant – it is among the most genuine harms that can be sustained. As virtually all parents would no doubt agree, the loss of or serious harm to a child is hardly the sort of fictional, fleeting, or easily feigned type of distress that historically made courts so leery of claims for emotional distress. It evokes the most severe sort of enduring psychic pain one can imagine.

B *Physical Nature of the Harm*

These observations about how physically intertwined and inseparable a pregnant woman is from her fetus lead to a final reason why our duty analysis in *Tebbutt* was erroneous: in characterizing the plaintiff's harm as purely emotional, it misapprehended the physical nature of the injury to a pregnant woman. The fetus and the woman are not two separate beings; the fetus is a physical part of the woman's body inextricably connected to and totally dependent on her physical and emotional well-being. Accordingly, when malpractice is committed in the course of treating her for her pregnancy and related medical conditions, and the malpractice harms the fetus, it is fundamentally an injury to her body, and not just an emotional injury. The physician is treating the woman, and the object of the treatment is to ensure the well-being of both the woman and the fetus. Any treatment intended to ensure the health of the fetus has to be performed on the woman's body, and has inevitable effects on her body, not just on her emotions. Similarly, malpractice that consists of failures to diagnose or treat physical conditions of the woman that threaten the health of the fetus has physical consequences for the woman. While the unique and profound relation between a woman and her unborn child has both emotional and physical dimensions, that does not undermine the fact that harm to the fetus from improper medical treatment of the woman is a physical harm to her. One court expressed it this way: Because the fetus is a physical part of the mother's body until birth, "injury to an unborn child in the womb of the mother is to be considered as physical injury to the mother" and recoverable damages include "the injuries and mental anguish suffered by her as the result of the fetal death occurring while the infant was a part of her." Modaber v. Kelley, 348 S.E.2d 233, 237 (Va. 1986).[2]

The facts in *Tebbutt* and the present cases readily illustrate the ways in which all three pregnant plaintiffs were physically injured. Marta Tebbutt had to be anesthetized, and her abdomen and uterus were penetrated by a large needle. This procedure led directly to intense pain, severe cramps, and profuse hemorrhaging as her body tried to expel the now-dead fetus, and she

[2] Indeed, that court rejected a challenge that the award was excessive, finding that the emotional distress and mental anguish was pronounced and persisted years after the stillbirth. *See Modaber*, 348 S.E.2d at 239.

had to endure an emergency hospitalization and drugs to induce labor. The physician's failure to diagnose and properly treat Debra Fahey's incompetent cervix caused her to experience intense pain and nausea and led to her body expelling a fetus while she was on the toilet, with the fetus still attached to her body by the umbilical cord. She had to endure an emergency ambulance ride to the hospital and an emergency medical procedure. Karen Broadnax had a bodily organ, her placenta, pull away from another organ, her uterus, and defendant's failure promptly to treat this dangerous bodily condition led to extensive bleeding, and major abdominal surgery. All of the women had their previously healthy developing fetuses inside of their bodies die. These consequences of the defendants' malpractice are every bit as much physical injuries to the women as were the similar injuries deemed physical in *Ferrara*. To label these injuries as purely emotional defies reality. Although the physical harms to the woman may be temporary, and may fully heal long before the psychic wounds are repaired, that makes the profound emotional harm no less deserving of compensation.

Cases that allege medical negligence toward a pregnant woman should be treated no differently by tort law than alleged malpractice toward nonpregnant persons. Healthcare providers owe a direct duty of care to their pregnant patient, and they should be responsible for all harms, physical and emotional, that are proximately caused by a breach of their duty. The tortured and inconsistent reasoning of previous decisions that have tried to fit these cases into the procrustean bed of "pure" emotional distress claims has led to serious injustices.

Our holding today takes account of the very real and immense psychic pain visited on a pregnant woman whose fetus dies *in utero* or during delivery, or is born in a severely damaged state, due to the negligence of her treating physician. Recognition of this cause of action acknowledges the physical reality of pregnancy and the all too genuine pain experienced by the pregnant woman.

C *Relationship to Claims of Fetal Rights*

Because some have argued that recognition of tort liability in these circumstances is necessarily linked to the claim that the unborn have a juridical existence, we feel compelled to address that issue and reject it. To recognize that a pregnant woman is harmed and thus has her own cause of action when a physician's malpractice toward her also results in harm to her fetus in no way undermines women's reproductive autonomy, nor does it require entering into the debate about when a fetus should be deemed a legal person.

A woman's right to control her reproductive life, and her constitutional right to terminate her pregnancy pursuant to relevant regulations, is at the heart of the cause of action we recognize today. While seeming on the surface to be at odds, in the reality of women's lived experiences they are wholly consistent. Both the newly recognized tort claim and the right to terminate a pregnancy (along with parallel rights to access to contraception and to reproductive healthcare) honor a woman's right to bodily integrity without interference either by the state or by the negligent conduct of a doctor. The cause of action we embrace today rests on the recognition that the fetus is part of the pregnant woman, and thus injury to the fetus necessarily entails injury to the woman. By recognizing this cause of action, we put the weight of tort law behind a woman's choice to pursue pregnancy and parenthood and enjoy the fullness of those experiences without bearing the cost of negligent conduct on the part of medical professionals.

IV CONCLUSION

Our decision today reflects two parallel and powerful insights emerging from the so-called second wave of feminist thought. The first is the recognition that women's full participation as citizens requires respecting the dignity interest all persons have in controlling decisions affecting their own bodies, decisions that should be made on fully disclosed information. The second is our growing understanding that tort jurisprudence has failed to acknowledge and compensate fully, or sometimes even minimally, harms suffered predominantly by women. See, e.g., Lucinda Finley, *Female Trouble: The Implications of Tort Reform for Women*, 64 TENN. L. REV. 847 (1997). This second problem is especially acute as to matters of pregnancy and childbirth, life events that women alone experience. Finley, *supra*, and Martha Chamallas, *The Architecture of Bias: Deep Structures in Tort Law*, 146 U. PA. L. REV. 463 (1998). The previous failure by courts to account for harm predominantly or exclusively suffered by women undercuts tort policies of compensation and deterrence of careless behavior, and discounts the lived experience of so many women. We have tended to trivialize nonpecuniary, relational harms as too speculative, insubstantial and subjective. See Finley, *supra*, at 851–55. By failing to value genuine, serious and profound losses, we have denied both women and men meaningful access to justice to vindicate significant interests.

Today, we take an important step to correct these inequities. By affording tort recovery for the mental anguish directly suffered by expectant mothers upon the loss of their pregnancy due to negligence on the part of medical providers, we acknowledge women's rights to make reproductive choices in the same way tort law protects the right of all patients to receive medical care free of negligence.

Accordingly, both *Broadnax* and *Fahey* are remanded for further proceedings consistent with this opinion.

12

Commentary on *Boyles v. Kerr*

LISA R. PRUITT

The Texas Supreme Court in *Boyles v. Kerr*[1] rigidly refused to extend the state's negligent infliction of emotional distress (NIED) precedents to permit recovery for a young woman, Susan Kerr, who alleged severe emotional distress when her lover, Dan Boyles, Jr., surreptitiously videotaped the pair having sex and then shared the video with college fraternity brothers, causing Kerr to become the object of derision. But Professor Cristina Tilley, rewriting the case as Justice Tilley, makes clear that the salient doctrines are more than capacious enough to have permitted Kerr's NIED recovery. In fact, the myriad opinions in *Boyles*, as well as their extensive discussion of NIED's history and precedents, reveal a highly malleable claim, the evolution of which reveals clearly gendered themes and trends.

THE *BOYLES V. KERR* LITIGATION

Susan Kerr was 19 years old, and Dan Boyles, Jr. was 17 in 1985 when they went on their first date and began a sexual relationship. Before Kerr and Boyles each went off to different colleges that fall, the two had sex a few more times. The Texas Supreme Court majority's characterization of Boyles and Kerr's relationship rings of judgment, noting that they were "not dating steadily" but "had shared several previous sexual encounters" in the "few months" they had known each other.[2] The majority acknowledges Kerr's testimony "that she had not had sexual intercourse prior to her relationship

[1] 855 S.W.2d 593 (Tex. 1993).
[2] *Id.* at 594.

with Boyles,"[3] though including this fact suggests a vulnerability the court did not elsewhere credit.[4]

One evening in August, Boyles arranged to pick up Kerr and take her to a friend's home where Boyles had plotted with three male friends to set up a hidden video camera in the bedroom. The friends first recorded crude remarks about the anticipated encounter and then left the home with the camera running. Boyles brought Kerr into the room, and the two had sex; she was unaware that the encounter was being taped. Soon after, Boyles started college at the University of Texas, and he showed the sex tape to fraternity brothers there. Word of the tape soon spread among students at the University of Texas and, eventually, also at the college Susan Kerr attended. Kerr became the target of humiliating ridicule and was labeled a "porno queen."[5]

Kerr eventually confronted Boyles, who admitted what he had done and gave her the only copy of the tape. Rumors and public ridicule nevertheless hounded Kerr for months. Kerr claimed that she suffered severe distress, impaired academic performance, and difficulty developing healthy relationships with men. She required psychological counseling and was diagnosed with post-traumatic stress disorder. But the court majority seemed dismissive of her allegations of emotional distress, noting that Kerr "had subsequent sexually-active relationships" after learning of the video and its circulation.[6]

While Justice Tilley's recitation of the facts in her feminist rewritten opinion is not dramatically different from that of the actual majority, she provides additional bits of context that evince more empathy for Kerr. Tilley notes, for example, that one fraternity brother enjoyed the video enough that he "forgave Boyles's repayment of a $20 football bet." Justice Tilley also tells us more about the parties' relationship, including that their first date was their senior prom and that their last "date" was the night the videotape was made. On the latter night, Justice Tilley details that Susan Kerr had invited Dan Boyles to be her date for a wedding, seeking to "spend non-sexual, social time with him ... during which they would presumably talk, dance, and share a

[3] *Id.*

[4] Interestingly, while media commentators and the drafters of Westlaw headnotes referred to Kerr and Boyles as former boyfriend and girlfriend, neither Tilley nor the Texas Supreme Court used that terminology. David Margolick, *Law: At the Bar; For Texas Firm, the Price of Circulating a Videotape Proves Quite Steep*, N.Y. TIMES, June 1, 1990, at B6. Oddly, Margolick also referred to what had transpired between the two as "ma[king] love," attributing a romanticism to the encounter that no one else does, which seems especially inappropriate given the hindsight with which the journalist wrote. *Id.*

[5] *Boyles*, 855 S.W.2d at 594.

[6] *Id.*

meal." Boyles declined the wedding invitation but arranged to pick Kerr up afterwards and take her to his friend's house for "purely sexual purposes." The majority does not reveal such details about Kerr's efforts to establish a meaningful relationship, writing instead simply that Kerr and Boyles "had made plans to go out on the night of the incident."[7] This distinction is salient to Justice Tilley's assertion that Boyles's attitude toward Kerr suggested his failure to see her as fully human, which she argues is highly relevant in relation to his mental state vis-à-vis Kerr's emotional distress. Tilley also shows feminist sensitivity to the reality of women's emotional lives when she notes that Kerr's sexual encounters with other men following Boyles's predatory behavior could show both that she struggled to form healthy intimate relationships, and that she experienced enduring emotional damage.

Kerr initially sued for negligent infliction of emotional distress (NIED) and invasion of privacy, seeking $48 million in damages.[8] Boyles framed the taping as merely "an impromptu, stupid, adolescent mistake,"[9] and his defense team minimized Kerr's emotional damage. Indeed, speaking to the press, they blamed Kerr's trauma on the lawsuit itself, which they said was her father's idea.[10]

Kerr eventually withdrew her cause of action for invasion of privacy, and only the NIED claim went to trial. A jury of seven women and five men awarded Kerr $500,000 in compensatory damages and $500,000 in punitive damages.[11] Among the four defendants, only Boyles appealed. Each of his male confederates either paid his share of the judgment or settled for a lesser amount.

The Texas Court of Appeals upheld the jury's decision in 1991, but in December 1992 by a 6:3 vote the Texas Supreme Court, composed at that time of nine men, overturned it, reversing a recent precedent that had recognized the tort of NIED. The ruling fueled a sense among women's groups that the decision was highly gendered at best, distinctly sexist at worst. Kerr filed a motion for rehearing, and the Women and the Law Section of the Texas State Bar, the Association of Women Attorneys, the Women's Advocacy Project, and the Texas Women's Political Caucus all filed amicus briefs protesting the reversal. The Women and the Law Section of the Texas State Bar argued that the decision had "turned back the clock to a time when the

[7] *Id.*

[8] *Woman Awarded $1 Million in Videotape Case*, United Press Int'l (June 9, 1989), https://www.upi.com/Archives/1989/06/09Woman-awarded-1-million-in-videotape-case/1129613368000

[9] Margolick, *supra* note 4.

[10] *Woman Awarded $1 Million in Videotape Case*, *supra* note 8.

[11] *Id.*

sexual exploitation of unwilling women was socially acceptable, without regard to negligently inflicted emotional distress."[12] More provocatively, the Women and the Law Section alleged that "if the tables had been turned, and Kerr had peddled the videotape as a vignette of Boyles' sexual performance . . . the all-male majority in this case would have reached a decidedly different result."[13]

In response to Kerr's motion for rehearing, the Texas Supreme Court withdrew its prior opinion and issued a superseding opinion in 1993, reiterating its reasons for reversal and responding to the accusations of gender bias lodged in the amicus briefs. The majority opinion called these charges "grave" and "wholly without merit," asserting that its analysis was gender neutral.[14] Concurring Justice Raul A. Gonzalez protested that the "case ha[d] nothing to do with gender-based discrimination or an assault on women's rights."[15]

The majority in that superseding opinion held that "there is no general duty not to negligently inflict emotional distress."[16] Kerr had relied on a then recent Texas Supreme Court decision in *St. Elizabeth Hospital v. Garrard*, which had recognized such a duty, and upheld plaintiff-parents' recovery for negligent infliction of emotional distress after the defendant hospital negligently disposed of the Garrards' stillborn baby without the plaintiffs' knowledge or consent.[17] The *Boyles* majority distanced itself from *St. Elizabeth Hospital*'s reasoning while preserving its result, ruling that "mental anguish damages should be compensated only in connection with defendant's breach of some other duty imposed by law."[18] The result in *St. Elizabeth* could stand, the court reasoned, because tort law had long recognized a duty of care toward surviving family members in handling corpses. The *Boyles* majority rejected the proposition that intimate personal relationships should give rise to a duty to avoid negligently inflicting emotional trauma because granting relief "for every instance of rude, insensitive, or distasteful behavior" would dignify most disputes far beyond their social importance.[19] The court emphasized that Kerr should have brought a suit for *intentional* infliction of emotional distress (IIED) rather than *negligent* infliction, and it granted her leave to do so.[20]

[12] *Boyles*, 855 S.W.2d at 605 (Doggett, J., dissenting).
[13] *Id.* at 602.
[14] *Id.*
[15] *Id.* at 604 (Gonzalez, J., concurring).
[16] *Id.* at 597.
[17] 730 S.W.2d 649 (Tex. 1987).
[18] *Boyles*, 855 S.W.2d at 596.
[19] *Id.* at 602.
[20] *Id.* at 603.

Justice Lloyd Doggett, joined by Justices Robert Gammage and Rose Spector, issued a strong dissent, endorsing the gender bias concerns expressed in the amicus briefs and agreeing with their characterization that what Boyles did to Kerr went well beyond "name-calling" and was "tantamount to rape."[21] He decried the overruling of *St. Elizabeth*, a precedent he characterized as affirming respect for human dignity.[22] Doggett also lampooned the majority's insistence that Kerr's only recourse should be an intentional infliction of emotional distress claim: "This is tantamount to concluding that a court should not hold accountable one who, through negligence, discharges a loaded gun within inches of another's head because there is a duty not to shoot intentionally."[23]

Justice Rose Spector, the sole female justice and new to the court at the time of the *Boyles* rehearing, also wrote a separate dissent.[24] Spector asserted that claims for NIED were gendered, an argument that had then recently been given academic voice by Martha Chamallas and Linda K. Kerber's 1990 law review article, *Women, Mothers and the Law of Fright: A History*.[25] Justice Spector noted that "[i]n the judicial system dominated by men, emotional distress claims have historically been marginalized ... From the beginning, tort recovery for infliction of emotional distress has developed primarily as a means of compensating women for injuries inflicted by men insensitive to the harm caused by their conduct."[26]

Indignant, Justice John Cornyn (who went on to become a US senator from Texas), wrote a separate opinion in which he undertook a simplistic empirical investigation of NIED claims, reporting that among the thirty-four "Texas appellate cases in which a claim for negligent infliction of emotional distress was alleged, thirteen were brought by women, twelve were brought by men, seven by husbands and wives jointly, one by an executrix on behalf of an estate, and one by a corporation."[27] Based on his bean-counting approach, Cornyn saw "no factual or legal basis for the suggestion that by choosing not to

[21] *Id.* at 607 (Doggett, J. dissenting).

[22] *Id.* at 605 (Doggett, J. dissenting).

[23] *Id.* at 606 (Doggett, J. dissenting).

[24] Her dissent was officially in the companion case to *Boyles*, *Twyman v. Twyman*, but it was offered as a dissent to both cases. 855 S.W.2d 619 (Tex. 1993). *Twyman* relied on *Boyles* to reject an NIED claim, while permitting an intentional infliction of emotional distress claim by one spouse against the other during a divorce.

[25] Martha Chamallas & Linda K. Kerber, *Women, Mothers and the Law of Fright: A History*, 88 Mich. L. Rev. 814, 819 (1990).

[26] *Twyman*, 855. S.W.2d at 642.

[27] *Id.* at 622–23. Justice Cornyn's opinion was the majority opinion in *Twyman v. Twyman*, the companion case to *Boyles*.

recognize this particular tort, the court demonstrates insensitivity to female claimants."[28]

Following the court's decision on rehearing, Kerr's attorney told the press that he had not pursued a claim of intentional infliction of emotional distress (IIED) because intentional acts were not covered by the homeowner's insurance policy on the house where the young men did the videotaping. He announced, however, that he was prepared to refile an IIED claim.[29] The need to do so was alleviated when Boyles settled with Kerr for $460,000.[30] With the $500,000 the other defendants had already paid, Kerr ultimately received most of the million dollars the jury had awarded her.

Indeed, because of an indiscretion by Boyles's trial counsel, Kerr settled for another $600,000 from the firm that defended Boyles. Further illustrating the Texas "good ol' boy" culture in which the case was litigated and appealed, that firm violated a court order to limit viewing of the videotape to absolutely necessary attorneys and staff.[31] So relieved was defense counsel that the verdict had been only one million dollars, that his firm indulged in a champagne-laced, post-trial celebration that lapsed into what one law firm employee characterized as a "stag" party, with the videotape screened to employees not involved in the case.[32] Interestingly, the trial judge fined the law firm a meager $2,000 for this indiscretion.[33]

THE EVOLUTION OF NIED CLAIMS

While the *Boyles* majority rejected what it called a "general" tort claim for negligently inflicted emotional distress, it endorsed many types of NIED claims that had evolved over decades. Despite Justice Cornyn's attempt to cast NIED as a genderless tort, as Chamallas and Kerber demonstrated in their germinal article, the major precedents through which the tort developed involved women claiming emotional harm related to disruptions to their roles as procreators or nurturers. Some of the oldest successful NIED claims were

[28] *Id.* At 623.

[29] Dominick Vetri et al., Tort Law and Practice 310 (4th ed. 2011) (citing Clay Robison, *Court Again Denies Damages for Secretly Videotaped Sex*, Houston Chronicle, May 6, 1993, at 33; Stephen Johnson, $500,000 *Settlement to Close Case Over Bedroom Videotape Saga*, Houston Chronicle, Aug. 26, 1993, at 22).

[30] *Id.*

[31] Margolick, *supra* note 4.

[32] *Id.*

[33] *Id.*

those based on miscarriages – stillbirth being viewed as a clear physical manifestation of a "fright" when a pregnant woman suffered "nervous shock" and stillbirth due to a defendant's negligent behavior.[34] The Texas Supreme Court in 1890 had decided one such case, *Hill v. Kimball*, in favor of a pregnant plaintiff who suffered a stillbirth after she saw her landlord carry out a bloody racial assault of two men in her "immediate presence."[35] Such cases represented an early exception to the old "impact rule,"[36] which privileged physical harms and recognized emotional distress, if at all, as parasitic on the former.[37] As Tilley demonstrates in her rewritten opinion, another category of cases, referred to in *Boyles* as "mishandled corpse" cases, frequently involved grieving mothers such as Garrard, the plaintiff in the 1987 *St. Elizabeth* case. Like miscarriage cases, such claims had become well established in many states' NIED jurisprudence, including the 1885 Texas decision in *Stuart v. Western Union Tel. Co.*[38]

In miscarriage cases, courts justified recovery because of the physical consequence of the negligence – the lost pregnancy. Indeed, the majority in *Boyles* rationalized *Hill* as a physical injury case, rather than a purely emotional distress claim. In the mishandled corpse cases, courts permitted recovery based on what one commentator had called the "mysticism or aura of death."[39] In both types of cases, courts relied heavily on the foreseeability of emotional injury in the face of the defendant's behavior.

Judicial conceptions of when emotional distress was sufficiently foreseeable to justify an NIED claim evolved to encompass two additional categories: "bystander" and "direct victim." In the former category, family members were permitted to recover for severe emotional distress when they saw a loved one injured in an accident. Relying on the 1968 California bystander case, *Dillon v. Legg*,[40] which allowed a mother to recover when she witnessed a negligent driver kill her child, the *Boyles* majority explicitly embraced bystander NIED recovery.

[34] *See* Chamallas & Kerber, *supra* note 25, at 832.

[35] 13 S.W. 59, 59 (Tex. 1890).

[36] *See, e.g.*, Mitchell v. Rochester Ry. Co., 45 N.E. 354 (N.Y. 1896).

[37] *See generally* Julie A. Davies, *Direct Actions for Emotional Harm: Is Compromise Possible?*, 67 Wash. L. Rev. 1 (1992) (noting criticism of the physical manifestation rule as having no clear link to emotional harm).

[38] 18 S.W. 351 (Tex. 1885).

[39] Charles E. Cantu, *Negligent Infliction of Emotional Distress: Expanding the Rule Evolved Since Dillon*, 17 Tex. Tech. L. Rev. 1557, 1565 (1986).

[40] 441 P.2d 912 (Cal. 1968).

As in bystander cases, "direct victim" NIED plaintiffs claimed foreseeable distress stemming from physical injury to a loved one. The Boyles majority relied on two key California precedents, *Marlene F. v. Affiliated Psychiatric Medical Clinic, Inc.* (1989),[41] and *Burgess v. Superior Court* (1992).[42] In *Marlene F.*, a psychologist was counseling several mothers and their sons when the mothers learned that the psychologist had sexually molested their children, and several asserted claims for NIED. The California Supreme Court upheld the mothers' claim because the psychologist owed a duty to them – and not only to their sons – based on their therapeutic relationship. In *Burgess*, the "direct" victim was also a mother, this time of an infant who suffered brain damage when the defendant physician's negligence caused the newborn to be deprived of oxygen during delivery. The mother could recover for NIED because the physician owed a duty to her, and not only to her infant child, based on their doctor–patient relationship.[43] In both bystander and direct victim NIED cases, courts reasoned that it was fair to impose a duty on defendants because emotional injury to the plaintiffs was eminently foreseeable. As in the miscarriage cases, judicial analysis of foreseeability relied on the plaintiffs' maternal role.

MATERNAL ROLES AND GENDER STEREOTYPING

Boyles v. Kerr tested whether the Texas court would be as solicitous of a woman who was made an object of scorn and ridicule because of her sexual practices as it had been of women injured in relation to maternal roles, e.g., by miscarriage, through trauma in relation to a deceased loved one, or because of physical injury to the plaintiff's child. The Texas court proved not to be as concerned about women's emotional well-being in relation to their sexual dignity. Instead, the *Boyles* majority declared foreseeability of harm a useless guideline that could lead to limitless liability.[44] Tilley's feminist rewrite, in contrast, embraces the traditional foreseeability principle and permits Kerr's recovery as *the* foreseeable sufferer of emotional distress that flowed from negligent behavior in the context of an intimate relationship. Recasting the actual *Boyles* majority as a dissent to her opinion, Tilley makes her most overtly feminist move in unpacking sexual stereotypes underlying the original opinion's selective embrace or rejection of NIED precedents.

[41] 770 P.2d 278 (Cal. 1989).
[42] 831 P.2d 1197 (Cal. 1992).
[43] *See id.* at 1201–03.
[44] *Boyles*, 855 S.W.2d at 599.

Tilley contrasts differing views of womanhood – that between women as wives and mothers on the one hand, and women as agents of their own sexuality on the other. Tilley compares the decisions in *St. Elizabeth* (mishandled corpse 1987) and *Hill* (miscarriage 1890) with the facts in *Boyles*. Moving beyond Justice Cornyn's simple census of whether NIED plaintiffs were female or male, Tilley observes that the offending behaviors in that successful pair of NIED claims were viewed by the court as "self-evidently capable of causing anguish" because female plaintiffs were seeking redress after their attempts to fulfill traditional womanly roles were thwarted by careless third parties. Tilley observes that Susan Kerr, in contrast, "strayed outside orthodox notions of caregiving womanhood."

Tilley suggests that imposing a duty of care on unmarried sex partners might facilitate greater responsibility in nonmarital relationships, and she concludes that fostering such sexual liberation may be the very outcome that the Texas Supreme Court fears. Taking a jab at the "nine middle-aged men, most of whom had long since left the dating world," who sat on the Texas Supreme Court at the time of the initial *Boyles* decision, Tilley notes that while they are entitled to their personal opinions about teen sexual behavior, they are not entitled to impose those views on all Texans. In this aspect of her rewritten opinion, Tilley draws from feminist insights that the gender composition and lived experiences of judges can make a difference in courts' understanding of and empathy for women's lived experiences. She also makes an eloquent plea for tort law to keep pace with evolving social behavior and societal expectations. Tilley acknowledges that while Kerr and Boyles may have been at the cusp of what we now call a hook-up culture and thus did not expect enduring romantic commitments, Susan Kerr did not discard expectations of respect for her privacy, dignity, and humanity.

Ironically, Kerr's attorneys were reluctant to be as blunt as Justice Tilley could be – writing in a feminist utopia – about the sexual revolution. In one of their filings, Kerr's attorneys played to the stereotypes of women's roles that they presumed comported with old white men's expectations of womanhood: "If this court holds that it is alright to film a woman in the act of lovemaking and then show that act to a howling mob then [plaintiff] fears that the traditional role of women in this society will be set back centuries. How can a woman expect to assume her traditional roles in society as mother, care-giver and primary exponent of morals if she is allowed to be portrayed as a porno-queen."[45] Kerr's legal team purported to seek preservation of a separate spheres

[45] Respondent Susan Kerr's Response to Amicus Curiae Brief of Phillips Petroleum Company, Sept. 25, 1992, p. 3.

ideology even as they also sought recompense for a harm more obviously associated with sexual liberation.

INTENT VS. NEGLIGENCE

A significant theme of the Texas Supreme Court majority and several concurring opinions was criticism of Susan Kerr and her lawyers for pursuing a claim of NIED rather than IIED. Justice Gonzales, in his concurring opinion, contemptuously accused Kerr's lawyers of pursuing the negligence claim instead of the IIED claim because all they cared about was the "deep pocket" of the insurance company.[46]

Tilley deftly responds to this debate by noting the perversity of requiring the plaintiff to meet the higher bar associated with doctrinal requirements that the defendant's behavior be both intentional and "outrageous."[47] Another of Tilley's feminist moves draws on dignity conceptions of personhood and the longstanding and pervasive male practice of objectifying women without any thought to the impact of male behavior on women's feelings, autonomy, or basic human dignity. Tilley's focus on how Boyles's conduct undermined Kerr's dignity is a theme that resonates throughout tort law.[48]

Tilley separates Boyles's intent to do the acts of videotaping and sharing the sex tape from any intent attendant to the consequences of the actions for Kerr. Tilley quotes Boyles's own testimony that he did not mean to hurt Kerr, and she then affirms the statement's credibility by reasoning that Boyles could not have had the requisite intent to cause Kerr severe emotional distress because he had no "emotional tie or meaningful relationship" with Kerr, who "seems to have been for him no more than an object of sexual gratification." Thus, Tilley asserts, the negligence claim more accurately captures Boyles's utter disregard for Kerr as a feeling human being, as well as his self-centered desire to amuse himself and his friends.

Finally, Tilley insists on Kerr's entitlement to a robust monetary award for her injury, which requires tapping into the homeowner's insurance policy.

[46] *Boyles*, 855 S.W.2d at 604.

[47] *See* Mae C. Quinn, *The Garden Path of Boyles v. Kerr and Twyman v. Twyman: An Outrageous Response to Victims of Sexual Misconduct*, 4 Tex. J. Women & L. 247, 248 (1995) (discussing the very high standard for IIED claims under Texas law).

[48] *See, e.g.*, Lisa R. Pruitt, *Her Own Good Name: Two Centuries of Talk about Chastity*, 63 Md. L. Rev. 401 (2004) (focusing on dignitary injuries in the context of sexual slander and false light invasion of privacy, particularly with respect to claims defeated as "opinion" under the rhetorical hyperbole doctrine).

She points out that Kerr legitimately was seeking far more than "heartbalm" or a moral victory of unrecoverable damages. Like any seriously injured plaintiff, Tilley argues, Kerr fully deserved monetary recovery rather than relegation to a feminized notion of "moral virtue" as "the coin of the realm." Moreover, she points out that Kerr's future economic prospects were impaired by her diminished college grades flowing from her emotional trauma. The often unappreciated economic consequences to women of harm labeled as simply "emotional" is an important feminist insight.

The majority opinion and Justice Gonzales in his concurrence were concerned about opening the door to too much liability, and they deemed it unseemly that Kerr's lawyer was focused on the best route to securing an actual monetary recovery for his client. While diminishing the importance of monetary recovery for Kerr, they expressed concern for the adverse economic impact on Texas homeowners from the presumed increased cost of homeowners' insurance policies should the NIED claim prevail. They viewed the "moral victory" of an unrecoverable IIED verdict as sufficient to vindicate Kerr's human interests, while protecting the larger economic climate.

Justice Tilley, in contrast, sees the economic and dignitary interests of the plaintiff as inextricably connected. Taking seriously the harm Kerr suffered, she notes that money matters to actually vindicate her. Tilley's feminist opinion reminds us that Susan Kerr is the victim – not Texas insurance companies. She puts the monetary focus on what Kerr deserves, rather than on external financial implications for corporate interests.

IMPLICATIONS FOR THE "REVENGE PORN" ERA

Tilley calls for tort law to recognize changing times, which in *Boyles* means recognizing new technology and the new opportunities for tortious behavior and the injury it facilitates. As Tilley notes, at the time Boyles and his buddies videotaped the sexual encounter, video cameras had been on the market for only two years. The potential of such new technology to wreak havoc was only beginning to be realized.

Indeed, *Boyles v. Kerr* was only the tip of the iceberg of technological transformations of the ways that men humiliate and degrade women in relation to their sexuality. The unauthorized public disclosure of sexual practices has become increasingly common in the digital age. Smartphones and social media now facilitate the proliferation of so-called revenge porn and other nonconsensual distribution of sexually graphic images, including those obtained with the subject's permission, e.g., images initially shared as "sexts," but without authorization for further dissemination.[49] Victims in such cases have sought civil redress through various tort claims, including NIED and IIED, along with defamation and invasion of privacy.[50] Some courts have proved very sympathetic to plaintiffs' claims. The district court in Hawaii, for example, awarded damages based on a "revenge porn" victim's claims of public disclosure of private facts, defamation, and NIED.[51] Texas courts, on the other hand, still lag behind, as illustrated by *Patel v. Hussain*, where an appellate court in 2016 rejected an NIED claim after a jury awarded the female plaintiff $500,000 when the defendant used the Internet to share sexual videos of her following their breakup.[52]

Despite the #MeToo movement and enhanced societal awareness regarding men's sexual misconduct toward women, a number of obstacles deter victims from recovering on tort claims.[53] Among these are the judicial resistance to recognizing NIED claims exemplified in *Boyles* and the high standards for proving an IIED claim.[54] Further, the tension between competing values underlying various privacy torts and First Amendment free speech guarantees may also limit a victim's options. Thus, while tort law continues to provide the best chances for recovery in cases involving nonconsensual "revenge porn," cases like *Patel* remind us that the more things change, the more they stay the same. If Justice Tilley's feminist opinion were available as a legal precedent, it would provide lawyers and judges with many powerful arguments for expanding the tort of NIED to recognize women's right to exercise sexual autonomy without selfish, thoughtless, and cruel men undermining women's dignity and fundamental humanity.

[49] *See* Danielle Keats Citron & Mary Anne Franks, *Criminalizing Revenge Porn*, 49 WAKE FOREST L. REV. 345, 346 (2014); Margaret Talbot, *Taking Trolls to Court: The Attorney Fighting Revenge Porn*, NEW YORKER (Dec. 5, 2016), http://www.newyorker.com/magazine/2016/12/05/the-attorney-fighting-revenge-porn

[50] Citron and Franks, *supra* note 49, at 357; *see also* Ashlee Hamilton, *Is Justice Best Served Cold?: A Transformative Approach to Revenge Porn*, 25 UCLA WOMEN'S L.J. 1, 15–16 (2018).

[51] Taylor v. Franko, No. 09–00002 JMS/RLP, 2011 WL 2746714, at *5 (D. Haw. June 12, 2011).

[52] Patel v. Hussain, 485 S.W.3d 153, 157–58 (Tex. App. 2016).

[53] *See* Hamilton, *supra* note 50, at 16 (discussing concerns about "not only the high costs of civil litigation, but also the high burden placed on the survivor in these suits and the message it sends to society at large about sexual freedom and expression"); Citron & Franks, *supra* note 49, at 358 (pointing out that "most victims lack resources to bring civil suits" and some "may be reluctant to sue for fear of unleashing more unwanted publicity").

[54] Hamilton, *supra* note 50, at 15 (noting how victims have had difficulty in showing that "their particular experience was emotionally distressful enough" or proving that "their feelings of embarrassment and humiliation constitute severe emotional harm").

BOYLES v. KERR, 855 S.W.2D 593 (TEX. 1993)

JUSTICE CRISTINA TILLEY ANNOUNCED THE DECISION OF THE COURT ON A MOTION FOR REHEARING[1]

I FACTS

As 17-year-old Dan Boyles, Jr. was preparing to begin his college career at the University of Texas in late May of 1985, he began a sexual relationship with 19-year-old Susan Kerr. The two attended her senior prom together; at the end of the evening, they had sexual intercourse. Every time they met thereafter, the two had sex. In August, Kerr asked Boyles to escort her to a wedding. He declined to go to the event with her but suggested they meet afterwards. Egged on by a friend, Boyles decided to covertly videotape himself having sex with Kerr that evening. The instigator of this plot, Karl Broesche, arranged for Boyles to bring Kerr to the Broesche home for the encounter. Broesche then enlisted Ray Widner and John Paul Tamborello to help him hide a video camera in a bedroom there, and taped some crude preliminary remarks about the scheme and what was about to occur. They left the camera running and secreted themselves so Boyles could execute their plan. Boyles brought Kerr to the prearranged bedroom, and the video camera was running while the two had sex.

Thereafter, on three separate occasions Boyles shared the tape with friends at the Alpha Tau Omega fraternity house at the University of Texas. A total of ten people watched the video. One friend apparently enjoyed watching the tape so much he forgave Boyles's repayment of a $20 football bet.

[1] The procedural complexity that has produced today's decision is emblematic of the doctrinal complexity it presents. The events that form the basis of the suit occurred in 1985. The jury completed its work on the case in 1989. The Texas Court of Appeals affirmed the judgment in January of 1991, and overruled two motions to rehear the case. Boyles v. Kerr, 806 S.W.2d 255 (Tex. App. 1991). We issued our first opinion in the case in December 1992, overruling the court of appeals and holding that there is no independent right to recover for negligently inflicted emotional distress. That decision included a majority opinion, an opinion dissenting and concurring (written by Justice Cook), and an opinion dissenting (written by Justice Doggett). After some dismayed responses to perceived insensitivity to women and the pervasive problem of sexual abuse in the original opinion, we received a motion for rehearing. We now grant the motion for rehearing, and issue a superseding opinion that affirms the Court of Appeals and the jury's award of damages to Kerr. Between our original and this superseding opinion, Justices Enoch and Spector joined the court, replacing Justices Mauzy and Cook, respectively. The original majority opinion and concurrences have been recast as dissents; the original dissents have been revised and recast as a concurring opinions, which have been joined by our new colleagues Justices Enoch and Spector.

As Boyles sought and received attention for this exploit, Kerr remained in the dark about the videotape's existence or these viewing parties. Rumors of the tape's existence eventually reached her at the end of the semester. When she confronted Boyles in December of that year, he admitted what he had done and gave her the single existing copy of the tape. Taking possession of the tape did not, however, close down this chapter of her life. Kerr testified that for months thereafter, gossip spread at both the University of Texas and her own school, Southwest Texas State University. She also testified that gossip about her and the tape had spread to friends who attended other colleges. At parties and other events, casual acquaintances sought her out to discuss the video, asking why she agreed to make a sex tape. Ultimately, she testified, she became known socially as a "porno queen." She was humiliated, stigmatized with an unwelcome notoriety, and unable to relate to men in a healthy or appropriate way. Her grades suffered. Ultimately, she sought psychological counseling, and her therapist diagnosed her with post-traumatic stress disorder.

Kerr sued Boyles, Broesche, Widner, and Tamborello. In her initial complaint, she claimed intentional and negligent invasion of privacy as well as negligent infliction of emotional distress. At the close of trial, and before the jury was charged, Kerr dropped the privacy causes of action and asked the court to send the case to the jury solely on the issue of negligent infliction of emotional distress. Despite Boyles's objection to this instruction, the court agreed to Kerr's requested charge. The jury returned a verdict for Kerr in the amount of $500,000 actual damages and another $500,000 in punitive damages. Of the punitive figure, $350,000 was assessed against Boyles and the remainder against the other three men. Broesche settled thereafter, and Widner and Tamborello apparently complied with the court's entry of judgment and did not appeal. Only Boyles has asked reviewing courts – first, the Texas Court of Appeals, and now us – to nullify the conclusion that he negligently inflicted emotional distress on Kerr.

The Texas Court of Appeals affirmed the jury's verdict. Boyles, 806 S.W.2d 255. In our first review of that opinion, we reversed. Kerr has now sought a rehearing, which we hereby grant and conduct. Determining whether to affirm the jury's verdict in this case requires more than a review and construction of Texas precedent. It requires us to think deeply about the purpose of assigning tort liability. It also requires us to unpack the comparative roles of torts based on negligence and intentional acts, and the subtle differences between "injury" and "damages" within tort. Finally, it invites us to consider the role the law can play in reinforcing or disrupting social stereotypes about interpersonal relationships between men and women.

II ISSUES PRESENTED

A *Recovery for Negligent Infliction of Emotional Distress in Texas*

The crucial question of doctrine we must decide is whether Texas recognizes a general cause of action for negligent infliction of emotional distress (NIED). Kerr contends that we do and points to our 1987 decision in *St. Elizabeth Hosp. v. Garrard* as its foundation. 730 S.W.2d 649 (Tex. 1987). Boyles contends that we do not, and says that *St. Elizabeth* created a narrow cause of action limited to its facts, which are not applicable here.

A little history is in order. Traditionally, Texas courts required that both intentional tort plaintiffs and negligence plaintiffs suffer some kind of physical impact or injury as a basis for recovery. Those who can prove a physical injury (along with the other required elements of the tort) are entitled to recover damages that compensate them for the harms that flow from that physical injury. In most cases, the plaintiff's injury and the actual nature of the harm for which damages are assessed are symbiotic – if the injury is a broken leg, the damages are the costs associated with the loss of the leg's use and with the necessary repairs to the leg. In some cases, though, the real damages to the plaintiff are only tenuously connected with the physical injury that operates to fulfill the doctrinal requirements. The disconnect between injury and damages tends to be most pronounced in cases where the defendant's wrongful behavior in the external world has repercussions for the plaintiff's internal emotional well-being and mental health.

In tacit recognition that recovery is often warranted even when injury and damages are disconnected, we have taken a somewhat flexible approach to what counts as an "injury" for doctrinal purposes. In a garden-variety intentional tort, such as battery, physical contact of some kind is sufficient. These contacts must be "offensive," but needn't impose permanent or profound changes to flesh or bone. For example, in *Fisher v. Carrousel Motor Hotel, Inc.*, 424 S.W.2d 627 (Tex. 1967), we found liable for battery a hotel whose manager snatched a plate from the hand of an African-American guest at a business lunch, while making racially derogatory comments. Although the man's physical body was unimpaired by the contact, his dignity was vitiated, and he was permitted to recover emotional distress *damages* that were parasitic on the negligible physical contact that we counted as an *injury*. We remarked there that "[d]amages for mental suffering are recoverable without the necessity for showing actual physical injury in a case of willful battery because the basis of that action is the unpermitted and intentional invasion of the plaintiff's person and not the actual harm done to the plaintiff's body." *Id.* at 630.

In negligence causes of action, where the defendant's behavior typically is not "willful," we have historically required more than a mere physical contact but instead some actual physical harm as proof of injury. Here too, though, we have taken a somewhat flexible approach. For example, in *Hill v. Kimball*, 13 S.W. 59 (Tex. 1890), the defendant landlord assaulted two African-American men in the front yard of his onlooking female tenant, who was pregnant. The defendant's attack drew blood from his victims and involved profane racial epithets. The tenant went into premature labor and suffered a miscarriage. The woman and her husband sued the landlord, and we held that she had a cause of action sounding in negligence. We allowed recovery even though the landlord's behavior was not the direct physical cause of the tenant's injury. We said there was "no doubt" that "operation of the mind" can produce physical injury, so that behavior triggering mental distress could plausibly be deemed the cause of the woman's physical injury. *Id.* at 59. This transitive approach allowed us to locate a physical injury caused by the defendant's negligence in order to satisfy the then existing doctrinal requirement of a physical impact or injury.

Hill represents an early understanding by this court about the purpose of assigning tort liability. We observed in *Hill* that "one who had been injured in his person ... by the wrongful or negligent conduct of another should ... get a redress of his wrongs." *Id.* at 60. In other words, tort law provides a forum in which a community can identify wrongful behavior on the defendant's part and restore the plaintiff to equal dignity by compelling a redress of the wrong at issue. Too cramped a view of what constitutes "personhood," and consequently what counts as an injury, can prevent tort law from fulfilling its social role. First, it prevents full plaintiff redress. Second, by shielding the defendant from the judgment of his peers, it signals that the underlying behavior is socially condoned. Consequently, one way to understand *Hill* and *Fisher* is that they prioritize the restorative and deterrent tort function over rigidly formalistic notions of physical injury. In both cases, we stretched the notion of "injury" within the doctrinal framework in order to generate just outcomes for blameworthy defendants. When technicalities of doctrine impeded the identification and compensation of wrongs, we massaged those technicalities.

These two lines of doctrine were married in *St. Elizabeth Hospital v. Garrard* to achieve the same goal in a more direct and transparent fashion. There, a woman gave birth to twins – one live, and one stillborn. Her husband and the attending physician agreed an autopsy was warranted, but the stillborn infant's body was instead "delivered to a mortuary and disposed of in an unmarked, common grave" without either parent's consent or knowledge. 730 S.W.2d at 650. The parents sued the hospital and the pathologist, alleging negligence and claiming as their sole injury mental suffering. Unlike *Hill* and *Fisher*, the plaintiffs did not attempt to claim or prove any physical manifestations of injury at all. Nevertheless, we recognized their claim as legitimate under Texas law.

In waiving the requirement that plaintiffs prove physical injury in order to recover for negligence that caused profound mental suffering, we held that "freedom from severe emotional distress is an interest which the law should serve to protect." *Id.* at 653. We described our decision as recognizing a general common law action for negligent infliction of mental anguish that did not carry a physical injury requirement. *Id.*

Our dissenting colleagues now seem to rue the high level of generality in that holding because they think this specific jury erred in applying its principles to authorize compensation for Susan Kerr. The dissenters suggest that *St. Elizabeth* intended a claim for negligent infliction of emotional distress to be available *only* within the context of mishandling of corpses. But this reading of *St. Elizabeth* is not supported by the text. We said in general terms that physical injury was "no longer required [in Texas] to recover for negligent infliction of emotional distress" where such distress was foreseeable. We never stated nor implied that mental anguish was foreseeable only in cases involving corpses. In fact, we purposefully left undetermined the precise fact patterns in which the probability of severe emotional distress was foreseeable. Instead, we stated that juries in individual cases were more competent than we were to "determine whether and to what extent the defendant caused compensable mental anguish." *Id.* at 654. The dissent now seeks to nullify that allocation of latitude to the jury and to rewrite *St. Elizabeth* so that it is limited to its facts.

This zigging and zagging is consistent with the halting progression of NIED over the past several decades. Tort law has historically privileged property interests and physical integrity over emotional well-being and relational ties. *See, e.g.*, Leslie Bender, *A Lawyer's Primer on Feminist Theory and Tort*, 38 J. LEG. ED. 3, 37 (1988). In this respect, tort doctrine has replicated American culture, which historically assigned men and women to two distinct "spheres." The market sphere, occupied by men, "structure[d] ... productive li[fe]," while the family sphere, occupied by women, "structure[d] ... affective li[fe.]" Frances E. Olsen, *The Family and the Market: A Study of Ideology and Legal Reform*, 96 HARV. L. REV. 1497, 1498 (1983). The family sphere was seen as a "safe repositor[y] for the virtues and emotions," and within it, women were expected to be "nurturant, giving, submissive, sensual, mother, housekeeper – all things that man wants her to be." *Id.* at 1499; Bender, *supra*, at 18. In fact, women who did not fit this mold were not considered "real or proper wom [e]n." Bender, *supra* at 18.

While this gendered understanding of the world prevailed, counting physical injuries that impair "productive" capacity as compensable, and emotional injuries that devastate "affective" life as uncompensable, matched doctrine with culture. Over time, both doctrine and culture have evolved. Our society has come to realize that emotional harm is quite real and can seriously impair human health and wholeness. Emotional well-being has similarly assumed an increasingly legitimate place within tort doctrine over time. Pain and suffering "parasitic" on bodily injury have long been recoverable damages. Bodily harm that arose absent an impact but following the infliction of mental anguish began to count as a legitimate tort injury early in the twentieth century. *See* Martha Chamallas & Linda K. Kerber, *Women, Mothers, and the Law of Fright: A History*, 88 MICH. L. REV. 814, 819–20 (1990). Eventually, those emotionally frightened by their own physical jeopardy at the hands of a careless defendant were said to have been injured. And, in some cases, those forced to watch their loved ones suffer were permitted to recover for their shock. *Id.* at 821. Notably, the majority of early "fright" claimants were women, often complaining of rough behavior or threats to unborn or living children. Leon Green, *"Fright" Cases*, 27 U. ILL. L. REV. 873 (1933), *cited in* Chamallas, 88 MICH. L. REV. at 842–44.

This path represents the law's increasing sensitivity to the lived experience of women, by expanding the notion of injury to include emotional and relational harms. But the path has too often privileged only a narrow class of female relationships and emotional interests.

For example, Garrard claimed in *St. Elizabeth* that she was injured by the botched burial of her stillborn infant, an injury to her role as mother and nurturer. To evoke the words of Professor Bender, the defendant's cavalier treatment of her deceased baby kept her from being the "things that man wants her to be." Thus, it is not surprising that the judges on this court, all of whom were men at that time, recognized and compensated her injury. In contrast, Susan Kerr claims injury from the taping and broadcast of her sexual relationships. Her injury was an obstacle to safe and dignified nonmarital sex. The defendants' actions and her subsequent humiliation kept her from being something that society traditionally did not think women should be (and the dissenting men on this court apparently still do not think women have the right to be), and her pain was not classified as a compensable injury in our original opinion. *St. Elizabeth* did not condition NIED access on expectations that female plaintiffs had behaved "properly" in the course of sustaining their injuries. It conditioned liability solely on a jury finding that the defendant's behavior would foreseeably cause the plaintiff emotional distress. Susan Kerr's jury thought she satisfied that condition.

Having established this cause of action, and having left the question of foreseeable distress to the jury, this court has no just reason to rewrite *St. Elizabeth* so that it offers succor solely to wives, mothers, and "good girls."

B *Boyles's NIED Liability*

1 Negligence or Intent?

Boyles argued on appeal that even if an NIED cause of action exists in the state, it is not the proper repository for Kerr's claims. Instead, he suggested that Kerr's suit was properly one for intentional infliction of emotional distress (IIED). Boyles argued that "the case [was] tried start to finish as an intentional tort." *Boyles*, 855 S.W.2d at 601. Our dissenting colleague Justice Gonzales seems to agree, observing that "[t]he young men who videotaped Ms. Kerr's sexual encounter *intentionally* positioned the camera to capture the event on film. They *intentionally* showed the videotape to their friends. There was nothing accidental or careless about their outrageous conduct." *Id.* at 603.

Of course, it benefits Boyles to frame this cause of action as one that sets higher bars on every element. Intentional infliction of emotional distress – a tort not explicitly recognized by this state until the companion case of *Twyman v. Twyman* was issued concurrent with our original opinion in this case – demands substantially more of a plaintiff than does NIED. 855 S.W.2d 619 (Tex. 1993). An IIED plaintiff must show that the defendant acted not just unreasonably, but "outrageously" and beyond all bounds of decency. She must show that the defendant intended or was substantially certain that he would cause the plaintiff severe emotional distress. She must show that the resulting distress was quite severe, and that no reasonable person could have avoided extreme suffering. *Id.* at 621–22. Our dissenting colleagues say that instead of holding Boyles to the jury's finding that he carelessly and thoughtlessly exploited Kerr, we should instead send her back to a second jury to prove her case under this more demanding framework.

Undoubtedly, the intentional infliction tort – a fairly new entry on the intentional tort menu – plays an important role in holding defendants liable for some instances of egregious behavior that transcend negligence. But the line between intent and negligence is not as crisp as it might initially seem. And it is not as self-evident as the dissenting justices suggest that Boyles's behavior here belongs on the more demanding side of that line for purposes of assigning liability. Kerr *might* be able to persuade a jury that Boyles had a conscious design to hurt her. But we suspect that is not exactly what happened here. Boyles testified that he intended to have sex with Kerr, intended for his friends to videotape it, and intended to share that tape with his circle of friends in Houston. But he also testified that "he . . . had *not* meant to hurt her." 855 S.W.2d at 616 (Doggett, J., dissenting, italics added). It does not strain credulity to take him at his word. It is believable that he did not mean to hurt Susan Kerr because the evidence suggests he did not see her as a full human being with dignity or emotions that could be hurt. She was not a person with whom he had an emotional tie or meaningful relationship. Rather, she seems to have been for him no more than an object of sexual gratification.

According to trial testimony, he did not have a single encounter with her that did not end in intercourse. *Boyles*, 806 S.W.2d at 257. In fact, when she sought to spend nonsexual, social time with him at a wedding, time during which they would presumably talk, dance, and share a meal, he turned down her invitation. *Id.* Instead, he arranged to retrieve her at the end of that emotionally meaningful portion of the night and take her to Broesche's house for purely sexual purposes. *Id.* He agreed to let his friends tape the encounter. He showed the tape to his friends in what appears to have been a celebration of his sexual conquest and, in one instance, a basis for bartering away a gambling debt. None of this suggests that he had any understanding of Kerr as a thinking, feeling person who would be anguished by this course of behavior.

Based on this evidence, a finding that Boyles intentionally inflicted anguish on Kerr seems misplaced. Juries tend to find defendants liable for IIED when they act out of some design or malice personalized to their victim. *See, e.g.*, PROSSER, THE LAW OF TORTS 56 (4th ed. 1971) ("The rule . . . is that there is liability for conduct exceeding all bounds usually tolerated by a decent society, *of a nature which is especially calculated to cause* . . . mental distress") (italics added).

Boyles seems not to have seen Kerr as sufficiently three-dimensional to merit any kind of calculated malice. Rather, he seems to have seen her as a fungible object whose role in his life was to provide physical gratification and – on the night in question – derisive amusement. In other words, his behavior seems to reflect a "thoughtless" failure to consider her rather than a "thoughtful" design to diminish her. Consequently, categorizing Boyles's behavior as a possible instance of negligence rather than as an intentional tort actually seems to capture the chain of events in a doctrinally principled fashion.

2 Duty

We explained in *St. Elizabeth* that since *Hill*, Texas has recognized a negligent infliction of mental anguish tort "to be administered using traditional tort concepts." 730 S.W.2d at 652. Accordingly, all that remains is to ask whether Kerr has satisfied those traditional concepts.

The threshold inquiry in a negligence case is duty. The plaintiff must establish both the existence and the violation of a duty owed to the plaintiff by the defendant to establish liability in tort. Moreover, the existence of duty is a question of law for the court to decide from the facts surrounding the occurrence in question. We have most recently been willing to "make changes in [our understanding of the duty owed in a particular fact setting] as the need [has arisen] in a changing society." El Chico Corp. v. Poole, 732 S.W.2d 306, 310–11 (Tex. 1987). This case is one where the scope of duty is directly tied to social changes. The dissent argues that a consensual nonmarital sexual relationship is not the sort of "special" relationship that should justify a duty to avoid carelessly inflicting foreseeable emotional distress on one's partner. This "no duty" position turns a blind eye to changes in social understandings about nonmarital sex. Our finding that a duty exists acknowledges a growing acceptance that such relationships are common, and that relational duties are owed within them.

Boyles argued below that as a matter of law, he owed no duty to Kerr. *Boyles*, 806 S.W.2d at 259. Our dissenting colleagues, in a rather perfunctory fashion, agree. Notably, they do so after pointing out the many circumstances in which defendants *do* owe duties to not to behave in ways that can foreseeably cause distress. Stuart v. Western Union Telephone Co., 18 S.W. 351, 352 (Tex. 1885), tells us that telegraph companies are obliged to timely deliver messages regarding the imminent death of a family member because missing the opportunity to say goodbye and comfort other mourners foreseeably inflicts anguish. *St. Elizabeth* tells us that hospitals are obliged to exercise care in interring corpses because depriving mourners of burial rituals inflicts anguish. 730 S.W.2d at 650. And *Hill* tells us that landlords are obliged to refrain from bloody racial assaults in the front yards of pregnant women because watching such violence inflicts anguish. 13 S.W. at 59.

This court concluded that the contested behaviors in *Stuart*, *St. Elizabeth*, and *Hill* were self-evidently capable of causing anguish. Why those wrongful behaviors were sufficient to impose a tort duty, but covertly taping and then ridiculing Susan Kerr was not, is never analyzed by the dissenters. One possible explanation, we think, is that the cases cited approvingly by the dissenters feature female plaintiffs seeking tort redress after their attempts to fulfill traditional womanly roles were thwarted by careless third parties. In contrast, Kerr sought this court's protection after behavior that strayed outside orthodox notions of virtuous or caregiving womanhood.

Justice Spears, concurring and dissenting in *St. Elizabeth*, remarked that permitting recovery for pure mental injury was only warranted when "anguish or distress is so probable that a [physical] manifestation requirement is unnecessary." 730 S.W.2d at 655. Identifying behavior that is highly probable to cause anguish is really an exercise in basic human empathy and the ability to imagine the inner lives of people who are sometimes unlike oneself. And it seems that the dissenters have limited imagination when it comes to the emotional lives of female plaintiffs outside the confines of motherhood. The existence of a duty of care has been *assumed* where the negligence at issue harmed female plaintiffs carrying out their socially approved roles as nurturers and caretakers. That the pregnant wife in *Hill* was likely to miscarry because the sight of racially motivated male brutality was so jarring to her quiet domestication seemed unremarkable to this court in 1890. ("[T]he defendant knew [that the wife was 'well advanced in pregnancy'] and . . . was also aware that any undue excitement to a lady in that condition was likely to produce a serious injury to her health." 13 S.W. at 60.) That a mother would be distraught when excluded from burial and mourning rituals for her infant was taken for granted by this court as recently as 1987. *See St. Elizabeth*, 730 S.W.2d at 650 (noting that Garrard's claim for anguish was based on being "unable to do traditional memorializations such as placing flowers on a grave"). In these cases, the court was able to empathize with the feelings of plaintiffs who were acting out traditional versions of family-oriented womanhood celebrated and shared in the popular culture.[2]

Our dissenting colleagues cannot make the same leap of empathetic imagination for Susan Kerr. Much like Boyles and his codefendants in this case, they ignore that she has an inner life capable of sustaining harm. Instead, they fixate on how her external behavior deviated from idealized notions of appropriate female sexuality. They note that although she was not dating Boyles "steadily," she nevertheless had sex with him repeatedly. *Boyles*, 855 S.W.2d at 594. This detail seems to separate her from the wives and mothers in previous NIED cases whose emotional lives took place solely within the confines of the family unit. The court could imagine the anguish that would follow when Hill and Garrard were stymied from mothering. But they cannot

[2] *Stuart*, the third in this trio, involved a male plaintiff whose effort to keep abreast of his brother's declining health was foiled by a careless telegraph operator who failed to deliver an update on the dying man's condition. 18 S.W.2d at 351–52. The court observed that the delay injured him by preventing him from a final goodbye, *and* by keeping him from comforting "the bereaved mother." *Id.* at 353. Thus, all three cases finding a duty to refrain from negligent behavior causing anguished turned, in whole or in part, on an interest in shielding a woman from grief caused by the loss of a nurturing relationship.

imagine the anguish that would follow when Susan Kerr discovered that a tape of her sexual encounter was being shown at fraternity gatherings.

Our dissenting colleagues raise – and immediately reject – a second route to locating a duty owed from Boyles to Kerr. They acknowledge that select categorical relationships that involve trust and the exchange of intimate information or action can be categorized as sufficiently "special" so as to generate interpersonal tort duties. The mortician–mourner relationship and the telegraph company–recipient relationship are highlighted as "special." Why consensual adult sexual relationships are outside this category is not explained. It appears that "special" duties are imposed on those who steward personal messages and beloved corpses, presumably because those relationships require trust and dependence. The imposition of a legal duty on message senders and morticians pacifies plaintiffs and allows communication and safe burial to thrive. Imposing a similar duty on unmarried sex partners might facilitate and recognize the social validity and importance of nonmarital relationships, and perhaps the dissenters fear this outcome.

For decades, the law has protected women against loutish male behavior primarily through torts that recognize duties of care running to women via their positions of wife, mother, fiancée, or daughter. In other words, female standing was essentially derived through the woman's relationship with a man. For example, the tort of seduction was originally predicated on the belief that men who reduced a daughter's virginal reputation and thus her "marriageability" had wronged plaintiff fathers, but not the women themselves. *See, e.g.*, Jane E. Larson, *"Women Understand So Little, They Call My Good Nature 'Deceit'": A Feminist Rethinking of Seduction*, 93 COLUM. L. REV. 374, 382–84 (1993). Similarly, the torts of alienation of affection and breach of promise were predicated on the belief that there was a social duty owed to avoid harming the marital relationship. *See, e.g.*, Nathan Feinsinger, *Legislative Attack on "Heart Balm,"* 33 MICH. L. REV. 979, 980–96 (1935). Susan Kerr has asked Texas to recognize that she has a right to be treated with a reasonable degree of consideration for her humanity and emotional well-being in sexual relationships outside of marriage. The dissent's rejection of that request suggests that if she wants to be treated well, she should not be having sexual relationships outside of marriage.

There is yet another reason the dissenters' "no duty" argument misses the mark. They conceptualize the duty at issue exclusively in terms of what Boyles owed Kerr as a sexual partner. They neglect to consider the duties that follow from the use of a video camera. Duty has long been identified as a platform for consideration of social policy concerns. *See, e.g.*, MacPherson v. Buick Motor Co., 111 N.E. 1050 (N.Y. 1916). In fact, the use of "duty" as a threshold element has allowed courts to adapt the role of tort law to address the growing recognition of risks presented by new technologies. *See id.* Deciding that those who use these technologies must take into account the impact they might have on others is a powerful mechanism for setting community expectations about the role of such innovations in daily life.

So, for example, when early courts assigned a duty of care to those who manufactured automobiles on an assembly line and marketed them to remote consumers through independent middlemen, they created a profoundly different car culture than we would have had if no such duty had been assigned. *See id.* And when this court decided that telegraph operators owed a duty to those sending and receiving messages, they set the stage for responsible use of this new communicative technology. *See Stuart*, 18 S.W. at 351. Video cameras like the one Boyles used went on the consumer market just two years before Kerr's ordeal. Our court owes it to the community to grapple in a real way with the question of the duty owed by video camera owners to their would-be subjects, especially those who are unwittingly filmed. The dissent says that Boyles owed Kerr no duty to refrain from capturing and broadcasting her intimate behavior without her consent. This conclusion risks creating a "gotcha" culture in which people may be filmed, and those films distributed, at the sole discretion of the camera owner. That rule would reinforce a problematic expectation that women exist to be seen and evaluated by men and are not entitled to control how their own images are captured and used.

3 Breach

We confirm the conclusion of the court of appeals that Boyles's conduct was sufficiently likely to distress Kerr that he owed her a duty. We must now review whether jurors correctly concluded that he failed to exercise reasonable care for her emotional well-being.

Tort law intends "reasonableness" to be an objective, uniform standard. But that aspiration can be a bit problematic, especially in a case like this. The metric for "reasonableness" originated as shorthand for the judgment of a "reasonable man." Although most jurisdictions today use a "reasonable person" test, the fact remains that the original notion of reasonableness was produced by male judges, male lawyers, and male jurors. Bender, *supra*, at 22. Some would say that the understanding of what is "reasonable" continues to reflect a worldview that may not be shared across gender. For example, in recent years, it has become fashionable to understand "reasonableness" in terms of utility, that is, to ask whether the level of care necessary to avoid invading another's right is cost-justified by the value of that right. Torts scholar

Leslie Bender has suggested that this way of understanding "reasonableness" draws primarily from economics, and purely abstract reasoning devoid of consideration for the complex reality of people's lives, ethical modes historically understood as male. *Id.* at 31–32. Another approach, she has suggested, is to understand "reasonableness" in terms of "concern and responsibility for the well-being of others." *Id.* at 31. This approach draws primarily from an ethic of empathy and care, ethical modes historically understood as female. It is a small leap to see that a concern-based notion of reasonableness would be friendlier to Kerr in this situation (and to plaintiffs generally).

Even without thoroughly reworking existing notions of reasonableness, we can affirm the jury's finding that Boyles breached the standard of care here. Applying the garden-variety reasonable person test – would a person of reasonable prudence in a similar setting have foreseen the possibility of injury – yields a resounding "yes." Remember that the question here is not whether Boyles should have foreseen that having sex with Kerr without the benefit of true affection would foreseeably cause her emotional distress. That is not at all what she alleges as the cause of her injury. Kerr consented to the sexual encounter at issue aware that Boyles was not interested in a full-fledged romance. This is a relatively common occurrence in the life of modern teenagers. Boyles would not have, and would not have been expected to, foresee that this alone would cause her anguish.

However, Kerr did not consent to be filmed during their encounter, or to having the tape shared with strangers. The term "kiss and tell," and the social disapproval of such a practice, has been with us for centuries. *See, e.g.*, William Congreve, Love for Love (1695) (Congreve's play was the first print use of the phrase, according to William Safire, *On Language: Kissing and Telling about Kiss-and-Tell*, N.Y. Times (June 5, 1988)). Whether engaged in out of love, or for less enduring reasons, sex may be the most private behavior known to human beings. It is precisely *because* most people would not wish to have these activities watched by strangers that the showings of the tape seem to have provided Boyles and his friends such an illicit thrill. To be filmed unawares during such an encounter and to learn that the tape made the rounds among strangers for purposes of amusement would foreseeably cause emotional injury to any person who does not willingly exhibit him or herself in such a circumstance. That is to say, it would foreseeably cause emotional injury to the vast majority of Texans.

It is possible that our dissenting colleagues have conflated Kerr's consent to a particular sexual encounter with a complete forfeiture of her sexual dignity and autonomy. In tort language, they seem to feel that by assuming the risk that Boyles would exploit her privately for an evening of sex, she also assumed the risk he would exploit her publicly for his amusement thereafter. This logic reminds us of the old saw in rape prosecutions that evidence of consensual sexual encounters with past partners operated as evidence of consent with the defendant. *See, e.g.*, Vivien Berger, *Man's Trial, Woman's Tribulation: Rape Cases in the Courtroom*, 77 COLUM. L. REV. 1, 15–16 (1977). Sexual agency does not work that way. Susan Kerr had the autonomy to choose what she would – and what she would not – do with Dan Boyles. She did not choose to be taped nor to have the tape distributed, and that the theft of her control over these choices would humiliate and distress her is eminently foreseeable.

This, at any rate, was the conclusion of the twelve Texans on the jury after a trial. Tort law gives the greatest deference to the jury on questions of reasonableness. In fact, jury instructions often equate "due care" with prevailing community views of what is reasonable. One study has indicated that courts often urge jurors to define care according to "everyday community norms." RANDOLPH E. BERGSTROM, COURTING DANGER: INJURY AND LAW IN NEW YORK CITY, 1870–1910, 134–36 (1992). Juries are uniquely suited to inject their daily experiences into deliberations about the relational and social norms that are at the heart of the tort enterprise. "Judges may not know a great deal about driving a farm wagon, boarding a streetcar, operating a ripsaw, or the other activities ... common during our period," according to eminent jurist Richard Posner. Richard A. Posner, *A Theory of Negligence*, 1 J. LEG. STUD. 29, 51 (1972). Jurors have a "better feel for the facts in many ... situations." *Id.* Indeed, jury verdicts often pull against judicial intuition in a way that raises the profession's consciousness, as in the many cases where juries appeared to render verdicts that nullified harsh contributory negligence and fellow servant doctrines. *See, e.g.*, Stephan Landsman, *The Civil Jury in America: Scenes from an Unappreciated History*, 44 HASTINGS L.J. 579, 610 (1993).

The people of Texas, represented by this jury, decided that a woman may consent to sex without consenting to being taped in the act. They decided that videotaping a sexual partner and repeatedly broadcasting the tape was an unreasonable course of action.

One reason we should defer to the jury on this issue has to do with its diversity and our homogeneity. As recently as 1954, this state (along with many others) barred women from jury service. AMERICAN CIVIL LIBERTIES UNION, THE CASE FOR EQUALITY IN STATE JURY SERVICE app. 3 tbl. I (1966). It was not until 1968 that all states permitted women to serve on juries. Rhonda Copelon et al., *Constitutional Perspectives on Sex Discrimination in Jury Selection*, WOMEN'S RTS. L. REP., June 1975, at 3. Even then, many extended automatic exemptions for women who sought them, until 1978 when the Supreme Court struck them down. Duren v. Missouri, 439 U.S. 357 (1979). Years ago, in *Ballard v. United States*, 329 U.S. 187, 193–94 (1946), the court told us that diversity of gender viewpoint is a unique strength of the jury: "The truth is that the two sexes are not fungible; a community made up exclusively of one is different from a community composed of both." This is especially true in tort, where jurors are asked to evaluate the meaning of contested behavior. Where the contested behavior arises specifically out of relationships between members of the opposite sex, a norm derived from a diverse institution is likely to be superior to a norm that arises from the male experience alone.

The Texas Supreme Court that originally overturned the verdict against Dan Boyles in December 1992 comprised nine middle-aged men, most of whom had long since left the dating world.[3] That court was not legally compelled to overturn *St. Elizabeth* and find that the jury should not have even been allowed to consider Kerr's claim for NIED. It chose to disturb the jury's verdict because it had a different opinion about what men and women should expect from each other as sexual partners. Our dissenting colleagues are entitled to their personal opinions about how young people should court, but they are not entitled to impose those preferences on Texans at large.

4 Injury

We suspect that our dissenting colleagues are also skeptical on the element of injury. As a matter of law, they may wonder whether emotional injury is sufficiently weighty to anchor this cause of action. Kerr claims to have been humiliated and traumatized, and while the dissenters tell us that is regrettable, they also intimate it is beneath the concern of the law. In their original opinion, the majority wrote that "[t]he tort law cannot and should not attempt to provide redress for every instance of rude, insensitive, or distasteful behavior, even though it may result in hurt feelings, embarrassment, or even humiliation." *Boyles*, 855 S.W.2d at 602.

Restricting legal injuries to those that could be physically proven seemed an efficient mechanism for screening out trumped up claims of injury when it was originally suggested by Oliver Wendell Holmes in 1902. Homans v. Boston Elevated Rwy, 62 N.E. 737 (Mass. 1902). But that doctrine was adopted at a time when physical damage and psychic damage were thought to be distinct, and when mental harm was poorly understood and presumed to be

[3] In the interim, we have welcomed Justice Rose Spector to this court.

easy to fake. Science has since adopted a far more nuanced understanding of the brain–body connection and of the diagnosable veracity and seriousness of mental harm. *See, e.g.*, Chamallas and Kerber, *supra*, at 834. Screening out illegitimate claims of injury can no longer be done by drawing a fallacious line between body and mind.

Further, defining legal "injury" to exclude emotional harm may be a holdover from a nineteenth-century legal system populated entirely by men. Cultural expectations that men act while women feel may have informed a legal conclusion that physical injuries are real and important, while emotional injuries are not. *See, e.g.*, Frances Olsen, *The Sex of Law, in* THE POLITICS OF LAW: A PROGRESSIVE CRITIQUE 453–65 (David Kairys, ed. 1990). Tort law originally defined injury to include the devaluation of property or body, both of which resources were leveraged by men as participants in the economic marketplace. It placed diminution of emotional well-being in a secondary position because emotional resources were not obvious drivers of a market system but were thought to belong to the female "sphere." *See* Lucinda M. Finley, *Breaking the Silence: Including Women's Issues in a Torts Course*, 1 YALE J.L. & FEM. 41 (1989).

NIED is tort's attempt to give a fuller account of experiences that can injure.[4] Notably, when we recognized the tort in *St. Elizabeth*, we did not supply a list of fact patterns in which we would accept claims of emotional injury without physical harm. Any such list would likely be both overinclusive and underinclusive. The gravity and genuineness of harm is highly fact-dependent. That is why we did not limit *St. Elizabeth* to its facts, and why we specifically delegated to the jury the task of identifying the kinds of behavior most likely to cause compensable mental anguish. Having opened the door as a matter of law to liability for negligently inflicting distress, we cannot now yank it shut because some of us may disagree with the jury's conclusion that the distress here was real.

Aside from appearing skeptical that humiliation counts as an emotional injury compensable in tort, the dissenters also seem skeptical that Kerr actually was humiliated. Boyles was her first sexual partner and he exploited that role to

[4] Again, it is no mistake that the plaintiffs in the leading NIED cases are women. Women have historically not been expected to use their bodies to generate wealth or take up space in the public world; but rather have been expected to use their bodies as vessels for the creation of life and thereafter to use emotional resources to nurture that life. Recognizing injuries to emotional life that grow out of these socially approved familial relations was an early step toward treating women as equally deserving of the law's protection in the event they had been wronged. *See, e.g.*, Chamallas & Kerber, *Fright*, *supra* at 816.

boost his own social standing at the expense of hers.[5] While the dissenters dutifully report her allegation that the trauma caused by the scandal "made it difficult for her to relate to men," they disparage it by gratuitously remarking that she had multiple sexual partners after the scandal. *Boyles*, 855 S.W.2d at 594. And they connect the two observations with the conjunction "although," which suggests that the two statements are in tension with each other. *Id.* They seem to disbelieve that she could *both* struggle to form healthy intimate relationships *and* engage in intercourse with men. That she continued to seek sexual partners after this trauma is construed by the dissenters as evidence she was not truly damaged. But, of course, it could also demonstrate the opposite.

C *Remedies*

Finally, our dissenting colleague Justice Gonzales complains that Kerr framed her complaint as one for *negligent* infliction of emotional distress rather than *intentional* infliction of emotional distress solely to access insurance coverage to pay the verdict. This is so, we are told, because homeowners' insurance policies like the one Boyles's parents carry cover negligent, but not intentional, torts. He chides Kerr for selecting the cause of action that presents the best chance of a full dollar recovery. *Id.* at 604. He seems to think she should be grateful for a possible moral victory on remand. *Id.*

In suggesting that Susan Kerr should content herself with a possible IIED verdict that is unlikely to lead to the actual ability to recover any significant money, the dissenters imply that the best remedy for her is a public declaration that she was not a willing "porno queen." The dissenters seem to think that moral virtue is still the coin of the realm for women, and this declaration might "rehabilitate" Kerr socially. But Kerr made clear by opting for the "deep pocket" NIED cause of action that she didn't want indirect access to money via a merely declarative judgment. She wanted actual money, and the actual deterrent impact of a real recovery. *Id.*

Kerr testified that her college performance suffered because of this ordeal. It takes little extrapolation to surmise that this would diminish her career prospects as well. She is a less viable participant in the job market than she would have been without the trauma of this event. She sees herself as

[5] Boyles's legal team acted no better than their client. The day of the verdict, attorneys and staffers at the firm representing him held a champagne party to celebrate the comparatively low award to Kerr. The centerpiece of the party was a raucous screening of the videotape, compared by a female employee of the firm to "a stag party." Confronted with evidence of this event, they preemptively paid Kerr $600,000. David Margolick, *For Texas Firm, the Price of Circulating a Videotape Proves Quite Steep*, N.Y. TIMES, June 1, 1990, at B6.

belonging to the sphere historically reserved for men – the public, economic sphere. She wants to be compensated accordingly.

By diverting her to a tort not covered by Boyles's insurance, the dissenters would restrict her to recovering her "good name," rather than recovering the financial wherewithal she has articulated as her true goal. They would deny her the cause of action she has selected. Instead, they promise her an alternate right, although it is one effectively without a remedy. This is a charlatan promise indeed.[6]

III CONCLUSION

We hereby grant the motion for rehearing, withdraw our opinion of December 2, 1992, reversing the jury's verdict in Kerr's favor and replace it with this opinion affirming that verdict.

6 F. Scott Fitzgerald, This Side of Paradise 236 (1920).

13

Commentary on *Emerson v. Magendantz*

LUCINDA M. FINLEY

INTRODUCTION

The desire to control fertility and childbearing has long been a human imperative. Recognizing how fundamentally the "decision whether to bear or beget a child" can affect one's life, in the early 1970s the US Supreme Court gave constitutional protection to this decision in landmark cases involving access to contraception and abortion.[1] Even before constitutional law recognized a woman's right to control her reproductive destiny, courts grappled with repercussions of medical negligence that impinged on this right. These cases fall into two distinct categories: cases involving women who did not want any children or additional children, and cases involving women who wanted children free from congenital disease or disability.[2] These cases typically present medical malpractice claims involving the failure properly to perform a tubal ligation or vasectomy,[3] or failure to inform a parent of the likelihood a pregnancy would result in a child with birth defects or a genetic disease, thereby depriving a woman of her right to make an informed decision about whether to conceive, or if already pregnant, to have an abortion.[4]

1 Eisenstadt v. Baird, 405 U.S. 438, 453 (1972); Roe v. Wade, 410 U.S. 113 (1973).

2 *See* Barbara Pfeiffer Billauer, *The Sperminator as a Public Nuisance: Redressing Wrongful Life Claims in New Ways (Aka New Tricks for Old Torts)*, 42 U. Ark. Little Rock L. Rev. 1 (2019).

3 *See, e.g.*, Custodio v. Bauer, 59 Cal. Rptr. 463 (1967) (failed sterilization procedure led to unwanted pregnancy and childbirth); Christensen v. Thornby, 255 N.W. 620 (Minn. 1934) (husband's failed vasectomy led to wife's unwanted pregnancy that threatened her health).

4 Many of the earliest cases in this category arose from the rubella epidemic and involved claims that a doctor negligently failed to inform the pregnant woman of the risks of having a disabled child due to German measles exposure. *See, e.g.*, Gleitman v. Cosgrove, 227 A.2d 689 (N.J. 1967); Jacobs v. Theimer, 519 S.W.2d 846 (Tex. 1975). Some states have statutorily banned wrongful birth actions that involve a claim that but for a physician's negligence a woman

Along the way, courts have used various names to identify these claims. The terminology, and judicial receptivity to the claims, varies according to whether the plaintiff is the child born with a disabling condition, or the parents who wanted to avoid having a child. When the claim is brought on behalf of a child who never would have been conceived, or would have been aborted, but for the defendant's negligence, courts have called the claim "wrongful life." All but a few states reject such claims, reasoning that "[w]hether it is better never to have been born at all than to have been born with even gross deficiencies is a mystery more properly to be left to the philosophers and the theologians."[5] In contrast, when the claim is brought by parents for damages resulting from an unwanted pregnancy and subsequent birth, courts commonly use the term "wrongful birth,"[6] and these claims are widely allowed. Some courts further refine the terminology, using the terms "wrongful conception" or "wrongful pregnancy" for those cases where a failed sterilization procedure results in the birth of a healthy child.[7]

THE MEASURE OF DAMAGES

While courts have overwhelmingly approved claims for wrongful birth, wrongful pregnancy, or wrongful conception, determining the measure of damages has been fraught with contention. Only one state high court has denied recovery outright, reasoning that the birth of a healthy child presents no compensable injury.[8] All the other state courts to have addressed these claims do recognize that there is some injury from an unwanted pregnancy, but the majority of courts allow only limited recovery, which generally includes the costs of the initial failed sterilization procedure and of the subsequent corrective procedure, medical expenses for prenatal care and the childbirth and

would have chosen to abort. *See* Cailin Harris, *Statutory Prohibitions on Wrongful Birth Claims and Their Dangerous Effects on Parents*, 34 B.C.J. L. & Soc. Just. 365 (2014).

5 Becker v. Schwartz, 386 N.E.2d 807, 812 (N.Y. 1978). Only California, Washington, and New Jersey permit "wrongful life" claims by the disabled child. *See* Curlender v. Bio-Science Labs., 165 Cal. Rptr. 477 (1980); Procanik v. Cillo, 478 A.2d 755 (N.J. 1984); Harbeson v. Parke-Davis, Inc., 656 P.2d 483, 495 (Wash. 1983). *See generally* Barbara Pfeiffer Billauer, *"Wrongful Life" in the Age of Crispr-Cas*, 142 Penn State L. Rev. (2020).

6 Speck v. Finegold, 439 A.2d 110 (Pa. 1981).

7 *See* James v. Caserta, 332 S.E.2d 872, 879 (W. Va. 1985); Chaffee v. Seslar, 786 N.E.2d 705 (Ind. 2003).

8 Szekeres v. Robinson, 715 P.2d 1076, 1079 (Nev. 1986).

immediate postpartum care.[9] Some courts also allow damages for emotional distress[10] and lost wages related to the pregnancy.[11]

The major disagreement involves the cost of raising the healthy child. Only two state courts allow full recovery for child-rearing costs. Courts denying full recovery raise public policy arguments such as resistance to categorizing a healthy child as a harm,[12] or allege difficulty in valuing these claims.[13] The most common rationale that courts give for denying full recovery for the costs of rearing a healthy child is based on what has been called the benefit-offset rule. This rule, derived from *Restatement (Second) Torts* §920, provides that the costs of rearing a healthy child should be offset by the benefits, either emotional or economic, that the child brings to the parents' lives.

The case of *Emerson v. Magendantz*[14] presents a classic wrongful pregnancy fact pattern of a failed sterilization operation, and sets forth the issue of the appropriate measure of damages in stark relief. This makes it an excellent vehicle to investigate the romanticized stereotypes about children, rooted in ideology that presumes the centrality and unmitigated joy of motherhood in women's lives, that permeate the reasoning of courts that bar full recovery. By the time *Emerson* was decided in 1997, thirty-six US jurisdictions had approved the validity of wrongful birth claims, including wrongful conception and pregnancy. In Rhode Island, however, the matter was still one of first impression, and the Rhode Island Supreme Court extensively surveyed the various approaches taken by other courts.

EMERSON V. MAGENDANTZ

Diane and Thomas Emerson already had one child and determined they could not afford another when Emerson sought a tubal ligation from obstetrician-gynecologist Dr. Henry Magendantz. The operation was a failure, and a year later Emerson gave birth to a daughter, Kirsten, born with congenital deformities. After the birth, Emerson underwent a second tubal ligation. She and her husband later brought suit, claiming that she suffered severe physical pain and emotional distress, required additional invasive medical treatment and sustained lost wages and diminished earning capacity.

[9] *See, e.g.*, James, 332 S.E.2d at 879.
[10] *See, e.g.*, Speck, 439 A.2d 110.
[11] *See, e.g.*, Miller v. Johnson, 343 S.E.2d 301, 305 (Va. 1986).
[12] *See, e.g.*, Johnson v. Univ. Hosps. of Cleveland, 540 N.E.2d 1370, 1378 (Ohio 1989).
[13] *See, e.g.*, McKernan v. Aasheim, 687 P.2d 850, 855 (Wash. 1984).
[14] 689 A.2d 409 (R.I. 1997).

Additionally, the Emersons sought recompense for their existing and future obligations to financially care for their daughter.

Defendant Magendantz moved to dismiss the complaint, contending that Rhode Island law should not recognize a tort claim for a failed sterilization procedure because the resulting child was a "precious gift." The trial court, seeking definitive guidance on the legal issues at the heart of the motion to dismiss, certified to the Rhode Island Supreme Court the questions of whether this tort claim should be allowed, and, if so, what damages should be awarded. After an extensive review of existing precedent, the Supreme Court, following the majority of American jurisdictions, held that a cause of action existed for negligent performance of sterilization when a patient subsequently becomes pregnant and delivers a child. The court, however, offered no independent analysis of the reasons for allowing the claim or of the nature of the interests harmed.

The court then turned its attention to the measure of damages, noting the three different types of remedies that other courts had allowed: limited recovery consisting of the expenses of and pain and suffering from pregnancy and delivery and the subsequent sterilization; full recovery for all foreseeable damages including the costs of child-rearing; and full recovery but with the costs of child-rearing offset by the benefits derived by the parents from having a healthy child.

Faced with these alternatives regarding the damage claim, by a 3:2 vote the court rejected both full recovery including child-rearing costs for a healthy child, and the benefit-offset approach, and instead adopted the limited recovery rule, albeit a variant which excludes the mother's emotional distress incident to the pregnancy. In support of their decision, the *Emerson* majority reasoned that "the public policy of this state would preclude the granting of rearing costs for a healthy child whose parents . . . have decided to retain the child as their own with all the joys and benefits that are derived from parenthood."[15] The fact that the parents decided to keep the child rather than pursue abortion or adoption "constitutes most persuasive evidence that the parents consider the benefit of retaining the child to outweigh the economic costs of child rearing."[16]

If the child, such as Kirsten Emerson, was born with congenital defects, the *Emerson* majority decided that the parents could recover the extraordinary costs of raising a disabled child that exceeded the costs associated with rearing a nondisabled child. The majority further expanded the allowable damages for

[15] 689 A.2d at 413.
[16] *Id.*

a disabled child when the physician had reason to know that there was a likelihood that any pregnancy resulting from a failed sterilization could result in a physically or mentally handicapped child. In these circumstances – which did not apply to the Emersons – the parents would be able to recover all of the costs of raising the child throughout its life, offset only by any governmental benefits received, plus emotional distress from the disability.[17]

Two justices, while concurring with the decision to recognize the wrongful pregnancy cause of action, dissented from the limitation on recoverable damages. The dissenters noted that the case was a straightforward medical malpractice action, and thus should be treated in accordance with the normal tort principle that all foreseeable damages are recoverable – and the costs of raising a child that results from a failed sterilization are certainly foreseeable. The dissent chastised the majority's treatment of parents' decision to keep a child rather than choose adoption or abortion as evidence that the parents considered the child a benefit. Such an equation, the dissent argued, amounts to a denial of a woman's constitutionally protected right to not have children.[18] The dissent stopped short, however, of permitting full recovery including all child-rearing costs, in all situations. They recommended following the decisions of the Supreme Judicial Court of Massachusetts in *Burke v. Rivo*,[19] and the Connecticut Supreme Court in *Ochs v. Borrelli*,[20] which denied recovery for child-rearing costs when the reason the parents sought sterilization was to prevent birth defects or a health risk to the mother, and the resulting pregnancy and child were healthy. In this instance, these courts and the *Emerson* dissenters reasoned, the harm the parents sought to prevent had in fact not happened, so for them the healthy child could not be considered a foreseeable and compensable injury.

THE FEMINIST JUDGMENT

Professor Katharine Silbaugh, writing as Justice Silbaugh, offers a rewritten majority opinion that in significant aspects tracks the reasoning of the *Emerson* dissent in adopting the rule of full recovery for all foreseeable damages, including child-rearing costs for a healthy child. But Silbaugh also significantly departs from the dissent, criticizing the *Burke* and *Ochs* decisions on

[17] *Id.* at 414.

[18] *Id.* at 416 (Bourcier, J., dissenting). The dissent cited *Griswold v. Connecticut*, 381 U.S. 479 (1975); *Eisenstadt v. Baird*, 405 U.S. 438 (1972), and *Roe v. Wade*, 410 U.S. 113 (1973), as establishing the right to decide to not have children.

[19] 551 N.E.2d 1 (Mass. 1990).

[20] 445 A.2d 883 (Conn. 1982).

which it relies as inviting an inquiry into a woman's reasons for wanting to avoid pregnancy that inherently undermines the autonomy of her choice, and risks basing recovery on paternalistic value judgments about her reasons for not wanting a child. Silbaugh's opinion is distinctly feminist in two significant ways: (1) she relies on liberal feminist theory to assert women's reproductive autonomy and choice[21] not to become a parent as a paramount value that is not only constitutionally protected, but should also be fully protected by tort law; and (2) she focuses on women's experiences, needs, and perspectives as the relevant lens for legal policy, rather than romanticized stereotypes divorced from reality about the costless joys of children.

In contrast with the *Emerson* majority, which simply concluded that it would recognize a cause of action because the overwhelming majority of other courts have allowed this claim, Justice Silbaugh analyzes the reasons why unwanted pregnancy, even when it results in a healthy child, should be considered a compensable harm. She notes that US constitutional law protects the right to decide not to become a parent not only because of abstract interests in autonomy, but also because of the recognition that pregnancy, and the mental, physical, and financial strains of child-rearing, can in fact harm women's physical health and economic prospects and ability to participate equally in society.

As Silbaugh points out, the joys of pregnancy and child-rearing blithely assumed by the *Emerson* majority are not unmitigated. Childbearing can lead to economic loss from child-rearing costs and diminished career opportunities, and also can be accompanied by physical harm and mental anguish. Silbaugh draws on the everyday lived experiences of women, for whom it is normal to go to great lengths to avoid pregnancy and its sequelae (i.e. having a child), as proof enough of its non-benign status. She deftly uses this aspect of women's experience to eviscerate defendant Magendantz's argument that having a child can never be a harm because children invariably bring precious joy. The efforts of the vast majority of women routinely to attempt to avoid pregnancy for most of their fertile years demonstrates that women do not see pregnancy and child-rearing as a precious joy that outweighs all its burdens.

Silbaugh's focus on the compensable injury as the impairment of reproductive autonomy is significant, because it keeps the focus on the interests of the plaintiff who wanted to not have a child, and avoids the conundrum that has tripped up judges of whether a healthy child should be considered an

[21] *See, e.g.*, Martha Chamallas, Introduction to Feminist Legal Theory 19–26 (3d ed. 2013) (describing liberal feminist legal theory and its focus on women's autonomy and reproductive choice).

"injury." Under Silbaugh's analysis, when a woman wants to avoid having a child for any reason, and seeks sterilization to prevent this outcome, the costs of rearing the child that results from the failed sterilization are foreseeable consequences of the physician's negligence toward the woman, regardless of whether the child is healthy or disabled.

Silbaugh's emphasis on women's reproductive autonomy and the experiential burdens of pregnancy and child-rearing brings into sharp relief the ways in which the majority approach denies women the full range of compensation to which they would otherwise be entitled by traditional tort law principles routinely applied in contexts other than pregnancy. In discussing why the so-called benefit-offset rule should be rejected, Silbaugh notes that conventional negligence law bars the use of a benefit to one type of human interest to mitigate damages from harm to a different type of interest, as in using emotional benefit to offset economic harm. As she trenchantly points out, even when a child does bring great emotional benefit to parents, they cannot take these benefits to the bank. That so many courts have misapplied this general rule in pregnancy-related cases is but another example of the law's difficulty in addressing the complex reality of pregnancy to women's lives, blinded perhaps by a moralistic preference for child-bearing.

Silbaugh's analysis suggests that the real motivating public policy that leads courts to limit recovery seems to be the notion that women are meant to be mothers, and that a woman's desire to avoid childbearing is inevitably misguided in retrospect, because she has failed to embrace the joy. As Silbaugh points out, the ideology underlying the cases that deny full recovery is that doctors who fail to sterilize a woman have actually done both that woman and society a favor. The burdens of children on women become invisible, and the logic of women's reproductive choice not to become a mother becomes, as she puts it, "idiosyncratic or selfish."

Silbaugh's feminist embrace of women's autonomy and respect for their reproductive choices also is apparent when she rejects the damages limitation endorsed by the dissenters in *Emerson*. The dissenters embraced full recovery for child-rearing costs only when the reason a woman wanted to avoid pregnancy was to avoid the economic burden of a child. But they rejected full recovery when the reason a woman wanted to be sterilized was to avoid a disabled child or adverse health effects of pregnancy, and she survived the pregnancy and had a nondisabled child. Silbaugh refuses to inquire into the motivations for pregnancy prevention and declines to stigmatize some choices. She expresses concern that once one starts down the slippery slope of privileging some reasons for wanting to avoid pregnancy over others, moralistic judgment can inevitably creep into the legal calculation. Her position is far more consistent with valuing autonomy, and it also recognizes that even when the wish to avoid pregnancy is based on one set of reasons that do not materialize, there can still be an adverse impact of even a healthy child on a woman's economic and social well-being

Silbaugh's rewritten opinion draws on this complex reality of mothering when she exposes the "sentimentality" of the actual opinion's view of the "benefit" of child-rearing, imposed at the expense of the mother who may experience it in an entirely different fashion. The original decision assumes that a woman's decision not to abort or put the child up for adoption is persuasive proof that she considers the child a joyful benefit, completely without any economic or emotional burden on her life. By imposing the Hobson's choice of receiving no compensation for the costs of rearing a healthy child from the negligent physician, or aborting the pregnancy or putting the child up for adoption – choices that may go against personal morality – the original *Emerson* opinion was completely divorced from any experiential idea of what pregnancy and mothering involves.

Silbaugh also recognizes the complex reality of mothering when she criticizes cases, such as the actual *Emerson* majority, and the Florida decision of *Fassoulas v. Ramey*[22] on which it relied, that deny damages for healthy children but permit damages for the extraordinary costs of raising a child with disabilities. Silbaugh points out that the assumption that a child with disabilities invariably presents burdens that outweigh any benefits is a "breathtaking double insult," both to parents who derive great joy from their children with disabilities, and to parents like the Emersons who had good reasons for determining that even a healthy child would present too great a burden in their lives.

GOING FURTHER AND IMPLICATIONS

If Silbaugh's reasoning that women's reproductive autonomy and lived experiences matter more than romanticized stereotypes about mothering had been adopted by a state's highest court in 1997, it could have influenced subsequent courts to align recovery in wrongful birth cases with traditional tort principles of full recovery for all damages caused by the negligence. Her articulation of why childbearing can adversely impact women's lives, even when they deeply love and value their children, has been fully borne out by subsequent sociological research. It is now fully empirically established that the emotional and

[22] 450 So. 2d 822 (Fla. 1984).

economic burdens of child-rearing affect women differently than men. Women bear a larger share of the child-rearing responsibilities.[23] Women also experience diminished earnings when they become mothers, while men tend to experience increased income when they become fathers.[24] This motherhood wage penalty is most pronounced in low wage jobs, which exacerbates overall gender inequality in wages for the women who can least afford it.[25] With the groundwork laid by Silbaugh, this research could lead even more courts to understand why permitting recovery of all the costs of rearing the child that results from a negligently performed sterilization is essential to redressing the harm and advancing women's equality.

In addition to discussing the burdens of child-rearing on women, Silbaugh could have gone further by more explicitly considering the significant relational aspects of motherhood on other family members. This concept is evidenced by concerns Emerson may have had regarding the impact of Kirsten's birth on her already existing child. Whatever family resources exist will now have to be split between the children, as will the parents' time and attention. These are consequences that Emerson went to great lengths to avoid, and they could be alleviated by the full recovery for child-rearing costs adopted in Silbaugh's feminist rewritten opinion.

Silbaugh's forceful advocacy for the full recovery principle also could have influenced courts in other countries, which, like the majority in *Emerson*, make concerted efforts to review preexisting cases in order to choose what degree of damages to allow. Prior to *Emerson*, in the United Kingdom, the prevailing view was that the normal tort principle of recovery for all foreseeable loss applied, and thus child-rearing costs were fully compensable. By 1999 the sentiment in the UK had changed, influenced by the accumulating weight of US authority as exemplified by *Emerson*. In 1999, the House of Lords, at that time the supreme appellate court that declared binding law for all civil cases in the UK, ruled in *Macfarlane and Another v. Tayside Health Board* (Scot.),[26] that compensation for child-rearing costs and diminished post-birth income would no longer be recoverable. This was a case where a

[23] Jill E. Yavorsky, Claire M. Kamp Dush, & Sarah J. Schoppe-Sullivan, *Production of Inequality: Gender Division of Labor across the Transition to Parenthood*, 77 J. Marriage & Fam. 662, 663 (2015).

[24] Michelle J. Budig & Paula England, *The Wage Penalty for Motherhood*, 66 Am. Soc. Rev. 204 (2001).

[25] Michelle J. Budig, *The Fatherhood Bonus and the Motherhood Penalty: Parenthood and the Gender Gap in Pay*, Third Way (Sept. 2, 2014) https://www.thirdway.org/report/the-fatherhood-bonus-and-the-motherhood-penalty-parenthood-and-the-gender-gap-in-pay

[26] [2000] 2 AC 59 (HL) (appeal taken from Scot.).

vasectomy performed on the husband failed, and the wife became pregnant and bore a fifth child that the couple alleged they could not afford. Since the *MacFarlane* court surveyed the American cases, one wonders what would have happened to law on the international scene if *Emerson* had been decided by the feminist Justice Silbaugh? Would it have turned the entire tide of British cases post-*MacFarlane* on its head?[27] If so, that in turn might have influenced courts in the United States to stop insulating negligent defendants from the full costs and effects of malpractice when it comes to pregnancy-generating harms.

The feminist voice of Justice Silbaugh, focusing on how women actually are affected by unwanted pregnancy and child-rearing, and valuing women's reproductive autonomy, could have changed the tide depriving women of their due, and shielding a defendant from foreseeable acts of malpractice. The rewritten feminist opinion reminds us that to accomplish this end, a diversity of judicial voices influenced by feminist theory certainly counts.

EMERSON v. MAGENDANTZ, 689 A.2D 409 (R.I. 1997)

JUSTICE KATHARINE B. SILBAUGH DELIVERED THE OPINION FOR THE COURT

On April 27, 1995, Justice Ragosta of the superior court certified two questions of law to this court pursuant to R.I. G.L. § 9–24–27:

1. Is there a cause of action under Rhode Island law when a physician negligently performs a sterilization procedure and the patient subsequently becomes pregnant and delivers a child?
2. If so, what is the measure of damages?

The facts giving rise to these certified questions may be summarized as follows from the pleadings and the documents filed by the parties in the superior court and in this court.

Following the birth of her first child, plaintiff Diane Emerson made a decision not to have more children and sought medical intervention to prevent any future conceptions. Emerson was motivated by a desire to avoid the expenses associated with supporting a larger family. She chose to undergo

[27] In 2003 Australia reversed the trend back when the court in *Cattanach v. Melchior*, (2003) 215 CLR 1 (Austl.), held the negligent doctor could be held responsible for the costs of raising and maintaining a healthy child.

a tubal ligation surgical procedure performed by defendant Henry Magendantz, MD, a gynecologist who advised Emerson about her sterilization options. Magendantz failed to advise Emerson about the risks of failure from a tubal ligation at any time before or after surgery.

A few months after her sterilization surgery, Emerson discovered that she was pregnant, despite her tubal ligation. She gave birth to Kirsten Emerson in early 1992, after which she chose to undergo a second tubal ligation surgery. Emerson and her husband filed a complaint against Magendantz alleging that his negligence both in performing the procedure and in failing to inform Emerson of any postsurgical risk of becoming pregnant led to significant damage to each of them. Emerson alleged that she suffered severe pain from pregnancy and childbirth as well as from additional invasive medical treatment pursuant to both the pregnancy and the second tubal ligation. In addition, both Emersons alleged that they have suffered mental anguish and distress arising from the unwanted pregnancy, as well as lost wages and earning capacity associated with both the pregnancy and the additional child-rearing burdens of a second child. Finally, the complaint alleges that Magendantz's negligence has imposed on the Emersons an obligation to expend substantial resources for the medical care and child-rearing expenses of Kirsten, who has already required substantial resources due to severe congenital health issues.

Magendantz moved to dismiss the complaint, arguing that there is no cognizable claim for wrongful pregnancy under Rhode Island law, and in response to that motion, Justice Ragosta certified the two questions to us.

I IS THERE A CAUSE OF ACTION UNDER RHODE ISLAND LAW WHEN A PHYSICIAN NEGLIGENTLY PERFORMS A STERILIZATION PROCEDURE AND THE PATIENT SUBSEQUENTLY BECOMES PREGNANT AND DELIVERS A CHILD?

The question posed is an issue of first impression in this state. Of the numerous courts that have considered the question, however, all but one recognize a cause of action for negligent performance of sterilization procedures whether performed on a woman or on a man.[1]

The thirty-five other states that have allowed the claim vary widely, however, in their treatment of the appropriate measure of damages. While the near unanimity of courts that recognize the claim might lead us to provide a cursory affirmative answer to the first certified issue, the relationship between

[1] The lone case to deny a cause of action for negligent performance of sterilization procedures is *Szekeres v. Robinson*, 715 P.2d 1076 (Nev. 1986).

the first and the second issue is too tightly woven to allow us this cursory answer. We conclude that an examination of the reasoning for and against a cause of action is essential to understanding the contours of the wrong, which in turn informs the appropriate measure of damages.

Defendant Magendantz argues in his brief that Rhode Island should decline to recognize a cause of action in these situations because viewing the birth of a child as a legally compensable injury is "offensive to the public sentiment that the birth of a child is one of life's most precious gifts." Yet according to this logic, Magendantz has taken it as his professional medical calling voluntarily to perform elective sterilization procedures that have as their sole purpose depriving adults of, in his own words, "one of life's most precious gifts." We cannot comprehend why Magendantz would offer sterilization services if he believed his own argument, and we consider his routine medical practice evidence that he does not. Further, extending the logic of his argument, were Magendantz to fail each time he contracted to perform a sterilization procedure, his medical ineptitude would actually have bestowed a precious benefit on his poorly served patients. Indeed, one Pennsylvania court that denied a cause of action *in contract* for these cases offered just such a rationale: "To allow damages in a suit such as this would mean that the physician would have to pay for the fun, joy, and affection which plaintiff[] will have in the rearing and education of [their] fifth child." Shaheen v. Knight, 11 Pa. D & C. 2d 41, 45–46 (1957). This reasoning seems to cast a woman's desire to avoid prospective parentage as always misguided retrospectively.

But the law firmly respects and protects a woman's autonomous decision not to have children, and recognizes that interference with this decision undoubtedly can lead to harm. In 1965, the United States Supreme Court recognized that a married couple's decision to prevent conception during sexual relations is a constitutionally protected right. Griswold v. Connecticut, 381 U.S. 479 (1965). The court did not explore in depth the reasons that a couple would decide against procreation, defending instead a privacy of decision-making in doing so. Yet it is difficult to see how the prevention of pregnancy can be a coherent decision worthy of constitutional protection if it were not possible for pregnancy – especially an unwanted one – to be a harm. Indeed, in *Roe v. Wade*, 410 U.S. 113 (1973), the court articulated the harm a pregnancy *can* impose on a woman who does not wish to bear a child, and that reasoning bears repeating in response to defendant Magendantz's argument that "the birth of a child is one of life's most precious gifts":

> The detriment that the State would impose upon the pregnant woman by denying this choice altogether is apparent. Specific and direct harm

> medically diagnosable even in early pregnancy may be involved. Maternity, or additional offspring, may force upon the woman a distressful life and future. Psychological harm may be imminent. Mental and physical health may be taxed by child care. There is also the distress, for all concerned, associated with the unwanted child, and there is the problem of bringing a child into a family already unable, psychologically and otherwise, to care for it.
>
> *Id.* at 153

When the Supreme Court later confirmed the basic holding of *Roe* in *Planned Parenthood of Southeastern Pa. v. Casey*, 505 U.S. 833 (1992), it again connected women's economic and social well-being to reproductive control, confirming that the "ability of women to participate equally in the economic and social life of the Nation has been facilitated by their ability to control their reproductive lives." *Id.* at 836. Applying this insight, Emerson's decision to prevent conception through sterilization could understandably be made to enhance her economic and social prospects, and so the pregnancy in question can inflict damages to those interests. Limiting future reproduction is an essential component of autonomy and liberty for women. Interfering with it through medical negligence therefore logically inflicts a grave harm.

The Supreme Court in *Roe v. Wade* carefully evaluated a balancing of interests, including women's right to control their own reproductive lives and the state's interest in protecting potential life, then confirmed that balancing more recently in *Planned Parenthood v. Casey*. Given these decisions, it would be remarkable were this court to accept Magendantz's argument that bearing a child that a woman had undergone surgery to prevent placed only blessings, and no countervailing burdens, on that woman. Magendantz's contention that it would offend public policy to recognize a cause of action precisely because it would "declare that a birth is a legally compensable injury," flies in the face of the very reasons articulated in *Roe* for protecting a woman's reproductive choice: bearing and raising a child *can be* injurious to a woman, and it is for her to evaluate the potential benefits and burdens to her of that pregnancy given her individual life circumstances and experiences, as well as her personal valuation of them based on her values and interests.

In short, a negligently performed sterilization that results in an unwanted pregnancy and birth of a child inflicts an "injury" because tort law defines injury as "invasion[s] of any legally protected interest of another." RESTATEMENT (SECOND) OF TORTS § 7(I) (Am. Law Inst. 1965). A woman's autonomous right to decide whether or not to become pregnant and have a child has been recognized as an interest legally protected by the US Constitution for over thirty years.

Defendant further argues that recognizing the Emersons' claim would be inconsistent with 10 R.I Gen. Laws § 7–1, which recognizes that the loss of a viable fetus is a compensable wrong. In his brief, Magendantz asserts that to "allow parents to claim that it is not the death or injury, but the *birth* of a child that is a wrong amounts to a seemingly insurmountable paradox." But it is no paradox at all when one recognizes that on balance some pregnancies confer a benefit and some a burden according to a woman's circumstances and values. The reproductive rights cases are premised on that logic.

In essence, defendant's reasoning that a child is *always* a blessing and a benefit would render a woman's exercise of her constitutionally protected right not to reproduce both illogical and invisible. We decline to ignore the clear implication of the rights afforded women to make reproductive decisions: often, the birth of a child does inflict an injury, one of enough significance to overcome the government interests expressed in those cases. Thus, a woman can have compelling and constitutionally protected reasons for wanting to avoid pregnancy by obtaining a tubal ligation. The failure of the medical procedure due to negligence inflicts a direct injury recognized in the articulation of the constitutional right of reproductive autonomy, and this right surely deserves recognition in the private law of torts. The interests invaded by Dr. Magendantz's malpractice have analogs across tort law, and appreciation of the right invaded helps us to evaluate the second certified question: how should damages for this cause of action be measured?

II IF SO, WHAT IS THE MEASURE OF DAMAGES?

Perhaps in anticipation of our decision to follow the overwhelming majority of states that recognize a cause of action for pregnancy resulting from a failed sterilization due to negligence, both parties focus their attention on the measure of damages. As a general matter, a defendant physician is liable for all foreseeable damages to a plaintiff patient for medical malpractice in the provision of medical care. On the issue of compensable damages for this cause of action, however, there is little consensus among other jurisdictions, yet the distinctions they have entertained provide us with a range of alternatives for answering this question. The larger set of jurisdictions allow for limited recovery, while a smaller set of jurisdictions permit more expansive recovery.

Standard rules of proximate cause and foreseeability point toward recovery for all categories of ordinary damages in a case where medical malpractice leads to losses. Medical malpractice actions frequently include recovery for medical expenses, pain and suffering, emotional distress, lost wages, and other foreseeable economic harm. We use as a starting premise in determining what measure of damages should be permitted to a victim of medical malpractice the same unquestioned basic common law rule of damages that we have applied in all negligence cases for centuries. We have always permitted the victim of a negligent tortfeasor to recover for all of the injuries and damages that can be proven to have been reasonably foreseeable and proximately caused by the tortfeasor's negligence. Atlantic Tubing & Rubber Co. v. International Engraving Co., 528 F.2d 1272 (1st Cir. 1976), cert. denied, 429 U.S. 817 (1976); Hueston v. Narragansett Tennis Club, Inc., 502 A.2d 827, 830 (R.I. 1986); Prue v. Goodrich Oil Co., 140 A. 665, 666 (R. I. 1928). *See also* Restatement (Second) Torts § 917 (1979); 1 Minzer, Nates, Kimball, Axelrod & Goldstein, Damages in Tort Actions, chs. 1, 2 (1996); 4 Harper, James, & Gray, The Law of Torts, §§20.4, 20.5 at 130–39 (2d ed. 1986).

In the case of failed sterilization procedures, however, a majority of jurisdictions have departed from this rule. Only two states, New Mexico and Wisconsin, follow traditional tort principles to permit the recovery of all damages foreseeably and proximately caused by the negligent defendant. Lovelace Med. Ctr. v. Mendez, 805 P.2d 603 (N.M. 1991); Marciniak v. Lundborg, 450 N.W.2d 243 (Wisc. 1990). The most common position across jurisdictions that recognize this cause of action is to allow recovery for a limited set of damages, primarily for expenses related to the unwanted pregnancy and birth of the child, but not including recovery for the costs of child-rearing.

Under the limited-recovery rule, jurisdictions frequently grant compensation to the plaintiffs for the medical expenses of the ineffective sterilization procedure, for the medical and hospital costs of the pregnancy, for the expense of a subsequent sterilization procedure, for loss of wages, and sometimes for emotional distress arising out of the unwanted pregnancy and loss of consortium to the spouse arising out of the unwanted pregnancy. They also generally include medical expenses for prenatal care, delivery, and postnatal care. In other words, these damages are highly limited in time, focused on the events surrounding the pregnancy and childbirth. The *type* of harm is not the sticking point for these states, but rather continuing the damages paid throughout the child's minority for ongoing expenses. We think that the length of time that the plaintiffs will suffer economic harm is hardly a meaningful limitation. If it is daunting for a court to imagine the awesome expenses associated with raising a child to the age of majority, we are cognizant that these expenses are in fact imposed on the plaintiff by the defendant's negligence.

The reasons for limiting recovery vary. Some courts claim that calculating the actual damage to parents requires an unacceptable level of speculation.

For example, the Supreme Court of Washington in *McKernan v. Aasheim*, 687 P.2d 850 (Wash. 1984), has made some pertinent comments:

> We believe that it is impossible to establish with reasonable certainty whether the birth of a particular healthy, normal child damaged its parents. Perhaps the costs of rearing and educating the child could be determined through use of actuarial tables or similar economic information. But whether these costs are outweighed by the emotional benefits which will be conferred by that child cannot be calculated. The child may turn out to be loving, obedient and attentive, or hostile, unruly and callous. The child may grow up to be President of the United States, or to be an infamous criminal. In short, it is impossible to tell, at an early stage in the child's life, whether its parents have sustained a net loss or net gain.
>
> *Id.* at 855[2]

This court's cautionary qualifier that "perhaps" child-rearing costs might be able to be calculated is entirely unwarranted. Actuarial tables and economic information about the costs of raising a child are readily available through numerous federal and state agencies. The United States Department of Agriculture (USDA) has produced an annual report since 1960 on the expenditure on children by families. The Bureau of Labor Statistics gathers consumer expenditure statistics often used by state level child welfare agencies to set a benchmark for child support. The costs of education are carefully tracked by governmental education departments and accrediting agencies and financial institutions, and are routinely calculated when making investment and financial aid determinations. When compared with pain and suffering damages, emotional distress damages, or loss of consortium damages, the lifetime cost of raising and educating a child is relatively easy to calculate. We are not persuaded that this element of damage requires so much speculation that we should depart from our ordinary practices.

As for the expressed concern about the speculative value to the parents of the child's accomplishments, the difficulty of commensurability pervades remedies in tort law. *See* Margaret Jane Radin, *Compensation and Commensurability*, 43 Duke L.J. 56–86 (1993). For example, we allow recovery for wrongful death, yet we know that no amount of money replaces a loved one whose life is ended due to the negligence of another. When we

[2] This argument assumes that a parent receives an economic benefit, a "net gain," from a child's accomplishment, such as becoming president of the United States. There was a time when the legal status of the child included ownership of the child's productivity, *see, e.g.*, Viviana Zelizer, Pricing the Priceless Child (1985), but the law of the family has developed beyond that kind of calculation, as we discuss at greater length below.

allow recovery for loss of consortium or for pain and suffering, we contemplate substituting financial payments under circumstances where we realize that those payments are not direct equivalents to the loss at hand. Only a failure of imagination lets us see the need for monetary damages for those losses, yet prevents us from grasping the harms and ongoing economic costs associated with a pregnancy by an individual who underwent surgery to prevent it.

Other jurisdictions explicitly depart from the normal proximate cause rules in medical malpractice actions based on faulty sterilization for policy reasons that aren't always clearly articulated. In *Johnson v. University Hospitals of Cleveland*, 540 N.E.2d 1370, 1377 (Ohio 1989), the Supreme Court of Ohio, after considering rules adopted by the various states, suggested that it would not mechanically apply the rules of proximate cause and foreseeability because the "strict rules of tort should not be applied to an action to which they are not suited, such as a wrongful pregnancy case, in which a doctor's tortious conduct permits to occur the birth of a child rather than the causing of an injury." *Id.* at 1378. In *Cockrum v. Baumgartner*, 447 N.E.2d 385 (Ill. 1983), the Supreme Court of Illinois stated that they would not "rigidly and unemotionally . . . apply the tort concept that a tortfeasor should be liable for all of the costs he has brought upon the plaintiffs," because, as Justice Holmes famously stated, "the life of the law is not logic but experience," and their experience led them to conclude that it was more reasonable to deny child-rearing costs than to "abstractly apply[] a rule not suited for the circumstances in this character of case." *Id.* at 390.

We are unpersuaded that requiring a physician who commits malpractice to pay for all foreseeable consequences of that malpractice demonstrates either an emotional or an unusually rigid, strict, or abstractly formalistic response to the circumstances of the case. We do agree, though, that the life of the law is not based solely on logic, but also on experience. In our experience, a person who seeks surgical intervention to avoid becoming pregnant has taken a difficult step consistent with her understanding, born of experience, that the birth of a child would dramatically alter her life course, emotionally, socially, and economically. When these significant and foreseeable costs are imposed on her as a result of medical malpractice, justice requires us to take notice.

While some courts consider the damages too speculative, and others argue that they should be rejected for policy reasons grounded in experience or reasonableness, most courts focus on the idea that the birth of a child following an unwanted pregnancy confers an emotional benefit of such value that it washes away the costs of raising that child. Joy is in equipoise with burden, nullifying losses associated with child-rearing against choice. The courts that take this approach do acknowledge that the costs of child-rearing can be a compensable loss, but balance against these costs the benefits derived by the parents, either economic or emotional, from having a healthy child. *See, e.g.*, Univ. of Ariz. Health Sciences Centr. v. Superior Court of Ariz., 667 P.2d 1294 (Ariz. 1983); Ochs v. Borrelli, 445 A.2d 883 (Conn. 1982); Burke v. Rivo, 551 N.E.2d 1 (Mass. 1990). Ordinarily, these courts intuit that the values are equal.

These courts refer to this offset as the "benefit rule." According to this rule, when, in addition to inflicting an injury on a plaintiff, a defendant also simultaneously confers a benefit on that plaintiff, the benefit should be subtracted from the burden in the calculation of damages. This reasoning would preclude granting rearing costs for a healthy child whose parents have decided to forego the option of adoption and have decided to retain and raise the child with all the joys and benefits that presumably are derived from parenthood. According to this reasoning, their decision to forego the option of releasing the child for adoption constitutes persuasive evidence that the parents consider the benefit of retaining the child to outweigh the economic costs of child-rearing. *See, e.g.*, Fassoulas v. Ramey, 450 So.2d 822 (Fla. 1984).

Courts that rely on this benefit rule cite to the RESTATEMENT (SECOND) TORTS § 920 (Am. Law Inst.1979), which provides:

> When the defendant's tortious conduct has caused harm to the plaintiff or to his property and in so doing has conferred a special benefit *to the interest* of the plaintiff that was harmed, the value of the benefit conferred is considered in mitigation of damages, to the extent that this is equitable. [emphasis added]

These jurisdictions reason that this provision provides for full recovery for all damages proximately resulting from a physician's negligence, while also permitting the factfinder to mitigate or reduce any damage award by what may be proven to be the value of the benefit conferred upon the plaintiff parent or parents by the birth of the child. Yet the RESTATEMENT only permits offsetting of damages by benefits to the *same interest of the plaintiff that was harmed*. That is to say, economic benefits may be subtracted from economic harms, emotional benefits from emotional harms. The RESTATEMENT does not support the offsetting of interests that are different in type, such as the economic loss of child-rearing costs offset with the emotional gains of having a child. Comment b to RESTATEMENT § 920 makes this explicit, giving as examples that a court cannot offset economic gain to reduce pain and suffering damages, nor can a court reduce damages for loss of consortium because a spouse is no longer obligated to economically support the lost loved one. As the Wisconsin Supreme Court noted in

Marciniak, "[p]roperly applied in the negligent sterilization context, the 'same interest' rule would require that the economic damages involved in raising the child be offset by corresponding economic benefits, and that emotional harms be offset by emotional benefits, and so on." 450 N.W.2d at 249. *See* Joseph S. Kashi, *The Case of the Unwanted Blessing: Wrongful Life*, 31 U. Miami L. Rev. 1409, 1415 (1977). This court reasoned that the parents presumably knew what emotional benefits they were foregoing by not having a child, and that it would be unfair "to not only force this benefit upon them but to tell them they must pay for it as well ." *Id.* The court also declined to offset economic benefits because it deemed any economic benefits that a child might bring to parents to be insignificant. *Id.*

This case illustrates the wisdom of the "same interest" limitation on the "benefit rule." To the extent that raising a child confers the emotional benefits so hoped for by these courts, there is simply no way to take those emotional benefits to the bank when a wronged plaintiff seeks to house, clothe, feed, and educate the child that results from defendant's negligence. Even at the most practical level, these jurisdictions ignore the reasons that the offset benefits must be limited to the same interests.

The "benefit rule" is problematic for additional reasons, linked to our answer to the first certified question. Courts that rush past meaningful evaluation of why there must be a cause of action in these cases – because there is a real harm to a fundamental constitutionally protected interest in reproductive autonomy – fail to recognize that the exercise of the constitutionally protected decision to avoid pregnancy is entirely routine in the experience of women. A woman who chooses not to become pregnant believes that for her, in her life circumstances, a child is a greater burden than benefit. By focusing on the benefits of raising children, some courts appear to minimize the burdens of caregiving, as if a labor of love is both priceless and costless. Caregivers know otherwise. Not only does the care of children require enormous financial resources of parents, but it also exacts additional financial opportunity costs, impairing a parent's earning capacity. Women's earning capacity is particularly adversely impacted by having children. In addition, the emotional content of caregiving is both joyful and burdensome, such that even the nonfinancial aspects of parenting cannot be assumed to keep a parent "in the black." Attachment and responsibility exact pain and suffering on parents just as they impart joy.

Courts that deploy soaring rhetoric to the effect that life's greatest joys are found in child-rearing make a person's decision not to have children, or additional children, seem idiosyncratic or selfish, as if it were an error from which she was fortuitously rescued by the defendant's malpractice. This belies how ordinary it is for people to seek to prevent pregnancy. Day in and day out, countless individuals, women in particular, go to great lengths to prevent pregnancy, not out of a large-scale miscalculation of benefits and burdens, but after a considered judgment about that balance. Although children can be joyful, the sheer regularity of the choice to prevent pregnancy suggests that the balance is often tilted toward burden. Those courts that invoke the "benefit rule" substitute their own feelings about children for the clearly revealed preference of every patient who seeks sterilization procedures. This is sentimentality, not justice.

Just as courts romanticize the benefits of children in order to deny malpractice victims compensation for their costs, some courts also demean the value of children with disabilities by recognizing that for them, unlike for a non-disabled child, a parent has been harmed by the imposition of an unwanted pregnancy and can recover for lifelong expenses. For example, in *Fassoulas v. Ramey*, *supra*, the Florida Supreme Court rejected child-rearing costs for a normal healthy child after a failed vasectomy, but observed that in the case of a child with a physical or a mental disability, special medical and educational expenses beyond normal rearing costs should be allowed because the "financial and emotional drain associated with raising such a child is often overwhelming to the affected parents." *Fassoulas*, 450 So. 2d at 824.

How quickly the Florida court turns from characterizing the birth of a child as a blessing and a joy, to comprehending that raising a child can pose a financial and emotional drain that overwhelms affected parents. According to the Florida court, a child with a disability is an injury, while a healthy child is not. We reject this reasoning because it is a breathtaking double insult, both to parents who derive tremendous joy from children with disabilities and to the many parents of healthy children who find that the financial and emotional strain of a healthy child is not worth the joys, and who therefore, like the Emersons, seek to prevent the birth of future children.

Magendantz seeks to avoid even the costs of raising a child with a disability. He urges that if we adopt the reasoning in *Fassoulas*, we should limit it by holding that only where a physician is placed on notice, in performing a sterilization procedure, that the parents have a reasonable expectation of giving birth to a child with a physical or a mental disability, should the entire cost of raising such a child be within the ambit of recoverable damages. While Kirsten Emerson was born with a disability that increases the Emersons' expenses compared with a healthy child, the Emersons were not motivated by fear of disability when they sought sterilization. They were motivated by economic concerns, feeling that they could not afford the ordinary child-rearing costs of a second child, whether perfectly healthy or not. By defendant's logic, because the Emersons sought to avoid *any* expenses from raising children, they should not be able to recover the *greater* expenses associated with Kirsten's disability, nor any of her ordinary child-rearing expenses.

Some courts have based their recovery rules on the reasons that a plaintiff wished to avoid a pregnancy. For example, in *Burke v. Rivo*, the court held that there is no harm when a patient seeks sterilization to avoid giving birth to a child with a disability, and a failed sterilization leads to the birth of a healthy child. The Massachusetts court allows recovery for child-rearing costs of a healthy child only if the plaintiff can show that she sought the sterilization for financial reasons. Ostensibly, this rule avoids paying child-rearing expenses where a patient might want to raise a child, but seeks to avoid pain and complications from pregnancy and delivery. *Burke*, 551 N.E.2d at 5–6.

We think the search for motivations for a sterilization procedure cannot be administered without inviting speculation or self-serving testimony, or a distasteful interrogation of patients prior to their seeking sterilization procedures. Accordingly, we decline to structure an inquiry into the motivations for preventing a pregnancy, just as we decline to base damages recovery on the value placed on one child over another. Given how widespread and routine the desire to prevent pregnancy is, we recognize that many individuals have multiple overlapping reasons to prevent a pregnancy, and an effort to sort out these reasons may unnecessarily stigmatize some reasons and pathologize this routine choice. We instead choose to follow the holdings in both New Mexico and Wisconsin, the two jurisdictions that follow traditional tort rules and allow recovery for all foreseeable damages arising from malpractice in this context by adopting a full-recovery rule without offsetting either the economic or the emotional benefits to be derived from having a healthy child. *Mendez*, 805 P.2d at 611–15; *Marciniak*, 450 N.W.2d at 247–50.

Understanding the reasons for allowing the cause of action in the first instance aids in considering the appropriate measure of damages. Once we appreciate that the benefit theory can be characterized as ideological rather than factual, in that it resists entirely the logic of exercising reproductive freedom by choosing sterilization, we can set aside its strained application to these cases and resort to the conventional rules of tort damages.

These cases have puzzled courts unnecessarily. One issue in particular, raised in a number of courts, requires our comment. Some courts go about assuming the benefit of a child to a plaintiff by noting that the plaintiff had an opportunity to either terminate her pregnancy or place her child for adoption. The fact that she chose instead to raise her child, say these courts, proves that the child is more benefit than burden. *See* Univ. of Ariz. Health Sciences Ctr.,

667 P.2d 1294; Jones v. Malinowski, 473 A.2d 429 (Md. 1984); Sherlock v. Stillwater Clinic, 260 N.W.2d 169 (Minn. 1977).

Emerson sought sterilization to avoid being presented with either of these options. She may have known she would not choose to terminate a pregnancy. The right recognized in *Roe v. Wade*, and reaffirmed in *Casey*, is the right to decide whether *or not* to terminate a pregnancy, and a woman should not be penalized by tort law for whichever she decides to do. Emerson is already parent to a child, and may not have wanted her child to experience the loss of a sibling placed for adoption. This hardly negates the costs of raising Kirsten. Emerson may have feared that given Kirsten's disability, she would not find care as dedicated as the Emersons would provide. Emerson may have predicted that despite the expenses of raising a child, she would experience an emotional attachment that would make placing the child for adoption impossible.

Courts who resist this cause of action also sometimes argue that it is a dignitary harm to a child to have a parent litigate their birth as an injury. Courts most often express this concern when the parents of a healthy child seek damages; their corresponding silence when parents seek compensation for an unwanted pregnancy that results in a child with a disability speaks volumes about the value judgments being made about children with disabilities. This professed concern about the psychological impact of a lawsuit on the child ignores the fact that the financial costs of child-rearing are real even to a parent with tremendous attachment to a child, perhaps even because of that attachment, which may fuel self-sacrifice for which the Emersons did not volunteer. As the court noted in *Marciniak*, the parents':

> suit is for costs of raising the child, not to rid themselves of an unwanted child. They obviously want to keep the child. The love, affection, and emotional support any child needs they are prepared to give. But the love, affection and emotional support they are prepared to give do not bring with them the economic means that are also necessary to feed, clothe, educate and otherwise raise the child.
>
> 450 N.W.2d at 246

It would be unrealistic and callous to recharacterize the parents' dilemma of attachment as a benefit pure and simple, much less a benefit cancelling out the extraordinary financial burdens of child-rearing. To do so would once again resist the logic that drives the overwhelming majority of women to, under some circumstances and for some period of time, seek out a variety of means to avoid pregnancy and childbirth. Cognizance of that logic requires that we fully compensate the Emersons for their damages.

For these reasons, we answer the certified questions as follows:

1. When a physician negligently performs a sterilization and there is a subsequent pregnancy and child, the patient has a cause of action for medical malpractice.
2. The measure of damages is the same as in any other malpractice action, and should include all foreseeable damages including the costs of rearing the child to adulthood, regardless of whether the child is born healthy or with a disability. Any emotional benefits that the child brings to the parents should not be offset against the economic costs of child-rearing.

14

Commentary on *McCarty v. Pheasant Run*

MOLLY WILDER

SETTING THE STAGE

When Judge Richard Posner wrote his opinion in *McCarty v. Pheasant Run*,[1] Ronald Reagan had been president for six years. Reagan's signature economic policy platform, "Reaganomics," had successfully transformed the dominant economic and political landscape into one that worshiped economic rationality, individual autonomy, and the free market. He was well on his way to appointing 402 federal judges – the most of any president to date[2] – to help secure his vision for years to come, including the appointment of Posner to the U.S. Court of Appeals for the Seventh Circuit. Although Reagan received acclaim for appointing Sandra Day O'Connor, the first woman Supreme Court justice, his overall record on appointing women was dismal. Of those Article III judges Reagan appointed, only 8 percent were women, compared to the 16 percent his predecessor Jimmy Carter appointed, the 19 percent his successor George H. W. Bush appointed, or, more recently, the 42 percent Barack Obama appointed.[3]

Posner would go on to serve for thirty-six years. Like Reagan, he leaned conservative, despite some more liberal stances on certain social issues; his guiding philosophy was that in judging, as in governing, wealth maximization was of paramount importance. As his judicial record shows, this philosophy led him to regularly support the economic interests of businesses and

[1] 826 F.2d 1554 (7th Cir. 1987).

[2] *Judgeship Appointments by President, Federal Judiciary*, https://www.uscourts.gov/sites/default/files/apptsbypres.pdf

[3] John Gramlich, *Trump Has Appointed a Larger Share of Female Judges than Other GOP Presidents, But Lags Obama*, Pew Research Center (Oct. 2, 2018), https://www.pewresearch.org/fact-tank/2018/10/02/trump-has-appointed-a-larger-share-of-female-judges-than-other-gop-presidents-but-lags-obama

employers at the expense of women's physical and emotional well-being. Among other examples, he found in favor of a department store that terminated an employee the day before she was to go on maternity leave,[4] interpreted substantial pay differences between male and female coaches of the same sport as economically defensible,[5] and trivialized a secretary's experience of sexual harassment to protect her employer from liability.[6]

At the other end of the political spectrum, second-wave feminism was in full force in the 1980s, focusing its criticism on sexual harassment, sexual objectification, and sexual violence. Just a year earlier, in 1986, Catharine MacKinnon had won a major feminist victory in *Meritor Savings Bank, FSB v. Vinson*, successfully convincing the Supreme Court to hold unanimously that sexual harassment counted as illegal discrimination under Title VII of the Civil Rights Act of 1964.[7] Because of the hurdles to recovery or conviction in both tort and criminal law, however, she and many others focused their efforts on making use of statutory anti-discrimination laws, such as Title VII's workplace protections and Title IX's protections in educational spaces.[8] Despite the advantages of this focus, it left women highly vulnerable to sexual harassment and violence outside of workplaces and schools and with little legal recourse in the event of a violation.

FRAMING THE FACTS

In that political atmosphere, Dula McCarty, a 58-year-old woman, sued Pheasant Run, Inc. after suffering a rape attempt while staying at the Pheasant Run Lodge in St. Charles, Illinois. In her feminist dissent, Professor Hannah Brenner Johnson, writing as Judge Hannah Brenner Johnson, shifts the focus from economic policy to the specific harm McCarty suffered as well as how that harm was exacerbated by structural discrimination she faced as a woman.

The first line of a judicial opinion often signals which issue the judge considers to be central to the case at hand. Posner begins his opinion, "The high crime rate in the United States has interacted with expanding notions of tort liability to make suits charging hotel owners with negligence in failing to

4 Troupe v. May Dep't Stores Co., 20 F.3d 734 (7th Cir. 1994).

5 EEOC v. Madison Community Unit School Dist., 818 F.2d 577 (7th Cir. 1987).

6 Baskerville v. Culligan Int'l Co., 50 F.3d 428 (7th Cir. 1995).

7 477 U.S. 57 (1986).

8 *See* Catharine A. MacKinnon, Sexual Harassment of Working Women: A Case of Sex Discrimination 171–74 (1979).

protect their guests from criminal attacks increasingly common."[9] This opening strongly suggests both that Posner is primarily concerned with large-scale economic trends ("expanding notions of tort liability") and that he considers the hotel to be the real victim in the case. This focus is all the more notable because the more typical opening of a case discusses its factual background – situating the case primarily in its own narrow and highly particularized context rather than in the expansive context Posner forefronts. Although Posner next moves on to the specific facts of the case, this opening line signals that he is more concerned with the case's economic effects on businesses than with the harm suffered by the plaintiff.

As first-year law students learn, a persuasive legal writer uses their presentation of the "facts" of a case to craft the narrative of the case.[10] Precisely because 'facts' carry at least a sheen of objectivity, subtle framing of facts provides a powerful means by which the writer may establish her version of the facts as the objective and authoritative account of what happened. Although the facts an appellate judge may present are constrained by the information available in the trial record, the judge still has significant discretion as to which facts to include, which to leave out, and how to frame those facts.

Posner's articulation of the facts emphasizes the size of the hotel ("a large resort hotel on 160 acres outside Chicago");[11] the safety features of the room ("door equipped with a lock and a safety chain");[12] and his skepticism about McCarty's testimony ("she claims that the incident caused prolonged emotional distress").[13] In contrast, Brenner Johnson's fact section tells the story from McCarty's point of view ("The sliding glass door, which was not used as the primary entrance to the room, was obscured behind a heavy curtain, and not readily visible to guests when they entered the room"); highlights the hotel's security failures ("the hotel provided no information to its guests upon check in about the existence of the sliding glass door, did not double check the rooms to ensure the door was locked, and did not warn its guests to do so"); and presents McCarty's testimony as fact ("[h]er emotional injuries were severe, and ultimately forced her to retire early from … Sears"). Whereas Posner sets up a story about a large hotel doing the best it could reasonably be expected to do, Brenner Johnson tells her narrative from the perspective of a female guest and victim.

9 *McCarty*, 826 F.2d at 1555.

10 Andrew Jensen Kerr, *Meta-Stories and Missing Facts*, 6 Cal. L. Rev. Cir. 69, 74 (2015).

11 *McCarty*, 826 F.2d at 1555.

12 *Id.*

13 *Id.*

POSNER'S LAW AND ECONOMICS APPROACH

Before and while he was a judge, Posner belonged to the cohort of professors at the University of Chicago that brought law and economics to prominence as the most important analytic tool for understanding law. The primary tenet of the law and economics approach is that economic efficiency is the appropriate standard by which all laws should be judged – not precedent, not corrective justice, not fairness, and certainly not moralized conceptions of "reasonableness." As applied to tort law, the law and economics approach tells judges to impose the costs incurred from accidental damage on the lowest cost provider. Essentially, in deciding a tort case, a judge's job is to treat the situation as a failed market, and to fix it by reallocating financial resources to where they would have fallen in an ideal market situation, where all parties could have bargained to the most efficient and therefore wealth-maximizing outcome for all. The law and economics approach is forward-looking; moral worth derives only from the expected worth of predicted consequences, unlike backward-looking notions of justice that aim to rectify or punish moral wrongs.

Although in theory a law and economics approach could be quite progressive in its approach to wealth maximization, its proponents have largely wielded it in favor of more conservative and libertarian positions. Posner, for example, has defended the right to abortion[14] and same-sex marriage,[15] winning him favor with liberals, but has taken positions on police power[16] and anti-trust laws[17] more in line with conservatives. Given his more liberal positions on certain social issues, one might wonder why his decisions in *McCarty* and other cases are so hostile to feminist legal positions. Most likely, Posner's sexism stems from a belief that consensual market transactions aimed at wealth maximization respect individuals' autonomous decisions. He likely justifies his opinions not only on the basis of their superior economic consequences but because he believes that the parties involved

[14] Planned Parenthood of Wis., Inc. v. Schimel, 806 F.3d 908 (7th Cir. 2015) (holding that statute requiring abortion doctors to have admitting privileges at nearby hospitals placed undue burden on women seeking abortions).

[15] Baskin v. Bogan, 766 F.3d 648 (7th Cir. 2014) (holding that statute banning same-sex marriage bore no rational relationship to legitimate state interest).

[16] Am. Civil Liberties Union of Ill. v. Alvarez, 679 F.3d 583, 608 (7th Cir. 2012) (defending a statute that would have prevented ACLU from videotaping police officers in public places).

[17] Roland Mach. Co. v. Dresser Indus., 749 F.2d 380 (7th Cir. 1984) (defending an exclusive-dealing arrangement).

have in some sense consented to the risk of whatever those consequences turn out to be.

Posner also holds an extremely broad conception of consent. In addition to express consent, where parties have in fact actively articulated their agreement, he considers *ex ante* compensation and hypothetical consent to be valid forms of consent that carry all the moral worth of express consent. *Ex ante* compensation occurs when the party has expressly consented to some transaction that implicitly encompasses the risk of whatever the loss the party suffers.[18] For example, under this view, when a homeowner's property value goes down because a waste facility is built next door, the homeowner implicitly consented because she was (or should have been) aware of the risk of devaluation when she bought the property. That risk is purportedly included in the price of the house, the assumption being that the price of the house is lower because it encompasses that risk, and that the homeowner preferred the lower price to avoiding the risk.[19] Hypothetical consent is even broader, including anything that rational people would consent to, were they actually asked.[20]

Posner's understanding of consent rests on his assumptions about the decisions rational independent people make. This calculating and atomistic conception of 'the economic man' has been the target of decades of feminist critique.[21] The understanding of 'rationality' or 'reason' as an emotionless impartial weighing of burdens and benefits has been criticized as a masculinist understanding that cuts out the role of feminine-associated emotion and relationships in our reasoning practices. As illustrated by the backlash President Obama faced when he suggested that judges should decide cases using 'empathy,'[22] this particular form of sexism continues to be deeply entrenched in the legal system. It is no accident that the furor reached a fever pitch around Obama's nomination of two women, Sonia Sotomayor and Elena Kagan, to the Supreme Court. Similarly, the isolated picture of the independent man ignores how men are only enabled to be 'independent' by the women who raise them and care for their physical and emotional needs throughout their lives.

[18] Richard Posner, The Economics of Justice 94 (1981).

[19] *Id.* at 90–94.

[20] *Id.* at 96.

[21] *See generally* Relational Autonomy: Feminist Perspectives on Autonomy, Agency, and The Social Self (Catriona Mackenzie & Natalie Stoljar eds., 2000).

[22] *See generally All about Empathy: Articles about Conservatives Attacking Empathy*, Center for Building a Culture of Empathy, http://cultureofempathy.com/references/Articles-Conservatives-Empathy.htm

ECONOMICS AND SEXISM IN *MCCARTY*

Posner's law and economics philosophy drives his opinion in *McCarty* and manifests as sexism at several points. He not only affirms the jury verdict for the hotel but sharply criticizes McCarty's behavior and arguments. He depicts Dula McCarty as incompetent, careless, and overly dependent, a direct contrast to the ideal economic *man*. For example, Posner undermines McCarty's testimony that she was unaware of the door behind the curtain in her hotel room, arguing that "[m]ost people on checking into a hotel room, especially at a resort, are curious about the view."[23] He suggests she may have been negligent or incompetent in leaving the door unlocked because she "was an experienced business traveler, so maybe she should have known better; and most people don't consider a safety chain an adequate substitute for a lock."[24] Finally, he ridicules her pleas for additional security as unreasonably needy, pointing out that the hotel "was a large place, and it is not to be supposed that it would be free of criminal activity no matter how careful (within the bounds of reason) the management was."[25]

At one point, Posner seems to take particular glee in knocking down McCarty's suggestion that Pheasant Run should have invested in more secure locks. He belittles her intelligence – though the theory was likely her lawyer's invention – writing, "Mrs. McCarty argues with some show of reason that the advertised locks appear to be more effective than the locks on the sliding glass doors at Pheasant Run," but then goes on to condescendingly explain that because the door in her case was unlocked, "[t]he world's fanciest lock – a lock to foil a Houdini – would thus have done her no good."[26]

Following Posner's *ex ante* compensation theory, a reader might well come to the conclusion that, given that McCarty voluntarily paid to stay in the Pheasant Run Lodge, she consented to the risk of almost anything that might happen to her there. Part of Posner's justification for his decision came from thinking that any reasonable traveler (and perhaps especially a seasoned business traveler) knows that she may be vulnerable to crime when staying in a hotel. Therefore, when McCarty paid for her room, she assumed that risk and therefore had no standing to complain *ex post facto* when the risk actually materialized.

[23] *McCarty*, 826 F.2d at 1557.
[24] *Id.* at 1559.
[25] *Id.*
[26] *Id.* at 1560.

Posner's approach to consent in *McCarty* employs the same logic courts used for decades to justify the doctrine that marital rape was impossible. Under this reasoning, knowing that marriage entails sex, a wife was deemed to consent *ex ante* to all instances of sex with her husband simply by marrying him. While feminists have made significant progress in excising this implied consent logic from legal doctrine, many vestiges remain.[27] Posner's understanding of consent in *McCarty* perpetuates the attitude that individual women are responsible for avoiding rape, rather than holding accountable those enterprises, such as Pheasant Run, that contribute to the heightened vulnerability of women.

THE FEMINIST JUDGMENT

In contrast to Posner's primary concern with the economic well-being of businesses and employers, Brenner Johnson's feminist dissent focuses on the health and safety of women victims of assault and sexual violence. While Posner's judicial philosophy is limited by a myopic focus on wealth maximization, Brenner Johnson takes into account how sexism is built into the structure of the legal system at every level. Where Posner focuses on the lack of physical injury, Brenner Johnson recognizes and emphasizes the emotional trauma McCarty suffered. Where Posner suggests that an 'experienced business traveler' like McCarty was negligent in failing to lock the door through which her attacker gained entrance, Brenner Johnson makes clear how unreasonable it is to expect any hotel guest to check their room for hidden unlocked doors – and how the suggestion of McCarty's negligence plays into the systematic victim-blaming suffered by survivors of rape and sexual assault. Overall, she characterizes Posner's attacks on McCarty's intelligence and character as a strategy that "deflected the attention of the fact finders away from the negligent conduct of the defendant and projected the defendant's negligence onto the plaintiff victim."

Brenner Johnson takes her concern with victim-blaming strategies and rhetoric one step further to object to Posner's treatment of the issue of plaintiff's comparative negligence in this case and in third-party rape cases more generally. Her dissent demonstrates that use of a comparative negligence defense in rape cases carries the risk of importing discriminatory norms, such as those that unfairly blame women for violence they suffer at the hands of men. Feminist scholar Ellen Bublick has documented the wide range of precautions juries

[27] Jill Elaine Hasday, *Contest and Consent: A Legal History of Marital Rape*, 88 Cal. L. Rev. 1373, 1483 (2000).

have found to be reasonable, cumulatively suggesting that, for a 'reasonable' woman, "fear of rape shapes every aspect of her life and conduct":[28]

> According to the cases, a reasonable woman does not go outside alone at night to hail a cab or walk to her car in a hotel parking lot, especially if a man is outside. She does not take four or five steps inside the door before closing it. She double checks her door locks and is certain that every window is closed. She does not open the door when someone knocks or invite a salesman into her home or a man into her hotel room. She never drinks alcohol with a man, particularly if he is older or streetwise or someone she has recently met. [internal citations omitted]

Apparently, Posner would add to that list that a "reasonable" woman must check her hotel room thoroughly for hidden doors.

At a broader level, Brenner Johnson uses her dissent to criticize the famous *Carroll Towing* case[29] and the brand of cost–benefit analysis that law and economics scholars such as Posner employ as the sole determinant of reasonable care. Objecting to such an "all-purpose economic formula," Brenner Johnson argues that such analyses fail to capture the severity of a "deprivation of personal autonomy that can occur without observable physical harm" and threaten to undervalue and trivialize sexual injury.

Brenner Johnson ends her dissent by noting that providing tort remedies for rape and sexual assault is all the more important because of the discrimination and obstacles women victims face in the current criminal justice system. While recognizing that tort law sometimes falls prey to these criticisms as well, tort also provides benefits criminal law does not: it gives victims more control over the process, reduces the burden of proof needed to secure a remedy, and provides the financial compensation that victims need to recover their mental and physical well-being. Moreover, the ability to sue third parties, as McCarty did in this case, often means that victims are more likely to recover substantial damages, since the defendants are more likely to be relatively wealthy corporations compared to individual perpetrators, who are often suffering from poverty themselves.

The preference for tort over criminal law is particularly important for women of color, as the criminal justice system has been demonstrated to be deeply biased against people of color, and especially black men. Black women scholars have written extensively about the conflict they often face between holding rapists and

[28] Ellen M. Bublick, *Citizen No-Duty Rules: Rape Victims and Comparative Fault*, 99 COLUM. L. REV. 1413, 1433 (1999).

[29] United States v. Carroll Towing Co., 150 F.2d 169 (2d Cir. 1947).

other sexual offenders accountable and throwing them to a system that disproportionately targets and convicts black men and punishes them more harshly.[30] It is often the women left behind who have to deal with the loss of economic resources and community destabilization caused by incarcerating nearly one-third of the black male population.[31] Tort law, though certainly still plagued by the same biases as criminal law, at least provides women of color with a form of accountability that they can better control, that can help them maintain their financial security, and that keeps their communities intact.

Had Brenner Johnson's opinion been the majority opinion in 1987, rather than Posner's, we can imagine that tort law could have become a haven for women wishing to avoid the criminal system. Such a decision from a prominent circuit court of appeals could have had a wide impact on the entire federal court system. While there likely would have been resistance to Brenner Johnson's overt feminism and her use of statistics, perhaps this one powerful judgment could have tipped the political balance in favor of a feminist approach, rather than the law and economics approach. Success in this particular area of tort law would likely have spread to other areas, and most significantly, might even have influenced the development of criminal law. Had it been the case that jurisprudence of sexual assault was addressed primarily through civil suits brought by the survivors themselves, rather than criminal prosecutors, a jurisprudence more in line with Brenner Johnson's approach might have developed. But the past cannot be changed. Still, looking forward, Brenner Johnson's opinion points toward a hopeful future for tort law. If the legal community capitalizes on the momentum created by the #MeToo movement, perhaps tort reform that successfully treats women with empathy and respect can become a reality.[32]

MCCARTY v. PHEASANT RUN, INC., 826 F.2D 1554 (7TH CIR. 1987)

JUDGE HANNAH BRENNER JOHNSON, DISSENTING

Dula McCarty, the plaintiff in this case, is a 58-year-old woman who was previously employed as a retail merchandise manager at Sears Roebuck, Inc.

[30] *See, e.g.*, Patricia A. Broussard, *Black Women's Post-Slavery Silence Syndrome: A Twenty-First Century Remnant of Slavery, Jim Crow, and Systematic Racism – Who Will Tell Her Stories?*, 16 J. Gender Race & Just. 373 (2013).

[31] *See* Cassia Spohn, *Race, Crime, and Punishment in the Twentieth and Twenty-First Centuries*, 44 Crime & Just. 49, 55 (2015) (noting that in 2001 "the chances of ever going to prison were highest among black males (32.2 percent) and Hispanic males (17.2 percent)").

[32] *See* Martha Chamallas, *Will Tort Law Have Its #MeToo Moment?*, 11 J. Tort L. 39 (2018).

McCarty v. Pheasant Run, Inc., No. 82 C 1310, 1985 WL 2069, at *1 (N.D. Ill. July 31, 1985). On October 27, 1981, she checked into the Pheasant Run Resort, an upscale hotel located in the suburbs of Chicago, where she had traveled to attend a business meeting hosted by her employer. The room in which she stayed was typical of those on the property. It had two entrances: the first entrance was a traditional hotel room door that opened into an interior hallway; the second entrance was a sliding glass door that opened onto an exterior walkway with stairs leading to a courtyard accessible to other hotel patrons and the public. The sliding glass door, which was not used as the primary entrance to the room, was obscured behind a heavy curtain and not readily visible to guests when they entered the room.

Despite the fact that the curtain blocked the view of the door that lay behind it, the hotel did not have a policy to provide information to its guests upon check-in about the existence of the sliding glass door, did not double check the rooms to ensure that the door was locked when a guest checked in, nor warn its guests to do so. On the night in question, consistent with hotel practice, McCarty was not advised of the door or the necessity to ensure it was locked. After checking in to her room, McCarty left to attend a work dinner and a meeting. While she was away, a man wearing a stocking mask entered her room and hid from sight. Upon McCarty's return later that same evening, she went into the bathroom to get ready for bed. As she exited the bathroom, the man came out of his hiding place and began physically assaulting and beating her. In the course of this attack, the masked man sexually assaulted McCarty and threatened to rape her.[1] After a struggle, McCarty fought him off and he eventually fled from the room. McCarty notified the hotel manager and local law enforcement immediately following the attack. Unfortunately, the perpetrator was never apprehended, and his identity remains unknown to this day.

The police investigation conducted after the attack revealed that the intruder entered into McCarty's hotel room through the sliding glass door, which had been secured by a safety chain, but was not otherwise locked. Because the sliding door's main lock was not engaged, the perpetrator was able to break the chain, enter the room and hide from sight until McCarty returned from dinner.

Fortunately, McCarty did not sustain serious physical injury at the hands of the intruder. However, she did suffer extreme emotional trauma as a direct

[1] The characterization of the harm experienced by McCarty, as described by the district court, was far more severe than the characterization by the majority in this appeal. *McCarty*, 1885 WL 2069, at *2.

result of the attack and attempted rape. Her emotional injuries were severe, and ultimately forced her to retire early from her career at Sears. McCarty subsequently filed a lawsuit against Pheasant Run, alleging the hotel was negligent in failing to protect her, as a hotel guest, from the criminal acts of this third-party attacker.

After a lengthy trial, the jury found in favor of the defendant hotel and the district court entered a judgment on the jury verdict. Immediately thereafter, McCarty filed a motion asking the trial court to enter a judgment notwithstanding the jury verdict. The trial court refused to grant her motion, and it is on this basis that she now appeals.

The majority, per Judge Posner, affirmed the ruling below. I respectfully dissent. The majority's decision relies on unwarranted speculation about the evidence presented to the jury and the parties' behavior. Both its analysis of the reasonableness of the defendant's conduct and its application of an economic test to determine reasonableness are untenable. Moreover, contrary to the majority, I agree with plaintiff's contention that the trial court's instruction to the jury on contributory negligence was improper. The instruction ignored crucial facts and was based on an erroneous application of the law. It was unduly prejudicial in that it reinforced rape myths, perpetuated victim-blaming, and likely inappropriately influenced the jury in its deliberations. It also erroneously injected a contributory negligence defense into a case involving the perpetration of an intentional tort by a third party. These errors were not harmless: they deflected the attention of the fact finders away from the negligent conduct of the defendant and projected the defendant's negligence onto the plaintiff victim in this case, McCarty.

I BACKGROUND

The kind of crime perpetrated against McCarty is all too common. According to the FBI Uniform Crime Report, there were 91,459 reports of rape or attempted rape in 1986. NATIONAL ARCHIVE OF CRIMINAL JUSTICE DATA, FBI UNIFORM CRIME REPORT (1986). Research reveals that over the past few decades in the United States, the number of rapes reported to law enforcement has increased significantly. David J. Giacopassi & Karen R. Wilkinson, *Rape and the Devalued Victim*, 9 L. & HUM. BEHAV. 367 (1985). Despite these significant numbers and the increased reporting trajectory, historically, rape has been a crime that largely goes unreported. Indeed, researchers have found that only 20 percent of forcible rapes are ever reported to law enforcement. Camilee E. LeGrant, *Rape and Rape Laws: Sexism in Society and Law*, 61 CAL. L. REV. 919, 921 (1973). Even when victims do come forward and make reports to the police, the related rates of arrest, prosecution, and conviction of perpetrators are very low.

Rape is now increasingly recognized as part of a continuum of violence that consists of different kinds of sexual violations. Illinois law reflects this reality by prohibiting rape, sexual assault, and attempts to perpetrate these forms of violence. 720 Ill. Comp. Stat. §5/11–1.20 (1984); 720 Ill. Comp. Stat. §5/8–4 (1984). However, the seriousness of all forms of sexual violence is often misunderstood and/or treated dismissively, and the long-term emotional impact on victims is not always readily apparent. Significantly, victims of *attempted* rape can be affected by the experience of having their bodily and personal autonomy threatened, often to the same extent as victims of completed rapes or sexual assaults. Libby O. Rusch & Susan M. Chandler, *Sexual Assault Trauma during the Acute Phase: An Exploratory Model and Multivariate Analysis*, 24 J. HEALTH & SOC. BEHAV. 174, 179 (1983) (observing that variation in factors such as injury to the victim, relationship of victim to assailant, and number of assailants may have an impact on the level of trauma experienced); Lynda L. Holmstrom & Ann W. Burgess, *Assessing Trauma in the Rape Victim*, 75 AM. J. NURSING 1288 (1975) (noting the varying impacts of sexual assault on the victim depending on contextual factors, including victims' subordination to the assault, or assaults that begin as a consensual encounter).

It is disconcerting that public perception and understanding of the impact of attempted sexual assaults is not well informed. Indeed, I suspect the decisions of both the district court and the jury were likely affected by what they regarded as the relatively "minor" harm McCarty experienced. After all, as the common narrative might suggest, she was not actually raped, and she successfully fended off her attacker before he could cause more significant or serious physical injury. Indeed, such a dismissive attitude toward the impact of attempted sexual assault is discernible in Judge Posner's downplaying of the seriousness of the attack on McCarty, at several points in his opinion, by referring to the sexual assault as a mere "mishap." *McCarty*, 826 F.2d at 1559. This inaccurate characterization of the assault minimizes both plaintiff's injuries and the severity of sexual violence. In my view, the law should better reflect the research and evidence-based reality that even an attempted rape is an attack on one's physical being that can trigger substantial and lasting emotional harm. And the law should hold accountable those who are in a position to prevent such crimes and fail to take reasonable steps to do so.

To be sure, the brutal physical attack and attempted rape of McCarty was not actually perpetrated by the Pheasant Run hotel, but instead by an unidentified criminal. Although the attack took place in a room located on the hotel's property, this does not automatically make the hotel liable for negligence. However, courts have long recognized that hotels and other similar businesses may be liable to victims when criminal activity – perpetrated by third parties – is foreseeable, and when there is a failure on the part of such businesses to act reasonably to keep the premises safe. *See* Mrzlak v. Ettinger, 323 N.E.2d 796 (Ill. 1975); Danile v. Oak Park Arms Hotel, Inc., 203 N.E.2d 706 (Ill. 1964). Indeed, the defendant hotel had experienced at least eleven breaches in security involving break-ins to hotel rooms through sliding glass doors in the two-year period preceding the attack on McCarty, and hotel staff had alerted management about concerns with the doors and their locks. *McCarty*, 1985 WL 2069 at *1.

Moreover, the law has long expected those who have a special relationship to the plaintiffs – such as common carriers and innkeepers – to exercise greater care than the ordinary person in protecting their patrons. *Id.* at *2. This special duty is not without limits, but it is significant. The innkeepers' heightened duty of care is not tantamount to strict liability, as suggested by the majority, but falls squarely within the established domain of negligence. The rule is stated succinctly by the Sixth Circuit in *Kveragas v. Scottish Inns*: Although an innkeeper is not required to provide a warranty of personal safety, a duty of due care to protect guests from third-party misconduct under all circumstances is required. 733 F.2d 409, 413 (6th Cir. 1984). The imposition of this standard of care is due in part to the vulnerability of individuals who are away from the safety and security of their own homes, and it dates back far in time.

Given this history, it is not surprising that courts across the nation have increasingly recognized the right of individuals to bring negligence claims against entities such as hotels, businesses, and landlords, for their failure to take reasonable precautions to protect against criminal attacks by third parties. Restatement (Second) of Torts § 324A (1965); Kline v. 1500 Massachusetts Ave. Apartment Corp., 439 F.2d 477, 482 (D.C. Cir. 1970). As an early legal scholar explained, "By the great weight of authority it is held that an innkeeper is not an insurer of the safety of the person of his guest, but that the innkeeper's obligations to protect and guard the safety of his guest is limited to the exercise of reasonable care for their safety, comfort, and entertainment." Joseph J. Hemphling, *Innkeeper's Liability at Common Law and Under the Statutes*, 4 Notre Dame Law Rev. 421, 428 (1929).

II DISCUSSION

Reasonableness is the cornerstone of the law of negligence. This venerable duty of reasonable care is easy to state, but difficult to define. A determination of reasonableness, which we routinely ask juries to make, entails making rational judgments informed by cultural norms. However, such a determination can also be infected by stereotypes and implicit biases. In this case, the question whether Pheasant Run acted reasonably in its efforts to ensure the safety of its guests is the central issue on appeal. Answering this question requires an assessment of what degree of care the hotel was required to exercise to ensure reasonably safe conditions for its guests.

At trial, McCarty put forth a number of different theories in support of her argument that Pheasant Run failed to act reasonably, and as a result failed to keep her, as a hotel guest, safe. According to McCarty, Pheasant Run should have: (1) ensured that the sliding glass door opening to the public walkway was locked at the time she checked into her room; (2) provided a warning to guests to keep the sliding glass door locked; (3) utilized better locks on its doors; (4) added a security force better matched to the large size of the hotel, which contained over 500 hotel rooms; (5) changed the structure of the walkway outside the room to make it inaccessible to the public from the ground floor; and (6) implemented protections to keep room keys out of the hands of people unauthorized to have them.

As the facts emerged at trial, some of these theories found evidentiary support, whereas others did not. According to the police investigation, McCarty was attacked by a man who entered her room through the sliding glass door, which was hidden by thick drapery, and provided direct access to her room via a public walkway. Of the various negligence theories offered by McCarty, three clearly apply to this unique set of facts. First and foremost is plaintiff's contention that Pheasant Run should have taken reasonable measures to ensure that the sliding glass door was locked at the time of check-in. Such a safety check could easily have been incorporated as part of the routine check-in protocol. Second, the hotel should have adopted the practice of routinely issuing warnings to its guests about the existence of the sliding glass door, and the importance of keeping it locked throughout the duration of their stay. Finally, Pheasant Run should have employed a stronger security force to match the scale of the resort property.

In evaluating McCarty's appeal, the majority maintains that the jury was entitled to decide whether to accept or reject any of plaintiff's proposed theories in evaluating the reasonableness of the hotel's behavior. In analyzing the jury's decision, the majority saw no legal problem with the jury's rejection of these theories and concluded that Pheasant Run acted reasonably in its efforts to address the safety of its guests. It must be borne in mind, however, that if any of plaintiff's proposed precautions are found, as a matter of law, to be reasonable precautions that would have averted her injury, the jury's ruling for the defendant may not stand.

I start my analysis with the awareness that there is no singular way to evaluate reasonableness. As evidence of its acceptance of this widely held truth, the majority acknowledges that courts in Illinois have not devised a firm definition as to what constitutes reasonable care or the failure to use reasonable care. Yet, in this case, Judge Posner and the majority have taken it upon themselves unilaterally to define reasonable care and negligence by smuggling an economic cost–benefit analysis into tort law where it is unwarranted. To this end, the majority relies – incorrectly in my view – upon the formula developed by Judge Learned Hand (the "Hand formula"), first used in *United States v. Carroll Towing Co.*, 159 F.2d 169, 173 (2d Cir. 1947) and employs it as the exclusive test to analyze reasonableness. The majority attempts to justify its reliance on this analytical and mathematical method by claiming that other courts in Illinois have done so. But, at the same time, the majority acknowledges that "Illinois courts do not cite the Hand Formula but instead define negligence as failure to use reasonable care, a term left undefined." *McCarty*, 826 F.2d at 1557.

The majority also fails to appreciate that the facts of *Carroll Towing* are significantly different from those present in this case, especially as relates to the kind of harm suffered by the respective plaintiffs. In *Carroll Towing*, an admiralty case, the negligence of a bargee charged with guarding the barge caused property damage, destroying goods aboard a sinking barge and damage to another shipping vessel. This stands in contrast to the harm sustained by the plaintiff in this case, i.e., serious physical and emotional injury to her person.

Those familiar with the *Carroll Towing* case know that the Hand formula was designed as a risk–utility test meant to measure the burden (B) of taking precautions to prevent harm against the likelihood or probability (P) the harm will occur as well as the gravity of the potential harm or loss (L), should it occur. The test is expressed algebraically in the famous equation, $B<P \times L$. However, the Hand formula does not fit all tort cases. It ignores the reality that many cases of negligence do not involve deliberate or explicit risk-taking, but instead are based on more ordinary instances of carelessness or thoughtlessness. Given the immense variety of negligence cases, we should hesitate to adopt an all-purpose economic formula and resist the temptation to radically steer the law away from precedent. Relying on the Hand formula is particularly problematic in cases involving sexual violence, where the "loss" being quantified (often a deprivation of personal autonomy that can occur without observable physical harm) is liable to be seriously undervalued and misunderstood. I fear that such undervaluation occurred in the present case, given the majority's description of sexual violence as a mere "mishap."

In my view, Judge Posner's insistence on applying the Hand formula to determine reasonableness in every case, and especially this case brought by McCarty, is a serious error and I write in dissent to underscore that Illinois courts have not and should not equate reasonable care to a strictly economic calculus of costs and benefits.

Moreover, Judge Posner's attempt to apply the Hand formula to the case at bar, combined with his unwarranted speculation about the jury's assessment of the facts, only ends up confusing the issues and fails to get at the potential negligence of the hotel. Unlike Judge Posner, I find it unnecessary to consider McCarty's theory of negligence based on the quality of the locks in the hotel rooms. Indeed, there is nothing in the record to suggest that the locks were faulty or inadequate, or that stronger locks would have prevented the assault. The majority goes to great lengths, however, to criticize McCarty for her failure to offer evidence on precisely how much it would cost to install new and presumably better locks. Such criticism is way off the mark, particularly because, as Judge Posner himself admits, the Hand formula does not require a plaintiff to quantify costs in such a way. More to the point, under the majority's analysis, the issue of providing better locks is not really relevant to this case. Instead, the majority takes the position that, regardless of the quality of the locks provided, it is ultimately the responsibility of the guests to use them. The court presumably is of the view that the jury could conclude that the hotel acted reasonably in simply providing doors that were capable of being locked. In my view, this assessment of the relative duties of hotels and guests is insupportable and flies in the face of a common law history that requires innkeepers to take reasonable measures to keep their guests safe.

Additionally, there was no evidence that McCarty herself unlocked and then later failed to relock the sliding glass door. To the contrary, the evidence suggests she did not even know of the door's existence. Absent such evidence, it is patently unreasonable to place the onus on a hotel guest to lock a door she may or may not know even exists. Such a view directly contradicts the long-held policy of holding innkeepers to a higher standard of care because they are more aware of the dangers and special features of the property than their guests.

In the final analysis, a proper evaluation of reasonable care in this case turns on the defendant's failure to ensure that the sliding door to the walkway was locked at the time of check-in. No one disputes that the sliding glass door was left unlocked. This immediately raises the question of whether making sure the door was locked was a reasonable precaution that the hotel should have taken. In my view, it clearly was. Checking the locks on the sliding glass doors in all hotel rooms poses neither a significant nor costly burden. It is a task that may easily be added to the responsibility of hotel housekeepers or bell staff as they escort guests to their rooms. The configuration of rooms at Pheasant Run differed from that of other hotels in that there were two entrances: a main door and a secondary sliding glass door. Nevertheless, guests at all hotels have a reasonable expectation that their rooms are secure upon check-in. As such, the guests who checked into Pheasant Run were entitled to expect that the secondary doors were also locked. Placing such a minimal burden on the hotel is entirely reasonable.

Because the hotel clearly failed to fulfill its duty to take a reasonable precaution to prevent plaintiff's injury, McCarty's motion to enter judgment notwithstanding the verdict should have been granted.

III CONTRIBUTORY NEGLIGENCE

In her appeal, plaintiff challenged the instruction on contributory negligence that the trial judge gave to the jury, arguing there was no evidence to support such an instruction. I agree with plaintiff and conclude that the trial court's action constitutes reversible error.

The instruction on its face was not inaccurate, as it reflects well-settled Illinois law that contributory negligence is no longer a complete bar to recovery. *See* 110 Ill. Rev. Stat. §2–1107.1, 2–1116; Davis v. United States, 824 F.2d 549, 551–52 (7th Cir. 1987). Rather, in this jurisdiction, contributory negligence is a partial affirmative defense that serves to reduce the defendant's liability by the proportion of fault borne by the plaintiff. However, an instruction as to plaintiff's contributory negligence should not be given unless the evidence supports a conclusion that plaintiff acted unreasonably.

As a procedural matter, the issue of plaintiff's contributory negligence arises only once the defendant's negligence is proven and must be kept separate from that initial inquiry. Before that stage, it is inappropriate to explore the quality of the plaintiff's conduct because it may distract or misdirect the fact finder's assessment of the reasonableness of defendant's conduct. I find unpersuasive the majority's assertion that it was "unlikely that the mere giving of the instruction somehow signaled to the jury the judge's belief that the verdict should be for the defendant." *McCarty*, 826 F.2d at 1559. Making such an assumption about what the jury "probably thought" does not mitigate the very real possibility they were improperly influenced by the substance of the jury instruction. To the contrary, researchers and scholars have found that juries in tort cases do in fact incorporate ideas of contributory negligence into their deliberations, and when they believe the victim actually contributed in some way to her victimization, are likely to render a verdict for the defendant. HARRY KALVEN JR. & HANS ZEISEL, THE AMERICAN JURY 242–43 (1966).

The negative impact of such a misdirected focus cannot be overstated. Permitting the contributory negligence defense brought with it extensive testimony about the plaintiff's negligence, or fault, which likely had a significant prejudicial effect. This is not a simple run-of- the-mill negligence case, but a case involving an attempted rape and a brutal attack on a woman. Sadly, it is still widely believed in our society that women who are victims of rape, or even attempted rape, are somehow to blame for what has happened to them. This attribution of blame is partly due to the proliferation of myths surrounding sexual violence. Common rape myths include the belief that women are at fault because of their appearance or what they wear, where and when they choose to go out walking, whether they are alone, or other choices they have made. The responsibility to avoid or prevent rape has often been unfairly placed on women, essentially holding the individuals who commit such crimes unaccountable. In this case, presenting the jury with evidence of the plaintiff-victim's purported negligence, while they grappled with the negligence of the defendant hotel, likely fueled and exacerbated these rape myths and misperceptions. Kurt Weis & Sandra Borges, *Victimology and Rape: The Case of the Legitimate Victim*, 8 ISSUES IN CRIMINOLOGY 71 (1973).

Finally, certain aspects of the majority's contorted reasoning relating to McCarty's behavior deserve mention. In refusing to credit McCarty's claim that she was unaware of the existence of the sliding doors, the majority simply assumed that all travelers, upon checking into their rooms, would take the time to pull back the curtains and admire the view. To be plausible, however, this farfetched assumption required several facts be true. First, that the guest was aware of the existence of a window or door, even though it was obscured behind the thick drapery. Second, that there was sufficient light outside to illuminate the supposedly picturesque view and entice the traveler to attempt to look outside. And, finally, that there was a view worth seeing. Anyone who has had occasion to travel to the flat and largely uninteresting Chicago suburb of St. Charles knows all too well that it is not mountainous, tree-filled, or otherwise all that view-worthy.

Therefore, I would conclude that there was insufficient evidence to justify giving a contributory negligence instruction to the jury. There is nothing in the factual record to suggest McCarty acted negligently. Nor is there anything to suggest that she had knowledge of the potential danger lurking behind a curtain in her room. To the contrary, she was simply the unfortunate victim of a crime while a guest at a hotel where she was staying to attend business meetings.

Although I do not believe the facts of this particular case support a finding of contributory negligence on the part of the plaintiff, there is a broader issue worth considering. I believe we should adopt a special rule disallowing the contributory negligence defense in cases in which a business or other entity is accused of negligence for its failure to protect the plaintiff against the foreseeable intentional criminal acts of a third party. In such cases, there are strong policy reasons for departing from the comparative negligence framework, thereby sending a strong message that rape victims and other victims of crime bear no legal responsibility for preventing their own victimization.

When the victim of a crime sues a perpetrator for the intentional tort of battery or assault, the defense of contributory negligence is not permitted, even in cases where the victim might have avoided the attack by acting prudently. In this respect, tort law tracks criminal law. Just as contributory negligence is no defense to an intentional tort, our system of criminal justice does not permit a rapist to point to the victim's behavior as a defense to the crime. Put another way, it is not a defense to a physical assault or attempted rape that the victim failed to take precautions, such as locking her door at night or installing an alarm system. Because such facts would not allow a defendant to escape criminal liability for committing a rape, it should follow that tort law should also disallow such a defense in cases like the one before us.

Individuals should not be expected to adapt their behavior to avoid becoming a victim of crime. More specifically, women should not be expected to act in ways to avoid the possibility of being raped. Such a requirement reflects a serious misunderstanding of the reality of rape and is at odds with fundamental conceptions of freedom, liberty, and autonomy. Appreciating the unfairness inherent in such an expectation is just as important in negligence cases as it is in intentional tort cases or criminal prosecutions. Disallowing a contributory negligence defense in third-party criminal attack cases would further protect crime victims and enhance their mobility and autonomy.

Simply put, contributory negligence should not be an available defense in cases like these. I recognize that this approach represents a deviation from settled law. But all settled law is not necessarily good law. As we learn more about the systemic blame levied against victims of sexual abuse and the unfairness and myths that often permeate the legal process, it is our responsibility to adapt tort doctrine to meet such pressing problems.

Finally, even assuming that giving the contributory negligence instruction was proper, the majority's analysis of McCarty's conduct is highly problematic. Importantly, it is well settled that reasonableness is evaluated by what an average or ordinary member of society knows and does. Courts generally have not created separate categories of reasonable people against whom to compare the conduct of the parties in a given case. In this case, the majority noted that the average guest might not have realized that a safety chain was an inadequate locking mechanism, yet remarked that "Ms. McCarty was an experienced business traveler, so maybe she should have known better[.]" *McCarty*, 826 F.2d at 1559. This not-so-subtle shift in the standard of care, from average guest to experienced business traveler, was unwarranted and unfairly suggested that plaintiff was negligent.

IV CONCLUSION

Tort law functions to provide monetary relief to individuals who suffer harm from civil wrongdoing. The fundamental goals of tort law are wide-ranging, but those especially relevant to our inquiry include making a victim whole through financial compensation, allocating responsibility for loss to appropriate parties, deterring future accidents and harm, and ensuring fairness.

Tort law has rightly become an increasingly valuable legal tool for victims of sexual violence. Society now recognizes that responsibility for sexual victimization is no longer limited to the perpetrators of such crimes, but also falls on those who fail to take reasonable steps to protect others from harm. Businesses such as Pheasant Run are in the best position to prevent harms like that suffered by McCarty. Holding them accountable not only accurately spreads the costs of injuries onto all responsible parties but also makes communities safer. Imposing liability also has a strong deterrent effect on businesses, as it puts them on notice that they must take reasonable precautions to avoid liability.

Assuring the availability of civil remedies is critical because the criminal justice system has often not been responsive to victims of sexual crimes. As one legal scholar notes, "[l]egal and social attitudes about rape have produced a network of formal and informal restraints on the actions of police, prosecutors, judges, and juries that hinder prosecutions for forcible rape." Legrant, *supra* at 928. Victims are frequently blamed for the crimes perpetrated against them, and often understandably do not feel comfortable reporting their attacks to law enforcement. Rape myths inform the perspectives of police, prosecutors, and jurors, and exacerbate the impact of violence on victims. Julia R. Schwendinger & Herman Schwendinger, *Rape Myths: In Legal, Theoretical, and Everyday Practice*, 1 CRIME & SOC. JUST. 18 (1974). Sometimes, as was the case with McCarty's attacker, the perpetrator is never apprehended, leaving no possibility for a criminal prosecution. Moreover, the criminal justice system is simply not designed to provide financial compensation to victims of crime.

Sadly, this entire case has been infused with myths, misconceptions, and misplaced blame regarding the attack and sexual victimization of McCarty. In cases such as this, courts should go to great lengths to be impartial and refrain from restating and reinforcing stereotypes or blaming victims of crimes for not protecting themselves or preventing harm. The jury should not have been permitted to reject McCarty's claims under the misguided view that she somehow failed to act "reasonably" in taking necessary precautions. Such an outcome is directly at odds with the goals of our tort system of compensation. The better approach is to shift the burden onto those actors who should regard it as a cost of their business venture and are much better situated to take preventative measures and ultimately absorb and spread the loss.

15

Commentary on *Lisa M. v. Henry Mayo Newhall Memorial Hospital*

CHRISTINE M. TAMER

INTRODUCTION

American tort law is largely fault-based,[1] save for notable pockets of strict liability for abnormally dangerous activities, animals, and defectively manufactured or designed products. Another important form of strict liability is vicarious liability, which imposes automatic liability upon a party – without regard to that party's fault – for a tort committed by another.[2] In her feminist judgment in *Lisa M. v. Henry Mayo Newhall Memorial Hospital*,[3] Professor Stacey Tovino uncovers the sexism behind application of the doctrinal tests used to invoke vicarious liability.

In the workplace, vicarious liability is encompassed in the doctrine of *respondeat superior* – meaning "let the superior respond." *Respondeat superior* provides that, as "a consequence of the employment relationship," the employer is held strictly liable for the employee's negligence or wrongful acts as long as such acts are committed "within the scope of employment."[4] This means that an employer cannot avoid liability for the wrongful acts of an employee "by ordering the employee to obey the law, by properly training or supervising the employee, or even by threatening to discharge employees who

[1] Dan B. Dobbs, Paul T. Hayden & Ellen M. Bublick, The Law of Torts § 426 (2d ed. 2011).

[2] *See, e.g.*, Kerl v. Dennis Rasmussen, Inc., 682 N.W.2d 328, 334 (Wisc. 2004) ("Vicarious liability is a form of strict liability without fault. A master may be held liable for a servant's torts regardless of whether the master's own conduct is tortious"); Alan O. Sykes, *The Boundaries of Vicarious Liability: An Economic Analysis of the Scope of Employment Rule and Related Legal Doctrines*, 101 Harv. L. Rev. 563 (1988).

[3] 907 P.2d 358 (Cal. 1995).

[4] Samuels v. Southern Baptist Hosp., 594 So. 2d 571, 574 (La. Ct. App. 1992).

act carelessly."[5] As the oldest form of strict liability, the doctrine of *respondeat superior* has been described as "an essential element in the tort system," justified by the principle that employers should bear the costs resulting from the risks of their business.[6]

Importantly, vicarious liability is imposed only for an employee's acts within the "scope of the employment." In struggling to determine just which acts are within the scope of employment, courts generally use one of two tests: (1) the more restrictive "motive to serve" test or (2) the more liberal "risks of the enterprise" test.[7] The *Restatement (Second) of Agency* and a majority of courts use the more restrictive "motive to serve" test,[8] which asks whether the employee was motivated to serve or intended to serve the employer at the time of the tortious action.[9] Other courts, such as those in California, employ a more liberal test that looks at the relationship between the employee's tortious act and the risks created by the enterprise. Courts using this more liberal test typically analyze whether (1) the employee's tortious act is "'engendered by' or an 'outgrowth' of his employment"; or whether (2) the employee's tortious act is "foreseeable from the employee's duties."[10] If the employee's tortious act falls within either prong, courts hold the employer can be vicariously liable for the plaintiff's injury.[11]

Under both tests, courts have regularly found an employee's negligent acts to be within the scope of employment. When it comes to an employee's intentional torts, however, some courts are more reluctant to impose vicarious liability.[12] Yet under the right set of facts, particularly in cases involving fights on the job or other nonsexual acts of misconduct, courts have imposed

[5] Apollo Fuel Oil v. United States, 73 F. Supp. 2d 254, 262 (E.D.N.Y 1999) (noting "[a]n employee who acts in direct contradiction of his employer's instructions can still be within the scope of his employment") (citations omitted); RESTATEMENT (THIRD) OF AGENCY § 7.07, cmt. c.

[6] Gary T. Schwartz, *The Hidden and Fundamental Issue of Employer Vicarious Liability*, 69 S. CAL. L. REV. 1739, 1745 (1996).

[7] Rochelle Rubin Weber, Note, *"Scope of Employment" Redefined: Holding Employers Vicariously Liable for Sexual Assaults Committed by Their Employees*, 76 MINN. L. REV. 1513, 1518 (1992).

[8] Martha Chamallas, *Vicarious Liability in Torts: The Sex Exception*, 48 VAL. U. L. REV. 133, 141–42 (2013); RESTATEMENT (THIRD) OF AGENCY § 228 (1957).

[9] *See* RESTATEMENT (THIRD) OF AGENCY (1957); Christopher E. Krueger, Mary M. v. City of Los Angeles: *Should a City Be Held Liable under Respondeat Superior for a Rape by a Police Officer?*, 28 U.S.F. L. REV. 419, 426 (1994).

[10] Lisa M v. Henry Mayo Newhall Memorial Hospital, 907 P.2d 358, 362–63 (Cal. 1995).

[11] *Id.*

[12] Fearing v. Bucher, 977 P.2d 1163, 1167 (Or. 1999) (noting that it is more difficult to apply *respondeat superior* to an employee's intentional torts); DAN B. DOBBS, PAUL T. HAYDEN, & ELLEN M. BUBLICK, THE LAW OF TORTS § 429 (2d ed. 2011) ("In many cases, perhaps most,

vicarious liability for an employee's intentional torts, ruling either that the employee's act was at least partially motivated to serve the employer[13] or, under the more liberal test, that the nature of the employment made employee's assault foreseeable.[14]

In contrast to cases involving an employee's nonsexual violence, courts have rarely held that an employee's sexual assault falls within the scope of employment.[15] Under the stricter motive to serve test, courts find it "almost inconceivable that a sexual assault furthers any employer's interest."[16] Even under the more liberal risks of the enterprise test, courts regularly hold that sexual assault is outside the scope of employment by characterizing a sexual assault as "purely personal," stemming from an employee's "lust" and, thus, not an outgrowth of his employment.[17]

The California Supreme Court's decision in *Lisa M. v. Henry Mayo Newhall Memorial Hospital* exemplifies this tendency to deny recovery and treat cases of sexual abuse differently from other tort claims. Since *Lisa M.* was decided in 1995, it has remained good law and has been cited repeatedly by courts to dismiss a plaintiff's claim against an employer for an employee's sexual violence.[18]

an employee's intentional torts are purely personal acts and thus not within the scope of employment").

13 *See, e.g.*, Patterson v. Blair, 172 S.W.3d 361, 372 (Ky. 2005) (holding employee was acting to further his employer's business interest when, while trying to repossess a truck, he shot at a truck being driven by a third party); Mason v. Sportsman's Pub, 305 N.J. Super. 482, 499 (App. Div. 1997) (employer could be vicariously liable where employee bouncer assaults third party in effort to remove patron and "serve the purpose of his employer in maintaining an orderly establishment").

14 *See* Carr v. Wm. C. Crowell Co., 171 P.2d 5, 6–8 (Cal. 1946) (employer vicariously liable when an employee threw a carpenters' hammer at a third party during an altercation). *See also* Kirlin v. Halverson, 758 N.W.2d 436, 447–48 (S.D. 2008) (genuine issue of material fact raised on scope of employment when employee assaulted a competitor because "use of force was foreseeable given his employment and the duties he undertook").

15 Daza v. L.A. Cmty. Coll. Dist., 202 Cal. Rptr. 3d 115, 121–22 (Cal. App. 2016); Chamallas, *supra* note 7, at 135 ("[T]ort law gives no crisp answer to the question of whether a business is vicariously liable for the sexual torts committed by its employees. Instead, the cases are conflicting and confusing, with a decided tendency to rule against vicarious liability in the sexual misconduct context").

16 Krueger, *supra* note 8, at 426.

17 *See* Doe v. Fulton-Dekalb Hosp. Auth., 628 F.3d 1325, 1333 (11th Cir. 2010).

18 *See, e.g.*, Z.V. v. County of Riverside, 189 Cal. Rptr. 3d 570, 581 (Cal. App. 2015) (holding social worker's sexual assault of 15-year-old child in foster care not within scope of employment); John Y. v. Chaparral Treatment Ctr., Inc., 124 Cal. Rptr. 2d 330, 338 (Cal. App. 2002) (holding no vicarious liability for counselor's sexual assault of a minor at a residential facility); *Daza*, 202 Cal. Rptr. 3d at 121–22 (holding school district not liable for guidance counselor's sexual assault of third party).

ORIGINAL OPINIONS

The majority opinion in *Lisa M.* held that, as a matter of law, a male ultrasound technician's sexual assault of a hospital patient occurred outside the scope of his employment at the hospital.[19] Applying the liberal "risks of the enterprise" test,[20] the majority made clear that, while the circumstances of the ultrasound (an invasive exam in a secluded, dark, private room without chaperones) made the sexual assault "possible," this was insufficient to impose liability, given that the technician (Bruce Wayne Tripoli) committed a "deliberate sexual assault" on the plaintiff which the majority characterized as "fairly attributed not to any peculiar aspect of the health care enterprise, but only to 'propinquity and lust.'"[21] The court also held that Tripoli's conduct was not foreseeable because "nothing happened during the course of the prescribed examinations to provoke or encourage Tripoli's improper touching of plaintiff, viewing the assault solely as "the independent product of Tripoli's aberrant decision to engage in conduct unrelated to his duties."[22] It distinguished the case from an earlier decision which had imposed vicarious liability when a police officer raped a citizen detainee.[23]

To support its holding, the majority cited the three policy goals of the *respondeat superior* doctrine: (1) preventing future injuries; (2) assuring compensation to victims; and (3) spreading the losses caused by an enterprise equitably.[24] It summarily dismissed the first two goals, stating that it drew "no firm direction" from considering either.[25] With respect to the third – spreading the risk of losses caused by the hospital equitably – it reasoned that the ultrasound technician's conduct was "so unusual or startling" that it was "unfair" for the hospital to assume the loss.[26]

Two dissenting justices argued that the case should not have been taken away from the jury. One dissenting justice explained that given that an ultrasound examination "inherent[ly]" requires "intimate contact" and puts pregnant women in a "vulnerable position," it would be reasonable for a jury to infer that Tripoli's "employment as an ultrasound technician did have certain 'peculiar aspects' that played a not insignificant role in the sexual

[19] *Lisa M.*, 907 P.2d at 367.
[20] *Id.* at 364–65.
[21] *Id.*
[22] *Id.* at 365.
[23] *Id.* at 365–66 (*citing* Mary M. v. City of Los Angeles, 814 P.2d 1341 (Cal. 1991)).
[24] *Lisa M.*, 907 P.2d at 366.
[25] *Id.* at 366–67.
[26] *Id.* at 367.

assault."[27] She noted that it would not be "unreasonable to infer that the intimate contact inherent in the job contributed to Tripoli's sexual arousal and incited him to engage in the misconduct," and, as such, it was inappropriate to take the question away from the trier of fact.[28]

Another dissenter complained that the majority "blink[ed] reality" in claiming to be able to "discern a particularized lust rather than work-related concupiscence"; and that the majority was "wrong" in refusing to acknowledge that Tripoli's "inspiration [for his sexual misconduct] arose from the mise-en-scène established by the hospital."[29] He also predicted that an "unfortunate but inevitable result of the majority's analysis [was] to exempt the health care employer, at least in part, from the doctrine of respondeat superior."[30] Unfortunately, in California, this prediction has come true with respect to not only healthcare employers, but all employers in sexual assault cases as "[c]ourts generally have held that an employee who sexually assaults a third party is not acting within the scope of employment for purposes of imposing liability on the employer under the doctrine of respondeat superior."[31]

THE FEMINIST JUDGMENT

Professor Stacey Tovino, writing as Justice Tovino, applies the same doctrine as the original opinion, but refuses to treat sexual violence differently than nonsexual violence. In reversing the trial court's grant of summary judgment and holding that a jury must decide if Tripoli's sexual assault was within the scope of his employment, Tovino's rewritten opinion incorporates several familiar feminist moves or themes.

The first feminist move Tovino employs is to attempt to remove male gender bias through the incorporation of women's experience. The original opinion held that it was not "generally foreseeable" that the ultrasound technician would sexually assault a patient and that Tripoli's conduct was "so unusual or startling" that it would be unfair to hold the employer hospital vicariously liable.[32] As noted by one feminist scholar, however, in applying the concept of foreseeability in tort cases involving sexual assault, courts often "end[] up meaning 'what is foreseeable to reasonable men,' rather than what it

[27] *Id.*
[28] *Id.*
[29] *Id.*
[30] *Id.* at 368, n.1.
[31] 3 Witkin, Summary of California Law (11th ed. 2018); Agency and Employment, § 201 (collecting cases).
[32] *Lisa M.*, 907 P.2d at 365–67.

is supposed to mean, that is, 'what is foreseeable to reasonable people,' a group that includes women and men with their differing experiences in our society."[33] The original majority opinion can be seen as a product of "a male-biased understanding of foreseeability interpreted to mean what men give attention to and focus on or protect against for their own well-being."[34] Armed with statistics and studies to prove that sexual violence against women is not only "generally foreseeable," but also frighteningly common, Tovino paints a vivid picture of the reality of women's experience. Her rewritten opinion forces "[t]ort law and foreseeability doctrine … [to] deal with the concrete reality of women's vulnerability to sexual violence."[35]

The second feminist theme in Tovino's opinion is her recognition of how a power imbalance can lead to sexual violence.[36] While the original majority opinion denied that Tripoli had "any power to exercise general control over plaintiff's liberty," the rewritten feminist opinion reveals the power imbalance present between a male healthcare professional and a female patient and explains how such a job-created power imbalance can lead to sexual assault.[37] Drawing from Catharine MacKinnon's dominance feminist scholarship,[38] the rewritten opinion recognizes that the power imbalance, coupled with the fact that the plaintiff was "a vulnerable young woman expected to submit to an invasive examination to preserve the health and safety of her fetus," "multiplied the chances of sexual assault." Paying close attention to the specific position Lisa M. found herself in – 19 years old, pregnant, vulnerable, and worried about the health of her baby – Tovino highlights that, from Lisa M.'s perspective, Tripoli's authority was bolstered by his medical scrub attire, advanced knowledge of the procedure and use of equipment, and the expectation that she would comply with what she thought was a valid request for an invasive exam.

33 Leslie Bender & Perette Lawrence, *Is Tort Law Male?: Foreseeability Analysis and Property Managers' Liability for Third Party Rapes of Residents*, 69 Chi.-Kent L. Rev. 313, 320 (1993).

34 *Id.*

35 *Id.* at 323.

36 Marjorie A. Silver, *Love, Hate, and Other Emotional Interference in the Lawyer/Client Relationship*, 6 Clinical L. Rev. 259, 267 (1999) ("The greater the degree of power-dependency, the higher the incidence of exploitative sexual encounters between professionals and the recipients of their services").

37 Jami Perez, *Keeping Sex Out of the Doctor's Office: A California Proposal to Stop Patient Sexual Abuse*, 35 Whittier L. Rev. 137, 139 (2013) ("There is an inherent power imbalance between patients and health care professionals largely because the patient seeks the health care professional for help. This immediately places the health care professional in a position of power that may intimidate the patient").

38 Catharine A. MacKinnon, *Feminism, Marxism, Method and the State: Toward Feminist Jurisprudence*, 8 Signs 650 (1983).

Tovino's opinion is also "mindful" that the sexual assault in *Lisa M.* occurred in a healthcare setting, a setting where studies show sexual misconduct is "not uncommon." She locates the case at the intersection of two areas where women have been oppressed in the law: (1) sexual violence; and (2) women's health – where, in comparison to men, the level of autonomy to make medical decisions given to women is less, and the level of care given to women is worse.[39]

Third, the rewritten opinion rejects sexual exceptionalism, i.e., "the tendency to characterize sexual desire or motivation as different from all other inducements to action."[40] In the original majority opinion, the court drew a bright line between nonsexual assault and sexual assault, holding that the latter was not "engendered" by the employment, but instead was a "result of only propinquity and lust."[41] It assumed that – unlike other forms of physical violence – sexual violence stems solely from the lust/sexual desire of the offender and failed to consider the significance of opportunity or job-created power – both linked to employment – as contributing to a foreseeable risk of sexual violence. In this way, the original majority opinion is a classic example of the "fundamental attribution error," defined as "a tendency to attribute an event to the character or disposition of the individual actors and to miss the significance or underplay the contribution of situational factors."[42] The original majority chose to fixate on Tripoli's character/motivation, thereby overlooking how the nature of his employment at the hospital (environment, location, job duties, power imbalance, etc.) facilitated a foreseeable risk of sexual violence.

Tovino's rewritten opinion eliminates the "fundamental attribution error" present in the majority's original opinion by refusing to treat Tripoli's sexual assault of Lisa M. as exceptional, unique, or different and goes on to apply the same legal analysis that prior California courts applied in cases of nonsexual assault. In such cases, the courts placed great weight on the fact that an employer required its employee to associate with third parties and on the fact

[39] Stephanie S. Gold, *An Equality Approach to Wrongful Birth Statutes*, 65 FORDHAM L. REV. 1005, 1008 (1996) ("Since its origin, the medical profession has been insensitive and even hostile to patient autonomy, especially female agency with respect to medical decisions"); Lisa Napoli, *The Doctrine of Informed Consent and Women: The Achievement of Equal Value and Equal Exercise of Autonomy*, 4 AM. U. J. GENDER & L. 335, 336 (1996) ("Although patients generally report having poor relationships with their doctors, studies have shown that women patients are consistently treated worse than men").

[40] Chamallas, *supra* note 7, at 160.

[41] *Lisa M.*, 907 P.2d at 364.

[42] Chamallas, *supra* note 7, at 168.

that the employee had no prior relationship with the third party. Tovino's rewritten opinion emphasizes these same "important situational factors."[43]

In rejecting sexual exceptionalism, Tovino's rewritten opinion also points out that there is no reason to differentiate between a man's propensity for "lust" and a man's "propensity for [nonsexual] violence," the latter of which courts have recognized as a "personal quality" that "[m]en do not discard ... when they go to work." By doing so, Tovino's opinion can be seen as rejecting a "pre-feminist world where sexual conduct is viewed as private behavior having nothing to do with the public sphere of work and employment."[44] Perfectly summarizing her rejection of sexual exceptionalism, Tovino proclaims: "We are unpersuaded that a man's propensity for nonsexual, physical violence toward another man should subject the employer to liability in *respondeat superior* ... but that a man's propensity for sexual lust with respect to a woman should not."

Lastly, Tovino's opinion challenges the conventional wisdom that sexual assault is a "private" crime or tort affecting only the victim, as opposed to something the "public" must take responsibility in preventing.[45] By showing that the three policy objectives of *respondeat superior* – spreading risk of loss; assuring victim compensation; and preventing reoccurrence of tortious conduct – all support the application of the doctrine in the case of an employee's sexual assault of a third party, the rewritten opinion requires employers to share in the responsibility to prevent sexual violence. The rewritten opinion not only helps assure a compensatory remedy for victims of sexual assault, but also serves to motivate employers, such as hospitals, to take the safety of women seriously, out of fear of potential liability. Tovino's opinion takes the opportunity to educate the public about the broader social costs to women of sexual violence and refuses to add to a woman's burden by insulating employers from vicarious liability just because the nature of the employee's wrongful action and the victim's resulting injury is sexual – and, therefore, society would say it is somehow deserving of less weight.

If Tovino's feminist rewritten opinion had been adopted by the California Supreme Court, not only would Lisa M.'s case have reached a jury for decision, but a message would have been sent to society's institutions

[43] *See id.*

[44] *Id.* at 170.

[45] Brande Stellings, *The Public Harm of Private Violence: Rape, Sex Discrimination and Citizenship*, 28 Harv. C.R.-C.L. L. Rev. 185, 216 (1993) ("Sexual assaults of women are not just transgressions against that individual woman or against women as a class, but also transgressions against the broader public").

(government, businesses, schools, hospitals, etc.) and the public at large that preventing sexual violence is not a "private" female problem, but a universal problem in dire need of a solution. It would have forced these institutions to be a part of the solution, as opposed to permitting them to "blink reality" – as the dissenting justices accused the original majority of doing.[46]

LISA M. v. HENRY MAYO NEWHALL MEMORIAL HOSPITAL, 907 P.2D 358 (CAL. 1995)

JUSTICE STACEY A. TOVINO DELIVERED THE OPINION OF THE COURT

I SUMMARY

Plaintiff Lisa M. was injured in a fall and sought treatment at defendant Henry Mayo Newhall Memorial Hospital. Under the pretense of conducting an ultrasound examination, an ultrasound technician sexually molested plaintiff. In plaintiff's action against the Hospital and others, the Los Angeles County Superior Court granted the Hospital's motion for summary judgment after concluding as a matter of law that the ultrasound technician's sexual misconduct occurred outside the scope of his employment.

The plaintiff appealed the trial court's ruling. The second district court of appeal reversed and remanded, holding that a genuine issue of material fact regarding the Hospital's *respondeat superior* liability precluded summary judgment. Morin v. Henry Mayo Newhall Mem'l Hosp., 34 Cal. Rptr.2d 535, 540 (1995). The Hospital petitioned the Supreme Court of California for review and we granted certiorari earlier this year. Morin v. Henry Mayo Newhall Mem'l Hosp., 886 P.2d 1252, 1252 (Cal. 1995).

A motion for summary judgment may not be granted when there exists a "triable issue as to any material fact." CAL. CIV. PROC. CODE § 437c(c) (West 1995). As discussed in more detail below, we hold that a genuine issue of material fact regarding the Hospital's *respondeat superior* liability exists and precludes summary judgment in this case. Accordingly, we affirm the judgment of the court of appeal and remand the matter to the trial court for further proceedings consistent with this opinion.

[46] *See Lisa* M., 907 P.2d at 368 (Mosk, J., dissenting).

II FACTS AND PROCEDURAL BACKGROUND

On July 9, 1989, plaintiff, then 19 years old and pregnant, sustained neck and back injuries when a movie theater chair she was occupying collapsed. An ambulance transported plaintiff to the Hospital's emergency room to determine the seriousness of her injuries. In addition to assessing plaintiff, a physician working in the emergency room also ordered an ultrasound assessment of plaintiff's fetus. Bruce Tripoli (Tripoli), the ultrasound technician who was on call to the Hospital's emergency room pursuant to a contract between Mediq Imaging and the Hospital, transferred plaintiff from the emergency room to an ultrasound room where he was alone with her.

The plaintiff asked Tripoli if her mother and boyfriend could be present with her during the examination. However, Tripoli refused the request. During the ultrasound examination, Tripoli turned out the room lights but left the adjacent bathroom door ajar to admit dim light. Other than the plaintiff and Tripoli, no one else was present in the room during the ultrasound examination.

Typically, an ultrasound examination conducted for purpose of assessing the health of a fetus consists of passing an ultrasound-generating wand over the exterior of the mother's stomach and abdominal region. The ultrasound waves must be mediated by a gel, which must be rubbed into the mother's skin to displace any remaining air. In this case, Tripoli testified that the exact placement and movement of the ultrasound wand varies with the mother's body type. On some women, according to Tripoli, images are best obtained by passing the wand as much as an inch below the pubic hairline. Tripoli stated that he found it necessary to pass the ultrasound wand one inch below plaintiff's pubic hairline.

After the ultrasound examination, Tripoli left the room for about ten minutes to develop the photographic results. Upon his return, Tripoli asked plaintiff if she wanted to know the sex of her fetus. Plaintiff consented to Tripoli's further use of the ultrasound instrument to determine the sex of her fetus. Tripoli told plaintiff, falsely, that to determine the sex of the fetus he would need to scan "much further down." With plaintiff's cooperation, Tripoli pulled plaintiff's shorts down and began to scan in her pubic hair. According to plaintiff, Tripoli also inserted the ultrasound wand in her vagina. After a while, Tripoli placed the wand down and fondled plaintiff with his fingers. Plaintiff testified he moved his fingers "around everywhere down there." While fondling plaintiff, Tripoli further stated that he needed to excite her to get a good view of the baby. Plaintiff found the touching uncomfortable, but Tripoli testified that he thought plaintiff was getting pleasure from it because she said it tickled.

Tripoli eventually stopped molesting plaintiff and returned her to the emergency room. Plaintiff wondered about the propriety of Tripoli's manual examination but, never having been through the procedure before, initially assumed that Tripoli was acting appropriately. Plaintiff was returned to the emergency room, from which she was discharged without further incident.

Still concerned about the propriety of Tripoli's manual examination, plaintiff spoke with her sister. Plaintiff's sister had undergone an ultrasound procedure for the same purpose while pregnant but told plaintiff she had not experienced the invasive finger examination suffered by plaintiff. Plaintiff then discussed the incident with her obstetrician. The obstetrician told plaintiff that the examination described by plaintiff was very inappropriate. Plaintiff reported the event and Tripoli was criminally prosecuted for sexual assault and pled no contest to a felony charge.

Thereafter, plaintiff filed a civil lawsuit, based on Tripoli's sexual assault, against Tripoli himself; Mediq Imaging, Inc. (Mediq), Tripoli's employer; and Henry Mayo Newhall Memorial Hospital (Hospital), contractor of the services of Mediq Imaging. Plaintiff's lawsuit stated a number of causes of action including battery, intentional infliction of emotional distress, negligent infliction of emotional distress, negligent supervision, and vicarious liability based on the doctrine of *respondeat superior*.

The Hospital filed a motion for summary judgment, asserting in relevant part that the actions of Tripoli did not fall within the normal duties of an ultrasound technician and therefore the Hospital could not be held vicariously liable for Tripoli's actions under the doctrine of *respondeat superior*. In opposition to the Hospital's motion for summary judgment, plaintiff asserted that there was a triable issue of fact regarding whether the Hospital was vicariously liable for Tripoli's actions committed within the scope of Tripoli's agency and employment. The trial court granted the Hospital's motion for summary judgment, ruling that the Hospital could not be vicariously liable for Tripoli's sexual assault of plaintiff.

The plaintiff appealed to the court of appeal, which reversed the trial court's grant of the Hospital's motion for summary judgment. *Morin*, 34 Cal. Rptr.2d 535 at 540. The court of appeal relied on Mary M. v. City of Los Angeles, 814 P.2d 1341 (Cal. 1992) (hereinafter *Mary M.*). In *Mary M.*, the female plaintiff was stopped for a traffic violation and then raped by an on-duty police officer who was eventually convicted of rape. The plaintiff brought a civil action against the officer and the city that employed the officer. The plaintiff alleged that the city was vicariously liable for the police officer's actions under the doctrine of *respondeat superior*. We held in *Mary M.* that the question "whether [the officer] acted within the scope of his employment was one properly left for the jury to decide." 814 P.2d at 1352. We further recognized that, despite its criminal nature, the rape in *Mary M.* was facilitated by the police officer's power and authority and should not be categorically ruled out as falling within the scope of his employment. We now review the court of appeal's reversal of the trial court's grant of the hospital's motion for summary judgment.

III DISCUSSION

A *The Doctrine of* Respondeat Superior

Under the doctrine of *respondeat superior*, an employer is vicariously liable for the torts of its employees committed within "the scope of the employment." Perez v. Van Groningen & Sons, Inc., 719 P.2d 676, 678 (Cal. 1986). Under California law, "scope of employment" is interpreted broadly and we have recognized that "[t]he fact that an employee is not engaged in the ultimate object of his employment at the time of his wrongful act does not preclude attribution of liability to an employer." Alma W. v. Oakland Unified School Dist., 176 Cal. Rptr. 287, 289 (Cal. App. 1981). Moreover, an employee's willful, malicious, and even criminal actions may fall within the scope of employment for purposes of the doctrine of *respondeat superior* even when the employer has not authorized the employee to commit the crimes or intentional torts. *See, e.g.*, Mary M., 814 P.2d at 1351; John R. v. Oakland Unified School Dist., 769 P.2d 948, 964 (Cal. 1989); Carr v. Wm. C. Crowell Co., 171 P.2d 5, 6 (Cal. 1946). In contrast to the standard used in some other states, for an employee's actions to be considered within the scope of employment, California law does not require that the employee's actions be motivated, in whole or part, by a desire to serve the employer's interests. *Carr*, 171 P.2d at 7. Instead, courts in this state have adopted a more modern approach that places emphasis not on the motivations of the offending employee but on the risks of danger or injury created by the business or enterprise. *Id.* (focusing on "the risks of the enterprise").

Under California law, the doctrine of *respondeat superior* reaches beyond those risks over which the employer has actual or possible control. The doctrine "rests on the broader ground that every man who prefers to manage his affairs through others remains bound to so manage them that third persons are not injured by any breach of legal duty on the part of such others' while acting in the scope of their employment." *Id.* In *Carr*, we held a defendant building contractor liable for injuries caused when the defendant's employee, angry at a subcontractor's worker for interfering with building-related work, threw a hammer at the worker's head, injuring the worker. *Id.* at 6. We rejected the defendant's claim that its employee was not acting within the scope of his employment when he threw the hammer, noting that the defendant's enterprise required the employee to associate with third parties, "attended by the risk that someone might be injured." *Id.* at 7.

Our approach to *respondeat superior* liability "is grounded upon 'a deeply rooted sentiment that a business enterprise cannot justly disclaim responsibility for accidents which may fairly be said to be characteristic of its activities.'" Rodgers v. Kemper Construction Company, 124 Cal. Rptr. 143, 148 (Cal. App. 1975) (internal citations omitted). One way to determine whether a risk is characteristic of an enterprise is to ask whether the risk is an "outgrowth of employment" and is "generally foreseeable." *See* Martinez v. Hagopian, 227 Cal. Rptr. 763, 767 (Cal. App. 1986) (examining whether the employee's assault was an "outgrowth of employment"); *Rodgers*, 124 Cal. Rptr. at 148 (assessing whether the risk was a "generally foreseeable consequence of the activity"). Generally foreseeable consequences are ones "'that may fairly be regarded as typical of or broadly incidental' to the enterprise undertaken by the employer." *Id.* at 149 (internal citations omitted). The consequences of an employee's conduct are generally foreseeable when the employee's conduct is "not so unusual or startling that it would seem unfair to include the loss resulting from it among other costs of the employer's business." *Id.* (internal citations omitted).

B *Application of the Doctrine*

Turning to the present case, the Hospital argues that the doctrine of *respondeat superior* does not apply because Tripoli's assault of plaintiff was outside the scope of his employment. We disagree. We hold that a reasonable trier of fact could conclude that Tripoli's assault of plaintiff was: (1) an outgrowth of his employment by the Hospital; and (2) a generally foreseeable consequence of the Hospital enterprise. Our holding is supported by three policy objectives that support the application of *respondeat superior* in this case. Each of these points is discussed in more detail below.

1 Outgrowth of Employment

A reasonable trier of fact could conclude that Tripoli's assault of plaintiff was an outgrowth of Tripoli's employment due to several interrelated facts. It is undeniable that the Hospital's enterprise required Tripoli to associate with third parties, including the plaintiff in this case. *See Carr*, 171 P.2d at 7.

Tripoli's assault occurred while Tripoli was at the hospital, performing the ultrasound duties he was hired to perform, on a patient of the hospital who was identified by the hospital as needing Tripoli's ultrasound services. Indeed, Tripoli's entire association with plaintiff arose out of his employment by the Hospital for his performance of ultrasound duties. Tripoli and plaintiff had never met and had no prior relationship before a physician in the Hospital's emergency department ordered plaintiff to submit to a fetal ultrasound by Tripoli. *See Rodgers*, 124 Cal. Rptr. at 151 (because the assailants and the victims were "complete strangers" until their work brought them together, their dispute could not have derived from "personal malice unrelated to the employment"); *Carr*, 171 P.2d at 8 (noting that employee's "entire association with plaintiff arose out of his employment" and that he had "never seen plaintiff before the day preceding the accident, and had never conversed with him before the dispute").

Tripoli's assault of plaintiff was connected to – and an unfortunate extension and abuse of – the power and control Tripoli had over plaintiff's body. During a properly performed ultrasound examination, a technician has direct power and control over the patient whose body structures are being imaged. In particular, the ultrasound technician is responsible for explaining the ultrasound procedure to the patient, answering any questions the patient may have about the procedure, spreading and rubbing the ultrasound gel onto the surface of the patient's body covering the internal area to be imaged, and performing the actual examination, which requires moving the ultrasound wand slowly over unclothed portions of the patient's body, such as the patient's lower abdomen, and sometimes even inside the patient's body, such as during the conduct of a transvaginal ultrasound. The authority of an ultrasound technician over a patient – bolstered by the technician's donning of medical scrubs, required identification name tag, training in anatomy and pathology, use of and comfort with technologically advanced equipment, and expectation of patient submission to intimate and sometimes invasive examinations – is substantial and necessary for the technician to perform his or her assigned duties.

In summary, Tripoli's assault of plaintiff occurred during the time period in which Tripoli was exercising job-created control and power over plaintiff's body for purposes of performing duties assigned to him by the Hospital. When he molested the plaintiff, Tripoli abused that power by engaging in the same type of action – controlling and touching the plaintiff's vaginal area – that Tripoli was employed by the Hospital to perform. By affording Tripoli such power and control over plaintiff, a vulnerable young woman expected to submit to an invasive examination to preserve the health and safety of her fetus, the Hospital facilitated Tripoli's abuse, and multiplied the chances of a sexual assault. A reasonable trier of fact could thus conclude that Tripoli's assault of plaintiff was an outgrowth of his employment.

Our holding today regarding outgrowth of employment is supported by other cases decided by this Court involving sexual assaults, particularly *Mary M.*, in which a female plaintiff was raped by an on-duty police officer during a traffic stop. 814 P.2d at 1342–43. In that case, we placed great weight on the formidable power and control police officers have over the citizenry as well as the potential for significant abuse of that power:

> [S]ociety has granted police officers extraordinary power and authority over its citizenry ... As visible symbols of that power, an officer is given a distinctively marked car, a uniform, a badge, and a gun ... Inherent in this formidable power is the potential for abuse. The cost resulting from misuse of that power should be borne by the community, because of the substantial benefits that the community derives from the lawful exercise of police power.
> *Id.* at 1349 (internal citations omitted)

We do not think *respondeat superior* liability should be limited to cases involving sexual assaults committed by police officers. Despite their different positions, the power and control an ultrasound technician has over a patient is similar in weight and effect to the power and control a police officer has over a citizen. For example, a patient who does not comply with a healthcare provider's request for an invasive examination, whether it be a mammogram, a pap smear, an abdominal ultrasound, or a transvaginal ultrasound, may prevent the provider from making a diagnosis (or result in a misdiagnosis) and may lead the patient to forego needed treatment, which in turn can jeopardize the health and safety (and even the life) of the patient or, in cases such as this, the patient's unborn child.

Other state supreme courts have come to the same conclusion regarding outgrowth of employment in cases arising in the healthcare context. In *Marston v. Minneapolis Clinic of Psychiatry and Neurology*, for example, the Supreme Court of Minnesota found that a material fact issue existed regarding whether a psychologist's inappropriate touching of a patient was within the psychologist's scope of employment. 329 N.W.2d 306, 311 (Minn. 1982). The Supreme Court of Minnesota explained:

> [T]he instant situation would not have occurred but for Dr. Nuernberger's employment; it was only through his relation to plaintiffs as a therapist that Dr. Nuernberger was able to commit the acts in question. Moreover, the acts occurred during or shortly after regular therapy sessions and were preceded by normal massages ... Thus, it should be a question of fact whether the acts

> of Dr. Nuernberger were foreseeable, related to and connected with acts otherwise within the scope of employment.
>
> *Id.*

Like the psychologist in *Marston*, it was only through Tripoli's relation to plaintiff as her hospital-assigned ultrasound technician that Tripoli was able to sexually assault plaintiff. Similar to the facts in *Marston*, Tripoli's sexual assault occurred during the same session, and immediately followed, the legitimate portion of Tripoli's treatment. *See also* Wells v. Bowie, 622 N.E.2d 1170, 1173–74 (Ohio 1993) (holding that genuine issues of material fact precluded summary judgment for hospital on the *respondeat superior* claim of a patient sexually assaulted by a hospital nurse); Samuels v. Southern Baptist Hosp., 594 So. 2d 571, 574 (La. Ct. App. 1992) (upholding as "not clearly wrong" a determination that a nursing assistant was acting within the scope of his employment when he raped a psychiatric patient); Stropes v. Heritage House Child. Ctr., 547 N.E.2d 244, 250 (Ind. 1989) (holding that a question of fact existed regarding whether a nurse's aide acted in the scope of his employment when he sexually molested a patient with severe intellectual disabilities).

The Hospital relies on *Lyon v. Carey*, decided by the US Court of Appeals for the DC Circuit, for its argument that Tripoli's assault was not an outgrowth of his employment but, instead, was the result of Tripoli's personal "propinquity and lust." *See* Lyon v. Carey, 533 F.2d 649, 655 (D.C. Cir. 1976). In *Lyon*, the defendant's deliveryman raped the plaintiff following a dispute regarding whether the goods sold by the defendant should be carried up the plaintiff's stairs and whether a check was an acceptable form of payment instead of cash. *Id.* at 651. The court stated that, "Where sexual assault is not motivated or triggered by anything in employment activity but is a result only of propinquity and lust on part of employee, there should be no liability on part of employer." *Id.* at 655.

Lyon is inapplicable in California, however, because the California Supreme Court has recognized that powerful personal emotions can motivate the offending employee, yet the employee's act can still be within the scope of employment. For example, in cases involving nonsexual assaults, we recognized that individual men may have personal qualities that lend themselves to "emotional flareups" and a "propensity for violence," yet we still found in favor of the plaintiff on the issue of *respondeat superior*. In *Carr*, for example, we stated that:

> Men do not discard their personal qualities when they go to work. They carry their intelligence, skill, habits of care and rectitude into the job. Just as

> inevitably they take along also their tendencies of carelessness and camaraderie, as well as emotional makeup. In bringing men together, work brings these qualities together, causes frictions between them, creates occasions for lapses into carelessness, and for funmaking and emotional flareups.
>
> 171 P.2d at 6

We are unpersuaded that a man's propensity for nonsexual, physical violence toward another man should subject the employer to liability in *respondeat superior* – as in *Carr* – but that a man's propensity for sexual lust with respect to a woman – as in the instant case – should not. The Hospital does not offer, and our review of the case law does not reveal, any reason to differentiate between the two situations.

2 Foreseeability

A reasonable trier of fact could also conclude that Tripoli's assault of plaintiff was foreseeable, and not unusual or startling. *See Mary M.*, 814 P.2d at 1350 ("the precise circumstances of [an] assault need not be anticipated [for *respondeat superior* liability to apply], so long as the risk is one that is reasonably foreseeable"); *Rodgers*, 124 Cal. Rptr. at 148–49 (applying *respondeat superior* liability to "generally foreseeable" risks); *Alma W.*, 176 Cal. Rptr. at 291–93 (excluding from the doctrine of *respondeat superior* risks that are "unusual" or "startling").

We begin with the sad reality that risk of sexual assault is a common feature of the lives of women in the United States. Three out of four American women will be victims of violent crimes, such as sexual assault, during their lifetimes and 97 percent of all sex crime victims are women. H.R. Rep. 103–395, at 25 (1993); William H. Hallock, *The Violence Against Women Act: Civil Rights for Sexual Assault Victims*, 68 Indiana L.J. 577, 577–78 (1993). As a young woman 19 years old, plaintiff falls into the precise category of women who are most likely to be sexually assaulted. The National Crime Victimization Study (NCVS) found that women who were in "younger age groups" were more likely to be victims of violent crimes. *Id.* at 1. Specifically, the NCVS found that women age 20 to 24 were the most likely to experience all types of violent crime and that women age 12 to 19 were the second most likely to experience all types of violent crime. *Id.* at 3, tbl. 3. The NCVS further reported that most female victims of violent crimes were attacked by lone (versus multiple) offenders. *Id.* at 5, tbl. 5. In particular, lone offenders committed 85 percent of simple assaults against women and 79 percent of aggravated assaults against women. *Id.* at 5, tbl. 6. In this case, plaintiff was a 19-year-old woman who was assaulted by a lone man. As such, she falls into each of the NCVS's "more likely to be victimized" categories.

We are also mindful that plaintiff's assault occurred in the healthcare setting. Recent studies reveal that sexual misconduct in the healthcare setting is not uncommon. *See, e.g.*, Thomas Fahy & Nigel Fisher, *Sexual Contact Between Doctors and Patients: Almost Always Harmful*, 304 BRITISH MED. J. 1519, 1519 (1992) ("Despite such unambiguous ethical and legal declarations [against sexual contact of patients by doctors] several sources suggest that violations are not uncommon"). One study reported that 18 percent of obstetricians, 13 percent of general practitioners, and 12 percent of internists confessed to or condoned sexual contact with their patients. *Id.* at 1519 (internal citations omitted). Given the not uncommon nature of sexual misconduct by healthcare providers and the power imbalance inherent in the provider–patient relationship, patients seeking both physical and mental healthcare are considered vulnerable to sexual abuse. *See, e.g.*, Nanette K. Gartrell et al., *Physician–Patient Sexual Contact: Prevalence and Problems*, 157 WEST. J. MED. 139, 140 (1992); Larry H. Strasburger, Linda Jorgenson, & Pamela Sutherland, *The Prevention of Psychotherapist Sexual Misconduct: Avoiding the Slippery Slope*, 46 AM. J. PSYCHOTHERAPY 545, 545 (1992). The American College of Obstetricians and Gynecologists (ACOG), anticipating the very kind of case we have before us, issued a statement clarifying that gynecological examinations "should be performed with only the necessary amount of physical contact required to obtain data for diagnosis and treatment." *See* ACOG, *Sexual Misconduct in the Practice of Obstetrics and Gynecology: Ethical Considerations*, 48 INT'L J. GYNECOLOGY & OBSTETRICS 239, 241 (1995).

In summary, we cannot say that Tripoli's assault of plaintiff was "unusual" or "startling." Indeed, in our society, a reasonable trier of fact could find that Tripoli's assault of his patient was foreseeable. Notably, other state supreme courts have come to the same conclusion regarding foreseeability in cases set in the healthcare context. In *Marston v. Minneapolis Clinic of Psychiatry and Neurology*, for example, the Supreme Court of Minnesota relied heavily on testimony that "sexual relations between a psychologist and a patient is a well-known hazard and thus, to a degree, foreseeable and a risk of employment" in applying *respondeat superior* liability. 329 N.W.2d 306, 311 (Minn. 1982). We believe that the mentally intimate nature of the psychologist–patient relationship is similar in kind to the physically intimate nature of the gynecologist – or ultrasound technologist–patient relationship. Sexual misconduct in both scenarios is foreseeable.

3 Policy Considerations

In prior decisions, we have identified three policy objectives that support the application of *respondeat superior*, including: (1) spreading the risk of loss among the beneficiaries of the enterprise; (2) assuring victim compensation; and (3) preventing recurrence of the tortious conduct. *See Mary M.*, 814 P.2d at 1347. Taken together, these policy objectives support the application of *respondeat superior* in this case.

(a) Spreading the Risk of Loss among the Beneficiaries of the Enterprise

An employer's liability under the doctrine of *respondeat superior* rests on the public policy that an employer should bear liability for acts committed by employees as a cost of doing business. *See, e.g.*, Farmers Ins. Group v. County of Santa Clara, 906 P.2d 440, 448 (Cal. 1995). That is, damages fairly attributable to the enterprise should be allocated to and spread among the beneficiaries of the enterprise. *Id.*

Hospitals benefit handsomely from the examinations performed by ultrasound technicians. In the hospital setting, ultrasound technicians do not directly bill patients for the ultrasound examinations they provide. Instead, the hospital in which the examination takes place charges the patient a fee for the facility component of the patient's hospital visit (called the "facility fee").[1] Among other items and services provided by the hospital, this facility fee covers the cost of the room or space in the hospital in which the ultrasound examination takes place, the technician's time in performing the examination, the equipment used by the technician during the examination, the development and interpretation of the images by the technician, and other hospital overhead. Depending on the part of the country in which the hospital is located and the cost of living in that area, ultrasound technicians are typically paid in the low-to-mid five figures.[2] Despite these relatively modest salaries, ultrasound technicians generate substantial revenue for the hospitals in which

[1] The physician who examines the patient prior to making a decision to order the ultrasound examination and/or who makes treatment decisions based on the results of the ultrasound examination will send a second, separate bill to the patient for the professional component of the visit (called the "professional fee").

[2] *See, e.g.*, The University of Texas System, Office of Human Resources Pay Plan, at pp.-4 (1994–95) (stating the salary range of Ultrasound Technician I as $18,408–$39,084; stating the salary range of Ultrasound Technician II as $21,048–$32,496; and stating the salary range of Senior Ultrasound Technologist as $26,292–$42,072; all salary ranges refer to the 1994–95 academic year).

they work. Depending on the body structure imaged, the hospital's facility fee for an ultrasound examination ranges from $200 to over $1,000 per examination, with technicians performing as many as twenty or more examinations per workday.

Because the Hospital benefits financially from examinations performed by technicians, such as ultrasounds, allocating the risk of loss to the Hospital is fair and supports the first policy objective underlying the application of *respondeat superior*, i.e., spreading the risk of loss among the beneficiaries of the enterprise. *See, e.g., Mary M.*, 814 P.2d at 1349 ("[T]he cost resulting from misuse [of police] power should be borne by the community, because of the substantial benefits that the community derives from the lawful exercise of police power"). The Hospital in turn has the ability to spread the loss among its patients and other users of the facility through its fees and other charges of service.

(b) Assurance of Victim Compensation

The second policy objective supporting the application of the doctrine of *respondeat superior* is to give greater assurance of compensation to the victim. In analyzing this particular policy objective, the court in *Mary M.* noted the Legislature's recognition that the imposition of vicarious liability on an employer is an appropriate method to ensure that victims of misconduct are compensated. *Mary M.*, 814 P.2d at 1348.

We find that the second policy objective also weighs in favor of the application of *respondeat superior* in this case. Hospitals employ a number of individuals with relatively low salaries and, therefore, shallow pockets. Allowing a patient who has suffered a sexual assault to proceed only against the individual technician will frequently leave the patient without compensation for her injuries, especially when the technician has been convicted of the crime of assault (as in the instant case) and may no longer be working or working at the same salary.

(c) Preventing Recurrence of the Tortious Conduct

The third policy objective that supports the application of *respondeat superior* is preventing recurrence of the tortious conduct. That is, the application of *respondeat superior* is supported when imposing liability on the employer may prevent recurrence of the tortious conduct by creating "a strong incentive for vigilance by those in a position 'to guard substantially against the evil to be prevented.'" *Mary M.*, 814 P.2d at 1347.

In the instant case, hospitals may without difficulty, and with no additional cost, implement measures that will protect hospital patients from at least some sexual assaults. These measures include allowing third parties, called chaperones, to be present during medical examinations, as requested by the plaintiff in the instant case. As background, the American Medical Association's Council on Ethical and Judicial Affairs recently stated that, "A policy that patients are free to make a request for a chaperone should be established in each health care setting" and "[t]he request by a patient to have a chaperone should be honored." Am. Med. Ass'n, *Use of Chaperones during Physical Exams: Recommendations*, 10 ETHICAL & JUDICIAL AFFAIRS 298, 300 (1995). A recently published opinion by the ACOG similarly states that, "The request by either a patient or a physician to have a chaperone present during a physical examination should be accommodated irrespective of the physician's gender" and that "the presence of a third person in the examination room can confer benefits for both the patient and physician, regardless of the gender of the chaperon." ACOG, 48 INT'L J. GYNECOLOGY & OBSTETRICS 239, 240 (1995). Likewise, a recent draft of a policy authored by the Committee on Practice and Ambulatory Medicine of the American Academy of Pediatrics states: "In some cases, either the patient, the parent, the pediatrician, or some combination of these persons may wish to have a chaperone present. In those cases, the chaperone protects the interest of the patient and the pediatrician." Am. Acad. Pediatrics, *The Use of Chaperones during the Physical Examination of the Pediatric Patient*, 98 PEDIATRICS 1202, 1202 (1995).[3]

In the instant case, Tripoli denied plaintiff's request to have her mother and boyfriend present in the examining room, thus deviating from the standard set by the national medical association policies referenced above. Although we cannot state with certainty that the presence of either the plaintiff's mother or the plaintiff's boyfriend would have prevented this assault, the record shows that Tripoli, while fondling plaintiff, stated that he needed to excite her to get

[3] *See also* Mark A. Penn & Claire C. Bourguet, *Patients' Attitudes Regarding Chaperones during Physical Examinations*, 35(6) J. FAM. PRAC. 639, 639–43 (1992) ("[Patients] should be given the option of having a chaperone present during an examination of the breasts, pelvis, or rectum"); TENN. ST. BD. MED. EX., SEXUAL MISCONDUCT STATEMENT AND POLICY, at 2, ¶4 (adopted Sept. 17, 1993) ("A physician may wish to consider having a chaperone present during examination of any sensitive parts of the body for the protection of both the patient and the physician"); Richard M. Buchta, *Use of Chaperones during Pelvic Examinations of Female Adolescents*, 141(6) AM. J. DIS. CHILD. 666, 666–67, tbl. 2 (1987) (surveying physicians who treat adolescents regarding whether they "ever perform a pelvic examination [on an adolescent patient] without a chaperone present," and reporting a 63% "no" response); *id.* at 167 (reporting that more than half (50.3%) of the physicians surveyed believed that having a chaperone present was "always essential").

a good view of the baby. Plaintiff's mother, having experienced similar examinations before, likely would have recognized the falsity of Tripoli's statement had she been allowed to chaperone her daughter. It is also possible that Tripoli would have feared that plaintiff's mother or boyfriend would recognize the falsity of the statement and would not have made the statement and/or would not have attempted to fondle plaintiff had a chaperone been present.

In summary, had Tripoli followed the national standard of care and allowed the plaintiff to be accompanied by a chaperone, it is possible that the sexual assault of plaintiff would not have occurred. Such a practice of allowing chaperones was designed in part to prevent sexual abuse and, if implemented conscientiously, is likely to do so. For this reason, we think the third policy objective – preventing recurrence of the tortious conduct – is supported by the application of *respondeat superior* in such cases.

IV CONCLUSION

We hold that a reasonable trier of fact could conclude that Tripoli's assault of plaintiff occurred within the scope of his employment. Our holding today will ensure that individuals who are injured by sexual acts have the same opportunity to recover under *respondeat superior* as individuals who are injured by nonsexual acts. California law has permitted men who are injured in physical workplace quarrels with other men to recover under the doctrine of *respondeat superior*. *See Carr*, 171 P.2d at 6 (holding a defendant building contractor liable under *respondeat superior* for injuries caused when the defendant's male employee, angry at a subcontractor's male worker, threw a hammer at the worker's head); *Rodgers*, 124 Cal. Rptr. at 146–47 (holding the employer of off-duty, male employees who had been drinking beer on their job site liable under *respondeat superior* for injuries caused when the employees attacked the male workers of another contractor). Individuals who are sexually assaulted are no less deserving of recovery. Stated another way, we are unwilling to take the position that nonsexual, physical quarrels are an outgrowth of employment, but sexual assaults are not. To do so would be to give less weight to sexual injuries than to nonsexual injuries, or to injuries disproportionately suffered by women compared to injuries suffered by men. Such a double standard is unwarranted, given that both sets of injuries can grow out of employment, involve injuries to third parties who associate with employed individuals, and cause those third parties considerable pain and suffering. Again, the Hospital does not offer, and our review of the case law does not reveal, any reason to justify such differential treatment.

Our holding today also recognizes the high educational,[4] professional,[5] and social[6] costs to women of sexual assault and other gender-based harms. We refuse to add to that list of costs by denying tort recovery for foreseeable abuse in the medical context.[7] By assuring that plaintiffs have a right to receive tort compensation for sexual abuse by medical professionals, we hope to alleviate any fear of accessing emergency and other forms of healthcare that patients may have, either for themselves or their future children. For too long, harms disproportionately suffered by women, including sexual assault, have been trivialized by labeling them personal or individual, with the result that the victims of such harms historically have had few remedies, even under civil rights law.[8] We hope our holding today will begin to reverse this trend and give victims of sexual assault, the majority of whom are women, an equal opportunity for compensation under tort law.

For the reasons discussed above, we find that a reasonable trier of fact could conclude that Tripoli's sexual assault occurred during the scope of his employment. Accordingly, we affirm the judgment of the court of appeal and remand the matter to the trial court for further proceedings consistent with this opinion.

4 *See* S. Rep. No. 101–545, at 44 (1990) (noting that the effects of gender-based crime are "often magnified for young women attending college" and that female college students who are victims frequently drop out of school and leave their studies to avoid their assailants).

5 *See* S. Rep. No. 103–138, at 54 (1993) (stating that almost half of all rape victims "lose their jobs or are forced to quit in the aftermath of the crime"); S. Rep. No. 101–545, at 33 (1990) (stating that those who remain employed after a rape may experience a prolonged period of decreased productivity).

6 *See* S. Rep. No. 102–197, at 38 (1991) (stating that many women victims of gender-based violence stop using public transportation, stop being alone in public spaces, stop going to public events, and stop participating in political forums).

7 *See generally* Women and Violence: Hearing Before the S. Comm. on the Judiciary, 101st. Cong., 2d Sess. 69 (1990) (statement of NOW Legal Def. & Educ. Fund) (listing the many, high costs suffered by women who experience gender-based violence).

8 *See* David Frazee, *An Imperfect Remedy for Imperfect Violence: The Construction of Civil Rights in the Violence against Women Act*, 1 Mich. J. Gender & L. 163, 167 (1993) ("Too often civil rights doctrines have worked in conjunction with other social institutions to trivialize the importance of gender based violence by labeling such violence as aberrant, private, personal, or individual and therefore outside of the realm of violence that merits serious legal remedies").

PART V

Damages

16

Commentary on *G.M.M. v. Kimpson*

TWILA L. PERRY

INTRODUCTION

The issue presented in *G.M.M. v. Kimpson*[1] is whether statistics based on the ethnicity of a child can be used to determine damages for lost future earning capacity. In 2015, Judge Jack B. Weinstein of the United States District Court of the Eastern District of New York held that the use of such statistics in determining damages for the lost future earning capacity of a Hispanic male child violates both due process and equal protection. *Kimpson* lies at the intersection of two issues: the assessment of damages for lost earning capacity when the injured party is a child, and the use of race, ethnicity, and sex-based statistics more generally in assessing damages in torts cases.

When an adult has been injured in an accident, the question of impaired future earning capacity is often a central issue. In assessing damages for that loss, the life expectancy, working-life expectancy (i.e., how many years the person would have worked if not injured) and predicted future wages of the injured person are taken into account. When the injured party is an adult and has a history of earnings, the individual's own history is an important part of the factual basis used to determine what the future earnings likely would have been.

When the injured person is a child, however, determining damages for impairment of future earning capacity is more complicated. Usually there is no history of earnings and no substantial record of life experiences that can be referenced to estimate what the child's likely future earnings would have been absent the injury. As a result, the law looks to other evidence, including statistics, and, as a result, damage awards can differ significantly, depending on the assumptions made about the future of the child. If it is assumed that the

[1] 116 F. Supp. 3d 126 (E.D.N.Y. 2015).

child would have gone to college, and possibly graduate school, and would have had a strong earning potential, the damages will be significantly higher than if it is assumed that the child would have attained a lower educational level resulting in a lower range of earnings.

Historically, and probably surprisingly to many people, it has been common in our legal system for courts to take into account the race, ethnicity, and sex of a person in measuring damages in torts cases. When actuarial tables based on race, ethnicity, and sex are used to calculate the variables of life expectancy, work/life expectancy, and likely future earnings, minority and female plaintiffs often receive lower damage awards than plaintiffs who are white and/or male.

HISTORICAL AND LEGAL CONTEXT

The use of race as a factor in determining tort damages has a long history in American law. Before 1950, assumptions about race and a judge's own racial bias could easily factor into damage awards.[2] For example, in a 1905 case, *The Saginaw and The Hamilton*,[3] involving a steamship collision, the court lowered the wrongful death awards of black plaintiffs based on data showing differences in life expectancy for white and black people.

The ability to rely on more sophisticated statistical tables to determine damage awards began in the 1950s when the United States Bureau of Labor Statistics began to publish tables containing statistics on the working-life expectancy of men and women.[4] Later, during the 1980s, tables included consideration of the factors of race and educational attainment.[5] Despite its importance, the use of race, ethnicity, and sex-based tables has not garnered the level of attention it might have otherwise received, perhaps because most tort cases are settled without a trial. But even in cases that are settled, the settlement is likely affected by the opinions of experts who have relied on race, ethnicity, and gender-based tables in forming an opinion as to the monetary value of a case.

There is a long history in tort law of devaluing harms suffered by people of color and women.[6] That history has been manifested in a number of ways,

[2] Jennifer B. Wriggins, *Damages in Tort Litigation: Thoughts on Race and Remedies, 1865–2007*, 27 Rev. Litig. 37, 56 (2007).

[3] 139 F. 906 (S.D.N.Y. 1905).

[4] *See* G.M.M., 116 F. Supp. 3d at 149.

[5] *Id.*

[6] Martha Chamallas & Jennifer B. Wriggins, The Measure Of Injury: Race, Gender And Tort Law 2 (2010).

including the award of lower verdicts to black plaintiffs in personal injury cases[7] and hostility to the recovery of damages for injuries that disproportionally affect women, including harms to reproductive capacity and negligently inflicted emotional harms.[8]

Only since the 1990s has the issue of using race and gender-based tables in the determination of tort damages started to receive more attention, beginning with the scholarship of law professors Martha Chamallas and Jennifer Wriggins.[9] The issue gained some visibility when Kenneth Feinberg, the Special Master for the September 11th Victims Compensation Fund declined to use race, ethnicity, and gender-based tables and instead used tables based on the experience of white men to calculate the damages for the families of those killed in the 9/11 terrorist attack.[10] Most recently, in the wake of the Black Lives Matter and #MeToo movements, there has been a substantial increase in the number of articles and news stories devoted to the issue, many by women scholars and journalists.[11]

Although sparsely litigated, some courts have refused to use race and gender-based tables. In *United States v. Bedonie*,[12] for example, the court directed the calculation of damages for lost earning capacity without regard to race or gender where the young male plaintiff was a Native American. In *Tarpeh-Doe v. United States*,[13] the court refused to allow racial statistics on loss of future income where the plaintiff male child had one black parent and one white parent. However, it was not until 2008, in *McMillan v. City of New York*,[14] that a federal judge rejected the use of race-based tables on the specific ground that they were unconstitutional.[15] The judge in that case was Judge Weinstein, the author, several years later, of the opinion in *Kimpson*.

Discrimination on the basis of race, ethnicity, and gender in the award of damages in torts cases is a timely issue. The Black Lives Matter movement has

7 Frank M. McClellan, *The Dark Side of Tort Reform: Searching for Racial Justice*, 48 Rutgers L. Rev. 761, 773–74 (1996).

8 Martha Chamallas & Linda K. Kerber, *Women, Mothers and the Law of Fright: A History*, 88 Mich. L. Rev. 601 (1990).

9 Martha Chamallas, *Questioning the Use of Race-Specific and Gender-Specific Economic Data in Tort Litigation: A Constitutional Argument*, 63 Fordham L. Rev. 73 (1994).

10 Chamallas & Wriggins, *supra* note 6, at 156.

11 *See, e.g.*, Kim Soffen, *In One Corner of the Law, Minorities Are Often Valued Less*, Wash. Post (Oct. 25, 2016).

12 317 F. Supp. 2d 1285 (D. Utah 2004).

13 771 F. Supp. 427 (D.D.C. 1991).

14 253 F.R.D. 247 (E.D.N.Y. 2008).

15 Kimberly A. Yurako & Ronen Avraham, *Valuing Black Lives: A Constitutional Challenge to the Use of Race-Based Tables in Calculating Tort Damages*, 106 Cal. L. Rev. 325, 328 (2018).

placed the issue of the devaluation of harms visited upon black and brown people at the center of national attention. Similarly, the #MeToo movement has highlighted women's work lives, including the diminished compensation women receive for the work they do and how they are devalued and disrespected.

THE ORIGINAL OPINION

The plaintiff in *Kimpson* was a young Hispanic boy who suffered permanent injury as a result of exposure to lead paint in his family's New York apartment before he was 1 year old. The family contended that the child's exposure to the lead paint was due to the negligence of the landlord in failing to abate the lead paint in the building in accordance with applicable law.

At the time of trial, the child was just under 4 years old. An important factor in determining the damages he would receive for lost future earning capacity involved an assessment of the probability that he would have obtained a college degree or advanced degrees had it not been for the injury. The family was a stable one with both parents holding steady, responsible jobs; the father had a bachelor's degree and the mother had an MA in fine arts. The defense strategy was to lower the award for lost earning capacity by basing its damage estimate on statistics indicating that the probability of a Hispanic male receiving a college degree was small and showing that the earnings of Hispanic men are generally much lower than those of white men. However, Judge Weinstein rejected the ethnicity-based evidence and held that the use of such data is unconstitutional. He ruled that "the specific characteristics of the family and the child, rather than the characterization of the child as a member of a particular ethnic group, must be used in determining the damages." The jury found in favor of the plaintiffs, awarding the child and his mother $2,005,000.

Judge Weinstein relied heavily on his earlier 2008 opinion in *McMillan v. City of New York* holding that it was a violation of equal protection to use racially based statistics to calculate a shorter life expectancy for a plaintiff identified as an African American than for other people in the general population.[16] The plaintiff in *McMillan* was an African-American adult male who was injured and became a quadriplegic as a result of a crash of the Staten Island Ferry caused by the city's negligence. In estimating the award for future medical expenses, the city sought to rely on statistics demonstrating that African-American men with spinal cord injuries have a lower life expectancy

[16] *McMillan*, 253 F.R.D. 247, 255–56 (E.D.N.Y. 2008).

than persons of other races with the same injury. Judge Weinstein held that the use of such race-based data to depress the award was impermissible and instead used a table for all spine-injured males to calculate the damages.

Judge Weinstein's ruling in *Kimpson* built upon *McMillan* and provided an extensive rationale for holding that the use of race-based statistics to calculate damages in torts cases violates both equal protection and due process. With respect to equal protection, Weinstein applied strict scrutiny, invalidating the race-based figures because they embodied "a disadvantageous estimate of damages solely on the basis of ethnic classification." With respect to due process, Judge Weinstein viewed the race-based estimates as constituting arbitrary and irrational state action. Declaring that compensation for negligently caused damage is a protected property right, he concluded that automatically burdening one group of litigants in seeking recovery violates due process.

In a wide-ranging opinion, Judge Weinstein detailed several objections to the use of the tables: they undermined the deterrence goal of tort law by providing incentives to potential injurers to impose greater risks of harm on minority persons and minority communities, and they assumed the continuation of current racial pay gaps when the reality is that minority groups are making significant progress against racial discrimination. Referencing "resiliency theory," Weinstein emphasized that race-based statistics do not take into account the fact that many children achieve at a much higher level than one might expect, given the challenging circumstances of their childhoods. For this purpose, he adopted the American Psychological Association's definition of resiliency as the process of successfully adapting in the face of adversities such as trauma, tragedy, threats, or other significant sources of stress.[17]

Kimpson dealt only with race-based data and did not explicitly hold that the use of gender-based data or tables was unconstitutional, although Weinstein cited legal scholarship that argued for that position and, at numerous points in his opinion, made references to gender as well as to race and ethnicity. In addition to holding that the educational and employment background of a child's parents may be used to calculate the child's damages, Judge Weinstein took note of another option: considering each person equivalent to the average person, unless there is evidence that takes that individual outside of the normal range.

[17] "The Road to Resilience" in American Psychological Association, http://www.apa.org/helpcenter.road-resilience (last visited May 8, 2019). *See also*, Mandie Shean, *Current Theories Relating to Resilience and Young People: A Literature Review*, VicHealth 2015, Victorian Health Promotion Foundation, Melbourne.

THE OPINIONS COMPARED

In many torts decisions rewritten from a feminist perspective, it is not difficult to see how the rewritten opinion reflects feminist values in ways that the original opinion clearly does not. Thus, the inclusion of *Kimpson* in this volume is unusual in that the original and the rewritten opinion reach the same conclusion, and through a very similar analysis. Additionally, because *Kimpson* is a recent district court opinion, it is impossible to know how influential it will turn out to be. Yet its comprehensive analysis of the constitutionality of race and ethnicity-based tables could make it an important precedent with respect to both race and gender discrimination.

It is not surprising that the two opinions share much common ground, since many of the objections to the use of the tables are the same whether they are being used for race and ethnicity or for gender. The fact that the two opinions employ such similar rationales suggests that an opinion addressing an issue from a feminist perspective does not necessarily differ dramatically from one addressing the same issue from a perspective that is not consciously feminist. Many of the same principles that animate the rewritten opinion also animate Judge Weinstein's opinion: acknowledgment of the need to address both past and present social inequalities; the need to eliminate stereotypes based on identities and to cease using measures that ignore socioeconomic and other relevant factors; the need to deter injurious behavior toward disadvantaged groups; and the desire to anticipate a future in which progress will continue to be made against racism and sexism.

Indeed, one might ask whether Weinstein's original opinion, is, itself, a feminist opinion. In a recent law review article, torts scholar Anita Bernstein argued that a number of Judge Weinstein's earlier opinions could be described as feminist.[18] The cases she offered as examples involved women with low incomes, female offenders, and women plaintiffs in civil rights and personal injury cases. Bernstein argues that Judge Weinstein's decisions in these cases further the interests of women in concrete, material ways and reveal the judge's empathy for the kind of issues and challenges present in the lives of many women.[19]

The question of whether a particular opinion should be characterized as feminist is a complicated one because there is no one agreed-upon definition of feminism. Instead of a single definition, there are multiple schools of thought. However, various schools of feminism do seem to embrace some

[18] Anita Bernstein, *The Feminist Jurisprudence of Jack Weinstein*, 64 DePaul L. Rev. 341 (2015).
[19] *Id.* at 365.

common themes, including a recognition of systemic gender inequality, the need for expanded opportunities for women and eradication of discrimination, as well as respect for women's lives and choices.[20] There also seems to be widespread acceptance of the idea that the achievement of these goals will require major societal changes.[21] Judged by these standards, Judge Weinstein's opinion in *Kimpson* certainly can be considered one that furthers feminist goals. Even without an explicit feminist analysis or a clear declaration that gender-based tables are also unconstitutional, *Kimpson* will be helpful to women plaintiffs in personal injury cases and will further the wider goal of gender equality.

However, there are at least two important aspects in which the rewritten opinion reflects feminist analysis in ways that Judge Weinstein's opinion, progressive as it is, does not. First, the rewritten opinion specifically holds that use of the gender-based tables is unconstitutional. This is an important contribution because it is not clear that rejection of race-based tables will automatically result in invalidation of gender-based tables as well. Indeed, forensic economists, who are in the business of generating loss appraisals used in personal injury cases, and often testify in such cases, are more comfortable and familiar with using gender than race in their calculations, perhaps because of the still-widespread belief that differences between the sexes are biological and enduring. Although the Weinstein opinion references gender at various points, the rewritten feminist opinion contains a detailed examination of equal protection's intermediate scrutiny test to the address whether use of gender-based tables is also unconstitutional.

A second reason the rewritten opinion is more clearly feminist is that it engages the issue of intersectionality, a central issue in feminist theory.[22] Intersectionality theory examines the ways in which some people's identities and treatment in society can be affected by not one, but multiple statuses, including possibly race, class, sexual orientation, religion, or disability. The rewritten feminist opinion is intersectional in that it explicitly addresses both race and gender in its analysis. Its analysis of gender-based tables mirrors its analysis of the race and ethnicity-based charts, using, however, as it must, the intermediate level of scrutiny. Similar to its analysis in the case of race, the rewritten opinion holds that the gender-based tables rely on outdated statistics

[20] *See, e.g.*, Deborah L. Rhode, *Feminist Critical Theories*, 42 Stan. L. Rev. 617, 619 (1990).
[21] *Id.*
[22] *See* Kimberlé Crenshaw, *Demarginalizing the Intersection of Race and Sex: A Black Feminist Critique of Antidiscrimination Doctrine, Feminist Theory and Antiracist Politics*, 1989 U. of Chi. Legal F. 139 (1989).

concerning women's educational attainment, work/life expectancy, and earnings and do not account for the growth of women's participation and advancement in the workforce. The feminist opinion also states that the tables reinforce the effect of past gender inequalities and project those inequalities into the future. Such a dual focus on race and gender is imperative if courts are fully to address the injuries of women of color who are doubly disadvantaged by their race and sex.

Finally, the rewritten opinion notes that there are alternatives to relying on race, ethnicity, and gender to yield a prediction of future earnings in a case involving the lost future earning capacity of a child. Similar to Judge Weinstein's opinion, the rewritten feminist opinion suggests using blended tables and relying on the educational, professional, and economic status of the child's parents as measures of the probability of success the child would have achieved absent the injury.

THE QUESTION OF REMEDY

Both the original and the feminist opinion touch upon the all-important question of remedy once a court determines that using race and gender-based tables are unconstitutional. Weinstein and the feminist opinion mention the use of blended tables and endorse the use of the parents' educational and employment history and status to determine the likely educational attainment of the injured child, although the rewritten opinion expresses reservations about that method. Another possible alternative, not suggested in either opinion, would be to award each injured child the amount of damages a child with the most privileged parental background would receive.

A *The Status of Parents*

While it is clearly not easy to predict a child's future earning capacity, relying on the parents' educational attainment and work status seems problematic because it can result in perpetuating the consequences of past racial and economic disadvantage. Addressing this problem under existing constitutional doctrine is difficult because classifications based on class and occupation receive only rational basis scrutiny rather than the heightened scrutiny reserved for race and gender-based classifications. This means that relying on parental data is probably not unconstitutional. Nevertheless, it is troubling that reliance on parents' status is likely to hurt certain minorities, such as African Americans and Hispanics, more that it hurts white females, who, as a group, are more dispersed at different class levels in the society. It would be preferable to find a solution that does not result in this kind of disparate effect.

In holding the use of the tables to be unconstitutional, both opinions note the relevance of the psychological theory of resiliency, which posits that there are many children who achieve far beyond expectations considering the challenges of their childhoods. Resiliency theory clearly supports the rejection of race-based tables because the tables assume that children are unlikely to exceed the achievements of their parents, while the reality is that many children achieve against the odds. However, incorporating resiliency theory into the determination of future lost earning capacity for children poses other complications. For example, would it require individualized determinations as to whether each particular child would be likely to exceed the educational and work status of his or her parents? If so, what kind of evidence would be relevant? Resiliency theory also seems a more comfortable fit in the case of race, than in the case of gender, again because of the wider dispersal of female children at all levels of the population. Other alternatives, such as using blended tables or treating all children in the same way the most advantaged children would be treated, discussed below, might avoid some of complexities posed by resiliency theory.

B *Using Blended Tables*

Neither Judge Weinstein's opinion nor the rewritten feminist opinion delves at length into the issues presented by the use of blended tables. Blended tables can avoid problems of speculation, stereotypes, and assumptions based on race or gender, but they present their own set of complications. For example, black men may benefit from blended tables on life expectancy, but women can be disadvantaged by those tables because, statistically, women live longer than men do. The inclusion of white men in blended tables predicting expected wages would benefit black men, but disadvantage female workers.[23] Thus, there is need for more explicit, detailed consideration of the effect of blended tables generally, and specifically of any differences in consequences depending on whether the blended table being used applies to life expectancy, work/life expectancy, or lifetime wages. A detailed analysis of the complexities presented by blended tables in the determination of loss of future earning capacity, of course, is probably more effectively addressed via legal scholarship

[23] *See* Yurako and Avraham, *supra* note 15, at 333.

than in a judicial opinion where the goal is to address the facts and law in the specific case before the court.

C *"Leveling Up"*

An alternative to using blended tables or relying on the status of a child's parents would be to treat all injured children the same, by either "leveling up" or "leveling down." In leveling up, all children would be treated as the most advantaged group of children are treated. In leveling down, all children would be treated the same as the most disadvantaged children.[24] As between these alternatives, it is likely that few would suggest leveling down, since the most advantaged children would receive less, while the situation of the least advantaged children would not be improved.

It is also interesting that neither Judge Weinstein's opinion nor the rewritten feminist opinion advocates leveling up. The hesitancy likely stems from a belief that leveling up is inconsistent with tort law's focus on individualized determinations and with the widespread view that the purpose of tort damages is to restore the injured person to the position he or she held prior to the injury. Clearly, leveling up would also result in more damages being awarded overall in cases involving diminished earning capacity than would be the case using blended tables. That result is also in tension with the widely held view that there should be a close nexus between compensation and the actual injury suffered by the individual.

Finally, there is the question as to what exactly would constitute leveling up in the case of children. Presumably, this would mean giving all children the amount of damages a white male child of educated parents would receive. Even so, the method for assessing these damages would still need to be determined.

In an essay some years ago, legal scholar Richard Abel posed the question, more generally, of whether the law should give the same damages to everyone who suffers an identical injury.[25] Such an approach treats all people as having equal worth and, further, acknowledges the reality that no one's future is certain. There is an even stronger argument for adopting such an approach in the case of children, because so much more of their future is in front of them than is the case with adults. The children of the most advantaged people in a

[24] *See* Deborah L. Brake, *When Equality Leaves Everybody Worse off: The Problem of Leveling Down in Equality Law*, 46 Wm. & Mary L. Rev. 513, 515 (2004).

[25] Richard L. Abel, *Torts*, in The Politics Of Law: A Progressive Critique 185 (David Kairys, ed. 1982).

society are not always successful. The children of the least advantaged sometimes beat the odds. While to some extent using blended tables also has the effect of treating all children the same, awarding all children the same amount of damages as those who are the most advantaged might also increase the chances of success for those whose childhoods present more challenges.

The idea of giving the same damages to all children that would be given to the most advantaged children who suffer the same injury would entail a fundamental shift in the law because it centers a goal of social justice over a number of other well-established values in tort law. The leveling-up approach is a controversial one but is one that, like the other two approaches, warrants further consideration. Feminist analysis, which has already done much to make tort law more responsive to issues of equality, would seem well equipped to undertake the task of continuing to seek the best solution to the vexing problem of determining damages for diminished earning capacity in the case of both adults and children.

G.M.M. v. KIMPSON, 116 F. SUPP. 3D 126 (E.D.N.Y. 2015)

JUDGE JENNIFER B. WRIGGINS AND JUDGE SARA CRESSY, DISTRICT JUDGES

I INTRODUCTION

This case raises the issue of whether the ethnicity and sex of a tort plaintiff who lacks an earnings history can be used to determine his or her damages. The plaintiff is a young Hispanic boy who was injured by lead paint exposure in his family's apartment during the first year of his life. Specifically, this case requires us to decide, for purposes of measuring the damages he sustained, whether it is permissible to consider the child's ethnicity and sex to estimate his likely educational attainment and earnings,[1] using expert testimony based on statistical tables showing past average educational attainments and earnings of Hispanic males.

At its core, this case involves the pressing question of whether the law may take into account the race, ethnicity, and sex of a person in valuing the degree of harm and the measure of damages such an individual suffered. This issue is

[1] For further discussion, see Section II.

especially important for men from minority groups and women of all races and ethnicities because their injuries are often devalued by the torts system. Although the plaintiff in this case is a young boy of Hispanic descent, our ruling today may carry particular significance for female plaintiffs, particularly female plaintiffs who are members of minority groups. This is because female members of minority groups whose identities are located at the intersection of race, ethnicity, and gender stand to be injured the most by the practice challenged here today.

It may surprise readers that in the twenty-first century, the race, ethnicity, and sex of injured tort plaintiffs is sometimes used to estimate their damages because virtually all other explicitly race- and sex-based classifications have been eliminated in law. The reasons for this are several, in our view. The use of race-, ethnicity-, and sex-based statistics are hidden in plain sight. Because most tort cases settle before trial, judges rarely see the statistical tables divided by race, ethnicity, and sex that are used by some experts to estimate damages. Further, plaintiffs' lawyers rarely raise the issue we decide today, perhaps because they have an incentive simply to get the maximum for their individual client rather than to litigate broad discrimination claims related to damages.

For reasons explained herein, we conclude that the use of such statistical tables in this context violates the Equal Protection Clause of the Fourteenth Amendment of the US Constitution and is, therefore, impermissible.

A *Facts*

Nikki Hernandez-Adams and her husband, Joshua Mendez, moved into the basement apartment of a building located at 490 MacDonough Street in Brooklyn, New York, when Hernandez-Adams was pregnant with her first child. The child, G.M.M., was born in the apartment and spent the first year of his life there with his parents. At the end of the year, his pediatrician discovered that he had high levels of lead in his blood – almost ten micrograms per deciliter. Until recently, this level has been regarded by the Centers for Disease Control (CDC) as a "level of concern." More recently, the CDC suggests that children with 5 micrograms per deciliter should be professionally monitored. CDC, *Blood Lead Levels in Children* (2015). https://www.cdc.gov/nceh/lead/acclpp/lead_levels_in_children_fact_sheet.pdf

Although Hernandez-Adams and her family moved out of the MacDonough Street apartment shortly after G.M.M.'s doctor discovered his high blood-lead level, G.M.M. developed permanent injuries that are common in children who have been exposed to lead. According to the CDC, children who are exposed to lead have an increased risk of "damage to the brain and nervous system, slowed growth and development, learning and behavior problems (e.g., reduced IQ, ADHD. . .), and hearing and speech problems." CDC, *Childhood Lead Poisoning Data, Statistics, and Surveillance*, https://www.cdc.gov/nceh/lead/data/index.htm

The plaintiffs assert that defendant Mark Kimpson, who owned and managed the building in Brooklyn where Hernandez-Adams and her infant son lived, is liable for G.M.M.'s injuries because he negligently and recklessly failed to abate the lead paint in the building in violation of the NEW YORK CITY CHILDHOOD LEAD POISONING PREVENTION ACT OF 2003, NEW YORK CITY ADMIN. CODE §§ 27–2056.1 et seq. Pursuant to the New York law, building owners must investigate and remediate lead-based paint hazards in buildings where children under the age of 6 reside. Federal law imposes further obligations upon owners, requiring them to provide tenants with information about lead-based paint hazards and to disclose the presence of lead-based paint in a building. 42 U.S.C. § 4852d (a)(1) (2012).

The defendant, on the other hand, asserts that the child's exposure to lead was not a result of his own failure to abate the lead in the building, but rather a result of Hernandez-Adams's dogs scratching thc walls and moldings in the apartment and exposing properly encapsulated lead-based paint. Regardless of the source of the lead, however, Kimpson further asserts that G.M.M.'s developmental disabilities resulted from other medical conditions, both during Hernandez-Adams's pregnancy and early in G.M.M.'s life, and not exposure to lead paint.

The plaintiffs claimed lost earnings and medical expenses for G.M.M. Both of G.M.M.'s parents hold degrees – his father a bachelor's degree and his mother an MA in fine arts – both hold steady jobs, and both are involved in G.M.M.'s care and upbringing. Nevertheless, the defendant asserts that any award for G.M.M.'s future earnings should be diminished by virtue of the fact that he is "Hispanic." Conversely, plaintiffs claim that a more accurate prediction of lost future earnings would be obtained by analyzing the educational attainment of G.M.M.'s parents and extended family and using "blended" earnings tables that are not divided by ethnicity and sex.

B *Context of Exposure to Lead-Based Paint*

It is important to consider the context of the plaintiff's alleged injury. Lead-based paint is the primary means by which children are exposed to lead. *See Preventing Lead Poisoning in Young Children*, CDC 1, 4 (2005). Lead poisoning is often caused by ingesting paint chips or dust, likely to be found in older buildings in low-income neighborhoods. *See* CDC, *Managing*

Elevated Blood Lead Levels in Young Children, CDC 4, 17 (Birt Harvey, ed. 2002). Ingestion of lead paint causes cognitive injury such as learning disabilities and lowered IQ. Karin Koller et al., *Recent Developments in Low-Level Lead Exposure and Intellectual Impairment in Children*, 112(9) ENVTL. HEALTH PERSP. 987 (2004). Although lead paint was banned for residential use in 1978, it is still found in old, poorly maintained apartments and houses, usually in pre-1950 urban dwellings where paint is peeling, chipping, or flaking, where low-income children tend to live. *Preventing Lead Poisoning in Young Children*, CDC 18 (1991).

Given the disproportionate number of low-income children living in dwellings where lead-based paint is common, it is unsurprising that lead paint poisoning affects minority children in numbers disproportionate to their numbers in the population. According to survey data published in 2003, fully 76 percent of children with elevated blood levels were African American or Hispanic. MARTHA CHAMALLAS & JENNIFER WRIGGINS, THE MEASURE OF INJURY: RACE, GENDER, AND TORT LAW 139 (2010). A large proportion of lawsuits brought for lead paint poisoning have, consequently, been filed on behalf of minority children. *Id.* at 140. The race, ethnicity, and socioeconomic status of plaintiffs have surfaced in complex ways in this type of litigation, particularly as relates to the causation inquiry, as well as in calculating damages. CHAMALLAS & WRIGGINS, at 138–53; Jennifer Wriggins, *Genetics, IQ, Determinism, and Torts: The Example of Discovery in Lead Exposure Litigation*, 77 B.U. L. REV. 1025, 1028–79 (1997).

II ISSUE

This case concerns how the law estimates damages for an injured child. Lost future earnings, also known as future economic loss, is a standard element of tort damages for physical injury. But how do we predict what a child would have been likely to earn had he not been injured? To make such a calculation, we need to rely on some sort of data. But what sort of data should be used in court for this calculation? The immediate question is whether, in this tort case where the injured child is a Hispanic boy, statistical tables based on sex and ethnicity may be used in determining the damages for future economic loss. The broader legal question is whether statistical tables based on race, sex, and ethnicity may constitutionally be used in tort litigation to predict the earnings that an injured child would have received in the absence of injury.

In considering these questions, it is useful to contrast the task of calculating future economic loss for an adult. The future economic loss calculation for adults who have an earnings history is relatively straightforward. All we need to do is estimate how long they would have worked if they had not been injured, what their salary each year would have been, and so on.

However, in cases where there is no individualized track record of earnings, such as in cases involving children, courts and experts need to rely on other less individualized data, generally statistics, to estimate future economic loss. The question is which set of statistics they should rely on.

Experts frequently rely on two sets of statistical tables. The first set of tables sets out educational attainment by race, ethnicity, sex, and age. Experts will plug a plaintiff's race, ethnicity, sex, and age into these tables and come up with an estimate of the educational attainment (e.g., high school education, college degree, post-college degree) that the plaintiff will likely achieve. Then, armed with that estimate of likely educational attainment, they will turn to tables showing earnings by race, ethnicity, and sex of people with a certain educational attainment to reach an estimate of the plaintiff's likely future economic loss. It is important to note that economists are selective in the factors they rely on. They typically do not take into account other factors that arguably might be predictive of future earning potential, such as socioeconomic status, geography, or even religion. Additionally, not all experts use the same methodology, as we shall see in this case.

Plaintiff's expert, Dr. Kenneth William Reagles, testified that in the absence of injury, G.M.M. would have been likely to earn a master's degree or perhaps a Ph.D. He based this opinion primarily on the educational attainment of G.M.M.'s parents and G.M.M.'s extended family. The lost earnings estimate of plaintiff's forensic economist did not incorporate any assumptions about what an "average Hispanic" male would have earned or the level of education an "average Hispanic" would likely have attained.

The approach of the defense expert, Dr. Lentz, was markedly different. He estimated the injured child's future economic loss using the following data from the National Center for Education Statistics: "2.1% of Hispanic adult males held a Master's degree or better in 2013 while 13.1% held a Bachelor's or higher degrees. It can also be noted that 73.1% of Hispanic males held a high school degree or better." *See* Daubert Hr'g, Ct. Ex. 8–F at 5, June 22, 2015. Based on these data, Dr. Lentz concluded that the injured boy was unlikely to have achieved a bachelor's degree or a higher degree if he had not been injured, because only a small proportion of Hispanic males receive bachelor's or more advanced degrees. Bear in mind that lower educational attainment correlates with lower earnings in general.[2] Thus, because the plaintiff child

[2] Dr. Lentz estimated if G.M.M. had only a high school diploma his economic loss would be $1,384,776. If he earned a baccalaureate degree his future economic loss would amount to

had a reduced educational expectation at the outset, Dr. Lenz calculated that his lost earnings were considerably less than that estimated by plaintiff's expert witness.

The experts' estimates of lost earning capacity track statistical data publicly available. Additional data from the Center for Education Statistics, for example, show that 37 percent of adult white men but only 13 percent of Hispanic men aged 25–29 had completed a bachelor's or more advanced degree in 2013. National Center for Education Statistics, *Spotlight: Disparities in Educational Outcomes among Male Youth*, THE CONDITION OF EDUCATION 2015, 12. Based on these data, if the injured boy had been a white male, rather than a Hispanic male, Dr. Lentz would have estimated the child to have a much higher likelihood of attaining a bachelor's or more advanced degree, translating into a higher earnings potential.

Unfortunately, Dr. Lentz's use of tables showing educational attainment based on race, sex, and ethnicity to estimate educational attainment and lost earnings is not an uncommon practice. In *Damages in Tort Actions*, for example, Jerome Nates advises as follows:

> In many cases, the plaintiff will not have a sufficient work history to permit the use of historical earnings in the establishment of a pre-accident earnings level ... The economist may consult data of the U.S. Department of Commerce to establish average educational levels by the sex and race of the plaintiff.[3]

Nates indicates that once the economist estimates the average educational level of the injured party based on that person's race and sex, the economist looks at the table setting forth the average earnings by a person of that educational attainment, race, ethnicity, and sex. In this widely accepted methodology, race, sex, and ethnicity are taken into account in determining a plaintiff's damages not once but twice: first, in estimating likely educational attainment, and second, in estimating earning capacity.

The race-, sex-, and ethnicity-based tables used by Dr. Lentz to estimate likely educational attainment are not the only types of race-, sex-, and ethnicity-based tables used in tort litigation. Experts often use tables divided by race, gender, and ethnicity in predicting future earnings, working-life expectancy, and life expectancy. Most courts have accepted the use of such

$2,509,542. If he pursued a career in the 'arts and design' field after earning one or more postsecondary education degrees he was estimated to earn $1,522,067.

3 JEROME H. NATES ET AL., DAMAGES IN TORT ACTIONS sec. 10.02[2][b] (2012). The referenced Department of Commerce tables also include "Hispanic" ethnicity as a category.

tables as a matter of course when determining damages. Some courts, however, have been troubled by the use of such tables. *See, e.g.*, United States v. Bedonie, 317 F. Supp. 2d 1285, 1315–19 (D. Utah 2004), aff'd sub nom United States v. Serawop, 505 F.3d 1112 (10th Cir. 2007) (rejecting lost earnings calculations that distinguished on the basis of race and sex, without reaching the constitutional question); Tarpeh-Doe v. United States, 771 F. Supp. 427, 455 (D.D.C. 1991) (holding that blended tables showing average earnings of all persons should be used in calculating lost wages where plaintiff was child of white mother and black father).

The most extended discussion to date of issues related to race-based tables used in tort litigation was presented by this court in *McMillan v. New York*, 253 F.R.D. 247 (E.D.N.Y. 2008), although that decision did not deal directly with ethnicity- or sex-based educational attainment or earnings tables. In *McMillan*, an adult African-American man was rendered a quadriplegic in a Staten Island Ferry crash in which New York City was clearly at fault. *Id.* at 248 (*citing* In re City of New York, 475 F. Supp. 2d 235 (E.D.N.Y. 2007), *aff'd* 522 F.3d 279 (2d Cir. 2008)). The plaintiff's future medical expenses were an important element of damages and calculating those future medical expenses required estimating the plaintiff's life expectancy. New York City used statistical tables showing that spinal cord-injured African-American men will live a shorter time than spinal cord-injured persons of other races, thus reducing the estimate for future medical expenses.[4] *Id.* The court concluded that "'[r]-acially' based life expectancy and related data may not be utilized to find a reduced life expectancy for a claimant in computing damages based on predictions of life expectancy." *Id.* The court used tables showing life expectancy for all spine-injured males in its calculation. This case presents a somewhat different but obviously related issue.

The issue here, as stated above, is whether in this tort case, tables based on race, sex, and ethnicity can be used to predict the educational level a Hispanic boy would have achieved in the absence of his injury, thus lowering the damages awarded to the plaintiff child. This is a question of constitutional dimension, and we answer it in the negative. The use of classifications based on race, sex, and ethnicity in our courts raises questions about the scope of the Equal Protection Clause. For reasons explained below, we hold that use of such tables in this case and more generally violates the Equal Protection Clause.

4 The tables were clearly sex-based as well as race-based as they only pertained to African-American men.

III ANALYSIS

A *State Action*

The Equal Protection Clause of the Fourteenth Amendment protects individuals only against state action or action by a private entity that "may be fairly treated as that of the State itself." Jackson v. Metro. Edison Co., 419 U.S. 345, 351 (1974); *see also* United States. v. Stanley, 109 U.S. 3, 11 (1883) ("It nullifies and makes void . . . State action of every kind . . . which denies to any [citizens of the United States] the equal protection of the laws"). Here, state action is present when an expert is allowed to testify about a plaintiff's damages using ethnicity-based and sex-based statistics, as explained below.

State action occurs "when private parties make extensive use of state procedures with 'the overt, significant assistance of state officials.'" Edmonson v. Leesville Concrete Co., 500 U.S. 614, 622 (1991) (*quoting* Tulsa Prof'l Collection Servs., Inc. v. Pope, 485 U.S. 478, 486 (1988)). The *Edmonson* court applied the two-step state action framework set out in *Lugar v. Edmondson Oil Co.*, 457 U.S. 922, 939 (1982) to decide the issue of whether a private party's exercise of a peremptory challenge in a civil action constituted state action. The first step of the framework asks whether "the claimed deprivation has resulted from the exercise of a right or privilege having its source in state authority." The second step of the *Lugar* framework requires the court to determine whether the private party who is acting "may be appropriately characterized" as a state actor. *Id.* The *Edmonson* court ultimately concluded that a private attorney who makes a discriminatory peremptory strike during jury selection in a civil action is a state actor for purposes of the Equal Protection Clause of the Fourteenth Amendment. *Edmonson*, 500 U.S. at 622. It also reasoned that, because a peremptory strike has no purpose outside of a courtroom, when a court enforces "a discriminatory peremptory challenge," it both makes itself a party to and places "its power, property and prestige behind" an act of discrimination. *Id.* at 624.

In this case, the process of certifying an expert witness, offering expert testimony at trial, and admitting the testimony and tables supporting the testimony undoubtedly has its source in state authority and therefore satisfies the first requirement of the *Lugar* state action framework. Professor Martha Chamallas has correctly argued that "[v]ery much like the regulation of peremptory challenges, there are statutes and rules governing the use of experts, and permitting them to express opinions and draw conclusions that other witnesses may not." Martha Chamallas, *Questioning the Use of Race-Specific and Gender-Specific Economic Data in Tort Litigation:*

A *Constitutional Argument*, 63 FORDHAM L. REV. 73, 107 (1994). Parties may not offer expert testimony without first going through the process of having that person's expertise evaluated and approved by the court. When the court admits the expert's testimony – including data on educational attainment and earnings divided by race, ethnicity, and sex – it communicates to the jury that those factors are not only relevant, but legally permissible. *Id.* As Chamallas notes, as is the case of a peremptory strike, "the special status of expert testimony has no parallel outside the courtroom." *Id.*

The second step of the *Lugar* framework – whether a party appropriately may be characterized as a state actor – is "often a factbound inquiry." *Edmonson*, 500 U.S. at 621. The court has, however, recognized three factors within this inquiry. First, "the extent to which the actor relies on governmental assistance and benefits"; second, "whether the actor is performing a traditional governmental function"; and third, "whether the injury caused is aggravated in a unique way by the incidents of governmental authority." *Id.* at 621–22. Each of these three *Edmonson* factors is satisfied here.

First, as stated above, a litigant must follow the procedures set out in state or federal evidentiary rules to certify an expert to testify at trial. After that expert is certified, the litigant relies upon the judge, a state actor, to admit the evidence. *See* Shelley v. Kraemer, 334 U.S. 1, 14 (1948). The judge's role is to exercise control over the presentation of evidence, thereby ensuring the effectiveness of the trial. *See, e.g.*, Fed. R. Evid. 611. The recognition of an expert as qualified to render an opinion on damages, in court, can only take place because of government action. By admitting discriminatory data, "the court 'has not only made itself a party to the [biased act], but has elected to place its power, property and prestige behind the [alleged] discrimination.'" *Edmonson*, 500 U.S. at 624 (alterations in original) (*citing* Burton v. Wilmington Parking Auth., 365 U.S. 715, 725 (1961)). Thus, the use of expert testimony in a civil case clearly depends upon "governmental assistance and benefits."

Second, the assistance that the court provides to the litigant in certifying experts and admitting expert testimony and the data on which that testimony is based, combined with the jury's application of the expert's data to the facts of the case, fulfills a traditional governmental function. Although the information being provided by the expert may have applications outside of the trial, when viewed in context "the objective of expert testimony is to help the jury apply the law to the facts, a process that is intricately connected to the choice of the governing legal standard." Chamallas, at 109. The expert's testimony, once admitted, cannot be separated from the court's "traditional governmental function" of applying and refining the governing legal standard.

The third *Edmonson* factor that asks whether the injury is aggravated by governmental authority is also present here. When a court admits educational attainment and wage data based upon ethnicity and sex to determine damages for a tort victim, the court "reinforces the view that race and gender differences are inevitable and enduring, rather than a product of political and social arrangements that are subject to change." MARTHA CHAMALLAS & JENNIFER WRIGGINS, THE MEASURE OF INJURY: RACE, GENDER, AND TORT LAW 169 (2010). Wage disparities based on race and ethnicity, many studies show, stem in part from intentional discrimination.[5] Thus, when the tables are used to justify lower damage awards based on ethnicity, sex, and race for plaintiffs who are Hispanic, black, and/or female, the court is furthering the effects of intentional discrimination.[6] Allowing these data to be used in court to make damages decisions, therefore, contravenes the court's instruction that "the law cannot, directly or indirectly, give … effect" to private biases. Palmore v. Sidoti, 466 U.S. 429, 433 (1984). The court's validation of those biases through the use of ethnicity- and sex-based data aggravates the injury to the individual in a unique way.

For these reasons, a decision to admit expert testimony that is grounded on race-based, ethnicity-based, and sex-based statistical tables involves state action.

B *Race, Ethnicity, and Sex-Based Classifications*

For equal protection purposes, statistical tables divided by race, ethnicity, and sex (and expert testimony based on them) must be treated as race-based, gender-based, and ethnicity-based classifications when used in tort litigation to determine a plaintiff's damages.

Race-based, ethnicity-based, and sex-based tables categorize and divide people by race, sex, and ethnicity. When they are used in tort litigation, the plaintiff's race, sex, and ethnicity are 'plugged in' to the tables and in turn the

5 *See, e.g.*, Devah Pager, Bruce Western, & Bart Bonikowski, *Discrimination in a Low-Wage Labor Market: A Field Experiment*, 74 AM. SOC. REV. 777, 785 (2009) (white testers in audit study received a call back or job offer 31 percent of the time, compared to 25.2 percent for Latino testers and 15.2 percent for African-American testers); Marianne Bertrand & Sendhil Mullainathan, *Are Emily and Greg More Employable than Lakisha and Kamal? A Field Experiment*, 94 AM. ECON. REV. 991, 992 (2004) (finding that "[a]pplicants with white names need to send out about 10 resumes to get one call back while applicants with African American names need to send out about 15 resumes").

6 In cases with white male plaintiffs, the tables are used to justify higher damage awards for them. In either instance, the court makes itself a party to discrimination by endorsing discriminatory damage determinations.

tables are used to estimate something significant about the plaintiff, whether it be education, earnings, or both. This method of calculating damages imposes a race, sex, and ethnicity-based frame on an individual and uses that frame to affect the individual's compensation. The use of such data constitutes a classification based on race, ethnicity, and gender, and must be treated as such.[7]

C *Constitutional Analysis*

1 Standards of Review

Under established law, race- and ethnicity-based classifications are subject to strict scrutiny, *Regents of Univ. of Cal. v. Bakke*, 438 U.S. 265, 291 (1978), whereas sex-based classifications receive only intermediate scrutiny, *Craig v. Boren*, 429 U.S. 190, 197 (1976). The distinction between the two kinds of discrimination, however, is in a sense artificial, given that all individuals have both a sex and a race. In persons' lived experience, these factors cannot be separated. Rather, as scholars have long recognized, "[r]acism and sexism are interlocking, mutually-reinforcing components of a system of dominance rooted in patriarchy." Paulette M. Caldwell, *A Hair Piece: Perspectives on the Intersection of Race and Gender*, 1991 DUKE L.J. 365, 371–72 (1991); Kimberlé Crenshaw, *Demarginalizing the Intersection of Race and Sex: A Black Feminist Critique of Antidiscrimination Doctrine, Feminist Theory, and Antiracist Politics*, 1989 U. OF CHI. LEGAL F. 139 (1989); Trina Grillo, *Anti-Essentialism & Intersectionality: Tools to Dismantle the Master's House*, 10 BERKELEY J. OF GENDER, L. & JUST. 16, 16–19 (1995); Darren Lenard Hutchinson, *Identity Crisis: "Intersectionality," "Multidimensionality," and the Development of an Adequate Theory of Subordination*, 6 MICH. J. RACE & LAW 285, 307–08, 311–13 (2001); Jennifer Wriggins, *Rape, Racism, and the Law*, 6 HARV. WOMEN'S L.J. 103 (1983). The "intersectionality" approach of

[7] Many scholars have argued that race is largely a social construct. *See, e.g.*, Ian F. Haney Lopez, *The Social Construction of Race: Some Observations on Illusion, Fabrication, and Choice*, 29 HARV. C.R.-C.L. L. REV. 1–62 (1994); *McMillan*, 253 F.R.D. at 250. Racial categories used in statistical tables are far from clear or undisputed. *See, e.g.*, *McMillan*, 253 F.R.D. at 249–53. The ethnic category of 'Hispanic,' for example, has changed over time reflecting the politics of the day. *See, e.g.*, IAN HANEY LOPEZ, WHITE BY LAW: THE LEGAL CONSTRUCTION OF RACE 7–14 (2006). Similarly, we now recognize that gender and sex categories also are not always clear and undisputed. *See generally* Julie A. Greenberg, *Defining Male and Female: Intersexuality and the Collision between Law and Biology*, 41 ARIZ. L. REV. 265 (1999). Regardless of whether and to what extent race, sex, and ethnicity are socially constructed, individuals' placement in these categories has a significant impact on their lives. People are advantaged and disadvantaged by them. And constitutional analysis requires their use.

such scholars appropriately draws attention to the reality that race and sex cannot be untangled.

In practice, race- and ethnicity-based tables are generally sex-based as well. In this case, for example, the child was Hispanic, and the expert used educational attainment tables for Hispanic *males*. Because the tables incorporated both ethnic and sex-based classifications, we must apply two, somewhat different, standards of constitutional review in this case.

To satisfy strict scrutiny, a race- or ethnicity-based classification must be "'narrowly tailored' to achieve a 'compelling' government interest." Parents Involved in Cmty. Sch. v. Seattle Sch. Dist. No. 1, 551 U.S. 701, 720 (2007) (*quoting* Adarand Constructors, Inc. v. Pena, 515 U.S. 200, 227 (1995)). The reason for subjecting race classifications to such close scrutiny is, as Justice Burger wrote, that "[a] core purpose of the Fourteenth Amendment was to do away with all governmentally imposed discrimination based on race. Classifying persons according to their race is more likely to reflect racial prejudice than legitimate public concern; the race, not the person, dictates the category." Palmore v. Sidoti, 466 U.S. 429, 432 (1984). Thus "[a] racial classification, regardless of purported motivation, is presumptively invalid and can be upheld only upon extraordinary justification." Pers. Adm'r of Mass v. Feeney, 442 U.S. 256, 272 (1979).

Intermediate scrutiny, in contrast, requires that sex-based classifications "be substantially related" to achieving "important governmental objectives." Boren, 429 U.S. at 197; United States v. Virginia, 518 U.S. 515, 533 (1996); Nguyen v. INS, 533 U.S. 53, 60 (2001). For example, "'archaic and overbroad' generalizations concerning ... working women ... could not justify use of a gender line in determining eligibility for certain governmental entitlements." *Boren*, 429 U.S. at 198 (*quoting* Schlesinger v. Ballard, 419 U.S. 498, 508 (1975)). Gender-based classifications "may not be used, as they once were, to create or perpetuate the legal, social, and economic inferiority of women." United States v. Virginia, 518 U.S. at 534. Further, "parties who seek to defend gender-based government action must demonstrate "an exceedingly persuasive justification for that action." Miss. Univ. for Women v. Hogan, 458 U.S. 718, 724 (1982).

Each standard of review will be applied in turn.

2 Applying Strict Scrutiny

(a) Use of Such Tables Does Not Serve a Compelling Governmental Interest

What possibly could be the compelling governmental interest for using race-based and ethnicity-based tables in tort litigation to determine a victim's damages? The only plausible governmental interest at stake is furthering "accuracy" in determining tort damages. For several reasons stated below, however, we conclude that the challenged practice does not promote accuracy in damages determination and thus does not further any compelling governmental interest.

At the outset, it must be appreciated that the notion of "accuracy" in determining tort damages, while superficially appealing, is a nebulous concept that does not hold up under close analysis. Tort damages have always been regarded as highly individualized determinations, often yielding different damage amounts for similar or identical injuries. Jennifer B. Wriggins, *Torts, Race, and the Value of Injury 1900–1949*, 49 HOW. L.J. 99, 102, n.13 (2005). In contrast to workers' compensation laws which mandate a preset amount of damages for particular types of injuries, tort damages can and do vary from individual plaintiff to plaintiff. DAN T. DOBBS, THE LAW OF TORTS, 1099–1100 (2000). The law of damages acknowledges this variability and accepts it in order to do justice in individual cases. As the form jury instructions for the US Court of Appeals for the Fifth Circuit state, "the law does not require that the plaintiff prove the amount of his losses with mathematical precision, but only with as much definiteness and accuracy as the circumstances permit." 3 FED. JURY PRAC. & INSTR. § 128:01 (6TH ED.). Moreover, in this and other similar cases, the particular object of the inquiry – what the future earnings of the injured person would have been if she had not been injured – is inherently uncertain and speculative. CHAMALLAS & WRIGGINS, at 167–68. Thus, there is often no single correct or accurate measure of damages.

In addition to the inherent uncertainty in damage calculations, there are particular problems relating to the use of tables divided by race and ethnicity. Their use is arbitrarily underinclusive because other factors also affect educational attainment and earnings, such as socioeconomic status, healthcare, and geography. CHAMALLAS & WRIGGINS, at 161–69. As noted above, because ethnic and racial boundaries between people are neither clear nor undisputed, it is perilous and often offensive to classify persons on such bases. *See supra* note 7. In practice, the tables used by experts are often outdated and do not reflect current data at the time of trial. Martha Chamallas, *Civil Rights in Ordinary Tort Cases: Race, Gender, and the Calculation of Economic Loss*, 38 LOY. L.A. L. REV. 1435, 1452 (2005). Finally, when tables based on past data are uncritically used and extended into the future, such practice erroneously assumes that we can know the rate of future social changes such as educational participation rates and wage earning by race and ethnicity. Instead, we should candidly admit that we cannot know these things and cannot precisely predict the future. *See*

Jennifer B. Wriggins, *Constitution Day Lecture: Injury, Race, Gender, and Equal Protection*, 63 ME. L. REV. 263, 274–75 (2010); Chamallas, *Civil Rights in Ordinary Tort* Cases, 38 LOY. L.A. L. REV. at 1435–50.

In short, "accuracy" in determining tort damages does not hold up as a coherent interest on its own terms, let alone qualify as a *compelling* interest. It clearly does not rise to the level of being a compelling interest when compared with previously recognized interests. The classic compelling governmental interest is national security. *See* Korematsu v. United States, 323 U.S. 214, 219–20 (1944). Other interests determined to be compelling include "safeguarding the physical and psychological welfare of . . . minor[s]," New York v. Ferber, 458 U.S. 747, 758 (1987); remedying past discrimination, *Adarand Constructors v. Pena*, 515 U.S. 200, 220 (1995); *City of Richmond v. J.A. Croson Co.*, 488 U.S. 469, 518–19 (1989); protecting viable fetuses and women's health, *Roe v. Wade*, 410 U.S. 113, 162–63 (1973); diversity in higher education, *Grutter v. Bolinger*, 539 U.S. 306, 329 (2003); *Bakke*, 438 U.S. at 311–12; and "preventing crime by arrestees," *United States v. Salerno*, 481 U.S. 739, 749 (1987). Any purported interest in "accuracy" that could possibly support use of the race- and ethnicity-based tables simply does not stack up against these governmental interests.

Moreover, even if "accuracy" in determining tort damages does cohere as an interest, making sure that tortfeasors (and their liability insurers) pay neither too much nor too little tort damages is an inherently private interest and as such would not qualify as a compelling *governmental* interest.

(b) The Classification Is Not Narrowly Tailored

Even if "accuracy" in determining tort damages was a compelling governmental interest, the use of an ethnicity-based classification must be narrowly tailored to further only that interest. Parents Involved in Cmty. Sch. v. Seattle Sch. Dist. No. 1, 551 U.S. 701, 720 (2007). In this case, the use of ethnicity-based tables is not narrowly tailored.

Data from the tables provide a very weak estimate of the actual losses suffered by any specific victim. As noted above, tables used in litigation are often outdated and reflect data about the past situation of group members (or those seen as part of a group) without taking into account changes that might happen in the future. Wriggins, *Constitutional Day Lecture*, 274–75. As blunt instruments, the tables fail to consider important factors affecting earnings and life expectancy, such as socioeconomic status and geography. Arline T. Geronimus et al., *Inequality in Life Expectancy, Functional Status, and Active Life Expectancy Across Selected Black & White Populations in the U.S.*,

38 Demography 227, 251 (2001); Robert S. Levine et al., *Black–White Inequalities in Mortality and Life Expectancy, 1933–1999: Implications for Healthy People 2010*, 116 Pub. Health Rep. 474, 482 (Sept.–Oct. 2001). In addition, use of such tables ignores the insights of "resiliency theory," a sociological theory which starts from the assumption that many children often succeed against the odds and focuses on factors other than ethnicity and race to predict a likelihood of a child's success in the future. Laura Greenberg, *Compensating the Lead-Poisoned Child: Proposals for Mitigating Discriminatory Damages Awards*, 28 B.C. Envtl. Aff. L. Rev. 429, 454 (2001).

For young African Americans and Hispanics of high socioeconomic status, the fit between the tables and both educational attainment and earnings is likely to be especially poor. Many such child tort victims can be expected to earn wages closer to the white average than their ancestors would have earned, given that the racial pay gap lessens with education. *See* Jeremy Pais, *Socioeconomic Background and Racial Earnings Inequality: A Propensity Score Analysis*, 40 Soc. Sci. Research 37 (2011).[8]

It is axiomatic that the Equal Protection Clause protects individuals, not groups (*Pena*, 515 U.S. at 227) and rigorously protects individuals from being disadvantaged by the use of group-based classifications, such as ethnicity and race. Here, reliance on tables encourages racial stereotyping and operates as a disincentive toward considering individual plaintiffs and their injuries in a thoughtful, unbiased fashion.

In determining whether a racial or ethnic classification is narrowly tailored, some courts have required that the state show that there are no practical ethnicity- or race-neutral means to serve the state interest. *Grutter*, 539 U.S. at 339. Such neutral alternatives exist in this case. Thus, rather than relying on race or ethnicity, experts could base their estimates on the educational level of the child's parents, the socioeconomic status of the family, and the region where the child lives to yield a prediction of earnings which would be at least as "accurate" as the ethnicity-based tables relied on by the defense expert in this case. *See, e.g.*, Geronimus et al., *supra* at 241; *McMillan*, 253 F.R.D. at 252. These would certainly be workable, ethnicity-neutral alternatives.

As we see it, the use of such tables to determine an individual's damages has broad deleterious consequences. Simply put, the practice discriminates on the

[8] This is true for life expectancy as well; socioeconomic status is an important predictor, yet one ignored by statistical tables used in tort litigation. For example, an important study found that "African-Americans in well-off urban areas had higher life expectancies than African-Americans in poor urban areas; and white residents of poor urban areas had somewhat worse mortality profiles 'than residents of relatively advantaged black urban areas.'" Geronimus et al., *supra* at 241.

basis of race and ethnicity against black and Hispanic people seeking recourse in the legal system and endorses the legitimacy of racial and ethnic divisions and disparities. It virtually assures that a Hispanic plaintiff will recover less than a similarly situated white plaintiff. The tables take past discrimination (which is at least partly responsible for the educational and wage-based disparities) and inscribes those disparities onto the future. Rather than furthering the governmental interest in ending discrimination, the practice perpetuates discrimination and inequality by race and ethnicity.

Finally, because the use of race- and ethnicity-based tables generates lower damage awards for injuries to minorities, their use has the "perverse result of encouraging torts against them," for example, by making it cheaper for tort defendants to injure residents of low-income minority neighborhoods. Michael I. Meyerson & William Meyerson, *Significant Statistics: The Unwitting Policymaking of Mathematically Ignorant Judges*, 37 PEPP. L. REV. 771, 808 (2010). Rather than promoting accuracy in damage awards, such practice likely reduces deterrence of injury to minorities and is clearly not narrowly tailored to promote a compelling governmental interest. We therefore conclude that the use of race-based and ethnicity-based tables to determine tort damages does not satisfy strict scrutiny.

3 Applying Intermediate Scrutiny

We now turn to whether the use of sex-based tables satisfies intermediate scrutiny. As noted above, "for a gender-based classification to withstand equal protection scrutiny, it must be established 'at least that the [challenged] classification serves important governmental objectives and that the discriminatory means employed' are 'substantially related to the achievement of those objectives.'" *Nguyen*, 533 U.S. at 60 (quoting *Virginia*, 518 U.S. at 533). In this case, the sex-based classification does not serve an important governmental objective and the discriminatory means employed is not substantially related to achieving the objective.

(a) Use of Such Tables Does Not Serve an Important Governmental Objective

In this case, our analysis of intermediate scrutiny largely tracks our analysis of strict scrutiny. The only possible "important governmental interest" that could be asserted in this case is the interest in "accuracy" of damages. However, such an asserted interest cannot pass constitutional muster under intermediate scrutiny. As discussed above, the concept of "accuracy" in determining tort damages is vague and illusory, given the nature of tort damages. Even if "accuracy" in tort damages coheres as a governmental interest, it is not an *important* governmental interest.

The interests asserted to support a gender-based classification must be actual, not hypothesized, and must not be based on "overbroad generalizations about the different talents, capabilities, or preferences of males or females." *Virginia*, 518 U.S. at 533, 535. The governmental interests deemed important in the context of sex-based classifications have included enhancement of traffic safety, *Boren*, 429 U.S. at 197; protection of legally created reliance interests, *Heckler v. Mathews*, 465 U.S. 728, 746 (1984); impartial trials, *J.E.B. v. Alabama*, 511 U.S. 127, 135 (1994); and, in the context of citizenship for children born abroad outside marriage, assuring biological and day-to-day parental relationships, *Nguyen*, 533 U.S. at 62, 64. All of these interests are located within the realm of broad public concern. Here, the asserted objective that an individual tort defendant (or its insurer) pay the "right" amount to a tort victim does not qualify as an important governmental objective.

(b) The Classification Is Not Substantially Related to the Achievement of the Objective and There Is No Exceedingly Persuasive Justification for the Use of Sex-Based Tables

Even if "accuracy" in determining tort damages were an important governmental objective, using sex-based tables is not substantially related to achieving that objective. The discriminatory means of using sex-based predictions to determine an individual's damages is at best tangentially related to that objective, if it is related at all, and there is no exceedingly persuasive justification for it.

The "fit" between the objective of awarding "accurate" tort damages and the discriminatory means of using sex-based tables is loose. The tables embody a broad-brush summary of patterns of educational attainment, average numbers of years spent in the workforce, and earnings by women in the past. Using such tables gives a poor estimate of any given individual's actual losses. In order to project future loss, at a minimum, the tables would have to be modified to reflect an estimate of the rate of societal changes. For example, earnings tables divided by sex contain assumptions that female workers will spend a certain amount of years out of the workplace to raise children. Yet the workforce participation of mothers has changed considerably over time. Chamallas, at 122. Assumptions about the rate of change of such dynamic social practices must be made in order to project the tables into the future, and such assumptions will vary depending on predilections and preferences of the expert making them. CHAMALLAS & WRIGGINS, at 167.

Moreover, as noted earlier, the sex-based as well as race- and ethnicity-based lines drawn by the tables do not always match social reality, rendering them even weaker sources of information and highlighting the lack of "substantial relationship" between the discriminatory classification and the governmental objective.

Further, using sex-based tables to project future losses of an individual has the effect of reinscribing the disparities of the past onto the future. Some of the inequality in earnings by gender is a result of exclusion and discrimination. *See* Califano v. Webster, 430 U.S. 313, 318–19 (1977) (discussing economic discrimination against women and noting that women "have been unfairly hindered from earning as much as men"). To use such data in our courtrooms to determine an individual's losses is to endorse that inequality and project it into the future. Michael I. Meyerson & William Meyerson, *Significant Statistics*, 37 PEPP. L. REV. at 807–08 ("[T]he use of race- and gender-based statistics will have the undesirable effect of 'reinforcing the underlying social inequalities of our society rather than describing a significant biological difference'") (quoting *McMillan*, 253 F.R.D. at 250). In tort litigation, use of tables showing lower lost earnings for women sends a message to tort defendants that they need to exercise less care for women – and, taking into account ethnicity and race, less still for some subgroups of women – than for most groups of men. This is a significant negative consequence that is directly supported by use of tables in litigation. For similar reasons, the Supreme Court has rejected the use of gender-based classifications based on use of statistics given their tendency to reflect and reinforce gender stereotypes. *Boren*, 42 U.S. at 201–04.[9]

Overall, no substantial relationship has been shown between the discriminatory classification and the asserted governmental objective in this case and no exceedingly persuasive justification for the discriminatory classification has been presented.

9 In *J.E.B. v. Alabama*, 511 U.S. 127, 135–36 (1994), involving sex discrimination in jury selection, the defendant argued that while race discrimination was not constitutionally acceptable in jury selection, sex discrimination was. The Supreme Court rejected this notion, recognizing that although the histories are different, government action on either basis in jury selection is anathema. *Id.* at 136–38. We add that African-American women have faced exclusions and discrimination based upon their race and sex and as African-American women specifically. *See generally* Jennifer Wriggins, *Note: Rape, Racism, and the Law*, 6 HARV. J. GENDER & L. 103 (1983); Kimberlé Crenshaw, *Demarginalizing the Intersection of Race and Sex: A Black Feminist Critique of Antidiscrimination Doctrine, Feminist Theory, and Antiracist Politics*, 1989 U. OF CHICAGO LEGAL. F. 139 (1989).

IV CONCLUSION

The use of race-based, gender-based, or ethnicity-based tables to determine an individual's tort damages is a violation of Equal Protection and is therefore unconstitutional. In this instance, the parties may offer testimony about the educational attainment and earnings of plaintiff's immediate and extended family to form an acceptable basis on which to estimate lost earnings of the child plaintiff. Testimony based on blended tables that include the whole population is acceptable as well.[10]

[10] The court is not entirely comfortable with using an extended family's educational attainment to predict an individual's probable educational attainment (and lost earnings) in all contexts given that myriad individual and societal factors contribute to educational attainment, and predicting an individual child's educational attainment is inherently uncertain. However, without massive reforms of the tort system, this is the best alternative.

17

Commentary on *Simpkins v. Grace Brethren Church of Delaware, Ohio*

JILL WIEBER LENS

INTRODUCTION

Motivated by concerns that the tort litigation system was starting to have deleterious economic effects, a tort reform movement started gaining steam throughout the United States starting in the late 1970s, and continuing in some states even past the turn of the century. Numerous states adopted measures to limit the filing of and the recovery of damages in tort lawsuits, including measures shortening the time limits in which lawsuits must be filed,[1] limiting the amount of damages a plaintiff could recover from each defendant,[2] and limiting the recovery of both punitive and compensatory damages.

This last measure, a limit on a plaintiff's recovery of compensatory damages, known as a damage cap, proved very popular among states, although variations exist. Some state legislatures were most concerned about medical malpractice claims, believing that high tort damage awards were making malpractice premiums too expensive for doctors and causing doctors to leave the state. Thus, those state legislatures passed damage caps applicable only to medical malpractice claims.[3] Some state legislatures were concerned about businesses generally, believing that high tort damage awards were making it too expensive

[1] *See, e.g.*, N.Y. C. P. L.R. § 214-a (Consol. 1990) (shortening the statute of limitations for medical malpractice suits from three years to two and a half years).

[2] Several states, for example, eliminated joint liability, in which other defendants could be required to pay the damages share of a judgment proof defendant, and instead adopted pure several liability, in which no defendant pays more than a proportionate share of the damages and the plaintiff bears the burden of any uncollectible portion. *See, e.g.*, Colo. Rev. Stat. § 13–21–111.5; Ind. Code § 34–51–2-8; Ky. Rev. Stat. § 411.182; La. Civ. Code Ann. Art. 2323.

[3] *See, e.g.*, Cal. Civ. Code § 3333.2 (West 1975); Tex. Rev. Civ. Stat. Ann. Art. 4590 §§ 11.02, 11.03 (1986) (held unconstitutional in *Lucas v. United States*, 757 S.W.2d 687, 687 (Tex. 1988)); Mich. Comp. Laws Ann. § 600.1483(1) (1986).

to do any business in the state and causing businesses to leave the state. Those state legislatures passed damage caps applicable to all tort claims.[4]

Although the applicability to the type of tort claim has differed, what almost all damage caps have in common is that they distinguish between economic and noneconomic losses and apply to only noneconomic damages. Economic damages, damages like lost wages and medical expenses, are those that are supposedly capable of objective measurement.[5] Noneconomic damages, damages for injuries like pain and suffering, loss of a relationship, or emotional distress, lack this objective measurement.[6] Tort reform advocates asserted that this lack of objective measurement makes these damages less predictable and more susceptible to abuse when awarded by juries. Thus, state legislatures capped the recovery only of noneconomic damages, meaning tort plaintiffs can recover noneconomic damages only up to the amount of the cap, but can still recover all of their economic damages.

It did not take long for legal scholars to question the efficacy and possible gendered effects of noneconomic damage caps. Many wondered whether noneconomic damage caps would actually keep doctors and businesses in the state. Many also expressed concern about the effects of noneconomic damage caps on different plaintiffs, whether some plaintiffs would be more affected than others. One answer was obvious – that plaintiffs with significant noneconomic damages would be affected more than plaintiffs with significant economic damages. Less obvious though is that those plaintiffs with significant noneconomic damages tend to be women, whereas men are more likely to have significant economic damages. And, thus, women tort plaintiffs will be likely to recover a smaller proportion of the damages awarded to them because their significant noneconomic damages will be capped. Male tort plaintiffs, on the other hand, will likely still be able to recover a significant proportion of their damages because their significant economic damages are unaffected by a noneconomic damage cap.[7]

Numerous plaintiffs have challenged the constitutionality of noneconomic damage caps, as did Jessica Simpkins in *Simpkins v. Grace Brethren Church of*

4 *See, e.g.*, Ohio Rev. Code Ann. § 2315.18 (West 2005); Alaska Stat. Ann. § 09.17.010 (2002); Okla. Stat. Ann. tit. 23, § 61.2 (West).

5 Anthony J. Sebok, *Translating the Immeasurable: Thinking about Pain and Suffering Comparatively*, 55 DePaul L. Rev. 379, 383 (2006).

6 *Id.*

7 *See, e.g.*, Thomas Koenig & Michael Rustad, *His and Her Tort Reform: Gender Injustice in Disguise*, 70 Wash. L. Rev. 1, 3–8 (1995); Lucinda M. Finley, *The Hidden Victims of Tort Reform: Women, Children, and the Elderly*, 53 Emory L.J. 1263, 1281 (2004).

Delaware, Ohio.[8] Simpkins attempted to show the specific, detrimental effect that noneconomic damage caps would have on victims like her – female victims of sexual assault – whose damages consist primarily of noneconomic harm. Arguably, she did so. Yet, the Ohio Supreme Court still found Ohio's noneconomic damage cap constitutional.

THE ORIGINAL *SIMPKINS* OPINION

Ohio was one of the first states to pass a damage cap in 1975.[9] Claiming that it would help curb the rising costs of medical malpractice premiums, which could deter doctors from wanting to practice in the state, the legislature passed a tort reform package that included a damage cap limiting the recovery of noneconomic damages to $200,000 in all medical malpractice claims.[10] Almost fifteen years later, the Ohio Supreme Court found that damage cap unconstitutional on due process grounds.[11]

In 2005, the Ohio state legislature again passed a comprehensive tort reform package to deter frivolous lawsuits,[12] which the legislature believed were increasing the costs of doing business, threatening Ohio jobs, driving up consumer costs, and hindering innovation.[13] The 2005 package included a cap on the recovery of noneconomic damages, which this time applied to all tort claims.[14] The cap limited recoverable noneconomic damages to the greater of $250,000 or three times the amount of the plaintiff's economic losses (not to exceed $350,000).[15] The legislature created an exception in the cap making it inapplicable to a plaintiff who suffered a permanent physical consequence.[16] This is the noneconomic damage cap at issue in *Simpkins*.

Nine years before *Simpkins*, the Ohio Supreme Court found this same 2005 damage cap facially constitutional in *Arbino v. Johnson & Johnson*.[17] Specifically, the Ohio Supreme Court found no violation of the right to jury trial enshrined in the Ohio Constitution because although a plaintiff would

[8] 75 N.E.3d 122 (Ohio 2016).
[9] Melissa C. Gregory, *Capping Noneconomic Damages in Medical Malpractice Suits is Not the Panacea of the "Medical Liability Crisis,"* 31 WM. MITCHELL L. REV. 1031, 1036 & n.38 (2005).
[10] Ohio Rev. Code Ann. § 2307.43 (West) (held unconstitutional in *Morris v. Savoy*, 576 N.E.2d 765, 770–71 (Ohio 1991)).
[11] Morris v. Savoy, 576 N.E.2d 765, 770–71 (Ohio 1991).
[12] *Simpkins*, 75 N.E.3d at 126.
[13] *Id.*
[14] Ohio Rev. Code Ann. § 2315.18(A)(7)) (West).
[15] *Id.* § 2315.18(B)(2).
[16] *Id.* § 2315.18(B)(3).
[17] 880 N.E.2d 420 (Ohio 2007).

not recover all of her noneconomic damages, the jury still decides the factual amount of damages; the court characterized the cap as just a legislative policy choice limiting the recovery.[18] The court also found that the cap was consistent with Ohio's constitutional right to open courts and the right to a remedy because the cap still allows a meaningful remedy, especially due to the statutory exception for catastrophic injuries and the availability of punitive damages.[19] Last, the court found no due process violation. The court deferred to the legislature's conclusion that the damage cap was needed to help Ohio's economic climate, and that noneconomic damages are subjective and speculative and thus susceptible to influence of irrelevant factors, like the level of defendant's wrongdoing.[20] The court also found that the damage cap was neither arbitrary nor unreasonable because of the statutory exception allowing uncapped noneconomic damages for plaintiffs who suffered permanent physical consequences, meaning the most severely injured would not bear the burden to improve the economic climate for all.[21]

Because of *Arbino*, *Simpkins* was not a facial challenge to Ohio's noneconomic damage cap. Instead, *Simpkins* challenged the constitutionality of the damage cap as applied to certain tort plaintiffs – minors who are victims of sexual assault.[22] These minors are mostly female and suffer extensive noneconomic damages, but minimal economic damages, because while the assault causes long-lasting trauma, it usually does not lead to extensive medical bills or lost time from work. The plaintiff, Simpkins, was raped by her pastor when she was 15 years old. Simpkins won her lawsuit against the church for its negligence in hiring, retaining, and supervising that pastor. The jury awarded her a total of $3,651,378.85 in damages, $3.5 million of which compensated her for her pain and suffering and mental anguish.[23] Applying the 2005 legislative noneconomic damage cap, the trial court reduced her $3.5 million in noneconomic damages to only $350,000.[24]

Simpkins challenged the constitutionality of the noneconomic damage cap as applied to minor victims of sexual assault like herself. At the time, the Ohio Supreme Court had a majority of female justices.[25] Two male justices agreed

[18] *Id.* at 432.
[19] *Id.* at 433.
[20] *Id.* at 434.
[21] *Id.* at 435.
[22] *Simpkins*, 75 N.E.3d at 126.
[23] *Id.* at 129.
[24] *Id.*
[25] *See generally id.*

with Simpkins, concluding that the cap violated Ohio's right to jury trial.[26] But those justices dissented. The majority of justices, including three of the four female justices,[27] rejected Simpkins's challenge and found no constitutional problem with capping the recovery of noneconomic damages for minor victims of sexual assault.[28]

Justice Judith French wrote the majority opinion, which relied heavily on *Arbino*. The court first found no violation of the right to jury trial for minors who are victims of sexual assault. They, like all other tort plaintiffs, still had the right to a jury determination of facts; the cap was then a separately applied legislative choice.[29] The court also found no violation of the state constitutional rights to open courts and to a remedy because a right to meaningful remedies still existed, mainly unlimited economic damages, up to $350,000 in noneconomic damages, and the possibility of punitive damages.[30] With respect to due process and equal protection concerns, the court deferred to the legislature's conclusion that unpredictable noneconomic damage awards adversely affect Ohio's economy,[31] and the court found that the cap was neither arbitrary nor unreasonable.[32] The court specifically noted the reasonableness of the statutory exception exempting "catastrophic injuries" from the cap. The legislature defined "catastrophic" to require a debilitating physical injury. The court deferred to the legislature's view that a physical injury offers more concrete evidence of the existence and extent of noneconomic damages,[33] meaning the differing treatment of plaintiffs with and without catastrophic physical injuries does not violate equal protection.[34]

And, thus, the Ohio Supreme Court concluded that the noneconomic damage cap is constitutional even as applied to tort plaintiffs like Simpkins, minors who are victims of sexual assault. These victims, who are likely female and have extensive noneconomic damages but minimal economic damages, will be limited to recovering only their capped amount of noneconomic damages. This same result is likely to occur in any state in which a

[26] *Id.* at 139–40 (Pfeifer, J. & O'Neill J., dissenting).

[27] Justice Maureen O'Connor would have dismissed the case as "improvidently allowed." *Id.* at 138.

[28] *Id.*

[29] *Id.* at 130–31.

[30] *Id.* at 131–32.

[31] *Id.* at 133.

[32] *Id.* at 134.

[33] *Id.*

[34] *Id.* at 135–36.

noneconomic damage cap is constitutional under the state constitution.[35] This result is also exactly what many scholars had predicted would happen – that the application of noneconomic damage caps would disproportionately affect women's tort recoveries, including in cases involving rape or sexual assault, cases that are predominantly brought by women.[36]

THE FEMINIST REWRITE

Professor Shaakirrah Sanders, writing as Justice Sanders, dissents from the majority opinion affirming the constitutionality of the noneconomic damage cap as applied to minors who are victims of sexual assault.

Unlike the majority opinion, Sanders extensively retells the facts of Simpkins's rape. She details Simpkins's life before Pastor Brian Williams sexually assaulted her, the details of that sexual assault, and her life after that sexual assault. Sanders also details the evidence of Delaware Grace's unreasonable conduct in hiring and retaining Williams, including Delaware Grace's knowledge of prior complaints of sexual misconduct against Williams. Justice Sanders's opinion also puts Jessica's case in the greater context of clergy sexual assault and sexual assault generally in the United States. Jessica is unfortunately just one example of thousands of victims of clergy sexual abuse, abuse that the churches possibly knew about for years and did nothing to stop. Simpkins is also unfortunately just one example of the thousands of victims of sexual abuse generally, and as Sanders points out, over 80 percent of juvenile rape victims are female.[37] Sanders describes the traumatic and devastating "noneconomic" injuries that these women will experience for the rest of their lives – including suicidal and depressive thoughts, depressive episodes, and post-traumatic stress disorder.

Sanders's emphasis on the facts of Williams's sexual assault of Simpkins is consistent with feminist legal theory that seeks to identify and accentuate the woman's experience. The *Simpkins* majority opinion claimed to "not doubt the reality and seriousness of Simpkins's emotional and psychological injuries," but it also minimized the injuries by labeling them as merely

[35] In 2006, the Alaska Supreme Court also affirmed the constitutionality of the state's noneconomic damage cap in a case brought by a female rape victim, rejecting her equal protection arguments based on her injury "involv[ing] a 'disproportionate amount of pain and suffering compared to monetary loss.'" C.J. v. State, Dep't of Corr., 151 P.3d 373, 381 (Alaska 2006).

[36] *See, e.g.*, Finley, *supra* note 7.

[37] Rape, Abuse, & Incest National Network (RAINN), *Child Sexual Abuse Is a Widespread Problem*, https://www.rainn.org/statistics/children-and-teens

"noneconomic" and explaining that Simpkins was still able to play basketball in high school and college and that she got good grades in college. Justice Sanders's meticulous emphasis on Simpkins's injuries – how her life has irretrievably changed – demonstrates that, even if noneconomic, her injuries are real.

Sanders's feminist legal perspective continues when she addresses Jessica's claim that the damage cap violates equal protection as applied to minor victims of sexual assault. Ohio's noneconomic damage cap, just like any other state's, appears gender neutral, and no evidence exists that state legislatures were deliberately intending to hurt women. Still, the inherent male bias can cause an unintended negative impact or effect on women. Relying on feminist torts scholarship examining the discriminatory effect of damage caps on women, Sanders's opinion demonstrates that impact. Women tort plaintiffs on average suffer less in economic damages than do men tort plaintiffs, as women's wages tend to be less than men's wages. Women tort plaintiffs are also more likely to suffer injuries that are compensated primarily by noneconomic damages – like the emotional trauma caused by sexual assault or reproductive injuries.[38]

The *Simpkins* case is just one example. As a female victim of sexual assault, her main damages are noneconomic – her pain and suffering and mental anguish. The jury awarded her over $3.5 million in noneconomic damages, but the cap severely reduced her recovery to $350,000. Had she had extensive economic damages, she would have been able to still recover all of them. But she, like most victims of sexual assault, did not have extensive economic damages. Damage caps may appear gender neutral, but they are not. Noneconomic damage caps severely limit damage recovery for female tort plaintiffs, but not male tort plaintiffs.

The damage cap's disparate impact is unintentional, yet still unconstitutional as Sanders concludes that it fails rational basis review. The legislature claimed to pass the damage cap to curb the number of frivolous lawsuits in Ohio, thereby supposedly improving the economic climate in Ohio. But severely limiting the damage recovery for victims of sexual assault does little to curb the number of frivolous lawsuits, and thus will have little effect on the costs of doing business in Ohio. Plus, these business interests seem trivial compared to the need for the civil justice system to preserve the rights of *child* sexual assault victims. As Sanders points out, there is no legitimate business reason to protect an employee who presents a known risk for sexually

[38] *Finley*, *supra* note 7.

assaulting clients. Here, the jury determined that Delaware Grace was negligent; despite knowledge of his sexually inappropriate prior behavior with other young female parishioners, the church placed Williams in a position to be able to rape Simpkins. No rational basis exists to support limiting her, and others like her, from recovering her only significant type of damages. Moreover, no rational basis exists for forcing victims like Simpkins, who suffer significant noneconomic damages and insignificant economic damages, to bear the brunt of the supposed beneficial economic effects – preserving Ohio jobs, reducing customer costs, and promoting innovation – of Ohio's noneconomic damage cap.

Sanders's highlighting of this inherent male bias and the disproportionate effect on women enables her to easily conclude that the noneconomic damage cap also violates Ohio's right to jury trial. Sanders first explains how the cap violates the right to jury trial for all plaintiffs in Ohio. The right to jury trial includes far more than what the *Simpkins* majority concluded, the mere "right" to the jury's factual determination of the amount of damages. To be meaningful, the right must also include the right to receive the amount of damages the jury determined – the same way the right to jury trial was understood for centuries before state legislatures started passing noneconomic damage caps. Specifically, in the Ohio Constitution, the right to jury trial is "inviolate," meaning it cannot be limited. At common law, the right attached depending on the plaintiff's claim and the remedy sought. Simpkins's tort claim for compensatory damages, both economic and noneconomic, would have been tried in front of a jury at common law, meaning she still has the same inviolate right to a jury trial today. The right to jury trial has always attached to claims for compensatory damages, and the jury has always awarded compensatory damages based on the particular plaintiff's injuries, both economic and noneconomic.

Justice Sanders concludes that the noneconomic damage cap is facially unconstitutional and thus, obviously, unconstitutional as applied to plaintiffs like Simpkins. As she already established, women's tort damages are more likely to include a substantially greater proportion of noneconomic damages than are men's tort damages. Thus, if noneconomic damages caps are constitutional, women are more likely to be deprived of a substantially greater proportion of their total tort damages than are men. Simpkins's case amply illustrates this: as Sanders points out, the damages cap law entitled her to receive only 13.7 percent of her total jury award. Yet under Ohio's constitution, Simpkins had a right to her entire jury determination, a right that was violated when the application of the noneconomic damage cap reduced her recoverable noneconomic damages to only $350,000. Sanders's dissenting opinion demonstrates how noneconomic damage caps will and do affect tort claimants differently depending on the claimant's sex and the nature of the injury, and demonstrates how Ohio's noneconomic damage cap is unconstitutional as applied to Simpkins.

If Sanders's opinion had been an actual dissent – or even more powerfully, the majority opinion – in *Simpkins*, it may have helped highlight the effect noneconomic damage caps have on female tort plaintiffs. Feminist legal scholars have written about this disparate effect, but state supreme courts have not yet relied on this feminist scholarship to invalidate noneconomic damage caps. Sanders's *Simpkins* opinion may have at least persuaded some state supreme courts to focus on or address this issue.

Perhaps even more importantly, Sanders's opinion may have influenced state legislatures considering whether to create or modify noneconomic damage caps. If state supreme courts find noneconomic damage caps constitutional, a better strategy for reform is through the state legislature as cap statutes can be rewritten to have less harsh effects on women. For instance, Florida's noneconomic damage cap included an exception making it inapplicable to another type of injury more often suffered by women – "[l]oss of reproductive organs which results in an inability to procreate."[39] After *Simpkins*, some Ohio legislators have attempted to create an exception to Ohio's cap for sexual assault victims, as Ohio churches that protected priests and ministers known to be abusive have largely been insulated from the accountability that tort law helped bring about in other states. Specifically, in 2017, two Ohio lawmakers introduced a bipartisan bill that would have made the cap inapplicable to a tort action brought by a victim of rape, felonious assault, aggravated assault, assault, or negligent assault.[40] Unfortunately, the bill did not make it out of committee. Again, in 2018, an Ohio lawmaker introduced a bill to make the cap inapplicable to cases of rape and assault.[41] But again, the bill went nowhere. Still, it is possible for state legislatures to craft noneconomic damage caps in a way that lessens the effects on sexual assault victims and other female tort plaintiffs. But that will happen

39 Fla. Stat. Ann. § 766.118(1)(6) (West) (2018) (the overall cap on noneconomic damages, of which this exception was a part, was held unconstitutional in *N. Broward Hosp. Dist. v. Kalitan*, 219 So. 3d 49, 61 (Fla. 2017)).

40 Jim Siegel, *Pair of Lawmakers Want to End Damage Caps for Rape, Assault*, Columbus Dispatch (Dec. 24, 2017), https://www.dispatch.com/news/20171224/pair-of-area-lawmakers-want-to-end-damage-caps-for-rape-assault

41 Jim Siegel, *Rep. Boggs: Ohio Law Should Stop Being Lenient to Those Who Let Children Get Raped*, Columbus Dispatch (Nov. 14, 2018), https://www.dispatch.com/news/20181114/rep-kristin-boggs-ohio-law-should-stop-being-lenient-to-those-who-let-children-get-raped

only if state legislatures realize the need to lessen those effects. Shaakirrah Sanders's opinion could have provided that awareness.

SIMPKINS v. GRACE BRETHREN CHURCH OF DELAWARE, OHIO, 75 N.E.3D 122 (OHIO 2016)

JUSTICE SHAAKIRRAH SANDERS, DISSENTING

I INTRODUCTION

This case involves a constitutional challenge brought by a minor victim of clergy sexual assault to Ohio's statute capping noneconomic damages in all negligence-based personal injury cases, R.C. 2315.18. The plaintiff, Jessica Simpkins, contends that as applied to her, the damages cap violates the Ohio Constitution's guarantees of equal protection and right to a civil jury, among other constitutional violations. Jessica was 15 years old when she was raped by her pastor, Brian Williams, during a counseling session in his office at Sunbury Grace Brethren Church. Williams pled guilty to two counts of sexual assault and received an eight-year sentence.

Jessica and her father, Gene Simpkins, sought civil damages for negligent hiring, supervision, and retention against Grace Brethren Church of Delaware, the parent church of Sunbury Grace. The Simpkins argued that Delaware Grace failed to report at least two past incidents of sexual misconduct between Williams and underage female congregants. The Simpkins also alleged that Delaware Grace failed to conduct any investigation before endorsing and installing Williams as the founding minister at Sunbury Grace in 2004.

After hearing all the evidence, the civil jury found that Delaware Grace negligently hired, supervised, and retained Williams. The jury awarded Jessica compensatory damages in the amount of $3,651,378.85. Jessica's compensatory damage award included $3.5 million for past and future noneconomic damages. The trial court applied R.C. 2315.18, which caps noneconomic damages in personal injury suits to the greater of $250,000 or three times the economic damage award up to $350,000. Applying R.C. 2315.18 reduced Jessica's $3.5 million noneconomic damage award to approximately 10 percent of the jury's verdict. The same jury awarded Gene $75,000 for loss of consortium. Gene's award did not exceed the $350,000 statutory cap set by R.C. 2315.18 and thus Gene was entitled to receive the jury's full award, unlike Jessica who was the actual assault victim.

Jessica appealed and argued R.C. 2315.18, as applied to minor victims of sexual assault, violated the Ohio Constitution's guarantees of equal protection, due process, and the right to a civil jury. In rejecting Jessica's claims, the majority essentially treats her as-applied challenge as little different from the facial challenge this court rejected in *Arbino v. Johnson & Johnson*, 880 N.E.2d 420 (Ohio 2007). The majority also fails to give serious consideration to arguments that R.C. 2315.18, when applied to Jessica and others like her, lacks any rational basis, effectuates a serious miscarriage of justice, and denies a meaningful remedy.

The majority opinion treats what happened to Jessica Simpkins as if it were merely an unfortunate isolated incident. But it is one of far too many instances of clergy sexual abuse of minors – a longstanding scandal of epidemic proportions that the tort system has helped uncover and bring to public attention. *See generally* TIMOTHY D. LYTTON, HOLDING BISHOPS ACCOUNTABLE: HOW LAWSUITS HELPED THE CATHOLIC CHURCH CONFRONT CLERGY SEXUAL ABUSE (2008). While much of the public attention has focused on abuse within the Catholic Church, Protestant denominations like Delaware Grace also have a sordid history of condoning or concealing sexually predatory pastors. *See generally* Associated Press, *Data Shed Light on Child Sexual Abuse by Protestant Clergy*, N.Y. TIMES (June 16, 2007), https://www.nytimes.com/2007/06/16/us/16protestant.html (reviewing data from insurance companies who represent the majority of Protestant churches, which shows over 260 claims annually for sexual abuse of minors by clergy, church staff, or volunteers). Clergy sexual abuse of minors and the tendency of parent church organizations to cover it up or pass abusers along to other parishes or branches is no less a problem in Ohio than in other states. *See, e.g.*, *Database of Publicly Accused Priests in the United States*, BISHOPACCOUNTABILITY.ORG, https://bishop-accountability.org/priestdb/PriestDBbydiocese.html#OH (database of publicly reported incidents of clergy sexual abuse broken down by state and diocese region).

The clergy sexual assault crisis is but one manifestation of a prevalent problem of sexual violence in the United States. Researchers estimate that one in five women and one in seventy-one men in the United States will experience sexual abuse at some point in their lives. Michele C. Black et al., *The National Intimate Partner and Sexual Violence Survey: 2010 Summary Report*, National Center for Injury Prevention and Control at *1 (Nov. 2011), http://www.cdc.gov/ViolencePrevention/pdf/NISVS_Report2010-a.pdf. Another study estimates that one in four girls and one in six boys experience sexual abuse before the age of 18. David Finkelhor et al., *The Lifetime Prevalence of Child Sexual Abuse and Sexual Assault Assessed in Late Adolescence*, 55 J. ADOLESCENT HEALTH 329, 329 (2014).

Young girls and women are especially vulnerable to and at risk from sexual violence. Approximately 82 percent of all juvenile victims of rape are female.

Howard N. Syder, *Sexual Assault of Young Children as Reported to Law Enforcement: Victim, Incident, and Offender Characteristics*, U.S. DEPARTMENT OF JUSTICE, at *4 (July 2000), https://www.bjs.gov/content/pub/pdf/saycrle.pdf. According to the US Department of Justice:

> Females were more than six times as likely as males to be the victims of sexual assaults . . . The relative proportion of female victims generally increased with age. Sixty-nine percent of victims under age 6 were female, compared with 73% of victims under age 12, and 82% of all juvenile (under age 18) victims. The female proportion of sexual assault victims reached 90% at age 13 and 95% at age 19.
>
> *Id.*

Just under 30 percent of women are between the ages of 11 and 17 at the time of their first experience of rape. Black et al., *supra*, at *25. Approximately 42.2 percent of women experience "their first completed rape before the age of 18." *Id.*

The effects of sexual violence during childhood are particularly acute and can affect the victim's mental health for a lifetime. Heidi M. Zinzow et al., *Prevalence and Risk of Psychiatric Disorders as a Function of Variant Rape Histories: Results from a National Survey of Women*, 47 SOC. PSYCHIATRY AND PSYCHIATRIC EPIDEMIOLOGY 893–902 (2012), https://psycho-trauma.nl/wp-content/uploads/2015/11/Zinzow-et-al-2012.-Prevalence-and-risk-of-psychiatric-disorders-as-a-function-of-variant-rape-histories_.pdf. The likelihood of suicidal or depressive thoughts increases after sexual violence. *Id.* Child victims are also more likely to experience depression, develop symptoms of PTSD, or abuse drugs. *Id.*

In upholding R.C. 2315.18's cap on noneconomic damages as applied to Jessica, the majority is effectively closing the door of the civil justice system on child victims of sexual assault. Curtailing their tort remedy not only deprives victims of just compensation, but also largely insulates churches and other employers that for far too long have condoned and covered up for the abusers in their ranks, and removes a powerful incentive for institutional reform. *See* LYTTON, *supra* at 163–89 (analyzing how tort suits for clergy sexual abuse have had a socially beneficial role in prompting institutional reform).

When placed in the context of the problem of rampant sexual assault and clergy sexual abuse of minors in the United States, Williams's rape of Simpkins, and Delaware Grace's dismissive attitude toward prior reports of his inappropriate sexual conduct with young female parishioners, is hardly an isolated incident. It is one of too many instances of heinous criminal and tortious conduct against vulnerable minors – conduct that no legislature could ever have any rational basis for insulating from accountability for the full extent of harm to its victims as determined by a jury.

I join my dissenting colleagues, Justices Pfeiffer and O'Neill, who argue R.C. 2315.18 violates Jessica's inviolate right to a civil jury under Article 1, section 5 of the Ohio Constitution. I write separately to address how R.C. 2315.18 specifically affects Jessica and other survivors of sexual violence, by significantly and arbitrarily underfunding recovery for the lifelong impact of this most grievous and traumatic harm. In short, R.C. 2315.18 deprives Jessica and other minor victims of sexual assault not only of their inviolate right to have a civil jury decide their claims, but also of equal protection of the law.

II FACTS

Brian Williams was a senior minister at Sunbury Grace Brethren Church when he raped 15-year-old Jessica Simpkins on March 6, 2008. Sunbury Grace was a constituent branch church of Delaware Grace Brethren Church, and where Jessica and her family worshipped. TR at 267, 284–85. Jessica was the youngest of five daughters in her family. *Id.* Her parents had recently divorced, and Gene Simpkins raised the girls as a single father. TR at 270–71, 279–80, 285–87. Prior to the rape, Jessica was an active and social teenager who had a close relationship with her father and sisters, a lot of friends, and a passion for basketball. TR at 269–70, 281–82, 289, 298.

Williams and Jessica met in his office at Sunbury Grace to discuss Jessica's declining grades. TR at 330–31. Instead of counseling Jessica, Williams forced sexual contact and intercourse. TR at 323–64. Williams exposed his penis and repeatedly asked Jessica to "suck it." TR at 332–33. Jessica said no and tried to avoid contact. TR at 333. Jessica testified about her fear and how she submitted to fellatio because she thought it was the only way she could get out of the room. TR at 333. When she tried to escape, Williams blocked the door and forcibly kissed Jessica. Over Jessica's pleas for him to stop, Williams pulled down her pants, forced her onto the floor, and repeatedly and forcibly penetrated Jessica's vagina without consent. TR at 333.

Jessica shared what happened with a friend and with school officials, and the latter informed Gene and the Sunbury Policy Department. TR at 258–61, 296–97. Jessica also participated in a call to Williams monitored by the Sunbury Police Department. During this call, Williams admitted that Jessica neither initiated nor consented to the rape. TR at 335–37. Williams was subsequently arrested and charged with two counts of sexual assault. TR at 258, 323–64. He pled guilty and was sentenced to eight years in prison. *Id.*

The Sunbury Police Department's criminal investigation exposed two previous complaints of sexual misconduct against Williams by underage female congregants between the late 1990s and 2002. Both victims testified at trial and reported that Delaware Grace officials "made light of" what had happened, treated them as if they were making it all up, did not seriously investigate, and considered an apology by Williams rather than any discipline to be sufficient. TR at 128–132, 151–58, 554–71. Delaware Grace failed to note either incident in Williams's personnel record. TR at 193–97, 203–10, 569–70, 590–92. In 2004, two years after the second report of sexual misconduct by Williams, Delaware Grace promoted Williams from youth minister to the founding minister of its new Sunbury Grace branch. TR at 193–97. Delaware Grace continued to supervise Williams in his new role and to provide financial assistance to Sunbury Grace. TR at 528–29.

Jessica returned to high school after the rape, but missed classes and had to endure disparaging gossip and rumors from other students. TR at 340–43. Williams's supporters confronted Jessica at school and stated their disbelief about the rape. TR at 341–42. Other students placed newspaper clippings about Williams's criminal case on Jessica's locker. *Id.* Due to these encounters, Jessica spent many days at school crying in the office of her guidance counselor, and her grades declined for two semesters. TR at 340–43. Jessica also struggled at home, where she was a shell of her former self. TR at 304. Jessica had repeated nightmares about "getting kidnapped" and "getting raped again" and she became socially withdrawn and angry. TR at 298, 343–44. Jessica's previously close relationship with her father and sisters deteriorated. TR at 298.

Jessica's trauma continued after high school. While at college, Jessica got "really scared" if she had "to walk from [her] dorm to the library in the dark." TR at 346. If friends were unavailable to accompany her, Jessica did not go to the library to do homework. *Id.* Jessica briefly dated only one boy during her time in college, and she pushed away most other boys in an effort to prevent a closer relationship. *Id.* Jessica left college during her sophomore year. At the time of trial, Jessica had not completed her undergraduate education. TR at 346–47.

Multiple witnesses testified about how Jessica continued to struggle, even five years after the rape. Jessica continued to be withdrawn, unable to discuss her feelings, and afraid to go places alone, including church. TR at 272–75. Jessica still feared the dark and was afraid of being left home alone or driving at night alone. Several times a week, Jessica's fears and unwelcome memories would overcome her to the extent that she had to walk away from work in the middle of her shift. TR at 348–49. The ongoing trauma from her rape prevented Jessica from forming trusting and loving relationships with men. TR at 272–75, 348. Notably, Jessica fears what Williams might do or try to do after his release from prison. TR at 350.

Dr. Jeffrey Smalldon testified as an expert at trial and diagnosed Jessica with post-traumatic stress disorder, including general mistrust, vulnerability, and fear of other people. TR at 410–11, 414–17, 446–47. Dr. Smalldon doubted Jessica's ability to move past her experiences, especially because of her age at the time of the rape. TR at 417–20, 429–30. Dr. Smalldon recommended long-term treatment and counseling for Jessica's mental health and low self-esteem. TR at 423–24, 426–29, 440–43. Delaware Grace presented no evidence on the issue of damages.

III ANALYSIS

A *Equal Protection of the Law*

Article 1, section 2 of the Ohio Constitution provides: "All political power is inherent in the people. Government is instituted for their equal protection and benefit." OH. CONST. art. 1, § 2. This section of the Ohio Constitution is the functional equivalent of the US Constitution's Equal Protection Clause. Am. Ass'n of Univ. Professors, Cent. State Univ. Chapter v. Cent. State Univ., 717 N.E.2d 286, 291 (Ohio 1999) ("the federal and Ohio Equal Protection Clauses are to be construed and analyzed identically"). The federal Equal Protection Clause "commands that no State shall 'deny to any person within its jurisdiction the equal protection of the laws,' which is essentially a direction that all persons similarly situated should be treated alike." City of Cleburne v. Cleburne Living Ctr., 473 U.S. 432, 439 (1985).

A party who challenges a statute on equal protection grounds must demonstrate "either that there was no rational basis for the creation of the class itself or that those within the class are not being treated equally in the furtherance of a legitimate governmental interest." Morris v. Savoy, 576 N.E.2d 765, 771 (Ohio 1991). Equal protection prevents Ohio from relying "on a classification whose relationship to an asserted goal is so attenuated as to render the distinction arbitrary or irrational." City of Cleburne, 473 U.S. at 446.

Under the rational basis standard of review, Simpkins's claim requires us to address two questions: (1) Does application of R.C. 2315.18 disadvantage her, as a minor victim of sexual assault?; and (2) Is R.C. 2315.18's disadvantageous treatment rationally related to advancing any legitimate governmental interest?

1 Disproportionate Impact of Noneconomic Damage Caps

In *Arbino*, 880 N.E.2d at 420, this court heard a facial challenge to R.C. 2315.18's $350,000 cap on noneconomic damages. The *Arbino* decision, which upheld R.C. 2315.18, constituted a departure from decades-old jurisprudence on the constitutionality of tort reform laws in Ohio. All prior decisions of this court had found severe state constitutional flaws in damage caps and other efforts to limit tort recovery for injured people. *See* Morris v. Savoy, 576 N.E.2d 765 (Ohio 1991); Sorrell v. Thevenir, 633 N.E.2d 504 (Ohio 1994); Galayda v. Lake Hosp. Sys., Inc., 644 N.E.2d 298 (Ohio 1994); Zoppo v. Homestead Ins. Co., 644 N.E.2d 397 (1994); State ex rel. Ohio Academy of Trial Lawyers v. Sheward, 715 N.E.2d 1062 (Ohio 1999).

Deferring to the legislative record, the *Arbino* majority cited the testimony of Bruce Johnson, Director of the Department of Development, about the unreliability of civil jury awards for noneconomic damages. *Arbino*, 880 N.E.2d. at 434. *But see id.* at 460, 462 (Pfeifer, J., dissenting). According to Johnson, who was not identified as an expert on the civil justice system and its empirical effects, noneconomic damages were difficult to calculate, lacked precise economic value, and were inherently subjective or susceptible to influence from irrelevant factors. *Id.* at 434. Relying on Johnson's testimony, *Arbino* found R.C. 2315.18 "sufficiently different [from previous tort reform laws] . . . to warrant a fresh review of their individual merits." *Id.* at 429. *Arbino* uncritically accepted the legislature's declaration that Ohio's "civil litigation system" threatened the state economy by hindering employment opportunities, employee productivity, wage and salary taxes, and the business decisions of companies. *Id.* at 434. *Arbino* concluded the General Assembly sufficiently tailored R.C. 2315.18 "to address the constitutional defects identified" by prior cases reviewing tort reform laws. *Id.* at 429. Thus, the *Arbino* majority concluded that the legislature had a rational basis for capping noneconomic damages, and that R.C. 2315.18 did not on its face violate the Ohio Constitution. *Id.* at 429–37.

In contrast to the facial challenge in *Arbino*, Jessica brings an "as applied" challenge to the damage cap. This type of challenge involves a claim that a statute is unconstitutional as it applies to, or impacts, a particular litigant or set of circumstances. 16 C.J.S. CONSTITUTIONAL LAW §187; Michael C. Dorf, *Facial Challenges to State and Federal Regulations*, 46 STAN. L. REV. 235, 236 (1994). In upholding the noneconomic damage cap in R.C. 2315.18 against a facial challenge, the *Arbino* majority did not need to consider how the damage cap profoundly alters the civil litigation system for Jessica, and others for whom noneconomic damages constitute the primary category of compensation for their injuries. In the present case, however, despite the fact that Jessica's as-applied challenge demands this particularized analysis, the majority still does not grapple with the actual impacts of the noneconomic damage cap on minor victims of sexual assault. Instead, my colleagues just repeat *Arbino*'s blanket assertions that noneconomic damage awards above $350,000 adversely impact the general business climate in Ohio. Jessica's case does not question whether noneconomic damage awards in general might affect the state's business climate. The gist of Jessica's challenge is that the damage cap, when applied to her as a minor victim of sexual assault whose injuries are psychological and emotional and thus compensated primarily by noneconomic damages, deprives her of a significantly greater proportion of her damages awarded by the jury than other tort victims. Her case requires us to consider whether the legislature had any rational basis for limiting the damages that she or other victims of sexual assault can recover from those like Delaware Grace who turn a blind eye to, cover up for, or protect and promote child abusers.

The particularized assessment of the impact of R.C. 2315.18 on Jessica and those like her leads to the conclusion that R.C. 2315.18 has a severely disparate impact on minor victims of sexual assault, and thus deprives them of equal protection of the law. Because the harm caused by sexual assault primarily affects the aspects of life that are compensated through noneconomic damages, the majority of Jessica's jury award – 96 percent – was for this type of damages. The application of the cap reduced her jury award by 86 percent, leaving her entitled to recover only 13.7 percent of her jury award. R.C. 2315.18 took away such a significant amount of what the jury thought was necessary to redress Jessica's harm that it left her with virtually no redress through the deterrent and compensatory functions of tort law. Effectively closing the door of the civil justice system on a class of injury victims, especially minor victims of sexual assault, hardly comports with equal protection of the laws.

The fact that Jessica's jury award was primarily for noneconomic damages is typical in sexual assault cases. Empirical research shows that in negligence-based tort claims by women sexual assault victims, juries allocate over 90 percent of the damages to the noneconomic category, as they did in Jessica's case. *See* Lucinda M. Finley, *The Hidden Victims of Tort Reform: Women, Children, and the Elderly*, 53 EMORY L.J. 1263, 1300–01 (2004). Consequently, caps on these damages take away a far greater proportion of sexual assault victims' tort recoveries than those of other classes of injured people. *Id.*

The reason why sexual assault victims like Jessica receive most of their jury awards for noneconomic damages is that the injuries from sexual assault do not primarily affect the aspects of life – lost wages and medical bills – that are compensated through economic damages. This is especially the case when minors are victimized, since they are not yet fully involved in the wage-earning economy, and will have little or no wage loss damages. Sexual assault robs its victims of an intact and healthy sense of self, of emotional security, and ability to relate to others in a healthy intimate way. It causes ongoing mental harm such as depression and post-traumatic stress disorder. *See generally* Lucinda Finley, *Female Trouble: The Implications of Tort Reform for Women*, 64 TENN. L. REV. 847 (1997).

For sexual assault survivors like Jessica, the primary compensable injury is damages for pain and suffering. Denise LeBoeuf, *Psychiatric Malpractice: Exploitation of Women Patients*, 11 HARV. WOMEN'S L.J. 83 (1988). Many of the "most precious [and priceless] aspects of human life" that are damaged by sexual assault, such as "altered sense of self and social adjustment, impaired relationships, or impaired physical capabilities such as reproduction [or intimacy], are not directly involved in market-based wage-earning activity." *See* Finley, *Hidden Victims of Tort Reform, supra* at 1281. In short, the aspects of a whole and healthy human life that are damaged by sexual assault are "virtually worthless" in the economic marketplace and can only be compensated through noneconomic damages. *Id.* In Jessica's situation, where her medical bills and wage loss were relatively minor, noneconomic damages were the only way the jury could show that her injury was serious and profound, and compensate her accordingly.

Because the damages for injuries arising from sexual assault overwhelmingly fall in the noneconomic category, R.C. 2315.18's $350,000 cap becomes a virtual ceiling on recovery, especially when litigation costs, including expert witness expense, and attorney fees, are deducted from the capped award. As Jessica's case shows, minor victims of sexual assault are likely to recover a shockingly low percentage of what the jury thought they needed and deserved for their trauma. Caps like R.C. 2315.18 can reduce the value of these cases to such a significant degree that taking the case is a losing proposition even for the victorious plaintiff or their attorneys. Consequently, as academic research has shown, "many grievously injured women will be unable to convince an attorney to take their case." Thomas Koenig & Michael Rustad, *His and Her Tort Reform: Gender Injustice in Disguise*, 70 WASH. L. REV. 1, 87 (1995).

The discriminatory effects of R.C. 2315.18, while particularly egregious in cases of minor victims of sexual assault, undermine fair access to the civil justice system for women tort plaintiffs in general. By limiting only noneconomic damages, while allowing an injured person to receive the jury's full award of economic damages, caps like R.C. 2315.18 inflate the importance of economic loss damages, making them an ever greater proportion of allowable tort recoveries. Finley, *Hidden Victims of Tort Reform, supra* at 1281. Empirical research demonstrates that noneconomic damages "comprise a significantly greater proportion of women's overall tort damage awards than for men's damage awards." *Id. See also id.* 1284–1312 (reporting on percentage of the average economic and noneconomic damages that women receive in different states). Consequently, noneconomic damage caps deprive women of significantly more of their jury awards on average than men. *Id.*

The gender discriminatory effects of noneconomic damage caps like R.C. 2315.18 have several origins. First, as Professor Lucinda Finley notes, women tend to receive less in economic damages than men because women on average earn less. Finley, *Hidden Victims of Tort Reform, supra* at 1280–81. *See also* Lisa M. Ruda, Note, *Caps on Noneconomic Damages and the Female Plaintiff: Heeding the Warning Signs*, 44 CASE W. RES. L. REV. 197, 231–32 (1993). The gender wage gap means that "[w]omen are significantly disadvantaged "when damages awards are based primarily on out-of-pocket costs and loss of earnings." Koenig & Rustad, *supra* at 87. Ultimately, the "[u]ndervaluation [of women's work and services] and sexual stereotyping 'can affect projections of future income [and] basing damages on future income can disadvantage women in an economy where they are on the whole paid significantly less than men.'" Ruda, *supra* at 232 (quoting Lucinda M. Finley, *A Break in the Silence: Including Women's Issues in a Torts Course*, 1 YALE L.J. & FEMINISM 41, 51 (1989)). When tort compensation systems favor "'pecuniary injuries over lasting emotional scars,' the undervaluation of women's economic services increases the differential in verdicts awarded to female and male plaintiffs. Caps on noneconomic damages will further contribute to this disparity." *Id.*

A second reason why noneconomic damage caps like R.C. 2315.18 disproportionately discriminate against women is directly applicable to Jessica's case. "Several types of injuries that are disproportionately suffered by women – sexual assault, reproductive harm, such as pregnancy loss or infertility, and gynecological medical malpractice – do not affect women in primarily economic terms. Rather, the impact is felt more in the ways compensated through noneconomic loss damages." Finley, *Hidden Victims of Tort Reform, supra* at 1281. "[P]ain and suffering, mental anguish, and loss of consortium are disparately awarded to women in order to reimburse for [sexual] injuries." Koenig & Rustad, *supra* at 85.

Noneconomic damage caps like R.C. 2315.18 discriminate against Jessica both as a minor victim of sexual assault and as a young woman. The Ohio legislature never considered these aspects of R.C. 2315.18 and therefore this discrimination may be unintentional. Nevertheless, in my view, no legitimate governmental objective is served by severely limiting the damages that minor victims of sexual assault can recover for the lifelong trauma that they suffer. Unlike the majority, I find it difficult to reconcile any basis for legislative authority to sacrifice Jessica's right to *enforce* a civil jury determination of damages.

2 Lack of Rational Relationship to a Legitimate Government Interest

Despite the disparate impacts on women and rape and sexual assault survivors, *Arbino* describes R.C. 2315.18 as nothing more than a "policy choice that noneconomic damages exceeding set amounts are not in the best interest of the citizens of Ohio." 880 N.E.2d at 432. *Arbino* also noted that "[t]he General Assembly's general justification for the tort reforms in [R.C..2315.18] was that the state has an interest in making certain that Ohio has a fair, predictable system of civil justice that preserves the rights of those who have been harmed by negligent behavior, while curbing the number of frivolous lawsuits," among other goals. *Id.* at 437, 442.

None of these justifications apply to Jessica's case or other sexual assault cases, especially when children are the victims. There is nothing fair about capping the primary category of damages that are awarded to sexual assault victims. In my view, any cap that deprives a victim of virtually all of the damages awarded by the jury hardly preserves the right to seek redress for harm. Jessica's case was far from frivolous. The jury's decision that Delaware Grace was negligent in ignoring and covering up Williams's misconduct and promoting him despite his troubling history was fully warranted on the record. The jury's conclusion that Jessica suffered from serious disabling trauma that was likely to continue to impair her well-being and future life prospects was also fully supported by the record. A principal reason why the *Arbino* majority found R.C. 2315.18 was not unfair to injured people in general was that it left economic damages uncapped and that it exempted cases of severe permanent physical injury. Thus, *Arbino* concluded, the most seriously injured people could still get full, or nearly full compensation. This rationale completely falls apart when the injury is sexual assault.

The damage cap in R.C. 2315.18 ensures that sexual abusers and those who cover up for them will get little more than a financial slap on the wrist for their egregious behavior. R.C. 2315.18 also undermines the tort system's deterrent incentive to remove sexual predators from jobs where they have responsibility over minors. *See* Lytton, *supra* (examining the positive deterrent effect of tort suits in raising public awareness of clergy sexual abuse, of prompting more criminal prosecutions, and of leading churches to undertake institutional reform). When placed in the context of the problem of rampant sexual assault and clergy sexual abuse of minors, Delaware Grace's dismissive attitude toward prior reports of Williams's inappropriate and unwanted sexual behavior is one of too many instances of heinous criminal and tortious conduct that no legislature could ever have any rational basis for insulating from accountability.

Protecting employers who cover up misbehavior and continue to place children in contact with sexual abusers serves no legitimate interest. In upholding R.C. 2315.18, the majority effectively closes the door of the civil justice system on Jessica and other minor victims of sexual assault. As previously discussed, economic damages for sexual assault are likely to be very low, and noneconomic damages are the primary form of recovery. As applied to minor victims of sexual assault, R.C. 2315.18 eviscerates their right to recover for their harm, while insulating those who condone or commit abuse from a meaningful threat of tort liability. This is hardly fairness, and it certainly is not equal protection of the law for the victims.

B *The Right to a Civil Jury*

I also join my dissenting colleagues in their view that application of R.C. 2315.18 against Jessica's noneconomic damage award eviscerates Jessica's inviolate state constitutional right to have all aspects of her case, including the amount of damages, decided by a civil jury. I write separately to more fully explain why *Arbino* is wrong, and why this wrong has a severe disparate impact when applied to plaintiffs like Jessica and others who are primarily compensated with noneconomic damages.

The purported problem the legislature sought to address by mandating a cap on noneconomic damages was "excessive" jury verdicts. But legislatively imposed caps are inherently arbitrary, excessive verdicts are not a general problem, and to the extent that any one jury might deviate from the evidence and award damages that are too high, the civil justice system already allows for judicial correction tailored to the facts of the individual case. The ability of Jessica's jury to tailor its decision to the facts and circumstances is a constitutional virtue. *See* Jeffrey R. White, *State Farm and Punitive Damages: Call the Jury Back*, 5 J. High Tech. L. 79 (2005). Yet R.C. 2315.18 implies juries are constitutional vices.

One year after *Arbino*, the US Supreme Court rejected the suggestion of a damage cap like R.C. 2315.18 as a way to deal with potentially excessive verdicts in federal maritime cases. Exxon Shipping Co. v. Baker, 554 U.S. 471, 506 (2008).

The court noted that a cap is an arbitrary and unfair way to deal with the problem of excessiveness. Because there is "no standard tort ... injury," it is nearly impossible to settle "upon a particular dollar figure as appropriate across the board." *Id.* Moreover, the "problem" of excessive compensatory jury verdicts is actually illusory. Legal scholars for decades have demonstrated how jury awards in personal injury cases have remained relatively stable. *See* Debora Hensler, *Trends in Tort Litigation: Findings from the Institute for Civil Justice Research*, 48 Ohio St. L.J. 479 (1987) (discussing tort reform and its premises that liability lawsuits have exploded and that civil juries were out of control). Other studies have shown how juries provide more stable estimates of noneconomic damages than arbitrators. *See* Neil Vidmar & Jeffrey J. Rice, *Assessments of Noneconomic Damage Awards in Medical Negligence: A Comparison of Jurors with Legal Professionals*, 78 Iowa L. Rev. 883, 884 (1993).

The majority, relying on *Arbino*, reasons that the damage cap in R.C. 2315.18 does not conflict with Ohio's *inviolate* civil jury trial right because Article 1, Section 5 of the state Constitution means nothing more than the right to have a jury determine issues of fact. Neither this court nor the court in *Arbino* viewed the right to include giving meaningful *effect* to the jury's determination of the amount of damages necessary to compensate for the harm. Rather, both courts analogize R.C. 2315.18 with judicial authority to reduce a jury's damage award and reason that it simply reduces the jury's award as a matter of law. But there is a meaningful constitutional difference between the legislatively imposed cap in R.C. 2315.18, and a trial court, as arbiter of the law, receiving and reviewing the evidence that supports a defendant's motion for a new trial on the ground that an award is excessive and deciding to grant the motion unless the plaintiff agrees to a reduced award. *See* Dimick v. Schiedt, 293 U.S. 474 (1935).

R.C. 2315.18 explicitly ignores the traditional, historical, and constitutional gatekeeping role of trial courts to check the jury. Under the traditional role, intervention by the court follows from a motion by the defendant and agreement by the plaintiff, and from the fact that the trial judge has heard all of the evidence and viewed all of the witnesses (unlike members of the legislature). R.C. 2315.18 reduces the jury's award even if the defendant has not objected to the amount of damages, even if the trial judge concludes that the jury award is fully supported by the evidence, and even if the plaintiff strenuously objects to a reduced award. R.C. 2315.18 requires the trial judge to disregard the jury's determination and the plaintiff's rights because R.C. 2315.18 imposes a one-size-fits-all cap set by the legislature.

Arbino misinterprets the state constitutional right to a civil jury as inferior and malleable to legislative judgment. The majority in this case continues and compounds *Arbino*'s error by ignoring the meaning of the word *inviolate* in the Ohio Constitution's guarantee of a jury to decide all factual matters. *See* OH. CONST. art. 1, § 5. Over thirty other state constitutions, including the Ohio Constitution, establish an inviolate civil jury trial right. "Inviolate" is defined as "free from change or blemish, pure or unbroken." WEBSTER'S THIRD NEW INTERNATIONAL DICTIONARY 1190 (1993). This meaning reflects the anointment of juries in the United States as "the normal and preferable mode of disposing of issues of fact in civil cases." *Dimick*, 293 U.S. at 486. *See also* St. Louis, Iron Mountain & S. Ry. Co. v. Craft, 237 U.S. 648. 661 (1915) (the power, duty, and responsibility for determining damages is "*a question of fact*" for the jury). *See also* CHARLES T. MCCORMICK, HANDBOOK ON THE LAW OF DAMAGES 24 (1935) ("from the beginning of trial by jury" the amount of damages was "a 'fact' to be found by the jurors").

Associate Justice Joseph Story, a revered constitutional prophet, described juries as the "great bulwark of their civil and political liberties." 2 JOSEPH STORY, COMMENTARIES ON THE CONSTITUTION OF THE UNITED STATES 540–41 (4th ed. 1873). Juries are among the most honored and constitutionally enumerated individual rights against arbitrary or capricious interference by the executive and legislative branches of government. Renee Lettow Lerner, *The Failure of Originalism in Preserving Constitutional Rights to Civil Jury Trial*, 22 WM. & MARY BILL RTS. J. 811, 842 (2014); Suja A. Thomas, *Blackstone's Curse: The Fall of the Criminal, Civil, and Grand Juries and the Rise of the Executive, the Legislature, the Judiciary, and the States*, 55 WM. & MARY L. REV. 1195, 1232 (2014). At the time of the founding, "civil juries decided cases without significant interference" from the other branches of government. Thomas, *supra* at 1209 (citations omitted). This lack of interference encompassed findings on damages. *Id.* at 1209–11.

In Ohio, and in most every territory to join the United States, the right to a civil jury attached to a particular cause of action in accordance with the dictates of the English common law at the time of statehood. Jessica's cause of action for negligence is undoubtedly the sort of common law claim traditionally brought in a court of law, not equity, to which the right of a jury would have attached. Jill Wieber Lens, *Punishing for the Injury: Tort Law's Influence in Defining the Constitutional Limitations on Punitive Damage Awards*, 39 HOFSTRA L. REV. 595, 601 (2014). Civil juries in the United States have awarded damages in tort cases involving sexual misconduct since the founding era. *See* Koenig & Rustad, *supra* at 14; Coryell v. Colbaugh, 1 N.J.L. 90 (1791). Both the economic and noneconomic loss components of Jessica's compensatory damages constitute a traditional legal remedy for which a jury is required. DAN B. DOBBS, LAW OF REMEDIES § 3.1 (2d. ed. 1993).

See also id. § 8.1(1) (discussing requirement that personal injury damages be proved and calculated at the trial). Both economic and noneconomic damages were a question of *historical or predictive fact* that varied with "the kind of harm suffered." *Id.* § 3.3(2) (explaining the lack of universal measurement for damages).

An enduring principle of the common law is entitlement to compensatory damages that are based on the specific circumstances of an individual case. Jill Wieber Lens, *Procedural Due Process and Predictable Punitive Damages Awards*, 2012 BYU L. REV. 1, 39 (2012). In the common law, the amount of a compensatory damage award was based on a finding by the jury about "the injury alleged and proved." Birdsall v. Coolidge, 93 U.S. 64, 64 (1876). In other words, compensatory damages must be commensurate with the injury suffered. *Id.* This comports with the Ohio's Constitution guarantee of a jury determination of liability and damages that must remain *inviolate*, absent a finding of jury misconduct or a finding that the evidence was insufficient to support the award. *See* OH. CONST. art. 1, § 5. By dispensing with the findings of the jury, and substituting the legislature's one size fits all determination of the upper limit on noneconomic damages, regardless of the degree and duration of injury, R.C. 2315.18 tramples on the *inviolate* right to have damages assessed by a jury. Jessica's civil jury award should not be so easily dispensable. According to the meaning of inviolate, the damages determined by her jury must be "free from change or blemish, pure or unbroken." WEBSTER'S THIRD NEW INTERNATIONAL DICTIONARY, *supra* at 1190. By decreeing the upper limit of noneconomic damages in personal injury cases, the legislature has attempted to break, change, and reduce the evidence-based factual determinations of Ohio juries.

For these reasons, R.C 2315.18 is unconstitutional on its face for violating the right to have a civil jury, rather than the legislature, determine damages in individual cases. But when applied to Jessica's case, and to those of other victims whose injuries are of the type that are compensated primarily through noneconomic damages, the severe disparate impact of R.C. 2315.18 makes its unconstitutionality all the more apparent. The majority rejects Jessica's as-applied challenge to R.C. 2315.18 by asserting, without analysis, that "application of the damage caps does not affect Simpkins's right to a jury trial any differently than it affects any tort claimant whose damages are capped as a matter of law." *Simpkins*, 75 N.E.3d at 131.

As discussed in the previous section analyzing equal protection, damage caps like R.C. 2315.18 affect sexual assault victims, and women with sexual or reproductive injuries, differently, and far worse, than tort claimants whose physical injuries are compensated largely through economic damages. For plaintiffs like Jessica, their injuries lead to minimal medical bills and wage loss that are compensated through economic damages, but devastating ongoing mental trauma, depression, altered sense of self and emotional security, and an impaired ability to form trusting relationships. Consequently, the overwhelming majority of these jury awards will be for noneconomic loss damages, and the cap will thus deprive them of a far greater extent of their jury award than other tort claimants. The inevitable effect of R.C. 2315.18 is to deprive victims of sexual assault of an overwhelming majority of the damages their juries determine to be warranted to compensate them for suffering a most horrific harm. Those who suffer other kinds of severe and debilitating physical injuries, however, will still be awarded nearly all or the full amount determined by their juries. Such a severely disparate impact on the ability of minor victims of sexual assault to effectuate their inviolate right to damages as determined by a jury renders R.C.2315.18 unconstitutional as applied to sexual assault tort claims.

In adopting R.C. 2315.18's "one-size fits all" approach to noneconomic damages, the legislature purported to respond to "threats" to Ohio's business climate. But a civil justice system that awards compensation without regard to the balance between injury and compensation, and that deprives sexual assault victims of their inviolate right to a jury, is far more of a threat to justice and fairness in Ohio. R.C. 2315.18 creates a distinct class of civil litigants for whom the traditional process for safeguarding jury awards does not apply. This is amply illustrated by the fact that Jessica's jury award was targeted for drastic reduction, while her father's award, determined by the same jury, remained untouched. Jessica's award was targeted because the jury found that she suffered the type of injury that caused more damages, which both on its face and applied to her and other sexual assault victims constitutes an infringement on the fundamental right to a civil jury in Ohio.

The result in this case may discourage some survivors of rape or sexual assault from seeking redress through the civil justice system. I pray their voices will not be silenced. "Darkness cannot drive out darkness; only light can do that." MARTIN LUTHER KING JR., STRENGTH TO LOVE 37 (1963).

IV CONCLUSION

As applied, R.C. 2315.18 deprived Jessica Simpkins of equal protection of the law under article 1, section 2 of the Ohio Constitution. R.C. 2315.18 also arbitrarily infringed on Jessica's inviolate right to a civil jury under article 1, section 5 of the Ohio Constitution. I respectfully dissent.

Index

For EU product safety concerns, contact us at Calle de José Abascal, 56–1°, 28003 Madrid, Spain or eugpsr@cambridge.org.

www.ingramcontent.com/pod-product-compliance
Lightning Source LLC
LaVergne TN
LVHW011658200926
848484LV00004B/986

* 9 7 8 1 1 0 8 4 8 4 2 9 9 *